DATE DUE

LIBRARY OF
RELIGIOUS AND PHILOSOPHICAL THOUGHT

THE CHRISTIAN DOCTRINE

OF

JUSTIFICATION AND RECONCILIATION

THE CHRISTIAN DOCTRINE

OF

JUSTIFICATION AND RECONCILIATION

By ALBRECHT RITSCHL

THE POSITIVE DEVELOPMENT OF THE DOCTRINE

ENGLISH TRANSLATION

EDITED BY

H. R. MACKINTOSH, D.Phil.

MINISTER OF THE FREE CHURCH, TAYPORT

AND

A. B. MACAULAY, M.A.

MINISTER OF THE EAST FREE CHURCH, FORFAR

REFERENCE BOOK PUBLISHERS, INC.

CLIFTON, NEW JERSEY

1966

Published 1966 by
Reference Book Publishers, Inc.

Library of Congress Catalog Number: 65-27052

Printed in the United States of America

EDITORS' PREFACE

———◆———

THERE is reason to believe that an English translation of
Ritschl's greatest work is not inopportune at the present
moment. The attention paid in Britain to this theologian's
doctrinal system has been steadily deepening for some years.
Such works as Denney's *Studies in Theology*, Orr's *The
Ritschlian Theology and the Evangelical Faith*, and Garvie's
The Ritschlian Theology, are enough to prove how profound
is the interest felt here in the methods and conclusions of a
movement which has had so remarkable an influence in
Germany. Of this movement the primary source was
Ritschl's monumental work, *The Christian Doctrine of
Justification and Reconciliation* (1870–1874). Not since
Schleiermacher published his *Christliche Glaube* in 1821
has any dogmatic treatise left its mark so deeply upon
theological thought in Germany and throughout the world.
Schleiermacher's masterpiece, unfortunately, is inaccessible
to the English reader ; and it was felt that were the *magnum
opus* of his most notable successor also to remain untrans-
lated, the loss to English students of theology would be
doubly regrettable. The first volume of the German work,
containing the history of the doctrine, was published in an
English rendering as far back as 1872. The third volume,
of which a translation is now furnished for the first time,
has the supreme interest of presenting us with Ritschl's own
theological system.

The translation has been executed by several hands.
Chap. V. and part of Chap. I. were translated by the Rev.

A. B. Macaulay, M.A., of Forfar; Chap. II. by the Rev. A. R. Gordon, M.A., of Monikie; Chap. VI. by the Rev. R. A. Lendrum, M.A., of Kirkliston; Chap. VIII. by the Rev. Jas. Strachan, M.A., of St. Fergus; and the Introduction, Chaps. III. IV. VII. IX. and part of Chap. I. by the Rev. H. R. Mackintosh, D.Phil., of Tayport. Dr. Mackintosh, however, is responsible in every case for the rendering finally adopted. The thanks of the Editors are due to the Rev. A. Grieve, Ph.D., for valuable advice, and especially to the Rev. A. R. Gordon, who read most of the work both in manuscript and in proof, and to whose ungrudging help and accurate scholarship it owes much.

The translation of the hymns on pp. 186, 187 is by Mr. Macaulay.

The references to Vols. I. and II. are to the paging of the second German edition.

AUTHOR'S PREFACES

FROM THE PREFACE TO THE FIRST EDITION

IN publishing this, the third volume of the *Doctrine of Justification and Reconciliation,* I think I may assume that many questions excited by the History of the Doctrine which appeared four years ago will find their answer here. In order to make what is the central doctrine of Christianity intelligible as such, I have been compelled to give an almost complete outline of Systematic Theology, the remaining parts of which could easily be supplied. No one who has given any attention to Vol. II. will be surprised at the fulness of the exposition. . . . I need not, it seems to me, make any statement in advance regarding what has been my aim in the positive explication of the doctrine. For one thing my path and the goal it leads to were marked out for me by what I have exhibited in Vol. II. as the Biblical material of the doctrine; while for the rest I think I have already made it sufficiently clear in Vol. I. that my theology has no place in the ordinary classification of theological parties.

GÖTTINGEN, *July* 10, 1874.

PREFACE TO THE SECOND EDITION

THE last remark in the Preface to the First Edition has not been understood by all who have thought fit to express an opinion on my theology. In proportion as for the past two years the question has been raised of using force against me, certain of my opponents have made it their aim to brand me with all possible heretical names, by perverting or even directly falsifying what I intended to convey. I find myself in a situation like that of the prophet Jeremiah, whose enemies said : " Come and let us smite him with the tongue, and let us not give heed to any of his words " (Jer. xviii. 18). I therefore decline to allude particularly to the kind of opposition which I have experienced in the majority of cases. In the present volume, which is almost two sheets larger than before, much will be found which, if read connectedly, strengthens my point of view.

GÖTTINGEN, *June* 4, 1883.

PREFACE TO THE THIRD EDITION

IT affords me satisfaction that after five years a new edition of this third volume of the *Doctrine of Justification and Reconciliation* has become necessary. Yet I cannot help saying that anyone who thinks he can dispense with a knowledge of the first and second volumes of this work increases his own difficulty in understanding the third. Apart from minor improvements in style, and alterations serving to make my views clearer, which have been adopted in this new edition, fresh material has been introduced only in §§ 27, 29, 34, 44, 56, 60, 61. The controversial situation which I described five years ago still lasts on ; my opponents, indeed, have quite recently extended the scope of their exertions, and in part have taken to a harsh and common tone of writing, which redounds not to my discredit, but to their own. At the same time I perceive that in a surreptitious and fragmentary way individual principles of mine which have been vehemently assailed are being admitted even by my opponents. Lastly, from the growing sale of my writings I may draw the conclusion that the number of those is increasing who are not to be intimidated from learning from me directly, by the methods which have been employed to falsify and cast suspicion upon my theological views.

GÖTTINGEN, *August* 24, 1888.

CONTENTS

INTRODUCTION

A.—THE CONCEPTION OF JUSTIFICATION AND ITS RELATIONS

CHAPTER I

ITS DEFINITION

CHAPTER II

THE GENERAL RELATIONS OF JUSTIFICATION

CHAPTER III

THE SUBJECTIVE ASPECT OF JUSTIFICATION CONSIDERED IN DETAIL

B.—THE PRESUPPOSITIONS

CHAPTER IV

THE DOCTRINE OF GOD

CHAPTER V

THE DOCTRINE OF SIN

CHAPTER VI

THE DOCTRINE OF THE PERSON AND LIFE-WORK OF CHRIST

C.—THE PROOF

CHAPTER VII

THE NECESSITY OF THE FORGIVENESS OF SINS OR JUSTIFICATION IN GENERAL

CHAPTER VIII

THE NECESSITY OF BASING THE FORGIVENESS OF SINS ON THE WORK AND PASSION OF CHRIST

D.—THE CONSEQUENCES

CHAPTER IX

THE RELIGIOUS FUNCTIONS SPRINGING OUT OF RECONCILIATION WITH GOD, AND THE RELIGIOUS FORM OF MORAL ACTION

INTRODUCTION

———◆———

§ 1. THE exposition of Biblical Theology contained in my second volume was undertaken in order to ascertain what idea of the forgiveness of sins, justification, and reconciliation—together with their relations—had been called into existence by Jesus as the Founder of the Christian Church, and maintained by the apostles as its earliest representatives. In view of the many distortions and obscurations which the intellectual content of Christianity has suffered in the course of history, my aim, in harmony with the theological principles of the Evangelical Church, was to discover the conceptions originally held of the religious relation of Christians to God which the above-mentioned notions express. Once this authentical exposition of the ideas named has been given, however, the interests of theology are satisfied. For succeeding thinkers have been guided, in part intentionally, in part unconsciously, by the models of the New Testament, or should not be followed when they in point of fact diverge from them.

Now it is not sufficient for my purpose to bring out what Jesus has said about the forgiveness of sins attached to His Person and His death. For even if His statements might seem perfectly clear, their significance becomes completely intelligible only when we see how they are reflected in the consciousness of those who believe in Him, and how the members of the Christian community trace back their consciousness of pardon to the Person and the action and passion of Jesus. For thus we are made aware that Jesus' purpose of pardon has not failed. Its success, however, not only serves to make more clear what His purpose was: it also forms an essential condition of our religious and theological interest in the matter. We should pay no special attention to this purpose of Jesus, nor should we seek to discover its value and its meaning, did we not reckon ourselves part of *the religious community* which first attested, through the writers of the New Testament, its possession of the forgiveness of sins as effected by Christ. On the other hand, the necessity of this connection with the Church is ignored by those who think themselves competent to arrive at or reproduce " the religion of Jesus "; as also by those who acknowledge in Jesus only the Author of new moral legislation, or one of those who have helped to perfect humanity's ideal. Those who comprise in the latter view the results of their historical criticism, either ignore Jesus' sayings about forgiveness as attached to His Person and His death, or regard them as merely casual expressions, or content themselves with supposing that in Jesus' view forgiveness flows directly of itself from moral obedience to the law (vol. ii. p. 50). The advocates of " the religion of Jesus " are quite well aware that some value belongs to the *religious* example of Jesus, apart from His moral legislation and His moral example. But in thinking that His significance can be stated completely in terms of personal imitation, they overlook the very fact that Jesus withdraws Himself from imitation when He sets Himself over against His disciples as the Author of forgiveness. The minds of His disciples are so far responsive to His teaching on this point, that they become convinced that pardon must first be appropriated before it is possible to imitate His piety and His moral achievement.

Authentic and complete knowledge of Jesus' religious significance—His significance, that is, as a Founder of religion—depends, then, on one's reckoning oneself part of the community which He founded, and this precisely in so far as it believes itself to have received the forgiveness of sins as His peculiar gift. This religious faith does not take an unhistorical view of Jesus, and it is quite possible to reach an historical estimate of Him without first divesting oneself of this faith, this religious valuation of His Person. The opposite view is one of the characteristics which mark that great untruth which exerts a deceptive and confusing influence under the name of an historical "absence of presuppositions." It is no mere accident that the subversion of Jesus' religious importance has been undertaken under the guise of writing His life, for this very undertaking implies the surrender of the conviction that Jesus, as the Founder of the perfect moral and spiritual religion, belongs to a higher order than all other men. But for that reason it is likewise vain to attempt to re-establish the importance of Christ by the same biographical expedient. We can discover the full compass of His historical actuality solely from the faith of the Christian community. Not even His purpose to found the community can be quite understood historically save by one who, as a member of it, subordinates himself to His Person.

Thence follows for our present task, however, that the material of the theological doctrines of forgiveness, justification, and reconciliation is to be sought not so much directly in the words of Christ, as in the correlative representations of the original consciousness of the community. The immediate object of theological cognition is the community's faith that it stands to God in a relation essentially conditioned by the forgiveness of sins. So far, however, as this benefit is traced back to the personal action and passion of Christ, His proved intention to adopt such means makes the mediation of the community more intelligible. Such being the position of affairs, we have now a basis for the practice of theology in attaching its terminology directly to the apostolic circle of ideas. It would be a mistaken purism were anyone, in this respect, to prefer the less developed statements of Jesus to the forms of apostolic thought. Nay more, we are justified in not paring down the most developed forms of the Pauline system, but preserving them in theological usage, for they serve to express most sharply the opposition between Christianity and Judaism. What urges us to this is not solely the predominant custom of the Western Church and the Reformed tradition, but the fact that by means of the Pauline formulas the uniqueness of Christianity is marked off from the Pharisaic falsification of the religion of the Old Testament, and thereby the Christian Church most securely protected against a recrudescence of the latter error.

The precondition, thus indicated as essential for the understanding of forgiveness, justification, and reconciliation, which are assured through Christ, holds good for every part of the Christian circle of thought. We are able to know and understand God, sin, conversion, eternal life, in the Christian sense, only so far as we consciously and intentionally reckon ourselves members of the community which Christ has founded. Theology is bound to take up this point of view, and only so is there any hope of constructing a theological system which deserves the name. For in order to comprehend the content of Christianity, as a totality composed of rightly ordered particular data, we must occupy one and the same standpoint throughout. The form in which theology has hitherto been elaborated—after the model of Melanchthon's *Loci*—disobeys this principle. It takes up its standpoint, first of all, in the far-off domain of man's original perfection, which it makes correlative to a certain rational conception of God, correlative that is to the necessary twofold recompense which God awards to men, bound as they are to conform to His law. The formula of the *foedus operum*, which Cocceius invented for this combination of ideas, is thoroughly well suited to the exposition of this doctrine given earlier and later by Lutheran and Reformed theology. The traditional doctrine of man's original state, consequently, implies that theology takes up its standpoint within either a natural or a universally rational knowledge of God which has nothing to do with the Christian knowledge of Him, and is consequently indifferent to the question whether the expositor who expounds the doctrine belongs to the Christian community or not. The nature and the extent of sin, accepted as a fact, is thereafter determined by the standard of the first man's original perfection. Passages of Scripture may be used as well, but that makes no difference, for they are not read in the light of the fact that the Apostle

Paul's view of the effect on the human race of the first trans-gression is determined by its contrast to the effect of Christ upon His community. Traditional theology, in using the passage Rom. v. 12, rather keeps to the lines of Augustine, who, on thoroughly rational grounds, deduced original sin from the sin of the first human pair. Next, theology takes up its standpoint on the fact of the universally inherited sin of the human race, and undertakes to deduce from this the necessity of a redemption, the method of which is brought out by comparing sin with the Divine attribute of retributory right-eousness in the purely rational style which Anselm has applied to this topic. Then follows, at the third stage of the traditional theological system, the knowledge of Christ's Person, and work, and its application to the individual and the fellowship of believers. Not until it has to deal with this topic does theology take up the standpoint of the com-munity of believers, but it does so in such a way that the above-mentioned rational conception of redemption is held to throughout the exposition of its actual course. No system can result from a method which thus traverses three separate points of view in accomplishing the different parts of its task. A method which is so predominantly inspired by purely rational ideas of God and sin and redemption is not the positive theology which we need, and which can be defended against the objections of general rationalism.

Advocates of this method, who are unaware of its defects and feel no need to get rid of them, are therefore likewise incapable of understanding an exposition of Christian doctrine which views and judges every part of the system from the standpoint of the redeemed community of Christ. When they confront a rounded exposition of theology, represented on a single surface, with their many-angled mirror, of course they get nothing but a broken reflection. But the blame falls not on one who has ventured to employ the systematic method in theology, but upon the critics who cherish the belief that their own fragmentary knowledge, which loses itself in a variety of tentative efforts, complies with the conditions of systematic thought.[1] But system proper must all the more certainly be conditioned by the fact that every part of theological knowledge is construed from the standpoint of the Christian community, since only so can the worth of Christ as Revealer be employed throughout as the basis of knowledge in solving all the problems of theology. This constituted the new principle which Luther set forth in various passages, collected in Schultz's treatise (cited vol. i. p. 219). Reference is made there to the fact that Luther admits no " disinterested " knowledge of God, but recognises as a religious datum only such knowledge of Him as takes the form of unconditional trust. This knowledge, however, is so exclusively bound up with Christ, that whatever knowledge of God exists alongside of it does not, as the Scholastics suppose, arrive at a neutral idea of God, but issues solely in contempt or hatred of Him. This line of thought is to be found not only in Luther's Larger Catechism,[2] but also in the Augsburg Confession, xx. 24.[3] In 1543 Melanchthon merely echoes in a feeble

---

[1] I refer to Kreibig's work, *Die Versöhnungslehre auf Grund des christlichen Bewusstseins dargestellt* (Berlin, 1878). In the introduction he identifies, in a trice, the authority of the Bible and the Church with his Christian consciousness, deduces the method of reconciliation before proving the act of reconciliation, and on p. 242 betrays his rationalism by recognising belief in a twofold Divine recompense—which he affirms is the content of the biblical idea of righteousness—as an idea common to all men, and present originally in the moral consciousness. In his scattered and often falsified representation of my views, Kreibig's method is to concede to me in one breath what previously and subsequently he disputes. He ignores altogether the researches in Biblical Theology contained in my second volume, but continues to assure us cheerfully that his assumptions are based on Scripture without even in a single word mentioning what I have proved to the contrary.

[2] "Quid est habere deum aut quid est deus? Deus est et vocatur, de cuius bonitate et potentia omnia bona certo tibi pollicearis et ad quem quibuslibet adversis rebus atque periculis ingruentibus confugias, ut deum habere nihil aliud sit, quam illi ex toto corde fidere et credere . . . Siquidem haec duo, fides et deus una copula coniungenda sunt."

[3] "Qui scit, se per Christum habere propitium patrem, is *vere* novit deum"; further, in the *Apology*, iii. 20 : "Per Christum acceditur ad patrem, et accepta remissione peccatorum vere iam statuimus, nos habere deum, hoc est nos deo curae esse, invocamus, agimus gratias, timemus, diligimus." II. 34 : "Humanus animus sine spiritu sancto (outside the community of believers) aut securus contemnit iudicium dei, aut in poena fugit et odit iudicantem deum." II. 18 : "Ratio nihil facit, nisi quaedam civilia opera, interim neque timet deum, neque vere credit se deo curae esse."

way the principle that God is knowable only through the mediation of Christ, a principle which in the *Loci* of 1535 he had recognised with a certain emphasis.[1] The while, he builds Christian doctrine on a foundation of natural theology, after the model of the Scholastics. All this is a result of his return of Aristotle. Not only does the close affinity between Humanism and Scholasticism betray itself here, but Melanchthon abandons the task of constructing theology according to Luther's principle. That task I essay in the full consciousness that my action is justified and rendered imperative by the standard writings of the Reformation. But if we can rightly know God only if we know Him through Christ, then we can know Him only if we belong to the community of believers. Not only, however, are God and all the operations of His grace to be construed through the revelation in Christ, but even sin can be appreciated only in virtue of the forgiveness of sins which is Christ's special gift : for, as the *Apology* puts it, ii. 62 : *Evangelium arguit omnes, quod sint sub peccato.* V. 29 : *Haec est summa praedictionis evangelii, arguere peccata et offerre remissionem peccatorum.*[2]

This theological method, too, is the legitimate solution of the dilemma in which Spener places us between *theologia regenitorum aut irregenitorum.*[3] That theology no less than the Christian faith should possess the marks of the regenerate life, is obvious ; as it is also intelligible that Spener should find those marks awanting in the pedantic theology cultivated in his day. But if the point was to prove that those supernatural characteristics were present, that was impossible so long as theology retained its traditional arrangement and form. For opponents might rejoin that, provided their system were materially correct, it came to them from the Holy Spirit.

---

[1] Cf. *Theologie und Metaphysik*, p. 57 ff. (2nd ed. p. 61 ff.).

[2] In the *Apol. C. A.* v. 53, it is true, we meet with the formula which Melanchthon in the *Visitationsbuch* defended against Agricola's objections : *Lex ostendit, arguit, et condemnat peccata. Evangelium est promissio gratiae.* This formula indicates that the ground for our knowledge of sin lies outside faith in Christ. But Luther admitted this only in the sense that general saving faith is included in the law (vol. i. p. 201).

[3] Cf. *Geschichte des Pietismus*, ii. p. 117 ff.

And Spener's principle that theology is to be learned through prayer and moral discipline either ends in fanaticism, or is susceptible of a practicable meaning only when it is taken as a suggestion for making a fruitful application of theology in the pulpit and pastoral work. Spener,[1] however, claimed for theology a yet wider point of view—it is to make good its derivation from the Holy Spirit in virtue of the truth that "whoever willeth to do the will of God will know the truth of Christ's doctrine" (John vii. 17). This implies a complete revision of the matter of theology; for the traditional system was and is not adapted to this ethical proof of the truth of Christianity. What Spener's principles indicate, however, is the way to such a conception of the Christian view of the world and of life as can hope for success only when it is attempted from the standpoint of the community of believers. This standpoint, however, conforms likewise to the maxim that theology must emanate from the Holy Spirit. But if anyone builds Christian theology on a substructure of pretended Natural Theology, the rationalistic arguments of Augustine about original sin, and those of Anselm about the nature of redemption, he thereby takes his stand outside the sphere of regeneration, which is coterminous with the community of believers.

§ 2. The form of systematic theology is bound up, first of all, with the correct and complete *idea of the Christian Religion*. The latter is reached by an orderly reproduction of the thought of Christ and the apostles; it is confirmed by being compared with other species and stages of religion. The specifically peculiar nature of Christianity, which at every turn of theology must be kept intact, can be ascertained only by calling the general history of religion to our aid. Schleiermacher was the first to adopt this method (vol. i. p. 440 ff.). It is this that makes his definition of religion so important, even though when more closely examined it by no means justifies its claims. "The Christian religion is that

---

[1] *Pia desideria* and *Allgemeine Gottesgelahrtheit* (1680), i. p. 36. *Consilia*, iii. p. 54.

monotheistic form of faith within the teleological (moral) class, in which everything is referred to the redemption wrought by Jesus." The relation between this special characteristic and the generic qualities of Christianity is not stated with the clearness we desire. For if the Divine final end is embodied in the Kingdom of God,[1] it is to be expected that the redemption which has come through Jesus should also be related, as a means, to this final end. But as this relation is not expressed, the result is that Schleiermacher construes the whole Christian consciousness of God by reference 'now to redemption through Jesus, now to the idea of the Kingdom of God, without coming to any decision regarding the mutual relations of this final end and the function of the Mediator. The natural consequence of this want of lucidity is that no topic receives less justice in the general argument of his *Glaubenslehre* than what he admits to be the teleological character of Christianity. The latter is constantly crossed by the neutral idea of religion by which he is guided, by the abstract Monotheism which he follows, and finally by everything being referred solely to redemption through Jesus. His obscure definition betrays the fact, at the very outset, that Schleiermacher had not taken his final bearings in the realm of the history of religion. Here he was impeded, beyond all doubt, by his underestimate of the religion of the Old Testament, which, as the stage prefatory to Christianity, is possessed of characteristics analogous to those of Christianity itself. For, in the Old Testament no less, the concrete conception of the one, supernatural, omnipotent God is bound up with the final end of the Kingdom of God, and with the idea of a redemption. But that end is conceived under the limits of the national commonwealth; while the condition of the ·

---

[1] *Glaubenslehre*, § 9, 2 : "Whatever in the domain of Christianity belongs to our consciousness of God, must also be referred, through the idea of a kingdom of God, to the totality of our activities . . . This figure of 'the Kingdom of God,' so significant, so all-inclusive in Christianity, is only a general expression of the fact that in Christianity all pain and all joy are religious only in so far as they are related to activity in the Kingdom of God, and that every pious emotion, which arises from a passive state, ends in the consciousness of a transition to activity."

end being realised is conceived, it is true, as purification from sin, but partly also under the garb of the chosen people's political independence ; partly it is accompanied by the hope of outward prosperity destined to arrive with the perfect rule of Jehovah. In Christianity, the Kingdom of God is represented as the common end of God and the elect community⎰in such a way that it rises above the natural limits of nationality and becomes the moral society of nations. ⎰In this respect Christianity shows itself to be the perfect moral religion. Redemption through Christ—an idea which embraces justification and renewal—is also divested of all conditions of a natural or sensuous kind, so as to culminate in the purely spiritual idea of eternal life. Nor do the outwardly sensible circumstances, amidst which Christ's passion took place, affect its redeeming significance. That significance attaches to His willing acceptance of His sufferings, to the obedience which, under these circumstances, He displayed in His God-given vocation. And inasmuch as redemption through Christ comprises justification and renewal, what is obtained is such an emancipation from evils as, being a spiritual process, is specifically distinct from Old Testament anticipations.

In both these respects we have in Christianity a culmination of the monotheistic, spiritual, and teleological religion of the Bible in the idea of the perfected spiritual and moral religion. There can be no doubt that these two characteristics condition each other mutually. Christ made the universal moral Kingdom of God His end, and thus He came to know and decide for that kind of redemption which He achieved through the maintenance of fidelity in His calling and of His blessed fellowship with God through suffering unto death. On the other hand, a correct spiritual interpretation of redemption and justification through Christ tends to keep more decisively to the front the truth that the Kingdom of God is the final end. Now theology, especially within the Evangelical Confessions, has laid very unequal emphasis on these two principal characteristics of Christianity. It makes everything which concerns the redemptive character of Christianity an object of the most solicitous reflection. Accordingly it finds the central point of all Christian knowledge and practice in redemption through Christ, while injustice is done to the ethical interpretation of Christianity through the idea of the Kingdom of God. But Christianity, so to speak, resembles not a circle described from a single centre, but an ellipse which is determined by two *foci*. Western Catholicism has recognised this fact in its own way. For it sets itself up not merely as an institution possessed of the sacraments by which the power of Christ's redemption is propagated, but also as the Kingdom of God in the present, as the community in which, through the obedience of men and States to the Pope, Divine righteousness is professedly realised. Now it has been a misfortune for Protestantism that the Reformers did not purify the idea of the moral Kingdom of God or Christ from sacerdotal corruptions, but embodied it in a conception which is not practical but merely dogmatical. Apart from Zwingli, whose views on this point are peculiar to himself, Luther, Melanchthon,[1] and Calvin define the Kingdom of Christ as the inward union between Christ and believers through grace and its operations. The dogmatic theologians of both Confessions unanimously propagate this view by deriving an argument for religious consolation from the protection against powers hostile to redemption enjoyed by believers in the Kingdom of Christ. Kant (vol. i. 412 ff.) was the first to perceive the supreme importance for ethics of the "Kingdom of God" as an association of men bound together by laws of virtue. But it remained for Schleiermacher first to employ the true conception of the teleological nature of the Kingdom of God to determine the idea of Christianity. This service of his ought not to be forgotten, even if he failed to grasp the discovery with a firm hand. For none of the theologians who found in him their master, with the exception

---

[1] Once, however, in the *Apology of the C. A.* iii. 68, 71, 72, he expresses the true idea. Similarly Luther, in his Smaller Catechism, sec. 2, art. 2, with which the parallel statement in his Larger Catechism really agrees.

of Theremin,[1] has taken account of the importance of this idea for systematic theology as a whole. Modern pietists are accustomed to describe their favourite undertakings, especially foreign missions, directly as the Kingdom of God ; but in doing so, while they touch upon the ethical meaning of the idea, they narrow its reference improperly. This circle, too, have brought the word into use, e.g. to describe the public affairs of the Church as discussed in periodicals. This use of the name, however, involves that interchange of "Church" and "Kingdom of God" which we find dominating Roman Catholicism.

Since Jesus Himself, however, saw in the Kingdom of God the moral end of the religious fellowship He had to found (vol. ii. p. 28); since He understood by it not the common exercise of worship, but the organisation of humanity through action inspired by love, any conception of Christianity would be imperfect and therefore incorrect which did not include this specifically teleological aspect. We must further remember that Christ did not describe this moral task, to be carried out by the human race, in the form of a philosophical doctrine, and propagate it in a school : He entrusted it to His disciples. At the same time He constituted them a religious community through training of another kind. For when good action towards our fellow-men is subsumed under the conception of the Kingdom of God, this whole province is placed under the rule and standard of religion. And so, were we to determine the unique quality

---

[1] *Die Lehre vom göttlichen Reiche* (1823), p. 2 : "Although, in view of the great multiplicity of moral ideas contained in Christianity, it is difficult to discover the most comprehensive, yet it is impossible not to perceive that its highest ideal is a society, and that its doctrines and precepts become luminous only when they are subordinated and related to it. For as a unity of essence and a moral unity of spirit exists eternally between the Father and the Son, so the Son must likewise become the Head of all humanity, in order that it may be raised to the perfection which is to be seen in Him, and be led through Him into a fellowship with the Father similar to that in which He Himself lives. This union is appropriately named the Kingdom of God." P. 4 : "When we consider the relation of God to man, and the work of redemption in the light of this idea, many doctrinal conceptions lose the appearance of arbitrariness which they may have, and gain a closer connection and a firmer foundation."

of Christianity merely by its teleological element, namely, its relation to the moral Kingdom of God, we should do injustice to its character as a religion. This aspect of Christianity, clearly, is meant to be provided for in Schleiermacher's phrase—" in which everything is referred to the redemption wrought by Jesus." For redemption is a presupposition of the Christian's peculiar dependence on God ; but dependence on God is, for Schleiermacher, the general form of religious experience as distinct from a moral relationship. Now it is true that in Christianity everything is " related " to the moral organisation of humanity through love-prompted action ; but at the same time everything is also " related " to redemption through Jesus, to spiritual redemption, *i.e.* to that freedom from guilt and over the world which is to be won through the realised Fatherhood of God. Freedom in God, the freedom of the children of God, is the private end of each individual Christian, as the Kingdom of God is the final end of all. And this double character of the Christian life—perfectly religious and perfectly ethical—continues, because its realisation in the life of the individual advances through the perpetual interaction of the two elements. For the life and activity of the Founder of Christianity issued at once in the redemption and the setting up of the Kingdom of God. The same fidelity in His Divine vocation enabled Him to preserve and secure both His own fellowship with the Father, and the power to lead sinners back into the same fellowship with God ; and the same effect has two aspects—His disciples acknowledge Him as the Head of the Kingdom of God, and God as their Father.

Christianity, then, is the monotheistic, completely spiritual, and ethical religion, which, based on the life of its Author as Redeemer and as Founder of the Kingdom of God, consists in the freedom of the children of God, involves the impulse to conduct from the motive of love, aims at the moral organisa- tion of mankind, and grounds blessedness on the relation of sonship to God, as well as on the Kingdom of God.

This conception is indispensable for systematic theology

if the material correctly obtained from Biblical ideas is to be fully used. The history of theology affords only too many examples of the construction of what is either merely a doctrine of redemption or merely a system of morality. But it must also be observed that we are not to base theology proper on the idea of redemption, and ethics upon the idea of the Kingdom of God. On the contrary, so far as theology falls into these two sections, each must be kept under the constitutive influence of both ideas. Dogmatics, that is, comprises all the presuppositions of Christianity under the form of *Divine operation*; ethics, presupposing the former discipline, comprises the province of personal and social Christian life under the form of *personal activity*.[1] Now since the revelation of God is directed not only to the goal of redemption, but also to the final end of the kingdom which He realises in fellowship with the redeemed, dogmatics cannot dispense with the latter guiding idea. And as the spiritual activity of those who are called to the Kingdom of God and redeemed does not manifest itself merely in their moral influence on others, but also in the peculiar functions of Divine sonship, ethics must be conditioned likewise by the idea of redemption.

§ 3. The scientific understanding of the several truths of Christianity depends on their correct definition. The first task of systematic theology is correctly and completely to outline and clearly to settle the religious ideas or facts which are included in the conception of Christianity. The so-called proof from Scripture has to do with the correctness of these ideas, but it does not really yield more than the correctness of the ideas of Christianity in their original sense. Theological form, however, requires that their correctness should be of another kind. And so we cannot reach dogmatic definitions simply by summing up the exegetical results of Biblical Theology. For the writers of the New Testament are not in the least guided by the wish to define their ideas; and when,

---

[1] Cf. Schleiermacher, *Christliche Sitte*, p. 23 ; Nitzsch, *System der christlichen Lehre* (6th ed.), p. 4 ; Harless, *Christliche Ethik* (6th ed.), p. 3.

as in Heb. xi. 1, we have for once a tendency to definition, yet the definition is not complete. The ideas of Christ and of the apostles, which we regard off-hand as substantially in agreement, often enough employ divergent means of expression, or link themselves to different Old Testament symbols. Now exegesis itself, certainly, deals with many particular passages in such a way as to reduce the cognate symbolical expressions they contain to one conception of the greatest possible clearness. For in part exegesis must view the particular in the light of its relationship to everything which resembles it, in part it has to fill up the chasm between our way of thinking and the Israelites' symbolical manner of speech, in part its task is to clear away false ideas forced upon certain Biblical symbols by exegetical tradition. Under these circumstances, the exposition of religious ideas furnished by Biblical Theology, which supplies the matter of theological knowledge, itself contains attempts to define these ideas. But it gives no guarantee that they are completely and distinctly defined in organic relation to the whole. * Each definition can only be made complete as it receives its place in a system of theology, for the truth of the particular can be understood only through its connection with the whole. This gives us the certainty that theological propositions, which have been defined with logical correctness, are not mutually contradictory.[1]

The formally correct expression of theological propositions depends on the method we follow in defining the objects of cognition, that is, on the theory of knowledge which we consciously or unconsciously obey. The theory of knowledge, in the sense here intended, is identical with " the doctrine of

---

[1] Cf. Dilthey, *Einleitung in die Geisteswissenschaften*, i. p. 5. By science is understood in ordinary usage a system of propositions, the elememts of which are conceptions, *i.e.* ideas completely determined, constant, and universally valid throughout the whole connection of thought. The conjunctions of ideas in the system must be based in fact ; and finally, its parts must be combined into a whole to facilitate teaching, either because a part of reality is completely construed in thought by this combination of propositions, or because some branch of human activity is determined by it.

the thing or things " [1] which forms the first part of metaphysics.[2] Different philosophers interpret metaphysics differently. I have therefore explained elsewhere what I mean when I use the word metaphysics by reference to Aristotle, whose usage determined philosophical terminology until Kant. And I cannot refrain from repeating that explanation here. " First Philosophy," according to Aristotle, " is devoted to an investigation of the universal grounds of all being. Now the things with which our knowledge deals are divided into nature and spiritual life. When we are investigating the grounds common to all being, we abstract from the particular qualities which constitute for us the difference between nature and spirit, and enable us to regard them as heterogeneous entities. Natural and spiritual phenomena concern metaphysics only in so far as they may be conceived as things in general. For the conditions of knowledge common to them both are crystallised in the conception of ' the thing.' Thus metaphysical conceptions, it is true, include and regulate all other acts of knowledge which involve the specific peculiarity of nature and of spirit. They explain how it is that the human mind, having had experientially perceptions of special kinds, differentiates things in consequence into natural things and spiritual beings. But it does not follow from the position of metaphysics as superordinate to experiential knowledge, that metaphysical conceptions give us a more profound and valuable knowledge of spiritual existence than can be gained from psychology and ethics." Compared with natural science and ethics, metaphysics yields elementary and merely formal knowledge. If others understand by metaphysics : not that elementary knowledge of things in general which ignores their division into nature and spirit, but such a universal theory as shall be at once elementary and the final and exhaustive science of all particular ordered existence, they do so at their own risk. At any rate my method is neither unjust nor

---

[1] *Die Lehre von dem Dinge und den Dingen.*

[2] With what follows compare *my* pamphlet, *Theologie und Metaphysik : zur Verständigung und Abwehr*, Bonn, 1881 ; 2nd ed., 1887.

unhistorical when I explain, with express reference to
Aristotle, what extent of knowledge I include under the
name.   For in the last resort the question is one more of the
thing than of the name.

The first consequence of this is, that there are no sufficient
grounds for combining a theory of things in general with the
conception of God.   That is done, however, when Aristotle
gives the name God to the idea of the highest end which
he postulates as winding up the cosmic series of means and
ends, and so as an expression of the unity of the world.
This conjunction of the two forms the content of the
teleological argument for God's existence constructed by
Scholastic theology.   We have a similar case in the cosmological argument.   It exhibits a metamorphosis of the Neo-
platonic view of the world, which rests merely upon the idea
of things and their causal connection.   Now in religion the
thought of God is given.   But the religious view of the
world, in all its species, rests on the fact that man in some
degree distinguishes himself in worth from the phenomena
which surround him and from the influences of nature which
press in upon him.   All religion is equivalent to an explanation of the course of the world—to whatever extent it may
be known—in the sense that the sublime spiritual powers
(or the spiritual power) which rule in or over it, conserve
and confirm to the personal spirit its claims and its independence over-against the restrictions of nature and the natural
effects of human society.   Thus the thought of God, when
by the word is understood conscious personality, lies beyond
the horizon of metaphysic, as metaphysic is defined
above.   And both these proofs for God's existence, whose
construction is purely metaphysical, lead not to the Being the
idea of which Scholastic theology receives as a datum from
Christianity, but merely to conceptions of the world-unity
which have nothing to do with any religion.   This use of
metaphysic, consequently, must be forbidden in theology, if
the latter's positive and proper character is to be maintained.[1]

[1] Flügel's instructive book, *Die speculative Theologie der Gegenwart*,

2

A theory of "things" is employed merely formally in theology as a method of settling the objects of knowledge, and defining the relation between the multiplicity of their qualities and the unity of their existence. The rules which it is possible to set up here form the conditions of experience by means of which the specific nature of things is cognised. In the theory of things it is taken for granted that our Ego is not of itself the cause of sensations, perceptions, etc., but that these peculiar activities of the soul are stimulated by its co-existence with things of which the human body is also reckoned one. Accordingly, ontology and psychology mutually presuppose each other, and their results harmonise. This is so even if the conceptions of *thing* and *soul* are denied in their current sense. For Buddhism concedes the validity of each of these entities only as a multiplicity of qualities or sensations, in which there is supposed to be no normal identity or self-equivalence.[1] Heraclitus has a similar thought, but it found no acceptance among the Greeks. Within the domain of European thought, however, we have to do with three forms of the theory of knowledge. The *first* is due to the stimulus received from Plato, and found a home in the realm of Scholasticism.[2] Wherever its influence extends, we find the idea that the thing *works* upon us, indeed, by means

---

kritisch beleuchtet (1881), has not convinced me that the rational theology involved in Herbart's metaphysics is right as against the arguments I have given above. Though the task of this metaphysic, according to Flügel (p. 323), may be quite the same as that of natural science, since it aims at exhibiting that which is given as free from contradiction, yet it moves within the limits of a conception of things, their multiplicity and their interaction, which is abstract and indifferent to the distinction between nature and spirit. Such a context offers us no prospect of any conception of God which might even resemble the Christian idea. When, with Herbart, Flügel uses the purposive nexus of things, as ascertained by experience, as a ground for the *probability* of a creative intelligence, that is, of God, the result he reaches is neither necessary from the standpoint of scientific knowledge, nor capable of being used as the starting-point of a philosophy of religion which should be just to Christianity. The latter assertion is confirmed, indeed, by the most important arguments of Flügel's book. For by his criticism of views which make the necessity of the thought of God equivalent to scientific knowledge of His reality, he shuts out the metaphysical argument of probability for His existence.

[1] Cf. Oldenberg, *Buddha*, p. 253 ff.

[2] Cf. *Theologie und Metaphysik*, p. 30 ff. (2nd ed., p. 32 ff.).

of its mutable qualities, arousing our sensations and ideas, but that it really *is at rest* behind the qualities as a permanently self-equivalent unity of attributes. The simplest example of this view to be found in Scholastic dogmatics is the explication given on the one hand of the essence and attributes of God, and on the other of the operations of God upon the world and for the salvation of mankind. Here there may still be seen an idea which is peculiar to this theory—the idea that we can know the thing in itself apart from its effects. The fact is forgotten that the thing in itself is merely the stationary memory-picture of repeated intuitions of effects by which our sensation and perception have been stimulated all along within one definite space. The fault of this conception of the thing or object of knowledge appears in the inconsistency that the thing is conceived to be at rest and at the same time is to work upon us by its manifested qualities. This inconsistency makes itself apparent in yet another form, when the thing, as at rest, is represented as occupying a plane behind the plane in which its supposed qualities are placed. This makes it impossible to understand these phenomena as qualities of the thing in itself thus separated from them. The *second* form of the theory of knowledge we owe to Kant. He limits the knowledge of the understanding to the world of phenomena, but declares unknowable the thing or things in themselves, though their interdependent changes are the ground of the changes in the world of phenomena. The latter part of the statement contains a true criticism of the Scholastic interpretation of a " thing." The first part, however, is too near the Scholastic theory to avoid its errors. For a world of *phenomena* can be posited as the object of knowledge only if we suppose that in them something real—to wit, the thing —appears to us or is the cause of our sensation and perception. Otherwise the phenomenon can only be treated as an illusion. Thus by his use of the conception of phenomenon Kant contradicts his own principle that real things are unknowable. The *third* form of the theory of knowledge is due to Lotze. He holds that in the phenomena which in a definite space exhibit changes to a limited extent and in a determinate order, we cognise the thing as the cause of its qualities operating upon us, as the end which these serve as means, as the law of their constant changes. I have essayed a discussion and proof of this theory, with which I agree, in my little book, *Theologie und Metaphysik*, to which I hereby refer the reader.

Theology has to do, not with natural objects, but with states and movements of man's spiritual life; in our arrangement of the conceptions which belong to theology, accordingly, we must leave a place for psychology. Here there are two colliding views, which correspond respectively to the first and the third forms of the theory of knowledge. With the idea of the thing as remaining at rest behind its effects and qualities is bound up the Scholastic psychology, which is a principal factor in the theory of mysticism. Its assumption is, that behind its special activities of feeling, thinking, and willing, the soul remains at rest in its self-equivalence, as the unity of its diverse powers, the faculties. This level of the soul's existence, further, is regarded as the region in which it experiences the operations of Divine grace. This self-enclosed life of the spirit, above all, is conceived as the scene of the *unio mystica*, that indwelling of the Father, Son, and Holy Ghost, in which culminate all the gracious operations which our spirit undergoes. Nothing else, it is maintained, can explain how the changing functions of the spirit, its feeling, knowing, and willing, take on throughout a religious character, and become active in the service of God. This separation between the activities of the soul and its self-existence having been enlisted in the service of theology, it becomes observable in the method of Dogmatics after the middle of the seventeenth century.[1] Now this theology culminates in its scheme of individual salvation, which dominates likewise the doctrines of the Church and of the Christian hope. Consequently what it has to prove is that, besides the enlightenment of the understanding, and the renewal of the will, there occurs an invisible

[1] *Geschichte des Pietismus*, ii. p. 29.

union with God at the basis of the soul—*i.e.* within the region of its self-existence—a union which is the ground of blessedness, even when, as quietistic mysticism bids us add, the feeling of blessedness is interrupted or in great degree fails. The separation of the activities of the soul from its unaffected faculties, thus introduced into the more modern form of orthodox theology, is an error of the same kind as the distinction between the phenomenal effects of a thing and the thing in itself, unknowable as the latter is apart from its qualities. We know nothing of a self-existence of the soul, of a self-enclosed life of the spirit above or behind those functions in which it is active, living, and present to itself as a being of special worth.[1] It is a contradiction when the faculties of the soul are supposed to exercise their effects, and at the same time to constitute in repose the proper being of the soul, thus cut off from its functions. Besides, the conception of the *unio mystica*, which without this false distinction is untenable, lies outside the horizon of our Church standards. To the question : *Quid est habere deum ?* Luther answers, not : *Inhabitatio totius trinitatis in·homine credente :* he answers with psychological correctness that for man the possession of God consists in his active trust in God as the highest good. While, therefore, God communicates Himself to man in order to his salvation, the experience is not an object of knowledge in such a way as to be fixed and explained in this form ; rather it is evidenced by an activity of the human spirit in which feeling, knowing, and willing combine in an intelligible order.

For all causes which affect the soul work upon it as stimuli of the special activity with which it is endowed. The relation of the soul to all the causes which work upon it is not one of simple passivity : all actions upon it, rather, it takes up in its sensation, as a reaction in which it manifests itself as an independent cause. The use of passive predicates to describe the human spirit is always an inaccurate mode of speech. Pain, which represents suffering in the soul, exists only in sensation ; sensation, however, is the elementary act

[1] *Theologie und Metaphysik*, p. 23 (2nd ed., p. 25).

by which the soul makes it known that it is reacting in its own way upon the stimulus received from another cause; and through the feeling of discomfort it represents to itself the fact that the painful sensation, corresponding to the stimulus, is a disturbance of its condition as a whole. Now sensations are not only the material of feelings of pain or pleasure, but likewise the necessary occasions of ideas and other acts of knowledge; feelings, further, are the immediate impulses leading to acts of will. ⎰All causes, therefore, which act upon the soul, are only excitations of the soul's activity, which even in sensation, as the element from which all else is born, reveals itself as independent and distinctive. Now the peculiarity of the soul, in comparison with other causes, is expressed by the dissimilarity between the sensation and the stimulus which causes it. Sensations of light and sound, indeed, are something quite different from the experimentally ascertained vibrations of the aether and the air by which these sensations are called forth. The sensation of pain is unlike the antecedents which arouse it, for it is the same whether one is struck or pushed or falls upon a stone. The sense of wrong may attach itself to the words of another who, probably with all sincerity, disclaims the intention to offend. From this fundamental rule of psychology, there devolves on scientific theology the task of verifying everything which is cognisable as belonging to the gracious operations of God upon the Christian, by the corresponding religious and moral acts which are called forth by Revelation as a whole, and by the particular means included in Revelation. We must give up the question— —derived from Scholastic psychology, but insoluble—how man is laid hold of, or pervaded, or filled by the Holy Spirit. What we have to do is rather to verify life in the Holy Spirit by showing that believers know God's gracious gifts (1 Cor. ii. 12), that they call on God as their Father (Rom. viii. 15), that they act with love and joy, with meekness and self-control (Gal. v. 22), that they are on their guard above all against party spirit, and cherish rather a spirit of union (1 Cor. iii. 1–4). In these statements the

Holy Spirit is not denied, but recognised and understood. Nor is this method of procedure anything new. On the contrary, it has been employed by Schleiermacher, and the explanation of justification by faith to be found in the *Apology of the Augsburg Confession* follows the same plan. If Christianity is to be made practically intelligible, no method but this can be adopted. For Christianity is made unintelligible by those formulas about the order of individual salvation, which are arrived at on the opposite view and prescribed to faith without a directly appended explanation of their practical relations and their verification. Luthardt declines to grant that divergences between different forms of theology are to be traced back to differences in epistemology and psychology. He prefers to argue that these divergences point to different kinds of Christianity. Waiving the fact that thus he erroneously confuses theology and religion, I can agree with him thus far, that the Christianity which is expounded with the help of Scholastic ontology and mystical psychology is unintelligible and Neoplatonic, while with the other method it is an intelligible and practical Christianity that is set forth.

The principles of logic, epistemology, and psychology constitute the *ratio* or *intellectus* without which, in Hollatz' judgment, Divine Revelation cannot be comprehended at all, and in any case cannot be made the subject of theological exposition. He adds very convincingly : *Sicut enim sine oculis nihil videmus, sine auribus nihil audimus, ita sine ratione nihil intelligimus.*[1] But the controversy regarding the metaphysic and psychology which are admissible in theology compels us to limit this principle. As we hear only with our own ears, and see only with our own eyes, so we can understand only with our own mind, not with that of another. But the Scholastic distinction between the thing in itself and its effects upon us, between the proper life of the spirit and its active functions, is alien to our minds. For it might easily be shown that even those theologians who in their scientific work go

[1] *Examen theologicum*, p. 69.

by this distinction, judge elsewhere of things and persons by principles which they would declare invalid in theology. The correct forms of the understanding, no less than the Scholastic forms, are subject to the truth of the principle that Revelation goes beyond reason (*revelatio supra rationem*). Revelation must be given in order that our experience of it may be apprehended and interpreted with ontological, logical, and psychological correctness. For if that principle meant anything else than this, it would contradict the defence of *ratio* in theology as offered above. *Ratio*, however, is given a different signification when the further principle is asserted that revelation goes contrary to reason (*contra rationem*). By reason here is meant a connected view of the world which interprets the order of nature and spiritual life with instruments of knowledge which have no relation to Christianity. The Christian view of the world and of life is opposed, therefore, both to that produced by Materialism and to those views which are presented in systems of monistic Idealism. These, however, are not the only cases in which this principle may be applied.

Theology has performed its task when, guided by the Christian idea of God and the conception of men's blessedness in the Kingdom of God, it exhibits completely and clearly, both as a whole and in particular, the Christian view of the world and of human life, together with the necessity which belongs to the interdependent relations between its component elements. It is incompetent for it to enter upon either a direct or an indirect proof of the truth of the Christian Revelation by seeking to show that it agrees with some philosophical or juridical view of the world; for to such Christianity simply stands opposed. And as often as systems even of monistic Idealism have asserted their agreement with Christianity, and its leading ideas have been worked up into a general philosophic view, the result has only been to demonstrate over again the opposition between even such systems and Christianity. The scientific proof for the truth of Christianity ought only to be sought in the line of the thought already singled out by Spener : " Whosoever willeth to do the will of God, will know that the doctrine of Christ is true " (John vii. 17). Here it is indicated that Christianity can be verified, not when our aim is to understand the domain of spiritual life and of social human action by means of universal grounds of speculation, but only when we mark off the know-ledge of that domain from the knowledge of nature and her laws. To subordinate the ethical to the idea of the cosmical is always characteristic of a heathen view of the world, and to its jurisdiction Christianity is not amenable; before it Christianity will never succeed in justifying itself. Even when such an explanation of the world starts from an idea of God, it offers no guarantee that it can prove the truth of Chris-tianity. Christianity includes as one of its elements the distinction of the ethical from the world of nature in respect of worth, inasmuch as it attaches blessedness for man, as the highest and all-dominating notion of worth, to participation in the Kingdom of God and lordship over the world. The theological exposition of Christianity, therefore, is complete when it has been demonstrated that the Christian ideal of life, and no other, satisfies the claims of the human spirit to knowledge of things universally.

§ 4. These presuppositions of systematic theology of neces-sity lie within the horizon of the following monograph, for (§ 13) everything that falls within the domain of redemption through Christ must be referred to the supreme end of blessed-ness in the Kingdom of God, if it is to be understood as a necessary element in the Christian view. The exposition of the doctrine of Justification and Reconciliation is given here in four principal sections. *First*, we ascertain what is meant by justification and reconciliation; through what attribute of God we are to conceive justification, in what relation to men, and how far extending; finally, in what subjective functions this Divinely-originated relationship expresses itself actively. *Secondly*, we develop the positive and negative presuppositions of the religious truth of justification, the idea of God, the view that is to be taken of human sin, and the religious estimate of the Person and lifework of Christ. *Thirdly*, we prove why the thought of justification by faith is necessary at all in Christianity, and why justification is dependent on Christ as the Revealer of God and the Representative of the Church. *Fourthly*, we show, by way of conclusion, why justification manifests itself precisely in those religious functions which come into view, and what the relation is between them and moral activity.

CHAPTER I

THE DEFINITION OF JUSTIFICATION

§ 5. THE Justification and Reconciliation of sinners with God, considered as an operation of God effected through the instrumentality of Christ, are strictly *religious conceptions.* By religious conceptions, we mean such as are comprised within the scheme of His operation on men—taking the word "operation" in its widest sense. The conception of sin committed by men is also, it is true, a religious one, as distinct from injustice and crime. But it expresses merely a judgment upon the unworthiness of such actions when contrasted with God's precepts and honour. Sin, therefore, is a religious conception of an indirect kind, as it does not lend itself to interpretation as an operation of God upon men. Those, therefore, who have supposed that this idea of sin should be assimilated in form to those that are directly religious, in order to produce a system formally homogeneous, have been in error. But the ideas which represent what Christianity puts forward as the fundamental operations directed by God against sin, necessarily take the form of directly religious conceptions. Moreover, two characteristics are perceptible in religious conceptions which must be stated at the very outset. They are always the possession of a community, and they express not merely a relation between God and man, but always at the same time a relation toward the world on the part of God, and those who believe in Him. All religions are social. And if in particular cases we may observe that the founder of a religion is for a time the sole supporter of his convictions, this circumstance is, for one thing, counterbalanced by the other, that he intends to share his possession with others, that is, to

form a community.   But then, before that has taken place, he
appears rather as the bearer of a revelation, and only in a
subordinate way as the subject of his particular religion.   To
come under our scientific observation, consequently, every
religion must take shape as the religion of a community
whose members agree in recognising certain Divine operations
on them, and show that they are thus conscious of a common
salvation.   If, therefore, we attach our more exact knowledge
of a religion to a single individual, whom we isolate from the
rest of his fellows, in that case we shall have to take care
not to leave out of account the given fact of fellowship in
religion.   For fellowship includes, among its preconditions,
more than the similarity of all its members.   It will not
do, therefore, after we have previously analysed the individual subject as a type of all the rest, to bring in, in a
merely supplementary way, the social character of religion.
On the contrary, when examining the typical individual subject, the complete conditions of fellowship must be taken
into consideration from the outset.   When this is neglected
in the scientific investigation and explanation of the phenomena of religion, mistakes are made which tell on the subsequent discussion of the social character of a religion.   If,
therefore, justification and reconciliation of sinners are the
leading features of the Christian religion, they can be correctly
examined and explained in the case of the individual only
when at the same time we take note of his place in the
Christian community.

From the social character of religion we can gather that, in
a complete view of it, its relation to the world must necessarily
be included.   For the majority of those who exhibit attachment to a common religion employ, in the commerce and
outward expression of it in worship, such means as are
characteristic of mankind's situation in the world.   But for a
religion this circumstance cannot be without importance.
On the contrary, since even the thought of God or of gods
includes some kind of relation to the world, every religious
society, as such, must take up an attitude, either positive or

negative, towards the world in which it exists. Every
religion, on closer examination, is found to consist in the
striving after " goods," or a *summum bonum*, which either
belong to the world, or can only be understood by contrast
with it.   And this striving rests upon belief in some Divine
Being who professes to possess a more comprehensive authority over the world than is within the reach of man.   For
these reasons no religion can be properly understood unless it
be interpreted on some other principle than the most usual
one, that religion consists in a relation between man and God.
Three points are necessary to determine the circle by which
a religion is completely represented—God, man, and the
world.   For the central point is always this, that the
religious community, as situated in the world, endeavours to
obtain certain goods in the world, or above the world,
through the Divine Being, because of His authority over it.
And even when, as in Brahmanism (or, for that matter,
Neoplatonism), it is sought to negate the world for the sake
of God, yet the framework of this religion embraces the
world, which exists by God, and for the sake of man, in order
to be negated by man's religious activity.   Christianity has a
right to ask to be interpreted on the same principle.   Theology, it is true, is not as a rule prepared for this.   It states
the problem of the content of religion, as Melanchthon stated
it, in terms of the position of the mystic, in which the soul
which sees God sees Him as though it alone were seen by
God, and as though apart from Him and it naught else
existed.[1]   Schleiermacher, too, so far from abandoning this
method, rather confirmed it.   His interpretation of religion
as the feeling of absolute dependence on God, involves in its
intention the complete neutrality of both factors towards the
world, the latter being held in reserve as the object of discrete
cognition and volition.   Only in a secondary way is the
world brought into relation to the religious faculty, inasmuch
as feeling must combine with knowing or willing if it occu-

---

[1] Bernhardus in *Cant. Canticorum*, 69, 8.   Cf. *Geschichte des Pietismus*, i.
p. 59.

pies a moment of time, or, in other words, enters into experience. But this is an assumption quite as obscure as the conception of religious feeling itself, and it has not succeeded in preventing this conception from being erroneously confounded with the principle of mysticism. These conditions lead us to conclude that the religious conceptions of justification and reconciliation, to be explained, must not be applied in isolation to the individual subject, but to the subject as a member of the community of believers. Nor do they express a change of standing relatively to God, without at the same time implying a change of attitude to the world on the part of those who aforetime were sinners. Theological tradition recognises this fact, for it makes justification equivalent to the forgiveness of sins, but explains the latter as the abrogation of the Divine penalties. And these penalties, as regards their substance, invariably consist in some relation on man's part to the world. It is objected to the principle we have just considered, that religion is a relation between man and God, while to refer it to the world is part of its application. This is an untenable distinction. The reference of religion to the world cannot be regarded as an accident which may be present or absent without altering its substance, for in Christianity, *e.g.*, we must conceive God as the Creator and Ruler of the world, and ourselves as parts of the same. Whoever overlooks this fact makes an imperfect commencement in the subject he wishes to understand, and so falls into error.

§ 6. The *Kingdom of God* likewise is a directly *religious conception*. This is clear when we consider the phrase as it stood originally—Sovereignty of God. For this combination of words distinctly expresses an operation of God directed towards men. The conception contains two different things. The Kingdom of God is the *summum bonum* which God realises in men; and at the same time it is their common task, for it is only through the rendering of obedience on man's part that God's sovereignty possesses continuous existence. These two meanings are interdependent. Here,

however, we have the reason why the conception of the
Kingdom of God has the appearance of being a religious
conception of a different order from justification and reconciliation.   In these operations of God upon sinners, so far as
they have already been elucidated, no room is left for a
corresponding self-determined activity on the part of man.
On the other hand, the moral action demanded by the
Kingdom of God or the Sovereignty of God, and therefore
itself a part of the latter conception, is committed to men as
God's independent and responsible subjects.   The range and
the character of the separate tasks, which make up the total
task of the Kingdom of God, are of such a kind that we have
to devote definite attention and continuous purpose to their
separate fulfilment, and to the ties which bind them together.
In this respect the conception of the Kingdom of God differs
in a peculiar way from those other operations of Divine grace.
The question remains whether this diversity in nature
amongst the chief ideas of Christianity does not put an
obstacle in the way of our vindicating the general Christian
view, and whether the definition I have given of this religion
(p. 13) can surmount the difficulty.

In our desire to get rid of the appearance of contradiction,
it is possible some may revert to the fact that the two sets
of ideas occupy different planes, inasmuch as justification and
reconciliation concern men as sinners, while the Kingdom of
God concerns them as reconciled.   Such a statement, however, is not quite exact.   For it would imply that at the
moment of justification, which logically precedes the call to
the Kingdom of God, the predication of sin loses its validity
altogether.   But this is not the case; for the meaning of
justification is that it encompasses the whole life of the
Christian, and in this constitutive sense forms likewise a
continual reminder of sin and guilt, and thus emphasises
the necessity for its own continued existence (p. 7).   If
what this means is that, as a direct result of justification, the
presence of sin is felt so long as a Christian lives, then the
call to participate independently in the Kingdom of God

arises simultaneously.   But in that case the proposed solution of the difficulty is inadequate.

Two lines of thought have been employed to establish the homogeneity of these two sets of ideas.   In the first place, human activity, conceived as independent,—be its aim salvation or good works,—is subordinated to the grace of God, or included in God's operation upon men.   Certain apostolic expressions point in this direction.   Paul (Phil. ii. 12, 13) summons every man to work out his own salvation with fear and trembling; because He who works in believers, both to will and to do, is God.   The author of the Epistle to the Hebrews (xiii. 21) expresses the wish that God would make his readers perfect in every good work to do His will, while He Himself works in them that which is well-pleasing to Him through Jesus Christ.   John (1 John ii. 5, iv. 12) sees in the exercise of love on the part of Christians the real consummation of the love of God to us, i.e. its complete revelation (vol. ii. p. 374).   This consummation, therefore, would not take place if God's action extended only so far as to give believers the mere potentiality of exercising love. Later teaching also has adhered to this religious estimate of moral action in Christianity.   In Catholic theology the validity of the conception of the merits of believers, which depends on their being voluntary, is ultimately counterbalanced by the proposition that all merit is but an effect of grace, understood in its full significance (vol. i. pp. 108, 111). In the same way in Lutheran theology the moral activity of believers is included, as an effect of *regeneratio*, under the gracious operation of God; and the same thought is still further emphasised by Calvin by his conception of *perseverantia gratiae.*   Now, the leading statements of the apostles have never been interpreted in these systems of theology as giving a mechanical explanation of the process in question, and as thus requiring us to abandon the idea of human self-determination formerly admitted.   The theology of Calvinism itself stipulates for the reality of human freedom, in contradistinction from nature as such, under the operations of

Divine grace. That is to say, the psychological fact is kept
in view throughout, that even the operations of Divine grace
merely stimulate man to appropriate them in the way which
is peculiar to himself. We may ask, consequently, what
cognitive interest is satisfied by the thought that one who
is working out his own salvation by his own effort, regards
God as the author of his purpose and his self-activity?
What suggests this twofold way of looking at the matter?
I think it is suggested by the claims both of the individual
case and of the moral order of the world as a whole. The
occupation of the individual in his life's task, his performance
of duty, and his formation of character, demand the form of
independence and responsibility. This always stands out in
the forefront, however definitely he leans on Divine grace.
But if, in his own estimation of himself, he merges himself
in the whole which his activity serves, if he spends his life
upon a service which can only be understood in the light of
that whole, and which he has come by without being able to
urge the existence of previous purpose due to himself, then
the judgment expressed by Paul is the true standard of the
humility which befits a Christian.

On the other hand, a closer examination of the conception of justification reveals the fact that this Divine operation
does not imply the occurrence of any mechanical process in
man. For part of the significance of its relation to faith is,
that this self-active faculty in man, without regard to which
justification cannot be fully understood, is included under
this Divine operation; part, that justification, as calling forth
the reaction of faith in man, is in this sense a property of
the believer, and continues to be the motive of the religious
demeanour which it behoves him to adopt. In both relations,
therefore, the conceptions of the Kingdom of God and justification are homogeneous. This holds true in so far as, for
one thing, both notions express operations of Divine grace;
and, for another, the results of these operations manifest
themselves solely in activities which exhibit the form of
personal independence. They offer, therefore, really no

3

obstacle to their being linked together in a complete view
of Christianity. But in Dogmatics this alternating use of
the two principles cannot be avoided. Dogmatics comprehends all religious processes in man under the category of
Divine grace, that is, it looks at them from the standpoint
of God. But it is, of course, impossible so thoroughly to
maintain this standpoint in our experience, as thereby to
obtain complete knowledge of the operations of grace. For
the standpoint of our knowledge lies in formal opposition to
God. Only for an instant can we transfer ourselves to the
Divine standpoint. A theology, therefore, which consisted
of nothing but propositions of this stamp could never be
understood, and would be composed of words which really
did not express knowledge on our part. If what is wanted
is to write theology on the plan not merely of a narrative of
the great deeds done by God, but of a system representing
the salvation He has wrought out, then we must exhibit the
operations of God—justification, regeneration, the communication of the Holy Spirit, the bestowal of blessedness in the
summum bonum—in such a way as shall involve an analysis
of the corresponding voluntary activities in which man
appropriates the operations of God. This method has been
already adopted by Schleiermacher. Now those who are
strangers to the work of theology urge against this method,
that what they are concerned about is the objective bearing
of theological doctrines and not the interpretation of them
as reflected in the subject, and that this method renders
the whole matter uncertain. Such a view is at variance
with the right theory of knowledge ; for in knowledge we
observe and explain even the objects of sense-perception, not
as they are in themselves, but as we perceive them. If
what is intended in Dogmatics is merely to describe objectively Divine operations, that means the abandonment of
the attempt to understand their practical bearing. For apart
from voluntary activity, through which we receive and utilise
for our own blessedness the operations of God, we have no
means of understanding objective dogmas as religious truths.

Objective knowledge in this region is disinterested knowledge. Such knowledge, it is true, is quite in place in natural science; but in theology, however coolly we may sketch out its formal relations, we have to do with spiritual processes of such a kind that our salvation depends on them. Merely objective delineation, therefore, far from exhausting theological cognition, does the work in a most inadequate fashion. Whoever thinks that the method to be followed in this book is such as to evaporate the truths of Christianity and expose them to the perils of doubt, betrays in the last resort the paucity of his religious experience, and especially his ignorance of the fact that the more objectively the truths of Christianity are handed down in narrative form, the closer at hand will doubt be found.

§ 7. Justification, reconciliation, the promise and the task of the Kingdom of God, dominate any view of Christianity that is complete. The outstanding ethical character of this religion comes out in the fact that the *summum bonum*—the Kingdom of God—is promised only as the ground of blessedness, while at the same time it is the task to which Christians are called. Now the teleological relation of justification to this aim may be understood either directly or indirectly. In other words, either we may interpret justification as the bestowal of ability to perform those moral offices towards men which make up the task of the Kingdom of God; and here the relation would be direct. Or we may interpret justification as the restoration of the religious relation to God which the sinner neither has nor of himself can attain; and this would mean his being endowed with an independent valuable quality which, while manifesting itself in its own peculiar functions, would stand related to moral activity towards men only as a *conditio sine quâ non*. Those interpretations are held respectively by the *Catholic* and the *Evangelical Church*. The controversy between the theologians of the two Churches turns on the question which of the two meanings is valid. True, as the controversy is usually carried on by the spokesmen of Catholicism, they generally show themselves ignorant of the fact that on the two sides different implications—which respectively prove Christianity to be a religion and a moral life—are associated with the same terms. For the Roman doctrine of justification professes to state the causes and the means through which a sinner becomes actively righteous; that is, it professes to explain how one who believes in Christ is made capable of his *moral* vocation. Consequently it likewise maintains the co-operation of human freedom with grace. On the other hand, the Reformed doctrine of justification professes to provide reasons *why*, to a Christian who has been regenerated, there is secured, in spite of the permanent imperfection of his moral achievement, communion with God, salvation, and blessedness, or in other words the actual realisation of that *religious* character which Christianity aims at; and *why* he is able to exercise that character by trust in God in all the situations of life (vol. i. pp. 142, 181). Accordingly, it looks as if the controversy between the two great Western Confessions could be brought to a close, if only the one were to see that the other applies the same term to different problems, or if we could expect either to alter its dogmatic phraseology. For the difficulty seems to lie merely in the Catholic error of supposing that we, with our different interpretation of justification, mean to get at the same fact as the Catholics express by their conception. Now, as we acknowledge under the rubric of regeneration and sanctification what the Catholics call justification, the Catholic rubric of "making righteous" (*Gerechtmachung*) might perhaps be accepted for the former, and our conception of justification be replaced by the rubric of reconciliation or restoration to God. Such a change in phraseology would allay the controversy, *if it really were a verbal one*. But a readjustment of the kind described would only make it more evident that a real discrepancy exists. For what we call justification or reconciliation, what we understand as the *religious* character of the individual's life and as *radically* independent of moral activity, and what we are able, therefore, to show at work in definite religious functions, Catholic doctrine includes under the conception of hope. This function, however, is placed subsequent to the functions of faith and love, in the exercise of which *iusti-ficatio* is attained. The Catholic system is primarily arranged so as to explain the moral activity of the Christian life. Since this activity properly arises from the effort put forth by the free will in harmony with *gratia co-operans*, so likewise hope, which may in an imperfect degree precede love, attains the perfection of its nature because we most confidently set our hope in those whom we know as friends. Now the essential object of hope is eternal blessedness. But in this highest object it embraces every operation of the omnipotence and compassion of God, in other words, the evidences of His providence.[1] On the other hand, the Evangelical conception of justification is intended to explain the *religious* character of the individual's life. That character includes the certainty of eternal life; and instead of dependence on the world through sin has obtained freedom over the world and trust in God's providence, and therefore forms the precondition of the discharge of moral tasks. This method of formulating the contrast between the two Confessions shows that that contrast is qualitative. At the same time, it proves that the saving operations of God can only be understood from the corresponding independent functions of those who receive them. This law, indeed, is stated in such general terms that as yet it does not embrace the grounds which condition the opposition between the religious independence of the Evangelical Christian and the dependence of the Catholic. Nevertheless, this practical version of the contrast between the two Confessions leads to a peculiar limitation of the problem presented to theology in the conception of justification. The Divine operation which it expresses must be interpreted as being such that the religious appropriation of it guarantees to the believer an independence which specifically distinguishes his position from the dependence which is imposed by Catholicism.

[1] Thomas Aquinas, *Summa theol.* ii. 2 qu. 17, art. 8.

If the opposition between the Confessions, which attaches to the controversy about the conception of justification, extends so far as this, then the divergence from the doctrine of the Reformation which Döllinger [1] perceives in certain formulae, used by Evangelical theologians, gives but little prospect of reunion between the Churches. For those Evangelical theologians who interpret justification as an analytical judgment upon the value of subjective faith, will hardly agree to those conclusions which, in the Catholic system, are bound up with the conception of "making righteous" (*Gerechtmachung*). Their apparent approximation to the Catholic form of doctrine is to be accounted for partly by Pietism and partly by dialectical difficulties attending the old Lutheran view of justification as a synthetic judgment regarding the individual sinner, and that, too, a judgment conditional on the sinner's faith, which springs out of regeneration (vol. i. pp. 304, 550). These difficulties, however, must and can be removed by another form of statement.

§ 8. Justification, as understood by the Evangelical Church, signifies in general the act of God which gives to believers in Christ their peculiar religious character. The Divine operation on the believer, indicated in this conception, is a positive one. Yet not only does Paul, to whom we owe this terminology, interchange at will the positive term— justification—with one which has a negative ring—*the forgiveness of sins;* but in the discourses of Christ (with the exception of Luke xviii. 14) we meet with the latter form alone. This is due to the fact that it rests directly on Old Testament modes of thought, while the conception coined by Paul is designed to oppose the Pharisaic perversion of the idea of active righteousness (vol. ii. p. 308). It was possible for Jesus, like the men of the Old Testament, to rest satisfied with the negative term, inasmuch as they alike employed it in estimating sinful phenomena in the life of the people of Israel. For however much the sins of the Israelites, for which forgiveness is either expected or bestowed, are regarded

[1] *Kirche und Kirchen*, p. 429.

as *ipso facto* disturbing their proper fellowship with God, yet the actual continuance of that fellowship for the people of Israel, according to the terms of the Old Covenant, is taken for granted both by Old Testament witnesses and by Christ. On the other hand, Paul was directly led to construct the positive conception of justification; for he opposes it to his view of the total sin of humanity, in which he on principle disregards the fact that, in the community constituted by the Mosaic law, the Jews possessed a form (though inferior) of fellowship with Divine grace. For while, in particular cases, he can hardly divest his mind of the impression he had of the advantages possessed by the Israelites over the heathen in virtue of their having the law (Rom. ii. 17–20, iii. 1, 2, ix. 4, 5), yet these advantages are ignored in his decisive utterances about the sin of the human race, and about the function of the law in multiplying sin. Since Paul, therefore, finds justification through Christ foreshadowed, not in the legal community of Israel, but only in the promise connected with Abraham and in the sayings of later prophets, and since he sees in justification a saving operation of God on the totality of mankind which is counteractive of universal sin, he prefers the conception which is unquestionably positive, and only employs the term "forgiveness of sins," which he borrows from the Old Testament, to clear up the meaning of his own.

Now the fact that the Reformers used these two conceptions by turns, and expressly ascribed to them complete equivalence and identical scope, is explained by the influence of their situation within the Church as the sphere of positive fellowship with Divine grace. When contrasted with this organisation of grace, even the sinfulness of men within the Church, however severely he judged it, appeared to Luther exceptional, so that he found the negative expression clear enough for describing the counteractive force. Yet the positive expression "justification" was recommended, not merely by Paul's usage of it, but also by its antithetical relation to universal sin; and so the Reformers did not

scruple to treat both terms as synonymous even in this connection. For while, to begin with, they steadfastly kept the
positive grace of God in sight as the basis of the whole
saving dispensation, and asserted in consequence that the
relation established by grace constitutes the acknowledged
standing of Christians before God, it seemed to them all one
whether grace, in the form of justification, stood opposed to
man's general state of unrighteousness, or, in the form of
the forgiveness of sins, served to remove the derangement of
Christians' gracious fellowship with God. The attempt to
distinguish the two conceptions appeared in Dogmatics for
the first time after there had been elaborated the idea of the
justice of God and of the law as the original dispensation
determining the relation between men and God ; and there-
upon grace retired into the position of a Divine dispensation
which is merely relative. Not until the circumstances had
thus changed do we find the forgiveness of sins discriminated
as the negative, and justification as the positive effect.
Nevertheless, side by side with this later view, there re-
asserted itself from time to time the contention of the
Reformers, that the two expressions differ only *verbaliter*,
while in respect of the fact which they denote they are
identical (vol. i. p. 279). Historical reasons therefore
demand that our definition of the idea of justification should
base itself on the assumption that justification is synonymous
with forgiveness of sins.

§ 9. Now orthodox theologians of the Lutheran as well
as the Reformed school understand by forgiveness of sins
the remission of those penalties which according to Divine
justice necessarily follow sins. Now, since the same theologians regard the whole human race in every single instance
as so sunk in sin that all particular actual transgressions
of the commandments of God can add nothing to the guilt
which descends from our first parent to all his posterity, the
forgiveness of sins through Christ is taken to signify the
removal of the penalties which our first parent brought on
himself and his race. They believe that a mere reference

to this hereditary connection entirely exempts them from the task of proving emancipation from penalties a fact in the life of believing and justified persons. What we must rather investigate is the connections of punishment in the doctrine of sin which is premised, and there we discover what immunity from penalties signifies for believers. The old theologians take the conception of guilt as a consequence of sin into consideration only in so far as it expresses the objective liability of sinners to suffer penalties (vol. i. p. 407). The latter are then described and divided into various categories. The penalties of sin, which ensue if they are not averted by the forgiveness of Christ, are, according to Hollatz, partly temporal and partly eternal, partly positive (*sive sensus*) and partly privative (*sive damni*), partly personal and partly public and common. The middle classification embraces the whole series of painful evils, and death in its threefold sense, as bodily, spiritual, and eternal. Hollatz [1] remarks about this customary division, that it is not logical; that for one thing bodily and spiritual death as phenomena in time are together opposed to eternal death ; that eternal death, again, must be conceived as the continuation of spiritual death ; and, finally, that bodily death is only a result of the separation of the soul from the body, and not a privation in itself as spiritual death is. It would, he thinks, be advisable to include bodily death among the evils of the earthly life, over against which stands spiritual and eternal death as *poena damni*. This is the view taken by Wendelin [2] when he divides punishment into temporal and eternal death, and the former again into bodily death, inclusive of every ill, and spiritual death, which embraces bondage to the devil, the world, and sin.

Nevertheless, if we try to discover from these theologians what the conception is which all these different phenomena of punishment exemplify, we shall hardly find it anywhere developed purposely and completely. It is true that so far

[1] *Examen theologicum*, ii. 2. 20, p. 504.
[2] *Christianae theologiae libri duo*, i. 9. 9, p. 204.

as the relation to God of punishment for sin is concerned,
it is conceived of as His counteractive to sin, demanded by
His retributory justice, and necessary to His honour. But
we also want to know what it is for men, and under what
common characteristic all the various penal phenomena may
be grouped. No one belonging to the old Lutheran school
has directed his attention to this problem. Instead, Baier[1]
offers us an even more detailed account, *de morte seu damnatione aeterna* and *de morte temporali.* It is only in Reformed
theologians and the later Lutherans, Hollatz, Buddeus,
and Fresenius, that suggestions of varied range occur which
serve to determine the meaning of the whole series of ideas.
They amount to this, that punishment of sin, in so far as
it is conceived as a permanent consequence of sin, and
is not annulled by redemption, expresses *the separation of
sinners from God,* the suspension of man's proper fellowship
with Him.[2] The statements quoted from these theologians
all more or less explicitly start from the Biblical view that
the proper welfare and common good of men lies in the
presence of God ; and in contrast therewith it is rightly
inferred that the greatest evil which follows sin as its consequence is the ultimate withdrawal of His presence. Supposing, then, that no other difficulty exists, it is in keeping

---

[1] *Theol. posit.* i. cap. 7, 8.

[2] *Conf. Helv.*, post. 8 : " Poenis subiicimur iustis, adeoque a deo abiecti
essemus omnes, nisi nos reduxisset Christus liberator.". Amesius, *Medulla,* i.
16 : "Consummatio mortis—est amissio boni infiniti. Spiritualis mortis consummatio est totalis ac finalis derelictio, qua homo separatur penitus a facie,
praesentia vel favore dei." Witsius, *De oeconomia foederum dei,* iii. 6. 5 :
"Mortui sumus in Adamo omnes, hoc est, a deo remotissime seiuncti, sive ut
Paulus loquitur, alienati a vita dei." Heidegger, *Corp. theol.,* Loc. ix. 59 : "Poena
mortis nomine comprehensa . . . Est autem in universum mors separatio
eorum, quae prima origine sua coniuncta fuerunt. Cum igitur homo integer
a deo creatus et ipse cum dei sanctitate per imaginem dei actu coniunctus
fuerit, . . . horum omnium separatio mortis nomen et omen habuit." Rodolf,
Catechesis Palat. p. 70 : "Non mirum, omnes istos unius poenae, puta mortis,
gradus id habere commune inter se, quod notionem privationis vel separa-
tionis animae totiusque hominis a bono, cuius possessio felicitatem affert,
includant." Hollatz, ii. 2. 20 : "Mors spiritualis est separatio a gratioso dei
consortio ; aeterna est separatio a visione et fruitione dei beatifica." Buddeus,
ii. 3. 13 : "Sequitur, damnatos omnibus istis, quae communionem cum deo
consequuntur, destitui." Fresenius, *Rechtfertigung,* iv. 7 : "the ground of all
punishment is separation from God."

with the facts to define the forgiveness of sins—as consisting in the removal of the total penalty attached to original sin —as that operation of God which restores sinners, separated as such from Him, to the presence of God and their proper fellowship with Him.   And this operation on God's part, too', would take place despite the fact that those who have been brought back out of a state of separation from God are sinners by their own action and hereditary nature.   This definition of forgiveness, it is true, was not arrived at by any of the old theologians.   Nevertheless, the interpretation we have given of the remission of sins is in harmony with their suggestions regarding the punishment of sin.

And yet, of the theologians referred to, none but Rodolf and Heidegger, properly speaking, are tied to this conclusion. This is due to their identifying the conception of separation from God with death in its general sense as punishment for sin.   The others put that interpretation solely on the privative penalties of spiritual and eternal death (*poena damni*), not on bodily death and the equivalent evils of our earthly life (*poena sensus*).   There is, however, no doubt that the identification of forgiveness with remission of punishment primarily implies the removal of evils, which, indeed, are not to be described as bodily, in the sense that they do not concern the spirit at all, but which are always marked by sensible excitations, and thereby differentiated from the privative or purely ideal character of the other species of punishment for sin.   The intense longing for forgiveness which we find in the Psalms regularly includes, as has been shown (vol. ii. p. 58), an expectation of the deliverance of the nation from political servitude.   Thus the demand of the righteous, that God would acknowledge their righteousness as such, always includes the condition that they shall be spared the, evils of persecution.   So far as these evils excite pain, they pertain to their feeling for the honour of the nation, or of individual righteous persons; but in this connection they are also invariably bound up with external circumstances.   The view which the old theologians take of *poena sensus* is undoubtedly determined by these experiences and impressions, so that the division of positive penal evils into outward and inward, which we find, *e.g.* in Heidegger (x. 83), neither gives a correct representation of the facts of the case, nor harmonises with the necessary psychology of the subject. Accordingly, the various evils of the earthly life, those which are individual as well as those which are common, in which an outward stimulus communicated through the senses is bound up with a feeling of pain at the contraction of life, are interpreted by most of the old theologians as punishment for sin, in such a way as to contrast it with the privative *poena damni*, ideal separation from God. And although Heidegger and Rodolf subsume the former species under the latter, instead of opposing them, and thus exalt *separatio a Deo* to the rank of a generic conception, including all punishments for sin, they have certainly not earned the right to do so by proof. Therefore the above-mentioned definition of forgiveness or remission of punishment, which makes it consist in the removal of the sinner's separation from God, and which has been maintained as following from their view, cannot yet be affirmed to be such as would express the mind of Protestant orthodoxy as a whole.

In the old theology, however, though the manifold evils of earth and bodily death are regarded as penalties for sin, yet this estimate is everywhere accompanied by a peculiar reservation. The leaders of the old school, while making this affirmation regarding earthly evils, lay down the principle that while these evils have *the significance of punishment* for sinners who remain such, on the other hand, for the redeemed, reconciled, believing, and pious, they possess *the value of chastisement and trial.*[1] To emphasise the importance of this dis-

---

[1] Gerhard, *Loci theol.*, Loc. x. 125 (tom. iv. p. 366): "Quamvis credentes originalis et aliorum peccatorum remissionem per Christum et propter Christum obtineant, nihilo tamen minus calamitatibus huius vitae et temporali morti manent obnoxii. Causae huius rei sunt, 1. ut peccatum in carne adhuc haerens mortificetur ; 2. ut peccati gravitate agnita simus remissionis grata mente perpetuo memores ; 3. ut exercitia fidei, patientiae et obedientiae in cruce nobis proponantur. Magnum interea discrimen est inter poenas impoenitentibus et incredulis, deo nondum reconciliatis debitas, et inter has paternas castigationes

tinction, let me add that it was not won at the first onset.
For Melanchthon, who devotes his attention to the subject in
a division of the third edition of the *Loci theologici*,—that is,
in what is clearly a supplementary way,—has not yet arrived
at the necessary demarcation. He distinguishes four kinds
of sufferings (*calamitates*), τιμωρίαι, δοκιμασίαι, μαρτύριον,
λύτρον. Of these the last term applies exclusively to Christ.
The first applies to believers and unbelievers alike; it is
differentiated, by the Divine purpose to incite to repentance,
from punishment as mere retribution, yet comes under the
principle of Divine wrath.[1]   Next, however, this element of
Divine wrath is expressly abandoned and replaced by *paterna
castigatio piorum*, Alting and Wendelin using, for believers,
alternately the terms τιμωρία and παιδεία, and differentiating
from them δοκιμασία and μαρτύριον.   Finally, later writers,
Cocceius, Heidegger, Baier, Hollatz, have, in the first place,
the term παιδεία, while they expressly reserve τιμωρία for
punishment as retribution, a species which does not apply to
believers.   The evils, therefore, which come upon believers
are not inconsistent with their state of salvation, but are the
progressive instruments and marks of its attainment.   Definite transgressions on the part of believers, it is true, give
occasion for chastisements (or educative penalties).   Nevertheless, these evils must be put down as relative goods from
the point of view of salvation, because God's guiding purpose
is to induce repentance· by their means.   Those evils which
serve to test believers may be viewed in the same light with
all the more certainty that they are not occasioned by distinct
instances of sin.   Finally, affliction in the form of martyrdom,
as direct testimony to the standing in salvation of those upon

---

piis et reconciliatis impositas ; illae enim procedunt ab irato iudice, hae vero a
benignissimo patre ; illae sunt initia aeternarum poenarum, hae vero cum hac
vita desinunt." Baier, ii. 1. 15, p. 426 ; Hollatz, ii. 2. 19, p. 503 ; Henr.
Alting, i. 9, p. 138 ; Wendelin, i. 12. 2, p. 234 ; Coccejus, *de foed. et test. dei*,
cap. xv. p. 608 ; Heidegger, Loc. x. 92, 94.

   [1] *C. R.* xxi. p. 953 : "Sunt opera iustitiae divinae, per quae vult deus com-
monefieri et nos et alios de sua iustitia. . . . Quamquam autem hae poenae sunt
opera iustissimae irae dei, tamen exstant in ecclesia promissiones, quae affirmant,
in hac ipsa ira deum tamen velle, ut ad filium mediatorem confugiamus."

whom it falls, contributes in the fullest sense to their honour.
And it is simply as an inference from the conception of
fatherly chastisement and of the abrogation of the penal
significance of *all* earthly ills, so far as concerns the person
of the quondam sinner, that certain of the Reformed divines
deny even to bodily death a penal character in the case of
believers.[1]   Finally, light is thrown on the distinction of *castigatio piorum* from *poena* by the fact that the Evangelicals
repudiate the Catholic doctrine of " satisfactions " in the sacrament of penance.   This doctrine, as found in the decree of
the fourteenth session of the Tridentine Synod, cap. viii., aims
at showing that the "satisfactions " which priests impose in the
sacrament of penance serve "non tantum ad novae vitae cus-
todiam et infirmitatis medicamentum, sed etiam ad praeteri-
torum peccatorum vindictam et castigationem "; and the 13th
Canon adds : " pro peccatis quoad poenam temporalem deo
per Christi merita satisfieri poenis ab eo inflictis et patienter
toleratis vel a sacerdote iniunctis."   Accordingly, those evils
which are to be considered consequences of sin are still viewed
as of a penal character, even for such as are reconciled
through the sacrament of penance, inasmuch as they are
either borne with patience or have their place supplied by
Church exercises prescribed by the priest.   In opposition to
this, Calvin and Chemnitz [2] bring forward that very distinction
between the punishment of unbelievers and the chastisement

---

[1] Baier, iii. 5. 11, p. 672, states the principle : " Reatus peccatorum, licet non
tollatur ab ipsis peccatis, quia hoc ipso, quod peccata sunt, poena quoque digna
sunt, tollitur tamen ab homine peccatore."   More distinctly, Wendelin, p. 234 :
"Pertinet ad παιδείαν mors corporalis piorum, quae non est satisfactio pro
peccato, sed peccati deo maximopere displicentis indicium et abolitio peccati,
necessarium ingressus in gloriam antecedens." Heidegger, p. 369 : " Neque mors
fidelium poena proprie dicta est, quia eorum, in quibus Christus est, corpus
dicitur mortuum propter peccatum (Rom. viii. 10).   Non enim corpus moritur
propter peccatum vindicandum vel expiandum, sed deponendum et abolendum."

[2] *Institutio christ. relig.* iii. 4, pp. 31, 32 : " Ubicunque poena est ad ultionem,
ibi maledictio et ira dei se exserit, quam semper a fidelibus continent.   Castigatio contra et dei benedictio est et amoris habet testimonium, ut docet scriptura."   *Examen conc. Trid.* (Genev. 1641) p. 400 : "Omnino statuendum est
discrimen inter poenas et afflictiones, quae infliguntur impiis et quae imponun-
tur reconciliatis. . . . Tales igitur temporariae poenae, quas deus reconciliatis
in hac vita imponit, nequaquam sunt ita interpretandae, quasi sint vel merita
remissionis peccatorum vel compensationes poenae aeternae."

of the pious, according to which no evil has for the latter the significance of punishment such as would legally counter-balance their sin.

§ 10. The older theology rested satisfied with the con-clusion that earthly evils, including death, as consequences of sin, have for those sinners who remain so the value of punishment, but for those who are reconciled the value of means of education and of trial. Both conclusions, the one as well as the other, were drawn from Holy Scripture, and no need was felt for knowledge which should advance beyond this standard. Both cases were, as Divine ordinances, viewed as subordinate to the universal end of the Divine glory ; for the rest, the question was not raised whether any other relation than that of opposition obtains between the two affirma-tions, and whether it is possible to observe, in the domain to which they belong, still other analogous but divergent bonds of connection. Nevertheless, an investigation of this kind, advancing beyond Scripture proof, is necessary, in order to test the correctness and the completeness of the above two propositions. These propositions, now, are unlike in form, and heterogeneous in their ruling principles. *Earthly evils* are conceived as *punishments for sin*, without any stress being laid on the consideration whether those who are punished feel and acknowledge them as punishments or not. For the guilt of sin (*reatus*) is understood as meaning merely the *obligatio ad poenam* imposed by the legislator and judge, not the subjective acknowledgment of the righteousness of the punishment. On the other hand, *earthly evils* are inter-preted as *educative penalties*, because the reconciled sinners necessarily view them in the same sense as that in which God inflicts them. In their ruling principles the two propositions are heterogeneous. For the view which regards evils as means of education and trial is governed by the idea of the Divine love, or the highest moral end ; the view which regards them as punishment denotes a simple legal procedure. For every end is determined as a moral end by the fact that it must likewise be conceived as a means to other ends which concern men. Those evils which, as consequences of sin, are inflicted on the reconciled, are conceived as being in themselves divinely purposed, but also and predominantly as means of their education; thus they are given the form of moral ends. On the other hand, the interpretation of evils as punishments carries with it the implication that, on the principle of retribution, they are an end in themselves. In this sense, too, it is considered a matter of indifference whether the penal value of evils is acknowledged by those who are punished or not; in the same sense, the only point of importance is the objective congruity between the degree of evil and the sin. Both features are characteristic of the judicial punishment of the single crime. For, considered in this limited range, punishment ranks as an end in itself, inasmuch as it is measured by the gravity of the crime, and has nothing to do with the question whether it is recognised by the punished person as punishment, or is felt as an untoward accident or a wrong. The older theology, moreover, treats those two so heterogeneous propositions in such a way that the judicial punishment of sin by God appears the rule, the moral education of the reconciled by suffering the exception. That is the sole relationship to one another in which the two propositions are placed.

But for that reason this form of doctrine, if it is to do justice to the problems which it recognises, requires both to be supplemented and to be limited from its own point of view. The statement that it is of no consequence whether or not the penal value of evils is acknowledged by the persons punished, and whether or not with their offence they join a sense of its unworthiness, cannot hold good to such an extent that conversion and the estimating of evils as means of education become unthinkable. For the reconciled, in whose experience and judgment evils are means of education and trial, move out of the circle of sinners upon whom evils are inflicted as punishments. Now, although in the traditional representation the relation of the two propositions is of such a kind that the penal value of evils for sinners forms the rule,

and their educative value for them the exception, yet from the
general character of theology we may deduce another relation
between them.   For all theological propositions have for their
aim the explanation of the phenomena of the Christian life.
Accordingly, the universal judgment affirming the penal value of
evils was formed because the reconciled, in whose experience
evils prove themselves means of education and trial, formerly
stood, as members of the fellowship of sin, under the doom of
punishment, and not only remember this but likewise gauge
the worth of their present status of salvation by contrast
with their former state of punishment.   Now it is a rule that
the change brought about by reconciliation does not rend the
personality in sunder, as is betokened by the fact that the
earlier and later states are combined in a single self-
consciousness.   Now it is essential for the status of reconciliation that the evils which are inflicted by God for our
education and trial should be known by us as such, and
therefore the transition from the earlier stage to the later
cannot be correctly conceived, unless at the former there has
existed a manifestation of self-consciousness appropriate to it.
That is, one who is later reconciled must, in the status of sin,
have been conscious of the penal value of evils, if later he is to
be conscious of their saving worth.   Without this the identity
of the person at both stages is not assured.   Thus, even if
we had to suppose that the status of sin in general is not
accompanied by a consciousness of guilt, there would at least,
in order to explain the transition to reconciliation, have to be
conceived a middle stage, at which those who are later reconciled manifest their tendency towards this goal by their
consciousness of guilt in the status of sin.   And the older
theologians do assume this middle stage.   But it is only in
the doctrine of *poenitentia* that they have made it valid.
Now, if their general view of the penal state of sinners is
correct, namely, that in the *reatus* as *obligatio ad poenam* there
is absolutely no question of subjective consciousness of guilt.
then between this proposition and the estimation of evils by
the reconciled as means of education, there would fall to be

4

considered the third case, that by those sinners who attain to reconciliation, evils are previously recognised as punishments, through their consciousness of guilt. Only so do we exhaustively cover the whole domain, and mediate a connection between the two other contrary cases.

For the present purpose this demonstration, as understood in the older Dogmatics, is enough to prove that, if the forgiveness of sins is likewise remission of penalty, those sinners who experience remission of penalty must previously be conceived as persons who trace back their punishments to their guilt through the consciousness of guilt, in which the right of punishment is acknowledged. Now the time has not yet come for inquiring what right Christian theology has to take for granted, as the supreme rule of the Divine world-order, the recompensing of human actions by rewards and punishments, thus explaining the world-order on the analogy of the State or civil society. While admitting here, provisionally and dialectically, the correctness of this theological view as a whole, I wish to show that in this very circle the exclusion of the consciousness of guilt from the necessary characteristics of human guilt against God is untenable, and that the merely objective interpretation of these characteristics does not harmonise with other necessary aspects of this general view. In this connection I *first of all* recall the fact that the conception of punishment and guilt which is before us is borrowed from the judicial punishment of the single crime. The meaning of this is that that conception does not exhaust the significance of punishment for civil society or the State. Certainly it is of no consequence to the judge who, in the name of the State, exercises the power to punish, whether or not those who are punished acknowledge their punishment as just, and whether or not they are conscious of their crime as guilt. But, as a whole, it is not a matter of no consequence to the State how its power to punish is regarded by its citizens, especially by the victims of punishment themselves. Civil society exists at all only through the moral disposition of its members in favour of law in general, and of the existing legislation as a whole. If this disposition is shaken by the revolutionary temper of the citizens, so that either the existent form of the State, or the form of the State in general, ceases to be regarded as binding, the danger of the situation comes out especially in this, that civil punishments are not regarded as being such, but as arbitrary acts of violence. From the relatively moral peculiarity of character belonging to civil society, therefore, it follows that it has to aim at punishments inflicted by the State being acknowledged by the punished parties' consciousness of guilt. Now, if fellowship between God and man is to be conceived as taking the form of civil society, it follows that the hitherto current theological inter-pretation of evils as punishments for sin is incomplete. The guilt of sinners ought not to be conceived merely as an objective *obligatio ad poenam*, but must also embrace the feature of subjective consciousness of guilt, through which sinners, who are under God's legal power, acknowledge His power to punish. If, on the contrary, sinners regularly accept the punishments inflicted by God as aimless accidents, or even as wrongs done by God to them, then the permanent legal fellowship between God and sinners would become con-fused and insecure, and thus the view of the world defended by the older theologians would collapse. But there is a second circumstance which, in the traditional theology, works counter to the above interpretation of guilt. It is just by the status of universal human sin that theologians prove the validity of the legal fellowship of God with men. But this necessarily implies that the sinners who experience at God's hand nothing but punishment, acknowledge it to be right. For otherwise the Divine legal order would not be valid for them. This part of Dogmatics is under the influence of the models of pre-Christian religions in which the State is directly assumed as the sphere and the standard of men's relation to God, and in which, accordingly, there are called forth lively expressions of guilt against the gods. But, further, this part of Dogmatics is so framed as to prepare the mind for under-standing redemption through Christ ; therefore, to the universal fact of sin is appended the universal need of redemption, the fact of which can only be proved from a lively feeling of guilt. From these considerations the accompanying interpretation of guilt, as a merely objective relationship, is unsatisfactory even for the older Dogmatics itself.

That this conception should be supplemented by the inclusion of the consciousness of guilt as a normal feature is rendered necessary, *secondly*, by the consideration that for sinners as sinners punishment is not to be exhausted by earthly evils and natural death ; these inflictions, on the contrary, are to find their continuation and consummation in spiritual and eternal death.   By spiritual death is meant that hardening of the sinful will which leaves no prospect of conversion to good.   Such a condition is conceivable only if we presuppose that the consciousness of guilt, which as a rule accompanies sin, and under certain circumstances makes conversion possible, is crushed out.   Nevertheless this process contains no guarantee that with a heightened degree of sin altogether the consciousness of guilt will entirely disappear.   It is at work, without doubt, in the unhappiness and despair of lost men, and that it is entirely awanting in the hardened, is improbable.   If, then, in orthodox theology it is assumed that those who are condemned to eternal punishment recognise its justice,[1] it is inconsistent to deny altogether to the hardened that consciousness of guilt, without which they cannot acknowledge their state of punishment before God.   If it be said that this knowledge of the damned is the effect of their condemnation, and permits us to draw no conclusion regarding phenomena of deep-dyed sin in this world, yet the feeling of guilt in which that knowledge takes its rise cannot be awakened where it has once been wholly eradicated.   But if this is to be regarded as being the rule with the hardened, then the above assertion of Baier becomes all the more uncertain.   At least the view of the world-order

[1] Baier, i. 7. 6 : "Damnati poenarum, quibus affliguntur, meritum animo reputant."

—based on the double retribution of God—which in the older theology is assumed as a self-evident truth, takes the appearance of a questionable hypothesis, unless it be admitted that even the hardened normally possess ultimately so much feeling of guilt as to glorify God's justice in their punishment.

This inquiry was set on foot in order to discover whether Rodolf and Heidegger had good reason for subsuming under the idea of separation from God not only the *poena damni*, the privative and purely ideal punishments of spiritual and eternal death, but also the *poena sensus*, while elsewhere these classes of punishment were opposed to one another under the categories of the positive and the privative, the sensible and the spiritual. Since we have seen that the penal state of sinners is not conceivable at all apart from the varied relations of its elements to the consciousness of guilt, and especially apart from the fact that the evils of the earthly life can be understood as punishment only when viewed in the light of the consciousness of guilt, the question is what, in this connection, is meant by consciousness of guilt. We must not anticipate a complete definition of it. But it always finds its immediate expression in removal from the person whom we know ourselves to have offended. Thus, in relation to God, it is ever a form of the separation of sinners from God, as contrasted with the universal destination of men for fellowship with God. If on this there depends the estimation of earthly evils as punishments, then these evils likewise come to stand under the principle of that separation of our life from God which runs counter to the destination of man. Thus, then, the view put forward by the theologians named above is confirmed. All kinds of punishment for sin are the expression of a separation of sinners from God which is counter to their ideal destiny. If, therefore, forgiveness of sins is the removal of the penal state of sinners, it follows that it brings back those who are separated from God by sin into nearness or fellowship with God. It is to be defined, then, as the *removal of the separation* which, in consequence of sin, has entered in between man and God.

§ 11. Among the relations which go to make up the separation of sinners from God, the rest are overtopped by the consciousness of guilt, partly as a condition of the varied gradations of punishment, partly in so far as it is not an objective attribute, but a subjective function of the sinner. We ought therefore rather to transpose " the removal of the separation of sinners from God" into *the removal of the consciousness of guilt.* In so far as God is conceived as its Author, it is, of course, to be understood as running counter to the process which takes place in hardening. Now, from the ethical standpoint which we owe to Kant, Tieftrunk contended for the interpretation of forgiveness as liberation from the consciousness of offence (vol. i. pp. 436, 466). The discovery of the consciousness of guilt as the consequence and the test of the freedom of the will and the absolute validity of the moral law, coinciding with the inexplicable fact of the radical strain of evil in man, enabled this disciple of Kant to perceive clearly the rule of common moral knowledge—that, if an injured benefactor remits to his thankless beneficiary outward penalties, but, nevertheless, consistently repudiates him with undiminishing contempt, such a species of pardon is simply worth nothing. In making this the measure of his claim upon the Christian meaning of the forgiveness of sins, he surrendered the contention that with forgiveness there is bound up a direct liberation from the penalties (evils) incurred in the status of sin, which work on in accordance with the universal Divine world-order. Accordingly, he likewise proves his agreement with the Christian estimate of evils upheld by the orthodox, by concluding that the amended person, who wins pardon and has attained to a love for the law, will gladly bear the punishments which he has merited. Even if this conception stops short of the precision of the Christian view of evils which continue to act, and drags in the fact of moral improvement in a strange fashion, yet even this theory witnesses to the truth of the result arrived at above. For as the consciousness of guilt, not suppressed yet also not relieved, is a precondition of evils being viewed as punishments, so there follows, from the removal by God of the consciousness of guilt, the reversal of our judgment about them, and the sense that they are relative blessings which we homologate.

The dialectic transformation of the earlier established conception of forgiveness into this conception of Tieftrunk, overleaps the distinction which served to draw Töllner away from the traditional form of doctrine (vol. i. p. 398), and around which there revolve the reflections of the *Aufklärung* theologians. In the process of the historical development of theology it is significant, indeed, that a distinction was drawn by Töllner between guilt and the obligation to endure punishment, and that, besides the discharge of the latter by the suffering of Christ, a special act of grace on God's part was insisted on for the former. For here there first appears an impulse to an ethical criticism of the problem of reconciliation, a problem which could not be exhaustively treated with legal conceptions. But this stimulus remained ineffectual, because it apprehended the moral idea of guilt merely objectively, without respect to the consciousness of guilt. For this reason Töllner himself could find no sure determination of the relation between the conceptions of guilt and punishment which he had distinguished, and Eberhard arrived at the idea that the aim of punishment is to convince men of their offence (vol. i. p. 403). This statement is incorrect and intrinsically obscure. If punishment, as has been indicated, is to be understood as a legal method of dealing with the single criminal, then the judge who imposes the punishment has, as a judge, nothing to do with the moral impression made by the punishment upon the person punished. Nor does the result in any way answer to the definition of punishment as stated. The conjunction of ideas which Eberhard has formed, however, confuses two domains of life, the legal and the moral. For the guilt of which punishment is to convince men, is not limited to these features of the case through which the judge arrives at his verdict of guilty. The judge has to confine himself to ascertaining whether the criminal is the cause of the given illegal action, as tested by his cognisable intention and his cognisable purpose. But if the criminal is to be made aware of his guilt through his punishment, this means that he is to interpret his act and its intention from the whole bearing of his conduct, from his general responsibility for himself, in other words, he is to interpret it as a datum of moral unworthiness. These elements of the situation converge in the feeling of guilt. Hence it follows just as distinctly that even moral guilt can never be completely conceived without the element of the feeling of guilt, but also that a judicial punishment may perhaps, under special circumstances, awaken or intensify the feeling of guilt in a condemned man, though this consummation cannot be proved to be the purpose of judicial punishment. He who has the true feeling of guilt will necessarily understand and acknowledge the punishment he has incurred; the opposite holds good only in accidental cases.

If we abstract from the connection between punishment and guilt, we shall find it impossible to form a complete, universal, and practically applicable conception of moral guilt without the element of the feeling of guilt. If we think ourselves into the case when " thy brother sinneth against thee," the ascertainment of this case is intended to move the other, by the awakening of his feeling of guilt, to acknowledge the offence he has committed. For that this is the character of his action can only be made out through a united and consentient judgment. If the other will not confess to having offended in his action, even though his attitude be due to obstinacy or a lack of sensibility, the accusing judgment of the injured person does not suffice definitively to subsume the case in question under the idea of guilt. We should be justified in finding anticipatively in the accusation a judgment affirming the guilt of the other only provided we ascertain that through negligence or wickedness he has disabled or suppressed his feeling of guilt. But even in this case our judgment has regard indirectly to the element of the feeling of guilt. Without this the assertion of the moral guilt of another is always uncertain. But what is wanted cannot be that we should form a conception of moral guilt so little determinate that it can never be used with any certainty, or only at the risk of filling with pride the man who finds such a conception satisfactory.

§ 12. If forgiveness, according to Töllner, is to be conceived as the removal by God of the guilt of man, it is certain that the conception of guilt is intended to be understood in the moral sense. For, as has been shown, even the acknowledgment of the punishment they have suffered by those who are punished, has its basis solely in their consciousness of moral guilt. All the more certainly is it the removal by God of moral guilt that is denoted in the Christian use of the term, because the religious-moral goal of the Kingdom of God forms the standard of our conception of sin and guilt. But moral guilt will necessarily come into consideration here along with the element of the feeling of guilt, since unless it is distinctly presupposed the forgiveness of guilt cannot be thought as operating on the guilty. For if, in the contrast between existent guilt and its forgiveness, the identity of the person in whom both are realised is to be preserved, then the guilty who receive forgiveness of their guilt must be distinguished first by their clear consciousness of their guilt and by a lively feeling of pain about it. Conversely, the removal of the consciousness of guilt must likewise be so interpreted that it includes the removal of real guilt. For were this not so, even hardening might be conceived as a species of forgiveness. But this is absurd, for hardening denotes that situation of the sinner which is farthest removed from forgiveness.

Guilt, in the moral sense, expresses the disturbance of the proper reciprocal relation between the moral law and freedom, which follows from the law-transgressing abuse of freedom, and as such is marked by the accompanying pain of the feeling of guilt. Guilt is thus that permanent contradiction between the objective and the subjective factor of the moral will which is produced by the abuse of freedom in non-fulfilment of the law, and the unworthiness of which is expressed for the moral subject in his consciousness of guilt. Guilt can be the expression of such a contradiction only provided that, even subsequent to a transgression of the law, both the law and freedom continue to operate, the former as expressing the extent of ends which ought to be realised by the subject, and which therefore necessarily have an attraction for freedom, while freedom is present in the feeling of pain at its having missed its proper direction towards the law. Now, in the Christian view of the world, God is conceived as the Author and the active Representative of the moral law, because the final end which He desires to realise in the world must be realised just through the human race, and because the moral law represents the system of ends which are the means to the common final end. In the Christian sense, therefore, guilt denotes that contradiction of God on which the individual as well as the totality of mankind has entered through the non-fulfilment of the moral law, and which is recognised as present through the consciousness of guilt in which the individual feels with pain the unworthiness of his own sin as well as his share in the guilt of all. By this statement the provisional explanation of the consciousness of guilt as expressive of that separation of men from God which enters in instead of their proper fellowship, is completed and clarified. The form of the idea of space, which lies at the foundation of the previous theory, is filled out by an expression of the logically defective relationship existing between the two factors which ought to be in harmony with one another.

But the *contradiction of God* and our own moral destiny which is expressed in the conception of guilt, and is felt with pain in the consciousness of guilt, is by this concomitant circumstance marked as a real disturbance of human nature. Duns Scotus (vol. i. p. 100) has asserted that, inasmuch as guilt is an ideal relation, it is nothing real, and therefore the forgiveness of sins is nothing real either, but the colourless presupposition of our being made righteous through grace. For even sin, he argues, destroys nothing good which exists, but only something which ought to exist; accordingly, even guilt denotes not a real defect in the soul, but a defect in the relation of the soul to its proper destiny.   But in this verdict no notice is taken of the witness given by the consciousness of guilt, the outcome of which is entirely of a contrary kind.   It does not make use of the distinction laid down by Duns.   Rather does it feel the logical contradiction of the will to God, which is contained in guilt, as a real contradiction, and as a real defect of will.   For the logical contradiction, of which we are guilty in an act of objective knowledge, betokens the fact that we have taken a wrong path in knowledge.   But in our knowledge of things according to their peculiar final end we come upon existing contradictions between individual mediating members and the end of the whole.   This fact makes itself apparent especially in evil as an effect of the will, since the essence of the will, or its freedom, consists in its working the good as its final end. If this is baulked by the production of evil, the accompanying consciousness of guilt attests both the lasting validity for the will of the good final end, and also the real injury which freedom has sustained through the production of evil.   Thus in the domain of the will, sin, as the disturbance of the ideal relation of the will to its final end, or to God as representing that end in the world-order, is a real contradiction.

§ 13. How is *forgiveness, as the removal of guilt by God,* thinkable?   In the Old Testament there is to be found the idea, significant in this connection, that God is willing to remember transgressions no more (Jer. xxxi. 34; Isa. xliii. 25), or to hide them from His sight and no more regard them (vol. ii. p. 195).   But the important point is that in the Divine act of forgiveness there is expressed an ideal relation, since likewise the real significance of sin clings to the subversal of the ideal relation of the will to its final end. The Old Testament figures, that God covers sin, veils it, blots it out, puts it away, express the ideal aspect of the fact, that He renders it inoperative in relation to Himself.   Now this type of representation works on likewise in the ecclesi-

astical tradition, even though it be with limited range, alongside of the interpretation of forgiveness as the remission of
penalty. This is the case, for instance, in the formula of
the Heidelberg Catechism, Question 56, where it is said that
" God will never more remember my sins, nor even the sinful
nature with which I have to struggle all my life long." The
validity of this idea, however, comes into collision with
Löffler's objection (vol. i. p. 408), that the thought of forgiveness, as expressive of an altered disposition, is incompatible with the immutability of God, and the forgiveness
of sins incompatible with His truthfulness, which prohibits
His regarding the guilty as innocent, or one who in details
is guilty as innocent in general. It is incompetent for this
objection as yet to bring into play the argument from the
immutability of God. But the second argument was supplemented on the subjective side by Döderlein and Knapp
(vol. i. p. 425), for they reason to the effect that even the
sinner's conscience will always testify to him that he has
sinned. Thus the removal of guilt and of the consciousness
of guilt would be in contradiction with the validity of the
law of truth for God and for the sinner's conscience.

The importance which the idea of Divine forgiveness has
in Christianity is as far as possible from demanding such an
eradication of the consciousness of guilt as would collide with
truth. Rather is it impossible to esteem the forgiveness of
sins the basis of the Christian religion, unless the memory
of that contradiction of sin to God which is expressed in
the consciousness of guilt continues to operate. On the
contrary, it is actually acknowledged that forgiveness itself
keeps awake the memory of sin and its unworthiness. One
who could so understand the forgiveness of sins as to forget
and consequently to deny his previous sins, would make God
a liar (1 John i. 10)—in other words, would eviscerate the
promise of forgiveness of its meaning. Nor does any contradiction arise from the fact that, in virtue of forgiveness, the
consciousness of guilt is removed, and the feeling of pain
thereat rendered inoperative for the future and the present,

while the memory of the guilt is preserved, and the recollection of the pain previously felt likewise held fast. It is even possible that this recollection itself may call forth pain directly ; but even that leads to no contradiction. For these echoes of pain at sin committed fill other parts of time than does the pleasure arising from forgiveness received, and in the oscillation of feeling to both sides the pleasure surpasses the pain in strength. Thus forgiveness must not be construed as the eradication of the feeling of guilt altogether, but as its removal in a certain aspect. On the other hand, it ought not to be maintained that God can forget the transgression of man if He chooses. For the will of God cannot be thought of as operative in any direction whatsoever which might seem to place Him in contradiction to the knowledge of the truth. This formula, borrowed from the Old Testament, appears, even in the older theologians, for the most part in the modified form that God is willing not to impute, not to estimate, the guilt of man (*non reputare*). This expresses the truth that the fact of man's transgression is preserved in God's memory, while the will of God renders invalid an aspect of that offence which of itself it asserts in the system of things. The question thus is to discover the aspect of guilt which God thus renders inoperative by His intention to forgive sin.

To this end it must be recalled that the discourses of Jesus (Mark xi. 25 ; Luke xi. 4 ; cf. Col. iii. 13) represent God's forgiveness as altogether of the same nature as *pardon* among men. Now the latter is not at all a truth-controverting denial of the fact of an injury ; it rather includes veraciously the recollection of the injury, although the degree of retentiveness which belongs to the human mind admits of our losing the memory of an injury altogether. Pardon rather is an act of will by which there is cancelled that aspect of an injury received which interrupts intercourse between the injured person and the offender. An injury is any action which either entirely destroys a man's honour, or diminishes or impairs it. A man's honour is his standing as an independent moral entity in moral society. The normal consequence of an injury is the cessation of intercourse, the severance of moral fellowship between the injured person and the offender. For the injured person repels the author of the action which has violated his honour. None but men of no honour are accustomed to let mutual injuries pass without any consequence of this kind. Now pardon is possible provided the injured person is really a man of honour, whose honour has unjustly been offended. In that case pardon is the expression of the honourable man's intention to resume intercourse, by the cancelling of which he has upheld his honour against the unjust offender—in other words, to resume moral fellowship with the other. That to this end the offender must have perceived and confessed his wrong and thus besought pardon, is provided for in the simplest injunction given by Christ regarding pardon (Luke xvii. 3, 4).

But we ought not to interchange the conception of pardon with the right of the magistrate to condone. For the latter has reference to civil society, and is manifested in the remission or abridgment of a penalty inflicted with the force of law. A crime leads to the annulment of civil society so far as concerns the will of the criminal himself, but not universally; and punishment does not imply that thereby civil society, as such, is reconstituted for the criminal. Rather would the infliction of a punishment by the power of the State be unintelligible unless, despite the subjective breach of civil society, it were so far indissoluble as not to be dissolved by a State mandate of punishment, e.g. by a decree of banishment. Thus, from the side of the State's power, punishment is really an action of the civil society of which the criminal still remains a member. Thus condonation cannot mean that one who, by his crime, has left civil society altogether, is again received into it. It means rather that judicial cognisance by itself, or a lesser degree of punishment than it has imposed, suffices to give expression to the civil fellowship existing between the State and the criminal.

Thence it follows that the analogy between moral pardon and State condonation is only a remote one. The former excludes all punishment, the latter merely modifies quantitatively the punishment which has already been expressed in the penal sentence; the former is the independent resumption of interrupted moral fellowship, the latter presupposes that the existing civil fellowship is really preserved by the penal sentence. Influenced by their interest in the universal and public significance of Divine forgiveness, orthodox theologians have compared Divine forgiveness to the State-power's right of condonation (vol. i. pp. 267, 337); and they believed that the path they took in this connection was all the safer that the remission of the penalties of sin was assumed to be the content of the conception in question. But not only has that confused mixture of heterogeneous principles lost the support which is to be found in this preconception, but it can no longer hold its ground at all against the distinction, expounded above, between moral pardon and State condonation.

On the other hand, the moral explanation of pardon harmonises with all the indications regarding the direct operation of the Divine forgiveness of sins which the writings of the New Testament attach to the sacrificial death of Christ. It has been proved that the forgiveness of sins and the bringing of men to God are both deduced in the same sense from the sacrificial value of the death of Christ (vol. ii. p. 213). Paul especially uses as equivalent the two propositions that one is justified by faith, and that one has reached in Christ the relation of peace with God (vol. ii. p. 342). If, therefore, the forgiveness of sins is interpreted after the analogy of human pardon, it is as far as possible from signifying such a removal of the guilt of sin and of man's consciousness of guilt as might come to be incompatible with truth. The forgiveness of sins as pardon, rather, merely renders inoperative that result of guilt and the consciousness of guilt which would manifest itself in the abolition of moral fellowship between God and man, in their separation or

mutual alienation. God, in forgiving or pardoning sins, exercises His will in the direction of not permitting the contradiction—expressed in guilt—in which sinners stand to Him,
to hinder that fellowship of men with Him which He intends
on higher grounds. And so far as this intention works
determinatively upon sinners, it does not, indeed, free them
altogether from the consciousness of guilt, but from that
mistrust which, as an affection of the consciousness of guilt,
naturally separates the injured man from the offender.
Granted, too, that the recipient of guilt incurs no new guilt,
his recollection of his transgression, with its indirect excitation of pain, will form a guarantee that the presupposed fact
of guilt is not unveraciously negatived by pardon. Thus
the definition of forgiveness which Steudel brings forward
(vol. i. p. 543) is confirmed, namely, that guilt, which indeed
cannot be forgotten, and therefore cannot altogether be
annihilated, at least forms no restriction upon our re-estab-
lished relation to God.[1]

§ 14. This definition, it is true, is not taken account of
by such theologians as think that a distinction should be
made between the forgiveness of sins and justification, as
between something negative and something positive. If we
had to conceive the forgiveness of sins merely as the negation
of the guilty state or penal state, then the idea of it certainly could not claim to be of decisive importance for the
existence of the Christian religion. For this end we should
rather have to set up a conception of positive content.
Duns Scotus (vol. i. p. 100) offers for consideration the
question whether God may not forgive sins through His
boundless perfection of power, and in doing so omit the
bestowal of habitual grace. He decides against the hypothesis,
possible as it is from God's point of view, on the ground
that One, who through pardon of an injury is no longer an
enemy, is not yet a friend, but is neutral. The forgive-

---

[1] This is not yet the place to inquire how the pardon of guilt *in concreto* is
possible for God, and especially how it harmonises with His character as Lawgiver and Representative of the law ; this aspect of the conception we shall
determine in § 17.

ness of sins, he says, is not the expression of any positive result of the well-pleasingness of a person to God; to this end there must be brought in, in addition, the idea of making righteous (*Gerechtmachung*). The same consideration is at the bottom of *the distinction* made by Lutherans and Reformed *between the forgiveness of sins and justification* (vol. i. p. 279). Even Schleiermacher expresses himself to the same effect (§ 109, 1). But as justification is no longer construed as equivalent to making righteous, but shares in common with the forgiveness of sins the form of a Divine judgment, those who take logic strictly come to the conclusion that justification precedes the forgiveness of sins. For a positive judgment is only apparently the supplement of the corresponding negative; in reality the negative presupposes it. Now justification carries with it the non-imputation of sins, because it is conceived as the imputation of righteousness—in other words, as the imputation of the righteousness which is contained in the twofold obedience of Christ for sinners who believe in Him.

This thought, characteristic of both orthodox schools, is not derived from Paul (vol. ii. p. 326); nor do Luther and Melanchthon give it the preference.[1] The imputation of the righteousness of Christ as a formula for justification, moreover, occurs in Calvin,[2] in whose *Institutes* it is to be found ever since the edition of 1539. Thereafter it is championed by the Lutherans and the Reformed, with the exception of Piscator and his followers. It is clear, too, that as a part of the theological system it forms a deduction from the presupposed legal world-order. It was assumed that the reciprocal relation between God and man is originally and

---

[1] In the *Apology of the Augsburg Confession* the formula occurs thrice, ix. 19, xii. 12 ; most clearly, iii. 184 : " Iustificare significat reum absolvere et pronuntiare iustum, sed propter alienam iustitiam Christi, quae communicatur nobis per fidem. Itaque hoc loco iustitia nostra est imputatio alienae iustitiae."

[2] In the edition of 1559, lib. iii. 11. 2 : " Iustificabitur ille fide, qui Christi iustitiam per fidem apprehendit, qua vestitus in dei conspectu non ut peccator, sed tanquam iustus apparet. Ita nos iustificationem interpretamur acceptionem, qua nos deus in gratiam receptos pro iustis habet. Eamque in peccatorum remissione ac iustitiae Christi imputatione positam esse dicimus." In the editions 1539–1550, cap. ii. (x.) § 2. *C. R.* xxix. p. 738.

5

necessarily bound to the standard of the law of good works. This principle likewise determines the conditions of redemption through Christ. For if men as sinners could not themselves fulfil the law, so as to answer to the righteousness of God and their own blessedness as their end, then Christ, the Founder of the order of grace, had to prove His congruity with the legal world-order by accomplishing in place of sinful humanity the righteousness which is due to the law, and bearing the punishment incurred by men, and both of these had to be imputed by God to each individual who was to be received into the new fellowship of grace with God. This is not yet the place for examining the leading thought of the significance of the law in this world-order. The question rather is, *first*, to ascertain the connection of thought which explains the imputation of the righteousness of Christ, and enables us to determine how the forgiveness of sins is related to this Divine act.

For the righteousness of Christ which is to be imputed to the believer is variously determined, according as there is ascribed to it the value of satisfaction for God or the value of merit on men's behalf (vol. i. pp. 249, 282–286). As *satisfaction* for God the righteousness of Christ consists in His passive and active obedience. The former serves to execute and discharge the penal demands of the law upon sinners, the latter serves to satisfy and discharge the legal demands of the law upon men, which are based upon the fact that the fulfilment of the law is the originally ordained means to blessedness. As *merit* the righteousness of Christ consists in His obedience as a positive whole, which was maintained even in suffering unto death. The righteousness of Christ comes to be imputed to believers in both aspects. When this takes place under the category of satisfaction, there results for believers this negative predicate, that they are released from their penal obligations to the law, as also from their legal obligations to it—in other words, from the necessity of attaining blessedness through fulfilment of the law. Only through the imputation of the righteousness of

Christ as merit does there follow the positive predicate of justification. Now, according to the presuppositions of this doctrine, Quenstedt is consistent in making the satisfaction-value of Christ's righteousness logically precede its merit-value. For the relations of sinners' guilty obligations to the law and men's general legal obligations to it had first of all to be met, ere God's order of grace could be put into operation. Now, if the imputation of the righteousness of Christ likewise follows in the same logical order, then the forgiveness of sins as remission of penalty and release from legal relations to God must precede, and justification as the reckoning to believers of the whole obedience of Christ must come after. But if, as a number of the older theologians demand, justification must logically precede the forgiveness of sins, this implies that the righteousness of Christ comes to be imputed, not as satisfaction, but as merit. For if the meritorious effect of the obedience of Christ, as formulated by Quenstedt, *nos in statum benevolentiae divinae restituit*, it follows that God imposes no more punishments upon believers, and no longer makes their attainment of the goal of blessedness at all dependent on their exercising a legal relationship to Himself.

These distinctions were not clearly realised by the older theologians, and therefore they did not view as a controversy involving the truth, the question whether forgiveness and justification follow in this or the reverse order, or whether, indeed, they are not synonyms. But if justification is once distinguished from the forgiveness of sins as something positive, if positive justification is the logically sufficient ground for the forgiveness of sins, and if, notwithstanding, positive justification can only be understood as the imputation of the merits of Christ, such an explanation cannot claim to differ in effect from the two diverse definitions of forgiveness we have discovered already. For these have themselves a thoroughly positive meaning. The forgiveness of sins as remission of penalties signifies the removal of that separation from God which has been brought about by sin. As separation is the negation of our proper fellowship with God, the removal of separation is to be construed as the positive re-establishment of the fellowship of sinners with God. This is the direct meaning of the definition of Steudel that, owing to the forgiveness of sins, guilt forms no hindrance to the relationship to God which has been established. Now, if through the imputation of the merits of Christ sinners are placed in such a status that God treats them with goodwill, such behaviour on God's part is an expression of the permanent character of the proper fellowship of believers with God. And when, in consequence thereof, He forgives sins, *i.e.* remits penalties, the proof of it is to be found in the fact that the goodwill of God invalidates the penal significance of the evils which believers have to bear in consequence of their sin, of which the further consequence is that believers likewise do not fall under the penalties of spiritual and eternal death.

This argument, it is true, was not completely stated by any of the older theologians. They did not attempt any accurate or complete analysis of the idea of forgiveness, and therefore they always ascribed to it a merely negative effect, and thought that the only way of expressing a positive result was through the imputation of the righteousness of Christ, whether this was added to the negative idea by way of supplement, or logically subordinated to it as its presupposition. Thus we must inquire, *secondly*, whether this positive idea of justification is thinkable. The objections raised to it by Faustus Socinus [1] have reference to the twofold significance of the righteousness of Christ as penal satisfaction and as positive fulfilment of the law (*iustitia*), for he had before him an ⸌rlier stage in the development of the Reformers' doctrine than is in view in the foregoing representation. But what he denotes by the *imputatio iustitiae Christi* has reference to the merit-value of the obedience of Christ, and his denial of the *imputatio satisfactionis Christi* is valid, not only as regards the bearing of the punishment imposed by the law, but also as regards the discharging of its legal claim on men in general.

[1] *De Christo servatore*, lib. iv. cap. 1–6.

For in this connection he declares, founding on a principle of Roman law, that satisfaction and imputation mutually exclude each other. Imputation takes place in legal matters, he says, only where no service has previously been rendered; if, therefore, Christ has accomplished satisfaction, the matter is done with, and no imputation is required (vol. i. p. 328). But the imputation of the righteousness of Christ, he maintains, is absurd, since in other respects believers are bound to acquire righteousness of their own. This basal presupposition of Christianity is annulled by the hypothesis of an imputed righteousness.

Nevertheless this principle of private right does not touch the presupposition of the Reformation doctrine. On the contrary, if it is true that the original world-order consisted in a legal relationship between God and man, answering to the pattern of the State, then the cancelling of it, whether in general or in respect of penal demands, must be imputed to believers, *i.e.* they must be expressly regarded by God in such a way that the standard of the State and of criminal law no longer holds good for their relationship to Himself. Moreover, the imputation of the positive obedience (merit) of Christ is not at all intended by the orthodox to mean that thereby the acquisition of righteousness of their own by believers is excluded. It is regarded only as the precondition enabling God to enter at all into positive fellowship with them for their salvation, or of His bestowing upon them, along with justification, eternal life or the prospect of it. This conviction is common to both Confessions, and finds expression in symbolical documents on both sides;[1] while, as against this, it is a matter of indifference, to begin with, how dogmatic theologians understand this connection. Now, that the imputation of the righteousness of Christ, in this limited reference, is unthink-

---

[1] *Apol. C. A.* ii. 5 : " Christus promittit remissionem peccatorum, iustificationem et vitam aeternam." *F. C.* iii. p. 585 : " Christo confidimus, quod propter solam ipsius obedientiam ex gratia remissionem peccatorum habeamus, sancti et iusti coram deo patre reputemur et aeternam salutem consequamur." *Catech. Pal.* 59 : " In Christo iustus sum et haeres vitae aeternae." *Conf. Helv.*, post. 15 : " Sumus absoluti a peccatis, morte vel condemnatione, iusti denique (donati iustitia Christi) ac haeredes vitae aeternae."

able or unnecessary, Faustus has not proved, as indeed he has not directed his attention to the matter at all.

Nevertheless this argument too is devoid of intrinsic utility; nor has it any real basis in Paul's typical circle of thought. For active righteousness, or obedience to the moral law, is so indubitably bound up with the personal intention and disposition of the acting subject, that we lose altogether the idea of determinate righteousness once we abstract from the subject by whom the righteousness has been produced. But this is the case when we conclude that the righteousness of Christ is imputed to others as though it were their own product. Thus this idea is altogether false, because it treats the personal moral lifework of a person as a thing which has no essential connection with its author, and may change its owner without having its essence and value altered.[1] More-over, it seems superfluous to conceive the imputation of the righteousness of Christ as a precondition of God's admitting believers to religious fellowship with Himself, when such an assertion, if made a rule, takes for granted the position that God enters into no real fellowship in religion save with morally perfect men. For the present case there is thence drawn the conclusion that God, to attain this purpose of fellowship with believers, creates the moral perfection which in themselves they lack, through the imputation of the right-eousness of Christ.

The formula of the imputation of Christ's righteousness can be extended so as to possess an excellent sense, if we interpret it in the light of other presuppositions than the system of legal relations employed for that purpose by the dogmatic theologians of the seventeenth century. If we take our bearings from the Gospel of John, the intention of Jesus is that His disciples should become one as the Father and the Son are in one another, or that they should become one in this

---

[1] Limborch, *Theol. christ.* vi. 4. 25 : "Unius iustitia alteri imputari nequit. Tota enim iustitiae natura et laus in eo sita est, ut quis libere et alacri animo eam praestet; illam autem perire necesse est, quamprimum imputatur illi, qui eam non praestitit. Nec transferri potest ab uno ad alium, ne ipso quidem conceptu mentis, si verus ille conceptus sit futurus."

fellowship of the Father and the Son; and that it should thereby be made known that the Father loves the Son, and the disciples as the Son ; the love of the Father, however, is directed to the Son before the creation of the world (xvii. 21–24). The nature and the existence of the Son are founded in the love of God. But now to this we must add, on the other side, that Jesus maintains Himself in His existence by carrying on the work of God for the salvation of men (iv. 34). This is exactly equivalent to the truth that, by the execution of the commands or commissions of the Father, He maintains His position in the love of God (xv. 9, 10). Among these commissions, His willingness to lay down His life in the service of the community of disciples is a ground of the Father's loving the Son (x. 17)—in other words, a condition of the continuance of the love of God as the basis of the unique character of Christ. Now, this is the material content of the righteousness of Christ—the execution of the work of God, the fulfilment of God's commandments, the sacrifice of life in the service of the called community. But these services are not measured by universal law and an all-embracing rule of compensation, but first of all by the end aimed at, that Christ should maintain the unique position which, as Son, He has in the love of the Father, and then further by the end that the community of disciples should be effectively taken up into the love of the Father. How this result is mediated is not expressed in the Gospel of John. But we can supply it if we represent to ourselves the process through which the transference of love from one to another is possible. That can happen only through a resolve, in which there is included a judgment; this judgment, however, takes the form that the worth, which one individual has as the object of love, is imputed to those who in themselves lack this worth, but belong to the person who is the primary object of love. The position of Christ relative to God is imputed to His disciples when God, for Christ's sake, takes them also up into His effective love. But Christ's position relative to God also depends on His righteousness. Indirectly, therefore,

Christ's righteousness is imputed to His disciples that they may be taken up into the love of God, even as the roots of Christ's being are there. But in this way the righteousness of Christ is not severed from His Person, and no prejudice is raised against our own practice of righteousness. And while the formula is made intelligible by these modifications, that very fact is proof of its previous obscurity. The point at issue is the imputation of the position relative to God which Christ likewise occupies through His practice of righteousness, to those who as His disciples belong to Him through faith, in order that they may be taken up effectively into the love of God. This thought, however, is not at all accurately expressed in the current formula, nor have those theologians who employ that formula, *e.g.* Calvin,[1] succeeded in making its meaning clear.

§ 15. In this analysis of the formula of the imputation of Christ's righteousness, the position of Christ, relative to God, which is determinative for the idea of justification, is construed otherwise than is done by Melanchthon. As he sees in the promise of the forgiveness of sins the compassion of God acting as cause, he interprets the precondition here provided for by Christ (*iustificare propter Christum*) as coming under the conception of satisfaction as the placation of God (*propitiatio, placatio dei*). Apart from this, he employs for " justify " and "forgive" a series of synonyms, by which considerable light is cast upon the idea, and at the same time every semblance is removed of making it the chief point in justification to transfer the predicate of active righteousness —in other words, to assert an untruth and cast uncertainty upon the task of life. For Melanchthon makes *reconciliation*

---

[1] *Inst.* iii. 11. 23 : " Hinc et illud conficitur, sola intercessione iustitiae Christi nos obtinere, ut coram deo iustificemur. Quod perinde valet, acsi diceretur, hominem non in se ipso iustum esse, sed quia Christi iustitia imputatione cum illo communicatur. . . . Vides, non in nobis, sed in Christo esse iustitiam nostram ; nobis tantum eo iure competere, quia Christi sumus participes, siquidem omnes eius divitias cum ipso possidemus. . . . Quid aliud est, in Christi obedientia collocare nostram iustitiam (Rom. v. 19), nisi asserere, eo solo nos haberi iustos, quia Christi obedientia nobis accepta fertur, acsi nostra esset." Edition of 1539, *C. R.* xxix. p. 745.

and acceptance or favour with God the equivalent of justification, as also acceptance as sons of God, and finally the opening
of access to God.[1]   The word *reconciliare* he uses in this connection only as applied to men who are brought back to God,
but never as applied to God.   The influence of Melanchthon's
view is still visible in Chemnitz.[2]   Moreover, the identity of
the forgiveness of sins, justification, reconciliation, and admission to communion with God, receives really classical expression
in Calvin,[3] despite the fact that before and after the passage
cited below he treats of that distinction between the forgiveness of sins and the imputation of Christ's righteousness which
is discussed above.   The influence of the combination of ideas
before us at present is also to be seen in the founder of
Lutheran dogmatism.   Leonard Hutter unites with the con-

[1] *Loci theol. C. R.* xxi. p. 742 : "Iustificatio significat remissionem peccatorum et reconciliationem seu acceptationem personae ad vitam aeternam. . . .
Sumpsit Paulus verbum iustificandi ex consuetudine Hebraeorum pro remissione
peccatorum et reconciliatione seu acceptatione. . . . Iustificari fide in Christum
significat consequi remissionem et iustum hoc est acceptum reputari propter
mediatorem filium dei." *Apol. C. A.* ii. 86 : "Sola fides iustificat, quia recon-
ciliati reputantur iusti et filii dei"; iii. 20 : "Per Christum acceditur ad patrem,
et accepta remissione peccatorum vere iam statuimus, nos habere deum"; v. 37 :
"Per Christum habemus accessum ad deum."

[2] *Examen conc. Trid.* (Genev. 1641) p. 158 : "Scriptura docet quicquid divina
iustitia ad iustificationem hoc est reconciliationem peccatoris requirit, a Christo
pro nobis impletum esse." P. 159 : "Habet fides suum proprium obiectum,
cuius respectu, merito et dignitate credens coram deo iustificetur, h. e. accipiat
remissionem peccatorum, reconcilietur deo, accipiat adoptionem et accceptetur ad
vitam aeternam." P. 161 : "Obiectum fidei iustificantis, cuius respectu et apprehensione iustificat, est gratuita promissio misericordiae dei remittentis peccata,
adoptantis et acceptantis ad vitam aeternam propter Christum mediatorem."

[2] Lib. iii. 11. 21 (1539, cap. vi. (x.) 12, 13. *C. R.* xxix. p. 744): "Nunc
illud quam verum est excutiamus, quod in definitione dictum est, iustitiam fidei
esse reconciliationem cum deo, quae sola peccatorum remissione constet. Audimus peccatum esse divisionem inter hominem et deum, vultus dei aversionem a
peccatore (Ies. 59. 1): nec fieri aliter potest, quandoquidem alienum est ab eius
iustitia, quicquam commercii habere cum peccato. Quem ergo dominus in con-
iunctionem recipit, eum dicitur iustificare, quia nec recipere in gratiam, nec sibi
adiungere potest, quin ex peccatore iustum faciat. Istud addimus fieri per peccatorum remissionem. Nam si ab operibus aestimentur, quos sibi dominus
reconciliavit, reperientur etiamnum revera peccatores, quos tamen peccato solu-
tos purosque esse oportet. Constat itaque, quos deus amplectitur, non aliter
fieri iustos, nisi quod abstersis peccatorum remissione maculis purificantur, ut
talis iustitia uno verbo appellari queat peccatorum remissio." § 22 : "Iustitiam
et reconciliationem Paulus promiscue nominat, ut alterum sub altero vicissim
contineri intelligamus. Modum autem assequendae huius iustitiae docet, dum
nobis delicta non imputantur."

ception of the imputed righteousness of Christ all the predicates which have been pointed out in the authorities just mentioned.[1]

Now this conjunction of ideas has disappeared from the writings of the Lutheran theologians. They have not even kept in view that direct teleological relation of justification to the bestowal of eternal life which characterises the view originally taken of the subject (p. 69). They are satisfied with adducing this aspect, like all others, under the heading of the effects of justification, and that, too, with no other interest than that of registering the various statements of Scripture. Especially with Gerhard this list exhibits the most motley variety of subjective phenomena and objective determinations of relation, of heterogeneous and synonymous expressions, as though we were dealing with a rubbish-heap. Later writers reduce this multiplicity to a few rubrics, but they think they have done all that is required of them in enumerating them.[2] Under these circumstances the thought of justification comes to be isolated from all practical relations by Lutheran theologians, and condemned to barrenness. We have here again the phenomenon which I have characterised as the pervading feature of the Lutheran theology of that epoch (vol. i. p. 270), that in it no use is made of the conception of end, but all relations are represented under the category of efficient cause. But along with this formal inadequacy, there is still another circumstance to which is due the fading of the idea of justification among the Lutherans. From Aegidius Hunnius onwards this idea receives exposition only in polem-

---

[1] Comp. *Loc. theol.* xii. 2 : "Iustificatio est opus dei, quo hominem peccatorem, credentem in Christum ex mera gratia sive gratis a peccatis absolvit, eique peccatorum remissionem donat, iustitiamque Christi ita imputat, ut plenissime reconciliatus et in filium adoptatus a peccati reatu liberetur et aeternam beatitudinem consequatur."

[2] Gerhard, Loc. xvii. 72. 8, tom. vii. p. 85. Baier, iii. 5. 14 : "Effecta iustificationis sunt pax conscientiae cum deo, adoptio in filios dei, donatio spiritus sancti, sanctificatio et renovatio, spes vitae aeternae." To the same effect Quenstedt, Hollatz.—Fresenius, *Rechtfertigung*, vii. 38 : "The benefits bestowed upon one who possesses forgiveness of sins, consist in free access to God, the right of inward fellowship with God, the right of Divine sonship, and the claim to the eternal inheritance. All this becomes his in Christ, his Surety, Head, and Saviour, who Himself also has taken possession of such glory, and as the Head gives His members a share therein."

ical controversy first with the Tridentine, and then with the Socinian doctrine. Thus it is apprehended only in those aspects which are directly challenged by these opponents; all lying beyond these aspects hardly receives any consideration.

In the Reformed theology of the sixteenth century, also, we meet to begin with a limited and pedantic treatment of the idea of justification. In the seventeenth century, however, a series of dogmatic writers advance to a more living apprehension of it, which consists in this, that the conceptions of reconciliation and adoption are placed in reciprocal relationship to that of justification. To begin with, Amesius declares justification or forgiveness identical with reconciliation, inasmuch as these different expressions describe the same thing only in different aspects.[1] Adoption, it is true, he declares to be a result of justification, and denies that it signifies an element in it, on the ground that those adopted are not yet accounted righteous. To this distinction he clings, although he recognises in justification its direct relation to eternal life, and finds the same character expressed in Divine sonship. His view, indeed, is that thereby believers possess a double title to anticipation of the blessing of life eternal. These latter interpretations are adopted by Heidanus, but he over-steps the scheme to which his predecessor held, in that he takes justification and adoption to be the two parts of reconciliation, and attaches to them the saving effects, both positive and negative. Thus it is brought about that adoption no longer appears as an accident, but as the fulfilment of the idea of reconciliation.[2] A somewhat different formulation of

---

[1] *Medulla*, i. 27. 22: "Absolutio a peccatis vario respectu sed eodem sensu dicitur remissio, redemtio et reconciliatio. . . . Quatenus status peccati consideratur ut inimicitia quaedam adversus deum, eatenus iustificatio dicitur reconciliatio."

[2] *Corp. theol. christ.*, Loc. xi. tom. ii. p. 299: "Reconciliationis nostrae duas partes fecimus iustificationem et adoptionem. . . . Nam peccatorum remissionem iustificationis beneficio consequimur, eoque in gratiam recipimur. Verum quisquis in gratiam recipitur, simul adoptionis particeps et filii loco haberi cognoscitur. Et quidem haec adoptio sequitur iustificationem. Neque nempe adoptione iusti constituimur, sed iustificati exaltamur ad dignitatem et ius filiorum. Si filii, haeredes; si haeredes, etiam ius consequimur ad vitam. . . . Hinc fideles, duplici quasi titulo vitam aeternam possunt a deo petere et

the matter is to be found in the youngest representatives of the Reformed orthodoxy, Fr. Turretin, Rodolf, and Heidegger, as also in Schleiermacher. They distinguish as elements in justification the forgiveness of sins and the award of a right to eternal life or adoption.[1] In general this is the result of the eagerness with which the majority of Reformed theologians have maintained the direct reference of justification to eternal life. The combination of this aspect of it with the conception of Divine sonship then resulted from the fact that the objective aspect of the latter likewise is eternal life. Finally, no difficulty could arise from the form of the idea of justification, for acceptance as the children of God must be conceived as a synthetic judgment. Why, now, has this conjunction of ideas not been accorded recognition on all hands ? In this connection an explanation given by Baier is very noteworthy. Baier [2] brings forward the fact that a minority of theologians extend the *terminus ad quem iustificationis* to the *ius filiorum dei et haereditas vitae aeternae*, while the majority see here effects of justification. Now he likewise concedes that it serves to recommend the former view that it is in formal agreement with the *terminus a quo*. For man is created with a destination to eternal life, but through sin this is converted into a destination to eternal death. Now if justification begins with the removal of this characteristic, it must be completed by the restoration of the original destiny. This, indeed, has been noticed by the majority of Reformed writers. Baier, however, decides against this formulation, because Scripture not infrequently represents the bestowal of Divine sonship as a new attribute over and

exspectant, titulo nempe redemtionis, quem habent ex iustificatione, et titulo quasi filiationis, quem habent ex adoptione."

[1] Heidegger, *Loc.* xxii. 59 : "Iustificatio remissionem peccatorum et vitae seu haereditatis adiudicationem complectitur." 72 : "Quae iuris vitae concessio realiter cum adoptione convenit, neque aliter ab hac distinguitur, quam quod vita aeterna in iustificatione ut debitum, in adoptione vero ut haereditas spectatur, et deus ibi iudicis, hic patris personam sustinet." Rodolf, *Cat. Pal.* p. 334. Turretini, *Theol. elenchtica*, tom. ii. p. 719. *Compend.*, ed. Riissen, p. 426. Schleiermacher, § 109 : "That God justifies one who is converted involves that He forgives his sins and recognises him as a child of God."

[2] *Theol. posit.* iii. 5. 4, 14, pp. 661, 677.

above justification, and proves this by making it subordinate to regeneration.

If justification places sinners in a positive relationship of congruence towards God, and if the declaration that they are righteous is not to make their destination to active righteousness wear a semblance of superfluity, it must find its limit in that fellowship with God which is expressed, to begin with and in an indeterminate way, by nearness to God, and then, further, by the right of communion with God. Not only, however, does this open a prospect that all that is still attainable for the salvation of believers and in opposition to their sin, will result from this new and peculiar relation to God; but these results, up to the goal of eternal life, are included by intention in justification, as surely as justification determines the lasting and unvarying character of believers. If Lutheran theologians have been dull enough to close their minds to this directly teleological aspect of justification, it is for them to inquire how far they are in agreement with the Formula of Concord, which identifies the bestowal of blessedness with justification. But further, if the right to eternal life is the objective aspect of Divine sonship, which is proved to be an abiding attribute of believers just through the certainty of this right of inheritance, then adoption must coincide with justification. True, Heidegger brings out this difference between the two ideas, that in justification God appears as Judge, in adoption as Father; but the question arises whether this distinction can be maintained. A conclusion on this point can only be reached at a later stage, and therefore we shall not seek here to state finally the relation between adoption and justification (*vide infra*, § 18).

In any case the conception of reconciliation has a more general sense than adoption, and therefore stands nearer to justification. By Paul, too, who as the author of the idea of justification is altogether decisive for its further ramification, it is set in the closest relation to that idea. As has been remarked before (vol. ii. p. 342), Paul describes man's peace with God as the specific effect of justification, while this effect directly coincides with reconciliation as the removal of man's enmity to God.   If we take account merely of this conjunction of ideas, we get the impression that the two conceptions are synonymous.   Nevertheless, the conception of reconciliation has a wider range and greater definiteness than that of justification.   For it expresses as an actual result the effect ever aimed at in justification or pardon, namely, that the person who is pardoned actually enters upon the relationship which is to be established.   By the idea of justification sinners are merely passively determined, and it fails to inform us what stimulus is acted upon them by the Divine treatment of their case.   On the other hand, the idea of reconciliation is expressive of the fact that those who formerly were engaged in active contradiction to God have, by pardon, been brought into a harmonious direction towards God, and first of all into agreement with the intention cherished by Him in acting thus.   From this point of view we may count on it that the justification which is successfully dispensed by God finds its manifestation and response in definite functions of the persons reconciled.

True, both ideas express the divinely-initiated fellowship of men with God which is no longer obstructed by sin ; but the sin which, to secure this end, is rendered inoperative is considered under the attributes of guilt or consciousness of guilt so far as it is related to justification or forgiveness, but in its essence as active contradiction to God so far as it is related to reconciliation.   Thus even from this consideration it follows that the idea of reconciliation has a more comprehensive range than that of forgiveness.   But it is in this wider scope that the matter must be apprehended, for unless the removal of guilt can be likewise conceived as the removal of the contradiction of the will to God, the former result would issue in a self-delusion on God's part.   Or if the removal of guilt must be thought only as God's determination of relationship in regard to sinners, and not as the completion of a reciprocal harmony, then there is not proved to exist here any sufficient basis for

a religion with moral aims. But now, that the thought of
the removal of guilt should be supplemented by the thought
of the removal of contradiction to God follows necessarily
from the relation of the consciousness of guilt to both ideas.
It has been proved above (p. 56) that the idea of guilt as
an attribute of sin possesses validity only in virtue of the
consciousness of guilt by which it is qualified. But this
consciousness is also the subjective expression of the fact
that sin is active contradiction to God. Further, it has
been shown that the removal of guilt and the consciousness
of guilt does not imply any unveracious denial of the existence of sin; that, rather, pain at the sin which has been
committed is present in memory even after the reception of
forgiveness. But the removal of guilt does signify that God
cancels the effect of sin, which is to make fellowship with
Him impossible; and that accordingly the consciousness of
guilt has its mistrust of God, to Whom we know ourselves
to be in contradiction, removed. Thus the removal of guilt,
conceived as an actual result, includes this change in the
consciousness of guilt—that in it there no longer works on
that opposition of the will to God of which sin is the consummation. That is, even while pain at sin committed is preserved in the memory, the effective removal of guilt on God's
part, namely, its non-imputation as a ground of separation
and alienation, appears in our newly-established confidence
towards God as the counterpart of our still surviving opposition to Him. Justification or forgiveness, conceived as
effective, thus is identical with reconciliation as expressive
of mutual fellowship between God and man. If this denotes
the basis of Christianity as a religion, the subjective functions
of reconciliation will be directly religious. On the other
hand, the functions of a moral kind, which spring from the
independence of the will that is in harmony with God, must
stand in a more remote relation to reconciliation with God,
for they cannot be deduced without taking into account still
other points of view.

§ 16. This conception of justification, which has been

developed in essential agreement with the intention actuating the Lutheran and Reformed theologians, *is, in form, a synthetic judgment.* This quality answers to the fact that justification, in the sense meant here, must be thought as a resolve or act of the Divine will. For every act of the will moves analogously to the synthetic judgment; especially can a creative act of God's will only be understood in this form. But such an act is conceived when God through the revelation in Christ receives those who are separated from Him by sin into fellowship with Himself, to the establishment of their salvation. Not even from the standpoint of Roman Catholicism can objection justly be raised to this position. For even if we interpret the act of deciding against sin as the real communication of the *gratia gratum faciens,* or as the material inspiration of love to God and men, yet this process, as a Divine act, can only be represented in the form that to the sinner whom God makes righteous there is added a predicate not already included in the conception " sinner." The opposition between the two forms of doctrine, therefore, in reality consists, not in the fact that the necessary form of the Evangelical conception of justification is altogether omitted in the Catholic mode of doctrine, but in the fact that the synthetic judgment on God's part, in the Evangelical sense, is conceived, not as having as its content the moral change of the sinner, but merely as the ground of his relationship to God as altered by God's will. The basis of this opposition, however, lies in this, that Catholic doctrine represents Christianity first and foremost as the form of a moral direction of the will set in opposition to sin, while Protestantism represents it first and foremost as the true religion, in contrast to the operation of sin as the ground of all irreligion and all false religion. But now Christianity in its genus is religion, in its species it is the perfect spiritual and moral religion. The Evangelical idea of justification, accordingly, is constructed so that in this special and peculiar relation of men to God the universal character of Christianity as a religion may attain expression. For that idea is in harmony with the desire to formulate Christianity as the true religion, in that the fellowship of men with God, in which lies their salvation, is made independent of sin, which is wont either to negate or falsify religion. On the other hand, the Catholic representation of making righteous (*Gerechtmachung*) as the decisive idea is wrong, for that idea is not modelled on the general conception of Christianity as a religion, but on its moral quality. And that to proceed in this way is also unpractical, may be seen from the fact that in Catholicism all possible falsifications of religion, the polytheistic and magical as well as the Pharisaic, enjoy official sanction, in spite of all pretended disclaimers.

The synthetic character of the judgment of justification is not denied even by the Socinians and Arminians, although these parties give the idea another reference than the Lutherans and the Reformed, and therefore also invest it with a different significance. They interpret justification and the remission of penalties as a judgment upon faith in Christ, in which is included active obedience to the law. Now as obedience, when compared with the law, is always imperfect, and does not of itself offer a basis for the predication of righteousness, and therefore, also, does not carry with it entire freedom from punishment, the judgment of God, that the believer is righteous, is not analytic. As the basis of the completion of salvation, of the remission of penalties, and of eternal life, therefore, it is synthetic, deduced solely from God's free resolve of grace ; nevertheless it is not to be looked for apart from the indispensable precondition of the moral obedience of faith.[1] This view, like that of the orthodox schools of the seventeenth century, is based upon the belief that the predicate of righteousness is properly attached to the faultless fulfilment of the law. If this is not to be looked for from believers, they must be invested with it by

---

[1] *Catech. Racov.* 452 : "Per fidem in Christum consequimur iustificationem." 453 : "Iustificatio est, cum nos deus pro iustis habet, quod ea ratione facit, cum nobis peccata remittit et nos vita aeterna donat." 418 : "Fides est fiducia per Christum in deum. Hoc est ut non solum deo, verum et Christo confidamus, deinde et deo obtemperemus, non in iis solum, quae in lege per Mosen lata praecepit, et per Christum abrogata non sunt, verum etiam in omnibus, quae Christus legi addidit."— *Fausti Socini Theses de iustificatione, B. F. P.* i.

6

Divine judgment. Now, according to the Socinians and Arminians, this is done, not by the imputation of the righteousness of Christ, but by a free Divine judgment, conditional upon the partial realisation of the obedience of faith. The decisive divergence between the two lies here, that the imputation of another's righteousness instead of our own is construed by the orthodox as the precondition of the opening of saving fellowship with God, while by the other parties the imputation of our own imperfect righteousness as perfect is viewed as the precondition of the completion of salvation. Thus conceptions expressed by the same terms are of unequal value for the two groups, and therefore do not directly correspond to one another.

What really corresponds to the Reformation idea of justification in the Arminian doctrine is the idea of reconciliation, in so far as it precedes faith and conversion.[1] This preliminary reconciliation is, as a consequence of the priestly work of Christ and the reconciliation of God, distinguished from the complete reconciliation of men, which coincides with justification. The preliminary reconciliation consists in the establishment of the new covenant, under which God is prepared to forgive sins and to bestow eternal life on condition of the obedience of faith described, and under which He provides that the word of grace shall be proclaimed until this condition has been fulfilled by men. Now it might seem as though what is here expressed were the same as what we have shown to be the content of the Reformation idea of justification and reconciliation. For that willingness of God and the proclamation of it might perhaps convey the impression that according to the Divine intention the sins of believers were forgiven in advance. Nevertheless, such an interpretation must be put aside, for

p. 603 : "Deus ex pura sua gratia et misericordia nos iustificat. . . . Est obedientia quam Christo praestamus, licet nec efficiens, nec meritoria, tamen causa sine qua non iustificationis coram deo, atque aeternae salutis nostrae."—The Arminians differ from this only in that they admit the validity of Christ's work of satisfaction (vol. i. p. 342). Otherwise all the conditions of the doctrine are in harmony with the Socinian doctrine. Cf. Limborch, *Theol. christ.* vi. 4. 14–32.

[1] Cf. Limborch, iii. 23.

thereby the very essence of the promise would be misconstrued. The promise of the forgiveness of sins, it is held,
is intended and is intelligible only on condition of the
appropriate faith and active obedience. But the mere proclamation, conceived apart from this condition, would be no
promise. Now this is really to introduce quite another connection of thought than is implied in the Reformation view
of reconciliation or justification. As the latter is always
implicite directed against the action of the consciousness of
guilt in separating us from God, it must necessarily be conceived in such relations that the justified person recognises
the change in his relation to God, or that he comes to be
directed towards God as his positive end. Even if, to begin
with, the individual functions through which this is done are
left out of account, yet it cannot be doubted that in them
there will be expressed the religious recognition of the fact
that the believer specifically belongs to God—a fact which,
as a result of justification, is included in the idea of justification, so certainly as reconciliation is the equivalent of that idea.
But the Arminian view of the new covenant established by
God describes merely a one-sided willingness on God's part,
the response to which on men's side is left to their purely
accidental resolution, and limits the invitation to take such
a resolution to a proclamation which is addressed to their
understanding. This interpretation of *reconciliatio*, however,
not only falls short of the simple sense of the word, which
denotes a reciprocal relationship, but even of the incontestable religious signification of the idea, the character of
which is shown by its relation to the idea of the consciousness of guilt. At bottom this belief regarding the preliminary reconciliation as a result of the priestly office of
Christ is expressed more openly and simply in the fundamental Socinian doctrine, that Christianity as a proclamation
of commandments and promises altogether rests exclusively
upon the prophetic office of Christ. If, therefore, the importance given to His priestly office by the Arminians seems
almost like an accommodation, designed to conceal their

Socinian tendency, conversely we may well suppose, with all the greater certainty, that the state of decomposition which this idea exhibits here is partly due to the orthodox theologians. Everywhere in the history of theology it appears that inaccurate and superficial forms of doctrine lead to the connections of thought which were originally intended being distorted or dissolved. Now, as orthodox theologians never clearly fixed the relation of justification or forgiveness to the consciousness of guilt, it became possible for the Arminians to form a conception of reconciliation without any relation to the fact of that consciousness, a conception which is entirely alien to the recognisable tendency of Reformation doctrine.

Another distortion of the idea of justification appears in the Pietistic hypothesis which, with manifold modifications, amounts to this, that justification is an analytic judgment upon the moral worth of faith, in so far as faith, as a result of conversion, includes the power of moral action.[1] It is clear that this thought is very far removed from that which was laid down as in harmony with the tendency of the Reformation. The fact that it was possible for the one to be substituted for the other, is to be explained chiefly by the attention which the Pietists gave to their own struggles and efforts to attain subjective assurance of salvation. Originally, the thing aimed at in justification was to look away from one's own states of mind, and to turn to the judgment which is pronounced in virtue of Christ's mediation according to the free grace of God. It is therefore an inversion of the Reformation point of view when Pietism makes the moral power of faith the object which God invests with the value which moral conduct would possess when carried out. Besides this, justification, when so apprehended, is conceived as an accident of the effective moral change brought about by regeneration, and therefore does not denote that turning - point from the status

---

[1] Cf. vol. i. pp. 359, 362. *Gesch. des Pietismus*, i. pp. 129 f., 158; ii. p. 403 ff.

of sin to the state of new life, which the Reformers desired to fix.

This comparison of the different explanations which have been given of justification is here intended only to show us where we are ; for at this point we attempt neither a proof of the necessity of one definition, nor a refutation of other theories. The definition we have reached only claims to be thinkable, and to stand nearer than any other to the view held by the men of the New Testament and the Reformers.

1. Justification or the forgiveness of sins, as the religious expression of that operation of God upon men which is fundamental in Christianity, is the acceptance of sinners into that fellowship with God in which their salvation is to be realised and carried out into eternal life.

2. Justification is conceivable as the removal of guilt and the consciousness of guilt, in so far as in the latter that contradiction to God which is realised in sin and expressed in guilt, works on as mistrust, and brings about moral separation from God.

3. In so far as justification is viewed as effective, it must be conceived as reconciliation, of such a nature that while memory, indeed, preserves the pain felt at the sin which has been committed, yet at the same time the place of mistrust towards God is taken by the positive assent of the will to God and His saving purpose.

CHAPTER II

THE GENERAL RELATIONS OF JUSTIFICATION

§ 17. It has been impossible to define justification without taking into account its relation to the subjective consciousness of guilt. In order, however, to determine with complete accuracy the place of this thought within the Christian religion, it is necessary both to know the Subject or Author of justification under the corresponding predicate, and to estimate the characteristic note of faith which is to be found in the objects of justification along with, and apart from, their consciousness of guilt. Then we shall be able to consider the scope and the definite sphere within which the Divine judgment of justification must be conceived as operative, in order to hold good as the special basis of the religious quality in the Christian subject.

The attribute of God through which the older theology seeks to understand justification is that of *Lawgiver and Judge*. It is precisely in ascetic representations of the doctrine that this preconceived idea of God receives special and intentionally strong emphasis.[1] The conception of God as Lawgiver and Judge, it is true, has no direct bearing on the general idea of pardon, or the forgiveness of sins: it belongs rather to the special means by which the older school attempted to

---

[1] Cf. Joh. Friedr. Fresenius, *Abhandlung über die Rechtfertigung eines armen Sünders vor Gott* (1747. New edition by A. F. C. Vilmar, 1857), p. 8: "As regards the Author of justification, He can be no other than the Supreme Lawgiver. For justification is a judicial act, which proceeds according to Divine law." F. A. Lampe, *Geheimniss des Gnadenbundes*, part i. (1726) p. 429: "Seeing that the expression 'to justify' refers to a judicial act, it will be most fitting to represent the whole scheme of justifying grace under the form of a judicial process."

solve the contradiction between the grace and the justice of God, in order to explain the forgiveness of sins which is received in Christianity.   But we meet the same preconceived idea of God also in Tieftrunk (vol. i. p. 462), although his idea of the way in which Christ mediates the forgiveness of sins departs from orthodox lines.   The special influence which works on Tieftrunk is the Kantian estimate of the moral law.   Recognising the facts of the transgressor's consciousness of guilt before the law, and his feelings of awe and shame in presence of the Lawgiver—feelings which are not removed by moral reformation—he explains the bestowal of pardon by the Judge as the chief need of the guilty person.   Here, therefore, we find a ground for the common assumption in a quite different motive from that assigned by the orthodox theology.

This assumption, however, when compared with the ideas with which it stands connected, is, to say the least, incomplete. We may at the outset concede to the orthodox theology that the imputation of the double obedience of Christ to the law, for the purpose of judging sinners as righteous, may be represented as a special instance of the application of law by the Judge.   We cannot, however, represent this act as isolated from the antecedent gracious purpose of God, His purpose, namely, to bless sinners ; nor must we lose sight of the fact that God has Himself brought into court the Righteous One, Whose obedience to the law, according to the presupposition, He judicially imputes to sinners.   On these two accounts, God, in executing the judicial act of imputing the righteousness of Christ to sinners, cannot be conceived as Lawgiver and Judge, but as the Dispenser of grace and love to men.   The act of imputation, moreover, when placed in its true connection with the whole, is only the means to an end. The judicial quality in God, therefore, can be admitted only as a co-operating element in the act of justification, or as a subordinate trait in the conception of His character as the Author of justification.   Even the above-quoted writers are compelled either to supplement their own representations by

saying that " in this work " God reveals Himself in the character of love, or, by actually designating justification as an
" act of grace," to indicate the real principle of the matter.
One may, of course, insist upon the fact that, in ascetic representations, paradoxes are used as means of stimulating the
attention. But the above-quoted expressions are not to be
regarded as mere harmless exaggerations. Their effect is
really the dislocation of one member of an organism, the
isolation of one proposition, which, we maintain, can only
be rightly represented in connection with quite different
propositions.

But if we fix our attention more closely on this analogy
of the power of the State, which has been applied to explain
God's method in bringing about the remission of guilt and
punishment, we find that justification cannot possibly be
represented as a judicial act. For the right of bestowing
pardon, which is vested in the head of the State, is no prerogative of his power as lawgiver and supreme judge; it is
a right, altogether independent of these attributes, explicable
from an entirely different aspect of the idea of the State. As
lawgiver, the head of the State unites the various members
thereof for the purpose of common organised action ; and as
holder of the power of punishment, he defends the legal
order of the community, preserving it against the violations
to which it is exposed. The right of pardon, on the other
hand, follows from the fact that the legal order is only a
means to the moral ends of the people, and that consequences
of legal action are conceivable, which are incongruous with the
respect that is due to public morality, as well as to the moral
position of guilty persons. In order to prevent such incongruous results of judicial condemnation, the right of pardon
is exercised by the authority to which the case of the moral
well-being of the community is officially entrusted. The
bestowal of pardon thus appears, it is true, always in the
form of a judgment of the head of the State—not, however,
a judicial, but an extra-judicial judgment. This relation of
different functions has remained for the most part hidden

from the older theologians,[1] partly because they were not accustomed to determine accurately the meaning of the symbols
they used, and partly because they combined two different
ideas in the act of justification, namely, the vicarious satisfaction of the law, and the pardon of sins through imputation of
the righteousness of Christ. A conception of justification was
thus formed, which should correspond, not with the simple
idea of pardon, but also with the judicial act of the execution
of punishment. By means of this conception, therefore, it
appears as though justification could be represented as at
least as much a judicial as an extra-judicial judgment. The
apparent contradiction was explained through the peculiarly
Divine character of the judgment, which transcends the analogies
derived from the notion of the State. But these two ideas
which have thus been brought into relation in the judgment of justification are not co-ordinate. The extra-judicial
bestowal of pardon can alone be regarded as the specific form
of the judgment of justification, the judicial acceptance of the
satisfaction of the law through a substitute being but the
presupposition of that judgment. In this way, therefore, we
cannot arrive at the conclusion that justification is judicial
in character. We should then have to decide, with the
Reformed theologians (vol. i. p. 302), that the imputation
of Christ's obedience to those for whom, as their Head,
He rendered that obedience, is an act of Divine justice.
But this view of the matter would be least of all able to
escape the force of the argument which Faustus Socinus urges
in refutation of the orthodox doctrine (vol. i. p. 326), namely,
that the ideas of satisfaction and forgiveness are absolutely
self-contradictory. If, as is assumed, justification be held
to be an act of Divine justice, then it cannot conceivably be regarded as an act of grace. But the scope of this
argument extends even further; for it raises the question

---

[1] Compare, however, Amesius, *Medullá*, i. 27. 10 : "Iustificatio est gratiosa
sententia, quia non fertur proprie a iustitia dei, sed a gratia. Eadem enim
gratia, qua Christum vocavit ad mediatoris munus et electos ad unionem cum
Christo attraxit, censet etiam eos iam attractos et credentes ex illa unione
iustos."

whether the judicial recognition of the satisfaction and the merit of Christ can possibly be the ground of their extra-judicial imputation in the act of pardon. For in the penal law absolutely no provision is made for the transference of punishment and personal obligations to other persons than those under such obligations. If such a procedure on the part of God be admitted in the mediation of justification, then the recognition of vicarious satisfaction as such would have of necessity to be understood, not as the act of the Judge, or the Executor of the law, but as an antecedent act of grace. And, finally, the formula directed against the Catholic doctrine, namely, that Divine justification is to be understood *sensu forensi*, is anything but complete and accurate. Justification, it is true, has the form of a judgment, not of a material operation; but the judgment in this case is the synthetic judgment of a resolution of the will. On the other hand, every judicial judgment is an analytic judgment of knowledge. The consequent decree of punishment or acquittal is equally an analytic judgment, being a conclusion from the prohibitive or permissive law involved and the knowledge of the guilt or innocence of the person accused. Therefore in whatever way we view the matter, the attitude of God in the act of justification cannot be conceived as that of Judge.

The justification of sinners by God, when explained by the analogy of the bestowal of pardon by the head of the State, can just as little be deduced from the attribute of *Lawgiver*. It could rather be shown that the bestowal of pardon is in direct contradiction to the attribute of Lawgiver. For the lawgiver as such is interested in the absolute validity and universal observance of the law, whereas through the bestowal of pardon exceptions are admitted. Nevertheless the combination of these two attributes in the full power of the State is perfectly rational. No real contradiction exists between them, because, as we have said, they are differently related ideas, and because they do not come into collision with one another at the same moment. For the legislative power, which insists upon the absolute validity of the law, is satisfied when the bestowal of pardon does not in any instance interfere with legal procedure, but only follows after a verdict of guilt has been legally passed. Seeing, however, that legal right is not itself the highest good, but in all cases only a means to secure the moral goods which further the true life of the people, the full power of bestowing pardon is, in order to attain this end, united with the right of legislation in the person of one supreme authority, so that, in individual instances of legal procedure, due regard should be paid to the question, whether or not the complete execution of the demands of the law and of the judicial sentence would be more detrimental to the public moral interests than their non-execution.

It is from this side also that Tieftrunk has explained the possibility of Divine forgiveness of sins, notwithstanding the strictly obligatory character of the moral law, of which he is convinced. God is recognised by Tieftrunk as the correlate of the final end of practical reason. This end is the common-wealth in which the moral laws alone are authoritative, the Kingdom of God. In order to make this end conceivable as the standard of one's own action, practical reason postulates the existence of God as Creator, Lawgiver, Judge, and Ruler. If, now, the moral end of the world is to be maintained in spite of the sinfulness of men, God must be thought as the Author of forgiveness, through which act compensation is made for the transgressions of the moral law. In this argument the point has been duly recognised, the validity of which we have above maintained, namely, that the attribute of lawgiver in the character of the head of the State is not the highest, inasmuch as the judicial legislation is only a means subserving the moral ends of the people. But the attribute in the character of the head of the State which corresponds to the moral destiny of the people, namely, the right of bestowing pardon, has a narrower sphere of opera-tion, and, so to speak, only accidental validity, because the head of the State cannot actually bring about the fulfilment of the moral destiny of the people, inasmuch as he cannot play the part of moral Providence for the people. On this point, therefore, the idea of God and His Kingdom transcends the analogy of State processes. The moral legislation of God is, under all circumstances, the means toward the moral commonwealth, the Kingdom of God. The attribute of God as Founder and Ruler of His Kingdom is therefore absolutely superior to His attribute as Lawgiver. If He recognises pardon as the fitting means for the maintenance of His Kingdom, no general objection can be brought against the possibility of such pardon from His attribute as Lawgiver. It follows then that pardon, or the forgiveness of sins, is connected, not with God's special attribute as Lawgiver, but with His general attribute as King and Lord of His Kingdom among men.

This result, which we have reached under the direction of Tieftrunk, is free from the contradictions involved in the thesis of the older school, that God carries out the act of justification as Judge, and therefore as Executor of the law given by Himself. The principle of the advance beyond the older position consists in this, that use has been made of the idea of the Kingdom of God as the common moral end for God and men, an idea altogether foreign to the representatives of the older school. And yet the idea of the all-comprehensive Divinely-instituted moral law, which formed for those theologians the inseparable correlate of their idea of God, can hold good only as a deduction from the notion of that moral commonwealth, as certainly as every moral and judicial law is deduced from the nature of the corresponding community. If, therefore, the thought of forgiveness of sins, or justification, is to have vital significance in the Christian view of the world, and if it is to be understood through comparison with the right of pardon which is enjoyed by the head of the State, it must be conceived only as standing in relation to the universal sovereignty of God over the completed moral commonwealth which is to be formed of men. Tieftrunk has, however, at the same time taken into consideration the fact that the Divine forgiveness of sins, as a deduction from the final end of the Kingdom of God conditioned by the continual transgression of the law, yet cannot be indifferent to the unconditional authority of the law.   He demands, therefore, that the Divine forgiveness be conceived, not merely as a result of the law, but also as an act in harmony with the law.   He finds the first pre-requisite fulfilled, when forgiveness leads men to love the law ; the second, when reconciliability becomes a commandment of outstanding importance in the law, and when irreconciliability, conceived as the law of a moral kingdom, would be self-contradictory.   Tieftrunk has here, it is true, raised an important problem, but his solution is sophistical.   Reconcili-ability is certainly a principle which claims paramount importance as between those who are equal in every respect, but which has no unconditioned validity as between those of whom the one is superior in authority to the other.   Else the result would be, that through unlimited application of this particular principle, the universal legal order of common life would be destroyed.   The solution of the question, how the Christian truth of the Divine forgiveness of sins can be reconciled with the unconditioned validity of the moral law, must therefore be reserved for future consideration.

§ 18. In the meantime our task is to ascertain in general the attribute of God through which the positively Christian conception of the forgiveness of sins is to be understood. Now it is almost inconceivable that the orthodox theologians, in spite of their endeavours to reproduce the ideas of Holy Scripture, have been entirely oblivious of the fact that Jesus explicitly connected this operation of God with *His attribute as Father*.   He directed His disciples to invoke God as Father when they prayed to Him for forgiveness of their sins; and, to bring home to them the necessity of their forgiving their fellow-men, He promised them that their Father in heaven would also forgive them their sins (Luke xi. 2–4 ; Mark xi. 25 ; Matt. vi. 9–15).   In so far, too, as the forgiveness of sins is mediated through the expiatory death of Christ, the apostles recognise the love, or the grace,

or the righteousness, that is, the self-consistent saving purpose, of God as the ground of that scheme (Rom. iii. 25, 26,
v. 8; Heb. ii. 9). Moreover, the Old Testament idea of
sacrifice, through which this whole circle of conceptions
must be understood, contains nothing analogous to the
judicial procedure of vicarious punishment; the sacrifices of
the law are rather the symbols of a Divinely-ordered scheme
for the appropriation of the Covenant-grace (vol. ii. p. 185).
It is true that the God whom we invoke as Father, has also
inherent in His nature the attribute of impartial Judge
(1 Pet. i. 7); but He acts as Judge only in vindicating the
rights of His people. The title of Judge as applied to God
has therefore for Christians no real place alongside of, or
over, the relation in which He stands to them as Father.
It is only, therefore, when the love of God, regarded as
Father, is conceived as the will which works toward the
destined end, that the real equivalence of forgiveness and
justification, which is represented in the religious conception
of things, can be made good. If, however, God be preconceived as Judge in the forensic sense, the two ideas come
into direct antagonism with one another, as was indeed explicitly maintained by the leading representatives of the older
theology. The man who has gone through the punishment
he has merited can, of course, be no more looked upon as a
criminal, but he cannot by any means yet be regarded as an
active and successful member of the moral community; in
order to attain this place, the discharged culprit must give
special evidence of his fitness for membership in the community. If, therefore, a judicial procedure on the part of
God is recognised in this, that He regards sinners as free
from punishment and guilt on account of the satisfaction
which Christ has made, He must also, in order to judge
them as positively righteous, impute to them the merit of
Christ. It has been shown (p. 89) that this train of
thoughts carries us beyond the limits of the conceptions
derived from the analogy of the human judge. But the
forgiveness extended by a father to his child combines in

one act the judgment that a fault committed by the child ought to bring about no alienation between father and child, and the expression of the purpose to admit the child, as a right and gracious action, to the unfettered intercourse of love.

The attribute of father stands in relation to the peculiar moral and legal fellowship of the family. Therefore all the preceding arguments regarding the attitude of God to the forgiveness of sins, which have been derived from the analogy of the head of the State, that is, the legal and only relatively moral society of the people, are found to be incongruous with the Christian idea of God. The representation of God under the attribute of Father corresponds exactly to the transference to the whole of mankind of His relative moral and legal Lordship over the people of Israel for the bringing about of the highest moral end. Now, not only does this universal destination of the Kingdom of God exclude comparison with the form of government of any definite people, but the designation of God as our Father shows expressly that the real analogy for the Kingdom of God should be sought, not in the national State, but in the family. The consequences which this principle involves for the representation of the Christian view of the world cannot yet be brought out. One result, however, is the confirmation of a formerly established position (p. 62), namely, that the forgiveness of sins by God as Father finds no real standard of comparison in the right of pardon which belongs to the head of the State. The difference between the two is seen in this, that the right of pardon is only exercised in individual instances of legal condemnation, which as such stand in no connection with one another and always form exceptions to the recognised legal order, while the forgiveness of sins by God as Father is a universal, though not unconditioned, fundamental law, established in the interest of the community of the Kingdom of God.

If, then, justification in the Christian sense is related to God under the attribute—to use a human analogy—of

Father, not of Judge, the ground on which Heidegger distinguished justification and adoption (p. 77) becomes untenable. The only valid distinction between the two ideas is that forgiveness, or justification, or reconciliation, refers generally to the admission of sinners to fellowship with God in spite of sin, whereas in adoption the confidential relation to God which is thereby established is specially described in terms of the normal relation of children to a father. The connection being such, the idea of reconciliation is shown to be of equal constitutive significance for Christianity with the name of God as the Father of our Lord Jesus Christ. But the ideas of *reconciliation* and *adoption* agree with one another also in a formal respect. For adoption must also be conceived as a resolution of will in the form of a synthetic judgment (p. 80). The Reformed theologians, who alone give the idea of adoption an independent place in the Christian system, occupy themselves with describing the distinctions between the notions of Divine and human adoption. But we ought rather to seek to ascertain the harmony between the two. Now such harmony cannot be found in the idea of the establishment of a right of inheritance for a person of alien descent. For those persons who have in the Christian sense been adopted by God as His children, attain that rank only under the presupposition that in a certain real sense they derive their being from God, that is, that they have been created in His image. In harmony therewith, and in contrast to the alienation which sin causes between God and men, the adoption of the believing signifies their reception into that peculiar fellowship with God which is represented under the analogy of the family. Now, the moral fellowship of the human family rests not only on national descent, but on a judgment of the value of this fellowship by the husband and wife, and on the purpose of the father to educate his children to become spiritual and moral persons. The father's moral relation to his children therefore rests in every case on an act of υἱοθεσία, so that this idea is not exclusively applicable to children of alien descent. The certainty of blood-relationship is not the sufficient ground of the father's care; for there are fathers who shirk their responsibilities. Therefore the resolution to bring up one's children does not follow from the analytic judgment that one is the author of the children's life. On the contrary, this resolution, like every other resolution, is a synthetic judgment, even though it usually appears as a logical conclusion from the recognition of blood-relationship. The latter, however, is the case only when the resolution to give moral education to the children is included in the resolution to form the marriage union. On the other hand, the resolution to assume charge of a natural child for the purpose of moral education is usually absent, unless the purpose or resolution to enter upon the marriage state be combined with the sexual connection. If, therefore, the Divine υἱοθεσία in the Christian sense is understood in reference to the closest conceivable spiritual fellowship between man and God, then the form of the resolution, which is a synthetic judgment, is in exact harmony with that of the analogous resolution in the relationship of the human family, which we have taken as our standard of comparison. Seeing, however, that the resolution to admit children to moral fellowship applies not only, as a general rule, to children of the blood, but also, in extraordinary cases, to alien children, and that the resolution can extend in these cases only to the transmission of property rights, the idea of the Divine υἱοθεσία cannot be held to be completely harmonious in these essential respects with its human analogue. For those who are admitted to the rank of children of God are all, by virtue of their innate moral destiny, " of Divine race," but all in reality, because of sin, " as alien children" to God. Through the paramount influence of this fact, therefore, the Divine υἱοθεσία appears as most closely analogous to the human legal form of adoption. If, now, justification is an operation in which God appears under the attribute of Father, then the adoption of men as God's children is a substantially equivalent idea. The latter

7

modifies the former only in this respect, that the fellowship
with God to which sinners are admitted, is conceived to be as
close as that which exists between the head and the members
of a family.   Therefore the functions in which the believing
make manifest their justification and reconciliation must also
be conceived as the functions of sonship to God.

The union (*Gleichheit*) with God, which must be included
among the privileges which the justified enjoy as the
children of God, finds expression in the formula, that justification brings the believing into possession of *eternal life*.
In Luther's proposition (in chap. v.), "Where the forgiveness of sins is, there is life and blessedness," this attribute
is conceived as a present possession.   It will be sufficient to
recall propositions of similar import in the *Apology of the
Augsburg Confession*.[1]   Calvin holds precisely the same
views.[2]   To take a final example, in the Formula of Concord,
Art. 4, the connection between justification and eternal life is
made so close, that good works are regarded as equally
invalid as the condition for eternal life as they are for
justification.   In these propositions, as contrasted with the
Catholic view, the possession of eternal life is brought from
the sphere of the future and the world-to-come into the
present state of the earthly life of the believing.   By this
interpretation of justification we also rise beyond the mystical
standpoint.   The mystics claim to enjoy the blessedness
of the future in moments of ecstasy in the present life.
They have, however, to suffer for their elevation of spirit at
such moments through subsequent lassitude, aridity and
barrenness of the feelings, and the sense of desertion by God.
The Reformers, on the other hand, live in the faith that
eternal life, and the joy which attaches to it, namely,

---

[1] iii. 176 : "Iustificamur ex promissione, in qua propter Christum promissa
est reconciliatio, iustitia et vita aeterna."   233 : "Sicut iustificatio ad fidem
pertinet, ita pertinet ad fidem vita aeterna . . . Fatentur enim adversarii,
quod iustificati sint filii dei et cohaeredes Christi."

[2] *Inst.* iii. 14. 17 : " Efficientem vitae aeternae nobis comparandae causam
scriptura praedicat patris coelestis misericordiam et gratuitam erga nos
dilectionem, materialem vero Christum cum sua obedientia, qua nobis iustitiam
acquisivit ; formalem quoque vel instrumentalem quam esse dicemus nisi fidem ? "

blessedness, are present gifts, continually enjoyed as the result of the forgiveness of sins. But yet this thought, although presented in a series of proof-passages, has not been made quite clear by them. From the Catholic use of the formula, which was familiar to the Reformers, we must conclude that "eternal life," in their view, denotes a peculiar union and fellowship with God. In the Greek Church, indeed, "deification" is used as an expression equivalent to "eternal life." This usage has extended also to the Western Church. Bernard, for example, started from this idea in his exposition of the doctrine (vol. i. p. 117). The mediaeval mystics, although they strove to attain blessedness in the ecstatic knowledge of God, or the annihilation of their own wills, were yet led through their Neoplatonic conception of God as the only Reality beyond the idea of blessedness as consisting in union with God, to that of blessedness as consisting in the losing of self in the Divine essence. But Luther had no such idea in his mind. This is evident from the fact that ever since 1518 he set himself in deliberate antagonism to all mysticism.[1] Moreover, the re-acceptance of the mystical view is out of harmony with the doctrine of justification (vol. i. p. 356). Therefore the original Lutheran sense of eternal life cannot be ascertained through the notion of the *unio mystica*. To determine the precise method in which we must conceive this relation of justification will, however, require a special investigation.

[1] See the corresponding expressions on this subject in his *Operat. in Ps.* v. (*Opp. exeg. lat.* xiv. p. 239), and *De captiv. Babylon. ecclesiae* (*Opp. lat. var. arg.* v. p. 104). Cf. also the fragment which Löscher, *Vollständ. Timotheus Verinus*, i. p. 31, communicates from a manuscript in his own possession : "Ad speculationes de maiestate dei nuda dederunt occasionem Dionysius cum sua mystica theologia et alii eum secuti, qui multa scripserunt de spiritualibus nuptiis, ubi deum ipsum sponsum, animam sponsam finxerunt. Atque ita docuerunt, homines posse conversari et agere in vita mortali et corrupta natura et carne cum maiestate dei inscrutabili et aeterna sine medio. Et haec certe doctrina recepta est pro summa et divina, *in qua et ego aliquamdiu versatus sum, non tamen sine magno meo damno.* Ut istam Dionysii mysticam theologiam et alios similes libros, quibus tales nugae continentur, detestemini tanquam pestem aliquam, hortor. Metuo enim, *fanaticos homines futuros, qui talia portenta rursum in ecclesiam invehant* et per hoc sanam doctrinam obscurent et prorsus obruant." Cf. *Gesch. der Pietismus*, vol. ii. p. 32.

§ 19. As an operation of God upon men, justification is correlative to *faith*. This is the condition which prevents justification, or the forgiveness of sins, being represented as a contradiction to the presupposed estimate of sin. Up to this point, in our definition of justification, man has been treated in his peculiar character as sinner, and the subject of the consciousness of guilt. It was presupposed that with sin a state of alienation between God and men was brought about through the existence of real moral opposition between them. Justification, then, signifies the bringing back of the sinner into nearness with God, the removal of the alienating effect of the existent opposition to God and the accompanying consciousness of guilt. If, however, man in his relation to justification were to be represented only as sinner, his alienation from God, both in the objective and in the subjective respect, would continue, and the opposite status, that, namely, of justification, could not even be conceived. The sinner must therefore be thought of likewise as the subject of faith. Here, it is true, a new difficulty may be found. For if the condition must be fulfilled before the result can be reached, the faith of the sinner really appears to precede his justification. The question then will be whether and how the sinner can fulfil this condition. This difficulty may, however, be waived in the meantime, if we take into account the opposite fact that the idea of reconciliation, in which justification is represented inclusive of its result, makes the faith of the sinner to appear precisely as the result of justification. Justification effects a change in the consciousness of guilt in this respect, that the feeling of mistrust towards God which is bound up with that consciousness, and the shrinking from Him which results therefrom, are replaced by a consenting movement of the will towards God (§ 15). This new direction of the will to God which is evoked by reconciliation is, in the Evangelical view, faith ; and, in so far as it expects to be determined solely by God, it belongs as a special class to the general idea of obedience (vol. ii. p. 324).

The meaning of the idea of faith, and the relation in which

it stands to justification, have indeed been accurately determined in Evangelical theology. From various passages in Melanchthon [1] we ascertain that faith means neither the acknowledgment of the correctness of traditional facts, nor the acceptance of orthodox propositions, but trust in God's grace. Calvin has elucidated the idea of faith with still greater care than Melanchthon.[2] He emphasizes the fact that the knowledge which is included in faith, having for its object the goodness of God, is of quite a different nature from our knowledge of the world, which consists in the explanation of phenomena and perceptions. Faith is emotional conviction of the harmony between the Divine purposes and the most intimate interests of man. A certain interest, it is true, attaches to our ordinary knowledge of the world, as is shown in the act of attention. But the interest which expresses itself in emotion—that is, interest not in the discovery of truth for itself, but in the feeling of moral pleasure and in the satisfaction of our own spirit—is of quite a different nature, inasmuch as it connects the maintenance of our whole personality with the highest standard of our life, the Divine good-

[1] *Apologia C. A.* ii. 48 : "Fides quae iustificat, non est tantum notitia historiae, sed est assentiri promissioni dei,—est velle et accipere promissionem remissionis peccatorum et iustificationis." 77 : "Sola fide in Christum, non per dilectionem, non propter dilectionem aut opera consequimur remissionem peccatorum etsi dilectio sequitur fidem." *Loci theol. C. R.* xxi. p. 744 : "Fides est assentiri universo verbo dei nobis proposito, adeoque et promissioni gratuitae reconciliationis, estque fiducia misericordiae dei promissae propter mediatorem Christum. Nam fiducia est motus in voluntate, necessario respondens assensioni, seu quo voluntas in Christo acquiescit."

[2] *Inst. chr. rel.* iii. 2. 7 : "Nunc iusta fidei definitio nobis constabit, si dicamus esse divinae erga nos *benevolentiae firmam certamque cognitionem,* quae gratuitae in Christo promissionis veritate fundata per spiritum sanctum et revelatur mentibus nostris et *cordibus* obsignatur." 8 : "Assensionem ipsam iterum repetam cordis esse magis quam cerebri, et *affectus* magis quam intelligentiae. Qua ratione *obedientia* vocatur fidei." 14 : "Cognitionem non intelligimus comprehensionem, qualis esse solet earum rerum, quae sub humanum sensum cadunt . . . Sed dum *persuasum* habet, quod non capit, plus ipsa *persuasionis certitudine* intelligit, quam si humanum aliquid sua capacitate perciperet . . . Unde statuimus, fidei notitiam *certitudine* magis quam apprehensione contineri." 15 : "Sensus plerophoriae, quae fidei tribuitur, est nempe qui dei bonitatem perspicue nobis propositam extra dubium ponat. Id autem fieri nequit, quin eius *suavitatem* vere *sentiamus et experiamur* in nobis ipsis. Quare apostolus ex fide deducit *fiduciam* . . . Ostendit, non esse rectam fidem, nisi cum *tranquillis animis* audemus nos in conspectum dei sistere."

will and our own blessedness. In this analysis of Calvin's main theses it will be seen that the strong emphasis which Melanchthon laid on the will has disappeared. Calvin does, however, also recognise the place of the will in the act of faith, when, in treating of the emotional character of faith, he brings out the significance of faith as obedience. But his treatment of the matter is not quite clear. Emotion is a modification of feeling; and many emotions, especially those with which we are here concerned, have a peculiar resemblance to the will. But in acts of will we recognise a clear purpose, and this characteristic mark is just what is wanting in movements of emotion. Here, then, a difference comes to light between Melanchthon and Calvin. This difference is clearly expressed in Calvin's statement that the apostles *derive* trust from faith. Luther and Melanchthon, on the contrary, define the idea of faith accurately, making it precisely equivalent to the idea of trust in God. We may understand Calvin's statement in the same sense if we conceive him to have meant " derivation " analytically. But Calvin's further explanations do not make this clear. In Calvin's school, as, for example, in the Heidelberg Catechism, § 21, the original Protestant interpretation of faith as trust continues, but by the high Reformed Orthodoxy Calvin was understood to maintain that *fiducia* stands in a synthetic relation to *fides*, and therefore does not in all cases accompany the latter.[1] But trust is a function of the will, and therefore also, in the case under discussion, conceived as trust in the saving will of God, bound up with the characteristic mark of a clear purpose. We trust in God, Who, through the promise of forgiveness, shows our blessedness to be His aim. This connection of ideas governs the self-consciousness of the believer, as well as all the characteristic marks of emotion, conviction, certainty, obedience, and pleasure, as Calvin has rightly shown.

That the will plays a part in the act of faith is recognised

---

[1] Gomarus, *Loci communes*, p. 425, maintains that *fiducia* is *effectus fidei*, and denies that it is *forma fidei*. Cf. *Geschichte des Pietismus*, vol. i. p. 323.

also by Thomas Aquinas, even when he attributes faith specifically to the *intellectus*, and defines it as assent to the truths revealed by God. For, in order to distinguish faith from knowledge, he lays down the principle that in knowledge one is moved to assent to the truth through the object itself, but in faith and opinion not through the object of knowledge alone, but therewith also through the co-operation of the will. If these be the common distinguishing marks, then knowledge is opinion, if it be accompanied by doubt, or fear of the opposite possibility; and the knowledge of revealed truth supported by the will is faith, if it be accompanied by certainty regarding what is known.[1] In the Tridentine Decree, Session vi., it is recognised that faith in this sense is *fundamentum et radix justificationis ;* it is acknowledged, however, that something else must accompany this initial act of faith, in order to attain justification. Here then it is admitted that a rational knowledge of Revelation, comprehended in a formal resolution of the will, is not a sufficient ground for justification. It is therefore further maintained that, in order to attain justification, love must accompany faith, and that in a relation so close that love becomes the very essence of faith. Now the argument which Thomas advances in support of his thesis goes directly to prove that love to God as the highest good gives its essential character to faith.[2] If the Catholic idea of *fides caritate formata* were here accurately and exhaustively described, I should see nothing therein to contradict the Evangelical idea of faith. For faith, regarded as trust, is no other than the direction of the will towards God as the highest end and the highest good. When, therefore, Möhler [3] represents to us that trust in the love of

[1] See *Summa theol.* ii. 2, qu. 1, art. 4.
[2] Qu. 4, art. 3 : "Actus voluntarii speciem recipiunt a fine, qui est voluntatis obiectum. Id autem, a quo aliquid speciem sortitur, se habet ad modum formae in rebus naturalibus. Et ideo cuiuslibet actus voluntarii forma quodammodo est finis ad quem ordinatur . . . Actus fidei ordinatur ad obiectum voluntatis, quod est bonum, sicut ad finem. Hoc autem bonum, quod est finis fidei, scilicet bonum divinum est proprium obiectum caritatis, et ideo caritas dicitur forma fidei, in quantum per caritatem actus fidei perficitur et formatur."
[3] *Symbolik* (6th ed. 1843), § 17, pp. 169, 170.

God is begotten from a corresponding movement of the human
soul, namely, love to God, he tells us nothing new or startling.
But the above-mentioned conclusion of Thomas is not the
whole Catholic doctrine.   In the elaboration of the thema in
the third article of the Tridentine Creed—*quod unumquodque
operatur per suam formam : fides autem per dilectionem operatur,
ergo dilectio caritatis est fidei forma*—" love " is indeed used
strictly in the sense of " love to God"; but it is undoubtedly
the fact, in spite of Möhler's fine colouring, that in the
Catholic doctrine this Pauline principle is used as the correlate
of *justificatio* in the sense of " active love to men." [1]   For this
is intentionally not distinguished from " love to God," as the
unrelated expression *caritas* shows.

Thomas, indeed, proceeds to argue that love to God and
love to men are not different acts, but one and the same act,
only with different extensions.[2]   The principle on which he
bases this argument is, that the specific character of an act is
determined by the essential ground of the object to which the
act relates.   According to this principle, the act which relates
to a given object, and that which extends directly to the
essential ground of the object, are specifically identical.   For
example, the seeing of light and the seeing of colours on the
ground of light, are specifically one act.   In the same way,
love to God and love to men ˙are represented as one act,
because God is the ground of love to one's fellow-men, and
because the aim of such love is that every man should be in
God, that is, should find his blessedness in God.   But in my
opinion the essential ground of an object is related to the
object as the universal to the particular.   Therefore the act

---

[1] *Conc. Trid.* Sess. vi. cap. 7.

[2] Qu. 25, art. 1 : "Habitus non diversificantur, nisi ex hoc, quod variant
speciem actus.   Omnis enim actus unius speciei ad eundem habitum pertinet.
Cum autem species actus ex obiecto sumatur secundum formalem rationem
ipsius, necesse est, quod idem specie sit actus, qui fertur in rationem obiecti et
qui fertur in obiectum sub tali ratione, sicut eadem est specie visio, qua videtur
lumen et qua videtur color secundum luminis rationem.   Ratio autem diligendi
proximum deus est.   Hoc enim debemus in proximo diligere, ut in deo sit.
Unde idem specie actus est, quo diligitur deus et quo diligitur proximus.   Et
propter hoc habitus caritatis non solum se extendit ad dilectionem dei sed
etiam ad dilectionem proximi."

which is directed to the particular on the ground of the
universal will always have its relation also to the universal ;
but not *vice versâ*. Therefore, if God is the ground of genuine
love to one's fellow-men, that is, love which desires for one's
fellow-men that perfection and blessedness which they will
find in God, every act of love to one's fellow-men will also be
an act of love to God ; but not *vice versâ*, every act of love
to God will not also extend to one's fellow-men. It may be
urged as an argument for the latter thesis, that the seeing of
light is always also the seeing of colours. But the analogy
is not valid. For light appears only in its colours ; but God
does not exist only in men. The passage 1 John iv. 21, too,
the meaning of which Thomas attempts to turn to fit in with
his own conclusion, only contains the commandment that he
who loves God shall love his brother also. That is, love to
God is not in itself bound up with love to one's fellow-men ;
but the latter is a special resolution of the will, quite distinct
from love to God.

We must accordingly, it is true, concede to the Roman
Catholic theologians that love to God constitutes the essence
of faith, if in that idea the thought is expressed that the will
is directed to God as its highest end. The determination of
the specific character of faith will then depend on such conditions as the attributes under which God is conceived, the
idea entertained regarding man's own power of will, and the
estimate of the present capacity of the will for faith, compared
with its former incapacity. Through these conditions, and
others yet to be considered, therefore through the necessary
modes of representing faith, it will be shown that faith is
in intellectu tanquam in subjecto. That is, faith has for its
material content the ideas which mediate the movement of
the will which is expressed in it. This material element of
faith, however, is not really faith in its specific character,
apart from the essential form of the love to God which is
related to it. The error in the Thomist theology consists only
in this, that *fides informis* is treated, contrary to the above
principle, as a real stage of faith, and that the qualifying

phrase *formatio per caritatem* is introduced as merely the complement of the hitherto imperfect faith. This method of procedure, of course, involves a contradiction in itself. For either *caritas* is *forma fidei*, in which case *fides informis*, regarded as *actus intellectus*, is formless matter, and therefore the possibility, not the reality, of faith ; or *caritas* is real *fides*, in which case the act of will in faith is merely accidental, not the essential element. If, then, *caritas Dei*, as Thomas has really shown, is to be conceived as the essence of faith, one is unable to see how this thought can be made to appear contradictory to the Evangelical idea of faith as *fiducia Dei*. The latter is only a specialised mode of conceiving the same idea. But the notorious Catholic interpretation of *caritas* as " the active exercise of love to men "—the identity of which with " love to God " has not been demonstrated by Thomas— stands in direct contradiction to the Evangelical idea.

The general ground on which this Catholic assumption must be rejected is that the characteristic marks which distinguish Christianity as a religion, and those which denote its ethical purpose, are therein confused with one another ; whereas, if Christianity is not to be distorted and falsified in both respects, they ought to be clearly distinguished. Justification depends solely on faith, that is, trust in God, as its direct correlate, because, in the Christian sense, it denotes the definite relation of men to God as their Father, which is necessary under the presupposition of sin, and possible in view of the consciousness of guilt. Now the active exercise of love to men does not enter as an element into this definite relation to God. The recognised Evangelical doctrine, it is true, maintains that the impulse to love one's fellow-men, which is the fundamental principle of active human life, is essentially bound up with the very idea of justification. For Christianity is the ethical religion ; and wherever entrance into the specifically Christian status before God is realised, Christianity brings into exercise also the corresponding moral impulse. But for the very reason that the religious character of Christianity and its ethical purpose are different, active love to men, which is directed towards the ethical end of Christianity, cannot hold good also as the direct condition for the religious relation to God which justification denotes. The Christian designation of God as our Father, it is true, comprises also the notion of His Lordship over the Kingdom of God. For under that title we pray to God that His Kingdom may come. Now, love to one's fellow-men is a deduction from the highest principle which dominates all moral action, namely, regard to the Kingdom of God. Therefore the impulse to such love stands also in relation to the idea of God as Father. But the mutual relation which exists between God as Father and believers means one thing when represented as the peculiar status . before the Father into which Christianity brings believers, and quite another when represented as their co-operation with the Father in advancing the common end of the Kingdom of God. The peculiar status before God into which Christianity brings believers, therefore, consists in this, that God receives believers, in spite of their sin and their consciousness of guilt, into that fellowship with Himself which guarantees their salvation or eternal life. This relationship extends to all Christians as such. In so far, therefore, as we are dealing with the entrance of each individual through faith, that is, trust, into fellowship with God, the question of the moral relationship between the believers, the impulse to which is given therewith, does not come directly into consideration : nor is it possible to see how this question should come into consideration.

Where the faith which is related to justification comes into exercise, it is related also to God. And as it is called forth by reconciliation on God's part, it must be considered, in its relation to justification, not as a work of man possessed of independent value, but rather as the act through which the new relation of men to God, realised in justification, is religiously recognised and actually established.[1] Therefore the Pietistic wresting of the idea of justification to mean an

---

[1] *Apol. Conf. Aug.* ii. 56 : "Fides non ideo iustificat aut salvat, quia ipsa sit opus per sese dignum, sed tantum quia accipit misericordiam promissam."

analytic judgment on the value of faith (§ 16), is an approach to the Catholic view. We must not, however, fail to observe, as a difference between the two, that in the Pietistic view the idea of love to men is not included as an element in faith. Rather, in that view, only the manifold strivings of love to God, the aspirations after full faith, that is, the desire for the knowledge of saving truth, the hungering and thirsting after righteousness, and, finally, the acceptance of Christ, through which the knowledge of and assent to the saving doctrine are raised from the sphere of intellect to that of personal conviction (vol. i. p. 359)——only these, regarded as worthy effects of union with Christ, are brought under the special judgment of justification. This view is in perfect harmony with the first application of the Thomist notion of *fides caritate formata*, namely, the proposition that love to God gives reality and value to merely intellectual faith. The Pietists, however, distinctly avoid the further step which Thomas takes, the attempt to pass off love to men as identical with love to God. The language they use, moreover, does not warrant our bringing any one of them into harmony with the Tridentine Creed.

§ 20. The ground of justification, or the forgiveness of sins, is the benevolent, gracious, merciful purpose of God to vouchsafe to sinful men the privilege of access to Himself. The form in which sinners appropriate this gift is faith, that is, the emotional trust in God, accompanied by the conviction of the value of this gift for one's blessedness, which, called forth by God's grace, takes the place of the former mistrust which was bound up with the feeling of guilt. Through trust in God's grace the alienation of sinners from God, which was essentially connected with the unrelieved feeling of guilt, is removed. This is evidence that the guilt, so far as it prevents access to God, is forgiven by God. The purpose of God to forgive sinners is represented by the Reformers, under the notions of *promissio* and *evangelium*, not only as an openly revealed volition, but also as one which lays the foundation of a *fellowship* among men. In the gradation of the bearers of this Revelation, Christ, as the Mediator of the Gospel, is reckoned first. The next place after Him is accorded to the community which He founded, every member of which has authority to proclaim the justifying grace of God, especially the official representatives of the Church, whose function is to transmit the *promissio remissionis peccatorum propter Christum*. Besides these human organs, who by their word make the revelation of God in Christ efficacious for the community which He founded, the sacraments are channels of the same sin-forgiving grace, inasmuch as they contain the Word or Gospel of God as their essence, and apply the Gospel in a peculiar way to the members of the community. Therefore the unity of the Church is essentially bound up with the pure preaching of the Gospel and the proper administration of the two sacraments, and in the same degree with nothing else. Now the pure Gospel is defined in the Augsburg Confession chap. vii., as the preaching of justification in the above-represented sense, namely, as depending on the merit of Christ, and thus excluding the idea of human merits.[1] This preaching of the Gospel is the distinctive mark of the exist-ence of a community of believers ; for, according to the same Confession chap. v., it is only through the Word of God, in preaching and sacraments, that faith is called into existence. It follows, then, that, through the operation of the Holy Spirit, faith is identical in each individual case, and common to all the members of the community. Against this repre-sentation, however, the objection has been made that faith may be awakened in men through their own efforts, without the regular instrumentality of the publicly preached Word.

But these fundamental views of the Reformation are not disproved by the fact that very many hear the preaching of the Word without being led through any mechanical compul-sion to the point of faith, and the contrary fact that very many attain to faith without being directly led thereto through the hearing of a preached sermon. The principle was not arrived at from the consideration of such instances.

[1] *Apol. C. A.* iv. 20, 21 ; ii. 101 ; viii. 42, 43, 58-60.

Therefore it ought not to stand in the way of a full investigation of the manifold experiences of life. The recognition of the principle, in reality, only involves the proviso, that one cannot arrive at and maintain individual conviction of faith in isolation from the already existing community of faith, and that that community is coextensive with the spread of the Gospel, that is, the public preaching of the forgiveness of sins. And even if a man's conversion were as far as possible from being occasioned by the hearing of such preaching, yet the thesis in the 5th Article of the Augsburg Confession would be proved true by the fact that all the spiritual ideas which are effective in bringing about a conversion are derived from the Gospel, and become known to the converted person only through the Gospel; that, therefore, his conversion is entirely dependent on the purpose of God revealed in the Gospel. The maintenance of this principle is necessary for the welfare of the Church, in order that the individual's own struggle for faith may not be esteemed as independent of, or opposed to, the public preaching of the Word. The effect of such individualistic ideas would be, as seen, for example, in the history of the Anabaptists, that the Church would be given over to the conflicts of sectarianism, and that the faith itself would be falsified. The connection of faith with the revelation of grace through the Word was also plainly recognised by Calvin.[1] If, therefore, the community of believers is coextensive with the influence of the Gospel, and if the Gospel has no other sphere for the proclamation of its glad tidings of God's readiness to forgive sins, then those striking statements of Luther are intelligible, namely, that " the Church is full of the forgiveness of sins "; that " within the fold of the Christian Church God daily and richly forgives me, the individual, all my sins "; and that " the Church, as a mother, bears and nurtures every individual through the Word " (vol. i. pp. 161, 176). Calvin repeats the latter statement (*Inst.* iv. 1. 4).

---

[1] *Inst. chr. rel.* iii. 2. 6 : " Principio admonendi sumus, perpetuam esse fidei relationem cum verbo, nec magis ab eo posse divelli, quam radios a sole, unde oriuntur."

Finally, Luther pursues the same thought in a characteristic way. He loves, namely, to represent the Church as the Bride of Christ, with whom, in accordance with marriage right, Christ joins in a mutual exchange of benefits, He taking upon Himself the sins of the believing, and Himself imparting His righteousness to them.[1] In this representation of the process of justification by faith, however, Luther insists on the fact that the blessings which accrue to the individual are only imparted to him in common with all the others with whom he is bound up, through the same salvation, in the unity of the Church.

This idea, that the benefit of justification accrues to individuals as constituting the community of believers, corresponds to the significant expressions used in the New Testament regarding the sacrifice of Christ. For the conception of Christ's sacrifice through the types of the covenant sacrifice and the yearly sin-offering of the Israelites brings the forgiveness of sins which results from Christ's sacrifice into direct relation to the community founded by Him (vol. ii. p. 216). The individual can therefore appropriate the forgiveness of sins by faith only when he unites in his faith at once trust in God and Christ, and the intention to connect himself with the community of believers. For the individual who is led to faith always finds the domain of human life which is determined and governed by the forgiveness of sins already marked out for him ; and, moreover, he has to attach himself to the community of believers all the more decisively that he is indebted to that community for the knowledge of salvation and for stimuli of incalculable strength urging him to appropriate salvation. The relation of justification to the community of believers has been recognised not only by Brenz, who followed strictly in Luther's footsteps (vol. i. p. 209), but also by successive ascetics and theologians from Spener to Jer. Friedr. Reuss.[2] The idea has disappeared, however, in the orthodox

---

[1] Cf. *Geschichte des Pietismus*, vol. iii. p. 122.
[2] Cf. *ibid.* vol. ii. p. 26 ff.

Lutheran Dogmatics, because Melanchthon, the founder of that Dogmatics, rejected the above-quoted statements of Luther. The first edition of his *Loci theologici* contains no article at all on the Church. Here, therefore, he explains justification as exclusively an experience of the individual. In the following editions he has appended a chapter on the doctrine of the Church. He has, however, preserved unaltered his former scheme of justification. Melanchthon has indeed kept in view the factor of the Gospel, or the Word, of God, or the Divine promise. But he has nowhere made it clear that the community, to which the ministry of the Gospel is committed, thereby comprehends within its scope the process which he analyses as the experience of the individual. He testifies on several occasions that the community is the bearer of the Gospel;[1] but he nowhere brings this idea into connection with the explanation of justification as mediated through the promises, or the Gospel, of God. The Reformed theology, on the other hand, following Calvin's example, has rightly understood and maintained Luther's view (vol. i. p. 205), and has accordingly represented the justification of the individual as conditioned by the existence of the community (vol. i. p. 309). In spite of this representation, however, the mystical conception of the scheme of salvation, which completely isolates the individual from connection with the Church, has gained a place within the sphere of the Reformed Church as well as the Lutheran.

Mysticism (vol. i. pp. 120, 356), which claims to lead men to the attainment of essential union with God, is quite different from the Evangelical doctrine of justification by faith; and its sentimental communion with Christ as the Bridegroom is quite different from trust in Christ as the Bearer of the Divine promise. The mystical communion of love with Christ, it is claimed, transcends trust in the merits of Christ. The true believers, says Wilhelm Brakel, receive

---

[1] *Apol. C. A.* iv. : "Ecclesia proprie est columna veritatis ; retinet enim purum evangelium." Tractatus de potestate papae, 24 : "Tribuit Christus principaliter claves (i. e. evangelium) ecclesiae et immediate."

the Lord Jesus into their hearts; they do not remain content
with the benefits guaranteed by Him, but turn for full satisfaction to the Source Himself.   Union with God, says Johann
Arndt, in agreement with Tauler, is found in one's own heart;
for "the Kingdom of God is within you." "In our heart
is the real school of the Holy Ghost, the real workplace of
the Holy Ghost, the real house of prayer in spirit and in
truth."   In this statement, so little account is taken by
Arndt of the authoritative instrument of grace, the preached
Word of God, that he expressly maintains the revelation of
the eternal Word within the pious soul, the communication
of God's mind within the loving heart.[1]   The *doctrine* of
justification in the usual orthodox representation is indeed
recognised by the mystics as the presupposition of these
inner experiences, but has no influence on their circle of
thought.   If that doctrine had been still rightly understood, they would not have returned to the mediaeval types
of religious life which had been condemned by Luther.
Wherever Mysticism is found, the thought of justification
no longer retains its true significance as the key to the
whole domain of Christian life, but is so depreciated as to
become a mere formal precondition of the immediate union
with God, or the immediate communion with Christ, which
Mysticism strives to attain.[2]   One of the chief marks of
distinction between the two opposite views, however, is that,
wherever men give way to mystical states or aspirations,
they imagine that the sphere of the preached Word and the
promises of grace, therefore the necessary subordination to
the public Revelation in the Church, is transcended and may
be forgotten.   The falsehood of this pretended immediate
communion with, or immediate relation to, Christ, in which
men endeavour to enjoy all possible forms of blessedness
apart from and beyond the forgiveness of sins, has also
been shown by Calvin in the passage: "*Haec vera est Christi
cognitio, si eum qualis offertur a patre, suscipimus, nempe*

---

[1] *Geschichte des Pietismus*, vol. i. p. 296, vol. ii. p. 50.
[2] *Op. cit.* vol. ii. p. 23.

8

evangelio suo vestitum" (*Inst.* iii. 2. 6). Now the Song of
Songs, from the allegorical exposition of which all those
plays of fancy are derived, does not belong to the Gospel
with which Christ is invested (*vestitus*). The whole mystical scheme, in fine, lies outside the spiritual horizon of the
Reformers; it has no point of agreement with their doctrinal
standards; it stands in contradiction to both the direct and the
indirect estimate of the value of the community of believers
and the public preaching of the Word of grace, which the
standards attest; and, judged in its own special character, it
is no improvement on the Reformed type of religious life, as
certainly as it is derived from the practice of Monasticism.

§ 21. With justification by faith in the Evangelical sense,
there is bound up the attribute of Christian *freedom from the
law*. Under the heading *libertas christiana* the older theologians
bring together various heterogeneous ideas. The place of the
doctrine in the theological system is thus rendered uncertain.
One hardly knows at the first glance whether Melanchthon,
in closing his principal theological work with the doctrine of
Christian freedom, means thereby to distinguish freedom as
the highest mark of Christian life, or is merely adding a
supplement, the content of which he was unable to insert
elsewhere. As he deduces the principal points in the doctrine of Christian freedom from the redemption mediated
through Christ, the place which he has selected for the
exposition of the doctrine is certainly not rightly chosen;
the section, indeed, actually appears to be merely a supplementary treatment of sundry hitherto forgotten points. In
any case the Lutheran divines have regarded the matter in
this way; for not only has the *locus* "*de libertate christiana*"
entirely disappeared from their systems, but they have
introduced the various elements of the idea scattered here
and there in all possible places, and mentioned only incidentally. Not only so, but later divines, like Hollatz and
Buddeus, omit the idea altogether. On the contrary, in
Calvin's *Institutio* the doctrine of Christian freedom immediately follows that of justification, and is related to it by

the express statement that it is necessary for the understanding of the meaning of justification.[1]   Therefore, in the great majority of the Reformed divines, the "*locus*" entitled "*de libertate christiana*" either appears in its true place, or the subject is treated in connection with the ideas of justification and adoption.

Melanchthon enumerates four grades of freedom—freedom from sin and the wrath of God, the freedom of the new life inspired by the Holy Ghost, freedom from the Mosaic law, and freedom from the yoke of human ordinances in the worship of the Church.   Under the aspect of freedom from the Mosaic law, Melanchthon also maintains the right of the different national legislations.   Now, if we compare this combination of ideas with Calvin's, we find that Calvin omits the first—freedom from sin and the wrath of God (and rightly, because this attribute is not co-ordinate with, but rather, as an expression of *redemtio*, the basis of the following), and also the third—freedom from the Mosaic law (again rightly, because the Mosaic law not only belongs to a quite different order of things from the Christian faith, but is introduced into the Christian system merely through an entirely false conception of the significance of the Old Testament for the Christian community).   While Calvin has thus retained only the second and fourth of those four grades of Christian freedom, he has put in the forefront another aspect of freedom, to which he was necessarily led from regard to the true nature of justification.   It is just the other side of justification by faith, that nothing of law or legal works should play a part in it.[2]   To this fundamental principle we

[1] iii. 19. 1: "Tractandum nunc de christiana libertate, cuius explicatio praetermitti minime ab eo debet, cui summam evangelicae doctrinae compendio complecti propositum est.   Est enim res apprime necessaria, ac citra cuius cognitionem nihil fere sine dubitatione aggredi conscientiae audent; praesertim vero est appendix iustificationis, et ad vim eius intelligendam non parum valet."

[2] iii. 19. 2: "Sublata legis mentione, et omni operum cogitatione seposita, unam dei misericordiam amplecti convenit, quum de iustificatione agitur, et averso a nobis aspectu, unum Christum intueri.   Non enim illic quaeritur, quomodo iusti simus, sed quomodo, iniusti licet ac indigni, pro iustis habeamur."

must reduce the last of the aspects of Christian freedom, the right, namely, to regard human ordinances in the Church as indifferent.   There remain, therefore, two principal forms of freedom—freedom from all considerations alike of Divine and of human law in the act of justification itself, and the freedom from legal compulsion, that is, the freedom of will in rendering obedience to the Divine law, which one enjoys as the result of justification in the status of faith.   Luther's treatment of the subject of freedom also leads to these two results.[1]   It is easy, however, to see that these two aspects of freedom are heterogeneous, and that the second does not belong to the explanation of justification as a religious relation to God.   For it describes the nature of the moral conduct which goes along with justifying faith, but yet cannot be derived solely from that faith—even though the Reformers, on grounds which cannot yet be considered, entertain that notion.   We have here, therefore, to take account only of the freedom from Divine law and from human Church laws which is asserted when justification is referred to faith alone.

As the definite form of this doctrine has without doubt been modelled on Paul's arguments in the Epistle to the Galatians, it might be asked what practical interest we have in still retaining it in mind.   For since the time when Jewish Christianity disappeared from history, the error of the "foolish Galatians" has only reappeared among the Pasagians in North Italy (in the eleventh century), and the Russian Sabbatniki (since the end of the fifteenth century); while against the temptation to relapse into Jewish Christianity we Protestants are quite secure.   If, then, the conception of

---

[1] *Opera latina ad reform. pertin,* ed. Schmidt, tom. iv. p. 225 : "Clarum est, homini christiano suam fidem sufficere pro omnibus, nec operibus ei opus fore, ut iustificetur.   Quodsi operibus non habet opus, nec lege opus habet ; si lege non habet opus, certe liber est a lege.   Atque haec est christiana illa libertas, fides nostra, quae facit non ut otiosi simus aut male vivamus, sed ne cuiquam opus sit lege aut operibus ad iustitiam et salutem."   P. 229 : "Non operando sed credendo deum glorificamus et veracem confitemur. Hoc nomine fides sola est iustitia christiani hominis et omnium praeceptorum plenitudo.   Qui enim primum implet, cetera omnia facili opera implet."

Divine law, from which by virtue of justification the believer is free, be understood in a less accurate sense than Paul intended, the thought of freedom from Divine law will mean that justification in the Evangelical sense does not include the conditions which the Catholic view of justification claims to be essential—in short, that the two homonymous ideas are directly incommensurable. For if active love to one's neighbour be an essential element in justification, as the Catholic view represents, then the law plays a part in the process of justification; and if the value of justification be enhanced through obedience to Divine and ecclesiastical commandments (*Trid.* Sess. vi. 10), then human Church ordinances are obligatory for justification. Therefore the notion of Christian freedom from the law has for us only this meaning, that justification, as we understand it, is quite different from justification in the Catholic view. Thus it is quite evident why Luther, in comparing his present with his former monastic life, and Calvin, like Luther, from his Reformed opposition to the Catholic practice, had so strong an interest in maintaining the principle that moral action is no part of the process of justification, and that justification has nothing to do with the performance of ceremonial rites, therefore that the believer as such is free from the law. On the contrary, where Evangelical life has gained possession of the field independently of Catholic types of doctrine, one may, as is actually shown to be the case, have no personal interest in the notion of freedom from the law, but regard it as merely the test of the difference between the two opposed conceptions of justification.

The matter, however, is not yet settled. The Pauline principle that " through the works of the law no man is justified," is indeed only the negative side of the prophetic expression that " the just shall live by faith " (vol. ii. p. 309). But Pharisaism, the falsification of Christianity by which is here guarded against, has a significance which has extended quite beyond its immediate historical appearance. The error of Pharisaism consists in this, that it transforms the religious relation of men to God into a legal relation, and represents ceremonial rites as the substantial elements in the formation of moral character, and therefore as works of merit for God and men (vol. ii. p. 277). This error was fallen into not only by that Jewish party, but also by many within the Christian Church. It is met with especially in various Catholic positions which are most closely connected with the idea of justification. It is Pharisaic, when the assertion is made that the justification which is grounded on grace is enhanced in value through obedience to the Church's commandments; for the Church's commandments have only a ceremonial content, which is of no value for the public well-being. It is Pharisaic, when increase of grace is derived from good works, reckoned as merits (*Trid.* Sess. vi. can. 32); for "merit" signifies, at least according to Thomas, a legal claim upon God, even though the claim be due to grace (vol. i. p. 71). Therefore the principle of freedom from the law and of freedom as against human Church ordinances is valuable as a standard for the recognition of the Pharisaic error in the Christian religion. Even Evangelical Christianity has not altogether avoided that error.

A specially significant application of the relation of freedom from the law to the idea of justification has recently been made by Schweizer. He arranges the whole history of religion according to that principle. Between the religion of nature and the religion of redemption he places a second necessary stage, namely, the religion of law, asserting that in that stage the pious soul, in harmony with the influence of the moral world, acknowledges its dependence on the wisdom, creative power, providence, and judicial authority of God.[1] This assumption, however, is of doubtful value. For the definition is not applicable to the religion of the Old Testament. The latter, moreover, did not degenerate into "mere religion of law and Judaistic holiness of works" through having first shut itself against the possibility of advance to the religion of redemption. For Pharisaism is

[1] Cf. *Christliche Glaubenslehre*, vol. i. p. 311.

older than Christianity. And again, it is not in harmony
with the description of Pharisaism as a " mere religion of law
and legal rights " that the religion of law is again recognised
as the positive historical preparation for the religion of
redemption, and also as an abiding element of that religion
in the act of penitence. When, however, Schweizer says
that once the religion has been fully revealed, the pious
consciousness is made absolutely free from the religion of
law, he is merely giving expression to the thought of *libertas
a lege*.[1] A special significance is not to be attached to this
negative statement. Schweizer is hardly justified, however,
in concluding from these facts that " the moral Rationalism
of which Kant was the founder, and also in some measure
the older Socinianism, were attempts to comprehend Christianity itself again as a mere religion of law, excluding all
that claims to be revelation and redemption as imagination or error." This characterisation does not adequately
describe even the Socinian position, far less the Rationalism
of the disciples of Kant. For both tendencies of thought are
averse to all ceremonial practices. They do not surrender
the significance of the grace of God, and they are far from
reducing religion to notions of law. As a general rule,
Protestantism is little exposed to the Pharisaic error. For
even where in Evangelical Christianity ceremonial practices
are esteemed too highly, there is found, as far as one can
observe, no accompanying claim of right before God. The
Sabbath rest, as observed in the Puritan habits of life in
Scotland and England, is indeed in entire harmony with
the Pharisaic conception of the Mosaic law ; but in as far
as the practice is maintained as a national custom it is free
from the suspicion of a claim of right upon God. It would
only become the occasion of a religious error, if, for example,
it were made the basis for the judgment that the Christianity
of Germany is imperfect because it is without that custom.
The case is similar when Pietists deny the existence of faith
in those persons in whom they miss the exact demeanour

[1] *Op. cit.* p. 321.

and modes of speech which they have made into a ceremonial law for themselves.

§ 22. Justification or reconciliation is the determination of God as Father to admit sinners, in spite of their sin and consciousness of guilt, to that relation of fellowship with Himself which includes the right of sonship and the inheritance of eternal life. This relation to God is subject from the other side to the condition that faith, that is, the direction of the will to God as the highest end, should be called forth in the sinner, and that the feeling of mistrust which operates in the consciousness of faith should be converted into trust in God as Father. And finally, since justification or reconciliation is the fundamental principle of Christianity as a religion, through which all other corresponding functions first become possible, and at the same time forms the content of the public preaching of the Gospel, it must not merely be officially represented by the existent religious community, but must also be realised in the experience of every individual within the community. With regard, however, to the question of the *extent* of God's purpose of *justification*, there still remains unsettled the controversy between the Lutheran and the Reformed theologians (vol. i. pp. 305—314). Both the contending parties can appeal to definite expressions in the Epistles of the New Testament in support of their views (vol. ii. p. 216). In the Reformed view, the Divine purpose of justification through Christ is limited to those persons whom God has eternally elected in their individual capacity as recipients of salvation. This true community of Christ is the primary object of justification, which is manifested in the resurrection of Christ; the individual experiences that grace only in so far as he belongs by election, call, and spiritual incorporation, to the true community of Christ. For the eternally reprobate there is neither a purpose of justification on the part of God, nor the corresponding purpose on the part of Christ, even although His work in itself might have had power to secure pardon for all men. In the Lutheran view (vol. i.

p. 308), the wish of God, in accordance with which He has provided for the reconciliation of His justice through Christ, is directed to the salvation of all men, and Christ has also in intention made satisfaction both for elect and reprobate. But the offer of salvation which is made to all men results in justification effectually only in the case of those who exercise faith. On account, therefore, of this necessary condition of an effective result, God has eternally elected from the mass of the sinful race the individual persons whose faith He foresaw.

Neither of these opposed views is true; for they have alike two errors in common. The Lutheran view, on the very face of it, shows inconsistency in its conception of God. For according to that view, God's openly-expressed will, as made known in the Gospel, is directed to the salvation of all men; while His secret will, which alone is really effective, limits salvation to a portion of mankind, those, namely, who fulfil the condition of faith. This inconsistency, it is true, does not appear in the Reformed system of doctrine, as officially represented. It is involved, however, in that system. For along with the particular purpose of election and justification, the law-giving will of God extends the promise of salvation to all men. The other, the fundamental, error in both theories consists in this, that the human race on the one side, and the community of the elect on the other, are represented as sums of individuals, and that on both sides the real destination of individuals to salvation is given out as an eternal act of God. Now, the only passage in which Paul speaks of an election of individuals (Rom. ix. 11) merely conveys the sense that the Divine act is superordinate in respect of relative temporal priority to the self-activity of men.[1] All the other expressions of the apostles on this subject (Rom. viii. 29; Eph. i. 4; 1 Pet. i. 1) refer to the community as a whole. Eternal election of individuals is

---

[1] According to the usual interpretation, Gal. i. 15 also belongs to this category. I am very doubtful, however, whether Paul is here speaking of his election by God before his birth.

neither a Biblical idea nor a religious conception, but merely a deduction of Augustine's from his abstract idea of God —an idea which makes all temporal history nothing but unreal appearance. Now, our intuition of time is arrived at through the distinction which we draw between our different ideas; our notion of time is fixed through the thought of the dependence of effects on causes. The reality of the world for God, as we must needs conceive it, depends on the condition that in the whole the individual also, which is subject to change, is willed by Him. If so, then the form of time also has its validity for Him. Now the individual man is dependent on a succession of middle causes. God can therefore conceive the individual only as he appears in time. Eternal predestination of individuals to salvation, whether unconditioned or conditioned by the faith which God has foreseen, is altogether contrary to reason.

In the Lutheran teaching, in particular, there is a peculiar limitation of the ordinary usage of words, by which justification is made to find its correlate in the individual believer as such. It has been already observed how the original close relation of justification to the end of eternal life, a relation through which the idea of justification receives a quite characteristic colouring, has been overlooked by the Lutheran divines (§ 15). In the Reformers these two thoughts appear as interchangeable ideas, which are not to be conceived apart from one another. The Lutherans, on the other hand, regard the Divine purpose to bestow eternal life upon all men as belonging to the domain of antecedent grace, without reflecting that that gift can only be conveyed as the result of justification. Moreover, when they represent the satisfaction which Christ has made for all men, both elect and reprobate, as the means whereby the antecedent universal gracious purpose of God is freed from the restraints due to His justice, they do not add the thought that the grace of God thereby becomes effective for all men. Rather, they deduce as the only consequence of the redemptive work of Christ the public proclamation of the Divine grace in the Gospel, along with the conditions brought into existence by the work of Christ. It is only here that the principle first finds expression, that he who fixes his faith thereon is justified. Now, in this scheme the idea of justification is so represented that the extension of the privilege of the new fellowship with God, which is no more fettered by sin, is made superordinate to all possible changes in the sinners, especially regeneration. But justification does not become effective in the case of the individual except through the condition of faith. Now faith is only possible as the result of regeneration. Therefore regeneration necessarily precedes justification. Therefore, also, the idea of regeneration is superordinate to that of justification. That is, justification can only be brought into relation with the individual as such by surrendering what the Lutherans are interested in maintaining, the superordination of justification to regeneration. The Lutheran theologians have sought to escape from their false position by defining regeneration through the Holy Ghost, which they allow to precede justification, in the strictest possible sense as *donatio fidei* (vol. i. p. 304), and by making *renovatio* or *sanctificatio*, that is, the capacity for good works through the Holy Ghost, follow justification. But even supposing this sequence of ideas were represented not in the form of time, but logically, there can be found within the idea of the Holy Ghost no conceivable ground why the establishment of religious susceptibility and that of moral capacity for good works should not take place in one single act. Moreover, faith, even when regarded as susceptibility to the Divine grace, is only conceivable as the positive direction of the will to God, and as such is no mere formal activity, but a real power with a definite content. Thus it is only by means of doubtful distinctions that the Lutheran divines apparently evade the difficulty which they incur through the exclusive reference of justification to the individual. If one continues to regard this method of conceiving the idea of justification as valid, while refusing to be bound by the recognised distinctions, then the thought of justification is distorted into an analytic judgment on the value of faith (p. 84).

The Lutheran representation of justification which we have just discussed harmonises with the Reformation conception of the problem in so far as the latter finds justification in the experience which necessarily falls within the limits of the individual life. On this depends another characteristic feature of the original Reformation view, namely, the representation of justification as the immediate result of the work of Christ. Dogmatic theology has, however, placed a wide gulf between the work of Christ and the justification of the individual, in respect not only of time, but also of the object. Inasmuch as justification is the content of the Divine purpose of grace, which results from the reconciliation of that purpose with the justice of God through the work of Christ, and is thereby distinguished from the antecedent grace of God, a formula comes into existence which is worthy of special attention, although it appeared in history only before the stereotyping of the Lutheran doctrine, and once more in the time of its decadence. The work of Christ is regarded, namely, not only as the efficacious means of reconciling God, but also as the expression of the gracious will of God directed to the redemption and justification *of the whole human race.* After Osiander, contrary to the original opinion of the Reformers, had differentiated both temporally and logically the ideas of redemption and justification (*Gerechtmachung*) through Christ, Strigel sought to maintain the identity of both ideas (vol. i. p. 241). To this end he had to distinguish between the successive justification (*Gerechtsprechung*) of individual believers and the value of the historical event which revealed the justifying grace of God in general.   He was thus led, through maintaining the Lutheran universalism, to construct the formula that through Christ the human race has been redeemed, sanctified, and justified, but that these benefits are applied to individuals only when they believe in Christ and

are baptized in His name.   This formula recurs in Fresenius.[1]
It is noteworthy in this connection that Fresenius arrives in
the last sentence at the view of Samuel Huber, which had
been rejected in its day by the Lutheran theologians.[2]   And
this is no mere accident.   For if we bring justification into
such close relation to the redemptive work of Christ as the
religious view of Luther and Melanchthon demands ; if, further,
we attribute no particular "reference" to the Divine purpose
of redemption and justification ; if, finally, we regard the
purpose to justify all men as the expression of the eternal
determination of the will of God in order to give decisive
weight to the temporal revelation of the will of God—then the
eternal destination of salvation, or election, holds good for all
men.   But if so, then the election of all men, being afterwards rendered inoperative through the decision of individuals
for unbelief, has the character only of a wish which remains
for the greatest part unfulfilled.   The flaw in the Lutheran
conception of the Divine scheme of salvation in the world,
therefore, appears also under these presuppositions, although
at a different point from that in which it appears in the
authoritative type of doctrine of the sixteenth and seventeenth centuries.

Although Huber's thesis, that God has eternally elected and
foreordained to life all men through Christ, cannot be established on exegetical grounds, and bears on the face of it the
character of a fixed idea rather than a theological proposition,
yet, as a protest against Calvin's classification of men as

[1] Cf. *Rechtfertigung*, v. 8 : "Since Christ has also become, by virtue of His
manhood, the Head of the whole human race, therefore one man is as much to
Him as another : therefore all may have equal part in His satisfaction."   vii. 32 :
"Although the real imparting of the righteousness of Christ to an individual
man can only take place when he has come into being and has fulfilled the
necessary conditions, yet he was reckoned as already present at the time of
the great atoning sacrifice of Christ, not through a necessary predestination,
but through a free imputation, not only believers but all men having been
included in this imputation. . . . The ground of the whole business of redemption and justification is the covenant of peace which the Father made with the
Son in the eternities.   In this covenant the multitude of all men and also the
all-sufficient sacrifice of Christ were regarded as present."

[2] Cf. Schweizer, *Protestant. Centraldogmen*, vol. i. pp. 501 ff., 532 ff.

either eternally reprobate or eternally elect, it is not without interest. It was from the very outset an unwarranted over-stepping of theological competency to define the Biblical thought of Divine election more precisely by filling out, through rational processes, the opposite thought of reprobation. For the religious interest is only concerned with the question whether oneself belongs to the number of the elect, while one's human sympathies, when not suppressed by dogmatism, will always rise in revolt against the idea of eternal reprobation as represented by Luther (*De servo arbitrio*) and Calvin. And besides, the cognitive interest is not satisfied by this idea of reprobation, since one is not competent to subsume definite men under this predicate. Therefore Huber is worth our remembrance, if only we confine our attention to the negative side of the *gratia universalis* which he proclaimed so inde-fatigably. Huber was, however, a very poor theologian, inasmuch as he did no justice to the thought of the election of the human race *in Christ*, which he deduced from Eph. i. 4, 5. The doctrine of twofold predestination, as held by Augustine, Luther, and Calvin, has absolutely no connection with the thought of election in Christ. Thus, when the later Reformation system-builders saw themselves compelled to come to an understanding with this formula, the orthodox Calvinistic school maintained that the predestination of re-demption through Christ was subordinate to the predestina-tion of the elect individuals to salvation, as the means to the end. But, as I have already shown (vol. i. p. 306), some of the most important Reformed theologians have determined the relation of the two ideas differently. They think of Christ, in whom the community as a whole is elected, under the attribute of His Lordship over the community, and accord-ingly regard the predestination of Christ as the chief Heir of God as preceding the election of the community to participa-tion in His inheritance, as the ground precedes the conse-quence.[1] This view, which is held by Amesius, Heidegger,

---

[1] To the note on vol. i. p. 306, I add the following supplementary remarks. When I there stated that Arminius was the first to lay stress on the thought of

and Witsius, involves, in truth, as much as the orthodox view, the validity of the idea of particular election with all its peculiar consequences, therefore also the thought of reprobation. The latter, however, no longer rightly. For the condition under which reprobation became co-ordinated with election has disappeared. The community is elected as a whole in Christ, its Head; the reprobate, on the other hand, are reprobated only as individuals. Amesius further, through his expressed comparison between the solidarity of the elect community in Christ and the solidarity of the human race in Adam, opens up a new view of the meaning and end of election. He represents the creation of men, namely, as completed through the Son of God, Whose communion with the human race was predestinated in the eternal election of God. This thought was already indicated

election in Christ, I knew quite well that the formula had already found a place in theological usage. I did not need to be taught that it already occurs in the Formula of Concord. But with what degree of clearness is it there used? The Lutheran formula, which Musaeus (in Baier, vol. iii. pp. 12, 14) draws up— "Quod est causa, cur deus in tempore nobis salutem conferat, id etiam causa est, cur ad salutem nos elegerit. Atqui meritum Christi est causa, cur deus in tempore nobis salutem conferat; ergo meritum Christi est etiam causa, cur deus nos elegerit"—became possible for the first time after the lines of demarcation had been drawn between the Arminians and the Calvinists. One sees quite easily, indeed, that the Lutheran development of doctrine, from the time of the Formula of Concord, proceeded on the way towards this goal. But at the beginning of this process the appearance of a difference on this point between the Lutherans and Calvinists was anything but clear, especially as Zanchi (in Gerhard, *Loci theol.* viii. 8. 149) expressed himself in a characteristically Lutheran way on the subject.—The formula of Amesius and the later Calvinists was also anticipated by Calvin. But it is very interesting to observe how little the latter, in the period of his strongest dependence on Luther, was able to discriminate his thought of the election of the community in the Person of its Lord, and Luther's thought that Christ is the ground of the knowledge of our election. In the *first* edition of his *Institutio* of 1536 Calvin says: "Cum Christus dominus noster is sit, in quo pater ab aeterno elegit, quos voluit esse suos ac in ecclesiae suae gregem referri, satis clarum testimonium habemus, nos et inter dei electos et ex ecclesia esse, si Christo communicamus. Deinde cum sit ipse idem Christus constans et immutabilis patris veritas, minime haesitandum est, quin eius sermo vere nobis enarret patris voluntatem, qualis ab initio fuit et semper futura est. Quando itaque Christum et quidquid eius est, fide possidemus, certo statuendum, quod ut ipse dilectus est patris filius haeresque regni coelorum, ita et nos per ipsum in dei filios sumus adoptati et sic eius fratres ac consortes, ut eiusdem simus haereditatis participes; ob id certi quoque simus, nos inter eos esse, quos dominus ab aeterno elegit" (*C. R.* xxix. p. 74). It is worth while to investigate the history of this point of doctrine in its whole context.

by Zwingli:[1] and it has since been more fully developed by Schleiermacher.

We have to take account of three ideas, in virtue of which Schleiermacher rose above the limits of theological tradition, and which act and react in certain definite ways on one another. Although the conception of redemption denotes comprehensively the whole work of Christ, yet it does not form a suitable expression of the Divine decree, inasmuch as it stands in direct relation to the fact of sin. The latter is indeed ordained by God, in order that men should realise the formerly-existent insurmountable incapacity of the God-consciousness as a personal activity, and thus acquire the longing after redemption. But as God is not the Author of evil, and as the latter is no creative thought of God, redemption denotes not so much directly the Divine decree concerning men, as rather the practical effect of that decree in harmony with the special circumstances. Therefore the Divine decree of redemption applies properly to the completion of the creation of men in the Person of Christ. In this idea there is expressly included the thought that the attainment of perfect human life was not to be reached along the lines of mere natural development from Adam (§ 89, 1). If, now, the privilege of sonship to God which is bestowed in justification is the positive new status in which men participate in the life of Christ and in His relationship to His Father, then we must not think of merely isolated acts of justification. These acts are only manifestations in time of the one eternal Divine decree of the justification of men for Christ's sake. This decree is identical with that of the sending of Christ into the world, and also with that of the creation of the human race, in so far as human nature is perfected and made pleasing to God in Christ (§ 109, 2. 3). Now the election

---

[1] *De providentia*, cap. 4, Opp. iv. p. 98 : "Deus hominem non in hoc solum condidit, ut imago et exemplum eius esset, sed in hoc quoque, ut ex his creaturis, quae de terra factae sunt, esset quae deo frueretur, hic commercio et amicitia, isthic vero possidendo et amplexando ; sed in hoc, ut umbram quandam praefiguraret eius commercii, quod aliquando per filium suum cum mundo initurus erat."

of those who are justified, and who as such enter into the
Kingdom of God which was founded by Christ, is an idea
which the common Christian feeling applies to all who are
already within the circle over which the influence of Christ's
work extends, or who may hereafter enter into that circle.
This idea, moreover, is regarded as an expression of the Divine
world-order, which demands, as necessary conditions for salvation, the freedom of each individual and his personal relation
to the world and to the history of the accomplishment of
salvation.   A judgment on the eternal and unconditioned
reprobation of individuals, therefore, cannot possibly be deduced from this idea of election, but only the judgment that
certain individuals have not yet been brought within the
sphere of the operations of Divine grace.   But if we follow
theological tradition in its idea that those who die outside of
the fellowship of Christ have no possible access to fellowship
with Him, this means that those persons are altogether non-
existent as regards the domain of the new creation of humanity
which was opened up by Christ.   But, seeing that even the
elect enter only gradually into this domain, the conception of
predestination cannot in any way be related to individuals.
The following proposition results instead: "There is one
Divine predestination, according to which the whole of the
new creation is called into being from out the whole mass
of the human race" (§ 119).   This is not only an essentially
new definition of the problem of election, but also the opening up of a way towards the settlement of the controversy
regarding the extent of justification.[1]

[1] Hofmann follows the same line as Schleiermacher; but he surpasses him
in the precision with which he relates the reconciliation which was brought
about by Christ's obedience to the new humanity, which he sees in the community of Christ (vol. i. p. 621).   Cf. von Zezschwitz, *Die Rechtfertigung des
Sünders vor Gott in ihrem Verhältniss zur Gnadenmittelwirkung und der ewigen
Erwählung* (*Die allgemeine lutherische Conferenz in Hannover*, 1868), pp. 95,
96.   Von Zezschwitz relates eternal election in Christ not to individuals, but to
a holy human race, as the realisation of the Divine creative purpose, in which
"each individual is elected, adopted, and justified as a member of the humanity
in process of perfection," but so that "one who has been already justified and
thus also predesignated in time, may through apostasy fall away from the path
of perfection," and his place in the eternal race be taken by another.

The writers of the New Testament, as a general rule, confine the definite application of the benefits of Christianity to the Christian community, that is, to those persons who therein represent a peculiar stage of humanity. Whenever Paul, for example, treats of predestination and eternal election, he has the community of Christ in view (Rom. viii. 29, 30 ; Eph. i. 4). This limitation of horizon is in harmony with the fact that redemption and justification, regarded alike according to Divine purpose, according to the purpose of Jesus Himself, and as matter of actual experience, are correlated to the community of believers (vol. ii. p. 216). Paul, indeed, in one instance (Rom. v. 18) relates justification to all men, in the same way as he has related the sentence of condemnation which attaches to Adam's transgression. But in the explanatory addition the thought is restricted to " the many," an expression which has been already used as a key-word in the comparison between Christ and Adam. The " all," whom God " has shut up under disobedience " in order again " to have mercy upon them " (Rom. xi. 32), refers, as the context shows, not to individual men, but to the nations, which were formerly opposed to one another as Gentiles and Jews. In 2 Cor. v. 14, 15, those for whom Christ died are described as " all," but in the following sentences this " all " signifies only the community of believers. In John (1 John ii. 2), Christ in His atoning death is recognised as the Propitiation, " not only for our sins, but also for the sins of the whole world." This antithesis, however, in order to be made good, must be supplemented by the qualification that the community to which the sacrifice of Christ stands in necessary relation, extends over the whole human race. There remain, then, only the two passages, Heb. ii. 9 and 1 Tim. ii. 4–6. In the former of these, the phrase ὑπὲρ παντός distributes the benefits of the death of Christ to individual men. In the latter, the expression " all men " is not to be understood, as it is by Augustine, as meaning " all kinds of men." Whether, however, the expression in the Epistle to the Hebrews is in real contradiction with the other line of thought, must be questioned. For the immediately following arguments of the writer in regard to the sacrifice of Christ maintain the strict relation of that sacrifice to the Covenant-community. Now, in comparison with those fully-developed arguments, the expression in ver. 9 appears merely as a preliminary and incompletely defined remark, suggested by the language of Ps. viii., which opens the discussion in which the sentence in question is found. The first Epistle to Timothy, again, is not by Paul. The statements that "God wills the salvation of all," and that "Christ is the ransom for all," were without doubt called forth owing to the Gnostic limitation of the benefits of Christianity to "the spiritual" ($\pi\nu\epsilon\nu\mu\alpha\tau\iota\kappa\omicron\iota$). On account of their entire divergence from the express word of Christ, as well as from the apostolical (especially Paul's) conception of Christianity, they are not to be accepted as theologically authoritative. The same holds with regard to 2 Pet. iii. 9.

These passages of the New Testament give no confirmation to the Lutheran theory of the application of the grace of God to all individual men. The Calvinistic doctrine of the co-ordinate relation of blessedness and reprobation to individual men is equally without support in the New Testament. Paul speaks, indeed, of "hardening," partly on the occasion of his introducing definite quotations from the Old Testament (Rom. ix. 13, 17), and partly, in reference to the Jewish people, as a temporary dispensation of God (Rom. xi. 7, 26). But these sentences are quite wrongly used, when mere temporal hardening is made equivalent to eternal reprobation. How little, alike in the latter context and in general, Paul is thinking of individuals, how much rather, when pursuing the theme of the application of the grace of God, he has large masses of mankind in view, is evident from the fact that he finds consolation for the present hardening of the people of Israel in the prophecy of their conversion. He has thus no interest in the destiny of the many individual members of this nation who depart life before that consummation. It is in the same light that we must understand his declaration that he has fulfilled his call to preach the Gospel from Jerusalem to Illyricum, and that he has no more place in that geographical region for his activity (Rom. xv. 19, 23). The apostle makes that assertion, not on the ground that he has brought the Gospel within the hearing of every individual man in every inhabited spot of that region, but that he has preached the Gospel and established a Christian community in the chief city of every province. He thus thought his task accomplished when he had made the knowledge of Christianity possible in every nation of men. He speaks of the universality of the extension of Christianity, accordingly, in view of all the different nations, Jews and Gentiles, who, when God has compassion upon them, are received into the community of Christ (Rom. xi. 28–32).

As against this scriptural limitation of the problem concerning the relation of the universality of Divine grace to the universality of human sin, the theology of both Confessions has failed to take sufficiently true bearings. In neither, whether in respect of sin or of pardon, are the different nations treated as portions of humanity. But for that reason the conception of humanity in these systems of theology is both obscure and fluctuating. In the peculiar expression he gives to the doctrine of original sin, Augustine views the descent of sin as a simple instance of natural propagation, and regards the human race as *massa perdita*, without at all attempting to distinguish the individual members of the race. He first forms his general notion of men under the attribute of the sinfulness transmitted from their ancestors; then, led by his Platonic mode of thinking, he makes that general notion equivalent to actual humanity. In order, however, to be able to fit in the quality of guilt into this general notion, he takes the human race to mean all the individual men who in Adam sinned with their own personal responsibility. These utterly heterogeneous propositions, the one of which results from a realistic, the other from a nominalistic conception, form together the common doctrine of original sin.

The idea of pardon, whether conceived as applicable to all men or merely to a portion of mankind, takes its form from the latter of the two propositions.   Pardon is conceived only as applicable to individual men, who are made the objects of Divine grace entirely in reference to their own particular sin, and in no other respect.

The notion of humanity, however, can be represented with certainty only when the idea of races and nations, of grades and species within the genus, receives attention, and when not merely the points of agreement and difference in natural endowment, but also the diversity in spiritual activity within these groups, are taken into consideration.   For the notions of genus and species are so mutually related that the individual belongs to the genus of men only as sprung from a definite nation, and further, from a definite family of nations or race.   In this respect the existence of man is subject to the same conditions as all organic nature.   For, in this realm of knowledge also, the notions of genus and species are not categories in the nominalistic sense, merely for the correct ordering of our experiences ; rather, the observation of natural objects leads us directly to these notions. Their objective validity, moreover, is not impaired by the fact that in natural phenomena variations from the special type exist, and that transitional forms between different species and different genera are found, which suggest the hypothesis that species have sprung from species, and genera from genera.   For by the conception of species we are not to understand an absolutely immutable complex of characteristic marks.   Rather, the peculiar characteristic of a species may be thought of as acquired, without our doubting the fact of its fixity for the sphere of present experience.

The notion of the human genus, now, comes directly within the sphere of Christian theology in so far as the Christian view of the world involves a destination of men to fellowship with God, and to a common moral development, which shall apply not to one nation, but to all nations. This presupposes that men, who differ from all other created beings by the capacity for rational thought and the gift of speech, carry in them also the marks of an original endowment, which proves their kinship with God. On the other hand, the anthropological problem of the origin of racial differences, which is decided now for, and now against, their originality, is of no consequence for theology. In referring the different nations and the individual members of these nations to the common destination of men in the Kingdom of God, Christianity takes for granted national differences, whether these are to be regarded as original or as historically developed. For this purpose, however, account is to be taken, not so much of the peculiar natural endowments of the nations, as of their spiritual character. Now this is always something acquired. Therefore, for the scientific treatment of the relation between individual men and the generic end of man as posited in Christianity, the undoubted fact must be taken into account, that every individual man attains the full development of his spiritual capacities within the limits of his national speech, and of the peculiar morale which his nation acquires, partly of necessity through the local conditions which govern the maintenance of the common national life, and partly in the free use of these. But in the same way, also, other historical experiences of the nations influence the peculiar type which Christianity assumes among the members of these nations. The Christianity of the Western nations, for example, is conditioned in a quite peculiar way by the fact that these nations at one and the same time became adherents of the Christian religion and entered into the spiritual inheritance of the classical nations. How strongly our Western Christianity has been influenced by the aesthetic and intellectual tradition of the Greeks, and by the continued operation of Roman models in law and State, one can prove even from certain errors which have been handed down in theology. We must therefore recognise the fact that the individual enters upon the common human task of Christianity, never merely as an individual, but always under the conditions, whether favourable or unfavourable, of his peculiar national

education. The truth here brought out is completed by
the further observation that, in order to fulfil its destined
end, Christianity must win over the nations as wholes. That
is, it can only really accomplish its universal human purpose
when it brings under its influence all the social conditions
under which the spiritual life of individuals exists. A Christianity which should remain anti-national in the minority of
a people would destroy the necessary foundation on which the
spiritual existence of its adherents rests, and thus itself sink
into a fruitless particularism. One hears, indeed, from Pietistic circles precisely the opposite view, namely, that since the
time of Constantine Christianity had been led into a path
quite foreign to its nature, inasmuch as the end sought was
no longer the conviction of individuals, but the reception of
whole nations into the Church. This result, then, having
been attained by force, the peculiar conditions came into
existence which had to be amended after so many centuries
by the conversion of individuals as such. This contradiction
of views ramifies to such an extent that we cannot here
pursue the subject further. If, however, the nations are
destined for Christianity, as we may assume also in accordance with the suggestions and the evangelistic method of
Paul, the universal destination of Christianity is not impaired
by the fact that the members of a Christian nation do not all
enter upon the destination which validly obtains for them.
This position has already been justified by a Reformed theologian [1] by the help of analogies, the significance of which
cannot be denied, even though the introduction of the idea of
reprobation is out of place.

---

[1] Wolfg. Musculus, *Loc. comm.* xvii. : "Scimus non omnes redemptionis
fieri participes ; verum illorum perditio, qui non servantur, haudquaquam im-
pedit, quominus universalis vocetur redemptio, quae non est uni genti, sed toti
mundo destinata. Resolutio illa telluris, qua passim omnia ad germinandum
aestate solvuntur, recte universalis dicitur, etiamsi multae arbores et innumera
loca nec germina nec fructus proferant. Sol ille generalis totius orbis illumina-
tor est, quamvis multi sint, qui nihil ab eo lucis accipiant. Ad eum modum
habet et redemptio ista generis humani, de qua loquimur, quod homines reprobi
ac deplorate impii non accipiunt, neque defectu fit gratiae dei, neque iustum est,
ut illa propter filios perditionis gloriam ac titulum universalis redemptionis
amittat, cum sit parata cunctis et omnes ad illam vocentur."

The significance of Christianity for the human race has to stand a much more difficult test in the 'ascertained facts of ethnology. These facts were unknown to the first advocates of Christianity, but they cannot be left out of account by us. Paul, speaking from the extent of his knowledge of the different nations of the world, could maintain that Christianity was as much appropriate and accessible to barbarians and Scythians as to Jews and Greeks. We, on the other hand, know that the diversity in the character of nations is very strongly conditioned by graded differences in their spiritual endowment and acquired moral disposition. This fact of graded differences is already cognisable in the different families of languages. For languages are regarded as more imperfect or perfect in proportion to the degree in which they express less or greater versatility of spirit, or make possible a less or greater extent of spiritual culture. And further, the lower or higher degree of moral development, whether of the community or of the individual, which appears tangibly in the difference between the nomadic and the settled nations, is conditioned by the nature of the land in which the nations live. These and similar ethnological conditions are the grounds of the distinction between the unhistorical, the particular-historical, and the world-historical nations. Now, there is not found an equal disposition towards the Christian religion at each of these different stages. With regard to the unhistorical nature-peoples, Martensen [1] expresses the opinion that, regarded from the natural point of view, they are still in an embryonic, and therefore imperfect, condition. On the other hand, Steinthal [2] declares his conviction that the difference between the unhistorical and the prehistoric nations (thus, for example, between the Australian negroes and the Germans before the " wandering of the nations ") is precisely the same as the difference between sickness and health. The former of these

---

[1] *Dogmatik*, p. 416.

[2] *Philologie, Geschichte und Psychologie in ihren gegenseitigen Beziehungen* (1864), p. 39.

opinions is evidently formed, quite naturally, on the universal-istic principle of the Lutheran doctrine.   But the second view depends none the less on theological considerations, inasmuch as it is based on the assumption of a special degree of moral corruption.   On different grounds, particular-historical nations like the Chinese and the Hindus lack the disposition towards Christianity as much as the nations which adhere to the other universal religions, Buddhism and Islam.   Therefore it is only, strictly speaking, the world-historical nations of the West— that is, those nations which, through inhabiting lands afford-ing the conditions which are favourable to mutual intercourse, have developed a common history—which have arrived at an idea of the natural and moral unity of the human race suffi-cient to enable them to embrace the practically thorough-going Christian idea of the unity of the race.   For the common highest task which devolves upon the world-historical nations which have embraced Christianity is essentially bound up with the idea that they are united together in the religious community of the one only true God.

No one, of course, is in a position to predict whether the nations which stand outside of the history of Western culture will be led to embrace Christianity, and whether Christianity will fulfil its universal destination in regard also to them.   In any case, such a consummation is only possible in the measure in which these nations enter, through their own effort, into the circle of culture of the world-historical nations. For the existence of the Christian religious community is historically bound up with this section of humanity..   But even if the possibility of such a consummation be denied, there is still no reason why we should doubt the universalism of the Christian religion.   Only, the extent of that section of humanity which is destined to take part in the highest spiritual task is to be conceived as narrower than is often done.   For that the Christian universalism does not cover the whole human race in its natural existence, is evident from the fact that certain nature-peoples, through contact with civilised Christian nations, have not advanced along the lines of national development, but rather have become enervated and died out. One would, accordingly, be disposed to judge that nations which show no prospect of going over to Christianity are prevented from doing so by their own abnormal character, in other words, by their remoteness from civilised humanity. I am far, however, from denying *a priori* the possibility of the extension of the Christian community over other peoples which have not yet reached the stage of the world-historical or particular-historical nations. For the means of arriving at a scientific demonstration are wanting. And thus the expression of a personal conviction on this subject is of as much or as little value as the expression of the opposite opinion.

If the nations fulfil their destined end, namely, their development into one whole supernatural humanity, through their reception into the religious community of Christianity, then this whole is also the object of the decisive operation of God which determines its peculiar origin and existence. Justification, therefore, is the operation of God in which He receives sinful men into fellowship with Himself, from the point of view that they shall at the same time, in the Kingdom of God, reach their destined human end, namely, the highest morality. Now, just as little as the individual, whether in a physical or spiritual respect, can be rightly represented outside of the sphere of his nationality, as little can the individual, regarded as an object of Divine justification, be represented outside of the Christian community— whether he be conceived as one justified equally with the others, or from the point of view of his education by the preceding generation, meaning by ." education " not legal determination, but organic development of character. Therefore justification is directly related to the religious community as a whole, which in God's thought is always antecedent to the individual members of the community. Thus justification is the expression of the establishment of the religious community, whose character consists in this, that sin forms no barrier to the enjoyment of fellowship with God. It is also, however, the expression of the maintenance of this community, which consists in this, that every individual who experiences justification within the community becomes, by virtue of this quality, an organic medium of the continued existence of the community in its peculiar character. For, in an organism, all the individual members work together as means to the welfare of the whole, and apart from this no member exists as a member of the whole.

1. Justification, or the reception of sinners into the relation of children of God, must be referred to God under the attribute of Father.

2. The justification of sinners by God depends on the condition of faith: in other words, justification results when, conceived as reconciliation on God's part, it calls forth in the sinners that faith which, conceived as the direction of the will to the highest end represented in God and as trust in God in Himself, does not include love to men, and, conceived as freedom from the law, excludes all ceremonial conditions, equally with any co-operating presupposition of a legal claim before God.

3. Justification, or reconciliation, as positively connected with the historical manifestation and activity of Christ, is related in the first instance to the whole of the religious community founded by Christ, which maintains the Gospel of God's grace in Christ as the direct means of its existence, and to individuals only as they attach themselves, by faith in the Gospel, to this community.

CHAPTER III

§ 23. JUSTIFICATION or reconciliation denotes the status before God into which sinners are brought .through the mediation of Christ within His community. We belong to God as a child does to his father, in spite of the abiding consciousness that, in virtue of the previously dominant tendency of self-will, we used to stand in contradiction to Him as sinners. We know ourselves to be, in our present relation to God, entirely dependent on His purpose of grace openly made known ; for the abiding recollection of the pain of the consciousness of guilt excludes not merely every legal claim to the Divine pardon, but also any possibility of our having earned it by any meritorious actions whatsoever. Now, as this status before God comprises none save purely spiritual relations, so also the form of its appropriation, faith, is a purely spiritual function which, as such, can be exercised without any sensible actions whatever being essential to it. Nevertheless the fact still remains, that the opposition between man and God which is solved by justification is not altogether eliminated from the experience of the believer. If in Christianity the range of forgiveness included merely the sins of our past years, or, in addition to that, merely individual transgressions of the Christian life, the felt opposition between the sense of guilt and what God claims from men would no longer normally hold a place among the experiences of a Christian. From this point of view the Socinians assign forgiveness, as remission of punishment, to the accidental side of Christianity. The Evangelical

Confessions, on the contrary, in so far as they find in justification the fundamental precondition of Christianity whether
personal or social, reckon on the regular continuance of the
consciousness of guilt in those who profess adherence to
them.   If one were to say, as a Christian, that he had no
sin, he would make God a liar; for through His promise of
the forgiveness of sins, which forms the fundamental characteristic of the Christian community, God affirms the presence of
sin in its members (1 John i. 8–10).   From this point of view,
according to Luther and Melanchthon (p. 7), our knowledge
of our own sin is to be drawn directly from the Gospel.
That fact makes daily prayer for forgiveness of sin a fitting
thing.   Such prayer is no more inconsistent with the general
assurance of this blessing which has been given to the
Christian community, than prayer for Divine gifts is barred by
the knowledge we have that God is willing to bestow them.
On the other hand, if we did not daily perceive occasion to
pray for it, we should lose sight of the importance of forgiveness as the foundation-stone of the Christian religion.
Thus the value we set upon this blessing demands the continual confession that every one needs it.   The consciousness
of this need, however, will in the Christian life normally
extend to nothing which is not forthwith covered by the
certainty of forgiveness bestowed by God.   Now the traditional form of systematic theology leads to the contention
that in his daily life every Christian must pass through the
whole interval between the need of redemption and the
acceptance of grace—an interval the magnitude of which
finds expression in the unconnectedness of the doctrine of
sin, as traditionally developed, with the doctrine of redemption (p. 5).   Such teaching gives special support to the
demand of Pietism, that we should compel ourselves to such
a comprehensive estimate of our own sin, and should impress
upon ourselves our own inborn hatefulness and worthlessness
or nothingness to such a degree, that we cannot consistently
attach thereto any well-founded assurance of grace, but must
wait for some incalculable deliverance from this state of

feeling. This monkish method of self-abasement is proved
false by 1 John iii. 19–21. Nor can dogmatic theology
concern itself with such movements of sentiment: they
belong to the province of pastoral theology. For Dogmatics,
which has to interpret the normal course of the elements of
the Christian life, can affirm man's permanent need of redemption in no other way than by recognising that the forgiveness of sins is the necessary basis of the Christian
religion, both as a whole and in detail. But that is to
assert, not to deny, that the need of redemption must be
presupposed.

Faith, which, as related to the promise attached to the
work of Christ, appropriates forgiveness, is to be understood
as trust in God and Christ (§ 19), characterised by peace of
mind, inward satisfaction, and comfort. The pain arising
from one's state as a whole, which formed an element of the
presupposed sense of guilt, is thereby removed. This pain,
however, is an expression of that opposition to God and to
the purpose of our being which forms the essence of sin—
and that as a personal certainty for the individual mind.
Trust in the justification imparted in Christ, therefore, is
attended by certainty of an opposite kind. The pain of the
sense of guilt is a matter of feeling; the certainty which
accompanies trust in the justification assured by Christ can
therefore only be interpreted as a feeling of pleasure.[1]
From the nature of this connection between Divine act and
promise and human trust, it follows that the subjective
certainty of justification springs only from a vision of the

[1] Melanchthon, *Loci theol. C. R.* xxi. pp. 749–751 : "Si fides non est fiducia
intuens Christum et acquiescens propter Christum, certe non applicamus nobis
eius beneficium. Necesse est igitur fide intelligi fiduciam applicantem nobis
beneficium Christi. . . . Estque fides virtus apprehendens et applicans promissiones et quietans corda." *Apol. C. A.* iii. 27 : "Sola fides, quae intuetur
in promissionem et sentit ideo certo statuendum esse, quod deus ignoscat,
vincit terrores peccati et mortis." 178 : "Piae conscientiae vident in hac doctrina uberrimam consolationem sibi proponi, quod videlicet credere et certo
statuere debent, quod propter Christum habent placatum patrem." 180 : "Si
ideo sentire debent, se habere deum placatum, quia diligunt, quia legem faciunt,
semper dubitare necesse est, utrum habeamus deum placatum . . . Quando
igitur acquiescet, quando erit pacata conscientia ?"

object of faith.[1]   But although this object of believing and
peace-bringing trust is clearly outlined, and fitted by its
Divine origin to call forth and to sustain the subjective
function of faith, yet experience shows that what we have
here is not a mechanically regular process of cause and effect.
The certainty of justification, without which faith does not
fully satisfy the conception of it as trust, is a characteristic
which in many cases is liable to change in quantity; it may
increase, just as it is liable to interruptions of uncertainty.
Now it is worth noticing that Melanchthon, when forming a
judgment on the latter case, does not take the view that the
fact of justification is rendered inoperative and invalid by the
want of continuous subjective certainty.[2]   No doubt, as his
whole mode of thought moves within the limits of the individual
life, it strikes one as contradictory when, on the one hand,
justification as a permanent status is brought into relation
to believing trust, and conceived as operating only in response to trust; while, on the other hand, justification is held
to be valid even when the subjective certainty of it varies.
Nor was Melanchthon able altogether to remove this appearance of contradiction in the argument on which I am now
commenting.   The remark of Luther, indeed, might have
been recalled (vol. i. p. 162), that in this struggle of repentance the very feeling of being at an infinite distance from
God is a product of His grace; but what is wanted here is
that this conviction, felt by an impartial observer of the
soul that is passing through repentance, should be appro-

---

[1] *Loci com.* 59 : "In hac promissione debent pavidae conscientiae quaerere
reconciliationem et iustificationem ; hac promissione debent se sustentare ac
certo statuere, quod habent deum propitium propter Christum, propter suam
promissionem." 141 : "Non est hominis, praesertim in terroribus peccati,
sine certo verbo dei statuere de voluntate dei, quod irasci desinat."

[2] *Loci com.* 229 : "Haec fides, de qua loquimur, exsistit in poenitentia.   Et
inter bona opera, inter tentationes et pericula confirmari et crescere debet,
ut subinde certius apud nos statuamus, quod deus propter Christum respiciat
nos, ignoscat nobis, exaudiat nos.   Haec non discuntur sine magnis et multis
certaminibus.   Quoties recurrit conscientia, quoties sollicitat ad desperationem,
cum ostendit aut vetera peccata aut nova aut immunditiem naturae !   Hoc
chirographum non deletur sine magno agone, ubi testatur experientia, quam
difficilis res sit fides."

priated by the latter, and thus his conscience be calmed. Only, the view of the matter taken above offers no ground for this. Therefore the admission that within the domain of justification faith may be uncertain, always depends on the presupposition that the struggle for assurance of Divine grace is only a transition stage, leading in all probability to the goal of that certainty which belongs ideally to actual justification. But as this conclusion is anything but self-evident, a kind of categorical imperative lays on us the task of gaining assurance of justification by faith. This is unequivocally expressed by Melanchthon in a remark quoted above (p. 143), and holds good even when, to aid the endeavour to gain the assurance of faith, we recall the evidences of Divine grace furnished, not merely by the sacraments, but by the good works we do.[1] The original view of this matter held by the Reformers, however, can hardly be expressed more accurately or more clearly than in the doctrine *de iustificatione hominis*, which was formulated by Cardinal Contarini at the Regensberg Conference (1541), and received the adherence of the representatives of both parties.[2]

---

[1] *Loci com.* 155 : "Ut baptismus, ut coena domini sunt signa, quae subinde admonent, erigunt et confirmant pavidas mentes, ut credant firmius, remitti peccata, ita scripta et picta est eadem promissio in bonis operibus, ut haec opera admoneant nos, ut firmius credamus. Et qui non bene faciunt, non excitant se ad credendum ; sed pii gaudent habere signa et testimonia tantae promissionis."

[2] *Corp. Ref.* iv. p. 200 : "Quanquam in renatis semper crescere debent timor dei, poenitentia et humilitas et aliae virtutes, cum renovatio sit imperfecta et haereat in eis ingens infirmitas, tamen docendum est, ut qui vere poenitent semper fide certissima statuant, se propter mediatorem Christum deo placere . . . Quoniam autem perfecta certitudo in hac imbecillitate non est, suntque multae infirmae et pavidae conscientiæ, quae cum gravi saepe dubitatione luctantur, nemo est a gratia Christi propter eiusmodi infirmitatem excludendus. Sed convenit tales diligenter adhortari, ut iis dubitationibus promissiones Christi fortiter opponant et augeri sibi fidem sedulis precibus orent." On this extract cf. the admirable treatise by Theod. Brieger, *De formulae concordiae Ratisbonensis origine atque indole*, 1870 ; also, by the same author, *Cardinal Contarini's Doctrine of Justification*, in *Stud. und Krit.* 1872, H. 1. Contarini is the Romish theologian who, as the Articles of Regensburg show, was most successful in transporting himself exactly to the point of view and the terminology of the Reformation ; thus he drew the most advanced inferences which could be reached, by one who remained Roman Catholic, from the experiences of grace enjoyed by a Bernard. But the Regensburg Formula shows clearly by the proposition : *fides iustificans est*

For purposes of comparison with what I have given as Melanchthon's doctrine, I add the following considerations from Calvin. As was shown above (p. 102), they differ from Melanchthon in regard to their conception of faith, in that trust (*fiducia*), as the effect in the will which follows from faith, is distinguished from faith in the sense of a peculiar kind of knowledge. Calvin cannot hide from himself the fact, nevertheless, that the will, as obedience, participates in this steadfast heart-mirrored knowledge, this emotional conviction. But he regards faith essentially as a kind of conviction, because he puts great stress upon the clearness of the object to which faith turns. That he does not include trust in his definition of faith is to be accounted for, further, by the fact that he never loses sight of the above-noted manifestations of incipient faith—a faith which, like Melanchthon, he regards as saving faith, though it lacks the quality of steadfast trust. But the true and full faith, which applies the promise of grace to itself, ánd in the feeling of the Divine sweetness realises the irrefragibility of this application, brings in its train the trust and fearless conviction that we may appear before God's face with inward peace. Calvin argues further, that he who has once reached this stage is not, indeed, safe from fluctuations in his certainty of salvation, but will not lose the trust through which that certainty can be reached again. But he knows, too, an incipient faith, not as yet combined with trust, which yet embraces the reconciliation through which

illa fides, quae est efficax per caritatem, that it was a compromise intended to be explained in either of two ways. For while the context of this proposition suggests a Protestant interpretation, yet this does not exclude the Catholic interpretation ; for according to mediaeval ideas in this domain of thought, it is possible to alternate between the thought of "making righteous" (*Gerechtmachung*) through *fides caritate formata,* and the trustful apprehension of the Divine compassion. Now since Contarini, as Brieger proves, while expressing the latter experience in a form which comes near Reformed doctrine, understands *iustificatio* also in the real sense of making righteousness, he has not abandoned the platform of Catholic dogma. But thereby an obscure veil is drawn over his approximation to the Protestants which shows it to be less valuable than Brieger represents. For by ignoring the kindred-spirited predecessors of his hero, he is led to regard as Protestant in character a number of Contarini's expressions which are also in agreement with Bernard and Thomas.

10

access to God is won.   Faith, at its first stage, has this in
common with perfect assurance of faith, that it keeps steadily
turned to a God of grace; but it is inferior to the higher
stage in this, that the vision of God it gives is clear, indeed,
but remote; while a sense of the Divine sweetness alternates
with a confusing impression due to the consciousness of guilt
—in other words, the individual appropriation of grace is as
yet imperfect.   For it is just from this fusion of faith and
grace that there springs that trust which constitutes the *fides
specialis*.   Now Calvin does not need, as does Melanchthon,
expressly to insist that we ought to advance from the earlier
stage to full believing trust.   He can wait for this development patiently, for he knows that saving faith from the very
outset engrafts the believer into the community of Christ,
and that by this means Divine election guarantees progress
to a complete faith.   For the rest, he acknowledges no less
than Melanchthon that the consciousness of good works done
by the believer serves to support and to confirm faith, because
in these fruits of our calling appear evidences of Divine
favour (iii. 14, 18, 19).

In the main point, therefore, both are agreed.   The subjective function which answers to justification is faith as trust
in God's individual pardon, a trust which arises solely from
the clear presentation of the universal promise of grace along
with the sureties for it which Christ has given, and which is
necessarily accompanied by that joyful sense of harmony with
God and with oneself which stands opposed to the pain of the
sense of guilt.   Moreover, both equally declare that this
function of faith, in the case of many who are to be regarded
as justified, is subject to a development indicated by the
fact that trust and the feeling of inward peace do not continuously accompany the intentional turning of the will to
God as the Promiser of grace, but may be either interrupted
or altogether restrained by doubt of His grace.   This stage
in the development of faith can only be overcome by a
deepened attention to God's gracious promise.   Now whether,
with Calvin, one waits quietly for this advance in those who

are elect and belong to the community of Christ, or, with Melanchthon, simply insists that the advance shall be made, in either case the courage to venture on full trust in God springs from the believer seeing in his ability to perform good works an evidence of God's special pardon which will overthrow his doubts.   This is to assert a closer relation between that exercise of the moral goodwill towards men which is essential in Christianity and the religious function of justifying faith, than we find expressed in the general Evangelical doctrine that the renovation or regeneration of the will always goes along with justification.   Indeed, only on this assumption can the consciousness of actions which spring from a renewed will serve as a proof of his justification to one who cannot gain assurance of it in feeling by the direct path of accepting the impression of the promise of grace.

But in order to understand the meaning and the importance of the assurance of faith contended for by Protestantism, we must compare its antithesis, the Tridentine dogma.   Our polemic, as commenced by Chemnitz, interprets the decree of the Sixth Session, the 9th chapter of which bears the title *contra inanem haereticorum fiduciam*, as though the doctrine of the Roman Catholic Church altogether vetoed the characteristic of *certitudo gratiae*, and in its place prescribed doubt of one's salvation as an essential mark of faith.   But if this were so, we should yet have to confess that in reality such a characterisation of the Catholic Church does not hold good generally.   For uncertainty about salvation cannot help one to a Christian character, while it is beyond question that examples of such a character have appeared in the Roman Catholic Church.   Besides, personal assurance of salvation is indispensable in order that the Roman form of the Church should be put forward by its champions as the only authentic form.   Now it is certainly a fact that the principle of the necessary uncertainty of salvation had been employed against the Reformers before the Council of Trent;[1] but alongside

---

[1] *E.g.* by Berthold of Chiemsee; cf. Lämmer, *Vortridentinische Theologie*, p. 161.

of it we find the opposite position maintained, not only by Contarini (p. 144), but also by Gropper.[1] Even Thomas Aquinas, in his own way, may be cited as a witness for the certainty of salvation enjoyed by one who exercises faith, hope, and love. Faith, as a definite kind of reflective knowledge of the articles of the creed, is certain of their truth, and therefore certain of the omnipotence and compassion of God on which hope, at its first stage, rests and bases the struggle to reach eternal blessedness. The hope of the individual, however, when properly complete, becomes certainty of this goal, if faith be informed by love to God. Now, although hope is an affair of the will, and in this respect subject to uncertainty, yet as an effect of faith it partakes in the certainty of the latter, inasmuch as its aim is the goal of blessedness. This goal, however, is made so sure by the Divine power and compassion, that those who fail to reach blessedness do so from their own will and not from any lack in the Divine compassion.[2] But the controversy carried on in Reformation times does not circle round this representation of the matter. The denial and the assertion that assurance of salvation accompanies faith are in keeping rather with the twofold conception of *justificatio* which pervades the Christianity of the Middle Ages. The doctrine which attaches *justificatio* to faith and works issues in the conclusion that faith does not give assurance of salvation, but that assurance, never more than approximate, can be reached by the exercise of moral action, especially action prescribed by the ceremonial law. On the other hand, absorption in the exclusive value of Divine grace is possible only in the form of trust in God ; trust, however, includes certainty of its object and satisfaction in it. The connection between them, therefore, appears most clearly in the

---

[1] *Enchiridion Coloniense* (1538), fol. 170 : " Ad iustificationem hominis omnino requiritur ut homo credat non tantum generaliter, quod propter Christum vere poenitentibus remittantur peccata, sed etiam, quod ipsimet homini credenti remissa sint propter Christum per fidem." Cf. Brieger in Ersch and Gruber, *Allg. Encyclopaedia*, Erste Section xcii. p. 218 ff.

[2] *Summa theol.* ii. 2, qu. 18, art. 4.

exposition of Bernard (vol. i. p. 113). Even at the Council of Trent this conception was so energetically championed by Ambrosius Catharinus (Archbishop of Minori, in the Kingdom of Naples), that even there no proper and complete decision of the question, in the comprehensive sense in which it was raised, was reached at all. For the chapter of the decree of the Sixth Session which is directed against the Evangelicals does not exhaust the subject, and does not allow us to draw any inference as to what assurance of salvation counts for in the Christian life of the Roman communion. This chapter was also defended by Catharinus against Dominicus a Soto.[1] Now it is usual, in consequence of the representations of Chemnitz and Bellarmine, to suppose that the Catholic doctrine altogether excludes assurance of salvation from justifying faith. But it must be noted that Bellarmine assumes quite a different *status controversiae* from that maintained by Chemnitz, and this merely in order to be able to contradict Chemnitz. The Evangelical position is that if the believer, who, as seriously changed in mind and regenerate, stands at the beginning of his renewed life, lays hold of the promise of grace, he can and must be assured of forgiveness.[2] With this, now, Bellarmine declares himself in agreement. He asserts, however, that the controversy concerns, not this faith conditioned by change of mind, but faith absolutely. Moreover, while he does not deny that assurance is an essential mark of *fiducia*, he yet makes the controversy circle round *certitudo fidei*, which, as distinguished from *fiducia*, is nothing but *fides in intellectu*. But to this last the Evangelicals themselves have no wish to ascribe any subjective assurance of salvation, simply because with them it does not reckon as justifying faith at all. Thus Bellarmine's controversial discussion is aimless.

As follows from what has been shown, the chapter cited from the Tridentine Decree, if read attentively, by no means

---

[1] Cf. Sarpi, *Histoire du Concile de Trente* (trans. by Amelot), pp. 188–190 ; Gerhard, *Confessio Catholica*, pp. 1501–1513.

[2] Chemnitz, *l.c.*, p. 140 (vol. i. p. 153) ; Bellarminus, *de iustificatione*, lib. iii. cap. 2.

betrays an intention altogether to deny the assurance of faith. For we must remember that the Catholics, in their dispute with the Evangelicals, took for granted that the Divine promise of grace, revealed as it is only in connection with the Church system, does not exist for heretics and schismatics, and that the believing trust of the Evangelicals is without an object. For this reason alone is it regarded as mere subjective imagination.[1] Further, it is denied that justification takes place only when the assurance of faith is not interrupted by doubt at all, or that only he is justified who possesses assurance of faith, or that assurance is so essential to complete justification that without it there remains merely doubt of the Divine promise. But all this does not at all touch the Evangelical doctrine, which regards justification as real in many cases where for the moment there exists no specific assurance, and admits that assurance can be disturbed by doubt. Finally, it is a perfectly straight-forward principle to hold that a pious man who does not doubt the compassion of God may yet, in view of his weakness, be in anxiety about his salvation; but the reason adduced, that we cannot know our standing in grace by an infallible assurance of faith, loses its point against the Evangelical doctrine, when we consider that it would imply thinking away the object of faith, namely, the promise, and regarding the subjective assurance of grace as its own sufficient ground. The two Canons, 13 and 14, which deal with the same subject, are not inconsistent with the interpretation just given; and while, at the same time, the possibility of assurance of eternal election, save when given by special Divine revelation, is denied, yet this declares invalid merely one particular form of assurance—not assurance in general. Yet again, the repudiation of assurance of election does not touch the Calvinistic doctrine, for the latter maintains that it is through Christ that we ought to become assured of our election, consequently through the medium of justification.

Both of the opposed views upon this question having

---

[1] *Trid.*, Sess. vi. Decr. de iustificatione, cap. 9.

been current before the Council of Trent, they could not but maintain themselves after it as well. And in fact the Romish Church succeeded in deriving thence the advantage, partly of affording satisfaction to different kinds of men, partly of controlling them so as to suit its purpose. For the sake of persons of energetic character, the possibility of assurance must be admitted for purely general reasons, and everyone who takes a leading position in the Church accepts it without asking many questions. On the other hand, for the sake of the discipline of the great mass, it is expedient to foster the feeling of uncertainty about one's salvation, in order to intensify the people's zeal for the works which the Church prescribes. So that this Church fares best by using a double measure and a double weight. The Evangelical principle, how-ever, not only strikes Catholic opponents as strange ; it seems no longer in any degree to command real confidence among ourselves, whether in theory or in practice. The fact is, very good Evangelical Christians would acknowledge as an expression of their own sentiments the opinion of Möhler, that we ought to embrace assurance of our own salvation, if we have it at all, very timidly and modestly.[1]   But, on the other hand, we decisively reject Möhler's view, that on Protestant principles we ought simply to ask everyone what he thinks of his own state, and that his answer would compel us to regard him as a saint, since the teaching of our symbols refuses to attach any weight to the doubt which others might feel of his reply. This misconception, which regards the Evangelical Christian as a wax figure, on which every single dogma is to be tried and proved, is one for which, unfortunately, the older theo-

---

[1] *Symbolik*, p. 195 : "Certainly, the Spirit witnesses to our spirit that we are the children of God ; but this witness is of so gentle a nature, and requires such tender nurture, that the believer, feeling as he does his own un-worthiness, draws near to it only timidly, and hardly dares to receive it into his consciousness. It is a holy joy, which hides its face in its own presence, and would remain a secret from itself. . . . Moreover, the same holds true in many other instances of the spiritual life. Innocence which becomes conscious of itself is usually lost in the very act, and reflection on the question whether a deed which one is on the point of doing is pure, not infrequently makes it impure. The life of the true saints unfolds itself quiet and still ; they do not call themselves blessed on that account, but leave that to God."

logians are to blame, for they represent religious feelings and emotions in a mechanical form as objects of empirical study by the understanding. But if anyone thought it his duty "on Protestant principles" to ask me whether I felt assured of my salvation, I should reply that that did not in the least concern him, for it is a matter between me and God. And so I perfectly understand Möhler's protestation that he would feel exceedingly uncomfortable in the neighbourhood of a man who declared himself *unconditionally* assured of his salvation, and that he could hardly escape the feeling of there being something diabolical in such a case. For such a man would be anything but a true Evangelical, were he to assert his assurance of salvation apart from the condition of *seria contritio*. But I should also have the feeling expressed by Möhler in the vicinity of people who indicated, even though it were indirectly by the exclusion of other Christians from the fellowship of salvation, that they themselves in their own way were quite certain of being saved.

Both Evangelical Confessions, in their practical treatment of the subject of personal assurance, follow the models which, as has been shown (§ 19), are set before them in Melanchthon on the one side and Calvin on the other. They assert in common that the Divine promise, as the object of faith, is at the same time the ground of the assurance which either is, or ought to be, combined with faith. They acknowledge that it is through the promise that the witness of God's Spirit leading to personal assurance exercises its power. But since in the promise, as historically given, no individual recipient is named, they look to faith to make special application and appropriation of the Divine intention. Even the Calvinists determine the idea of faith chiefly by the idea of *fiducia*, as the opposite of *dubitatio;* but as a distinction must be drawn in real life between weak and strong faith, they differentiate from trust, as the general notion, a higher stage of itself, which carries with it *certitudo*, which is the assurance and seal. Further, the Divine promise is regarded by Lutherans as *universalis*, as referring to all individuals, by Calvinists as *indefinita*. Therefore the Lutherans make its appropriation the subject of a categorical imperative, compared with which all other arguments count merely as persuasives. The Calvinists, on the contrary, calling to their aid the assumption of the eternal election of individuals, treat the problem with the instruments of theoretical reflection. The Lutheran, therefore, who keeps before him the universal promise of grace in the Divine word, has to make the practical experiment of subsuming himself by faith under this universal rule; then the witness of the Holy Spirit, which operates through God's universal word of promise, extends itself likewise to him; for the individual is determined in and with the universal. On the other hand, the Calvinist knows the promise to be valid for those who believe; through self-observation, therefore, he makes sure that he believes, and infers accordingly that he personally may feel assured of the promise of grace. The witness of the Holy Spirit operates in this form likewise, for upon it faith relies when reporting to itself on its relation to Divine grace. This theoretical method of obtaining a basis for assurance through a regular logical inference (*syllogismus practicus*) is a peculiarity of Reformed theology. But even the Lutheran " ascetics " were unable to refrain from employing this method. For when they attempt to help trembling faith to the right path, Arndt, Scriver, and Fresenius of necessity draw attention to the hidden traces of faith which indicate that the individual concerned ought to apply the promise to his own case; and Ph. D. Burk, in his *Lehre von der Rechtfertigung und ihrer Versicherung*, combines Lutheran and Reformed forms of statement without seeming to be surprised at the formal syllogistic method noted above. These writers chiefly urge that we should give heed to the comfortable invitations of Scripture, but the didactic style which they follow leads them also incidentally to adopt the syllogistic method. Both methods therefore take for granted that the witness of the Divine Spirit is immanent in the conviction of the human mind. Bellarmine (cap. 8), it is true, is willing to grant that this conviction is divinely grounded only provided that not merely the major premise is

given in the Divine word, but that the minor premise too—
that I have faith—is certified by Divine revelation, and not
based on human experience. But it is easy to repel this
sophistical suggestion if we remember that the reception of
Divine revelation is always humanly conditioned. This means
that there does exist a possibility of delusion in this sphere;
but in regard to personal assurance, what is in question is not
infallibility or the impossibility of error—for in no relation
can this be claimed by any human mind—but the possibility
of sufficient certainty subject to the conditions under which
the human spirit becomes conscious of its relation to God.
Precisely in accordance with the meaning we ascribe to the
Holy Spirit, therefore, moral certainty and Divine certainty
come to coincide. For the Spirit means anything but an
inexorable mechanism, running athwart the laws of the
human mind, but rather a principle which leaves these laws
in full validity.

Nevertheless the discussion of this earlier stage of faith,
at which assurance of salvation and the feeling of comfort are
absent, is carried out both by systematic theologians and
"ascetic" writers with a certain want of lucidity. They
firmly maintain that saving faith, in the full sense, is *fiducia
cum certitudine salutis*, and that it includes the feeling of
comfort and of satisfaction with God and with oneself. Now,
if justification is granted to weak and uncertain faith also, it
must be possible to bring the latter under the conception of
fiducia. And this is what they try to do; for otherwise
such faith, as being *fides informis*, would not avail to justify.
But how can we recognise weak faith as trust if the certainty
of salvation given by feeling is not present at all? Now I
find that the older theologians quite failed to make this
difficulty clear to their own minds; only in Maccovius have
I met with any attempt to solve it.[1] That attempt issues

---

[1] *Loci communes*, p. 689 : "Fidei sensus non est fides; hoc est, actus ille
reflexivus in ipsam fidem, quo credo me credere, non est ipsa fides, sed potius
sensus quidam fidei." P. 716 : "Quemadmodum dum homo deliquium
animi patitur, aut in ecstasin rapitur, sensu omnino non privatur (ubi enim
vita est animalis, ibi sensus est, sed hoc tantum incommodi patitur, quod non

in his making a distinction between the general feeling of
self which is inseparable from every vital act, and the feeling
of this self-feeling which he regards as the higher and clearer
stage.   But as he entirely fails to inquire into the conditions
under which this distinction emerges, no complete and clear
insight into the matter is attained.

It would not be in accordance with ecclesiastical Protestantism to remove the treatment of these experiences from
the province of the preaching of the Word, which is the
general promise of grace.   But *à propos* of Gerhard's discussion of this point (vol. i. p. 354), it has been already shown
that, from the standpoint of the preacher, the personal
application of justification seems to be possible merely, but
not necessary.   And that is inevitable ; for the general truth
of the forgiveness of sins leaves its actual compass still
undetermined, and therefore that compass cannot form a
sufficient ground of assurance in the case of those whose
actual assurance depends on further special conditions.
Hence arises the right claimed by Pietism to stimulate in a
different way the assurance of salvation given in the consciousness of justification.   But in Pietistic circles those special
conditions are imposed on every individual, and their validity
is made independent of those general principles which were
previously regarded as decisive.   Though their interest in
justification is not wholly given up, and though sanctification
in the sense of formal self-abnegation or the struggle after
good action is not pressed into the foreground,[1] yet the
consciousness of justification, or assurance, is made to depend
upon an acute experience of conversion.   Here what happened
in the case of A. H. Francke is typical.   Once he becomes
convinced that he has no standing in living faith, he goes
astray, in his hypochondriacal struggle to secure it, from what
of faith he formerly possessed ; doubts God, yet continues in

sentit se sentire), ita etiam fit, dum homo fidelis tentationibus sic abripitur, ut
extra se positus videatur.   Non desinit quidem ille vita spirituali vivere, et
sensu, qui cum vita hac indivulso nexu coniunctus est, praeditus esse, sed hoc
mali patitur, quod non sentit se sentire."

[1] As by Jodocus van Lodensteyn, *Geschichte des Pietismus*, i. p. 158.

prayer to the God Whom he no longer believes, and is finally surprised by the return of conviction with a full measure of assurance, and dates from that moment his being pardoned by God and the forgiveness of his sins.[1] The antecedents of this consummation may vary in different cases, but in every instance the Halle Pietism, in the conversion which it demands, insists on a similar experience of the intense consciousness that *my* sins are forgiven, and on the commencement of a concomitant feeling of joy, which puts an end to any unhappiness that may have gone before. Alexander Schweizer (vol. i. p. 558) has thrown this demand into dogmatic form ; and in Pietistic biographies similar experiences are described. Nevertheless we have no right to deduce a general rule from these cases, since we cannot conceal from ourselves the fact that the Reformers and the divines who follow them do not insist on any such element when thinking of personal assurance. For those who experience the kind of conversion which leads to this consciousness of forgiveness relate it only in the loosest possible way to the general credentials of salvation. They are forced to admit that any such conversion is preceded by the preaching of the Gospel, but the latter they regard as only its occasion, or as a source of information regarding the matters involved. But they exclude from the province of preaching the act of grace in which God operates on one who is being converted, and oppose it to preaching regarded as a purely theoretical means of grace. Spener, indeed, still holds firmly by Luther's principle that the individual's experiences all point back to his baptism, and are to be explained as the consequences, or the renewal, of baptismal grace. Francke, in reviewing his conversion, ignores this view altogether. Pietism, so far as it holds at all to the fundamental significance of forgiveness, totally ignores the fact that the community of believers, which every new convert finds previously existing, and in which conversion only gives him a firmer footing, is based upon the forgiveness of sin. A converted man is not, by his special experience, isolated from or

---

[1] *Op. cit.*, ii. p. 250.

opposed to this body; rather it awakens within him that common sentiment which holds to the Word of God and the sacrament of baptism as the distinguishing features of the community of believers. Instead of this, Pietism recommends its devotees to hold by the society which, by its special attainments in piety, proves itself to be the true community. On this point, therefore, as in their whole teaching, the Church and Pietism are utterly opposed in the way they guide men to assurance. The Church asserts merely the possibility, not the unfailing actuality, of personal assurance; Pietism asserts only exceptional instances of conversion, which indicate no general rule, for the simple reason that in principle they bear no relation to the Evangelical conception of the Church. What would be the result if we were to adopt simultaneously the point of view of both?

Löhe, in a short *brochure*,[1] has described the epoch of "Revival" as past. He testifies that Pietistic excitations of feeling are regarded—even by those who have striven to gain assurance through them, and, through the change that came over their impressions, have attained it—as youthful experiences whose return is not to be looked for in maturer years. He sees in Pietism of this kind a Pharisaic and self-willed mysticism, and finds in it the characteristics of an enervated age, which knows no joy but that of feeling, and understands no greatness but that of the labours accomplished by institutions and societies, etc. He denies that the approval of the Apostles or the Reformers can be claimed for so sentimental and Roman Catholic a method; he even doubts whether feeling should be given a normative place alongside of knowing and willing. I am not called upon to discuss this verdict upon modern Pietism; I prefer to leave it to others, who are more nearly concerned, to settle the disputed question whether the "Revival" was the product of an enervated generation, or a fresh return of springtime for the spirit of man. Only it appears to me that in the question before us Löhe has shaken himself clear of the Pietistic

---

[1] *On the Divine Word as the Light which leads to Peace*, 5th ed., 1869.

solution without getting rid of the Pietistic problem. For he considers it justifiable to address to individuals the question whether they are born again, whether they are children of God, whether they are assured in faith of their salvation. That is the view of the matter, indeed, which Möhler holds to be specifically Evangelical, but which took practical shape for the first time in the different phases of Pietism. Löhe, it is true, rests with only one foot upon Pietism, the other he places on the soil of doctrinaire Lutheranism, by giving the advice that awakened souls, who long for assurance, should accept with blind trust the immutable promises of the Word of God. This, he considers, was the meaning of the fact that in the age of the Reformation, alongside of knowledge and will, not feeling but memory was regarded as a principal function of the mind. For the memory ought to keep in active operation bright and clear texts of Scripture, so as to awaken believing confidence ; in a case of necessity, however, all doubts are to be beaten down by the believing confidence of the pastor.

But is memory, then, the power which fills up the gap between intellectual knowledge of the general truth of God's grace, and the personal satisfaction and pacification of the conscience ? And how long will the authoritative assurances of a believing pastor retain their power ? Can his words really produce more than that transient impression which Pietists gain anyhow by their tempestuous prayers for assurance ? Does the continuance of the frame of feeling desired really depend more on the imperious words of another than on the *syllogismus practicus*, or on the straining of the fancy to lay hold of the general promises of grace ? Feeling, as a matter of fact, is unaffected by the will, by logical reasoning, by the action of the fancy or the memory. But we are told that feeling ought not to enter here at all ; feeling—that discovery of post-Reformation times, that standard of an enervated generation, pretending to a scientific character which faith simply contradicts when it fills us with its proper power ! But unfortunately a pastor, even though he be as masterful in his ways as Löhe, must accommodate himself to the way of thinking of those on whom he wishes to work; he has no right to carry men away by claims so grotesque; for the impression which may be thus momentarily produced does not last, and the outcome of this method probably is to compromise Christianity. Now feeling is simply that function of mind in which the Ego is present to itself; and reconciliation with God must imply a modification of the feeling of self, if the assurance thereof is to occupy the mind at every moment and become a motive impelling the will.   But now, according to the Lutheran view, the course of events depends on the following syllogism.   The major premise—namely, the truth of the universal promise of grace—is presupposed as a judgment of theoretical cognition; the minor premise—that we are trusting firmly enough in the grace of God—is to be pro-duced by putting a strain upon the will: and from these there is to follow, as a perpetual gain for the feeling of self, the conclusion that we are assured of justification.   This exercise in reasoning, embracing all the three basal functions of mind, is not rendered any easier by the attempt which is made to explain the conclusion by comparing it to the success of moral effort.   For even if the latter ought to be inter-preted as an effect of grace, yet it is not sufficiently akin to trust in justification through Christ to give us any light upon assurance, when assurance does not arise directly of itself. Either that, or we run the risk of exchanging for justification a form of self-righteousness.

§ 24.. When Luther set up his view of justification by faith in opposition to the Catholic sacrament of penance (vol. i. p. 159), he not only bound up the conception of justification with the value of the Church for the individual believer, but with equal distinctness secured it against the predominantly legal practice of the Catholic system.   The predominant import-ance of the law in the sacrament of penance depends on the fact that from the penitent's confession the priest has to ascertain his definite sinfulness, in order to gauge absolution and penalties accordingly.   If, therefore, the priest's method is conscientious, he will hold the penitent firmly to *contritio*, or the terrors of the law. Against this Luther maintained in his earliest reforming period that the only genuine repentance is that which springs from faith, and that the penitent ought not to be detained under fears inspired by the law, but should be encouraged to cherish that believing conviction which appropriates forgiveness from the absolution of the Church (vol. i. p. 163). This is the sense of the new meaning given to the sacrament of penance in the Augsburg Confession, Art. xii., and in the *Apology*, Art. v. Since the *poenitentia* of those who commit sins after baptism is meant to produce *contritio* and *fides*, Melanchthon in the *Apology* regards the subsequent absolution as *sacramentum poenitentiae* in respect of those actions which confession brings to light (v. 41, vi. 13). Nevertheless, in contradistinction to the Catholic practice, what is here aimed at is to confirm the penitent's faith.   Now, in the *Apology* the Gospel, *quod arguit peccata* (ii. 62, v. 29), is repeatedly described as the motive to *contritio*, but alongside of it the same function is ascribed to the law (v. 53), so that the two parts of ecclesiastical *poenitentia* are connected with the two heterogeneous and graded parts of Divine revelation.   This view which, though only obscurely, lies at the basis of the 12th Article of the *Confessio Augustana*, approximates to the Catholic representation of the matter in a way that is not altogether favourable to the Evangelical character of the counsel intended.   For one who stands in need of special forgiveness for sins committed, really affirms the continuity of his believing status in the Church when, from the Gospel of forgiveness, he accepts the truth of his guilt.   Were he to betake himself exclusively to the law for this purpose, he would land himself in serious uncertainty.   For in the last resort this path will conduct him to the genuine repentance which is essential, only when by faith he sees in the Lawgiver the God of his salvation.   Here, therefore, within the narrow province of the *quasi* sacramental system of penance, we find the influence of that innovation of which Melanchthon gave an exposition in the *Visitationsbuch* (vol. i.

p. 200) in order to make the universal dispensation of justification intelligible to the laity.   The doctrine of justification, as exhibited also by Luther in the same sense,[1] narrows the problem to the case of individuals as such, and weakens its direct reference to life within the Church.   The Church remains in the background as the teacher of law and Gospel (vol. i. p. 189).

What disposed Luther to make this violent change in his teaching was the fact that he leaves the believer's standing as a Christian exposed to those agitations of feeling which he had experienced as a monk, owing to his erroneous attitude to the law.   Not finding in the prophets of Zwickau the same terrors of hell for sin, he thinks that he ought to conclude that they are untrustworthy.   Melanchthon, too, is the first to insist on these most torturing feelings as an element in *poenitentia* in the narrower sense;[2] they were next prescribed by both Reformers as a precondition of *justificatio* in general.   The orthodox theologians perpetuate this view. By combining the narrower conception of *poenitentia*, as equivalent to *contritio*, with *justificatio*, they finally come to discard the positive and comprehensive conception of *poenitentia*, with which Luther had opened his Theses of 1517, though it still receives recognition in the *Apology* (iii. 229).   In all these respects Calvin (vol. i. pp. 204, 214) keeps to Luther's original positions.   Justifying faith, as presupposing the regenerate status and *poenitentia*—which last covers the whole of life— and conditioned by the corporate existence of the community of which Christ is the Head, he represents as consisting in the imputation of Christ's righteousness; he makes room for the terrors of conscience only so far as to say that *many* experience them as preparatory to obedience, while he admits mortal terrors to be a precondition of conversion only in the case of those who have formerly been alienated by the devil from the fear of God.   Among the Lutherans

---

[1] E.g. *Commentarius in ep. ad Galatas* (1535), ed. Erl. tom. i. p. 186.

[2] *Apol. C. A.* v. 46: "Mortificatio (=contritio) significat veros terrores, sicut sunt morientium, quos sustinere natura non posset, nisi erigeretur fide.

Spener was the first to maintain a similar moderate view of the matter.[1]

The doctrine which Melanchthon made authoritative for the Lutherans had for a long time no pernicious effects. In practice it was counterbalanced by the survival of Luther's idea that baptism guarantees our standing in grace, and especially the forgiveness of sins. A. H. Francke, and besides him the Gotha Pietists in their Confession of 1693, was the first to insist on contrition, or the pain which accompanies the sweeping away of inherited lust, as a precondition of living faith; and they appeal to the *Apology of the Augsburg Confession.* But meantime the mysticism adopted by Joh. Arndt and Jodocus van Lodensteyn had led to a still more incisive precondition being prescribed than that expressed in the "conflict of penitence" (*Busskampf*). Formal self-denial, insistence on the hatefulness and loathsomeness of all sin whatsoever, is brought by them to such a pitch as to make man contrast himself in his creaturely nothingness with God, the only Lord and the only Existent One, in order that his heart may open to the grace which compensates him for the surrender of his own will by making him one with God. But this is to demand far more than pain excited by the feeling of one's own guilt. And while Luther may have inferred from his own experience that terrors of conscience arise spontaneously at the remembrance of the law, yet when the practice of monkish self-humiliation is revived, meditation upon sin in general and insistence on the nothingness of the creature become tasks which induce a constant tendency to morbid fancies. The Pietistic conflict of penitence points us also to the same methods. The uselessness of these methods, however, is plain from the fact that they really render uncertain the attainment of joyous trust in God as the mark of being pardoned, and that if it is attained at all, it is not continuous.[2] Besides, the Pietistic or mystical directions are always so stated

[1] *Geschichte des Pietismus*, ii. p. 113.
[2] Semler, *Lebensbeschreibung*, i. p. 48 ff.; Ph. D. Burk, *Die Rechtfertigung*, i. p. 152 ff.; Albert Knapp, *Lebensbild*, pp. 133, 140, 166, 179.

as though the Christian existed only for contemplation, and as though work, which interrupts his meditations, were worth nothing.   But this is a denial of the principle of the Reformation, that justification in actual fact becomes matter of experience through the discharge of moral tasks, while these are to be discharged in the labours of one's vocation.   And Heinrich von Bogatsky tells us in his biography that for the half of his lifetime all his pious exercises yielded him no lasting peace; not till he undertook the work of devotional writing did he attain to what he had been seeking.[1]

Spener repudiated both the conflict of penitence and the testing of justification by feeling; and taught instead that. we have to assure ourselves of the vitality of our faith and the certainty of our justification through the practice and the consciousness of moral action.[2]   This argument had already been put forward by Melanchthon and Calvin (p. 144); it came to possess a peculiar importance in Calvinism, which teaches that good works are to be regarded as evidence of *perseverantia gratiae*.   This view, moreover, not merely is inculcated in the Heidelberg Catechism (Qu. 86), but also explains the efforts made by the strict Calvinists to attain extreme precision in conduct.[3]   But the principle is likewise recognised in the Formula of Concord (iv. 15), and reiterated

---

[1] *Geschichte des Pietismus*, ii. p. 538.   Knapp, too, testifies to the same thing in his own way, *op. cit.*, p. 166.   His ceaseless conflicts in prayer had brought him only an insignificant gain, when one afternoon it seemed as though a gentle voice were urging him to work.   At the end of an hour of quiet study his heart overflowed with the blessed peace of God, so that with triumphant adoration he gives vent to his wonder in the question : How is it possible, my God, that Thou givest to me such heavenly peace in the midst of this dry work ?   Thence he draws the doctrine that the prayers even of an awakened man are evil and vain without work, thorough fidelity to his vocation, and honest industry.

[2] *Consilia latina*, i. p. 32 : "Ad sensum fidei internum provocare, res ambigua est.   Quoties enim eo destituentur, qui fide valent maxime, et in ipsa sua imbecillitate, cum se tentati fide vacuos vociferentur, robore coelesti conservantur, ut etiam vincant.   Si iam ex sensu iudicium, desperabunt aut desperare iubebuntur ac morti adiudicabuntur, qui vivebant ac vivere debebant . . . Cum ergo a priori, ut loquuntur, ea dicernere nequeamus, a posteriori cognitio nostra capienda est, videlicet a fructibus arboris indoles agnoscenda." Cf. *Geschichte des Pietismus*, ii. p. 97 ff.

[3] *Geschichte des Pietismus*, i. p. 112.

by Lutheran theologians, such as Quenstedt.   Nevertheless
this test of the justified status, when put into practice, turns
out to be unreliable.   The extreme precision of the Reformed
leaves an impression as though the thought of justification
had been swallowed up in attention to the trivialities of life.
But Spener (vol. i. 360) lets us see that partly he was reduced
to uncertainty when he asked himself what actions the glory of
God calls on us to perform or to omit, and partly came to
take an indulgent view of his sins.   At bottom, too, the
argument which concludes from good works to the truth of
the consciousness of justification by faith is very suspicious.
We ought, we are told, to look away from the good works
which we perform as regenerate, since they are always imperfect, and turn in faith to the perfection of Christ as the
ground of our standing before God.   And if, though we thus
turn, we become the prey of uncertainty, we ought again to
reflect that we still have good works, and have in them an
evidence of our standing in grace.   If this be so, it seems as
though we might spare ourselves this roundabout route, and
simply hold to the last-mentioned consideration.   The mistake
in the argument lies in this, that the category of good works
cannot be applied here, for when we are sitting in judgment
on ourselves, the real question always is whether our life-
work is manifested in the individual visible actions which we
have before us (vol. ii. 292).   But we cannot set up this
achievement alongside of justifying faith, or in opposition to
it ; on the contrary, that faith is an element in the true
conception of a man's lifework.   We cannot, however, discuss
at present how this comes to be so.

On the other hand, insistence on a "conflict of penitence,"
under the conditions laid down by Luther and Melanchthon
—conditions which Spener himself refused to acknowledge as
a rule for all—is, to begin with, inconsistent with that idea of
education through Church fellowship to which all the other
principles of the Reformers point.   Feelings of pain at one's
own sin, which are compared to the terrors of death and hell,
thereby fall under the category of emotions which belong to

the domain of the purely natural life. Natural feelings of pleasure and pain, as an original endowment of man, are the immediate impulses of his activities, but at the same time obstacles to the regular and continuous movement and direction of his will. Now all education consists in setting limits to natural and aimless emotions by exciting feelings of moral pleasure and pain, and in making possible the consecutive direction of the will to the good. This set of feelings is different from the other, for they are acquired and orderly. They are at the same time necessarily more peaceful, for they are modified by accompanying reflection. Now, if the transition from repentance to the assurance of pardon forms a self-consistent process, it must belong to the realm of education, and therefore cannot be experienced in those shifting feelings which, by the very strength demanded of them, would prove that the person concerned was destitute of all education. The moral pain of repentance cannot therefore consist in terrors comparable to the natural fear of death or the thought of hell. Such an hypothesis, besides, is rendered impossible by the mere fact that the *laetitia spiritualis*—which is an expression, in the religious feeling of self which God's grace has restored, of the reception of forgiveness—is shown by the epithet *spiritualis* to be moral pleasure. Or are we to suppose that this contrast between the moral pleasure which forms part of faith and the merely natural emotion which characterises repentance, is really a true one? That supposition would simply imply that we surrendered the self-consistency of the process. If the prescription of *poenitentia* is taken literally, we cannot escape this danger. The demand for a " conflict of penitence," in the sense of an excitation of natural emotions of anxiety and despair, simply suggests an aimless attitude of mind, in which one only removes oneself further from the possible peace offered by grace. And it is the same with the exaggerated insistence on the duty of our regarding ourselves in our creaturely nothingness as utterly unworthy before God. But just as *laetitia spiritualis* does not mean an emotion of the highest intensity, similarly the disapproval of oneself involved in repentance does not entail stormy sensations. Otherwise we are in danger of falling into the mistake of introducing storm and stress into our feeling of *laetitia* also, and so forfeiting that self-purification which yet ought to be attained if *poenitentia* is in general a moral experience.

The same result follows when we consider that, according to Luther's original position, repentance itself is an effect of faith, and when a penitent suffers from terrors of conscience he ought to have it made clear to him that he is really under the educative grace of God by which his faith is set free. And if what calls forth these experiences is his comparison of the sins he has committed with the Divine law, yet this points back to faith in the Lawgiver as the Benefactor and the Author of man's salvation. For if this thought be absent, if the Lawgiver be regarded as indifferent or as an object of mistrust, then there results no repentance at all. But he who is advised to go to the Gospel for the knowledge and condemnation of his sins, is from the outset supposed to be the subject of specific faith. Now this principle of the Reformers has hitherto been made use of as meaning that God's promise of forgiveness is intended to be our ground of knowledge in estimating our own sin. When looked at more closely, this conception requires to be drawn out into the further thought that the sight of Christ in His perfecting on the Cross both elicits from us condemnation of our sins, and makes God's grace to sinners certain. Such a conception has a deeper bearing on repentance than the law has, for it offers us the ideal of the God-pleasing life exhibited by Christ as the standard by· comparing ourselves with which we come to know and repent of our sins. For that model of what life should be embraces, in the unity of an ordered whole, all those relationships which are set forth separately in the law. And this, the model of our own faith and effort, excites our condemnation of those instances of unfaithfulness of which we have been guilty, in the same degree as, by its moral perfection and beauty, it impresses on us the revelation of God for our

salvation as the supreme motive of our faith in Him.   For
part of the meaning of repentance is that the sense of our own
moral dignity, too, should be a motive to condemnation of our
sin.   This fact is ignored when the demand is made that we
should learn our sin from the law, and estimate it by the
standard of the law; but it is acknowledged when we
draw our knowledge of our sin from a comparison of it with
the ideal.   For by recognising a model we do homage to our
own ideal, and that, too, from the standpoint of our own
honour and dignity.

I shall recapitulate the results attained up to this point,
in order to determine accurately the question still awaiting
solution.   Justification is God's forgiveness or pardon,
reconciliation with Him, adoption into the position of
children ; and, in God's revelation of grace through Christ, it
operates as the imputation of Christ's righteousness in such a
way that the position, given to Him and maintained by Him,
as Son of God and original object of God's love, is also imputed to those sinners who belong to the community of Christ
by faith, and thus they are accorded the *accessus ad patrem.*
Trust in God's grace, which includes emotional, *i.e.* personal,
conviction of what is thus connected with grace, and which
takes the place of the mistrust involved in the feeling of
guilt, is possible to every individual, provided that by this
faith he ingrafts himself into the community of Christ, which
presents to all its members, under the conditions described, the
promise of forgiveness as the proximate reason of its own
existence, and offers it to them for their salvation.   Since forgiveness through Christ is the fundamental form in which each
one receives the guarantee of his salvation, so likewise the
continuance of the consciousness of sin and of the need of
forgiveness, and therefore, too, repentance for our recurring
offences, are called for by the very fact that in Him Who
brings us the revelation of grace we recognise the moral ideal
—but in such a way that our education in the Church as a
rule excludes that passionate and acute form of conversion
which occurs in special cases.   What we still need to

discover is how the general truth of the promise of grace, for which each individual has the testimony of the community, is to become a personal conviction in every believer. The conditions of this have not yet been found. For as trust, in regard to justification, may change from stronger to weaker, a weaker trust is evidence of a lack of personal conviction which cannot be supplied by an intellectual acknowledgment of the general truth, cannot be confirmed by passionate and morbid effort, but is rather rendered impossible by the heightening of the feeling of guilt present in the " conflict of penitence," and in any case cannot be gained through feelings which are isolated and liable to change. All these methods assume that we are to receive assurance passively as an operation of God or through the influences of the Holy Spirit, perhaps even in a fashion definitely marked off from the normal context of mental life, or, in other words, through inspiration. But every point which we have hitherto been able to establish has gone to signalise the spiritual activities of the sinner. He exercises faith, he accounts himself a member of the community of Christ, he feels trust towards God, and no longer mistrust ; in recognising his ideal he condemns his sin, he seeks personal conviction of his salvation, in order that amid all other changes of his action and feeling he may hold fast to the *accessus ad patrem*. How are these two aspects to be reconciled with one another ?.

§ 25. If justification by faith is the basal conception of Evangelical Christianity, it is impossible that it can express the relation of men to God and Christ without at the same time including a peculiar *attitude of the believer to the world* founded upon that relation (p. 29). This fact is recognised by Paul when, in Rom. v. 1–5, viii. 3 2–39, he describes the application of justification (vol. ii. pp. 343, 349, 353). It creates in man a peculiar feeling of self which evidences itself in his hope of permanent acknowledgment by God and in patience under suffering, and which is charged with a power superior to all the forces and dispensations of this world. But the world is likewise the correlative of patience and hope. For

sufferings arise out of the believer's position in the world, and
his acknowledgment by God—which is the final verdict on
him—is always conceived, on the Old Testament model, as
installing him in his right relation to the world.   This aspect
of the matter was not forgotten by the Reformers.   Only,
the two classical expositions of this subject are not given in
connection with the statements of Paul.   On the contrary, in
his *de libertate Christiana* Luther uses Rev. v. 10 as the text
of his argument that those who are righteous by faith are
made kings and priests—priests, through the opening of the
accessus ad patrem and the right of prayer to God; kings,
through their trust in God Who governs all things for the
best, and will help the believer to surmount all obstacles
(vol. i. p. 181).   This line of thought, it is true, though without its leading terms, finds the clearest echo in the *Confessio
Augustana*, xx. 24, 25 (vol. p. i. 184).   On the other hand,
Melanchthon, in the *Apology of the C. A.*, relates justification
to the fact that it renders possible the fulfilment of the
Commandments of the first Table of the Decalogue, which
are beyond the ability of the natural man.

This doctrine, which pervades the whole of the *Apology*,
stands in a peculiar connection with the other parts of the
system.   It does not recur in any other of Melanchthon's
theological writings, and it had no influence on his successors.
It is all the more fitting, therefore, to attempt to elucidate its
meaning.   A new interpretation is put upon the first three
Commandments—according to the Lutheran enumeration—
when their content is reduced to true reverence, love,
invocation, trust in God under all sufferings, patience and
endurance in them;[1] though certainly the First Commandment must be explained in this sense.   Nevertheless,

---

[1] *Apol. C. A.* ii. 8: "Decalogus requirit non solum externa opera civilia,
quae ratio utcunque efficere potest, sed etiam requirit alia longe supra rationem
posita, scilicet vere timere deum, vere diligere deum, vere invocare deum, vere
statuere, quod deus exaudiat, et exspectare auxilium dei in morte, in omnibus
afflictionibus, denique requirit obedientiam erga deum in morte et omnibus
afflictionibus, ne has fugiamus aut aversemur, cum deus imponit." 18. "Ratio
nihil facit, nisi quaedam civilia opera, interim neque timet deum neque credit
se deo curae esse" (the same expression as in *C. A.* xx. 24, 25).

Melanchthon's interpretation agrees with Luther's Larger Catechism; for he, at least in his exposition of the First Commandment, has interwoven statements which approximate to Melanchthon's view (Pars i. 64, 70). On the other hand, the place of the Christian virtues just enumerated is, under the head of Christian Perfection, described by Melanchthon in the *C. A.* xxvii. 49, 50. Now, in the latter's position noted above, it is observable, first of all, that he draws a distinction of worth between the content of the first and the content of the second Table of the Decalogue. The first transcends reason, the second corresponds with reason. The Commandments contained in the latter, therefore, as embodiments of *iustitia civilis*, it is possible for the natural man to fulfil, at least relatively; the former are beyond him. The natural man cannot exercise reverence or trust in God, not to speak of the further obligations of patience, for as a sinner he is altogether *sine metu dei, sine fiducia erga deum*. These characteristics had first of all been enumerated under the head of original sin in the 2nd Art. of the *C. A.*, before *concupiscentia* in the Latin text, after it in the German. In the 1st Art. of the *Apology* Melanchthon had endeavoured to refute the objection raised in the *Confutatio pontificia*, that none save actual sins are to be understood under *concupiscentia*. We may pass over this aspect of the matter just now. Nevertheless the article of the Augsburg Confession itself, for all its dependence on Augustine, exhibits a change in the conception of sin which is all the more worthy of remark that it is not adopted in the later theology of the Lutherans.

In regarding inherited sin as equivalent to *concupiscentia*, Augustine conceived the basal relationship of men to God, which sin has overthrown, as being constituted by the law, and the field of unlimited desires as being the domain of moral action which God's law is to regulate. On the other hand, Luther does not consider the relation of the first man to God as ordered by the law; for him it consists in the reciprocation of Divine goodness and human gratitude. And therefore he finds the chief evil of original sin in the perversion of man's original reverence for God into its opposite.[1] He reproaches the Scholastics for neglecting this feature, but he might have passed the same censure on Augustine also. In his treatment of this point Luther is epochmaking, for he distinguishes between the irreligious and the immoral aspect of sin, and subordinates the latter to the former. It is possible for him to do so, because, when explaining the perfection of the first man, he lays more stress upon his free and spiritual religion than upon all his other *sapientia et iustitia*. With this agrees, finally, that articulated conception of Christian perfection to which Melanchthon gives most felicitous expression in the Augsburg Confession. For if the end contemplated is the restoration of original perfection through Christ, the religious aspect of things takes precedence of the moral. Moreover, though the Reformers allow that it is possible for the sinner to attain a certain measure of *iustitia civilis*, namely, the fulfilment of the Commandments of the second Table, yet grace is needed to produce reverence and trust towards God in sinners who have hitherto lived in indifference or mistrust towards Him. For these virtues, looked at in the light of their state as sinners, are *supra rationem*. The opposition held to exist between this fulfilment of the first Table of the law and the antecedent perversion of man's relation to God through sin, serves to explain the Lutheran interpretation of *poenitentia*. The latter experience, as set forth in the Augsburg Confession and the *Apology*, is meant as a substitute for the Catholic sacrament of penance, and

[1] *Enarrationes in Genesin. Opp. exeg. lat. Erl.* i. p. 133 : " Deus Adae verbum, cultum et religionem dedit nudissimam, purissimam et simplicissimam. Non enim praecipit mactationem taurorum, non fumum thuris, non vota, non ieiunia, non alias afflictiones corporis : hoc tantum vult, ut laudet deum, ut gratias ei agat, ut laetetur in domino, et ei in hoc obediat, ne ex vetita arbore comedat. Huius cultus reliquias habemus per Christum restitutas . . . quod nos quoque laudamus et gratias ei agimus de omni benedictione spirituali et corporali." 142 : " Sophistae cum de peccato originis loquuntur, tantum de misera et foeda libidine seu concupiscentia loquuntur. Sed p. o. est vere totus lapsus naturae humanae, quod est intellectus obscuratus, ut non amplius agnoscamus deum et voluntatem eius, ut non animadvertamus opera dei ; deinde quod etiam voluntas mire est depravata, ut non fidamus misericordiae dei et non metuamus deum ; sed securi, omisso verbo et voluntate dei, sequimur concupiscentiam et impetus carnis." Cf. pp. 77, 78, 82 on the content of the image of God.

receives that title even in the *Apology* (v. 41) as well as in the *Loci* of 1535. Now it is striking that in the Confession (xii.), and in the *Apology* (v. 28, 45), good works, as *fructus poenitentiae*, are distinguished from its two elements, *contritio* and *fides*. Though in the passage cited from the *Apology* Melanchthon makes no objection to their being regarded as a third element in *poenitentia*, he nevertheless conserves their character as *fructus poenitentiae*. For the former view is admissible, provided that *poenitentia* is interpreted in the comprehensive sense which it has in Luther's first thesis, a sense deliberately adopted by Calvin. On the other hand, we have *poenitentia* used again (vol. ii. 45) in a sense limited in the narrowest way to the *terrores*, and therefore equivalent to *contritio*. But the very limitation of *poenitentia* to *contritio* and *fides*—a sense which it received in later Lutheranism, as being incumbent on saints and backsliders alike, as both the beginning of justification and a daily duty—possesses a practicable meaning only when sin is regarded primarily as a defect in reverence or trust in God, and only in the second place as an offence against the moral law. Save on this presupposition, the doctrine is unintelligible.

But what relation has the idea of justification or forgiveness to the capacity of rendering to God reverence, love, and trust; of interpreting all worldly dispensations in this spirit, and of bearing sufferings patiently as Divine means of education? The difference between the Evangelical and the Catholic view was reduced above (p. 36) to this, that the latter is designed to explain the moral capacity of the justified sinner, the former to explain his religious character. Now the outcome of Melanchthon's statement in the *Apology* is that forgiveness renders possible obedience to the commandments of the first Table.[1] This may be proved by combining the

---

[1] One statement seems inconsistent with this. We read, iii. 228 : "Ideo iustificamur, ut iusti *bene operari et obedire legi* incipiamus. Ideo regeneramur et spiritum sanctum accipimus, ut nova vita habeat nova opera, novos affectus, timorem, dilectionem dei, odium concupiscentiae," etc. 229 : " Haec fides, de qua loquimur, exsistit in poenitentia. Et inter bona opera, inter tentationes et pericula confirmari et crescere debet, ut subinde certius apud nos statuamus,

following propositions from the *Apology :*—ii. 34 : " Humanus animus sine spiritu sancto aut securus contemnit iudicium dei (sine metu), aut in poena fugit et odit iudicantem deum (sine fiducia)." 36. " Impossibile est diligere deum nisi prius fide apprehendatur remissio peccatorum. Non enim potest cor, vere sentiens deum irasci, diligere deum, nisi ostendatur placatus." 44. " Promissio nobis affert gratis reconciliationem propter Christum, quae accipitur sola fide." 45. " Haec igitur fides specialis iustificat nos, regenerat nos, et affert spiritum sanctum, ut deinde legem dei facere possimus, videlicet diligere deum, vere timere deum, vere statuere, quod deus exaudiat, obedire deo in omnibus afflictionibus, mortificat concupiscentiam," etc. In this argument it is to be noticed, first, that Melanchthon illustrates the operation of forgiveness or the process of justification exclusively by bringing out the aspects of the correlative faith ; and further, that he uses *regenerare* as interchangeable with *iustificare*. This is the case also in ii. 72, 78, 118, with this additional difficulty, that even *iustum efficere* is employed as equivalent to the other two terms.

Wherever the formula, that faith justifies, occurs in the *Apology*, it is added that such language is not to be taken literally. Properly speaking, justification is bestowed by God for Christ's sake ; faith merely accepts it. But clear as the latter statement seems, it introduces a difficulty into the argument when a formula not meant to be taken literally is used alongside of the true description. Might this formula not have been avoided by the exercise of a little care, especially when it was so liable to be misconstrued by opponents ? And yet it is indispensable, for the operation of God, which is called justification, works a change in the person concerned. That this change has taken place, that the Divine cause has produced its

quod deus propter Christum respiciat nos, *ignoscat nobis*, exaudiat nos." Yet, as the second statement, agreeing with the first, shows, even in this connection Melanchthon means merely the Commandments of the first Table as the aim and end of *iustificatio* or *regeneratio*. The *nova opera* are only to be understood as instances of that trust in God and patience which are opposed by the *tentationes*. Through the overcoming of *tentationes*, by means of such religious actions, faith is represented as growing stronger even in its direct relation to the forgiveness of sins.

effect, has its evidence only in the faith *excited* by God's pardon, and in those various relationships which faith embraces. Here we have the inevitable psychological character of this conception (p. 21) from which no explanation of the matter can escape. For however earnestly we may strive to bring out man's passivity in this respect, yet we can never get over the fact that he receives and apprehends the unconditioned operation of God. And that means that he is spiritually active, whether as experiencing lively joy at the thought of pardon, or as listening to such a statement as, " Thy sins are forgiven thee." These possibilities, however, do not enter into Melanchthon's view, in so far as he includes obedience to the Commandments of the first Table under the faith which is the correlative of our being declared righteous. A man does not experience the fact of his justification so much in a contemplative act which presents to his mind justification or Divine pardon in an isolated way, but rather in trust in God, which embraces likewise the believer's situation in the world. He has a right to feel this trust, and is led to exercise it, just because he acknowledges Christ as the Reconciler of the community which He founded, of which he deliberately reckons himself a member. As it is most simply expressed in the *C. A.* xx. 24, faith verifies the forgiveness of God experimentally when it reaches out to grasp God's care and providence over the whole of life, and relies thereon even under those sufferings involved in the believer's situation in the world. For in his changing aspects as sinner and believer, man is not only face to face with God; he is also in relationship to the world. This is indisputable so long as he remains in a state of sin ; but neither can it be denied or thought away even in the believer as justified, unless we are to land ourselves in a fatal obscurity. The sinner who, by his former mistrust of God, shows himself to be dependent on the world, can be proved to have undergone a change through his trust in God's forgiveness, only if with that trust there is combined a new lordship over the world due to confidence in God's all-embracing care. Thus, too, this exercise of faith in providence and of patience under divinely-ordained sufferings is the form in which the believer attains assurance of the salvation guaranteed to him through Christ alone.   For since the dominion over the world, exercised through faith in the Reconciler, brings with it its corresponding feeling of pleasure, the *laetitia spiritualis* contains in itself the conditions of its continuity and inward equipoise.   Apart from these functions of trust and patience, we can find no place for assurance of our justification by faith.   Auditory hallucinations conveying anything of the kind have nothing to do with the case.

There are theologians who meet an explanation such as this with a charge of Pelagianism.   They are of opinion that if the conception of grace be the principle which is determinative for the data of the Christian life, man must be thought of as occupying a purely passive attitude towards it. Every interpretation of Divine grace which moves within the limits of the subjective functions determined and set in motion by it, they regard as a negation of Divine grace altogether.   For they detect the errors of Pelagius wherever the human subject is represented as possessed of self-dependence. Unfortunately, they themselves alone are guilty of these errors, for they forbid us to combine in thought the grace of God and the self-dependence of the human spirit.   The Pelagian conception of human freedom is that which makes it the sufficient ground of religion and morality in such a way as to abstract the subject from his connection with the religious and moral community.   But in the view given above there is this reservation, that the justification of the individual takes place only within the community of believers, which, as bearer of the promise of grace, proves itself an educative influence on those who are to belong to it (p. 109), and so this doctrine is not Pelagian.   If, on the other hand, it is asserted that the human spirit does not consist merely in feeling, knowing, and willing, but exists behind all these as a definite kind of being and life—in other words, as a kind of substance (*Natur*)[1]— that this dark background is acted on by grace in a purely

---

[1] Cf. *Theologie und Metaphysik*, p. 42 ; 2nd ed., p. 45.

passive way, and that this relationship must first be ascertained before its consequences can be observed in spiritual actions—then this mystical psychology is simply useless, whether for theoretical or practical purposes. This kind of mysticism takes upon itself to explain intelligible processes by unintelligible formulae ; it is a fruitless juggling with words. It is utterly alien to Melanchthon's style of thought, or rather, the charge of Pelagianism strikes also at the *Apology of the Augsburg Confession.*

Lastly, the fact that in the document just mentioned the expressions *iustificare, iustum efficere, regenerare* are used as equivalents in describing the connection, explained above, between justification and the functions of religious freedom, does not imply a relapse into Catholic methods of thought. The Formula of Concord, iii. Epit. 7, 8, Sol. decl. 17, 18, provided against *regenerare* in the *Apology* being understood in any other sense than as *absolvere a peccatis.* But this does not explain how Melanchthon not only comes to use as equivalents those expressions which elsewhere he differentiates, but also gives the same meaning to *iustum efficere.* He does not understand this latter phrase in the Catholic sense of *caritas infusa ;* and anyone who charged him with doing so would do him as grave an injustice as Fricke[1] does to me when, in spite of my express repudiation of this Catholic conception, he represents it as my view. By speaking of *iustificatio* as *iustum efficere,* Melanchthon can only mean to remove the impression, which might be created by the *imputatio iustitiae,* that by the latter is meant the predication of an imaginary attribute. But the real change in the sinner is proved by the fact that he is impelled, by the forgiveness of his sins, by the Divine decision that for Christ's sake he is *deo acceptus* (p. 73) to exercise that reverent trust in God which is the characteristic activity of the new life. This change at the same time depends on the Holy Spirit, yet not in such wise that His working is mechanical like that of a

---

[1] *Metaphysik und Dogmatik,* p. 7.   Cf. the first edition of this volume (Germ.), p. 531.

supernatural physical force, but in such a way that His action
on the individual can be shown to exist only when the individual is a member of the community of believers.   The Holy
Spirit necessarily coincides with this relationship.   Melanchthon's usage was not repeated by himself, for he did not
again state the direct practical relation of justification to the
religious functions.   In reasserting the rights of this important doctrine, I reserve the question whether the conception
of *regeneratio*, which it involves, demands or permits a more
extended use.

Reverent trust in God's protection and providence in
every situation in life, the invocation of God in prayer, and
patience under the sufferings which He ordains, constitute,
according to the teaching of Luther and Melanchthon in the
two documents under discussion, the content of the religious
freedom over the world in which the believer experiences his
justification; they constitute the activity which is called
forth by the pardoning grace of God, when it moves one
who was formerly a sinner to lay aside the mistrust of God
which goes along with the unrelieved sense of guilt.   This
religious change, which establishes the believer's independence
of the world, in addition makes it possible for him to attain
to moral independence of character.   The corresponding
element in Catholicism is not to be sought under the heading
of faith.   For faith, in the Catholic sense, means knowledge
accepted on God's authority, and, as related to justification
(*iustum efficere*), consists essentially in active love of one's
neighbour.   Through the exercise of this love, moreover,
hope comes to its proper perfection; and hope, as directed
to eternal blessedness, embraces also the other evidences of
God's compassion furnished by the believer's situation in
the world (p. 37).   But according to the delineation of hope
given by Thomas Aquinas, it is subjected to a peculiar
limitation, due to the sense attached to *timor filialis*.   On
this point the teaching of Thomas is as follows (Pars ii. 2,
qu. 19).   Fear has for its direct object some evil which is
to be avoided.   Now God is not an evil, and therefore

12

cannot be feared directly; but He can be feared in so far
as some evil impends which comes from Him or is in contrast
to Him.   And this is either punishment or guilt.   Punishment, as the deprivation of a particular good, is an evil,
though in the light of the final end it is in itself good;
guilt is essentially evil, for it is incompatible with a proper
relation to the good final end.   One fears punishment as
inflicted by God; one fears guilt as contrasted with God.
Fear of punishment is slavish; fear of guilt is childlike, for
a child fears to wrong his father.   A mixture of the two
kinds is *timor initialis,* as it occurs at the beginning of the
Christian life.   Slavish fear is bad, so far as its aversion to
punishment rests upon the lust of the world: it is essentially
good when what is feared in punishment is its coming from
God, and proof is thus given that love to God is bound up
with it.   But this does not annul the generic difference
between slavish and childlike fear.   This is shown by the
fact that both may be regarded as the beginning of wisdom.
Slavish fear, however, turns human life away from sin out of a
regard for the punishment of sin; childlike fear governs life
directly by the Divine motives of reverence for God, surrender to Him, and shame of abandoning Him.   Childlike
fear, therefore, is a gift of the Holy Ghost, and identical with
being poor in spirit; inasmuch as one who surrenders himself to God seeks no glory for himself and sets no value on
external goods.

    The last-named characteristic indicates that childlike
fear of God is meant to be regarded as the principle, not
only of action, but of our estimate of self and our view of
the world.   This aspect betrays its similarity to the freedom
of the Christian.   But at the same time the opposition between
the two standpoints comes out clearly.   For the Catholic
mode of feeling looks exclusively to the ever-threatening
possibility of offending against God: that of the Reformers
looks to the divinely-guaranteed certainty that guilt has been
blotted out, and the recurring sense of guilt deprived of its
power to separate us from God.   I do not say that Christian

liberty, in Luther's view, implies the certainty in advance
that all offences which we may conceivably commit are
forgiven ; but while the liberty of the children of God does
not express any such prospect, it is just as little a prey to
the fear of new offences. But though Christian liberty be
maintained as a standpoint both possible and necessary,
this does not make it impossible that any man's *poenitentia*
may long enough be attuned to the tone of *timor filialis*, and
that while life lasts this tone may enter momentarily into
the feeling of reconciliation.   But the liberty of the children
of God implies that the standpoint of childlike fear is not the
highest possible goal, but at best enters into experience as a
transitional stage.   In the education of children one must on
occasion take measures to prevent certain bad habits or faults
of disposition from breaking out : to this end, the children's
attention must be so directed that they come to be on their
guard against such offences, and therefore, when temptation
arises, remember the possibility of their committing them.
But education would defeat its own object if it were to aim
at producing, as the dominant tone of children's minds, a
terror of disobeying the commands of their elders.   Such
children would never attain independence of character :
according to their temperament, either this kind of education
would render them timid and useless in life, or their anxious
attitude of mind would swing round into shameless im-
·morality.   The superiority of Christian freedom, however,
may be seen from the fact that no rounded religious view of
the world is compatible with childlike fear, in the sense in
which Catholicism makes the latter a pervasive characteristic
of the Christian life.   For one who has always to be on his
guard lest in one of the multifarious situations of life he
should transgress against the highest end, and so against the
moral order, cannot take a survey of his own attitude towards
the world, nor estimate it as a whole in relation to himself,
as it is necessary and possible to do when, on the basis of
reconciliation, one feels unconstrained trust in God.   Lastly,
in childlike fear we have a positive expression of that

uncertainty about one's own salvation which is prevalently recommended in Catholicism.

Catholicism, however, furnishes yet another counterpart to the religious freedom which springs from justification by faith. This is the freedom of familiar intercourse with God, Who reveals His love in Christ, and it is accorded to perfect Christians, to monks and nuns, as the crown of their sanctification.[1] This freedom consists in the contemplative exercise of responsive love, which arises from compassion infused into the soul at the sight of God humbling Himself out of love. Such freedom, however, implies for its exercise a footing of equality with God as thus contemplated. Christ, the Bridegroom, is divested of all the qualities of loftiness and sublimity, and all considerations of reverence are laid aside, in order that the believer may exchange with God in this form all the delights of sensuously - coloured tenderness. Such freedom, which strives after mystical union and distinctionless identity with God, becomes the basis of an assurance of salvation which leaves *timor filialis* far behind it ; but, as being a deliberate straining of feeling, is only too quickly dispelled by the sense of desolation, desertion, and dryness of soul. In two respects such freedom of intercourse with God is differently constituted from that which arises from justification by faith. The latter is experienced by the Evangelical Christian when by his trust in God he incorporates himself into the community of believers, and makes its public standing in the pardoning grace of God his own. The monk, on the other hand, gains the right to the freedom of intercourse described above when he has climbed the heights of active sanctification, or, in other words, when he has marked himself off from others. Besides, the Evangelical Christian is called on to exercise the freedom arising from justification amid the trials and hardships of life ; the monk has no occasion for anything of the kind, for he has withdrawn himself from them.

[1] See *Geschichte des Pietismus*, vol. i. p. 46 ff., for the features of this style of piety as described by St. Bernard (vol. i. p. 116).

Is it permissible to regard these two forms of piety as equivalent ?

§ 26. It has been already shown (vol. i. p. 348) that the connection between justification and the religious functions of the new life, which Melanchthon expounds in the *Apology of the Augsburg Confession*, and which is an answer to the question about the nature of personal assurance, does not recur in the Reformer's later writings. The same thing happens here as with Luther's attachment to justification of positive world-dominating freedom. In all his later writings he limits the freedom which flows from justification to its negative sense of freedom from the law and from sin. In the same way, hardly anywhere save in Luther's Catechisms is the individual's experience of forgiveness made dependent on his connection with the Church. The most practical ideas of the Reformation, therefore, disappeared from later Lutheran theology. And this defect made its appearance even in the writings of the Reformers themselves, until the mischief was brought to an acute stage by Johann Gerhard's making faith in God's providence a part of Natural Theology. The fidelity of this orthodox divine to the Augsburg Confession is such that he declares possible to the natural, that is, sinful man, that very trust in God which the chief standard of the Church expressly denies to him ! Nevertheless, ascetic writers continue to take the same estimate of these religious functions, though they are influenced by different motives—Arndt, for instance, by the example of Christ, Scriver by our Divine sonship. By Stephan Praetorius alone is the joy of the Christian's view of life and personal attitude directly deduced from justification. Founding on the view of the Apostle Paul, the Reformed divine Peter Dumoulin the younger [1] develops the connection which Melanchthon had indicated. He starts from the fact that reconciliation through the merits of Christ has won peace

---

[1] Canon of Canterbury, died 1684. *Traité de la paix de l'âme et du contentement de l'esprit*, Amsterdam, 1675. Of the five books of this work, the first, *de la paix avec dieu*, has to do with our subject. The contents of the others are ethical. A reprint of this treatise appeared in Paris in 1840.

with God for all those who turn to Christ with true faith. In reconciliation they have received the forgiveness of sins and the rights of the children of God, and thereby are filled with joy. Even though they need to pray for forgiveness daily, yet that does not disturb their peace with God, for He to whom they pray is their Father. As sin, however, laid the foundation not only of enmity between man and God, but likewise of discord both between man and the world and between man and himself; so the peace with God which is gained through reconciliation brings in its train, first of all, man's peace with himself, then peace with the creatures and with other men. The latter appears in his readiness to forgive; the former, in his enjoyment of every temporal blessing as evidence of the goodness of a reconciled God. Thus we make experimental proof of the fatherly care of God throughout the whole of life; welfare and calamity are felt to be equally good as dispensations of His goodness; for, as Paul says, all things are ordered for our good, and sufferings when endured in this spirit heighten our love to God. In order to maintain peace with God, service to Him, or prayer, is needed. Prayer, issuing as it does from the assurance that we are reconciled to God through Christ, and manifesting as it does our subjection to God, is at the same time an exercise of the freedom to approach God which we have gained through Christ. When by it we seek to preserve the peace of God throughout all the wants and needs of life, it produces faith, love, hope, patience. The chief use of prayer, however, is to praise God for His benefits in general, and for the manifestation of His saving compassion in particular; and in this we have the beginning of eternal life. Peace with God is founded, through Christ's work, in the love of God. Now, as this love calls forth our responsive love, this attitude of our will continually strengthens the believing trust which embraces the peace won for us by Christ. That trust is supported by hope, exercises itself in a good conscience, and finally attests its genuineness by the practice of good works.

In the meantime, however, the idea of justification had, in tradition, lost its practical theological aspect and become unintelligible. Consequently, among both Lutherans and Calvinists the mediaeval methods of communing with the Saviour as with a Bridegroom, of formal self-denial, and of mysticism, were, for the purposes of edification, brought into operation again. Johann Arndt revived this method, and at the same time found in the example of Christ a prefiguration of the active religious virtues of Lutheran Protestantism. In this we may detect a mixture of views, uninfluenced by Luther's decision against mysticism. Already at the beginning of the seventeenth century there is to be found in general the commencement of that falsification of the history of the Reformation which was due to the inferences drawn from Luther's commendation of the *Theologia Germanica*, and his approval of Tauler. From his acting so people thought they could prove that Luther had really led mysticism to victory,[1] but they failed to observe that subsequent to 1518 we have declarations of an opposite character by Luther on the subject of mysticism (p. 99). Later, the hostile attitude adopted by the Catholic authorities towards the Quietists misled people into supposing that, as Zinzendorf says (vol. i. p. 595), the Molinist doctrine of disinterested love to God is in exact agreement with the 20th Article of the Augsburg Confession. Gottfried Arnold and Tersteegen, too, lauded the Quietistic hermits and nuns of Spanish, Italian, and French blood as the spiritual kindred of the Lutheran Reformers. Alongside of this, it is true, in those hymns which came to be used in public worship, an emphasis not in the least corroborated by the public teaching of the Church continued to be laid on the providence of God. Even those hymn-writers who devote themselves chiefly to expressing the various aspects of the Church's bridal love, and to sensuous contemplation of the wounds and blood of

---

[1] On the other side, it is still instructive to read Gottl. Wernsdorf, *Aufrichtige und in Gottes Wort gegründete Meinung von der mystischen Theologie*, Wittenberg, 1729. Cf. *Geschichte des Pietismus*, vol. ii.

Christ after mediaeval models, are likewise capable of giving full expression to gratitude for Divine benefits. But no one of all these sacred poets asks himself the question, from what principle their trust and their submission to God, their thanksgiving and their avowals of patience, are to be deduced. For that very reason they are far from taking for granted, with Johann Gerhard, that they are merely giving expression to the rights of the natural man. But this of itself is sufficient proof of the fact that the practical gain involved in Luther's view of the world and of life was not lost by the Church which bore his name. The same character pervades the Pietism which sprang up on the soil of Lutheranism. It is the most prominent feature of Francke's life. Evidences of the providence of God constitute the chief theme of the autobiographies and diaries which make their appearance with Pietism, by Petersen, Canstein, Joh. Jak. Moser, Bogatsky, Jung-Stilling. *Inter alia* all kinds of trivialities find their way into their pages, and occasionally even selfishness, as when Petersen points out how God has visited his enemies with sudden death or other calamities. Even Edelmann, when he went over to Natural Religion, retained this style of thinking from his Pietistic days. Originally this sort of " conduct of life " was alien to the Pietism of the Reformed Church ; its dominant note is awe rather than trust in God.[1] Stilling therefore follows rather the path of Lutheran Pietism.

The hymns adopted by the Lutheran Church, which celebrate the Divine Providence, furnish the clearest proof of what, in this Church's view, constitutes personal and social piety. I should become tedious, I fear, were I not to limit myself to the hymns of Paul Gerhardt in bringing out the characteristic features of these writers' circle of thought. In a chronological series of hymns, covering what lies between birth and death, Gerhardt gives repeated expression to that special faith in Providence which brings every experience of joy and sorrow under the goodness of God. In this series

---

[1] Cf. *Geschichte des Pietismus*, vol. i. p. 309.

there likewise appears a thankful acknowledgment of redemption through Christ, as one item among others. But
this does not in the least mean that, apart from redemption,
the poet is convinced of Divine Providence as an object of
natural cognition, as was assumed by the theologians. On
the contrary, every hymn of the kind is written from the
standpoint of redemption through Christ as an incontestable
presupposition—a fact which is sufficiently indicated even
by such slight allusions as those contained in saying that
" God is my God," or that " I am His child." The numerous
imitations of the Psalms to be found among Gerhardt's
hymns hardly admitted of any other kind of character. But
in two hymns it becomes palpably evident that for him
fellowship with God through Christ is the true basis of his
knowledge of God's general Providence, and that reconciliation is the fountain of that religious sense of freedom in
which the soul enjoys salvation. I refer to the hymn,
*Warum sollt' ich mich denn grämen ? hab' ich doch Christum
noch ; wer will mir den nehmen ?* and the hymn drawn from
Rom. viii.: *Ist Gott für mich, so trete gleich alles wider mich.*
True, the scholastic conception of justification is not echoed
by any of these hymns; and, indeed, I do not know how
that conception would look in a poetical guise. But who
can deny that these hymns form the classical expression of
the practical faith which takes its stand upon justification
and reconciliation through Christ ?

In what may be said to consist the difference between
the spiritual poems of Gellert and those of Paul Gerhardt ?
It would be a great mistake to regard the later poet merely as
a representative of Rationalism. On the contrary, as regards
dogma he is absolutely orthodox, and his hymns dedicated to
the great Christian festivals express his agreement with the
traditional views of Christ's birth, death, resurrection, and
exaltation to lordship over the world, with great warmth
and indisputable sincerity. Now alongside of these hymns
we find others which praise God as the Governor of the
world and the gracious Ruler of human fortunes : they, too,

commend themselves to us by their freshness of feeling and the earnestness of their trust in God.   But Gellert's Christianity issues from the school of dogmatic theology; and in the tradition of this school the truth of God's government of the world and special Providence simply stands on the same level with the truth of His reconciliation through Christ in order to the forgiveness of sins.   The one is an article of faith, and so is the other.   But the truth of God's Providence is not merely claimed by Dogmatics as a part of Revelation; it is also declared to be a product of natural cognition.[1]   Now it would be inconsistent with the character of poetry if, in the hymns celebrating the Divine Providence and government of the world, we were given a reflective treatment of either source of knowledge; and this is the less to be expected, since even the series *Ehre Gottes aus der Natur* definitely follows the model of the Psalms.   But the want of connection between these hymns and those which deal with the history of redemption is unmistakable; so much so, that if the latter are put aside, the poet who wrote the former might actually be a Deist.   This impression, however, is due to the fact that Gellert's hymns on the Providence of God lack that positive background of reconciliation from which Gerhardt draws his peace - pervaded view of the world.   A second feature of the difference between the two is this, that Gellert's mind is in process of transition from the dogmatic orthodoxy, in which he had been educated, to Rationalism; for to some extent he mixes up incentives to virtue with his treatment of God's redeeming grace, and to some extent subordinates experiences of this Divine grace to these incentives.[2]   It might be said, indeed, that the in-

---

[1] Baier, i. 5. 3: "Dari providentiam divinam, praeterquam quod ex lumine naturae constat, ex scriptura clarissimum est."

[2] In his collected works (1775), vol. ii. pp. 199, 200, the following strophes are to be found in the beautiful Passion - hymn, *Lord strengthen me, Thy Passion to remember* :—

> "Eternal Joy! For us Thou wast reviled,
> Even me Thy precious blood hath reconciled,
> Thou on the Cross, for me a free oblation,
> Earn'dst my salvation.

stances I have cited are not dogmatically erroneous, inasmuch
as our assurance of forgiveness is to be trusted only provided
we are at the same time devoting ourselves to moral activity ;
since, too, the elements of experience through which we
become certain of Divine pardon through Christ belong to
the active life.   In general, indeed, it is clear that devotion
and Dogmatics are guided by different interests.   In devotion we look at ourselves altogether in the light of subjection
to God ; and every thought, be it never so limited, which
is given to our personal activity, interrupts devotion.   On
the other hand, a hymn like the second quoted below is
not a religious poem at all, for it depicts the independent
moral activity of the saint.   The fact that such moral reflections are thought identical with devotion betrays that
intermingling of religion and morality which is characteristic
of Rationalism.   But this is still far beyond Gerhardt's
horizon.

This is not the place to revert to the rise of Rationalism
(vol. i. p. 366), but I cannot refrain from observing that the
position taken up by Gellert is not favourable to the hypothesis
that Rationalism is simply an apostasy from dogmatic belief.
For in his personal convictions Gellert combines elements
which subsequently fell apart everywhere ; and that he does
not interpret the general providence of God in the light of

> Is bliss then mine even here through faith prevailing?
> Secure my crown 'gainst every foe assailing?
> One day shall I within these courts supernal,
>   Gain life eternal ?
>
> Yes, if I stray from virtue's pathway never,
> Fight faith's good fight, keep watch and pray for ever:
> Since Jesus lives, my victory stands assured,
>   As now procured."

On the other hand we read, p. 128—

> "His peace alone is great, who aye God's way pursueth,
>   Vile passions yield before his zeal ;
> He fights, he knows God's prize which to the strife accrueth,
>   Rejoices in his virtue leal.
> Ever before his eyes and in his heart God reigneth,
>   A daily suppliant at the throne ;
> His faults he oft repents, his sins remission gaineth
>   Through grace of Jesus Christ alone."

reconciliation through Christ, is to be laid to the charge of orthodox Dogmatics. When the theology of the *Aufklärung*, however, renounced dogma in order to place the moral character of Christianity in an untroubled light, it yet kept its foot firmly planted upon faith in providence as the properly religious function. The emphasis with which this truth was brought to the front as *the* expression of religion is enough to refute the supposition that we have here at work the theoretical reflection which elsewhere dominates this movement. The faith in providence which Rationalism proclaimed before and after Kant, is a continuation of the subjective Christianity to which Luther originally gave expression.[1] It is true, indeed, that Rationalism makes an alteration in the form and contents of this function. For one thing, we have the erroneous belief that the love of God is a truth of Natural Religion (vol. i. p. 403), and thus the acknowledgment of God's Providence is robbed of its connection of reconciliation through Christ. A further consequence of this is that surrender to God's will takes on an altered tinge of sentiment. What intensity and courageousness of feeling are theirs who take for their own the declaration of Paul that nothing, neither life, nor death, things present nor things to come, can shake the believer, to whom everything belongs as his possession! The feeling which accompanies the *Aufklärung* faith in providence, on the other hand, is in many cases trivial, weak, sentimental. Lastly, from the reason indicated above, it follows that the *Aufklärung* became entangled afresh in the Old Testament dilemma between merit and felicity, and could only solve it by postulating compensations in the future life; while the Christian consciousness of reconciliation already transcends the antinomy of merit and happiness in every moment of the present life.

Unfortunately German theology, in its reaction from

---

[1] Cf. J. F. W. Jerusalem, "*Fortgesetzte Betrachtungen über die vornehmsten Wahrheiten der Religion,*" Posthumous Works, Pt. I. 1792. Heinr. Sander, "*Ueber die Vorsehung,*" three Parts (2nd ed. of Parts I. and II.), 1784, 1785. Especially Wegscheider, *Institutiones theologicae*, ii. 5. 107.

Rationalism, has almost entirely failed to appropriate, in a comprehensive and genuine way, that whole circle of thought which so unfolds into the doctrine of justification by faith, as to become the basis of religious independence of the world through trust in the Father of Jesus Christ. Schleiermacher limits himself to expressing in the conception of reconciliation —the second characteristic of Christ's work, redemption being the first—the abrogation, for those who are redeemed, of the penal significance of evil (vol. i. p. 515). This is to do no more than add to the doctrine of the work of Christ a feature which older divines had appended as an incidental note to the doctrine of the punishment of sin. Nitzsch,[1] on the other hand, touches on the subject in its entire range ; and it is all the more to be regretted that he has not developed it in detail from the subjective point of view, as might have been expected from the plan of his work. Recent theologians, so far as they have been guided by the form of Lutheran Dogmatics in the seventeenth century, were bound to miss the connection between justification by faith and the religious functions described above. Now we might expect that these functions would find their place in Ethics, especially when such theologians as Harless mean by Ethics an exposition of Christian self-knowledge and of our knowledge of subjective Christianity. But in the *Christian Ethics* of the writer named I have not found the least indication of how the believer knows himself to be a child of God, or what view of the world and estimate of self follow from justification and reconciliation. This topic appears to find a place neither in Dogmatics nor in Ethics; probably because it ought rightly to be discussed in both. This Martensen admits,[2] though strangely

---

[1] *System der Christlichen Lehre* (6th ed.), § 144 : "Faith in the name of the Lord, as the precondition of all acceptance with God and all blessedness, always includes the adoration of the God of grace and truth, and in every case consists in an abandonment by self-feeling of the feeling of one's own power and worth and right, and in recourse instead to the ever attested mediatorship of God, and is not merely related to our original trust in God's invisible action, but produces from itself, even in the presence of calamity and the trials of need and death, all trust and fidelity and comfort."

[2] *Christliche Dogmatik*, p. 427.

enough he makes it a consequence of the doctrine of election.
He describes the elect as the real *foci* which reveal the Divine
Providence, and in illustration of, this view he quotes Rom. viii.
28–39. But he fails to trace prayer back to this connection,
and he ignores the fact that it is the thought of their justification, not the thought of their election, which Paul makes the
basis of the assurance which raises believers superior to all
things. Ch. Fr. Schmid,[1] on the other hand, finds a place for
the doctrine of Divine sonship in Christian Ethics. Here he
brings in resignation, thankfulness, and trust in God, then
prayer, and finally humility, as the functions of the Christian
life, and lays down their scriptural basis. It is unessential for
our purpose to ask whether the particular virtues of Christian
self-preservation and self-culture ought rightly to be derived,
as is done by Schmid, from those religious functions. But
that he should have dealt with the subject as an *ethical* one,
proves how well founded his reputation was as a Biblical
theologian in the best sense. Hofmann, too, shows his independence of the forms of theological tradition by giving a
place to the religious functions in his *Schriftbeweis*. In the
7th Division, 2nd Half, §§ 2–4 of that work, he describes the
Christian's attitude towards God as consisting in this, that
he proves his freedom by his love and humility towards God,
and proves his blessedness by his joy in God and thankfulness
to Him; further, as concerns his own human nature, he
proves his freedom by his hatred of sin and his faith in God,
and he proves his blessedness by the pain he feels regarding
death and by his hope toward God. This scheme is likewise
applied to the Christian's relation to the world, thus—
humble love for the world and thankful joy in it are combined with hatred of sin and pain at it, and with faith and
hope for the world. Finally, to these there is appended
prayer, as the manifestation of this disposition in direct
relation to God. In this scheme homeless religious functions
find a resting-place. But they are bound up with things of
an alien character, such as hatred of sin, and pain felt in

---

[1] *Christliche Sittenlehre*, p. 638 ff.

view of death—which last, besides, is put forward as a proof
of blessedness.   On the other hand, we miss a statement
of the truth that the Christian's relation to the cross of
suffering is the reverse of that of the natural man.   Now
what was wanted was that the scriptural proof for these
statements of Hofmann should be drawn, fully and correctly, from the ideas of the apostles.   But to this side
of the matter Hofmann has failed to give an adequate
representation.

In defining justification or reconciliation, and in fixing
their relations, I have made use of materials drawn partly
from the dogmatic theologians of the classical age, partly
from the Reformers and the Lutheran symbols.   It has
been impossible to combine and arrange these materials
without modifying particular aspects to which importance
has always been attached from the very outset.   Conceptions, which we find alongside of each other in the pages of
the theologians without correlation, have at the same time
either been reduced one to the other or sifted out altogether.
But on the whole the doctrine of justification set forth in
these three chapters stands in the line of direct continuity
with the intention of the Reformers and the standards of
the Lutheran Church.   Especially is this the case as regards
the practical aspect of justification, its significance as explaining the peculiar character of that view of the world
and of life which we owe to the Reformation.   On this point
we get no help from the theology which is haunted by
the prejudice that it must follow the symbolical books at
every step.   And yet it has shown itself, and that not
merely in the present case, very indifferent to the standards
of the Reformation.

Accordingly, 1. The problem of personal assurance is
insoluble if it be conceived in a form which represents the
subject as passive.

2. Personal assurance can be attained neither through
the active "conflict of penitence" (*Busskampf*) nor by observation of the moral activity which accompanies it.

3. Personal assurance, springing from justification, is experienced in and through trust in God in all the situations of life, and especially in patience, by him who through his faith in Christ incorporates himself into the community of believers.

CHAPTER IV

§ 27. THE endeavour to construct *theology* in the Gentile-Christian Church arose from the belief that the positive conception of God as the Father of Christ, and of Christ as the Son of God, must be demonstrated as a universal truth of reason, in relation to the knowledge of the world which men had then attained. This belief has been, not confirmed, but rather shaken to the very foundation, by the manifold turns which the history of theology and philosophy has taken. For one thing, we can no longer conceal from ourselves the fact that the Greek Fathers carried the thought of God and Christ out into notions of the ultimate and the mediate ground of the world, which are peculiar to the later eclectic philosophy of Greece, and neither cover nor exhaust the original sense of the former conceptions. On the other hand, Gentile-Christian theology always insists on the reservation that the Christian religion presents an element which transcends all merely secular knowledge, namely, the end and the means of the blessedness of man. Whatever content may have been ascribed to this word *blessedness*, it expressly denotes a goal, the knowledge of which is unattainable by philosophy, and the realisation of which cannot be secured by the natural means at the command of men, but depends upon the positive character of Christianity. Consequently, the theology of the Greek Fathers is not merely cosmology, but, above all, a doctrine of redemption ; the cosmology upon which the doctrine of redemption is built, however, is developed by means of ideas borrowed from Plato and the Stoics. The Scholastics carry on this method, and Thomas

13

Aquinas makes a statement on the point which harmonises
with the foregoing criticism of Greek theology. For, in the
assurance of blessedness given by Christianity, he sees a
destiny for men which was not provided for in their creation
by God, nor included in their natural constitution, and which
cannot be understood merely by the use of their reason. But he
does not make this special feature of Christianity the key to
his view of the world as a whole ; rather, it is underpropped
by a thoroughly rational theology, the material of which has
no relation to Christianity, and which is unmistakably derived
from Greek Philosophy.   The same procedure is still adhered
to by the traditional theology among ourselves (p. 4).   Nevertheless the division of the material of theology into propositions given by reason and propositions given by revelation is
a method whose validity can no longer be maintained. In
opposition thereto there has gradually come into force the
contrary principle, that religion and theoretical knowledge are
different functions of spirit, which, when they deal with the
same objects, are not even partially coincident, but wholly
diverge.   This heterogeneity must be accurately established
ere it can be decided what use is to be made of general
theoretical knowledge in the scientific exposition of Christianity.

If religion in every case is an interpretation of man's
relation to God and the world, guided by the thought of the
sublime power of God to realise the end of this blessedness
of man, advancing insight into the history of religions has
forced on us the task of formulating a universal *conception of
religion*, under which all the particular species of religion
might find their peculiar features determined.   But this task
involves no slight difficulties, and contributes less to the
understanding of Christianity than is often expected.   The
formula by which this very thing, religion in general, has
just been described, makes no claim to be a definition proper
of the generic conception of religion.   It is too definite for
that.   The ideas which it employs—God, world, blessedness
—have so directly Christian a stamp, that they apply to

other religions only in a comparative degree, *i.e.* in order to indicate the general idea of religion, we should have to specify at the same time the different modifications which they undergo in different religions. For, besides belief in the One God, there falls to be considered the ascription to the Godhead of multiplicity, or duplicity, or difference in sex, and there is, further, the recognition of superhuman power in the spirits of the dead. Again, the relation of the Godhead to the world undergoes modification according as the world is conceived as a unity, or this point is left obscure, or the immediate surroundings of a particular wild tribe are taken as its world. It is modified, further, according as the Divine beings are identified with the forces and phenomena of nature, or distinguished from nature and creation, or, in the latter case, occupy a more negative or more positive relation to the world. Lastly, as regards blessedness, we have to consider the different cases in which what is sought through adoration or adjuration of the superhuman powers is merely some chance benefit, or the idea of a supreme good is formed, and this again is sought in the world, or apart from the world, or in a combination of both forms. As, therefore, the historical religions offer, under each of these heads, a rich supply of specific and sub-specific characteristics, which have no place in the general conception of religion, language can furnish no terms sufficiently neutral and indeterminate to express the general conception of religion desired. But, besides, it would be impossible to state in their proper place the above-discussed modifications of the several parts of the definition, without making obscure the very point which is professedly of importance.

If, however, we have once arrived at a general conception of religion more or less distinct in outline, it serves, as do all general ideas, as a clue by which to determine the chief characteristics of the various species of religion. Now we have no difficulty in ascertaining by an examination of all other religions, that the secular knowledge which they involve is not disinterestedly theoretical, but guided by practical ends.

This circumstance, therefore, when given a place provisionally in the general conception, suggests, first, that objection may justly be taken to the exactly contrary use of secular knowledge which has made its way into the Christian Church; and next, that the later should be expelled, as something accidental, from the idea of the Christian religion. In the investigation of Christianity the general conception of religion should be used *regulatively*. I desire to distinguish myself very precisely in this respect from those who, in interpreting Christianity, make a *constitutive* use of the general conception. For when this method is employed, no longer as Scholasticism employes it, but in such a way that the influence of the general conception of religion makes one even for a moment neutral towards the Christian religion itself, in order to be able to deduce its meaning from the conditions of the general conception, then the only effect of this is to undermine Christian conviction. Christian conviction, however, is necessarily left intact when, as a theologian, one forms a general conception of religion, whatever the nature of that conception may be, for regulative use. For the observation and comparison of the various historical religions from which the general conception is abstracted, likewise shows that they stand to one another not merely in the relation of species, but also in the relation of stages. They exhibit an ever more rich and determinate manifestation of the chief features of religion; their connection is always more close, their aims more worthy of man. Such a way of looking at them opens up more fruitful vistas than are offered by the abstraction of a general conception of religion, followed by the comparison of the historical religions as species of this genus. For in this case the various religions are treated merely as natural phenomena; in the other case they are viewed as elements in the spiritual history of humanity. To prove that religions are related to one another as stages, is a scientific problem which still awaits an impartial and unprejudiced solution. Consequently we have to consider that several religions, such as Christianity and Islam, claim to occupy the highest stage above all others ; and that Buddhists and Hindus who have become acquainted with Christianity put forward reasons which are meant to demonstrate the superiority of their faiths over the Christian. When, therefore, as Christians, in reviewing the series of stages presented by the religions of the world, we judge them by the principle that Christianity transcends them all, and that in Christianity the tendency of all the others finds its perfect consummation, the claim of the science of religion to universal validity may seem to be sacrificed to the prejudice arising from our own personal convictions. But it is aimless and impracticable to attempt to prove the universal validity of the view that religions can be arranged in an ascending series. Do people expect to discover thus a way of demonstrating scientifically to a Mohammedan or a Buddhist that the Christian religion, and not theirs, occupies the highest rank ? In carrying out the task we have indicated, we have no such aim. It were indeed a desirable result, in the case of people who have been born Christians, and now, *e.g.*, declare the verdict of their scientific knowledge to be the inferiority of Christianity to Buddhism, if we could detach them from their error. But it is impossible for us, when arranging religions in a series of stages, to shut our eyes to the claim of Christianity to occupy the highest place. For those qualities in other religions by which they *are* religions are intelligible to us chiefly as measured by the perfection which they assume in Christianity, and by the clearness which distinguishes the perfect religion from the imperfect. The arrangement of religions in stages, consequently, amounts to no more than a scientific attempt to promote mutual understanding among Christians ; and assent to the statement that Christianity is the highest and most perfect religion is therefore no obstacle to the scientific character of the theory.

Here, therefore, our task is not to elaborate the serial arrangement of religions, but to seek a solution of the question how Christianity, as a religion, is related to general philosophical knowledge. Consequently, it is desirable that the qualities by which *Christianity reveals its religious character* should be brought out with that distinctness which they claim to possess at the level of Christianity.   If in doing so we glance at other religions, our business will just be to point out the modifications for the worse which they exhibit when compared with Christianity.   The various historical religions are always of a social character, belonging to a multitude of persons.   Thence it follows that to assign to religion a merely psychological complexion, in particular to refer it to feeling, is not a solution, but only an abridgement of the problem.   In a community the influence of the individual is conditioned by two factors, inasmuch as he is both like and unlike the others, alternately dependent on them and affecting them actively.   Consequently a psychological explanation of religion is inadequate, for it deals only with those phenomena of spirit in which all men are alike, and one is the type for all.   The above-mentioned dissimilarity of men within the common life of a religion falls under the scope of ethics.   Now the multiplicity pertaining to a religion is one of distribution, partly in space and partly in time.   An illustration of the latter is presented by the successive stages of life.   Thence it follows that every social religion implies a doctrinal tradition.   The dispersion in space of the members of the same religion is a direct obstacle to their fellowship, but it is compensated for when the religion takes real shape in the gathering for worship.   Feeling, as pleasure or pain, as blessedness or suffering, is the personal gain or the personal presupposition which impels individuals to participate in religious fellowship.   Nor in all religions does this aspect stand out so clearly and distinctly from the other functions as it is customary to suppose.   In orgiastic faiths, contending emotions of feeling are the very material of worship ; in the Roman, religious feeling assumes the form of painful attention to the correctness of ceremonial actions; in the Greek, the same factor appears in the serenity and the seriousness which affect, and are affected by, the worship.   Hence it follows that for different reasons the historical religions claim service from all the functions of spirit—knowledge, for the doctrinal tradition, *i.e.* for a particular view of the world ; will, for the common worship ; feeling, for the alternation of satisfaction and dissatisfaction, moods by which religious life is removed from the ordinary level of existence. No religion is correctly or completely conceived when one element of this succession is regarded as more important or more fundamental than the others. At the same time the question is reserved whether our scientific explanation of the total fact of religion shall give the preference to one or other of the functions of spirit.

In every religion what is sought, with the help of the superhuman spiritual power reverenced by man, is a solution of the contradiction in which man finds himself, as both a part of the world of nature and a spiritual personality claiming to dominate nature. For in the former *rôle* he is a part of nature, dependent upon her, subject to and confined by other things ; but as spirit he is moved by the impulse to maintain his independence against them. In this juncture, religion springs up as faith in superhuman spiritual powers, by whose help the power which man possesses of himself is in some way supplemented, and elevated into a unity of its own kind which is a match for the pressure of the natural world. The idea of gods, or Divine powers, everywhere includes belief in their spiritual personality, for the support to be received from above can only be reckoned on in virtue of an affinity between God and men. Even where merely invisible natural powers are regarded as Divine, they are conceived in a way analogous to that in which man distinguishes himself from nature. For the rest, the ease with which definite stupendous natural phenomena, whether beneficent or destructive, are personified, proves that it is in the spiritual personality of the gods that man finds the foothold which he seeks for in every religion. The assertion that the religious view of the world is founded upon the idea of a whole [1] certainly holds true of Christianity : as regards the other religions it

---

[1] Lotze, *Mikrokosmus*, iii. p. 331.

must be modified thus far, that in them what is sought is a supplementary addition to human self-feeling or to human independence over against and above the restrictions of the world. For in order to know the world as a totality, and in order himself to become a totality in or over it by the help of God, man needs the idea of the oneness of God, and of the consummation of the world in an end which is for man both knowable and realisable. But this condition is fulfilled in Christianity alone. For in the religion of the Old Testament the presuppositions, indeed, are given, but the world-end aimed at is merely the perfecting of the one chosen people in moral, political, and economical independence; the human perfecting of the individual Israelite, each in his own personal character, is not kept in view, as it is in the Christian conception of life and blessedness. Nevertheless, in heathen and even in polytheistic religions there is always a tendency at work towards belief in the unity of the Divine power, and in the measure in which this is the case the supplement to his own resources which man seeks in religion becomes more clear and more worthy. When, as in Brahminism, the world which has sprung from the original Being is so constituted that it returns to the distinctionless unity of real existence, what takes the place of the maintenance of selfhood is its absorption in the Divine Being. In its own way, this too is a kind of unity, for it is viewed as the consummation of asceticism and quietistic piety.

Christianity, by its completely rounded view of the world, guarantees to believers that they shall be preserved unto eternal life in the Kingdom of God, which is God's revealed end in the world—and that, too, in the full sense that man is thus in the Kingdom of God set over the world as a whole in his own order. Not only the Christian's tone of feeling, but also his estimate of self is determined by this highest and all-inclusive good. For this religion offers no passionate impulse, no vacillation between changing tones of feeling arising from confused ideas, no voluptuous alternation of aesthetic pleasure and pain; on the contrary, such emotions must be viewed in the light of the antitheses of sin and grace, of bondage as to what is good, and liberty to give God thanks and to act aright.   The temper produced by these conclusions, therefore, normally issues in the reverence for God proper to the level reached by Christianity.   This combination is the rule in other religions also.   Those religious affections of feeling which are called forth by the effort to secure blessings obtainable from the gods, and which have a complexion of their own, universally manifest themselves solely in correlative acts of worship.   At this point, however, in the sacrifice of acquired property, and in religious and moral self-abnegation, there comes into view a universal characteristic of all religions.   In this way the domain of religious action is marked off from secular life as a sacred domain ; at the same time, however, the value of the blessings bestowed by the gods is gauged by pleasurable feelings of another class than those which accrue to man naturally or as a result of work.   Religious feeling, with or without the accompaniment of a clear estimate of self, will always be found to be the material of worship ; but the form which such feeling assumes witnesses at the same time to a decision of the will, which gives reality to the acknowledgment of God and the personal satisfaction this entails.   The idea of God is the ideal bond between a definite view of the world and the idea of man as constituted for the attainment of goods or the highest good.   Worship is the realisation of the blessing sought by the practical acknowledgment of the power that bestows it.   In Christianity, thanksgiving for God's grace, prayer for its continuance, and service of God in His Kingdom, have attached to them eternal life and that blessedness which corresponds to the highest good, the Kingdom of God.

Common worship has a still closer relation to the revelation which forms the organic centre of every connected religious view of the world.   This factor, too, appears with various modifications at the various stages of religion.   In the religion of sorcery, acts of worship are employed to elicit revelations from mysterious superhuman powers. In Christianity, revelation through God's Son is the *punctum stans* of all knowledge and religious conduct. In the developed natural religions, success in obtaining Divine revelations is bound up with their being regularly acknowledged in worship. No idea of a religion complete after its own order can be formed if the characteristic of revelation which belongs to it is either denied or even merely set aside as indifferent. True, this very method has long been customary. People think themselves justified in abstracting from the characteristic of revelation found in every religion, inasmuch as they regard the myths of natural religions, and the doctrines of the religions of the Bible, as veiled or undeveloped philosophy. But the original purpose of myths is to explain why particular acts of worship, intended to do honour to Divine self-manifestations, are performed at some definite spot and at regularly recurrent intervals. What we may regard as the doctrinal material of the religion of the Old Testament—the free creation of the world by God, and His intention that man, who, as spirit, is the image of God, should bear rule over it—denotes the presuppositions of the belief that the Israelites are called by God in an especial covenant, under which they have to achieve their historical destiny in the world under the government of their Divine King. The speciality of the spot at which a god has ordained that he shall be adored, the speciality of the times at which the gods move through the land and summon their worshippers to celebrate their festivals, the speciality of the choice of Israel by the Lord of all nations—in short, *speciality* is the element which impels men to grasp the different aspects of religion, and to combine them practically in worship. The significance which revelation thus has for common worship also indicates an indispensable precondition of our understanding Christianity. The Person of its Founder is not only the key to the Christian view of the world, and the standard of Christians' self-judgment and moral effort, but also the standard which shows how prayer must be composed, for in prayer both individual and united adoration of God consists. At the same time the acknowledgment of the revelation of God in Christ yields this pre-eminent excellence of Christianity, namely, that its view of the world is a rounded whole, and that the goal it sets to life is this, that in Christianity man becomes a whole, a spiritual character supreme over the world. For speciality is ever the condition under which a universal end is realised through the combination of individual things and relations.

§ 28. How, then, is *religious knowledge* related to theoretical or philosophical knowledge ? This question, indeed, has already been raised by the very fact of Greek Philosophy ; still, much more tangible and comprehensive reasons for raising it are to be found in the mutual relations of Christianity and philosophy. Accordingly, it is best that we should limit the question to Christianity in so far as it is a religion, intelligible as such from the characteristics noted above. The possibility of both kinds of knowledge mingling, or, again, colliding, lies in this, that they deal with the same object, namely, the world. Now we cannot rest content with the amiable conclusion that Christian knowledge comprehends the world as a whole, while philosophy fixes the special and universal laws of nature and spirit. For with this task every philosophy likewise combines the ambition to comprehend the universe under one supreme law. And for Christian knowledge also one supreme law is the form under which the world is comprehensible as a whole under God. Even the thought of God, which belongs to religion, is employed in some shape or other by every non-materialistic philosophy. Thus no principle of discrimination between the two kinds of knowledge is, at least provisionally, to be found in the object with which they deal.

Now, in order to elicit the distinction between the two from the realm of the subject, I recall the twofold manner in which the mind (*Geist*) further appropriates the sensations aroused in it. They are determined, according to their value for the Ego, by the feeling of pleasure or pain. Feeling is the basal function of mind, inasmuch as in it the Ego is originally present to itself. In the feeling of pleasure or pain, the Ego decides whether a sensation, which touches the feeling of self, serves to heighten or depress it. On the other hand, through an idea the sensation is judged in respect of its cause, the nature of the latter, and its connection with other causes : and by means of observation, etc., the knowledge of things thus gained is extended until it becomes scientific. The two functions of spirit mentioned are always in operation simultaneously, and always also in some degree mutually related, even though it be in the inverse ratio of prominence. In particular, it must not be forgotten that all continuous cognition of the things which excite sensation is not only accompanied, but likewise guided, by feeling. For in so far as attention is necessary to attain the end of knowledge, will, as representing the desire for accurate cognition, comes in between ; the proximate cause of will, however, is feeling as expressing the consciousness that a thing or an activity is worth desiring, or that something ought to be put away. Value-judgments therefore are determinative in the case of all connected knowledge of the world, even when carried out in the most objective fashion. Attention during scientific observation, and the impartial examination of the matter observed, always denote that such knowledge has a value for him who employs it. This fact makes its presence all the more distinctly felt when knowledge is guided through a richly diversified field by attention of a technical or practical kind.

But even if we have made up our mind that religious knowledge in general, and therefore Christian knowledge too, consists of value-judgments, such a definition is as lacking in precision as it would be to describe philosophical knowledge contrariwise as disinterested. For without interest we do not trouble ourselves about anything. We have therefore to distinguish between *concomitant* and *independent* value-judgments. The former are operative and necessary in all theoretical cognition, as in all technical observation and

combination.   But *independent* value-judgments are all perceptions of moral ends or moral hindrances, in so far as they
excite moral pleasure or pain, or, it may be, set in motion the
will to appropriate what is good or repel the opposite.   If the
other kinds of knowledge are called " disinterested," this only
means that they are without these moral effects.   But even
in them pleasure or pain must be present, according as they
succeed or fail.   Religious knowledge forms another class of
independent value-judgments.   That is, it cannot be traced
back to the conditions which mark the knowledge belonging
to moral will, for there exists religion which goes on without
any relation whatever to the moral conduct of life.   Besides,
in many religions religious pleasure is of a purely natural
kind, and is independent of those conditions which lift
religious above natural pleasure (p. 165).   For only at the
higher stages do we find religion combined with the ethical
conduct of life.   Religious knowledge moves in independent
value-judgments, which relate to man's attitude to the world,
and call forth feelings of pleasure or pain, in which man
either enjoys the dominion over the world vouchsafed him by
God, or feels grievously the lack of God's help to that end.
This theory is almost more easily intelligible if it be tested
by religions which possess no moral character.   Orgiastic
worships represent contending natural feelings with extraordinary intensity and with abrupt changes, in virtue of their
recognition of the value which the identity of the Godhead
with the vegetation as it decays and again revives, has for the
man who modifies his attitude towards the world of nature in
sympathy with the Godhead which he adores.   The peculiar
nature of religious value-judgments is less clear in the case of
religions of an explicitly ethical character.   Nevertheless, in
Christianity we can distinguish between the religious functions
which relate to our attitude towards God and the world, and
the moral functions which point directly to men, and only
indirectly to God, Whose end in the world we fulfil by moral
service in the Kingdom of God.   In Christianity, the religious motive of ethical action lies here, that the Kingdom of

God, which it is our task to realise, represents also the highest good which God destines for us as our supramundane goal. For here there emerges the value-judgment that our blessedness consists in that elevation above the world in the Kingdom of God which accords with our true destiny. This is a religious judgment, inasmuch as it indicates the value of this attitude taken up by believers towards the world, just as those judgments are religious in which we set our trust in God, even when He condemns us to suffering.

In its day the Hegelian philosophy represented theoretical knowledge as not merely the most valuable function of spirit, but likewise the function which has to take up the problem of religion and solve it. To this Feuerbach opposed the observation that in religion the chief stress falls upon the wishes and needs of the human heart. But as the latter philosopher also continued to regard professedly pure and disinterested knowledge as the highest achievement of man, religion, and especially the Christian religion—which he held to be the expression of a purely individual and therefore egoistic interest, and a self-delusion in respect of its object, God—was by him declared to be worthless, as compared not merely with the knowledge of philosophic truth, but also with purely moral conduct. But an interest in salvation in the Christian sense, when rightly understood, is incompatible with egoism. Egoism is a revolt against the common tasks of action. Now, people might say that faith in God for our salvation, and a dutiful public spirit towards our fellows, have nothing to do with one another, and that therefore there is no conceivable reason why religion, as a rule, should not be egoistic. But in Christianity precisely faith in God and moral duty within the Kingdom of God *are* related to one another. As a rule, therefore, it is impossible that Christian faith in God should be egoistic. On the other hand, theoretical knowledge in itself, as has been shown, is not disinterested; but moral conduct is still less so. For in the latter domain the vital point is that one realises as one's own interest the interest of others to whom the service is rendered. The

moral disposition can nowhere strike root save in such
motives.   It is true that, contrary to the rule, faith in God
may be combined with egoistic arrogance towards others.
But the same danger attaches to both of the other kinds of
activity which have been compared.   It is possible for one
occupied with theoretical knowledge to be vain and haughty,
and for one devoted to the moral service of others to be
tyrannical or sycophantic.

Scientific knowledge is accompanied or guided by a
judgment affirming the worth of impartial knowledge gained
by observation.   In Christianity, religious knowledge consists
in independent value-judgments, inasmuch as it deals with
the relation between the blessedness which is assured by God
and sought by man, and the whole of the world which God
has created and rules in harmony with His final end.   Scientific knowledge seeks to discover the laws of nature and spirit
through observation, and is based on the presupposition that
both the observations and their arrangement are carried out
in accordance with the ascertained laws of human cognition.
Now the desire for scientific knowledge carries with it no
guarantee that, through the medium of observation and the
combination of observations according to known laws, it will
discover the supreme universal law of the world, from which,
as a starting-point, the differentiated orders of nature and
spiritual life, each in its kind, might be explained, and understood
as forming one whole.   On the contrary, the intermingling and
collision of religion and philosophy always arises from the fact
that the latter claims to produce in its own fashion a unified
view of the world.   This, however, betrays rather an impulse
religious in its nature, which philosophers ought to have distinguished from the cognitive methods they follow.   For in
all philosophical systems the affirmation of a supreme law of
existence, from which they undertake to deduce the world as
a whole, is a departure from the strict application of the
philosophic method, and betrays itself as being quite as much
an object of the intuitive imagination, as God and the world
are for religious thought.   This is the case at all stages and

in all forms of Greek philosophy, especially in those forms in which the ultimate universal grounds of existence, through which the universe is interpreted, are identified with the idea of God. In these cases the combination of heterogeneous kinds of knowledge—the religious and the scientific—is beyond all doubt; and it is to be explained by the fact that philosophers who, through their scientific observation of nature, had destroyed the foundations of the popular faith, sought to obtain satisfaction for their religious instincts by another path. In a certain respect, too, they were able to follow this tendency with especial confidence, so far as they succeeded in making out the unity of the Divine Being to be the ground of the universe. But in another respect they failed to satisfy the essential conditions of the religious view of the world, partly in so far as they surrendered the personality of the Godhead thus identified with the ground of the world, partly because they had to give up the active influence of a personal God upon the world. Nor, under these circumstances, could any worship be deduced from the idea of God. Thus the collision of Greek philosophy with the popular faith was twofold, and in both respects inevitable. For one thing, the actual observation of nature and her laws is incompatible with the religious combination of popular views of nature and the idea of God. Further, the rigidly unified view of the world held by philosophers is incompatible with the religious view of the world which is only loosely developed in polytheism. But the real force of the latter incompatibility is to be found in the fact that, under the guise of philosophic knowledge, what was really only the religious imagination has been operative in designing the general philosophic view of the world, the supreme principle of which is never proved as such, but always merely anticipatively assumed.

The opposition to Christianity which has been raised by Pantheism in its various modifications and by materialism, arises likewise from the fact that the law of a particular realm of being is set up as the supreme law of all being, though the other forms of existence neither would nor could be explained by its means. It may be admitted that natural science is right and consistent in explaining the mechanical regularity of all sensible things by the manifold movement of simple limited forces or atoms. But within this whole realm of existence, which is interpretable by the category of causality, observation reveals to us the narrower realm of organisms, which cannot be exhaustively explained by the laws of mechanism, but demand, besides, the application of the idea of end. But among organic beings, again, one section, differentiated in manifold ways, is animate, that is, endowed with the capacity of free movement. Finally, a still smaller section of animate beings is so constituted as to act freely from the conception of ends, to discover the laws of things, to conceive things as a whole, and themselves as in ordered interaction with them, further to identify all these activities with their own Ego by means of the manifold affections of feeling, and to exchange their spiritual possessions with others through speech and action. Now the claim of materialism to invalidate the Christian view of the world rests on the belief that it must succeed in deducing the organic from what is mechanical, and similarly the more complex orders of being from those immediately below. The materialistic interpretation of the world busies itself with the pursuit of these empty possibilities. Its scientific character is limited, however, by the fact that it can only suggest chance as the moving force of the ultimate causes of the world, and of the evolution of special realms of being out of those which are more general ; for this is really to confess that science cannot penetrate to the supreme law of things. In all the combinations exhibited by the materialistic theory of the genesis of the world, there is manifest an expenditure of the power of imagination which finds its closest parallel in the cosmogonies of heathenism— which is of itself a proof that what rules in this school is not scientific method, but an aberrant and confused religious impulse. Thus the opposition which professedly exists between natural science and Christianity, really exists between an impulse derived from natural religion blended with the scientific investigation of nature, and the validity of the Christian view of the world, which assures to spirit its pre-eminence over the entire world of nature.

The same holds true of the various forms of Pantheism which have alternately assumed the guise of the Christian view of the world, and entered the lists against it. The deceptive power of the imagination has to be called in to deduce all the diversified orders of reality from the laws either of spatial construction, or of vegetable life, or of lyrico-musical sensation, or of logical thought. None of these laws is the key to an adequate view of the world as a whole; none has been elevated by the use of properly scientific method, *i.e.* by means of observation and orderly inferences, into the supreme principle of interpretation; but philosophers have been surprised into accepting one or other by the religious desire for a complete view of things which they did not distinguish from their scientific cognition. The claims, adverse to the Christian view of the world, which have been made as a consequence of this self-deception, are further supported by the assumption, by which philosophical idealism is dominated, that the laws of theoretical knowledge are the laws of the human spirit in all its functions. From the standpoint of such a principle many aspects of the Christian view of the world and of the Christian estimate of self appear contradictory, and consequently untrue. But as certainly as feeling and will cannot be reduced to ideational knowledge, the last-named is not justified in imposing its laws upon the former. Feeling is admittedly not susceptible to what are called the " reasons of the understanding," and the verdict of logic upon a contradiction, that it denotes something which is impossible and therefore unreal, is incommensurate with the moral verdict we pass on a bad will. It is true, the responsibility for the pretensions addressed by philosophy to the Christian religion often lies in part with the champions of Christianity themselves. It is so when they represent as the Christian faith some imperfect form of theology, that is, some system of the ideas of God and humanity which is as far away as pos-

sible from expressing the whole view of the world implied
by the religious estimate of self which Christians are known
to exercise, and by the character of their worship of God.
Under these circumstances, philosophy often enough regards
it as sufficient to demonstrate that the law of faith outlined
in theology collides with laws of experience, and then declares
religion untenable as an illegitimate trespass of the fancy
upon the field of rigorous science.   But the fact is, Pantheism
is very far from rising to that estimate of the destiny and
worth of human personality which is determinative in
Christianity.   Whenever the boundary-line between the
Divine nature and the world is erased, whenever the universe
in any one of its aspects is defined as the Absolute, there is
nothing for man but to regard himself as a transient emana-
tion of the World-Soul, or as an element in the spiritual
development of humanity, whose progress leaves him behind
and degrades him to a position of dependence.   Nor is this
result of the pantheistic view of the world sufficiently compensated for by the permission it accords us to cherish
aesthetic sympathy with the universe, or to exercise ethical
resignation in presence of the ceaseless advance of intellectual
culture.   These sentiments have already appeared on the soil
of heathenism, and they indicate no reason why we should
interest ourselves in free-thought.   He who thinks that this
view of the world is to be preferred to the Christian, ignores
the principle of the Christian estimate of self — that the
individual is worth more than the whole world, and that
each soul can test and prove this truth through faith in
God as His Father, and by service to Him in His Kingdom.
For the Christian view of the world, disclosing as it does
the all-inclusive moral and spiritual end of the world,
which is also the proper end of God Himself, evidences
itself as the perfect religion.

§ 29. That religious knowledge consists of value-judgments is brought out in a felicitous way by Luther in his
Larger Catechism, in the explanation of the First Commandment: " Deus est et vocatur, de cuius bonitate et potentia

omnia bona certo tibi pollicearis, et ad quem quibuslibet
adversis rebus ac periculis ingruentibus confugias, ut deum
habere, nihil aliud sit, quam illi ex toto corde fidere et
credere. . . . Haec duo, fides et deus, una copula coniungenda
sunt." In these sentences are expressed various truths of
which the theology of the schools both earlier and later has
taken no account, and which its modern successors combat
even yet. Knowledge of God can be demonstrated as religious
knowledge only when He is conceived as securing to the
believer such a position in the world as more than counter-
balances its restrictions. Apart from this value-judgment
of faith, there exists no knowledge of God worthy of this
content. So that we ought not to strive after a purely
theoretical and "disinterested" knowledge of God, as an
indispensable preliminary to the knowledge of faith. To be
sure, people say that we must first know the nature of God
and Christ ere we can ascertain their worth for us. But
Luther's insight perceived the incorrectness of such a view.
The truth rather is that we know the nature of God and
Christ only in their worth for us. For God and faith are
inseparable conceptions; faith, however, confessedly does not
consist in abstract knowledge, or knowledge which deals with
merely historical facts. On the contrary, it cannot be
conceived save as possessed of those qualities which Luther
vindicates for it. But, finally, his explanation of the First
Commandment is bound up with the revelation of God
in Christ, and is unintelligible apart from it. For the
" goodness and power " of God, on which faith casts itself, is
in Luther's view revealed in the work of Christ alone.
Apart from Christ, apart from the reflection of God in
Him, Luther finds the idea of God to be accompanied by
terrors and annihilating effects. This dilemma (pp. 6, 7)
absolutely excludes the possibility of " disinterested " knowledge of God, as in some way correlative to the idea of the
world.

While I am explaining that I maintain the religious conception of God as conditioned in the way Luther describes, I

should also like to adduce these further remarks of his : " quemadmodum saepenumero a me dictum est, quod sola cordis
fiducia deum pariter atque idolum faciat et constituat.   Quodsi
fides et fiducia recta et sincera est, deum rectum habebis,
contra si falsa fuerit et mendax fiducia, etiam deum tuum
falsum et mendacem esse necesse est. . . . Iam in quacunque
re animi tui fiduciam et cor fixum habueris, haec haud dubie
deus tuus est." For here the religious character of the knowledge of God seems to be reduced to the arbitrary feeling of the
subject, and we seem to be furnished with a corroboration of
the maxim that a man's God varies as his faith.   But this
interpretation of Luther's words cannot be the true one, for
this reason, that he distinguished between two kinds of faith,
that which is sincere, and that which is infected with
illusion.   If he reduced everything to arbitrary caprice, he
would not make this distinction, which depends on whether
one takes or does not take the right way to knowledge of
God, namely, through Christ.   For faith which is genuine
and sincere can be exercised only in response to the true
revelation of God.   This is as far as possible from the case
referred to in Luther's last sentence above, when it is said
that everything on which a man sets his heart, be it
sensual pleasure, or honour, or power, has the value of an idol.
Between the two stands the case of trust infected with self-
deception, with which an illusory idea of God is so combined
as to show clearly that the person concerned will only consent
to believe in a God Whose nature he can first determine in
general by disinterested knowledge through analysis of his
experience of the world.   Not only is such an idea of God
false, but it is contrary to truth to separate, in relation to
Him, between knowledge and trust.   Now theology is not
devotion ; as a science, rather, it is " disinterested " cognition.
But as such it must be accompanied and guided by a sense
of the worth of the Christian religion.   The theologian, in
his scientific work, must so far keep this degree of " interest "
in sight as to conserve all those characteristics of the
conception of God which render possible the trust described

above. All other theological ideas—*e.g.* the idea we have to form of Christ and His Divinity—must be treated either in quite the same way, or with the most careful reference to the nature of these supreme ideas.

Thus we secure a criterion by which to judge the so-called *proofs for the being of God.* Since the Middle Ages these arguments have been intended to prove that the idea of God, presupposed as given in Christianity, is scientifically valid. When people set about proving the existence of God, they did not thereby assume that the reality of God for faith was not sufficiently certain, or that as a religious idea it excited doubts of its own truth which a different kind of knowledge was needed to allay. On the contrary, to the Scholastics who adduce these proofs, the correctness and truth of the judgment of faith, that God exists, are absolutely indubitable. But they wished to prove that the Christian idea of God is valid likewise within the realm of science. This enterprise, again, does not imply the intention to exhibit the specifically Christian idea of God as that of universal reason. This distinction, which might have given a useful sense to a scientific demonstration of the Christian idea of God at the beginning of theology, has not been drawn by the Scholastics up to the present time. Christian thought about God, and scientific thought about God, it is supposed, will coincide and harmonise. Only it becomes clear later, that besides the characteristics that are common to both, Christianity carries with it a further and special knowledge of God. The traditional proofs of the being of God are themselves the expression of this confusion. Here we have to deal with the cosmological, the teleological, and the ontological arguments. They are not co-ordinate, it is true, but, as Duns Scotus observes, are so related to one another that the first two must be supplemented by the third. But even when so arranged, it is not difficult to see that they fail to prove the *objective existence* of God as contrasted with His existence in thought, that they fail to prove the existence *of God,* and that they cannot be constructed save in dependence on the very presupposition which distinguishes the Christian view of the world.[1]

The import of the cosmological and teleological arguments is that, at the stage of the interpretation of the system of things given by metaphysics, when things are not yet differentiated as nature and spirit, disinterested science, if it is *to comprehend the world as a whole*, is led to conceptions of God which coincide with the Christian idea of Him. The wish to comprehend the whole is itself something additional to disinterested science, and betrays the interest religious faith has in conceiving the world as a rounded unity. This interest, it is true, already appears in Greek Philosophy, and thus is not exclusively Christian. But in Greek thought, it is an expression of that religious way of looking at the world which could no longer rest satisfied with the popular worship. Now it is customary to state the cosmological argument thus—that if we seek a conclusion for the series of causes and effects in which things are arranged, we must conceive the first cause as *causa sui*, which is not also a *res causata*, and which therefore is God. And the teleological argument runs as follows, that if we seek a conclusion for the series of means and ends in which things are arranged, we must think the final end, which is no longer itself a means, as God. Now it is true that the Christian idea of God, our Father in Christ, includes in itself the ideas of First Cause and Final End, as subordinate characteristics. But, posited as independent things, the conceptions of first cause and final end fail to transcend the conception of the world, and therefore fall short of the Christian idea of God. For, to begin with, the idea of *causa sui* is not at all a specific notion, capable of rounding off the world as a whole. Every single thing is *causa sui* as the unity of its qualities, and this notwithstanding the fact that at the same time everything must be conceived as the effect of other things. We can reach a conclusion of the series only by assuming or postu-

---

[1] With what follows cf. Julius Köstlin, *Die Beweise für das Dasein Gottes*, in *Stud. u. Kritiken*, 1875, Heft 4 ; 1876, Heft 1.

lating a cause which is likewise *causa omnium* in the same respect as it is *causa sui*. For this alone excludes the possibility of this thing being the effect of other causes. But the thing thus fitted to be the cause of all other things is simply the world-substance, the multiplicity of things regarded as a unity. And this has no resemblance to the idea of God. For while we must conceive the world as a unity, in order to explain interaction between things, yet in this sense the world-substance becomes more intelligible when viewed as a universal law of the connection of its parts than when viewed as a cause. The teleological argument is surrounded by similar difficulties. If its construction is the outcome of *a priori* metaphysical reflection, there is in this implied a preconception which has still to stand the test of experience. Granted, now, that it stands this test better than we can assert it does, yet it is premature to make the conception of Final End equivalent to the Christian idea of God. For what Aristotle calls God not only falls far short of the Christian idea of God in definiteness and richness, but the metaphysical conception of the World-End (*Weltzweck*) to which the series of means leads up, altogether fails to transcend the idea of the world, the unity of which it expresses. But even if we could overlook the distance which separates the results of both arguments from their intended goal, they require to be supplemented before they conduct us to the objective existence of God. For they are merely the expression of the idea that, *if* we wish to cognise the world as a whole, we must *of necessity think* God in addition as its First Cause and Final End. This, however, gives us no guarantee that anything real corresponds to the thought in our minds, which is necessary on the condition stated.

According to Duns Scotus, the ontological argument is adapted to fill up this hiatus. Anselm constructed it, it is true, independently of any such motive, but it can be accommodated to the circumstances without trouble. For the conception of a Perfect Being—Anselm's term for God— must include the results of the other arguments: if the form

of proof, therefore, is at all correct, it covers also the validity
of the two arguments discussed already.   Anselm's ontological argument runs thus: The conception of a Perfect
Being, than which nothing greater can be thought, is impossible, unless Its existence is certain; the quality of
existence, consequently, follows from our idea of a Perfect
Being.   But this inference is true only for our ideas, not
for the reality which stands opposed to our thought: the
argument therefore fails of its purpose.   The attempt made
in the same direction by Descartes is no more convincing.
He holds that we could not have the idea of the positively
Infinite unless it existed in reality.   For, said he, as this
idea includes no negation, we do not gain it by abstraction;
it is therefore called forth in us by the Infinite itself; it is
therefore in itself proof of the reality of the Infinite.   But
this train of thought is merely an analysis of the pretended
innate knowledge of God asserted by the Scholastics.   Such
knowledge, however, is nothing but what is gained by abstraction from the world, and is therefore of a negative kind.   The
argument itself establishes nothing save the way in which
every form of religious faith expresses the reality of its gods.

This mode of reflective thought, which can go on within
the sphere of religious knowledge, is exceedingly often regarded as the product of general theoretical cognition.   In
this respect the example of Descartes has perpetuated
confusion among philosophers and theologians.[1]   For the
proposition, that we are compelled to posit the thought of
God as real in order to explain our own belief, is merely an
analytic judgment, which is deduced from religious belief
because it is already contained there.   But it is not the
synthetic judgment of theoretical knowledge, which is what
people undertake to make, or fancy they are making.   In
fact, that is unattainable by the method in question.   But,
on the other hand, no theoretical negation of God has the
right to reject the reality of God or gods affirmed by religious cognition; for the relation between these entities, and

---

[1] Examples in Flügel, *op. cit.*, p. 157.

the attitude to the world taken up by the believer in the feeling of blessedness produced by his trust in God, does not fall under the jurisdiction of theoretical cognition when conscious of its own limitations. For religious cognition the existence of God is beyond question, for the activity of God becomes to us a matter of conviction through the attitude we take up to the world as religious men. And while, from the standpoint of Christianity, we must maintain that the interpretations of this relation afforded by heathen religions do not correspond to the reality, yet at the same time they are to be regarded collectively as proofs of a striving after the true solution. Further, while theoretical cognition must for this reason take religion into account as a normal fact of the human spirit, it must regard these very circumstances as among its essential characteristics.

Since, whenever religion appears, it is subject to the presupposition that man opposes himself, as spirit, to surrounding nature, and to human society acting on him through the media of nature, it is a mistake to employ the idea of God as Author or Creator of the forces of nature in order to compel natural science, aware of its limits, to recognise God's existence. Inferences drawn from the observation of nature lead us to consider the multiplicity and interaction of material forces as the causes of natural things; many therefore suppose that they are justified in concluding further that this multiplicity of forces—which must all be conceived as limited—is derived from one creating and limiting Will. But this special modification of the cosmological argument for God's existence is just as incorrect as its metaphysical and academic form. Were the presupposition of the elements of nature, thus sought, really conceived as God, such a conclusion could not be justified by natural science. Besides, the affirmation of a creative Will, desiderated as the ground of the elements of nature, would not be a religious judgment, and to use the name God to designate the entity thus sought would be premature. For we never exercise religious cognition in merely explaining nature by a First Cause, but always and only in explaining the independence of the human spirit over against nature. The same confusion, therefore, as that of which Scholasticism is guilty when it treats the idea of of God as an element in metaphysical science, is to be detected in the combination we are now discussing of natural science with the idea of God.

In religious cognition the idea of God is dependent on the presupposition that man opposes himself to the world of nature, and secures his position, in or over it, by faith in God. Consequently no proof of God's existence starts properly save that which accepts as given man's self-distinction from nature, and his endeavours to maintain himself against it or over it. This condition is satisfied in the case of the so-called moral argument, stated by Kant in his *Critique of Judgment*. It is true that Kant directly attaches to this theistic argument the cautious limitation, that *it is necessary to think God* in order strictly to explain the existence in the world of rational beings under moral laws, who view their own action, when worthy of their nature, as the final end of the world. For this involves likewise, as its precondition, the hope of felicity: the supreme good, therefore, which shall express the final end of rational beings under moral laws, is the combination of virtue and felicity, of moral and physical good (vol. i. p. 439). Both orders of existence, which follow laws quite different in kind, are conceived as meeting in this goal. The supreme good, thus determined, depends neither on our use of freedom nor on natural causes; consequently, in order to set the final end before us as the moral law directs, we must assume a moral Creator of the world. That is, it is necessary to think God as vouching for the satisfaction of the moral necessity we are under of conceiving the supreme good as a combination of virtue and felicity or lordship over nature (*Critique of Judgment*, § 87). To begin with, there can be no doubt that Kant is in agreement with the Christian idea of God in his description of the Moral Creator and Ruler of the world. For everywhere in this connection God denotes the ethical Power Who assures to

man the position above the world befitting his ethical worth,
and this, too, as the final end of the world. Moreover, the
argument is not merely the outcome of the reflection of
religious knowledge upon the connection of its own elements.
For its starting-point—the estimate of moral action as
springing from freedom, and the hope of the union of felicity
and virtue—is conceived independently of the authority of
God. But, lastly, it appears from Kant's further explanations that he himself puts considerable limitations upon the
necessary validity of this conception of God as the explanatory ground of the supreme good above described. He
insists that the necessity of the thought of God can be
adequately demonstrated solely for the practical Reason, for
the idea of final end itself is rooted solely in the use of freedom according to moral laws, and does not arise out of the
investigation of nature, and thus possesses only subjectivo-
practical reality. He asserts that the argument in question
does not comply with any form of theoretical proof, not even
with that of an hypothesis set up to explain the possibility
of a given fact. For we lack the material for the idea of a
supersensuous being; and therefore it is impossible to determine such an idea specifically, and employ it as a basis of
explanation. He maintains, accordingly, that the idea of
God is only a conviction of personal faith, *i.e.* necessarily to
be conceived as standing in relation to the dutiful use of the
practical Reason. So also the idea of the final end of the
world, by which we judge the use of freedom, can claim
reality for us solely in a practical sense, and is therefore a
matter of faith (*Critique of Judgment*, § 88). These explanations of Kant are for one thing in accord with the dualism
which in general he maintains between the theoretical and
the practical Reason, and at the same time obey the principle that the reflective judgment attains merely to subjective
truth.

Under these circumstances Kant's line of thought implies
that, as his philosophy is incapable of combining into one
whole the two heterogeneous theories of practical reason and

of nature, he hands over the task of solving the problem to the Christian religion. I have already remarked (p. 207) that philosophical systems secure the unity of their view of the world either directly by introducing a tentative idea of God or by employing conceptions of the world, which, being neither proved nor provable, belong to the imagination, and are therefore to be assigned to the sphere of religious knowledge rather than to that of theoretical cognition. It is instructive to observe how Kant's procedure diverges from such methods. He does not start dogmatically from the idea of God, nor from a preconceived idea of the world; rather, he finds the final unity of his knowledge of the world in the Christian idea of God, and that, too, expressly in such a way as to limit that idea to the sphere of religious knowledge. Whether this procedure wins for him the suspicion of philosophers or the gratitude of apologists, at all events the moral Theistic argument, thus limited, adds nothing to the proof of the reality of God as distinct from the necessity of thinking Him in order to explain certain relations of man to the world—nothing, that is, to the proof of the reality of God as ' an object of theoretical cognition. The latter purpose Kant had not the least desire to accomplish. Even when he declares that he has proved the *reality* of a supreme Moral Legislator Who is also Creator of the world, yet the limitation of this proof " to the merely practical use of our reason " (*Critique of Judgment*, § 88) simply means that for religious knowledge the reality of God is self-evident. But this limitation hangs together with his separation of the spheres of the theoretical and practical Reason, in which Kant failed to estimate the practical Reason at its proper value. If the exertion of moral will is a reality, then the practical Reason is a branch of theoretical cognition. These two positions Kant never reached. The reason of this failure lies in the fact that with him sensibility is the characteristic mark of reality. Therefore, too, he declares the conception of God to be theoretically impossible, and abandons it to the practical Reason. For, says he (*Critique of Judgment*, § 90), we

possess no material for determining the idea of the supersensuous, seeing we should have to derive it from the things
of sense, and such material is absolutely incongruous with the
object in question.

If it is possible at all to give a proof, first of all, of the
scientific validity of the conception of God, which shall not
merely be an utterance of the religious consciousness reflecting on its own contents, it can be done only by the proper
delimitation of that sphere of experience which nothing save
the religious conception of God can adequately explain.
What I mean by this is that, besides the reality of nature,
theoretical knowledge must recognise as given the reality of
spiritual life, and the equal binding force of the special laws
which obtain in each realm.   With respect to this, theoretical
cognition must simply accept the fact that while spiritual life
is subject to the laws of mechanism so far as it is interwoven
with nature, yet its special character as distinct from nature
is signalised by practical laws which declare spirit to be an
end in itself, which realises itself in this form.   Kant wrongly
let himself be persuaded, by this specific quality of spiritual
life, to oppose practical Reason as one species of Reason to
theoretical Reason as another.   And yet knowledge of the
laws of our action is also theoretical knowledge, for it is
knowledge of the laws of spiritual life.   Now the impulses
of knowledge, of feeling, and of aesthetic intuition, of will in
general and in its special application to society, and finally
the impulse of religion in the general sense of the word, all
concur to demonstrate that spiritual life is the end, while
nature is the means.   This is the general law of spiritual life,
the validity of which science must maintain if the special
character of the spiritual realm of existence is not to be
ignored.   In so far as we consider spiritual life in itself, this
law holds good in a subjectivo-practical way, for spirit exists
in the form of subjects alike in character.   But since men, as
spiritual beings who exercise through their natural organism
particular effects on nature and on one another, constitute a
special realm of reality in the world, and since the moral

goods they call into existence are no less real than the natural world, therefore knowledge of the practical laws obtaining in this sphere falls under theoretical cognition no less than natural science does.   But it is likewise the task of cognition to seek for a law explaining the coexistence of these two heterogeneous orders of reality.   Kant, however, abandons the attempt to discover, by the methods of theoretical cognition, a principle which will unite spirit and nature in one, and bids us explain the combination of both in a single world through practical faith in God, conceived as endowed with the attributes which Christianity ascribes to Him.   One circumstance which co-operated to produce this conclusion is doubtless the fact that all knowledge of nature, as subject to law, depends on the practical presupposition that nature exists for the human spirit.   Now religion is the practical law of the spirit, in accordance with which it sustains its fundamental character as an end-in-itself against the restrictions it suffers from nature.   This practical law attains its complete development in Christianity, for Christianity lays down the principle that personal life is to be prized above the whole world of nature, which is the realm of division (Mark viii. 36, 37); and consequently repudiates that intermixture of nature and spirit by maintaining which the heathen religions betray their comparative failure.   For in the Christian religion the soul gains the assurance of its peculiar value as a totality through the consciousness of blessedness—a consciousness conditioned by the idea of the purely spiritual God, Who as Creator of the universe governs all things on the principle that mankind are ordained to be the final end of the world, through trust in God and as members of His spiritual kingdom.   Now we must either resign the attempt to comprehend the ground and law of the coexistence of nature and spiritual life, or we must, to attain our end, acknowledge the Christian conception of God as the truth by which our knowledge of the universe is consummated.   In the former case, science would disobey the impulse to complete itself which arises from the perception of the fact that nature is knowable and is known only because it exists for spirit. Such a renunciation of the systematic completion of theoretical knowledge would not impair the practical validity of religious faith in God in the Christian sense. But still, as all cognition of nature is subject to the precondition described above, knowledge has laid on it the task of comprehending the coexistence of nature and spiritual life. If so, however, nothing remains but to accept the Christian idea of God, and that, too, as an indispensable truth, in order that we may find both the ground and the law of the real world in that Creative Will which includes, as the final end of the world, the destination of mankind for the Kingdom of God.

While, then, by following this path we find that science is bound to accept the Christian idea of God, it is likewise true that this argument is directly based upon necessary data of the spiritual life of man which lie outside of the religious view of the world, and must be explained either by recognising the Christian idea of God or not at all. Now, when we mark the attitude taken up by the human spirit towards the world of nature, two analogous facts present themselves. In theoretical knowledge, spirit treats nature as something which exists for it; while in the practical sphere of the will, too, it treats nature as something which is directly a means to the realisation of the common ethical end which forms the final end of the world. The cognitive impulse and the will both take this course without regard to the fact that nature is subject. to quite other laws than those which spirit obeys, that it is independent of spirit, and that it forms a restraint on spirit, and so far keeps it in a certain way in dependence on itself. Hence we must conclude either that the estimate which spirit, as a power superior to nature, forms of its own worth—in particular, the estimate which it forms of moral fellowship, which transcends nature—is a baseless fancy, or that the view taken by spirit is in accordance with truth and with the supreme law which is valid for nature as well. If that be so, then its ground must lie in a Divine Will, which creates the world with spiritual life as its final end. To accept the idea of God in this way is, as Kant observes, practical faith, and not an act of theoretical cognition. While, therefore, the Christian religion is thereby proved to be in harmony with reason, it is always with the reservation that knowledge of God embodies itself in judgments which differ in kind from those of theoretical science.

The meaning, therefore, of this moral argument for the necessity of the thought of God differs altogether from the aim of the other arguments; and for that reason the success it attains surpasses that of the others. The cosmological and teleological arguments are intended to show that the conception of God—necessary to complete the circle of knowledge—is similar in kind to the results of science. A truth which for religious faith is certain is thus proved, it is held, to be at the same time the result of scientific cognition as it advances from observation to observation and crystallises into conclusions, and should be set up as the criterion of theological science. But this method ends in failure, partly because neither argument takes us beyond the limits of the world, partly because their pretended results, even if they were correct, differ from the Christian conception of God in this, that they fail to express His worth for men, and in particular His worth for men as sinners. On the other hand, while Kant regards practical faith in God, conceived as endowed with the attributes which Christianity ascribes to Him, as necessary to complete our knowledge of the world, yet he does not posit this idea—which is an object merely of practical faith, and cannot be proved apart from such faith—as a conception which is theoretical or rational in the sense of general science. On the contrary, he maintains it in its original and specific character. Now it is the duty of theology to conserve the special characteristic of the conception of God, namely, that it can only be represented in value-judgments. Consequently it ought to base its claim to be a science, when looked at in itself, on the use of the method described above (p. 15), and, when looked at in its relation to other sciences, by urging that, as Kant was the first to show, the Christian view of

15

God and the world enables us comprehensively to unify our
knowledge of nature and the spiritual life of man in a way
which otherwise is impossible.   When we have once got a
true conception of this point, a review of the moral constitution of man, based upon the principles of Kant, will serve as
the *ratio cognoscendi* of the validity of the Christian idea of
God when employed as the solution of the enigma of the
world.   Such an argument would form a close analogy to the
declaration of Christ (John vii. 17), that whoso willeth to do
the will of God, shall know whether His doctrine is of God or
of merely human origin.   Probably, too, this saying of Christ
has quite as wide a range.   For if, through actively fulfilling
the will of God, one becomes convinced that Christ has really
revealed God, that implies that it is by the same path that
we come to perceive that the practical end set before men in
Christianity is at the same time the final end for which the
world is created and governed by God.   This is the essential
characteristic of the idea of God valid in this domain.[1]

§ 30. The conception of God with which Scholastic
theology, whether mediaeval or Protestant, sets to work, is
very different from that which we find in Luther's *Larger
Catechism*.   To begin with, Scholastic theology posits as God
the conception of limitless indeterminate being, a conception
which is already current in the earliest Apologists.   In its
origin, this idea is simply the general conception of the world,
the predicate which belongs to all things alike, and which,
therefore, when abstracted from them, constitutes according to
Platonic standards the idea of the world.   But being in
general is so different from the concrete fulness of the world,
that it rather impresses the mind as *not* being the world.
And this impression leads to indeterminate being in general
being posited as God.   Now this idea has to be verified as

---

[1] The line of thought set forth here has been met by the contemptuous objection that it bases Christianity upon morality.   The sapient persons who thus
prefer the charge that I, like Kant in his *Religion within the Limits of Mere
Reason*, make religion a subordinate appendix to morals, though my mode of
doctrine shows the very opposite, would do better to acquire a thorough knowledge
of the elementary distinction between the *ratio essendi* and the *ratio cognoscendi*,
instead of sitting in judgment on me,

scientifically true in its relation to science in general. Accordingly, the cosmological and teleological arguments are employed to prove that the conception of First Cause and Final End is equivalent to the conception of indeterminate being. Nothing, indeed, was to be gained by keeping to the Platonic theory ; for the *abstraction from* the world, of which it is the expression, of course serves any purpose rather than that of *explaining* the world. Accordingly, the conception of cause was foisted upon it, and this again, by a similar interpolation of the conception of final end, raised to the level of personality—since, according to Aristotle, the perfection of the Final End consists in His thinking of Himself. Lastly, there was ascribed to these conceptions, which have no affinity with one another, the whole content of the Christian idea of God, although no necessary connection could be shown to exist between them and the Divine attributes of self-revelation and love to man. This false conjunction of ideas, with its four different stages, does not give even a semblance of scientific necessity to the Christian idea of God. In reality, what a doctrine of God so constructed does is merely to introduce an explication of the content of the Christian view of the world which has no affinity with the scientific notions of limitless being, first cause, and self-conscious end. The theology of the Middle Ages and Protestant orthodoxy, therefore, can claim a positively Christian character only so far as they neglect the scientific presuppositions of their doctrine of God. But when these presuppositions are taken seriously, there arise out of this element in " ecclesiastical " theology the different species of Rationalism—Deism and Pantheism. We must not permit ourselves to be blinded to this fact by the circumstance that the champions of Positivism and Rationalism derive mutual hatred from a mutual comparison of their respective tendencies. For as these hostile brethren have a common origin, so they are also bound together by the value which each sets upon the other. Neither will admit the possibility of a third kind of theology, for each, besides believing in itself, believes only in the other, even though it be with trembling, as the

demons believe in God. Circling round one another in endless controversy, they only further unintentionally each other's
interests ; and the champions of both schools, as would
appear, can as little dispense with mutual service as with
mutual vituperation. A specially conspicuous place in this
circle of speculators is occupied by those who follow Jacob
Böhme in construing the nature of God apart from the world.
Yet they ought to know, from the experience of Mysticism on
which they plume themselves, that he who abstracts from the
world so becomes one with God both in knowledge and in
will, that even his personal individuality, his thinking and his
speaking, cease to be. To describe the inward evolution of
God outward into the world is therefore, to say the least, to
use language without thought.

The explanation offered in § 29 has made it clear why
theology takes as its fundamental truth the full conception of
God as a Person, Who establishes the Kingdom of God as the
final end of the world, and in it assures to every one who
trusts in Him supremacy over the world. Such a conception
may be differentiated without further remark from limitless
being, regarded as the substance of the universe, from the idea
of a First Cause which need not be personal, and from the
self-conscious but self-enclosed Final End of the world. The
conception of God thus set up is of such a nature that it
simply cannot be distorted into Pantheism or Deism. A
theology based upon it, therefore, is not rationalistic. On the
contrary, it is positive, for it starts from the Christian idea of
God ; and it is scientific, for the Christian idea of God must
be acknowledged to be the fundamental principle which
explains the coexistence of nature and morality—morality
being viewed as the final end of the world—if their coexistence admits of any explanation at all. We have yet,
however, to justify the claim of theology to be a science, by
proving that the conception of *personality* can, without contradiction, be applied to God.

The aversion felt to this truth is due to the change in
aesthetic criteria which began about a hundred years ago.

In the previous era the feeling of the beautiful was guided by stereotyped traditions of artistic form. In particular, the presuppositions which legitimately influence architecture dominated taste also in regard to the music of the fugue and dramatic poetry, bound as the latter was to the unities of time and place. To this preponderance of *a priori* theory, by which artistic taste has been shackled since the Renaissance, corresponds that physico-theological estimate of the relation of the world to God by which it was sought to test the conception of His personality. The rapid growth of this mode of thought as a consequence of the philosophy of Wolff is full of significance, in the first place, as indicating the lines which feeling and taste followed in that age, and, in the second, as throwing light on the conception of religion current at that time. The tendency just noted has, since Goethe, been superseded by an unfettered feeling for the naturally beautiful, and thus lyrical poetry and lyrical music have gained supreme influence over the regulation of aesthetic taste. Lyrical feeling, which adapts itself to the various aesthetic objects by which amid all the changes of impression its continuity is sustained, and which, by producing subjective harmony, balances the varying values of objective things, is a powerful impulse towards a pantheistic view of the world. Under the influence of this feeling people think they have discovered a sufficient explanation of the real world, when they find in the impersonal principle of development the force which produces equilibrium amid all the shifting phenomena of nature, and see the moral order of the world in the actual purposiveness of human society, which unconsciously brings all the aberrations of moral forces into accord with their substantially concurrent tendency. These presuppositions lead to the view that "the universe" is the highest conception of all.

There is hardly anything better fitted to throw light upon this conjunction of ideas than Strauss'[1] unadorned statement of the notion of the Universe, on which he undertakes to

[1] *Die alte und neue Glaube*, p. 140.

found his new faith, his substitute for religion. He finds
that the Universe, on which we are absolutely dependent, is
constructed not *by* supreme reason, but *for* supreme reason.
If, arguing that every effect must have a cause, we incline to
the former belief, this, he maintains, is only to betray the
limitations of our intellect, for the Universe is really at once
cause and effect, inner and outer. In these disclosures the
mask of science is finally laid aside, and the successor of
Romanticism displays his true physiognomy. For his sub-
stitution of the conception of the Universe in place of the
conception of a personal God is now no longer set up, as a
pretended result of science, in opposition to the religious
fancy: it is opposed as the content of one faith to the
certainties of another. We are not permitted, however, to
decide between the two on the principle of knowledge that
an effect must have a cause which corresponds to it. The
new faith, it is true, repudiates the idea of the personality of
God, on the assumed ground that the implications of the
Absolute and of personality are contradictory. But we must
regard this argument merely as the expression of a fixed
aversion, for otherwise this creed finds no difficulty in
maintaining contradictions. A universe which is at once
cause and effect, inner and outer, is already by those descriptions withdrawn from the very conditions of scientific
knowledge. It is an object of the imagination, a generalisa-
tion of aesthetic feeling, due in fact to the lyrical, especially
the musical, balancing of feelings of pleasure and pain excited
simultaneously—that is, without a clear interval of time
between them—and by the influence of identical objects.
Here cause and effect, inner and outer, vanish into one
another! In particular, the position—inevitable once this
line of thought has been entered on—that the laws of reality
are at the same time the forces at work in reality (and this,
looked at logically, is as much as to say that what is passive
is *ipso facto* active), is only the reflex of an aesthetic emotion.
For artistic enjoyment represents an impression of phenomena
connected together in an orderly way, of a unified multi-

plicity which operates as such, *i.e.* on the feeling of the observer. But in this way of looking at things it is altogether forgotten that a law, as imposed, refers us back to a legislative and imposing Spirit and Will, and that the moral order of the world implies a Creator Who lays down laws and governs according to a fixed purpose. For such considerations would interrupt the feeling of artistic or natural beauty and of poetic justice. But it is only a leap of the imagination when the aesthetic effect upon our feeling of a law discerned in nature and history is thrown into objective form as the principle that every known law of reality is *eo ipso* the efficient force and sufficient ground of that which is real. Nor need we let ourselves be intimidated by the further assurance that it is a mark of limited intelligence to demand an ordaining Will as the *prius* of a law, and from that Will to deduce likewise the active force exhibited in the phenomena embraced by the law. Our thinking certainly has its limitations, but in the department of scientific thought we are called upon to set bounds to the aesthetic fancy, and to forbid it to intrude into a realm where it has no jurisdiction. The idea of a universe which should be at once cause and effect, inner and outer, which should be constructed for supreme reason, on which man should feel himself absolutely dependent and yet never be tempted to think that possibly it had its origin in an independent Mind—such an idea accords very well with one of Beethoven's symphonies, by which one is wholly carried away without ever reflecting on the question by whom and how it was composed, or how many are performing it. But we cannot but have ideas, other than those which visit us when enjoying a romantic piece of music, about the universe in which we exercise moral freedom in the consciousness that each of us is a whole in his own order, and no mere part of the world. For the principle of lyrico-musical feeling is not the principle of the universe.

An objection to the personality of God, which Strauss is never weary of repeating, is that the predicates of the Absolute and of personality are mutually exclusive. " Personality is that selfhood which shuts itself up against everything else, which it thereby excludes from itself; the Absolute, on the other hand, is the comprehensive, the unlimited, which excludes nothing from itself but just the exclusivity which lies in the conception of personality." [1] This idea of the Absolute is simply that of space, and that one cannot combine the idea of space with the idea of personality is undeniable. On the other hand, we define personality incompletely when we limit it to the characteristic it possesses of distinguishing between everything else and itself; for this is merely the precondition which renders it possible for human personality to comprise its multitudinous contents. We find, too, that the personality of man is more developed the greater the compass of his knowledge, the more susceptible his feeling to diverse impressions, the stronger his will in the capacity to change the form of things and to rule other persons. Personality, as we have it in our experience of manhood, is conditioned, it is true, by the natural endowments of the individual. The development of personality from this foundation, in the directions mentioned above, always issues likewise in that peculiar cast of character which proves the original endowment of each to have been different from that of all others. A person's peculiar cast of character, however, always indicates his *acquired* difference from all other persons. For that very reason it cannot coincide with that formal and original self-distinction of the individual from all others, to which Strauss limits his conception of personality. Every healthy human being, indeed, oversteps this function of personality perpetually, whenever he assimilates any material for his spiritual development. One who succeeded in living such a self-enclosed life as to shut himself off against everything that was not himself, would display none of the marks of spiritual life at all. Consequently, for the purposes of the present discussion he simply would not exist. Or if a man, in his spiritual

---

[1] *Die christl. Glaubenslehre*, i. p. 504.

appropriation of things, lived an exclusive life—even though only for the most part—lived, that is, indifferent to the problems of knowledge, insensible to the different values of things, irresponsive to stimuli of the will, regardless of the common interests of mankind, current terminology would not account him a personality at all.　When his reason is not affected, these characteristics may, in a perceptible degree, be traced to a selfish opposition to the social conditions of moral action, and then we speak of bad individuality.　Or they are accompanied by mental derangement; and no one professes to find the ideal of personality in the maniac or the imbecile. On the other hand, acquired individuality of character is the form assumed both by the highest possible degree of receptivity to the general relations of things and the common interests of mankind, and by the highest possible degree of spiritual influence over other men in any direction. Individuality, therefore, certainly denotes an impassable limit of human personality, for the single soul can be pervaded with the common elements of spiritual life, and the universal norms necessary for their appropriation, only when the form assumed is particular.　But the fact of acquired individuality is, for that very reason, not inconsistent with the subjugation of the world by spirit, with the appropriating reception of very diverse contents into " the self-comprising Ego," or with the latter's operating efficaciously upon a certain portion of the world, and a more or less extensive section of human society.　Thus Strauss' criticism of the notion of personality is not in harmony with ordinary usage, and is as far as possible from being based on that complete and precise observation of phenomena which usage points to.

The conceivability of the personality of God is to be reached rather through the study of what is so worthy of esteem among men—independent personality.[1]　For those objections to the personality of God which rest upon the contention that we only know personality as a product of the interaction between our Ego and the given world, or as a self-evolution

[1] Cf. Lotze, *Mikrokosmus*, iii. p. 565 ff.

of the Ego which is essentially conditioned by the stimulus of the environment, point to the fact that we are created *for* personality, and that even under the category of " persons " we are limited, growing, mutable.   But such considerations are more than balanced by the fact that an independent personality, when acquired, has open to it a range of activity beyond the sway of the above-mentioned conditions.   What we have become during life, through the interaction of experience and native endowment, the Ego opposes through memory as a connected reality to all possible stimuli arising from the world.   Further, the Ego draws a multitude of incentives from the reciprocal action of its own memories and from the principles it has acquired, and is thus able both to repel the synchronous stimuli it receives from surrounding persons and things, and to demonstrate its independence by influencing others.   Developed personal individuality consists in the power to take up the inexorable stimuli of the environment into one's plan of life, in such a way that they are incorporated in it as means under firm control, and no longer felt as obstacles to the free movement of the self.   In such a case, the emotions can no longer be regarded as passive mental experiences, but come rather to involve principally an exercise of power which the independence of one's character is felt to justify.   The stage of spiritual and moral culture, to seek and to maintain which gives human life its true worth, likewise brings with it that specific experience of eternity for which our spiritual constitution in general is adapted.   The idea of eternity would mean absolutely nothing for us, and even as an attribute of God would be for us an empty name, if the two current conceptions of it, as timelessness and as time without beginning or end, were correct.   For neither can we abstract from time during waking consciousness, nor in the idea of time without beginning or end can we distinguish God from the world.   Indeed, we can conceive neither the beginning nor the end of the world, since if we abstracted from the existence of the world we should also have to abstract from our thought, for as thinking spirits we are parts of the world. Time is our intuition and idea, in which we first distinguish our ideas from one another, then arrange our experiences according to the relations of cause and effect. But we abrogate it again in every act of knowledge, when we combine words heard consecutively in the unity of the judgment, qualities perceived consecutively in the unity of the conception, and experiences acquired consecutively in a view of the world. The positing and the abrogation of time in our simplest and most habitual acts of knowledge is itself an instance of the eternity of spirit. It manifests itself still more characteristically in the power of the will actively to pursue a single end throughout the ordered succession of intentions and resolves derived from it, and this even when some of the latter have to be modified or withdrawn. For eternity is in general the power of spirit over time. Nor is this general conception affected by the fact that this characteristic cannot be verified with equal facility in the realms of knowledge and of will, and that this difference is connected with the distinction in worth which exists for personality itself between theoretical knowledge and moral will.

These facts are enough to prove that the human spirit, designed as it is for personality, even though in its activity and development it is conditioned by stimuli received from things—that is, by the non-Ego—must still be supposed to exist anteriorly in its own peculiar character, if its evolution by means of these conditions is to be understood. It is true that the human spirit always remains conditioned by these external stimuli, even when it has reached the stage of independent personality, and thereafter, guided by its own principles and impulses, utilises things for its own ends, and exerts an influence upon the society of its compeers. For in both directions independent action must be guided by the laws which have been found to obtain in the natural and moral worlds. Moreover, the conscious connection between one's acquired individuality and one's fixed plan of life is limited at every moment by movements of feeling and vague ideas which form an accompaniment to the rest; and even though we know as a whole what we are and what we desire, yet the manner in which we have come to possess our nature is present to our memory only in a very defective form. From these characteristics we learn experimentally that, as persons, we are always in a state of becoming, and that this is what we are created for. But the personality of God is thinkable without contradiction just because it stands contrasted with the restraints which we find by experience imposed on our personality. As the cause of all that happens, God is affected only by such forces of influence as He has conferréd upon His creatures, and as He sees transparently to be the effects of His own will. Nothing which affects the Divine Spirit is originally alien to Him ; and there is nothing which, in order to be self-dependent, He must first appropriate. Everything, rather, that the world means for Him is at bottom an expression of His own self-activity; and whatever of the movement of things reacts upon Him He recognises as the recurrent sweep of that reality which is possible through Himself alone. As comprising all that happens in the unity of His judgment and the unity of His purpose, He is eternal ; and no break in this being or this consciousness is conceivable, for no impression can arise either from things or from ideas which He has not taken up beforehand into the unity of His knowledge and His will. Our mind, it is true, can lend no colour or music to this conception, for sensuous vivacity belongs only to perceptions acquired within that limited circle to which our creaturely nature confines us. Yet neither the truth nor the validity of our ideas depends on whether they are reinforced by perceptions of a sensuous or an aesthetic kind. The truth of the idea of the personality of God rather is verified just by our finding in it the standard which determines whether, and in what degree, the same predicate is to be ascribed to us. For that we are independent personalities we judge by reference to the conception of that Personality which, inasmuch as it has the whole ground of its activity within itself, is normative. At that stage of human development, therefore, which we describe as independent personality,

it becomes clear that the disputed idea, so far from being
alien and remote, is vitally bound up with the specific worth
which we ascribe to spiritual culture.

Personality is the form in which the idea of God is given
through Revelation. As theology has to do with the God
revealed in Christ, this is justified scientifically as the only
practicable form of the conception of God. The content of
the Divine will is to be deduced from the revealed reciprocal
relations between Christ and God, and from no other principle. Thus a full elucidation is given of the starting-point
of theology, as fixed by Luther. One would have thought
that this method of procedure would have been safe from the
objections of those who generally pique themselves on their
loyalty to the symbolical books of the Lutheran Church. Yet
Frank has contended against me that when stating the
theological doctrine of God we ought to begin with the conception of the Absolute, in order to keep the attributes of
love and personality in God distinct from their existence in
man.[1] This scholar understands by the Absolute, the qualities of existence in, through, and for self, in which, he
maintains, God must be conceived before we can ascribe to
Him the predicates of love and personality. This Absolute,
however, may be described as God because, under the qualities named, we conceive Him in Whom we make our refuge.
Now, when judged by the *Larger Catechism*, the trustful
confidence thus attested by Frank is hardly right, for it sets
up an idol instead of God. For his Absolute is nothing but
an incomplete conception of a thing, in which abstraction has
been made from its cognisable relations to other things. So
little is this conception fitted to ensure the distinction between God and the world, that there is nothing to which one
might not attribute the qualities which he enumerates, though
in doing so one would be further off from real knowledge of
it than ever. And even if in either case we fancy that by
their means we have reached a complete conception of something in its true character, yet no attributes of relation such

[1] Cf. *Theologie und Metaphysik*, p. 13 ff. ; 2nd ed. p. 15 ff.

as personality, love, or righteousness can be combined with such a subject without the conception of it being abrogated. For the qualities of the Absolute which Frank gives include likewise the quality of lacking external relations. The whole conception, therefore, when relations such as love and righteousness are combined with it, is transformed into the conception of the Relative. But that Personality which is love is the conception which Luther describes as God. Personality, indeed, is likewise a predicate of man; but, as has just been proved, only in a derivative fashion. Again, men too exhibit love; but the fulness of the idea is applicable to God alone, for, according to Christian ideas, all man's love springs from the revelation of God in Christ. And this every theologian ought to know; indeed, I have taken it for granted as a familiar truth (vol. ii. p. 99). Finally, the method which Frank adopts simply betrays a disinclination or an incapacity to think spirit as self-dependent. When, therefore, he wishes to comprehend God, Who is Spirit, he manufactures first of all an indeterminate Thing, a kind of frame or skeleton on which, if he is going to maintain their validity, he must then hang the attributes of spirit. But this framework, the Absolute, is an idol; and if Frank makes it his refuge, his trust is different from that of all the saints of the Old and New Testaments—a trust which Luther describes by saying that it builds upon the goodness of God. Now things are either spirit or matter. There exist no things-in-general, which are neither the one nor the other. When contrasted with the reality given in experience, "a thing" in the merely metaphysical sense is a conception indeterminate *as to its kind*. Now, if the Absolute is to be taken as real, and yet not to be taken as spirit, it must be a material thing. And this shows all the more clearly that the Absolute, which Frank posits as God, has the form and impress of an idol. I do not say that Frank has any inkling that this is implied in his position; but to my mind there is an element of materialism in his view.

§ 31. The Christian conception of God, with which theo-

logy sets out, has combined with it an idea of the world, and
of the destination of man—who is made in God's image—in
the world, or above it, which is at the same time God's final
end of the world. Without these implications, which the
Larger Catechism also indicates, the Christian conception of
God is quite incapable of being expressed. The assertions
which are made regarding God, as He was before the world
and before the moral order existed for man, are either purely
formal determinations which have no force until the content
of Revelation is taken into account—*e.g.* the conception of
the personality of God—or they are words without meaning.
Now, save where theology has taken on a pantheistic colour,
the general relation of God to the world is conceived as that
of creation and preservation, and His free omnipotent will is
given as the sufficient ground for these operations. On the
other hand, theology has in two ways made the attempt to
supplement the idea of God by the idea of a moral world-
order. The one theory depends on the position that God as
the unrestricted Sovereign over all His creatures, out of His
mere good pleasure treats mankind with equity (*Billigkeit*),
though in themselves they have no rights against Him. The
other theory defines the relation of God to humanity thus—
that He regulates the inter-relations of the reciprocal rights
subsisting between Himself and men by a law and dispensation of justice which is a necessary outcome of His own
nature. The former theory is dominant in the theology of
the Middle Ages, attains its classical expression in Duns
Scotus, develops its consequences in Socinianism, and, with a
diminished lucidity of inference, is adopted by Arminianism.
The other theory appears in the orthodoxy of the Lutheran
and Reformed Churches, in the latter case assuming a form
such that at the same time one position which follows from
the first theory is affirmed in the Reformed doctrine
of the twofold predestination.[1] Both theories, though they

[1] The various forms of the first theory are dealt with in my "Studies
towards the Christian Doctrine of God" (three articles), in the *Jahrbücher
für deutsche Theologie*, 1865, 1868.

build upon different elements in the Biblical mode of thought, yet betray the form and features of natural theology; and each of them likewise claims to expound what a rational criticism of the moral order takes to be self-evident. In both conceptions, the idea of God represents both the law of the moral world and the power which realises it. As the Christian doctrine of reconciliation is judged by these criteria, they also determine the decision of the question whether it and the mediatory processes involved in it—processes for which different kinds of proof are offered—are in harmony with reason.

The first theory, which represents *baseless Will*, caprice, *dominium absolutum*, as the supreme law of the world in general and the moral world in particular, has never received such consistent expression as the other. Its employment, on the one hand by the theologians of the Middle Ages, and on the other by the Socinians and Arminians, led to its being modified in various ways. The reason was that the latter sects had before them the Lutheran and Calvinistic theory of the *a priori* validity of law even for God, and only succeeded in carrying out their contrary view by making concessions to the correctness of the other. The average position taken by those who adopt the first theory may be summarised as follows. The relation of God to the world is based on His arbitrary will. That is, God could have made the world otherwise than He did, and no decisive ground can be discovered why He created it such as it is. Moreover, as against all His creatures, even man, He is unfettered Lord. They have no innate right against their Creator and Lord, but as contrasted with Him are as destitute of rights as slaves. If, nevertheless, they are not treated by God as chattels, this rests on a free resolve, a positive ordinance which He has made, and which imposes on His own action the principle of equity (*Billigkeit*) towards men.[1] The Scotists and

---

[1] Within this general framework there appear modifications. The Nominalists represent God as having the power to grant or not to grant salvation to any one ; the Socinian Crell limits the Divine omnipotence over the creatures at

Nominalists even illustrated the unrestricted omnipotence of God by the hypothesis that He might have given the moral law a directly opposite content to that which it actually has. The Socinians and Arminians avoided this inference by conceding that the Divine omnipotence is limited beforehand by regard for public order, both as concerns the permissible and the obligatory. And although the attempt was made to maintain the guiding conception of the arbitrary will of God, by contending that " the permissible," as the more general conception, is superordinate to " the commanded," yet Socinianism could not altogether ignore the only true view, that " the permissible " denotes in extent those actions which, while not commanded, are yet not in contradiction to that which is commanded. Socinians decline, however, to draw from this the inference that the relations between God and man are determined by the *a priori* rules of universal justice incumbent on God, and thus by the necessity of the case. For this would be to corroborate the opposite theory and renounce controversy with it. To obviate this difficulty, recourse is had to the position that men, as slaves, have originally no rights in common with God. For thence it follows that God treats them in accordance with special justice—which holds good alongside of general justice—*i.e.* He deals with them in accordance with His special purpose of *equity* (*Billigkeit*). Thence follows, further, that God is under no necessity to punish human transgressions of His laws, but is free to forgive them as injuries or as infractions of His private rights. Thomas is guided by this principle when he remarks, *à propos* of the Christian doctrine that the forgiveness of sins depends on the satisfaction and merit of Christ, that God could have attained the same end in another way ; similarly Duns considers it possible that a man might merit forgiveness for himself had God not determined otherwise ; the Socinians, finally, declare that to render forgiveness possible the satis-

least thus far, that God may not bring into existence any innocent creature destined to eternal torments ; the Arminian Episcopius views the lordship of God over men as limited *a priori* by respect for His own dignity, and for the natural situation of men.

16

faction of Christ is superfluous (vol. i. pp. 49, 69, 300). Moreover, Duns views the equity of God as the ground of His reckoning voluntary good actions as deserving of salvation; while on God's treatment of men thus the Socinians base the principle that He regards the obedience of faith, imperfect though it be in each particular case, as sufficient to win eternal life.

The conception of the Divine equity, which links the Socinian view of the order of the world to the Scotist conception of merit, serves to impose restrictions on the attribute which has been premised—namely, the *dominium absolutum*. This denotes the exclusive right possessed by God as Creator, the consequence of which is that originally men have absolutely no rights. This legal conception is now modified and supplemented by the introduction of the moral conception of equity, which recognises men not only as the subjects of rights, but, still further, as possessed of moral worth. For usage generally connects " right " and " equity " (*Recht und Billigkeit*) with one another, and thereby indicates a varying line of conduct accompanied by the desire to supplement the one by the other. The right which equity comes in to supplement always signifies the right arising out of a compact, in which human action is regulated by the ascertained interdependence of two individual aims. Now, one who strictly adheres to the standard of right ignores the fact that the legally obligated subject, as a moral personality, is entitled to be viewed otherwise than merely in the light of the compact. The legal obligation to perform a service which has been contracted for, however, never denotes more than a small element in the man's whole nature, considered as a person capable of action. When, therefore, the superior to the contract judges of the service contracted for in the light of the helpful or hindering influences which the inferior's whole situation exerts upon his performance, and when the view thus taken by the superior is not subsumed under the principle that each is bound to do the other all the good he can, then we have an instance of equity. For equity expresses itself either in forbearance, when a man's other obligations or his unfavourable circumstances impede the discharge of his legal obligation, or in the bestowal of a reward when, by the special promptitude with which he performs the service agreed upon, he shows that he is in earnest. In both cases the legal standard is supplemented by a moral standard, inasmuch as account is taken either of the man's moral freedom, or of the probable obstacles which it encounters in his discharge of the contracted service. But the standard which equity applies is in its nature purely relative, and does not exhaust the possible methods of moral judgment. For it confines itself to the same field as is prescribed by the relations of private right, and abstracts from the highest criterion of morality, which is based on the principle that the society of moral agents ought properly to be as comprehensive and as open as possible. Indeed, we refrain from criticising self by the conception of moral duty, just when, by exercising equity, we express such a private and moral concern for a neighbour as dovetails into the presupposed relations of private right.

A moral order, then, which makes the equity of God its highest criterion, splits up necessary human action, as we actually find it, into simple cases of private relations between God and the individual, and can therefore be regarded as a moral order only in an erroneous sense. This result of the Socinian theory, even with the otherwise clear opposition between law and equity, accords in a singular way with the presupposed Divine *dominium absolutum* over man. For if, from this point of view, men are to be conceived as slaves, then God is represented as the owner of property. Such a relation, however, can only be estimated from the standpoint of private right (*Privatrecht*), and cannot of itself become the source of public law (*öffentliches Recht*). Now, if God bestows rights upon men out of equity, it is only in appearance that we can deduce from this the existence of public law. For the idea of public law always depends solely on the existence of common aims; but common public aims are precisely what is excluded by the supreme principle of God's equity in deal-ing with individual men.

The development of this Socinian theory is occasioned, it is true, by certain similitudes used by Christ (Luke xvii. 10), and therefore stands in a certain analogy to the feeling of interest by which the Christian religion is sustained. The doctrine of man's dependence on God, in fact, is strained to its utmost possible limit. Everything which raises man above the level of things, exactly so far as it is not ascribed to his original endowment, is traced back to the Divine bestowal. Even man's destination to eternal life—a privilege transcend-ing the nature he receives at birth—is granted him merely through God's free resolve. In the most extreme contrast with this, however, stands the fact that this view regards human life, even though subject to universal moral law, as always dependent on the Divine equity alone—an equity which passes judgment on each individual as such, and that by a fortuitous and relative standard, which just for that very reason is neither necessary nor universally valid. But it is an absurdity that the definite principle of moral fellowship, when traced back to God, should be made subordinate to the incal-culable private considerations of mere equity, while equity can be brought into play only by neglecting the strict obliga-tions of the moral law. Equity, which is admissible only as an exception, under special circumstances, to the universal validity of duty, cannot, even as an attribute of God, form the basis of an obligation binding men to God and to one another. Consequently, this theory would justify men in taking a view of themselves which is utterly devoid of inward consistency. The very persons who have to regard themselves as originally destitute of rights against God, are then again to be convinced that they stand to God in a private relationship, such that they may count on His indulgence and His rewards. The sense of being as far from God as the utter difference between Creator and creature implies, is to give way to a feeling of co-ordinate equality, such as obtains between subjects capable of rights, and such as awakens the expectation that each will regard the other also as the subject of equal moral freedom. This theory, therefore, as combining the Divine attributes of *dominium absolutum* and *aequitas*, not only is composed of heterogeneous elements, but, so far as it represents a moral order, it is intrinsically absurd ; for no adequate basis for a public and universal order can be found in the indeterminate private moral relationship of equity (*Billigkeit*). To be strongly convinced of this, one only needs to remember the factors which confessedly go to make up the argument. A slaveowner, who out of equity treats the men who are his chattels as persons capable of rights, who in this confidence imposes on them a law of reciprocal behaviour, but indulgently tolerates infractions of it except when they are characterised by obstinacy, and rewards the well-meant fulfilment of his law, however imperfect it be—here, in this domestic *régime*, we have the model of the Socinian moral order ! But it is more than probable that a *régime* of this kind would simply break down when confronted with cases of obstinate transgression which must be punished.[1] There is only one argument which could make this moral order credible, the argument, namely, which the orthodox employ when they find themselves embarrassed in theology—that what is impossible for men is for that very reason befitting God ! But in this way, as is well known, any absurdity can be proved.

§ 32. The other theory regards the destiny of eternal life as forming part of the inborn nature of man, and therefore puts man forward from the outset as the subject of personal rights even against God. But the right to eternal life has

---

[1] Although Socinianism is an obsolete form of theology, the theory it offers deserves to be reviewed here. Another inference drawn from the *dominium absolutum* of God is quietistic mysticism, which derives its principles from Duns Scotus. From the same conception of God as the orthodox of the Reformed Church have extracted from the doctrine of predestination, the Pietists of the Reformed Church have drawn the same quietistic inference—that the believer ought to lose himself in God through formal self-abnegation, *i.e.* as judging that before God we are nothing, and that our own will as such is not steadfast. The way to this goal should be sought in loving interplay with God after the mode of the Song of Solomon. In this method, therefore, there are also combined unwarranted equality with God, and an utter absence of rights against Him in the status of grace.

first to be realised, and that too under the condition that the moral law, in its relation to God's authority and His fellowship with men, shall be fulfilled by action. Without this the right to eternal life, the basis of all personal rights, would be lost. In this scheme of the moral world-order, also, it would seem at first as though the form of private contract alone were employed. To counterbalance this impression, however, we have the fact that the law, the fulfilment of which is required, is not one of arbitrary content, but the expression of the Divine will—such, indeed, as is essential to God Himself, must of necessity be ascribed to Him, and is ordained to be in all its concreteness the indispensable and universal rule of the moral order. Not only is the moral law represented as the mirror of the Divine justice, to which men can become subject only through obedience, but its fulfilment or non-fulfilment is brought into close connection with the Divine justice, seeing that the rewarding of good works and the punishment of transgressions are unconditionally necessary for God. Thus the Divine law (*Gesetz*) is given the form and impress of public law (*Recht*). That this is implied is clear enough, though Cocceius traces it back to the *foedus operum*, a contract between God and man ; for that is only an expression of the tendency displayed in the seventeenth century to derive the State from a private contract. In any case, this form of representation neither intentionally nor necessarily eliminates the distinction between public and private law. Now, public law is an expression of the fact that the rights which individuals have against society are inferior to the rights which society has against individuals, and that their permanence depends on the performance of social duties. But, under these conditions, individuals are recognised as the subjects, even as against the State, of rights which the State does not create, but can only acknowledge. The conception of the moral order now under discussion, accordingly, is modelled on the idea of the State. For God, as Maker and Executor of the law—though He creates man as the subject of rights against Himself—represents the State with its acknowledgment of the rights of its citizens ; while

men, in their capacity as members of the State, are so subordinated to the Divine law that it depends on their fulfilment or non-fulfilment of it whether they realise their
personal right and claim to eternal life, or lose it altogether.
The civil character of this conception of the moral world-
order, further, appears clearly enough from the assertion that
God must, out of His justice, both reward the fulfilment of
His law and punish men for its transgression, and that of
Himself it is simply incompetent for Him to display that
indulgence and forgiveness which a private individual may
exercise.   For the legal community of the State can continue
to exist only if it asserts itself against the law-breaker by
the infliction of a judicial penalty.[1]

These criteria, derived from *public law*, are now applied
to a system of things which transcends civil relationships.
The question at issue, in the Divine ordering of human life
which we are now discussing, is the realisation of eternal life,
the realisation, that is, of a good very different from the ends
which, in the State, are controlled by public law.   But in
order to produce the impression that the civil order, thus
conceived, is likewise adequate to realise this supra-civil end,
every infraction of the Divine law is represented as being
visited, like treason, with the severest possible penalty, the
penalty of death or everlasting damnation.   Finally, the
doctrine of original sin is called in, and the position taken up
that all men whatsoever, who enter this world, are straightway subject to the sentence of death.   Thus is conceived the
order of human life, an order from which, it is true, reconciliation liberates us.   But, on the foregoing presupposition, the
fact of reconciliation is interpreted in such a way that the
action of the Reconciler is regarded as illustrating the legal
world-order, which therefore works on indirectly even in the
Christian life.   The conclusion drawn from this connected
series of ideas is conditioned by the doctrine of original sin,

---

[1] I borrow this general conception of punishment as a legal institution from
Heinze,—"Strafrechtstheorien und Strafrechtsprincip," in *Handbuch des deutschen Strafrechts*, vol. i. p. 321 ff.

accepted on scriptural authority but interpreted by reason; the earlier judgments composing the arguments, however, are affirmed in quite a rationalising way; and whenever any position of the Apostle Paul gives them support, his statement is credited with the value of a universal truth of reason (p. 4). Accordingly, we are called upon to investigate the rationality of this theory, *i.e.* its consistency with itself and with experience.

The *first* question is, whether the conception of God on which it is based accords with the presuppositions which must be fulfilled ere that conception can form the highest conceivable criterion of all reality. Now the Socinians have already raised the objection,[1] that the justice of God which furnishes the immutable principles of the Divine legislation, and which imposes upon the Divine will the necessity of punishment, indicates a power superior to God, and that, as Will, He is subject to this justice as a natural necessity. Now we cannot escape this difficulty, even by making this very power a part of the Divine attribute of justice. For then the conception of God falls asunder into two strata, distinguished by the superordinate attribute of passivity and the subordinate attribute of active will. Such a diremption of the idea of God, however, is incompatible with the necessity we are under of thinking God as the unity posited by religious experience. Neither is the Lutheran and Reformed theory justified by the fact that the conception of God held by the Scotists and Socinians involves the opposite error, namely, that of supposing that the groundless will of God can will, create, or command either of two opposites, and that He deals with men, not on a fixed plan, but according to His arbitrary *aequitas*. Both of these positions, that a thing is good because God wills it, and that He wills a thing because it is good, are equally unsatisfactory. The rare attempts made by orthodox theologians to support their view by reasons [2] only prove that,

---

[1] Cf. *Jahrb. f. deutsche Theologie*, 1868, p. 286 ff.

[2] *Op. cit.* p. 291: I there brought forward from Hoornbeck, *Socinianismus confutatus*, an attempt of the kind, which utterly failed.

with the materials of thought at their command, it was impossible for them to reach that unity of the conception of God at which they aimed. For if it follows strictly from the assumed personality of God that He is real only in the form of will, then it is bad metaphysics to attribute righteousness to Him as a passive quality possessed by Him apart from His form as will. What means a passive quality at all, if the qualities of things must necessarily be conceived as their particular ways of acting, and especially of acting on our perception? The idea of a passive quality is due to the self-delusion which arises when our attention is uninterruptedly enchained by the way in which something acts on us continuously. For our idea of action and cause is always called forth originally by the changes of phenomena, and unless we give stricter attention to the ways in which we get our knowledge, it is only from intermittent similar perceptions that we receive the idea of the action of a thing. But though our vision cannot discern the changes of phenomena at a distance as it can those near at hand, it does not follow that the remoter objects are really at rest, as they seem to us to be. The error in the conception of God now under discussion is occasioned specially, it is true, by the imprudent use of the analogy of human personality. Our consciousness of personality teaches us that it depends upon natural endowment, and that it is further guided by acquired principles, of which we know that, even apart from our assent, they possess certainty for others. And therefore our inaccurate way of judging marks off character, as a self-enclosed entity, from every individual action which proceeds from it, in such a way that—to use the spatial terms " near " and " remote"—we think that what is remote is in this case just as much at rest as to our limited vision it appears to be. Now our natural endowments determine beforehand the kind and range of our action, and we become conscious of our acquired character as a second nature, so that we thus know ourselves to be created personalities. But it is wrong to repeat these characteristics in our conception of God. For even our own character we do not really possess in passivity, but in its proper activity; and if it were not ever being reproduced anew by activity, it would not exist at all, or would be lost. To affirm a necessity for God, which cannot be intelligibly derived from His will but is deduced from some latent "natural" quality, is to describe Him as a finite and growing personality.[1] The orthodox doctrine of God, therefore, is altogether impracticable.

The *second* question is, whether the form of public law harmonises with the assumed contents of the Divine law, and whether it is at the same time fitted to embrace within itself the necessary relations between man and God. In regard to the former point, it must be remembered that the principles of love to God and to our neighbour to which, as the supreme commandments of the Mosaic law, Jesus ascribed fundamental authority in His Church, are regarded by the older school as forming the content of the universal law which God not only implanted in human reason, but publicly proclaimed in the prohibition He addressed to our first parents, and then later through Moses and through Jesus. The righteousness in which man was created, it is held, satisfied this standard, the covenant of works was based upon obedience to these commandments, and the bestowal of eternal life would then have followed as a common right. Now law is the ordering of social action with a view to the realisation of those ends which combine a people into a State, and in order to ensure that freedom which each individual has to exercise in pursuing those aims which lie beyond the province of the State. Law is either private law or public law. Private law controls the mutual commerce of individuals, which is due to the fact that several individuals (or groups, which may be treated as individuals) may simultaneously make the same articles or the same particular work the object of their desires. Public law controls reciprocal or social action, which arises from the fact that, in the State, men are combined for universal ends. The ends controlled by public law, however, never possess

---

[1] For this reason the theosophical assertion of a "nature in God" is likewise false. But I cannot enter upon a special examination of such theories.

more than relative universality. For the highest end which can be proposed to action forms the basis of the domain of morality. It proves itself the highest end conceivable, in that it prescribes rules not merely for action, but also directly for our purposes and intentions and disposition, and regulates action by regulating these determinants of the will. It proves itself the highest end conceivable, moreover, because it embraces all law and all action conformable to law. For thus law is seen to be a means to the end of moral action, or a precondition of the exercise, by each member of the community, of the freedom to pursue moral ends ; while at the same time law is intelligible as a product of the principle of moral freedom. Lastly, it thus becomes possible to regard law, and the association of a people under law, as a relative moral good, and to found it upon such a degree of moral disposition as is necessary for the continued existence of any civil society. So far as it is possible to regard civil society as an end in itself, the validity and efficacy of law, it is true, is independent of the question whether its provisions are submitted to voluntarily, or are enforced by fear and compulsion. But the derivation of all law from moral freedom, and the, in general, moral character of civil society are proved by the fact that, if civil society is to be permanent, its foundations must be laid in the moral disposition of its members (p. 50). This disposition the law of the State can neither demand nor enforce ; indeed, on the lines of State-law nothing more can be secured than legality of action. Only when law is regarded as a product of moral will can we perceive the possibility and the necessity of moral disposition for the existence of law.

Law, therefore, has to do with a material of narrower extent than morality. Nothing is subject to law but those conjoint or mutual actions which render possible the existence of the State. Morality, on the other hand, likewise embraces the inward tenor of the will as such, which may be discerned behind visible action ; it embraces, besides, all actions which the standard of law leaves undetermined, or are merely permissible. To it belongs everything which concerns the intercourse of men as moral beings, as distinct from the fact that in the State they have to take each other into account as fellow-countrymen. When the State is described as the social form of morality as such, an utterly confused and incorrect conception of its nature is the result. For the production and the criticism of moral disposition lie just as much outside the competency of the State—*i.e.* the nation as a civil society—as the duty of universal love to man transcends the limits of nationality. Moral fellowship as such neutralises national distinctions, for it springs from the subjective motive of love, which differs from that natural hereditary friendliness of fellow-countrymen to one another which is, as a rule, an accompaniment of civil society. Moral fellowship, viewed in these two characteristics of possessing the widest possible extension and being animated by the most comprehensive motive, can only be conceived as the *Kingdom of God*. This idea Christ expresses in such a way that He transcends the view of the national State, and takes up an attitude essentially opposed to it. In harmony with this is the following distinction. Civil law is the system embracing those actions which necessarily follow from the ends for which a particular State exists. Moral law is the system which embraces those dispositions, intentions, and actions which necessarily follow from the all-comprehensive end of the Kingdom of God, and from the subjective motive of universal love. It is clear that these two conceptions are not co-extensive. Since the one has a narrower compass than the other, it must be confessed that we might have a kind of action which would satisfy the civil law, and yet, more or less, might be immoral. Not only is it the case that action in accordance with State law may be barely legal and destitute of moral consideration for civil society—and therefore, so far as disposition goes, egoistic—but it may happen that the whole disposition is preoccupied with ends of State, and accompanied by indifference to the more universal ends of humanity. Conversely, the general moral disposition will also embrace the disposition to obey the laws of the State.

But even in this connection, we could conceive a case where we have a single infraction of the laws of the State, taking even the form of crime, while yet the general moral disposition of the offender is beyond all question. Those are the cases of tragic inward conflict, which in the highest degree engage the interest of those who combine the most educated moral disposition with insight into the difficulty of carrying it into practical effect.

Our discussion has shown that it is a self-contradiction to conceive the moral law under the form of public law. This error, however, is chargeable to that view of the world which forms, in the theology of the Lutheran and Reformed Churches, the presupposition of the doctrine of reconciliation. To say that God rewards obedience to the law by promoting man's personal end, *i.e.* by bestowing on him eternal life, is not a position in harmony with the law of love, the authority of which is based in the very nature of God. However, the connection of thought here is so obscure in the ordinary exposition of the theory under discussion, that a special analysis of its relevant aspects is still necessary to vindicate the judgment I have expressed.

When orthodox theology teaches that the law of love, by which the action of men to one another and to God is regulated, is a reflection of God's essential righteousness, this is to give an extremely imperfect account of its origin. Any law of action can be explained solely from the final end of the society which the law is designed to serve. If that end is to render a nation capable of the social life through which a nation as such exists, and through which protection is secured for every citizen and for every society possessing conjoint interests to pursue their particular aims, limited as they are by the common interest of the nation, but otherwise legitimate, then the law in question is the civil law of the State. If the end is to unite men in the closest conceivable way by disposition and by action, then we come to the law of love as the law of morality. The moral law affords no basis for any expectation, such as follows from the civil law, that obedience to the universal law will be rewarded by the protection and furtherance of our individual rights; on the contrary, the moral law forbids us to reckon thus on a reciprocal relation between duties and rights. Even though such an expectation were accidentally bound up with the permanence of a moral community, yet it is not an essential condition of the individual's performance of duty. He who acts dutifully, finds his enjoyment rather in the action itself: at all events, he does not count on being recompensed for his moral acts by others reciprocating what he has done. Now if, in the theory before us, God represents the society in relation to which men have to act as the law commands, it is impossible to combine in thought these two positions—that they are to discharge the obligations of love, and that they may expect a legal compensation for them in the satisfaction of their personal claim to eternal life. For of necessity it is only in civil society that men receive rights as a compensation for duties; in the moral fellowship, based on action prompted by love, such a compensation may occur accidentally, but it is not necessary as a precondition. In the theory before us, therefore, the fundamental principle of the moral world-order is composed of heterogeneous and incompatible elements.

Lastly, the following circumstance goes to prove the same thing. While, in this theory of the moral world-order, God represents the commonwealth, yet there must also be ascribed to Him His proper significance as the personal Power on whom man is religiously dependent. This requires that nothing by which the estimate of human nature is conditioned, shall be left outside the compass of man's acknowledged dependence on God. Now the theory is so constructed that it assumes a graduated relationship of dependence upon God. That men have a right to eternal life is deduced from their creation by God: that this right can be made good only through fulfilment of the Divine law, depends on God as the Sustainer of the moral order. Thus it is solely in reference to creation that dependence on God is considered complete; as regards the moral order, it is limited by a relative co-ordination of men with God, corresponding to the reciprocity which holds within the State between duties and rights. This scarcely gives expression to the Christian view of the world; but, apart from that, we cannot admit without more ado the rationality and self-evidence of the theory. For the Socinian view makes exactly the same pretensions (p. 241). It derives every right possessed by man within the moral order not from his creation, but from the special grant made to him by God out of equity (*Billigkeit*), and this last it likewise regards as the basis of the moral order. This gives consistent expression, such as is wanting in the other theory, to the complete dependence of man upon God in moral respects. But we shall have to consider later the elucidation of this contradiction of the two theories—a contradiction which was never fought through to the end.

If we look, *thirdly*, at the conditions under which this moral order is applied to man, no point shows more clearly how inadequate for its expression is the analogy of civil law, than the assertion that God is compelled to punish infractions of His law. This necessity, which arises from the Divine justice, is equally pressing with the necessity He is under to recompense the obedience of man with eternal life. The co-ordination of these two exemplifications of the Divine justice corresponds to the two branches of public civil law, the so-called police force and the penal law, and their employment positively to further and defensively to protect the common-weal. But since Divine justice, in relation to human sin, operates merely in a one-sided way, namely in its character as penal power, the juridical complexion of this theory comes out still further in the notion that the primitive justice of God manifests itself in the same positive impartiality as befits a judge when hearing each particular case of accusation. Just as a judge, when forming his opinion of a punishable act, must disregard everything of the nature of moral dis-advantage which the punishment of the criminal will entail upon his relatives and himself, so God, it is maintained, is bound so strictly by His punitive justice that He is entirely indifferent to the form which the fate of the human race may take as a result of punishment. The proverb which is used to illustrate the impartiality which ought to characterise any particular sentence—*fiat iustitia, pereat mundus*—is literally applied to the alleged Divine dispensation. It is impossible to prove that this theory, in and by itself, is in harmony with reason. For it is unintelligible how God could be compelled by His justice to punish our first parents with eternal death on account of their disobedience on a well-known occasion, and at the same time to consign the whole race for their ancestors' trangression to a state of punishment directly contrary to His plan. Among the standards of civil society by which this theory is dominated, there is also to be found the principle of penal law, that punishment must be determined by the degree of crime. The basis of the whole argument is abandoned, consequently, when the transgression of our first parents, which was anything but wicked, is represented as being visited by the heaviest of all penalties, and that, too, embracing their whole posterity. There may be a religious necessity for such a position, but the structure of the theory before us supplies but poor reasons for it. But if that theory, thus constructed, constitutes the proper criterion of the moral order, it has no connection whatever with the view that the first transgression was punished by the condemnation of the whole race.

But this view reckons as punishment not merely the eternal condemnation which embraces the whole race for their ancestors' sin, but also all evils which come upon individual men, including physical death. It is, however, very far from being proved that the conceptions of evil and punishment are equivalent. The slightest observation is enough to show that the former conception is used with a wider extension than the latter ; but if we were to regard punishment, for that reason, as a species of evil, we should be at once confronted with the question, what the two conceptions really have in common. In general that which ministers to our end is good, and so that which impedes our end, by injuring our means, is evil. Natural evils are either such effects of mechanical natural causes as render our bodily organism wholly or partially useless for its purpose of executing our ends, or such as spoil or destroy the property which we have acquired as the regular means for accomplishing our ends. Social evils are such disturbances of our freedom to follow out our ends, or of the intended result of our activity, as arise from the actions or expressed opinions of our fellow-men. Now punishment, as a civil institution, is always a social evil, for it is inflicted by other men. As put in force by civil society against a criminal, however, it is a special kind of social evil, for it encroaches upon those blessings which in ordinary circumstances are protected by the State, namely, personal rights of property and liberty. Punishment is that social evil which consists in a diminution of rights, and that not merely in virtue of the execution of a sentence, *i.e.* the deprivation of property (money fine) or of freedom (imprisonment, exile), but in virtue of the very fact of condemnation, the ideal negation of rights which are ideal attributes of personality. Now this conception of civil punishment certainly admits of being applied to the relation of man to God. If man be conceived as entitled to eternal life in fellowship with God, then banishment from God and exclusion from our proper fellowship with Him—which we have found to be the all-inclusive conception of Divine punishment (p. 42)—may be subsumed under the general notion of " diminution of rights." But just as the conception of civil punishment is not complete unless it be acknowledged by the criminal as a legitimate retaliation on the part of society, so there is nothing which can detect the presence of Divine penalties but the consciousness of guilt of the man who counts an evil a punishment sent by God, because he acknowledges the opposition of his will to God which broke forth in his transgression (p. 49). This introduces a complication with which the authors of the orthodox theology did not reckon, but which threatens to destroy our belief in its general truth.

17

It is certainly a fact that, in the circle of pre-Christian religions, it was common to combine the ideas of evil and Divine punishment. Through great calamities men were led to believe that some great enormity had been committed against the gods : and conversely, they expected or demanded that penal ills should light upon the foes of God or of human society. And so these currents of thought, appearing equally among the Israelites and the classical peoples, seem directly to favour the dogmatic theory. These considerations seem to prove it thoroughly in harmony with reason. However, another fact counteracts this impression. In the pre-Christian religions no application of the connection between the ideas of evil and Divine punishment is made, save to special and specially conspicuous cases of misfortune and of human wickedness. The insignificant sufferings of life, and death as a normal phenomenon, were not regarded as Divine punishment, but as something quite natural. This is true even of the religion of the Old Testament, where the record of the conjunction of death with sin is as far as possible from laying down a dogma. Though the fate of death is considered a special calamity by the psalmists, this does not imply a specific consciousness of guilt, but rather, on the contrary, a specific consciousness of innocence, accompanied by the feeling that, through their fellowship with the true God, they are raised above the ordinary level of mankind by nature. It is thus within that civilisation which is independent of Christianity and of Old Testament conceptions of a Divine revelation of grace, that we find the idea of evils, especially natural ills, combined with that of Divine punishment in connection with specially conspicuous degrees of wickedness and misfortune. But this "natural" view of the matter is not all equivalent to the principle, assumed as natural by Dogmatics, that the conceptions of evil and Divine punishment are coincident. Dogmatic theologians, it is true, treat the phenomena described above as though they could draw this general principle from them by a trustworthy induction. But this is an unjustifiable assumption. For while *special* cases of wickedness followed by striking misfortunes are interpreted by *religious* thought in the light of the conception of Divine punishment, slighter ills are in point of fact not viewed in the same way; for no attempt is made to reach a general rule. And this very combination of ideas betrays its religious character by the fact that it does not presuppose the theoretical principle of Dogmatics, that all evils are Divine punishments. We shall find (§ 42) that it is likewise impossible to represent this principle as an element in the view of the world which Christianity justifies us in holding. Nowhere, therefore, in the range that is claimed for it, does it possess practical validity. But it cannot claim theoretical truth, if it has no practical validity in the sense that any religion exists in which the consciousness of guilt is so comprehensive as to acknowledge all evils, felt as such, to be consequences of personal sin. Consequently, if anyone, relying on this theory, expects to succeed in convincing men of the truth of Christianity by the force of argument, he will find that the conception of the moral order now under review is accepted by no one.

For when, *fourthly*, we investigate the origin of this theory, we find that its dominant idea, that God must requite the diverse actions of men in one of two ways [*i.e.* by reward or punishment], is not the fundamental conception of Christianity. Even the writers of the New Testament, when dealing with the wider ramifications of the moral order, may show their belief in the Divine requital of human action, yet Christ fills out God's attribute of perfection with an exactly opposite content. God, He says, causes the sun to rise on the evil and the good, and lets the rain fall on the just and the unjust. This being the Divine perfection which Christ declared, He can prescribe love to one's enemies as a Christian duty (Matt. v. 44–48). This truth is ignored by those who harp upon the fact that penal retribution is a general ethical idea which had been realised in history long before the institution of civil and legal society was ever thought of.[1] This idea, it is

---

[1] Kreibig, *Versöhnungslehre*, p. 142.

asserted, theology found present to begin with as an element
of conscience, and transferred it to God under the guise of the
attribute of justice.   But the question for Christian theology
is not what idea of God can be shown to be the presumptive
content of natural conviction, but what declarations of Christ
we have.   In the present case it is simply a falsification of
Christianity to maintain that the attribute, from which the
twofold co-ordinate requital is derived, is that fundamental
element in the conception of God which should dominate all
other aspects ; and it proves but little acquaintance with the
Bible to assert that such an idea is Scriptural without
attempting to bring it into harmony with the sayings of
Christ adduced above.   Lastly, it would be worth while to
prove that the idea of punishment had appeared before the
existence of civil society !   Theologians who are accustomed
to copy second-rate models, might learn from Calvin (*Inst.* i. 2)
that the natural religion of our first parents before the Fall
did not rest at all upon the attribute of Divine retribution, for
the latter has no meaning until God has given His law.   But,
according to Calvin, the recognition of God as Lawgiver is
properly to be derived from the fact that God's goodness and
providence are reckoned the source of all blessings for men.
Not till we come to the third rank of the Divine attributes
do we meet with the attribute of retribution.   Foremost of
all stands, as Christ testified, the goodness of God.   And
that is as it should be : for the religion of our first parents
is nothing but the prophetic shadow of Christianity.   What
Calvin says upon the subject, however, is based upon Luther's
discussions of Genesis (p. 171).

The tendency to fill up the idea of God with the attribute
of a twofold co-ordinate requital, is not so innate or so
universal as Kreibig imagines ; for we can localise it historically in the religion of the Greeks.   Here it fundamentally
determines the relation between gods and men, who are not
regarded as dependent on the gods through creation.   That is,
to punish and to reward, as co-ordinate acts, are the functions
of the State as conceived by the Greeks ; and they are ascribed

to the gods, because in this religion the State constitutes the *summum bonum*. In these functions the Greeks discern the justice of the State, and the justice of the gods.[1] It is characteristic of them that they viewed the punishment of crime and the rewarding of merit as the co-ordinate duties of civil justice.[2] That is not a self-evident view, nor is it a view which obtains everywhere. For, according to our ideas, the single duty of the State is to maintain public law and order, and so assure everyone of protection in the pursuit of his legitimate ends, in order to promote which purposes the State likewise employs the forces of punishment against criminals. But the rewarding of individual merit is only an accidental addition to its functions ; the fulfilment of their civil duties is, rather, the very condition of all enjoying the protection of the State. This more mature conception of the State betrays itself even in the idea of God's justice which obtains in the Old Testament (vol. ii. pp. 107, 138); for here, too, the foundation is supplied by the civil order. But in the Old Testament the bestowal of rewards and the infliction of punishments are not co-ordinated under the Divine attribute of justice. Rather, the justice of God is regarded as assuring the righteous of their rights and of protection within normal civil society ; the destruction of the godless, however, effected as it is by God's wrath, is the means used to enforce law and order to the advantage of those, too, who hitherto have been deprived of their full rights. Thus to suppose that the conception of the twofold retribution of God, as an innate idea and as an element of natural religion, is likewise the fundamental conception of the moral order which must be presupposed in Christianity—to suppose this, is in reality to acknowledge the Greek idea of the relation between gods and men as the supreme criterion of every part of the Christian system. As has already been shown, therefore, the God who is conceived under this attribute is an idol, and so also the

---

[1] I refer the reader to Leopold Schmidt, *Die Ethik der alten Griechen* (1882), 2 vols.

[2] *Op. cit.* ii. p. 258.

trust placed in Him by His theological devotees must be false and deceptive. But how comes it that every attempt to correct this falsification of the Christian idea of God is so obstinately resisted as we find to be the case ? The primary cause is the slovenly and thoughtless use of the Bible which prevails in theology. If any statement whatever of God's retributive justice can be pointed to in its pages, then that is taken as constituting the Divine attribute of justice which is fundamental in Christianity ! Thus Kriebig says, in concluding the remarks to which I formerly adverted : " Even though the Biblical idea of God may differ in different passages, yet the idea of a God Who, as such, is a holy dispenser of justice, is incontestably Scriptural." But the point at issue is whether this Scriptural idea is the fundamental element in the conception of God. In the second place, theologians of this school are influenced by the fact that the twofold co-ordinate retribution, in the eschatological form which Plato had already given it, was represented by Justin Martyr as a leading feature of Christianity, and a correlative of its legalistic character. This doctrine of the Apologists, which we can likewise perceive to have been the Christian conviction of the earliest community in Rome (vol. ii. p. 317), implies that the chief idea of Hellenic religion is being carried over into Christianity. Thus it is that theologians of orthodox repute, who at bottom are rationalistic, foster the prejudice that they must believe in God under this attribute first of all, before they can agree upon the further attributes which the revelation in Christ offers to their faith.

§ 33. Such a moral order, which is based upon the Hellenic juridical conception of Divine justice, and which, moreover, in virtue of our first parents' sin issues in the condemnation of the whole human race, leaves no room for *the possibility of the reconciliation* of man with God. So far from being a positive presupposition of the governing idea of Christianity, it is an obstacle to our understanding the Christian faith. This conclusion is still further confirmed by the following considerations. Reconciliation with God may be

taken as the basis of the perfect religion. But we are told
that the original dispensation consisted in a reciprocal legal
relationship between God and man. Now law and religion,
at least in the experience of evangelical Christians, are conceptions quite opposed to one another in species. Species
cannot be derived the one from the other; they are mutually
exclusive. The species of fellowship with God which we
know as reconciliation, therefore, cannot be derived from the
presupposed reciprocity of rights between God and men.
Accordingly, if the religion of reconciliation is derived from
God, it must be based upon a different conception of God's
relation to man from that on which stress has been laid
hitherto, namely, upon His *grace*. This thought, however, is
treated by Protestant orthodoxy in such a way that, instead
of repudiating altogether the ideas which follow from the idea
of Divine retribution, it endeavours to preserve them in force
alongside of the inferences from Divine grace. This is
accomplished by means of a compromise, the artificiality and
pretended profundity of which are no guarantee of its truth.

An artificial solution of the contradiction contained in the
premises was already offered by the theory of Anselm, the
result of which is to remove the contradiction to a different
point from where it stood originally. For the presupposition
of this theory is that the honour of God forms, with equal
necessity, the ground both of His condemnation of the sinful
human race and of His intention to bless them with salvation.
In order to exhibit this intention as attainable and attained
despite the sway of condemnation, he demonstrates that satisfaction to God for sin is necessary, and that, through the
Person and the Death of Christ, it is possible and effectual.
But he derives the necessity for satisfaction from a conception
of the justice of God which implies an equality in private
rights between God and man. It is impossible, however, to
combine this relationship in thought with the truth that God
is the absolute end of man; consequently, the first contradiction is solved only by the admission of a second (vol. i.
p. 39 ff.). Moreover, a plain contradiction is involved in the

way in which Luther derives reconciliation from the love of God, but at the same time derives from the wrath of God the satisfaction which Christ has to work out through the vicarious endurance of punishment (vol. i. p. 221). For it is impossible to conceive sinners, at the same time and in the same respect, as objects both of God's love and God's wrath.

The doctrine of the scholastic theologians of the Reformation exhibits no inconsistencies so plain and open as these. To be sure, they start with the assumption of an antinomy in God. In His justice He must condemn the sinful race of man; in His goodness and grace He desires to bless them. But for God Himself these two attributes have not equal importance: in their simultaneous reference to one and the same object, therefore, they form no contradiction. Rather, from the very outset greater importance is ascribed to justice than to grace. The same may be said of their explanation of the mediatorial *rôle* in which Christ brings into operation for sinful man the order of grace instead of the order of law. The decree by which Christ is sent forth, it is true, springs from the Divine grace; but if that decree were conceived to include all the consequences of His mission, the result would be the outlining of a series of Divine operations which would come into collision with the necessary results of His justice. But the gracious purpose of Christ's mission is limited to this, that He should satisfy Divine justice for sinners by enduring punishment and fulfilling the law, and thus realise the essential precondition of their pardon. This act of grace is made subordinate as means to the Divine justice in such a way that, even when it is no longer put in force against sinners directly, justice still obtains satisfaction for its claims in a roundabout way. Moreover, this implies that the dispensation of grace, which springs from Christ, does not run counter to the dispensation of justice. For the Mediator of grace, in achieving satisfaction, is subject throughout to the standard of Divine justice, and He opens the door of the realm of grace only through bearing testimony, by His twofold satisfaction, to the inviolability of the justice of God. While the dispensation of grace remains dependent on His person, it likewise remains permanently bound up with the validity of Divine justice in virtue of the aforementioned significance which belongs to what He suffered and did.

The twofold satisfaction rendered by Christ imports that the law makes no claim to punish such sinners as are believers, and does not demand from them obedience to it as a precondition of salvation. Thus the direct authority of the original Divine law over believers is put in abeyance. If, now, the mission of Christ, as an effect of grace, were given its properly unlimited significance, then, as the satisfaction rendered by Christ would have set aside for believers the dispensation of law, the impediment in the way of Divine grace would have ceased to exist, and Christ would have to be described as the Mediator of grace to believers, in consequence of God's first decree. In the theory under discussion, however, this is not the case. God's first gracious resolve to send Christ is not conceived as including its possible consequences. For the merit of Christ is the moving power which first puts in force for men the Divine dispensation of grace, which is dependent on Him. Through endurance of punishment and entire obedience to the law, He vicariously satisfies both of the legitimate demands made on sinners by Divine justice, and abrogates for believers the dispensation of law, to the end that they may attain blessedness. Thus, *by the meritorious value of His whole righteousness*, He determines the resolve of God to open through Him for believers the dispensation of grace.

But what means the employment of this notion of merit when we are comparing the Person of Christ with the dominant conception of God ? Merit is the necessary correlate of equity (*Billigkeit*). This discovery of Duns Scotus meets us again in the less lucid theory of Thomas Aquinas. The Divine grace towards believers, which the merit of Christ puts in operation, is nothing else than arbitrary goodwill, which as such implies no inconsistency with the assumed justice of God. Here the scholastic theology of the Reformation appears to coincide with Socinianism, and it seems as though the circuit-ous paths which it follows to reach this goal might have been spared. Yet their agreement is very limited, and more theoretical than practical. To begin with, we ought to observe that grace in the sense of equity, as a concomitant of the dispensation of public law, wears another form when likened to the right of pardon which resides in the State, than when it is taken as supplementing a prior private relationship existing between God and man. The right of pardon as a correlative of the penal law, is certainly also a manifestation of equity arising out of consideration for the moral circumstances of the condemned criminal (p. 91); but the opposite standpoints occupied by public law and private right lead, in the two theories which we are comparing, to the drawing of different inferences from their common conception of grace as equity. On the basis of private right sins reckon as injuries, the equity of God is taken to be a matter of course, and the forgiveness of sins to be a private affair between God and the individual. When the form of public law is followed, sins reckon as crimes : the exercise, prompted by equity, of the right of pardon, must next be artificially secured as a concession from the inviolability of penal justice, which then forms the basis *de novo* of a general dispensation for the Christian community, in virtue of the merits of its Founder. The only question is, whether the conception of equity, as fixing the value of grace, is strong enough to justify its being applied in this way.

By employing the arguments I have described, this theory prevents any inconsistency between the grace and the justice of God from appearing at any point. By using the conception of equity to express the grace of God, the latter is made to appear as an accident of His justice which can be exercised without the essence of that justice being in any way altered. But this benefit is counterbalanced by a peculiar disadvantage. It has been remarked already that Divine justice, in the traditional sense, cannot be a positive presupposition serving to explain the Christian dispensation of grace (p. 263). As grace is now explained to be an accident of justice, it at once becomes clear that this accident is called into action in the will of God from without, by the merits of Christ. Now it comes to the same thing whether we trace the dispensation of grace to this cause, or maintain that it rests upon God's arbitrary volition. A contradiction between the Divine attributes of justice and grace had been avoided earlier by saying that God *has* to act according to justice, but *might* act according to grace if He chose. With this the conclusion, that the dispensation of grace rests upon God's arbitrary will, is in entire agreement. This is really as hostile to the true interests of Christian theology as the Socinian representation of grace as being arbitrary will unaccompanied by universal laws. We are brought here again merely to the same conclusion as before, that the conception of God which dominates the argument is not thought as a unity. Necessity and freedom are not comprised within the conception of the Divine will as elements which mutually condition one another; but necessity is maintained to be at work in His action as prompted by justice, freedom (arbitrary) in the method by which His grace is put in motion. Their correlates in the work of Christ, satisfaction and merit, are materially identical indeed, but formally they are as disparate as necessity and freedom in God. As rendering satisfaction, Christ is both subject to Divine justice and indebted for His mission to the grace of God; as possessing merit, the range of His influence is not determined beforehand by God's action; in this *rôle*, rather, He is regarded as putting in motion the Divine grace. But this is to offend against a fundamental presupposition of theology. It was right, by denying merit to man, to ensure the recognition of the essential unity of the Divine world-order, but this principle is as fatally endangered by the apocryphal formula, " the merits of Christ," as by any belief in human merit which existed in the Middle Ages. For even though the merits of Christ are based materially on His Godhead, and thus made subordinate to the being of God, yet formally they are referred to His human freedom, and through their being recognised as *merits* a range of activity is ascribed to Him which is not *a priori* subjected to the government of God.

This criticism of the way in which Lutheran and Reformed theology has derived the Christian dispensation of grace, is not to be confounded with the objections which have been raised by Faustus Socinus.   What I mean is that this theory, in spite of a tendency opposed to that of Socinus, is not sufficiently far removed from the Socinian view of the world, but has too much in common with it.   I trust, therefore, that I shall not be misunderstood if I homologate particular objections which Socinus has raised (vol. i. p. 326).   *Duo si dicunt idem, non est idem.*   The world-order which lies at the foundation of the theory in question is the moral law under the form of public law.   It has already been shown that this combination of ideas involves a contradiction (p. 250).   This contradiction naturally influences those inferences which condition the view taken of reconciliation through Christ. That is, if the moral law as such constitutes the original dispensation under which God deals with man, then the necessity of punishing, which follows from the moral law, will be no hindrance to God's resolving to forgive sins, and carrying out that resolution in a dispensation open to all.   Sinners, upon whom educative penalties are laid, may without inconsistency be conceived as objects of pardon.   But that the need for punishment is regarded as an obstacle in the way of pardon, and that in order to reconcile them the punishment of a substitute is accepted, is simply a consequence of the presupposed judicial character of the law.   There is no immediate relation, however, between moral good and the moral act of pardon and legal punishment, whether it is borne by the guilty themselves or by their substitute.   What legal punishment does is to expunge legal guilt, without anything remaining over which civil society can forgive ; and therefore the moral judgment of pardon has nothing to do with it.   For we can pardon criminals although we lay punishments on them, while we do not pardon every criminal because he has been punished.   These conceptions and no other we must apply to God's dealings with men, for we must keep moral law and civil law altogether distinct. Moreover, according to the moral law, it is conceivable that an innocent man should feel the legal punishment which falls upon a relative—a member of his family or a friend—to be a legal diminution of civil rights also for himself, since in consequence of the punishment of the other he has to suffer certain evils. But in civil society it would be a plain offence against judicial equity to inflict penalties upon an innocent man in order to spare the guilty. When punishment takes the form of fines, the innocent, it is true, can pay for the guilty; but that does not mean that the former is punished for the latter. For the pains and penalties intended by the judge fall, *quâ* sentence, upon the guilty man; and when the innocent man discharges the fine, the action does not imply a compulsory deprivation of civil status, but only a voluntary surrender of property. But from this we can draw no valid inferences regarding punishments which concern liberty and life, in which deprivation must be executed on the person of the guilty. In holding it possible to draw such inferences (vol. i. p. 334), orthodox theologians have fallen into the Socinian error of supposing that sin possesses the character of an offence which can be wiped out by a fine. According to civil law, punishment which affects the liberty of the subject can fall on no one but the offender himself, and cannot justly be transferred by the judge to one who is innocent. Just as little possible is it, according to the moral law, to reckon the moral achievement of one man's life to another as his own, in such a way as to dispense the latter in any respect from striving after it for himself. For moral action is not a thing which can even be conceived as detached from its author (p. 70). And it is impossible according to civil law likewise, for moral actions do not, as such, fall under civil law. For these reasons the theory of the twofold satisfaction of Christ, which characterises the scholastic theology of the Reformation, is a confused inference from contradictory presuppositions.

§ 34. The theories of the Socinians and of the scholastic
theologians of the Reformation regarding the original dispensation of fellowship between God and man, from which
they sought to derive the special dispensation of fellowship
between them in Christianity, are intended by their authors
to be understood as wholly based on reason, though points of
support for both were found in the New Testament. We
have seen that the Socinian theory was directly designed to
express the character of Christianity as the religion of forgiveness. But the conception of the Divine equity which
dominates it does not furnish a basis for a universal order of
moral action, nor can it form the foundation of Christianity as
a general dispensation taking its rise in forgiveness. It
really leads to a splitting up of the moral and religious
dispensation desiderated, into purely private relationships
between God and individual men. The theory of Protestant
scholasticism bases the general order of human action upon
the conception of Divine justice as a presupposition of reason,
while it bases forgiveness as a general dispensation on the
Christian Revelation. But it does not find in Divine justice
the positive ground of forgiveness; it rather sees in forgiveness merely an exception to Divine justice which, while
certainly controlled or conditioned by the latter, is yet
combined with it in the conception of God in a merely
accidental way. Lastly, in the normative view of the law
which answers to God's justice, the properties of the moral
law and of the civil law are conjoined in so absurd a way,
that the presuppositions, thence resulting, of the significance
of Christ as the organ of Divine grace issue in contradictory
conceptions. The basis of this train of thought is to be found
in the Hellenic idea of the twofold requital dispensed by God;
it is intelligible, therefore, that Christianity should not be
deduced from that idea, but proved to be an exception to the
rule. This is a misfortune which can neither be concealed
nor compensated for by using the conception of vicarious
satisfaction to explain the position of Christ within this
order. For that conception has no essential relation to the

moral law, it contradicts the civil law and even the moral
law at times, and least of all can it be proved sound by
confusing these two standards together.

The formal error, from which this theory of the Divine
world-order suffers, lies in its neglect of the question, what
end God has, or can have, in common with the human race.
For the nature of fellowship is determined by the end
common to both parties; and the law of action emanates
from the will of the lawgiver not arbitrarily, nor from any
other necessity than that of the preconceived end of the
fellowship which the law is meant to serve as a means.
Theologians of the older school have set these considerations
aside because, under the influence of the Areopagitic conception of God, they cannot bring themselves to assume a
real fellowship between God and man. The God who is
conceived only as not being the world, must always be
negatively related to everything that is real.   Thus, even
when He is conceived as a spiritual Person Who thinks
Himself and wills Himself, this idea—an idea which is
superinduced upon the Areopagitic theory, and, so far from
being specifically Christian, is Aristotelian—is really robbed
of all its force by the remark of Thomas Aquinas that
God's personal end lies incomparably above and beyond the
end or purpose of the world (vol. i. p. 62).   Therefore
the creation of the world, even when explained by Divine
love, is yet derived from God's arbitrary volition.   The
revelation of Him given in Christianity, moreover, appears
equally arbitrary; and though it leads men to the vision of
God, yet this end, transcending human nature as it does, has
as little relation to man's essential being as God's end has to
the world which He has created.   The scholastic divines of
the Reformation break through this rigid conception of
mediaeval theology by contending that the purpose, embodied
in Christianity, to realise the spiritual and blessed fellowship of man with God, is originally included in the notion
of human nature.   This truth had to be fought for and
won, if monasticism was to be deprived of its claim to be

the perfect Christianity, because it realised the supernatural life, the life of the angels, in fellowship with God. But these divines did not clearly understand how much this involved for their whole doctrine of God. If the proper destiny of the human race includes spiritual and blessed fellowship with God, this end cannot be unrelated to God's personal end. Between the creation of man for this end and the creative will of God it is impossible to think the relation as accidental; it must be necessary. The conception of God, therefore, which consists simply in thinking Him as equivalent to *what is not the world*, is not exhaustive. Or rather, He is not thought at all, until we gain that positive conception which ensures His differentiation from the world. Instead of perceiving this, the leaders of the theology which is extolled as loyal to the Church never offer us anything more than the shadow-play of Areopagitic negations and affirmations, which explain absolutely nothing, which constitute neither scientific nor Christian knowledge, and which simply must be thrown aside if the Christian view of the world and the practical interests of Protestantism are to be exhibited as necessarily and universally valid.[1]

Theology, in delineating the moral order of the world, must take as its starting-point that conception of God in

[1] Instead of this, Philippi (*Kirchliche Dogmatik*, ii. p. 20 ff.) arranges the attributes of God according to the " three moments in which the Divine nature discloses itself to us in an ascending series " : God (1) as absolute Substance, *a.* eternity, *b.* omnipresence ; (2) as absolute Subject, *a.* omnipotence, *b.* omniscience ; (3) as holy love, *a.* wisdom, *b.* justice, *c.* goodness. The first of these strata is the Areopagitic conception of God, in so far as, through affirmation, it is brought into relation to the world ; the second is the Aristotelian conception. Now this "Church" theologian assures us, indeed, that "there is here no development successively from lower to higher ; rather, we merely separate out the lower from the higher for preliminary examination." For what purpose this is necessary, he does not say : in my opinion it may be used to prove that this kind of theology contains the germ of all rationalism. The Socinian Crell (*Jahrb. für deutsche Theol.* xiii. p. 256) proceeds exactly as does Philippi. Now if Philippi meant the remark seriously, that the prior strata in the conception of God are separated out merely provisionally, in order to exhibit their defectiveness, then he ought to have deduced all the attributes of God afresh from the conception of holy love. As he does not do so, he has no conception of the unity of God, and leaves open to rationalism the possibility of accepting only so much of the Christian conception of God as harmonises with the first or the second stratum.

which the relation of God to His Son our Lord is expressed, a relation which, by Christ's mediation, is extended likewise to His community. For when the Apostles, in the Epistles of the New Testament, describe God as our Father, that is an abbreviated expression for the Christian name for God, which when fully stated runs, " the God and Father of our Lord Jesus Christ " (2 Cor. i. 3, xi. 31 ; Rom. xv. 6 ; Col. i. 3 ; 1 Pet. i. 3 ; Eph. i. 3). As the name of God is always used in Scripture as a compendious description of His revelation, it is clear that, when God reveals Himself as Father through His Son Jesus Christ, the process is only completed when the community accepts the revelation by acknowledging the Mediator who brings it as its Lord. Any attempt, therefore, to construct a scientific doctrine of God must be wrong which fails to keep in view all the aspects of this name. The name God has the same sense when used of Father, Son, and Holy Spirit (Matt. xxviii. 19). For the name denotes God in so far as He reveals Himself, while the Holy Spirit is the power of God which enables the community to appropriate His self-revelation as Father through His Son (1 Cor. ii. 12). That the revelation of God through His Son, however, embraces the community which acknowledges His Son as her Lord, and how it does so, is explained by saying that God manifests Himself to the Son and to the community as *loving Will* (vol. ii. p. 96 ff.). As this conception of God is recognised as coming from the source of knowledge which is authoritative for the Christian community, it likewise follows that the goodness of God to all men, in bestowing on them the good things of nature (Matt. v. 45 ; Acts xiv. 17), is an inference which Christ drew from the knowledge He possessed of the love of God to Him and to His community. Thus the goodness of God, as the general presupposition of everything, is embraced in the specific attribute of the Divine Fatherhood; or, in other words, the truth that He has revealed Himself to the Christian community as love. There is no other conception of equal worth beside this which need be taken into account. This is especially true of the concep-

18

tion of the Divine holiness, which, in its Old Testament
sense, is for various reasons not valid in Christianity, while
its use in the New Testament is obscure (vol. ii. pp. 89, 101).
Even the recognition of the personality of God does not
imply independent knowledge apart from our defining Him
as loving Will. It only decides the form to be given to this
content, for without this content of loving Will the conception of spiritual personality is not sufficient to explain the
world as a connected whole. The step, therefore, which we
take now in bringing forward the truly Christian view of God
ought not to be understood as though in His contrast to the
world God were conceived, first of all, in general, as personality, and secondly, in particular, as loving Will ;—and this in
such a way that while consistent knowledge of the world might
be drawn from the first conception, the second would yield
simply more knowledge of the same sort. What I mean is
rather this, that the conception of love is the only adequate
conception of God, for it enables us, both to understand the
revelation which comes through Christ to His community,
and at the same time to solve the problem of the world.
For this purpose the merely formal conception of personality
is insufficient : for it leaves us free to ascribe all possible
kinds of content to the Divine Will. Now, if an entirely
different sort of world were just as possible for God as the
world which actually exists, there is no perceptible reason
why the actual world was ever raised by God above the
level of possibility. And therefore, either the formal conception of the Divine personality is as unserviceable as a
pantheistic notion would be, or it can be successfully
employed only as the form whose special content is love.

It cannot be doubted, as a historical fact, that individuality (*Besonderheit*) is everywhere a characteristic of the
religious idea of God.   But the Scotists on the one hand, and
the Spinozists on the other, regard with distrust and aversion
the suggestion that a conception of God marked by this
characteristic is an appropriate expression of a scientific principle of knowledge.   Both follow the maxim : *omnis deter-*

minatio est negatio, and negation seems altogether incompatible with the idea of God. Scotism, however, fails to explain the fact that there is a real world, while Spinozism fails to explain the world as it really is. But modern Pantheism is not at all averse to the view that the Absolute forms the reality of the world by the gradual particularisation of itself, so as to reach its full realisation through the special organ of the human spirit and its special functions of intuition and methodical knowledge. If we think God as the universal ground of all reality, we cannot avoid ascribing individuality to Him in some way or other. For even in logic the particular comes under the universal only because it comes under the individual. The will, too, becomes the universal ground of particular real acts only by keeping to a definite direction, and simultaneously refraining from other possible directions. On the other hand, the Spinozistic principle that every special determination implies negation, amounts to no more than the logical law that the conceptions of the individual and the *differentia* always hold good together, or that we distinguish things by their species. If, therefore, the conception of individuality is inapplicable to God, God cannot be distinguished from things, nor things from God. Either everything is God, or everything is world. Either the distinction of things from one another and from the universal substance is a delusion, or it is a self-deception to assume the existence of an intelligent Creator of the world which is distinct from Him, and differentiated within itself. But this latter assumption was found necessary to explain the world, differentiated as it is into nature and spiritual life, with this further circumstance, that men regard their common moral life as the final end of the world (§ 29). To eliminate individuality from the conception of God, therefore, is wrong, for it leads to absurd conclusions.

God's personal will, like any other force, can be thought as the cause of effects only when acting in a definite direction. As Will, God can be thought only as in conscious relation to the end which He Himself is. Nevertheless, this formal truth is inadequate to explain anything which is not God; it is inadequate, therefore, to explain the world. Unless it can be shown that, and how, the world is embraced in the personal end which God sets before Himself, then even this analysis of the Divine Will leads to nothing. We shall find that the conception of love, which is the key to the revelation of God in Christianity, carries us past the difficulties which accompany that analysis. Still, the preliminary question arises, whether to determine the Divine Will in this specific way is not to menace the value of the conception of God. For if God, conceived under the special attribute of love, is subordinated to a generic conception of will, it might be argued that this generic idea, as the higher, might claim to be in value the equivalent of God. Here the difficulty solved above returns in another form. Nevertheless, the specific character assigned to God's Will is not such that the affirmation of it is the negation of some other specific character which in itself might possibly belong to Him, nor is it such that some other being might have to be viewed, under some other category, as deserving comparison with God. The truth rather is, that only through the special attribute of love is it possible to derive the world from God; this quality of love, therefore, serves in general to discover to us in God the ground of the unity of nature and spirit, and the law of their co-existence. It cannot, therefore, be regarded as lessening the cosmic significance of God. The logical superiority of the genus to the species never implies that the genus has an existence apart from the species. The conception of God, therefore, when it is specifically determined as love, is not to be regarded as being subordinated to some hypothetical substance, called " Will in general " or " indeterminate Will," and thus possessed of the absoluteness which does not belong to Will when defined as love. For we have seen that indeterminate Will is incapable of explaining anything.

The word " love " is frequently used to denote the feeling of the worth of an object for the Self. But as such feeling always sets the will in motion, either to appropriate the loved object or to enrich its existence, ordinary usage comprises these kinds of movement of the will also under the designation of love. Nor is common usage ambiguous in doing so, for the two aspects of the emotion are closely related to one another. Love, as feeling, fulfils its nature when it excites the will ; and love, as will, includes the feeling of the same name. The conception of love, therefore, is completely expressed by combining both. Love is will aiming either at the appropriation of an object or at the enrichment of its existence, because moved by a feeling of its worth. But this definition needs to be supplemented by special qualifications. *First*, it is necessary that the objects which are loved should be of like nature to the subject which loves, namely, persons. When we speak of love for things or animals, the conception is degraded beneath its proper meaning. *Secondly*, love implies a will which is constant in its aim. If the objects change, we may have fancies, but we cannot love. *Thirdly*, love aims at the promotion of the other's personal end, whether known or conjectured. To render assistance in ordinary matters does not require love, but only good-feeling, a less definite thing. Love, however, is not merely interested in the loved one's affairs, which may perhaps have simply an accidental connection with him. What love does is rather to estimate everything which concerns the other, by its bearing on the character in which the loved one is precious to the lover. Whatever valuable spiritual acquirements the other may possess, or whatever is still necessary for his perfection, becomes the content of the definite ideal which the lover sets before himself. Love desires either to promote, to maintain, and through sympathetic interest to enjoy the individuality of character acquired by the other, or to assist him in securing those blessings which are necessary to ensure the attainment of his personal ideal. *Fourthly*, if love is to be a constant attitude of the will, and if the appropriation and the promotion of the other's personal end are not alternately to diverge, but to coincide in each act, then the will of the lover must take up the other's personal end and make it part of his own. That is, love continually strives to develop and to appropriate the individual self-end of the other personality, regarding this as a task necessary to the very nature of its own personal end, its own conscious individuality. This characteristic implies that the will, as love, does not give itself up for the other's sake. To take up this position is not, as some have objected, to introduce the element of egoism into the conception of love. For the will is egoistic when it sets itself in opposition to the common aims of others; but in the present case, the will is directed to the closest fellowship with another and to a common end. This conception of love may without difficulty be tested by being applied to all sub-species of love, such as friendship, conjugal affection, paternal affection, and love for one's parents.

When, now, we apply this conception to God, it becomes clear that neither the indeterminate notion of a cosmos, nor the notion of the natural world, can be conceived as the correlate of this particular aspect of the Divine will; for in them there is nothing akin to God. The proposition, that God created the world out of love, is useless to begin with, so far as it can bear the meaning that God communicates Himself to mere creatures, and gives their existence realisation as though it were the ultimate aim of His personal end. We can find an object which corresponds to His nature as love only in one or many personal beings. We cannot, of course, decide from the conception of love itself whether the forthbringing of one loved person, or the forth-bringing, education, and perfecting of a world of spirits, constitutes the end which, under the conception of love, must be thought as embraced within the personal end of God. But the world also is for us a given fact, and an examination of the various aspects of the conception of God cannot but have some bearing upon the existence of the world, in which a multiplicity of persons exist as members of a race. These come into existence as a multitude of individuals, participating, as they do, in material and organic nature. For matter is the original expression of the multiplex, and the precondition of all multiplicity; while organic matter is the expression of the differentiation of a living multiplicity conditioned by the nexus of species and genus. Consideration of the world, therefore, shows that a multiplicity of persons, together composing a race, may be the object of the Divine love; while, apart from this empirical observation, it is at least as conceivable that God's personal end should be bound up with that of a single kindred spirit as with that of a multiplicity of spirits.

Now, if we follow out, in the first instance, the connection given in experience between the world of spirits and nature, we find that we may draw, from the relation between the world of spirits and God's character as love, a necessary conclusion regarding the origin of the world of nature. If it be an essential part of God's personal end that He should create a multitude of spirits, formed after their own kind, and that He should bring them to perfection in order to manifest Himself to them as love, then the world of nature, viewed in its separate formation as distinct from the world of men, cannot be viewed as a mere arbitrary appendix, but must rather be regarded as a means to the Divine end. The rest of nature might be an arbitrary appendix to the existence of the human race, were it not called into existence by a Divine Will whose character is love—were it, in other words, the creation of a purely indeterminate Divine Will. But absolutely nothing definite or real can be derived from such a ground as this. Nature, therefore, must likewise be explained from the Divine Will in its self-given character of love. But, owing to its lack of kinship with God, it cannot be the direct object and the last end of His loving will. And so nothing remains but to conclude, that nature is called into being to serve as a means to God's essential purpose in creating the world of spirits. In this way the statement that God has created the world out of love receives its proper limitations, and the creation of nature by God is given the value of a relative necessity, the necessity, namely, of serving as a means to God's previously chosen end of calling into being a multitude of spirits akin to Himself. Granted, therefore, that the world of nature in general cannot be known directly as the creation of God, and that, on the other hand, the moral development of men as individuals, and their union through progressive fellowship in good, demand for their explanation the idea of God, it must still be remembered that these results cannot be attained save through the means furnished by our natural endowment. For the apparatus by which the individual life and all commerce in things spiritual is carried on, presupposes for its permanent existence the whole immeasurable system of the world, mechanical, chemical, organic. Consequently, if we must conceive God as necessary to guarantee our personal morality and our moral fellowship, we must recognise that the entire universe is designed to serve this Divine end ; for otherwise we could not view even our moral life as an object of Divine care. The whole universe, therefore, considered thus as the precondition of the moral kingdom of created spirits, is throughout God's creation for this end.

We have now provisionally recognised a multitude of spirits, together forming a race, as a possible object of the Divine love. But the question may be asked whether, since multiplicity is a necessary characteristic of them, they can really be akin in nature to the one Divine Will. For the human race, in virtue of its attribute of multiplicity, is involved in the conditions under which the genera and species of all organic creatures exist. _Quâ_ multiplicity, therefore, the human race is akin to nature and not akin to God. In order to prove its kinship with God, it would be necessary to conceive the human race as a unity in spite of its natural multiplicity, a unity which is other than its natural generic unity. The conception we are in search of is given in the idea of the Christian community, which makes the Kingdom of God its task. This idea of the moral unification of the human race, through action prompted by universal love to our neighbour, represents a unity of many which belongs to the realm of the thoroughly defined, in other words, the good will. The multitude of spirits who, for all their natural and generic affinity, may yet, in the practical expression they

give to their will, be utterly at variance, attain a supernatural
unity through mutual and social action prompted by love,
action which is no longer limited by considerations of family,
class, or nationality—and this without abrogating the multiplicity given in experience. It is an essential characteristic
of the Kingdom of God that, as the final end which is being
realised in the world and as the supreme good of created
spirits, it transcends the world, just as God Himself is supramundane. The idea of the Kingdom of God, therefore, gives
a supramundane character to humanity as bound to Him, *i.e.*
it both transcends and completes all the natural and particular
motives which unite men together. Consequently, the unity
of the human race thus reached is so far akin to the unity of
the Divine Will that in it may be seen the object of the
Divine love. But the community, which is called on to form
itself by union into the Kingdom of God, and whose activity
consists in carrying out this assigned task, depends entirely
for its origin on the fact that the Son of God is its Lord, to
Whom it renders obedience. The community, as the object to
which God's love extends, cannot even be conceived apart from
the presupposition that it is governed continually by its
Founder as its Lord, and that its members go through the
experience of being transformed into that peculiar character of
which their Lord is the original, and which, through Him, is
communicated to them (2 Cor. iii. 18 ; Rom. viii. 29). The
community of Christ, therefore, is the correlative of the love of
God, only because the love in which God embraces His Son
and assures to Him His unique position (Mark i. 11, ix. 7 ;
John xv. 9, xvii. 24 ; Col. i. 13 ; Eph. i. 6), comes through Him
to act upon those likewise who belong to Him as His disciples or
His community (vol. ii. p. 97). Every aspect of this relationship to Christ, however, is comprised under the principle, that
the Son of God is acknowledged as the Lord of His community, and under this condition transfers to it His own
relation to God. The perfect name of God, by which He
reveals Himself to this community, owes its interpretation,
accordingly, to these progressive manifestations of His love.

God is love, inasmuch as He reveals Himself through His Son
to the community, which He has founded, in order to form it
into the Kingdom of God, so that in designing for men this
supramundane destiny He realises His own glory, or the
fulfilment of His personal end.   Herein is the love of God
perfected, that we love our brethren in the Kingdom of God
(1 John iv. 12).   But as, from our point of view, this consummation always appears as one yet to be attained, our
progress towards it is guided by our perception of the truth
that for us the love of God, in His relation to His Son our
Lord, is an assured fact.   Lastly, it becomes clear in this
connection that the destination of man for the Kingdom of
God, in the form of the community of God's Son, is to be
included in the Christian conception of man, and not to be
distinguished from it as something lying above and beyond it.

    If, now, the creation and government of the world are
accordingly to be conceived as the means whereby created
spiritual beings—men—are formed into the Kingdom of God
in the community of Christ, then the view of the world given
in Christianity is the key to solve the problem of the world in
general.   The fact that this religion, in its origin, wears a
particular historical guise, is no hindrance to its being destined
to become the universal faith of humanity.   The conception
of God, however, through which this result is reached, avoids
the difficulties in which is entangled the conception of God
held by the older school of theologians (§ 32), and rises above
the dilemma in which the orthodox and the Scotist theories
circle aimlessly round one another.   When God is conceived
as love, through the relation of His will to His Son and the
community of the Kingdom of God, He is not conceived as
being anything apart from and prior to His self-determination
as love.   He is either conceived as love, or simply not at all.
If anyone thinks it necessary, after the analogy of human
personality, to conceive God first as infinite Being, or as indeterminate Will, or as quiescent Character, which may advance
within itself to self-determination as love, what he conceives
under these prefatory ideas is simply not God.   For they mean

something that *becomes*.   But God is conceived as loving Will, when we regard His Will as set upon the forth-bringing of His Son and the community of the Kingdom of God ; and if we abstract from that, what we conceive is not God at all.   At the same time, the eternity of God is guaranteed by the very fact that we are compelled to think God in that self-deter- mination as love in which we actually do think Him ; for the content of our thought would not be really God, if we still posited something as prior in order to deduce from it His character as love.   Nor is the act of thought which I am describing at all difficult.   It has its analogy in the feeling of self and the judgment upon self of which we are conscious in exalted moments of moral will, and in which we discover ex- perimentally our power of self-determination towards good, and rise above all the obstacles which are present within us and without.

Lastly, these results decide the twofold question, whether God wills the good because it is the good *a priori* for Him also, or whether a thing is good merely because God wills it. Both suppositions are false.   We cannot at all conceive a will which is not definitely directed to some end.   The Scotists held that God could as easily command as forbid deceit ; the will, however, which they thus ascribe to Him is a will with- out direction.   And a will which should receive its direction from an *a priori* substantive righteousness is not the self- determination befitting God.   Now the conception of good employed in the twofold question stated above ought to be deduced exclusively from the consistent aim of the highest human fellowship, *i.e.* from the law of the Kingdom of God. But if the Kingdom is the necessary correlate of God's personal end, to which the Divine will is directed, then it is inconceivable that God could command deceit or theft, for they are contrary to the personal end of God as expressed in His Kingdom.   On the other hand, the thought of the Kingdom of God as the content of His personal end is a *datum*, it is true, for our knowledge, but not for God before He determines Himself in His own Will.   The truth is rather that it is brought forth eternally in God's self-determination as love; it holds good for God, therefore, not before, but *in* His self-determination, as expressing the direction His self-determination cannot but take in order to realise His purpose. And we simply cannot have a right conception of the good as defining the relations of the multitude of persons who compose the Kingdom of God, if we abstract from the form of the Divine Will, and from its content as love.

§ 35. The Christian idea of the Kingdom of God, which has been proved the correlate of the conception of God as love, denotes the association of mankind—an association both extensively and intensively the most comprehensive possible —through the reciprocal moral action of its members, action which transcends all merely natural and particular considerations. Now it has been shown (vol. ii. p. 295) that this, the ruling idea of Jesus, failed to maintain itself as central in the 'practical interest of the apostles, and came to possess only the limited sense of the redemptive consummation expected in the future. Cares about the formation of congregations came so much to the front, that the entire moral interest was concentrated on their internal consolidation. In order to preserve the true articulation of the Christian view of the world, it is necessary clearly to distinguish between viewing the followers of Christ, first, under the conception of the Kingdom of God, and secondly, under the conception of the *worshipping community*, or the Church. This distinction depends on the difference which exists between moral and devotional action, despite the fact that in Christianity moral action likewise can claim the value of service to God. Now every devotional act, in the technical sense of the word, is an end in itself to this extent, that it never can be at the same time a means to an act of the same kind. One may intend sacrifice and prayer to be the means of winning Divine favour and Divine gifts; but, among all the various possible devotional rites, it is neither conceivable nor justifiable to subordinate any one of them to another as a means to an end. Each devotional act, rather, just like artistic action, possesses in itself its end and its power to satisfy the human heart. On the other hand, every moral act, whatever its range, has this peculiarity, that it must be conceived at once as an end and as a means to all other possible moral acts. This is true even when the agent's original intention does not include the thought of morality as a means to itself, but the fact is brought out only subsequently that those moral goods, which are produced by action, always stimulate action afresh. Those who believe in Christ, therefore, constitute a Church in so far as they express in prayer their faith in God the Father, or present themselves to God as men who through Christ are well-pleasing to Him. The same believers in Christ constitute the Kingdom of God in so far as, forgetting distinctions of sex, rank, or nationality, they act reciprocally from love, and thus call into existence that fellowship of moral disposition and moral blessings which extends, through all possible gradations, to the limits of the human race.[1] The fellowship of Christians for the purpose of religious worship manifests itself in the sphere of sense, and therefore betrays its peculiar nature to every observer. On the other hand, the moral Kingdom of God, even while it manifests itself sensibly in action, as a whole reveals its peculiar nature to Christian faith alone. Moreover, the fellowship of Christians for worship gives rise to legal ordinances which it requires for its own sake ; but the Kingdom of God, while not injuriously affected by the fact that moral action under certain circumstances assumes the garb of legal forms, does not in the least depend on them for its continued existence.

The importance of this distinction, for theology as well as for practical life, will appear if we remember what confusion and obscurity have gathered round this point. The early Church, it is true, was saved from confounding the two conceptions by the fact that, following the example of the apostles, it regarded the Kingdom of God as denoting in general the

---

[1] To both may be applied Schleiermacher's distinction between action that is symbolic (representative), and action that is organising (disseminative).

object of the Christian hope, but the Church as a present institution, representing the task to be accomplished during the period of earthly life. Instead of this view, which is incomplete and yet not positively incorrect, Augustine introduced into the Western Church the fatally erroneous opinion, that the Kingdom of God, which stretches down the whole of human history parallel with the kingdom of sin, exists at present in the form of the Catholic Church, and that Christ's reign of a thousand years, which occupies the last epoch of the world's history, does not still lie in the future, but has begun with the founding of the Church. In the Kingdom of God, he teaches, true righteousness is realised; the State, on the other hand, as the kingdom of this world, has sin for its principle, and can be brought into harmony with the Divine order only by subordinating itself to the government of the Church. This theory has determined the policy of the Papacy in opposition to the State up to the present moment. History, however, has brought to light the fact that in this "Kingdom of God," governed by His earthly vice-gerent, righteousness consists in the most selfish quarrelsomeness, and in the employment of all means, whether of violence or of falsehood, which may be found of use for this purpose.

Nothing shows so clearly that the Reformers have broken with this theory, in which culminates Augustine's view of the world, as their recognition of the State as a directly Divine institution, and of civil justice as a positive moral good. They offer no deliberate criticism upon the above-mentioned theory, especially as Augustine's argument, as such, does not seem to have been known to them. The truth is, they wholly lose sight of the idea of the Kingdom of God so far as its eschatological sense was not forced upon them by the New Testament. But, on the other hand, they construct an idea analogous to it under the title of the "Kingdom of Christ." From this idea sprang the theoretical opposition, and the more important practical alienation, which arose between Luther and Zwingli. Luther, as a theologian, had arrived at a clear-cut antithesis between religion and the State; and so by the Kingdom of Christ he understood the inward union between believers and the Mediator, which subsists exclusively through the Word of God and faith, and is bound by no law or legal government: *regnum Christi est spirituale.* Zwingli, on the other hand, was so far influenced by the theocratic aspirations of the later Middle Ages, in line with Wiclif, Huss, and Savonarola (vol. i. p. 134), that he directly assigned to the State the function of realising the true religion by means of its laws and government. Accordingly, in conscious opposition to Luther and his followers, he defended the principle: *regnum Christi est externum.* This is the standard by which his reforming and political activity must be gauged; this also explains the tragic close of his life. The principle he asserted, however, has not remained determinative for the ecclesiastical constitution which owes its origin to him, nor for that which Calvin founded, but was brought into operation again only by the Puritans, and that under completely altered circumstances. Calvin, rather, holds to a theory in evident agreement with Luther's. He regards the Kingdom of Christ as the inward spiritual union of believers with Christ, which means that Christ, through His Spirit, guarantees to them the certainty of eternal life, leads them to victory over all obstacles hostile to salvation, and ministers support to them for the patient endurance of all their cares and sufferings. But as Luther's idea of the spiritual Kingdom of Christ did not suggest any legal constitution for the Church, and the State had to be called in to assume this latter responsibility, Melanchthon, Luther, and Calvin come back to this, that they admit the Zwinglian principle that the State has a religious function, and concede its validity as a practical measure, alongside of the theoretical distinction between the State on the one hand and religion and the Church on the other. This comes out in the theory put forward first of all by Melanchthon, that the State is called upon to protect both tables of the Divine law, and therefore has not only to prevent the false worship of God, but also to provide for the true. The only way in which it was possible to avoid the plain inconsistency between these two positions was by holding that the legal constitution of the Church, which it receives from the State, forms no part of the conception of the Kingdom of Christ, and that the only organs of Christ's Kingdom are the religious factors, the preaching of the Gospel and the administration of the sacraments. It was only from the point of view which affirms that discipline *maxima ex parte a potestate clavium et spirituali iurisdictione pendet*, that Calvin ventured to vindicate that also as an essential note of the Church; while he omitted to consider theoretically the important practical influence exercised upon discipline by the civil power.[1]

Luther's conception of the Kingdom of Christ also coincides with the general Reformation conception of the Church as the fellowship of believers, in so far as the latter conception is taken in a purely religious sense, and defined exclusively with reference to the creative action of God upon believers, and not as relating to their corresponding activity, namely, the worship of God. But this conception of the Kingdom of Christ is very far indeed from expressing the fellowship of moral action prompted by love. This, the content of the original idea of the Kingdom of God, is simply not apprehended at all in this form by the Reformers and their orthodox successors, with the single exception of Luther's *Catechism* and the *Apology of the Augsburg Confession* (p. 11). This indicates an essential defect in the Reformers' compass of thought and in the scholastic theology which is counted loyal to the Church, when we compare these with the authority of Christ Himself. Besides, there is a tenet, peculiar to Melanchthon, which might end in assigning to the Church or the Kingdom of Christ such a significance as

---

[1] Cf. Köstlin, *Luther's Theologie*, ii. p. 380; Melanchthon, *Loci theol. C. R.* xxi. pp. 519, 920; my lecture on "Ulrich Zwingli" (*Jahrb. für deutsche Theol.* xvii. pp. 109–137); *Zwinglii Opera*, viii. pp. 174–184 (Letter to Ambrosius Blarer); *C. R.* iii. pp. 240–258 (*de iure reformandi*); Schenkel, *On the original relation of the Church to the State within the bounds of German Protestantism* (*Stud. u. Krit.* 1850, pts. 1, 2); Calvini *Inst. chr. rel.* ii. 15. 4, 5; iv. 12. 1; 20. 1–3, 9; Weingarten, *The Churches of the English Revolution*, pp. 35 f., 128 ff.; *Conf. Scoticana* (1560), cap. 24, in Niemeyer's *Coll. Conff.* p. 355.

to smuggle in Roman Catholic error regarding the legal authority of the Church in matters of faith. Melanchthon, that is to say, in his conception of the Kingdom of Christ, expressly accepts preaching as a means. Now preaching is a legal institution of the Church, incongruous therefore with the spiritual and inward nature of the union of the believers with Christ expressed in the notion of His Kingdom. But to assert this connection between preaching and the Church, as is further done by Gerhard and Quenstedt, and also by Reformed divines, is to maintain in principle the same idea as is implied in the claim made by the Catholic Church to be the fellowship of godly righteousness and blessedness, on the ground that she is constituted a unity through the hierarchy as a legal institution. If, following the Reformers, we regard the Kingdom of Christ or the Church, understood in a purely religious way, as the fellowship of believers brought into existence by God through the preaching of His Word, and essentially characterised by that fact, then, in harmony with Melanchthon's Smalcald Confessional tract, *de potestate et iurisdictione episcoporum* (§ 68), we conceive the community of believers as the subject by which the Divine Word is proclaimed, without thinking of any special office for the discharge of this task. But when we think of this special office as a means essential to the Church, this is to conceive the Church as a society of a legal character. And so Melanchthon, in connecting the office of preaching as he did with the Kingdom of Christ, committed an indiscretion erroneous in theory, and in practice calculated to have serious consequences. A legally constituted Church, be it Catholic or Lutheran, is not the Kingdom of God or the Kingdom of Christ, for the simple reason that the Church is not the Kingdom of God. Activity of the most important kind for the service of the Church may be of no value whatever for the Kingdom of God. Nor is devotion to the Church a virtue which could in any way compensate for the absence of conscientiousness, justice, truthfulness, uprightness, tolerance. While we must at present put up with a great deal which contradicts this principle, I have always counted what Christ says in Matt. vii. 21–23 as part of the consolations of the Gospel.

According to the canons of the New Testament, then, we find that the self-same subject, namely, the community drawn together by Christ, constitutes the Church in so far as its members unite in the same religious worship, and, further, create for this purpose a legal constitution; while, on the other hand, it constitutes the Kingdom of God in so far as the members of the community give themselves to the interchange of action prompted by love. These two modes of activity, however, are not unrelated to one another. They rather condition one another reciprocally. For Christians must get to know one another as such in the exercises of Divine worship, if they are to make sure of occasions to combine together in mutual action from love. On the other hand, the whole range of this loving activity serves to support the maintenance and extension of fellowship in Divine worship. For there is nothing from which the latter suffers more than from slackness in discharging the tasks of the Kingdom of God, even though that Kingdom consists in righteousness and peace and joy in the Holy Ghost (Rom. xiv. 17, 18).

§ 36. The Kingdom of God, then, is the correlate of God's love in so far as it is the association of men for reciprocal and common action from the motive of love— an association which is determined, no longer by the natural conditions of affinity in the narrower sense, but by the unity of man's spiritual constitution. So far as this association comes to be a reality through the mediation of Christ in His community, it is always due to the operation of God, and only subject to this condition can it be completely conceived. And this does not mean merely that the individuals combined in the Kingdom of God are subject to Divine action as creatures and members of the natural world; it means, besides, that, as possessed of moral freedom and in accordance with their spiritual constitution and destiny, they stand in the line of that purpose which, from our interpretation of love, we have found to be the content of God's personal end. Accordingly, the instances of human action from love which are comprehended under the Kingdom of God constitute, as the correlate of God's personal end and as His specific operations, the perfect revelation of the truth that God is love. What is here stated by way of deduction is anticipated by John, when he says that if we love one another, God dwelleth in us, and His love is perfected in us (1 John ii. 5, iv. 22 ; cf. vol. ii. p. 376). The creation of this fellowship of love among men, accordingly, is not merely the end of the world, but at the same time the completed revelation of God Himself, beyond which none other and none higher can be conceived. This principle supplies a basis for that religious and theological way of looking at the world, which sets itself in opposition to those Areopagitic conclusions whose baneful after-effects are present in all forms of orthodoxy. Instead of holding with Thomas Aquinas that God's personal end has no relation to the end of the world, we find not only that God's personal end and the end of the world are one, but also that the knowledge of the end of the world attainable by us coincides with the Christian idea of the nature and the completed revelation of God.

On the basis of these results we may approach certain difficulties which spring, partly from a closer examination of the theory we have arrived at, partly from a comparison of it with our historical experience. The first question is, how *dependence* on God, as the form of human action from love, is compatible with *freedom ;* for not only is it necessary to conceive such action as free, but freedom is attested by the immediate feeling of self (§ 6). I should not venture to touch upon this classical question of theology, were it not that by pursuing the path we have adopted it is possible so to limit it as to facilitate its solution. The controversy between Pelagius and Augustine has become the regular model for theological discussion of the problem, but on these lines, certainly, no solution of it is to be looked for. For the dilemma, between freedom of choice (*Wahlfreiheit*) and the Divinely-imposed necessitation by original sin and electing grace, involves merely a small section of the problem in its philosophical form; and the shifting opinions, which appear in ecclesiastical theology, regarding the relation between grace and freedom, have never been determined by the principles which suggest themselves most readily in theology. For within Christianity experience teaches that it is just in and through a special kind of dependence on God that we possess freedom to do good. Theology, therefore, is only concerned with the question whether the law of freedom cannot be found by an analysis of this special experience; whereas Pelagius, by his general conception of freedom of choice, excluded *a priori* every law of the kind, and Augustine merely maintained as against freedom a law of sin and predestination. Between these two positions there is no medium, and a theology shut up to this dilemma is condemned to help itself out by a circumvention of the difficulty, which certainly takes a different form with Thomists, Scotists, Lutherans, and Calvinists, but is always equally unsatisfactory.

If freedom signifies that in which personality is unlike nature, although in virtue of its bodily organisation personality is interwoven with nature and receives from it impulses of a coercive kind, yet freedom is not the indeterminate in general, or that which is incapable of determination. Freedom, rather, is something quite as determinate as the system of nature, for only so can it be conceived as decidedly distinct from or opposed to the latter. Freedom, to begin with, is the quality of self-determination by universal ideals. Conscious self-determination in general would not, by itself, be an adequate expression for freedom : for even the coercive operation of particular impulses assumes in the soul the form of conscious self-determination. Nothing short of self-determination by universal ideals constitutes that capacity of the spirit which sets a limit to the propensities and their compulsion, and thus makes itself known as a force opposed

to them.   If now the spirit determines itself uninterruptedly
by a single end, then, as a power ruling over its individual
impulses, it is free.   For freedom from compulsion—the
negative sense of the conception—is actually realised only
when, in a positive sense, power is attained over such
influences as can in themselves, or under certain conditions,
exercise a compulsion which has its basis in nature.   Freedom, as the power of self-determination supreme over our
impulses, is not attained, however, when the end which
dominates our self-determination is bad, or when it consists
in the satisfaction of a single impulse.   For in that case
we have only a partial power over our impulses, while the
pursuit of a bad end implies a defect of freedom as against
the single dominant impulse.   Even though the general
ends of our family, or class, or nationality form our personal
end, self-determination exclusively by regard for family feeling, the interest of a class, or patriotism, may be bad if it
sets itself in opposition to common ends that are higher still.
In such cases what binds the will is certainly not a form of
personal selfishness; but yet the limitation of our moral
interest to these ends of merely relative universality implies
a refined or idealised selfishness, and therefore a defect of
freedom as against the impulse arising from natural partiality
for one's relatives, for those who follow the same occupation,
or for public law and the State.   Freedom, therefore, consists
in self-determination by that end which, by possessing the
most universal content, makes it possible to subordinate to it
all individual impulses and all moral aims which may be
particular in their range.   In other words, freedom is permanent self-determination by the good end, the standard of
which is to be found in the law of universal love for man, or,
in Christian terminology, permanent self-determination by
the Kingdom of God as final end.   The Kingdom of God,
however, is at the same time the end of the world in general;
accordingly, action which is guided by its aims proves itself
free in the positive sense likewise, in so far as it is controlled
by the consciousness that all interaction between surrounding

nature and one's own natural character is to be estimated solely as a means subservient to the agent. If, now, this action within the Kingdom of God be regarded in its completeness, viewed, *i.e.*, according to its religious idea, then the man who perceives himself to be free in the relations alluded to, must at the same time conceive himself as dependent on God throughout the whole range of his activity. For the Kingdom of God, in which we come to know freedom experimentally, being as it is the highest universal end by which our self-determination can be guided, is included as the object of Divine love in God's personal end; in other words, it is dependent upon God as a *whole*, and therefore also in all the particular relations which go to make up the whole. Thus there is no inner contradiction in this theory. And if, nevertheless, human knowledge in this field can conceive freedom of action and dependence on God only as alternatives, this is so because men cannot, like God, survey simultaneously the system of the whole in all its parts and connections. It is their part, therefore, to aim in their individual action at the final end of the whole, and thus become conscious of their freedom; and, while doing so, they may hope to come to possess the sense that, as members of the whole, they are dependent on God, and that in particular, as active members of the Kingdom of God, they form part of God's highest revelation of Himself.

Hence arises a new reason why we should criticise both the Lutheran-Calvinistic and the Socinian theories of the moral order. Both are out of harmony with Christianity exactly in so far as they are not guided by the Kingdom of God as a positive end which, as common both to God and man, follows from the conception of Divine love. It is for this reason that both schools have failed to reconcile, at any single point, moral freedom and dependence upon God. In various forms they give fixity to the customary experience that freedom and dependence are mutually exclusive. The Socinians begin with the position that men are created by God like slaves without rights, and therefore, as mere chattels, are dependent on His pleasure.   It is added that He has given them a claim upon His equity (*Billigkeit*), and the result is a dispensation in which God and men co-operate, alternately free and dependent on each other, just as in a private relationship one who has more power compounds with those who have less.   The theory of the Lutherans and Calvinists begins with the position that men, created by God with an innate right to blessedness, have a range of action not embraced in any knowable Divine end, but only limited by the condition of good works imposed by God.   True, one might say that this domain of human life, directed as it is to the goal of blessedness, is still subservient to the glory of God, and therefore to His personal end.   But a consideration such as that is in its nature ineffectual; for this reason, that the punishment of Adam's sin by the condemnation of his race, or at least the eternal rejection of the greater part of mankind, is declared to be as appropriate a means to God's glory as the salvation of mankind, or of the eternally elect.   In fact, we find here no concrete idea of the Divine end, in and through which a specific relationship between God and man is essentially involved, and a basis given for some necessary form of Revelation.   And so, after man's relative freedom and relative dependence on God had been affirmed as the original form of the world-order, the latter, in consequence of the treatment awarded to Adam's sin, veers round into an assumption of human dependence on Divine arrangements, so complete that neither in the status of sin nor in the status of grace is freedom conceded, or, as in Lutheranism, conceded only by an inconsistency.   However irrational these positions turn out in particular respects, yet the starting-points of both theories are rationalistic, in the same way as the opposed theories of Pelagius and Augustine are dominated by the common experience that freedom and dependence are mutually exclusive.   But it is not for Christian theology to start from such commonplaces of superficial experience ; otherwise it cannot interpret those special experiences, belonging to the Christian life, in which moral freedom and dependence on God coincide.   But if we start, as we must, from the analysis of freedom as subservient to the final end of the Kingdom of God, then we are not only forced to regard this use of freedom as being *eo ipso* entire dependence on God, but there results this further rule, that we must employ these two ways of looking at things alternately, because we cannot, like God, include in one view the whole of the Kingdom of God and our incorporation in it.   Simultaneously, however, this practical principle emerges, that, provided we continually guide our action, in all its special relations, by the highest and universal end, we thereby take our place in the system of the Kingdom of God, the object of Divine love.

§ 37. A peculiar difficulty arises, however, when we institute a comparison between this principle and the history of the human race.   What we are in search of is a moral order for mankind in general; the order represented by the Kingdom of God, however, holds good merely for the Christian portion of mankind.   Accordingly, the general truth that God is love seems to be imperilled if the correlate of the Divine love, the Kingdom of God and its law, is realised merely in a particular, temporally and spatially limited, domain of human history, and has not governed the development of humanity from the beginning.   The theological schools, whose theories we have rejected, deserve to be pardoned, at least for this reason if for no other, that they have undertaken to exhibit a moral order which shall embrace all mankind as related to the one God.   Without this, we are apt to repeat Marcion's error and make the God Who is love, and has created His Kingdom through Christ, distinct from the God Who made the world, and rules over natural humanity, or at least over the Jewish people.

Now it is worthy of remark that Augustine escapes from this dilemma by assuming that the Kingdom of God, of which Christianity is the completion, has always existed ever since there were men, that it constituted the dispensation under which our first parents lived before the Fall, that after the Fall it resumed its course with Abel and then again with Seth, and that it has had a connected, though oftentimes a hidden, existence during the whole course of human history. Augustine vindicates this conception by pointing to the fact that righteous Israelites, in believing the promises of their religion, really exercised faith in Christ; and at the same time he infers, from the example of Job the Idumean, that even those belonging to other peoples could live according to God, could please God, and belong to His Kingdom (*De civitate dei*, xviii. 47). Now we cannot, it is true, follow him in this view of history; it does not solve the difficulty as to how the universal significance of the Kingdom of God for the relationship between the human race and God is to be reconciled with its temporal limitations, as commencing with Jesus. And this difficulty Augustine himself felt still more deeply; for he puts to himself the question how God can be thought as Lord under all conditions, if He did not always have creatures to serve Him. This question he answers by referring to the world of angels, which existed eternally, even though created in time and not equally eternal with God (xii. 15). But just in this theory we find a precise expression of the difference between time and eternity, which in part seems to admit merely of a casual relationship between God and creation, and in part throws upon God the semblance of temporal change. How to escape this difficulty is the peculiar problem which arises out of the course, as hitherto followed, of our investigation into the relation which exists between the conception of God as love and the Kingdom of God which has been called into life by Christ. Augustine thinks that the difficulty described above is due to an imprudent use of the analogy of human life. In this he is right; but the brilliant antitheses in which he describes the conditions of the Divine volition and action have no meaning save the negative one, that these conditions lie beyond our powers of thought.[1]

If any further knowledge whatever on this point is possible, it can be attained only by distinguishing accurately those elements in the idea of the *eternity of God* which are

[1] *De civ. dei*, xii. 17 : "Non aliter deus afficitur cum vacat, aliter cum operatur. . . . Novit quiescens agere et agens quiescere."

treated by Augustine himself.   For him, the eternity of God implies, first, the inward continuity and identity of God's purpose ; secondly, existence without beginning or end.   These two ideas are heterogeneous, and have no necessary relation to one another.   If by eternity we understand the unchang-ing continuity and identity of the Divine will in relation to its goal, then we cannot place existence without beginning or end on a par with the former element, for it does not necessarily ex-clude a change of will.   Besides, this formula, for one thing, is not a positive conception ; for another, it must in a certain sense be predicated of the world, just as we are accustomed to apply it to God (p. 234).   For in every act of knowledge we presuppose that the world and its orderly system always exist, for if we were to suppose the world non-existent, our knowledge would cease.   And this holds true not merely of our knowledge of parts of the world, but also of our know-ledge of God.   For there, too, we cannot abstract from the world.   If, therefore, we are unable to place ourselves in thought before the beginning or after the end of the world, without being forced to think ourselves away and cease to think, we are shut up either to conceiving the world as without beginning or end, or to holding that it always exists. But such a conclusion has only the negative value of saying that we cannot represent to ourselves the characteristics which would actually belong to the beginning of the world, and that we cannot abstract from its existence.   Now, the existence of God without beginning or end likewise signifies that, in comparing the world with God and explaining it as arising from His will, we cannot think God as non-existent. But just as the conception of endless existence, when applied to the world, merely expresses the limits of our faculties, and accordingly does not exclude the possibility that on other grounds the world has a beginning, so one might discover grounds showing that God, Who always exists, nevertheless has a beginning in Himself.   This, at least, is what the theosophy of the school of Böhme comes to.   No guarantee, therefore, which would ensure the essential distinction between

God and the world is to be got by following this line of thought. Besides, if we express that distinction by applying the predicate " eternal " to God, then it is inadmissible to speak of the eternity of the world. For the world, besides existing, is always liable to change, and to say that the world always exists implies merely that we cannot conceive its beginning or its end. If, on the other hand, the idea of the eternity of God is taken as referring to the continual and immutable aim with which His will is directed towards His purpose, and towards the Kingdom of God as within that purpose, then the positive meaning of this conception of eternity is given when we compare it with the changing action of God in time, from which we can no more abstract in theology than in religion. If we tried to escape from this idea, we should have to deny the reality of all individual existence. On the other hand, it is impossible to explain the world successfully either from the conception of a universal substance, or from that of an indeterminate will. Any attempt at such explanation can succeed only if we conceive the Will of God, the presupposed ground of the whole, as set in a certain direction. God's Will, permanent and certain of itself, directed towards the realisation of the Kingdom of God as the ethical and supramundane unity of a multitude of souls, forms, for the sake of this end, the ground of everything, whether multiplex or individual, which serves as a means to its accomplishment. We must therefore conclude that God creates in time the multiplicity of things, which, as superior or inferior to each other, become causes and effects.

But now, is it a defect for God that the Kingdom of God is realised only at an enormous distance of time, not only from the beginning of the human race, but still further from the beginning of creation ? For it was under this impression that Augustine felt himself compelled not merely to date the beginning of the Kingdom of God from the creation of the first man, but to carry back its existence to the original creation of the angels—both to the detriment of the religious value to be put upon the claims which Christ makes for His unique work.   But the goal of human history and of creation, though, measured from the beginning of both, it is late in being reached, does not therefore stand in a more remote relation to the permanently identical will of God than do the acts by which His diverse creations are called into existence.   On the contrary, the end, embraced as it is in the Divine self-end, stands nearer to His eternal will than the creatures, which are merely means to its realisation.   Moreover, in every act of creation and of government performed by Him as a means to this end, God, as omnipotent will, is equally certain, not only of His end in an ideal sense, but also of its being realised by every means employed, however diversified and remote.   This may be seen from the fact that we are conscious of the very opposite, as a defect arising from our creaturely position.   When we are carrying out a plan piece by piece, we may have a sure and firm grasp of it in thought ; and though it should be that each successive link in the chain is not yet thought out in advance with perfect clearness, even this may leave us still unconscious of our imperfection.   But when we remember our manifold dependence on nature and society, or the weakness of our will, we see that the attainment of a preliminary aim by no means implies that thereby we enjoy already the realisation of the whole enterprise.   On the contrary, partial satisfaction makes us, likewise, always the victims of unrest and fear for the completion of the intended whole.   On the other hand, through the very arrangement of our conduct in accordance with a plan of life, we gain experimental knowledge of the fact that our spirit is destined for eternity : and just as certainly we come to know the eternity of God from this, that through the continuity of His will as directed to the end of the Kingdom of God, there is cancelled for Him the significance of time, in which, to serve that end, He calls the individual into existence or causes it to appear— in other words, that the temporal interval between His preparatory creations and the realisation of the goal of revelation, means nothing for Him.   The realisation of each subordinate means by the Divine will is reflected in God's self-feeling or blessedness as the realisation of the whole. For this reason, too, there lies no inconsistency for our knowledge in the fact that the Kingdom of God is contained in the eternal purpose of God as the correlate of His loving Will, while our historical experience tells us that it is realised only at the close of the first era of the world's existence. The religious reflection— arising out of the Christian view of the world—which affirms that God " has chosen us," the Christian community of the Kingdom of God, " in Jesus Christ our Lord before the founda- tion of the world " (Eph. i. 4 ; cf. 1 Pet. i. 20), no doubt merely asserts the truth that the final end of the world— which is contained within the purpose of the supramundane God as its essential object—is for God assured of fulfilment, quite apart from the creation of the whole system of things which stands to that end in the relation of means. At the same time the statement just cited from the New Testament, by also employing the temporal idea " before the foundation of the world," indicates the interval of time which lies between the Divine decree and its accomplishment. Possibly this leaves the impression that the duration of the world forms an obstacle to the accomplishment of the Divine decree, and we seem to be asked to do what is impracticable, viz. to call up an idea of time existing before time, while as a matter of fact we never can think the world as non-existent. But all that the positive conception of the Divine eternity contains is the logical superordination of the election of the community over the creation of the world. Accordingly, the idea of the community's eternal election denotes only the value which belongs to the community of the Kingdom of God, as the Divine final end, in contrast with the world, which is, in comparison, merely a means. We therefore reject the misuse which is made of this idea, as though the world formed an obstacle even for God, as so often it does for us ; for we recognise that at every step of creation God not only remains sure and certain of His plan, but enjoys the consciousness of the realisation of the intended whole as such.

For though the idea of time must so far hold good for

God also that He distinguishes the individual thing as such
from its causes, its effects, and all similar existences (p. 122),
yet we do not assert that our idea of time should, in all its
aspects, be imputed to the Divine knowledge.   For our idea
of time is conditioned by the fact that we find ourselves
occupying a place in the series of causes and effects which
come and go in time.[1]   So that, although the form of
temporal succession is overcome and abrogated by our
cognition in the unification of impressions, and by our will in
the imposition of a plan upon a multitude of objects (p. 235),
yet the self-consciousness of each individual as a whole
remains chained to the form of time.   This is manifest from
the fact that we regard ourselves and surrounding things as
real only in the present, while that which has been and that
which will yet be are regarded as non-existent.   No doubt
reflection rises superior to this impression by recollecting
that very much that has been, and no longer exists in exactly
the same form, still survives as a cause in its recognisable
effects.   Still, we do not venture to apply a similar mode of
looking at things to the future, in which things now present
will continue to exist as causes even though their present form
is altered.   Thus it is only in our presentiment of the future,
and when reviewing the past in a very fragmentary way, that
we are able transiently to escape from the subjection of our
self-consciousness to time, and to raise ourselves above those
limitations of our knowledge which arise from the fact that,
as individuals, we are only parts of the system of the world.
But the very circumstance that, at least in this degree, we
can understand the system of things, compels us to suppose
that a similar abrogation of the idea of time is the rule for
the Spirit to Whom, as the Creator of the system of
individual things, that system is perfectly transparent.   So
far as the world is subject in all its individual facts to a
process of becoming, it can be represented by God only under
the form of time ; and so far also the distinction of past and
future necessarily holds good for God's knowledge of things.

[1] Cf. Lotze, *Microcosmus*, iii. 599 ff.

But so far as individual things are, through God, parts of the world's system and organically related to its purpose, their reality for God consists precisely in their being members of the whole, for through His prevision of individual things and His insight into them as persistent causes, He is conscious of the realisation of the whole. On the other hand, if the future formed a limit to the knowledge and self-feeling of God, they would not attain satisfaction and equipoise until the end of the ages. On this presupposition, we should be forbidden even to believe that satisfaction with the world, previously lacking, had arrived for God with the historical commencement of the Kingdom of God; for then God would be dependent on His Kingdom for the completion of the possible satisfaction still awaiting Him throughout all the future. But if this is an absurd supposition, then no limit of time can be affirmed to exist in the life of God, after which He should be more certain of His goal than before. Rather must we abide by the statement that God not only is certain of His self-end and His world-plan at every point in its realisation, but that, through the congruence of His knowledge, which penetrates the whole, with His will, which moves the whole, He is continuously conscious of the realisation of the whole at every single point.

§ 38. But what inferences, now, does the conception of God as love allow us to draw for the affirmation of a moral order? This conception of God has as its correlative the association of mankind in the Kingdom of God, while the latter, so far as our experience goes, forms a special section of universal human history, more limited in space and in time than that history as a whole. Consequently, from this idea of God we can directly derive such a conception of the relations which obtain between human life and the world as holds good for those who are members of the Kingdom of God. Within this special sphere the supreme principle of the Divine love is to be applied on the analogy of the paternal education of children. Thence it follows that all evils which fall upon members of the Kingdom of God have, as Divinely decreed, the significance of educative punishments, and therefore of relative benefits; while, on the other hand, we have the assurance that all things work together for good to them that love God (Rom. viii. 24). It cannot be doubted, however, that to this there contributes the influence of the reconciliation likewise proclaimed in Christianity. But we are not concerned just now to follow out this special dispensation of human life, for we are interested in the doctrine of God only in so far as it forms a general presupposition which makes reconciliation possible. The question just now is, whether the knowledge we have, that the Kingdom of God as grounded in the Divine love is the final end of the world, throws any light on the character of the existence which the nations led up to the entrance of Christianity into history, and which even Christian nations lead, so far as we can abstract from their belonging to the Kingdom of God. For if the moral association of nations in the Kingdom is the end which God is pursuing in the world, then the inference is unavoidable, that the previous history of the nations must have stood in some teleological relation to that higher stage of development, and in some positive degree prepared the way for its advent, and that a similar order of things must obtain also in every Christian nation as a pre-condition of its Christianity. Observation, therefore, would have to verify the indications of the connection thus suggested, by demonstrating with some measure of certainty that *the human race is educatively prepared for the Kingdom of God.* When that was done, perhaps principles might thence be drawn explaining God's dealings with individual men.

The writers of the New Testament do not expend reflection upon this problem. The history of the Jewish people alone presented them with the spectacle of a government by God so extraordinary that it could be regarded as a positive preparation for the Christian Kingdom of God. Only two statements of Paul in the Acts of the Apostles (xiv. 15–17, xvii. 25–30) deal directly with the rest of the nations. They indicate a very remote relationship between the general history of the nations and the Divine government. God is represented as having worked upon the Gentiles only through the blessings of nature and through the temporal and spatial delimitation of their territories, in order to move them thereby to search after Him; in the activities of their moral history He left them to themselves without interference. The standard, measured by which the condition of the nations is made out to be corrupt, is not moral goodness, which is the real question, but their defective knowledge of God, while yet very meagre opportunities had been given them of acquiring it. The authentical statements of Paul in the Epistle to the Romans express a still more unfavourable judgment, for they depict the entire life of the Gentiles as given over to sin, nay, to unnatural vices. Nay more, Paul takes so dark a view of the character of the Jewish people, that he represents the law as given merely to enhance sin, not to afford moral guidance. But his judgment is imperfect; it is, especially when tested by the contents of the Mosaic law, historically incorrect, and it has never been seriously adhered to by theology. For what we have to concern ourselves with at this point is not Paul's formulation of the contents of the Christian religion, but his reflections upon history in its contrast to Christianity, which had just embarked upon its course. These would have taken a different form if the apostle could have surveyed the history of the Christian Church as we can. But, finally, these positions affirmed by Paul are not decisive in the question at present before us — how the general history of the nations is related to the final end of the Kingdom of God — for this reason, that Paul, viewing mankind exclusively as the subject of sin, takes Christianity merely as a dispensation of reconciliation.

If that is the point at issue, then, it is true, the universal sin which we find in pre-Christian history is only a negative presupposition of reconciliation. But the Kingdom of God, in the Christian sense, can be proved the final end of human history only if there existed even previously standards somehow analogous, which determined the worth of human life and prepared the way for the appearance of the perfect moral

20

standard.   The judgment pronounced by Paul upon universal sin is a reflection of the value he attached to the Christian reconciliation; but it is no less a reflection of the value we attach to the moral and religious content of Christianity when we speak of God's education of the human race, guiding them to the Christian ideal of morality.   For by this hypothesis the religious interpretation of the moral development of the individual which is involved in Christianity—an interpretation derived from the presupposition of Divine sonship —is further applied in a wider sense to God's leading of the nations to the supreme good.   I use the phrase—the education of the human race—in another sense, it is true, than Lessing has given it in his interpretation of the history of religion.   For one thing, Lessing has in his eye merely the narrower domain of Israelitish and Christian religion; next, he limits the idea of education to instruction through the medium of revelation; finally, his idea of this medium is such that it cannot fail to lose its applicability when Christian culture has reached the stage of maturity.   This is, no doubt, a quite consistent view to take, if the idea of education is limited to instruction given in school.   Every man who reaches a mature age grows out of school; if revelation, therefore, is defined as a kind of school-teaching, it becomes superfluous for one of independent character.   But in thus following the customary theological prejudice which looks on revelation as instruction, Lessing ignores the fact that the value which Christianity places upon human life, in virtue of the mutual relations between God as our Father and us as His children, bids us view education by God as the highest and the unsurpassable criterion.   Moreover, it is certainly a part of education that at the proper time the pupil should have disclosed to him both the aims and the conditions of personal life; but education consists still more in the timely restraint and stimulus of his volitions by the authority of the teacher.

It is in a much more comprehensive sense that Lotze [1] discusses the applicability of the phrase " the education of

[1] *Microcosmus*, iii. p. 20 ff.

humanity " to the course of history.   Under that conception
he comprises all the material of culture which is the product
of man's spiritual nature, and is handed down from generation
to generation.   But he expresses a doubt as to whether what
these conditions produce is the education of mankind as a
whole.   It is always the individual, he contends, whom we
must conceive as the subject of education ; humanity, whose
spiritual acquisitions we see augmenting with time, is divisible
into a sum of individuals ; but of that sum those who come
earlier know nothing of the progress achieved by their successors ; while the latter, it may be, receive the acquisitions of
their predecessors in the form of prejudices, and thus are put in
the possession of the very opposite of what is really imparted
by education, and makes it valuable to the individual.   Besides, progress in assimilating the materials of culture and
advance in their formal elaboration are never observable save
in the minority of men, while crudity and dulness remain
the lot of the great mass in every generation.   Finally, even
though we take no account of the many interruptions and
retrogressions exhibited by the history of culture, and allow
the minority of really educated persons to count as humanity,
yet even these are incapable of surveying the course of the
education of the whole race with such certainty of vision as
gives the individual assurance of the success of his own education.   For that would demand an amount of knowledge
such as is possible, indeed, for scholars, but is not, at every
moment, at the command of those who in a particular age may
rank as men of culture and education.   There is an obvious
objection that, if we suppose ourselves to have unravelled
the meaning of history by styling it the education of the
human race, the above observations might rather produce an
impression of the unconnectedness of the individual's existence
with the life of humanity, and of the vanity of all things.   It
is true, he admits, that the sentiment of fidelity in work is
directly opposed to this despair of comprehending the course
of human vicissitude, and that it is closely accompanied by an
estimate of the worth of individual activity for the whole,

which is the basis of faith in the success of such activity in the present and the future. But that very fact makes it certain that the idea of "the education of humanity" does not guarantee our insight into the laws of historical life as a whole.

This self-feeling, which belongs to patient and public-spirited moral work, and which repudiates the idea of the vanity of all things, testifies to the validity of the fundamental truth that the fellowship which arises out of these individual contributions is the supreme good, the final end of the world. Moreover, the hope we base thereon, that the effect of one's personal work for the whole will not be lost even in the future, always springs from a religious view of the whole as a purposive order. The attitude, therefore, which forms our substitute for insight into the course of history is, stated plainly, that of practical activity in the Kingdom of God. But in that case the question recurs whether the idea of an "education of humanity," by being limited in another way, might not be found suitable for interpreting the historical preparation for the stage we have reached in our estimate of self and the direction of our will.

We must not, it is true, expect to be able to embrace every nation in the framework of a theory fitted to solve the problem before us. We can pass no judgment whatever on nations which have played no part in history. Since the question concerns the meaning of the history of the world, none but the nations which have participated in that history can be taken into account. But even when considering these, we do not find that though one or other of them may have taken a step in the direction of the goal, it must therefore of necessity have reached the goal of its development, and maintained itself at the height of that attainment. Finally, in the answer we seek, we shall not consider it an objection to the idea of "the education of humanity" that the acquisitions of the preparatory generation should actually assume, for the generation which follows, the form of prejudices; though in the case of the education of the individual that

form might as easily be taken to imply a hindrance as a help.
What I mean is that the idea of the Kingdom of God, as the
moral fellowship of men proper to their nature, had its way to
influence prepared by the fact that it was preceded by the moral
fellowship of the *Family*, national fellowship in the *State*, and,
lastly, the combination of several nations in the *World-empire*.
The Christian conception of the Kingdom of God in part
stands in the closest analogy with all these graduated forms,
and in part it is genetically derived from them. So that it
could not be understood had these forms not previously
entered into human experience, and their peculiar value been
recognised. In every case the family is the original form of
human fellowship; but if the healthy conditions of independent
moral conduct are to be realised, it requires to be supplemented by the civil fellowship of the State.[1] For nothing
but intercourse with those whom one gets to know, not as
members of the same family, but rather as strangers, affords
that fulness of reciprocal social relationships by which our
respect for others and for our own rights can be tested. The
tendency towards equality of rights regularly manifests itself
even in the relation between brothers and sisters; but it
depends very much upon the form assumed by the father's
power over the children, whether it does not rather reduce
them under itself in an equality destitute of all rights whatsoever. In the history of the world, at any rate, the task of
supplementing family existence by the civil order of the
State has not been of such easy accomplishment as seems
necessary to us. Nomadic tribes exist only in an extended
form of the family, without distinct ideas of law being
developed, or fixed legal ordinances being extorted from the
caprice of the chief of the tribe. Nomads, therefore, either
remain outside history, or come into prominence only as
destroyers of higher culture, while they maintain their existence
in the form of the family only at the price of the corruption
of marriage, polygamy. In order to rise above this level at all,
and in any degree become a State, a nation must be numerous

[1] Lotze, *Microcosmus*, iii. p. 380 ff.

enough, and must settle down in a comparatively narrow territory. The importance for a purely nomadic people of this advance cannot be more clearly indicated than by the fact that the tribal legends of Israel make the acquisition of a fixed abode the proximate aim of the Divine revelation to Abraham. This people is distinguished from their Oriental neighbours by the energetic expression given in their law to the consciousness of right; and the theocratic principle confines even the rights of the monarchy over the people within very definite limits. For among the settled peoples of Asia which play a part in history, the conception of the public powers possessed by the king is modelled so predominantly on the patriarchal type of the nomadic chieftain, that among them the private rights of the subject, even in their reciprocal relations to one another, had no chance of developing. Within this circle only a loose and uncertain support is given to the idea of special rights by the fact that, under the *régime* of the Oriental world-empires, subject peoples were permitted to retain their customs and their social system. Now the Israelites did not exert an opposite influence of a different kind, for they never gained an extensive and permanent dominion over other nations; on the contrary, the monarchy in their case rather diverged from its prescribed path to follow the models of the surrounding nations. The Roman people was the first to establish the community of the State on a solid framework of ordinances securing private rights, and thus it also imparted to its world-empire a different character from that which previous enterprises of the kind had borne. For even the Hellenic world-empires relapsed into the Oriental type, the reason being that the Hellenic idea of the State maintained the entire dependence of the citizen on the State, and allowed no proper play within the State to the moral rights of individual families and individual persons. But the Romans, by elaborating a large number of institutions which reposed on private rights, succeeded in conferring on the individual citizens of the State the assurance of personal independence as against one another, and a higher

proportion of rights even as against the State; by their strict
and noble conception of marriage they infused a deeper
content into the power of the father over the family; finally,
by legally investing aliens with rights of their own, they
diminished the prejudice of antiquity which held that the
alien is a foe, and, as such, destitute of rights. The history
of the world, all down the succession of world-empires until
that of the Romans, is at bottom the outcome of self-seeking
and violence; but the moral sense finds a compensation for
this in the fact that the nations, even under these conditions,
arrived at a consciousness of their affinity as integral parts of
humanity. For the injustice of each conquest was certainly
atoned for by the benefits of a higher culture conferred upon
the subjugated peoples. The other nations which in antiquity
dominated the world cannot, it may be, claim this merit; but
it does belong to the Romans, in spite of all the oppression and
extortion which their provincial populations had to endure.
Their government called forth in the peoples that dwelt on
the shores of the Mediterranean a common sentiment of their
historical affinity, though in varying degree; and, by the
extension of the sway of Roman law, confirmed by the progressive bestowal of Roman citizenship, they paved the way
for the recognition of the individual as an independent
personality. These results of Roman supremacy are important
enough to be reckoned as a positive preparation for the
ethical tendencies of Christianity, even though as victories of
humane feeling they were lamentably counterbalanced by the
prevalence of slavery, that fountain of every kind of immorality. A further fact is that educated society in the Roman
Empire was still more directly influenced by the Stoic
philosophy towards belief in the moral solidarity of the
human race, and in the obligation to respect the individual,
and that in these principles the Hellenic spirit made its
contribution to the culture of the Roman Empire, while
remaining inferior in political force to the spirit of the
Roman people.

These results of classical culture, indeed, are not sources

from which the Christian idea of the Kingdom of God is directly drawn. For it finds its presuppositions proper solely in the religion of the Old Testament; in the fact, that is, that the One God is, to begin with, the Ruler, as He is the Father, of the chosen people, and that He stands Surety for that personal, independent, religious morality which follows from His righteousness. Jesus elevated these features into validity for all nations. But the understanding and acceptance of them by the nations within the Roman Empire was conditioned by the fact that the claim to act independently and with personal responsibility presuppposes the legal recognition of the individual, that the idea of the moral government of God demands a measure of common moral sentiment between nations, and, finally, that the principle of brotherly equality in the Christian community could count on a responsive feeling of the same kind in the people of that time. The very presence of these favourable prejudices among the population of the Roman Empire—even when men were unaware of the special grounds of their influence and of their origin—must be viewed as the outcome of a very highly complex historical development, which, when looked at in the light of the goal revealed by the foundation of Christianity, may be regarded as " the education of humanity."

These considerations might possibly find a place in the framework of traditional theology, as evidences of the Providence of God. But I think that for the purposes of a theological system they claim more serious attention, even though they cannot be proved to have come within the observation of any New Testament writer. The traditional form of theology only admits incidentally the hypothesis of a positive preparation for Christianity. The reason is that, following explicit trains of thought in Paul, it seizes only upon the factor of reconciliation in Christianity; and for reconciliation there is no precondition to be found in the prior history of mankind, save the negative one of universal sin. But Christianity in its last and loftiest aspect aims at the final end of the Kingdom of God; the authority of Jesus, which deserves to be set above that of Paul, makes this conception supreme. In the light of the significance which Christianity thus receives, the dominion over man gained by law must be recognised as a positive preparation. Law, as a system directed to the realisation of common ethical ends of a subordinate order, must be reckoned as a dispensation established by the purposive will of God, not as though legal conduct possessed equal worth with moral conduct prompted by religious motives, but in such wise that the former must be recognised as a precondition of the latter. And indeed this does not merely follow for the past from the view taken above of history in general; it holds good even in the present for the Christian conduct of every individual. For were this not so, then even the historical continuity of development which has been proved could only in a very problematical way be ascribed to the Providence of God.

The Evangelical system of doctrine includes the elements of this argument in two respects. I refer, first of all, to the view it takes of the possibility of *iustitia civilis* as contrasted with original sin, and the loss of freedom which that implies. Roman Catholic controversialists usually proceed as though they derived a great advantage from their assertion of the reality of freedom in the state of sin, as opposed to its denial in the Evangelical system. But when looked at more closely, this denial of freedom proves to be not absolute but relative, in so far, that is, as it refers to the discharge of duty from religious motives. On the other hand, a relative freedom is acknowledged to belong even to the state of sin, in regard to what is relatively good, *i.e.* the possibility of *iustitia civilis* is recognised. Whether, now, it is fitter to ascribe to the state of sin a relative freedom in regard to that which is completely good, or to limit the acknowledged relative capacity of sinners to that which is relatively good, is a question I shall not here discuss further.[1] The topic of *iustitia civilis*,

---

[1] *Conc. Trid.* Sess. vi. Decr. de iustificatione, 1 : " Etsi in eis (servis peccati) liberum arbitrium minime exstinctum esset, viribus licet attenuatum et inclina-

however, is treated in a merely one-sided way by the Reformers and the theological tradition dependent upon them. They discuss the conception merely as correlative to the state of sin, and as in its nature contrary to *iustitia spiritualis*. We must, however, further view both kinds of *iustitia* in their analogy to one another and in respect of their difference of degree, apart from the conditions of their realisation. This they omitted to do, clearly for the reason that they looked at the relations between the two exclusively in the light of the current antithesis between law and the promise of grace. For, in accordance with the usual conception of law, they took *iustitia civilis* in the sense of legality, without combining with it the idea of a law-abiding disposition, though the latter is one stage of the moral disposition.

The reason why the theology which is loyal to the Reformation cannot but attribute to the conception of *iustitia civilis* a significance which involves more than merely the correct determination of the notion of freedom in the state of sin, lies in the consistent estimate of the State as a positively Divine institution. It was only because he recognised the independent significance of the State as a direct institution of God, that Luther was able to construct his conception of *iustitia civilis* at all, and to wrest a domain for its exercise from the Augustinian theory of original sin. The opposite theory taught by the Papacy is rooted in the view which Augustine held of the *civitas terrena*. This *civitas* he finds realised in the existence of the Roman Empire, which, as reposing upon violence and conquest, perpetuates the character of the fratricide and city-founder Cain, and which, through its dependence on heathen idol-worship, is marked with the stamp of unrighteousness. Augustine never perceived that to the Roman people was due the creation of private rights. And so it actually leaves quite a comical impression to find him demonstrating, at the very climax of his exposi-

---

tum." *Conf. Aug.* xviii. : "Humana voluntas habet aliquam libertatem ad efficiendam iustitiam civilem et deligendas res rationi subiectas, sed non habet vim sine spiritu sancto efficiendae iustitiae dei seu iustitiae spiritualis."

tion (*De civitate dei*, xix. 21), that the Roman commonwealth, according to Cicero's own definition of it as a society united by uniformity in law and by common interests, never really existed. For, he argues, law (*Recht*) implies righteousness (*Gerechtigkeit*); now, righteousness can be had only through faith in the true God; the Romans, consequently, could not claim to have a legal or civil commonwealth, for in particular they had violated the legal maxim *suum cuique* by making man, who belongs to God, the slave of impure demons. We may learn the real value of this verdict on the Roman State—a verdict which lies at the basis of the mediæval view of the State in general—from the fact that Augustine also defends the opposite opinion. For he is not so perverse as to represent the empire as simply a devilish counterpart of the Kingdom of God, and civil laws as expressions of established injustice, or the law of property, for example, as veiled robbery. Rather, he recognises peace, aimed at internally by the State, as a mark of that struggle after good which men cannot abandon even in sin. However strongly he may emphasise the truth that the attainment of this peace can be purchased only by much violence and oppression of the weak, yet he does not reckon these means as necessary elements in the conception of earthly peace. And so Augustine finds that there is an ascending succession from the peace of the home to the peace of the State and the peace of the heavenly Kingdom —· a succession which expresses the generic unity subsisting among the aims of every human society, and therefore proves that each of the spheres thus compared is, in its own way, independent of the others. He therefore states it as his conclusion that God has ordained for men temporal peace and the means necessary thereto, and this as a stage preliminary to religious morality and a preparation for eternal life in loving fellowship with God and men. Whoever abuses the means of temporal peace, indeed, fails to attain the stage of peace with God, and misses the humbler goal as well.[1]   Here

---

[1] *De civitate dei*, xix. 13 : "Deus dedit hominibus quaedam bona huic vitae congrua, id est pacem temporalem pro modulo mortalis vitae in ipsa salute et

we have the principle stated which, in my opinion, the meaning
of Reformation theology requires us to add as a supplement to
the conception of *iustitia civilis.* However defective the latter
may prove in reality, yet it ought not to be regarded merely
as a possible accident of the state of sin, but as a necessary
and integral part of God's moral order. Viewed in isolation,
it wears a character opposed to religious morality. For the
disposition which limits itself to the domain of law may for
that reason come even to be in contradiction to the disposition which aims at the highest end of all. But of the successive kinds of human fellowship, that defined by law is of
narrower limits than that of moral action, and is so constituted
as to need the latter as its supplement ; for law is intelligible
only as a means to morality, and requires for its success a
measure of moral feeling. It merely confirms this conclusion,
and at the same time suggests the necessary limitation of the
doctrine of universal sinfulness, which is usually determined
exclusively by the idea of reconciliation, when we find Peter
and Paul (1 Pet. ii. 13–16 ; Rom. xiii. 1–7) prescribing obedience to the State absolutely, and this too as expressive of
religious conscientiousness.[1] Such teaching would be impossible unless the State and the law were magnitudes of permanent moral value when viewed from the standpoint of
Christian reflection on the world, and unless the capacity to

incolumitate ac societate sui generis, et quaeque huic paci vel tuendae vel recu-
perandae necessaria sunt : eo pacto aequissimus, ut qui mortalis talibus bonis
paci mortalium accommodatis recte usus fuerit, accipiat ampliora atque meliora,
ipsam scilicet immortalitatis pacem, eique convenientem gloriam et honorem in
vita aeterna ad fruendum deo et proximo in deo : qui autem perperam, nec illa
accipiat et haec amittat."

[1] In the above-cited passage Paul says expressly that whoever resists the government is opposing what God has ordained. The *Augsb. Conf.* xvi. here subjoins
the exception, *nisi cum magistratus iubent peccare, tunc enim Christiani magis
debent obedire deo quam hominibus.* But no command to sin is to be found in
State laws which make the privileges of definite denominations dependent on
positive legal conditions. The Christian owes obedience to these laws as indirect Divine ordinances, and it is a misuse of Scripture to oppose them, as
human ordinances, to any Divine commandment whatsoever. For Peter's declaration in Acts v. 29 is aimed, not at State laws as human and infra-Divine, but
at an injunction of the Church authorities ; bishops and pastors' conferences,
therefore, fall under the principle that we ought to obey God rather than
them.

satisfy the demands of the State were still preserved even in the state of sin.

The question which has given rise to this discussion was whether, from the interrelations between the love of God and the Kingdom of God, there results such a moral order that it prepares the way for the Kingdom of God among men. Our conclusion, that law and the State in general are preconditions of the Kingdom of God, is of a form different from that of the sketches of a world-order which we owe to the orthodox and the Socinians. What they attempt is to furnish information in regard to the individual's original relation to God, and the principles which God follows in His treatment of him. The theory put forward here to determine generally the relation between law and the Divine Kingdom has nothing to say to this interest in the fate of the individual. Yet it harmonises with the conception of an education which places men under special institutions, in order to render them capable of the free appropriation of the most universal principle of life. This is what is meant by saying that the reciprocity of private rights and the obligations which bind men to civil society have both to be impressed on the mind before we can order our behaviour to those farthest off, as well as to those who are nearest, by the motive of love. Now we find that if the only motive of an action be a legal one, it cannot be considered as coming under the head of our religious relation to God; but we also find that the motive of religious morality yields the principle of obedience to law, which raises an action done in the particular sphere of civil law into the domain of moral law and the Kingdom of God. Thus it becomes all the more clear that individual legal works *as* individual—and in this light the doctrine of the *foedus operum* views them—cannot, save incorrectly, be regarded as the material in which man's religious relation to God takes shape, and by which it can be judged.

The only question which might still arise is whether the result we have reached is not invalidated by certain of Jesus sayings. For in Matt. v. 38–42, He pronounces against the legal principle of retaliation in the intercourse of men with one another, and demands from His disciples, as proof of their belonging to the Kingdom of God, that on all conceivable occasions they should surrender their private rights. This section of the Sermon on the Mount is lacking, indeed, in the lucidity of expression and connectedness to be desired; nevertheless, it is quite impossible to doubt that it does not intend the subversion of the institution of private rights altogether. What is forbidden, rather, is that in our intercourse with fellow-members of the Kingdom of God, we should insist on our private rights unconditionally, on the principle that services must be reciprocal; and the command is given to surrender one's rights in particular cases for the sake of moral fellowship. That is to say, recourse to law between members of the Kingdom of God is thereby modified; but the validity of law for their life is not abrogated altogether. Its validity is of necessity presupposed; for the independence of moral action and of personal virtue in general is unthinkable apart from legal independence. The exhortation addressed to slaves, that they should patiently submit to being without rights (1 Pet. ii. 18—20; Col. iii. 22—25), is to be regarded as an exception dictated by circumstances, for the existence of slavery in the Christian world is a standing menace to public and personal morality.

§ 39. We have found that the institution of the State is a means to the Kingdom of God, and that it is not to be applied, contrariwise, as a standard of Divine authority by which to gauge the possibility of realising His Kingdom. In this consideration, therefore, there lies no obstacle to our *deriving reconciliation from the love of God*, as well as from His justice, when properly understood as denoting the method in which He carries out His loving Will for the salvation of all mankind, as well as of individuals (vol. ii. p. 113). If it is conceivable at all that God should bestow His love on sinful man, then the justice with which that love has to reconcile itself is not such as it would be if God originally stood to man in the relation of reciprocity characteristic of private right or civil law. Rather is it God's perfection, according to Christian ideas, that He does good to men even when they are His enemies (Matt. v. 44, 48). In this respect He is set up as a model to men. Thus Christian love to one's enemies, or forgiveness to one's debtors, is not dependent on their rendering satisfaction. No more can Jesus have found any difficulty in the fact that God, intent on reconciliation, should love men even though they are His foes. Nevertheless, we have not yet completely solved the question (§ 17) how the principle of forgiveness, and the attribute which issues in moral legislation, can be combined in our conception of God. Tieftrunk's contention that Divine pardon accords with the moral law, because irreconcilability, conceived as the law of a moral kingdom, would be self-contradictory, we found to be unconvincing. For reconcilability is a principle of moral duty which is binding only between equals, and even then not unconditionally, while, between one possessed of moral authority and a subordinate, it holds good only in a conditional way. If the moral law is the highest expression by which we can define the relation between God and man, then it is only in an accidental fashion that pardon or the forgiveness of sins can be conjoined with it. For that reason, however, the solution proposed by Kant (vol. i. p. 456), namely, that the forgiveness of sins is determined by the individual's amount of moral performance, does not harmonise with the Christian view of the matter. On the other hand, the path which we must take is indicated by the other theory put forward by Tieftrunk, that pardon and law are not contradictory if pardon be bestowed for the sake of the law—if, that is, the realisation of the universal ethical end, especially love to the law, is impossible without previous forgiveness (vol. i. p. 463).

For if God is conceived in general as love, in order to explain the Kingdom of God as the final end of the world and therefore the world itself (§ 34), then, from the significance which the Kingdom has for God, there follows the content of the moral law and its absolute stringency for the

members of the Kingdom. The practical union of a multitude
of persons, so that as homogeneous with God they become
the object of His will manifested as love, is effected by
obedience to the law of love to God and our neighbour.
The love of God is already intent upon men, in so far as His
aim is to elevate them to the Kingdom of God, even though
at the time their will may not actually be directed to the
highest moral end. For love ever aims first of all at the
possible ideal of another's self-end, and its proper strength
resides in the other's improvement and education. If, therefore, God eternally loves the community of the Kingdom of
God (Eph. i. 4, 6), He also loves already the individuals who
are to be gathered into it, in so far as He purposes to bring
them into the Kingdom. Now, if we must assume that they
are sinners, then God loves even sinners in view of their
ideal destiny, to realise which He chooses them. Why sin
should make this relationship unthinkable it is impossible
to see. For even though sin is active opposition to God's
final end, yet persistence in such a course would make the
love of God to sinners impossible only if in all cases sin were
definitive and conscious opposition to His final end. But if,
on the other hand, the degree of sin in individual cases is less
than this, and if it is therefore possible that the direction of
the will in this respect may be altered, then the love of God
may operate on sinners through His purpose to realise their
ideal destiny. Now, if we may thus presuppose that sin
involves different degrees, the founding and the existence of
the Kingdom of God cannot be deduced from God's love,
unless God removes the separation from Himself which
operates in the sin which is common to men. For as the
moral perfection of man in the Kingdom of God must at the
same time be regarded as God's final end in the world, sin is
an obstacle to its realisation. And it is so not merely as
immorality, but above all as a defect in reverence towards and
trust in God (to use the words of the *C. A.* ii.), or, to use a positive
expression, as indifference and mistrust of God. Viewed in
this light, the pardon which is a precondition of the Kingdom,

the forgiveness of sins which invalidates the guilt and the consciousness of guilt which separates men from God, likewise flow from the love of God, as a universal dispensation for behoof of the members of the Kingdom. Forgiveness, however, cannot come into collision with God's moral legislation. For the latter, as the moral order prevailing in the Kingdom of God, comes to be valid only for those whom God, through His forgiveness, has led to trust His love. The result of this discussion, therefore, is that pardon or reconciliation, as a fundamental precondition of the Kingdom's coming into existence and as presupposing universal sin, can be conceived in harmony with the love of God, and that it is in no way inconsistent with the Divine attribute of moral legislation.

But the question arises, whether still other reasons than the rejected notion of civil justice are not likely to call forth objections to this conclusion. This consideration makes it necessary to examine the sketch of the doctrine of reconciliation put forward by Schoeberlein, to the importance of which I have already drawn attention (vol. i. p. 650). He and I agree in our general definition of the problem of reconciliation, in holding, that is, that its ground is the love of God and its end the Kingdom of God, and that to estimate its possibility by the principles of civil law involves a doctrinal aberration. Schoeberlein starts so decisively with the idea that God is love that he will hear nothing of a Divine righteousness exercised in relation to the world of morality, and either preceding or accompanying it. However, he allows the conception of righteousness to operate as a modification of love as related to sinful humanity, inasmuch as the entrance of sin altered, not indeed the basal tendency of Divine love, but its method of revelation. For, as a recognition of the independence of man, respected by God, he contends that God manifests to sinners His love, which pain has altered, by the wrath and curse which make themselves felt in the consciousness of guilt and the ills of life. But as wrath is not the opposite of Divine love but a modification of it, these manifestations of wrath possess a significance of

21

their own as means preparatory to reconciliation. For when looked at completely, the wrath of God is accompanied by compassion for human sin; thence springs grace; and in grace the pain of God's love is eternally swallowed up in His blessed joy in humanity, beloved by God in His Son. These are the principal features of the theory, so far as it concerns the doctrine of God. The inferences it is made to yield for the interpretation of Christ's life are not in place here.

There can be no doubt whatever that a very imperfect view was taken of God's spiritual personality in the older theology, when the functions of knowing and willing alone were employed to illustrate it. Religious thought plainly ascribes to God affections of feeling as well. The older theology, however, laboured under the impression that feeling and emotion were characteristic only of limited and created personality; it transformed, *e.g.*, the religious idea of the Divine blessedness into eternal self-knowledge, and that of the Divine wrath into the fixed purpose to punish sin. The revolt against this, which finds vent in Schoeberlein's analysis of the Divine emotions, is on the whole fully justified. But it seems to me imperative to proceed very cautiously in this respect. The blessedness of God is a lucid and intrinsically clear conception, as expressive of His own feeling of His eternity. Now, as God's eternity is knowable by us through the continuity and immutability of the necessary relation between His nature and His world-plan, Schoeberlein rightly declares that the blessedness of God likewise includes eternally joy in the humanity which He loves in His Son. We must judge thus, if we are to give a theological representation *sub specie aeternitatis* of the whole domain covered by the Christian view of the world. On the other hand, all our reflections about God's wrath and compassion, His long-suffering and patience, His severity and sympathy, are based upon a comparison of our individual position with God's, under the form of time. However indispensable these judgments may be in the texture of our religious experience, still they stand in no relation whatever to the theological conception of the whole from the view-point of eternity. That these different lines of thought do not merge in one another, is precisely the truth expressed by Schoeberlein's principle, that the pain suffered by God's love is eternally taken up by the good pleasure of His grace into the unity of His blessed joy in mankind. For by taking this view we eliminate from our thought the pain which, as an act in time, we formerly conceived as resulting from the contrast between the love of God and the sin of man. From the point of view of theology, therefore, no validity can be assigned to the idea of the wrath of God and His curse upon sinners as yet unreconciled; still less, from this theological standpoint, is any special mediation between the wrath and the love of God conceivable or necessary in order to explain the reconciliation of sinners with Him.

Nevertheless, the following consideration serves to make the matter clearer. According to Scripture, we are not justified in regarding God's wrath as an altered form of His love, nor in relating it to sin as such (vol. ii. pp. 129, 137); according to the New Testament, God's wrath signifies His determination to destroy those who definitively set themselves against redemption and the final end of the Kingdom of God (vol. ii. p. 154). The authority of Holy Scripture gives us no right to relate the wrath of God to sinners as such, for *ex hypothesi* we conceive sinners to be known and chosen by God, as partakers in His Kingdom and objects of His redemption from sin. If we assume that God foresees their final inclusion in His Kingdom, as theologians we have no alternative but to trace their redemption back to His love in an unbroken line, even though these very redeemed ones may, as their ideas take a temporal form, have the impression of a change from Divine wrath to Divine mercy (vol. i. p. 163). We must come to the same conclusion, too, regarding the phenomena of those cases where men are conscious of guilt and regard evils as the effects of God's curse. For while these experiences, looked at from God's side, may also be regarded as means to conversion, yet from the standpoint alike of reconciliation as an accomplished fact and of God's overruling will of love—that is, from the only standpoint of interpretation open to theology — they appear with their meaning reversed, as dispensations of God's goodness and grace. The notion that there is a temporal change in God's attitude and even in God's feeling towards us may therefore remain safe and intact within its own domain, for our individual lives being parts of the whole, we cannot like God survey the entire world-order. But when in our theological study of the whole we place ourselves, even temporarily, at God's standpoint, we cannot combine the idea of a change in His tone of feeling towards the individual situation of individual men with the conception of the Divine knowledge and government of the whole. And so even Paul clothes the idea of God's wrath against those who are lost in the guise of a perpetual determination of His will, all the characteristics of a passing emotion being stripped away—even though, from the standpoint of experience in time, he also recognises a manifestation towards them of Divine long-suffering (Rom. ix. 22). Conversely, the knowledge of God as Father possessed by those who must ultimately be viewed as children of God, implies that every evil they experience even in consequence of sin should be reckoned, never as a destructive penalty, but as a means of education (§ 9). Whatever in this respect may excite a different feeling for the moment may—when we look at it later from the standpoint of the reconciliation and Divine sonship we have gained—be traced back to the antecedent and never-failing love of God, any feelings we may have of an opposite kind being set aside as delusive. But according to this view—and it is the ultimately valid one—any theology which keeps to the standpoint of the reconciled community must assert that into the life of the reconciled there can come from God's side no curse or damnatory punishment, and that God's love, as the antecedent ground of reconciliation, cannot be modified by any such feeling or action on His part towards those who are to be reconciled. For it is unthinkable that there should be for God a gulf between His intention and its accomplishment, such as might prove a ground of uncertainty or of an alteration in His judgment and His attitude.

It is of the greatest importance for the systematic procedure of theology that this difference, between our individual religious thinking and the form of theological cognition *sub specie alternitatis*, should never be forgotten. Our self-consciousness is bound up with time, and it is never given us to survey the whole of the Divine order within which we move as parts, so that we simply cannot but regard and judge our relation to God under the form of time; and thus we reproduce, in the idea that God's relations to us change, the alterations of our own experience. But if this way of looking at things were made determinative for theology too, either we should never get further than a history of Divine revelations, or we should drag the being of God down into the process of historical change. In orthodox theology itself this error is found in combination with its attempt to represent God as pure Being and as the latent moral character of perpetually self-identical justice. By the very fact that to these presuppositions is added a delineation of God's revealing acts, the conception of God is made subject to the form of becoming (§ 32). This procedure was facilitated by the fact that eternity was likewise regarded as equivalent to endless time, in which God is just as much liable to change as the world, while neither can we ever conceive the world as non-existent (§ 37). Not till the conception of God had been correctly defined as the love of a Will perpetually directed to the eternally beloved community of the Kingdom of God, was there attained a positive idea of eternity according to which temporal change in God's action does not appear as change in His being. Now it is not to be wondered at that this should mean the rejection of all those theological theories which introduce change into the essential relations of the Divine will. For a method which in one respect is inevitably followed by unsophisticated religious thought, is not determinative for the systematic construction of theology, even though the Biblical writers simply could not avoid attaching their lines of religious thought to temporal change in the Divine intentions and operations.

(1) The conception of God which is given in the revelation received through Christ, and to which the trust of those who are reconciled through Christ attaches itself, is that of a loving Will which assures to believers spiritual dominion over the world and perfect moral fellowship in the Kingdom of God as the *summum bonum*.

(2) This final end of God in the world is the ground from which it is possible to explain the creation and government of the world in general, and the interrelations between nature and created spirits.

(3) The reconciliation of sinners by God, if it is to be conceived, is conceivable without inconsistency as the means used for the establishment of the Kingdom of God by God's love.

CHAPTER V

THE DOCTRINE OF SIN

§ 40. SIN is the negative presupposition of reconciliation. Or, to put it more accurately, since in the Christian religion reconciliation is recognised as an attribute of the humanity which Christianity is to unify, it must be presupposed that all men are sinners. Even those who enjoy reconciliation must acknowledge that they are sinners who never cease to need it. These judgments are necessary parts of the Christian view of the world and the Christian estimate of self. Since we have *to comprehend the fact of sin from the standpoint of the reconciled community,* the Gospel of the forgiveness of sins is actually the ground of our knowledge of our sinfulness (p. 7). And this agrees with the statement of John, that we should make God a liar if we as Christians affirmed that we had no sin. Now, the sin of which one is conscious when one believes in forgiveness or reconciliation as presented in Christianity is conceived as actual. In the New Testament we invariably find that only offences and transgressions are indicated as the object of Divine forgiveness, while the point to which reconciliation refers is the active disposition of enmity to God (vol. ii. pp. 222, 230). We must reserve the question whether there is any indication that the fellowship of sin among men should and can be conceived in another form than that of actual sin. The assumption of sin as common to all, however, is one which, supplementing as it does the personal guilt of the individual, can only be arrived at in the connection just indicated, when we have ascertained our individual sin as such for ourselves.

That we are sinners, as individuals and in conjunction

with all others, is a necessary part of the view of the world
and of life which we share with the community of Christ.
And, following our practice above, we have to derive the
proper definition of sin from the New Testament. That does
not imply, however, that the fact and the explanation of sin
were first made certain by revelation, or that they are
articles of faith like other elements of the Christian view
as a whole. For men were familiar with the fact of sin even
apart from Christianity. But the determination of its nature,
and the estimate of its compass and its worthlessness, are
expressed in a peculiar form in Christianity; for here there
obtain ideas of God, of the supreme good, of the moral destiny
of man, and of redemption, different from those which are to
be found in any other religion. As a sinner every man has
to judge himself rightly and completely in the light of the
realities and blessings just named, and thereby also to determine
the nature of the interconnection of sin within the human
race. But we have not to believe in sin in general, or in a
definite general conception of sin such as would fall outside of
experience. Luther deviates from this principle when, in his
Smalcald Confession (iii. 1), he puts forward the notion of
original sin as a complete expression of the matter, with the
qualification, *ut nullius hominis ratione intelligi possit, sed ex
scripturae patefactione agnoscenda et credenda sit.* If, therefore,
this conception is an article of faith, then we have to believe
in original sin in the same way as we believe in God, etc.;
but that is absurd, for original sin is not a channel of salvation. But if original sin is an article of doctrine which we
believe, then this belief, if it cannot be tested by experience,
is a mere opinion both as regards its relation to theological
knowledge and in its bearing on the religious view of the
world. And so the sense of that dogma veers round into the
opposite of what it was intended to convey. In reality, the
notion of original sin was adopted by Augustine in no other
way than the above discussion has suggested for the notion
of sin as such—namely, as an inference from his estimate of
the worth of the Christian salvation. Augustine, in fact,

framed the conception of original sin in order to uphold the sacramental character of infant baptism, in other words, as an inference from the special worth of this instrument of the Divine revelation of salvation (vol. i. p. 504). This connection, however, was forgotten, when the thought to which Augustine had given his *imprimatur* became supreme in tradition.

The only way in which an idea of sin can be formed at all is by comparison with an idea of the good. The more or the less complete the latter, the deeper or the shallower will be our conception of the worthlessness of sin. Now for the Christian faith it is certain that, as the compass and the obligatoriness of the good first come out into full cognisability in the task of the Kingdom of God, especially as that task was faultlessly discharged in the life-course of Jesus, so likewise sin can only be understood as the contrary of this, the highest moral good. Hence it is absurd to expect that we can reach the Christian estimate of sin, in general as well as in the individual, in practical self-judgment as well as in theory, before grasping and appreciating that moral ideal. As far as individual experience is concerned, Luther first, and after him Calvin, maintained the opposite and true principle, by the explicit maxim that hatred of sin proceeds from love of the good, a love which entirely coincides with faith in reconciliation through Christ.[1] Before we attain to faith in Christ, it is perhaps possible to acquire from the law a theoretical knowledge of the characteristics of sin, but not that estimate of it which should express itself in the decisive estrangement of the will from it. For such a movement is thinkable only as the negative reverse-side of the good will. If, then, Luther's principle, originally discovered by him in his

---

[1] Cf. vol. i. pp. 163, 199, 214. Cf. also Spangenberg, *Idea fidei fratrum*, p. 246: "Although an individual, who turns to God from his heart, is immediately conscious of his sinful misery and forthwith obtains forgiveness, yet we must not think that he is sensible of his corruption all at once. For after pardon has been granted him, he is given more and more light from time to time; and so it happens that a man, after fifty years of faithfulness in the ways of the Saviour, is a much greater sinner in his own eyes than he was at the moment of his conversion."

controversy against the sacrament of penance, proves itself right as against Melanchthon's alteration of it, then the theological doctrine of sin will also need to adjust itself accordingly. Or if, on the other hand, the practical as well as the theoretical interpretation of sin is held to be both possible and necessary apart from the knowledge and valuation of the Christian good, every Christian will be bound to follow the method which leads to "the conflict of penitence" (*Busskampf*), although past experience shows that it issues in either despair or hypocrisy (p. 164).

Traditional Dogmatics avoids determining the idea of sin by comparison with the life-portrait of Christ or with the instruction He gave in the righteousness of the Kingdom of God, by affirming the *iustitia originalis* of our first parents before they sinned. In this connection we still have a divine of modern times recording of the progenitors of the human race that their self-consciousness was a pure unclouded consciousness of God, their will positively good, and the inclination of their heart childlike love to God. The higher these predicates run, the more profound appears to be the state of sin which has come about in them and their descendants through the transgression of the known prohibition of God. The record in Genesis, however, partly contains no trace of this characterisation of our first parents, and partly contains its very opposite ; and it is foreign to Paul's knowledge of Scripture as well, certain as it is that the comparison he draws between the first and the second Adam is as far as possible from indicating that the first was originally the counterpart of the second (1 Cor. xv. 45–47). But the theology which carries back to the beginning of human history that normal condition which Christianity has first made possible for man, and declares it to be the natural state of human life, entails upon itself the disadvantage of having to conceive the Person of Christ as an anomalous phenomenon in human history. For on that basis Christ can be understood only as the Bearer of God's operation against sin. But if sin is a fortuitous and abnormal fact in human history, we are bound

to pass the same judgment even on Christ Himself.   Thus the
plan of orthodox Dogmatics serves to make the historical
appearance of Christ unintelligible.   But if, on the contrary,
in the Christian religion Jesus Christ is the standard of His
believers' view of the world and estimate of self, then in
Dogmatics His Person must be regarded as the ground of
knowledge to be used in the definition of every doctrine.

Hence even the dogmatic doctrine of man must not be
filled up by adducing elements from the Biblical creation-
document, but by that spiritual and moral conception of man
which is revealed in the life-course of Jesus, and His intention to found the Kingdom of God.   The doctrinal statements
in the Confessions, too, regarding the original state of man,
have no other significance than that of antedating the
Christian ideal of life.   When this fact is recognised, they
are seen to be characteristic representations of the Catholic and
the Evangelical conceptions of that ideal.   In other words, the
Evangelical doctrine of *iustitia originalis* expresses the thought
that the Christian ideal should form an element of the conception of man.   On the other hand, the Catholic interpretation of
the subject, according to which original righteousness was added
to human nature as a gift of grace, implies that the Christian
ideal falls outside the essential constitution of man.   Therefore the alleged marks of the perfect Christian life, namely,
renunciation of the family, of private property, and of the
entire circuit of personal honour, are not demanded from all
Christians, but only from monks; and what they are expected
to lead under these conditions is not a human life, but the *vita
angelica*.   The Evangelical assumption, on the other hand,
that our first parents were created with righteousness as the
content of their nature, is an expression of the fact that the
Christian ideal falls within the limits of man's constitution,
and that in Dogmatics the general nature of man ought
to be interpreted in the light of this standard.   Conceived
in this fashion, the idea of *iustitia originalis* is confes-
sionally important and dogmatically significant; it is in
comparison a matter of indifference that no ground exists

for supposing that our first parents were endowed with this attribute.

This supposition is also rejected when Schleiermacher strives to view the sending of Christ for the purpose of redemption as at the same time the completion of God's creation of man (p. 128). This is an important step towards vindicating the conception of Christ's Person as the all-round principle of knowledge in Dogmatics. To be sure the expression used by Schleiermacher is not altogether felicitous. Since we usually define the idea of creation by distinguishing it from Divine preservation and government, the expression suggests the idea that it is intended to cover the birth of Jesus, and nothing more. But that cannot be the point in question, since Jesus in respect of His birth is not distinguisable from any other man. His unique worth lies in the manner in which He mastered His spiritual powers through a self-consciousness which transcended that of all other men, and by His will brought them all to bear upon His personal destination. Now, as this activity of His personal force must be conceived as embraced by the peculiar operation of God in Him, it ought to be acknowledged that in Him we have a manifestation of Divine creation; but, in that case, in " Divine creation " we include what we otherwise distinguish from it as preservation and government. Further, it must be taken into account that the transformation of the human race which is traceable to the peculiar work of Christ fulfils itself in individuals, whose existence is due to natural descent, in a manner compatible with their freedom, while to be free and to be created are contrary notions. Thus the expression chosen by Schleiermacher is paradoxical. What is meant by it is more suitably expressed by saying that the common destiny of men, through which they attain their distinction from nature and their lordship over the world, was first realised in its full compass in the self-consciousness of Christ, and through Him made manifest and effective. As compared with earlier known degrees of possible moral fellowship and spiritual freedom over against nature, Christ experienced the latter in perfect measure, and realised the former to the highest imaginable extent, inasmuch as He passed His life in the vocation of founding the Kingdom of God, without once deviating from it — and both in the strength of a fellowship or unity with God such as no one before Him had ever known.⌋

⌈The Christian ideal of life, as the opposite of which we have to conceive sin, includes two different kinds of functions, the religious and the moral—trust in God, by which we rise superior to the world, and action prompted by love towards our neighbour and tending to produce that fellowship which, as the *summum bonum*, represents at the same time the perfected good.   When we make it our personal end—as far as time and place and calling demand or permit—to second and assist all others in respect of their true destiny, we act from a good will and according to the law of God.⟩ In the conception of sin there will therefore have to be distinguished the two sides which are respectively opposed to these functions.⌋ Now this view is indicated in the *Confessio Augustana*, Art. II., and in its *Apology* when, as the content of universal or inherited sin, there is brought forward first man's being *sine metu, sine fiducia erga deum*, while in the second place *concupiscentia* is mentioned.   Probably both expressions denote the religious defect, which brings the moral defect in its train.[1]   At all events the emphasis laid upon these religious defects introduces an innovation in the hitherto accepted tradition, which is in harmony with other features of the Reformers' view as a whole.   Stress has already (p. 170) been laid on the fact that if the principal thing in Christian perfection is reverence and trust in God, the opposite of both must be affirmed as the leading characteristic of sin ; and further, that the Lutheran doctrine of *poenitentia* can issue in the regaining of faith only provided what is pre-eminently regarded in sin is its anti-religious side.

---

[1] Eichhorn, *Die Rechtfertigungslehre der Apologie*, in *Stud. u. Krit.*, 1887, p. 420 ff.

Augustine knows nothing of these considerations, inasmuch as he defines original sin simply as *concupiscentia*, selfish desire. Now, as the Reformers prove, it is indeed possible to find in this conception likewise an anti-religious attitude towards God, and to give specific expression to it accordingly. But yet Augustine and all his successors have not taken this step. And the explanation of this circumstance is to be found in the fact that Augustine assumes the moral law as the original dispensation between God and men, a dispensation which is violated by the entrance of sin. Luther, however, recognised the kind providence of God and man's trust in it as the basal form of religion, in which men lived and moved before the fall. Accordingly, a defect in reverence and in trust in God, or indifference and mistrust of Him, was proved to be the basal form of the sin of our first parents, and, if that sin is transmitted to all men, as the basal form of original sin, which then has as a special consequence selfish desire directed against the claims of the moral society. We can interpret sin exhaustively if we use this doctrinal position as a clue, for its worthlessness can only be measured by the perverted attitude which the sinner adopts towards God. For the point of importance is to distinguish sin from wrong-doing and crime. A given action, in the light of human society and the law of the State, is a wrong and a crime. But the same action is sin when it springs from indifference towards God, as the Benefactor and Governor of human life. By bringing out this aspect we stamp sin as a religious idea, as a characteristic value-notion.

§ 41. A more complete estimate of the anti-moral aspect of sin than is expressed in the conception of the *concupiscentia* of each individual, is to be found by comparing it with the common good which, according to Christian standards, ought to be realised through the co-operation of all. (The good in the Christian sense is the Kingdom of God, in other words the uninterrupted reciprocation of action springing from the motive of love—a Kingdom in which all are knit together in union with every one who can show the marks of a neigh-

bour; further, it is that union of men in which all goods are
appropriated in their proper subordination to the highest
good   Now sin is the opposite of the good, so far as it is
selfishness springing from indifference or mistrust of God, and
directs itself to goods of subordinate rank without keeping in
view their subordination to the highest good.   It does not
negate the good as such; but, in traversing the proper
relation of goods to the good, it issues in practical contradiction of the good.   Now, if we are to find in the
conception of the Kingdom of God the standard for the
full determination of sin as its opposite, then sin cannot be
completely represented either within the framework of the
individual life, or in that of humanity as a natural species.
[The subject of sin, rather, is *humanity as the sum of all
individuals*, in so far as the selfish action of each person,
involving him as it does in illimitable interaction with all
others, is directed in any degree whatsoever towards the
opposite of the good,.and leads to the association of individuals
in common evil.] This definition, which is in the closest
formal agreement with Schleiermacher (vol. i. p. 503),
transcends the dilemma which hovers between Pelagius and
Augustine, and to which the problem of sin has always been
restricted.   Pelagius recognises exclusively the individual
will as the form of sin.   He reflects, indeed, on the fact that
through example and imitation sin comes to be something
common to many.   But example operates only when one
receives and welcomes it from another, and thus by the path
described the dissemination of sin does not transcend the
limits of the individual will.   Moreover, the imitation of
moral or immoral actions is a rare phenomenon in maturer
years.   It is limited, rather, to the stage of childhood and
youth, and consequently it cannot be a universal basis for the
fellowship of sin.   But even though that fellowship came
into existence by means of example and imitation, yet it
would rather imply merely a similarity of all individuals in
possessing a sinful will: sin would thus be proved to be
something logically, but not really, common.   On the other

hand, Augustine takes the subject of sin to be humanity as a natural species, in its original embodiment in the person of the original parent, the first sinner. Now since the sin pertaining to the whole race is conceived as marked by the highest possible degree of worthlessness—a degree which no actual sin can possibly enhance—since, further, the individual members of the race, unless conceived as acting, are absolutely independent of each other as persons, Augustine's doctrine of original sin has for its outcome the thought that each individual descendant of our first parents is of necessity burdened with the highest degree of sin, and that in this respect all men are alike (p. 132). Since in relation thereto no notice whatever is taken of the interaction of actual sins, Augustine's form of doctrine no more than that of Pelagius succeeds in giving expression to the idea of the fellowship of many persons in sin ; what it expresses is their similarity in this respect—only that this similarity is transferred to another point than that favoured by Pelagius. Nor is the tenor of the Augustinian doctrine corrected at any stage of orthodox theology, as for instance by consideration being given in the doctrine of redemption to the thoroughgoing reciprocation which marks sinful action throughout the human race. Rather do we invariably find the idea of redemption or reconciliation formed exclusively in view of original sin and the actual sins of the individual.

Granted, then, that the conception of original sin is an intrinsically clear and necessary thought, yet, to say the least, it cannot express the highest possible sense of sin. Actual sins are more than manifestations or accidents of original sin in the individual. If we first of all realise how superficial a view of things it is which limits itself to the categories of being and appearance, substance and accident, we shall find it necessary to lay less stress on the Augustinian formula of original sin. Individual actions, which are traced back to the will as their source, are not phenomena of will which may or may not exist without changing its nature ; rather, through actions, according to the direction they take, the will acquires its nature and develops into a good or an evil character. This view is directly opposed to that which is expressed in the conception of original sin.   Nevertheless, it is the principle which governs our practical judgment of evil, and apart from which we never set ourselves to counteract evil in ourselves or in others.   In the *first* place, on it rests every kind of responsibility for evil which we impose upon ourselves. Only if we discern in the individual action the proof-mark of the independence of the will, can we ascribe to ourselves, not merely individual actions, but likewise evil habit or evil inclination.   But this is tantamount to denying that the individual action is the involuntary accident of a determining force of inborn inclination.   Even if we find radical evil working within us to the extent affirmed by Kant, responsibility for it can only be vindicated if it is assumed to be the result of the empirical determination of the will, for it can be derived neither from the natural origin of every man, nor from a pretended intelligible act of freedom (vol. i. p. 449). *Secondly*, education is possible only on the presupposition that existing bad habits or evil inclinations have come to exist as the products of repeated 'acts of will.   On the other hand, from the standpoint of original sin education is quite unthinkable.   Education strives to direct the child to the good as a whole, by offering inducements to what is good in all the particular relations of life, and by severally combating all bad habits.   It rests on the presupposition that there exists in the child a general, though still indeterminate, impulse towards the good, which just falls short of being guided by complete insight into the good, and has not yet been tested in the particular relationships of life.   This is the exact opposite of the tendency of the child's will to evil and of the determining power of evil, as asserted in the doctrine of original sin.   *Thirdly*, the assumption we make of distinct degrees of evil in individuals—an assumption rendered indispensable by practical considerations—is incompatible with the dogma of original sin, which asserts of all the descendants of Adam an equally high degree of sinful inclination, and that the highest

22

possible, namely, that they have fallen into universal and
obstinate resistance to the Divine good, and into the possession
of the devil. Nevertheless, from the degree of wickedness
which we call devilish we distinguish vice, selfish and
insolent imperiousness, vain and astute indifference to common
moral ends, and, lastly, self-seeking forms of patriotism, pride
of rank, and family zeal, which indeed are based upon particular moral goods, but pursue them in a way which comes
into contradiction with universal morality.

All these grades of habitual sin we include in the vast
complexity of sinful action when we form the idea of *the
kingdom of sin*. And indeed we can only regard ourselves as
sharing its guilt when we not only attribute to ourselves our
own sinful actions as such, but at the same time calculate
how they produce sin in others also, although we may possess
no complete or distinct idea of the extent of these effects.
On the other hand, we also feel the reaction of this power of
common sin, not only through example or the production in
us of sinful opposition to the sins of others, but especially by
the blunting of our moral vigilance and our moral judgment.
For whereas the Kingdom of God as the supreme end rises
above all that falls within the compass of the world, and is
destined to regulate and embrace every relationship of life, a
bondage and a false dependence on the world are the fruit of
that friendship for the world which runs counter to that
final end. This form of sinful federation with others, however, affects everyone, at least in this way that we become
accustomed to standing forms of sin, at any rate in others, and
acquiesce in them as the ordinary expression of human
nature. To be sure, no individual, from where he is placed,
surveys more than a narrow section of this federation of
humanity, and his feeling of worthlessness is further modified
by the influences of different stages of life, rank, calling, and
his degree of personal culture. But wherever, within the
domain in which the Christian view of the world prevails, the
idea is formed at all according to the standard of the value of
the Kingdom of God, it will be qualitatively identical. The

special causes by which each man is led to form the common conception serve in comparison actually to strengthen our conviction of the gravity of the sinful fate into which human life conducts us. For in moral matters those motives are always the most effective in which the general principle attaches itself to the individual's particular situation and particular experiences. Now it is without doubt a merit in Schleiermacher to have formed the above conception of common sin, in which are to be included all particular actions (vol. i. p. 503). Only he did wrong in inserting it under the traditional heading of original sin, to which it bears very little resemblance. This proceeding, however, is due to the fact that he undertook to expound Dogmatics as a representation of the system accepted by the Church—which it ought not to be.

Nothing is better calculated to emphasise the difference between the idea of common sin, as conceived to include all sinful actions, and the idea of original sin, than a knowledge of the motive which first prompted Luther to adopt the Augustinian conception. For his reasons were not the same as those which led Augustine to formulate the notion of original sin. To the latter it presented itself as a means whereby the sacramental character of infant baptism might be upheld. But with this Luther was not at all concerned, as may be seen from his official declarations on the subject of infant baptism, which partly exclude and partly evade the Augustinian point of view.[1] Augustine's doctrine of original sin found favour with Luther more as a ground for the negation

[1] It is true, indeed, that Luther occasionally affirms quite unreservedly the eternal damnation of unbaptized children, but, on the other hand, he counts it to their advantage that they have not committed actual sins. The fact is that, speaking generally, Luther never took quite seriously to the above inference from original sin. In connection with this problem he utters a warning against seeking to penetrate into matters which God has not revealed ; and hence he is not in favour of trying to solve the problem, as Augustine did, by purely theoretical arguments. He rather awakens hope in God's mercy towards children who die unbaptized, and, in short, clearly puts aside in this question the interest which actuated Augustine. For Luther, therefore, baptism becomes in part an act which proclaims the promise of grace to children, partly an act by which they are dedicated to God (*C. A.* ix. *Art. Smalc.* iii. 5). Cf. Köstlin, *Luther's Theologie*, ii. pp. 88–100, 375, 511.

of human merit before God, and as an argument against the freedom of the will.[1] This, however, is both to exaggerate and to minimise the idea of sin. For to assert the doctrine of original sin in order to refute the validity of merits before God is just as appropriate as it would be to use a boulder to kill a gnat. On the other hand, this affirmation of the doctrine in its present application serves rather as an argument for human weakness than for human guilt. In Augustine's teaching, however, the latter is the point of supreme importance. But this aspect of sin, which unquestionably enters into the connotation of "the kingdom of sin," can never be proved to belong to original sin; the two, in fact, are mutually exclusive. This can easily be demonstrated if only we recall Augustine's line of thought. He first deduces inherited sin from the natural relation between children and their sinful parents. This, however, does not involve any guilt on the part of the former. Consequently, to prove that the quality of guilt is theirs, he affirms that Adam's descendants have an active share in the guilt of their first parents, by dint of combining his erroneous exegesis of Rom. v. 12 with Heb. vii. 9, 10. Granted that this position is true, then the sin with which men enter upon life is not inherited at all, but belongs to each in virtue of his pre-existence. Hence inherited sin and personal guilt cannot be combined in thought without inaccuracy or a *sacrificium intellectus*. And this is confirmed by the literature of asceticism. Anselm and Johann Arndt alike, when treating of hereditary sin, regard it as misery, deformity, loathsomeness; guilt, however, they never connect with anything but actual sins.[2]

Now, however strongly the guilt of original sin may be expressed in the second Article of the *Confessio Augustana*, yet this very Article seems to awaken doubts regarding the admissibility of the doctrine. It has been shown above p. 333) how momentous it was for Luther's religious theory

---

[1] *C. A.* ii. : "Damnant Pelagianos et alios, qui vitium originis negant esse peccatum, et ut extenuent gloriam meriti et beneficiorum Christi, disputant, hominem propriis viribus rationis coram deo iustificari posse."

[2] *Geschichte des Pietismus,* ii. pp. 45, 70.

as a whole that he should have affirmed the characteristics *sine metu, sine fiducia erga deum* alongside of *concupiscentia.* If, then, original sin be really the basal conception of sin, the next step called for was to describe these manifestations of indifference and mistrust towards God as characteristics of original sin. But Melanchthon in his *Apology* stops short of so including the said defects in original sin that the attribute of guilt could be proved to attach to them. He rightly deems it an omission on the part of the Scholastics that they do not speak of these defects inherent in the status of sin.[1] But he finds it possible to assert them as attributes of original sin only by accepting the negative definitions of it framed by the Scholastics in direct divergence from Augustine. Now, so far as original sin has to be verified in the newly-born, what Melanchthon uses the formula *sine metu, sine fiducia erga deum* to express is either a defect which in the case of children is necessarily blameless, or a positive something which he cannot prove.[2] By comparing certain statements in the New Testament (1 Cor. ii. 14 ; Rom. vii. 5), however, he reaches all that can really be ascertained in the matter, namely, that the anti-religious aspect of sin, in so far as it implies guilt, not merely is present in single actions, but is habitual.[3] But Melanchthon here no longer maintains that this antipathy towards God is inherited, not acquired in the individual's life-time. We cannot, therefore, escape receiving the impression from this discussion, that if those characteristics of sin are to be accepted as constitutive for the idea of sin and as grounds of its worthlessness judged by the religious standard, original sin can no longer be maintained as the basal form of

---

[1] *Apol. C. A.* i. 8: "Cum de peccato originis loquuntur, graviora vitia humanae naturae non commemorant, scilicet ignorationem dei, contemptum dei, vacare metu et fiducia dei, odisse iudicium dei, fugere deum iudicantem, desperare gratiam, habere fiduciam rerum praesentium etc. Hos morbos, qui maxime adversantur legi dei, non animadvertunt scholastici."

[2] *L.c.* i. 29 : "Hugo ait, originale peccatum esse ignorationem in mente et concupiscentiam in carne. Significat enim nos nascentes afferre ignorationem dei, incredulitatem, diffidentiam, contemptum, odium dei."

[3] *L.c.* i. 31 : "Facile iudicare poterit prudens lector, non tantum culpas actuales esse, sine metu et sine fide esse ; sunt enim durabiles defectus in natura non renovata."

this idea. Or, if it is still sought to maintain this, then the above defects in religion fall under the heading of actual sins, which alone, along with original sin, enter into consideration. As regards the latter alternative, Luther's Smalcald Articles (iii. 1) confess that the Catholic opponents of the Augsburg Confession are in the right. Original sin is only described metaphysically as *corruptio naturae*, and amongst its effects —the *mala opera*—the religious defects are very strongly emphasised in the first place, and that with a greater wealth of description than is bestowed later on the moral offences. This bears out the great importance we have ascribed to this conception of sin for Luther's religious theory as a whole. But the very authors of the Formula of Concord showed themselves incapable of understanding this side of the subject, and in the Lutheran theology all sympathy with these positions has disappeared, although apart from them the doctrine of *poenitentia* is unintelligible. For it is really a disjunctive relation that obtains between the two statements —(1) that *concupiscentia*, *i.e.* immoral desire contrary to the law of God, constitutes, in the form of original sin, the basal form of the conception of sin, and (2) that it is the indifference and mistrust towards God which are involved in unlawful and criminal conduct that mark such conduct as sin according to the religious standard. Theologians have taken their stand upon the first view, and therefore they have lost sight of the other valuable idea of the Reformers, just as they ceased to realise that trust in God is the practical expression of justification (p. 181). For another reason why these anti-religious functions do not harmonise with the idea of original sin is that they are not coincident, but occupy different planes. Want of reverence towards God involves, no doubt, want of trust in Him, but in the status of sin we may also discern a want of trust in God coexisting with reverence towards Him. From this too we may learn that these defects indicate forms of active sin. But these forms must be regarded as the basal forms of sin and as determinative of its worth, if we are to have a correct and complete interpretation of sin at all. For if by *con-cupiscentia* we understand selfish desire contrary to the moral law, then this presupposes indifference and mistrust towards God, just as the recognition of that Divine law must be based upon the religious functions of reverence and trust. But if these anti-religious functions can be proved to be merely habitual, not hereditary defects, then by laying the emphasis upon them we wreck the notion of original sin.

The transmission of spiritual endowments, qualities of temperament, and emotional traits, which, guided by the resemblance between parents and children, we trace back to natural descent, carries with it no clear idea of how these capacities, apart from their action, can be set in a wrong direction and invested with guilt. Still less is it true to experience to say that every man begins life with that extreme measure of opposition to God which would result in eternal damnation. By assuming this, Augustine was led to commit an error in the formal expression he gave to the idea of original sin, because as a Platonist he made the condi-tionedness of knowledge a measure of the conditionedness of the will. In the sphere of knowledge contradiction arises when predicates which are furthest removed from one another in the series of predicables, and so far stand opposed, are affirmed of the self-same object at the same time and in the same respect. But contradiction in the will, or sin, arises even when some aim is striven after or some particular good realised which is not duly subordinated to the universal good, since the latter should be realised in every act of will. Accordingly sin, unlike the notion of logical contradiction, does not come to exist in the first instance as the extreme opposite of the good which ought to be realised; moral contra-diction, rather, comes about even when the will does not do, or does something other than, what corresponds to the perfect good. Even a particular deviation from obligatory truth for a selfish purpose is sin ; we do not need to wait for a general conscious intention to be untruthful and to suppress the truth. But in the conception of original sin this general tendency to untruthfulness as such is as distinctly predicated of each individual as the like tendency to oppose every other form of the good.   Accordingly, the conception is quite useless as a guiding principle in judging our own conduct, just because the intensity of our consciousness of moral opposition to the good is much less, and exaggerations of that kind could only serve to make us untrue to ourselves.

The notion of original sin, regarded as the expression of a bias exhibiting the extremest opposition to the good as a whole, which exists in every individual by a natural necessity, and as expressing likewise a corresponding degree of personal guilt of the highest kind, does not secure to us the complete Christian conception and estimate of actual sin in its entirety, and is negatived by the practical self-judgment which we exercise in regard to our own sin.   This notion, therefore, in the form in which it has hitherto been discussed, is likewise useless for the purpose of making the idea of the kingdom of sin more distinct or intelligible.   The kingdom of sin, however, is a substitute for the hypothesis of original sin which gives due prominence to everything that the notion of original sin was rightly enough meant to embrace.   For Luther's view, that the doctrine of original sin is revealed in Scripture, is based upon an inaccurate exegesis of particular expressions. It may be taken as beyond doubt that the personal confession in Ps. li. 7 cannot form the basis of any universal doctrinal truth.   Further, the predicate " children of wrath " (Eph. ii. 3) refers to the former actual transgression of those who now, as Christians, have the right to apply to themselves that Divine purpose of grace which is the very antithesis of wrath (vol. ii. p. 147).   Finally, Augustine's exegesis of Rom. v. 12 is admittedly false.   Paul does not say that all have sinned in the person of Adam ; and this thought finds no more support in the grammatical and rhetorical aspects of his language, than does the inference that all the descendants of Adam consequently begin their individual life with a sinful bias and the deepest guilt.   What Paul was actually thinking of when he wrote this verse and its parallel in ver. 19, not only is still a matter of dispute amongst exegetes, but perhaps is incapable of being determined at all. But in that case the theological norm of the older school itself makes it impossible to maintain the dogma of original sin. For dogmas can be based only on clear statements of Scripture. But what is clear in Paul's presentation of the subject is rather the fact that he says not a word about the transmission of sin and the inheritance of bias by natural generation.

On the other hand, Paul distinctly asserts that, in consequence of the one transgression of Adam, death is appointed by Divine decree for all his posterity, as a doom which has the value of a penal sentence. The sin of individual persons, as Paul declares, then arises only because the doom of death is already valid for all individuals in virtue of the Divine judgment.[1] For, as he adds, were the actual sin of each individual in all cases a transgression of a Divine command or prohibition, death would necessarily prevail as its consequence. But sin had no such character during the whole epoch which preceded the Mosaic legislation ; therefore the fact that in that epoch all men were subject to death was not dependent on their own sin. Now, however, as Paul assumes, death is in every case the consequence of sin ; if it is not brought about by one's own sin, it must be incurred by another's. And this according to the Biblical record can only be the transgression of Adam ; hence the doom of death imposed upon all men is dependent on the sin of Adam. Paul, however, does not look upon the relation between this cause and that effect as being mediated by the law and bond of natural descent. He takes the mediating factor to be the positive Divine appointment (ver. 16). But the question is whether, after all, another consideration should not lead us to take Paul's words as involving likewise the transmission of the sinful condition from the father of the race to his posterity. For he speaks of Adam's single actual trans-

---

[1] Cf. Dietzsch, *Adam und Christus*, p. 68 ff. The relative clause ἐφ' ᾧ πάντες ἥμαρτον refers to θάνατος. The preposition is here used as in Heb. ix. 15 ; 1 Thess. iii. 7 ; 2 Cor. vii. 4, ix. 6 ; Eph. iv. 26.

gression as the means by which sin entered the human race.
By sin he means just the phenomenon in its entirety, and
accordingly he speaks of the first action of a sinful kind as
inaugurating that state as a whole which is distinctly perceptible in the later phenomena of universal transgression.
But he still does not say that *sin*, which in its comprehensive
sense becomes real on the first act of transgression, becomes
universal otherwise than by the active transgression of every
descendant of Adam.   In the statements which follow, it is
never anything but the diffusion of the doom of death that
he connects with Adam's transgression, until at last, in the
concluding 19th verse, he comes to speak of the sinful state
of "the many," which, in his opinion, is latent in Adam's
disobedience.

Now, as the comparison in ver. 19 is really an explanation of the previous comparison (in ver. 18), it necessarily
expresses, in both its clauses, a relation different from that
expressed in ver. 18.   In the latter Paul is speaking of the
consequences of death and of life which have flowed, and are
to flow, to all men from Adam and Christ.   This thought,
then, cannot be repeated in ver. 19.   This of itself is enough
to prove Dietzsch wrong in translating κατεστάθησαν by
"are made" (*gemacht werden*), and he is further wrong in
making the second clause refer to the perfecting of moral
righteousness, to which believers attain as a future consequence of their oneness with Christ.   For the future tense
is only meant to express the logical necessity of the inference
from the analogy of the facts compared, and the righteousness
of "the many" is the righteousness by faith established by
God's decree.   Ver. 19, therefore, serves to explain ver. 18
thus : the effects of death and of life flow from Adam and
Christ respectively, in virtue of the value-content subsisting
in the disobedience of Adam and the obedience of Christ
apart from these effects.   The value-content of Christ's
obedience lies in the fact that it constitutes those who
believe in Him righteous by the judgment of God and *for
that judgment* (vol. ii. p. 327).   This being so, we are now

in a position to ascertain the sense of the first clause of the verse. (The value-content of Adam's disobedience consists in this, that his descendants are constituted sinners by the judgment and *for the judgment* of God) The relations between the parallel sets of conditions being such as we have described, we are at once dispensed from choosing between the possible meanings of καθιστάναι distinguished by Dietzsch (namely, to represent or demonstrate as, to treat as, to assign a place to, to make). Since it is God who judges that believers are righteous, and righteous for Him, it is impossible that this relation can be merely apparent, but not real. Hence, if God, by conjoining Adam's descendants with the father of the race in the common doom of death, decrees that all men are sinners, then for Him that predicate must belong to them not merely in appearance but in reality. An evidence of the correctness of this argument Paul sees in the fact that the doom of death is imposed upon men by Divine judgment before they have sinned on their own account. Now, if we looked merely to the law that death is a characteristic mark of the status of sin, we might frame a human judgment to the effect that God, by decreeing death prior to sin of the individual's own, invests Adam's descendants with no more than the semblance of being sinners. But human judgment cannot be taken as a criterion in this matter. On the contrary, what is signified by the decree of death, which we perceive in operation prior to the individual's own commission of sin, is that by the judgment of God Adam's descendants are really constituted sinners for God's judgment. Now, while this very conjoining of Adam's posterity with himself by God's judgment is valid for God's judgment, yet it is to be observed that revelation gives us no further light upon the point. We must neither regard it as mere empty appearance, nor strive to read its secret by the hypothesis of the natural entail of sin.

Paul was manifestly led to this exegesis of the Mosaic record by his interpretation of justification through Christ. True, the nature of the passage in Romans is such as to indicate a desire on his part to elucidate the process of justification through Christ by means of the analogy between it and the process of death in Adam's race. Genetically, however, it was undoubtedly the converse relation that obtained ; Paul's exegesis in regard to Adam was due, by analogy, to his conviction of the worth of Christ. So we must conclude —not merely because the Apostle's estimate of Christ is the foundation of all that goes to form his religious conception of the world, but also because the idea of justification in Christ is as distinct as the idea of mankind's sinfulness in Adam is obscure. The fact that God counts as righteous, by His judgment and for His judgment, the community which is bound up with Christ, is at the same time a revealed truth for the Christian faith, inasmuch as the specific character of that faith rests solely on the fact that God in Christ regards believers as righteous before Him. On the other hand, the fact that God, in decreeing death to the descendants of Adam, counts them as sinners in relation to Himself before they have committed sin on their own account, remains mysterious and obscure unless some key to this conception can be found from the other side. Now the correctness of the former thought needs no elucidation whatever from the analogy of the Adamic humanity. Our justification through Christ being so certainly a datum of our religious conviction, the mystery formulated by Paul, that God should regard the descendants of Adam as sinners, can lay little claim to rank as equal in value to the truth of our justification in Christ. And finally, since Paul neither asserts nor suggests the transmission of sin by generation, he offers no other reason for the universality of sin or for the kingdom of sin than the sinning of all individual men. For the sinful bias, which he discovered as present in himself when the negative commandment drew him into his first conscious act of sin (Rom. vii. 7–11), is not described by him as inherited, and can with perfect reason be understood as something acquired.

Sin is not an end in itself, not a good, for it is the opposite of the universal good. It is not an original law of the human will, for it is the striving, desiring, and acting against God. In the individual it comes to be the principle of the will's direction, for it establishes itself as the resultant of particular appetites and propensities. For as a personal bias in the life of each individual it originates, so far as we are able to observe, in sinful desire and action, which, as such, has its sufficient ground in the self-determination of the individual will. But as it actually exists in each individual and in all collectively, the normal conditions of spiritual life in men, as single individuals and as mutually associated, furnish it with materials for operating according to law in a way which is foreign to it in and for itself. This is the fact which the doctrine of original sin is meant to represent, though it does so in an exaggerated fashion and with means of explanation which are inadequate when it is adduced as proof of the bondage of the will. But the " law of sin " in the will is a result of the necessary reaction of every act of the will upon the direction of the will-power. Accordingly, by an unrestrained repetition of selfish resolves, there is generated an ungodly and selfish bias. Through involuntary reflex action, which a will unconfirmed in the good way exerts upon our experience of the influences received from others, sin is transmitted from one to another. And here we have to think not only of the facts of compliance and weakness which appear in the imitation of a bad example, but also of manifestations of that strength of impassioned resistance to will which itself misses the proper standard of action. Both these forms of temptation to sin are kept in view by Jesus and Paul in their warnings against σκάνδαλον. This term presupposes that a person, who is seduced by the conduct of another and ensnared thereby, has not developed the corresponding sinful intention in himself. This holds good even of the conduct and the lot of Jesus Himself, which, in virtue of the fact that neither His adherents nor His opponents had a true understanding of Him, became to them the occasion of a sinful misapprehension of Him, or of a sinful decision against Him (Mark vi. 3, xiv.

27, 29 ; Matt. xi. 6, xv. 12. xvii. 27 ; Gal. v. 11 ; 1 Cor. i. 23 ; Rom. ix. 33 ; 1 Pet. ii. 8). In this form, then, the innocent person gives an impetus to the consummation of sin, which has first of all been so far prepared for by varying degrees of ignorance and self-will that the impulse to sin finds an entrance. And *vice versâ* the indiscreet and careless manner in which we behave towards others is for them an occasion of sin, whether it consist in weak compliance (Matt. xvi. 23 ; Mark ix. 42 ; 1 Cor. viii. 13 ; Rom. xiv. 13, 21, xvi. 17 ; Rev. ii. 14), or in impassioned resistance (2 Cor. xi. 29). In the former case one incurs the danger of acting against his convictions, and consequently, of committing sin (Rom. xiv. 23). But in the other case also the very first step bespeaks the danger of a selfish and uncharitable tendency, unless moral watchfulness is maintained against it (1 John ii. 10). This whole web of sinful action and reaction, which presupposes and yet again increases the selfish bias in every man, is entitled " the world," which in this aspect of it is not of God, but opposed to Him. It is not necessary that everyone should be implicated in this sinful web, to the extent of contributing to it his own share of wickedness and untruth, for the selfish bias can also be associated with the appreciation of particular goods, with family pride, the spirit of caste, and patriotism, or with loyalty to the Church's creed. For the Church, as constituted by law and infested with partisanship, is not the Kingdom of God at all. The legal organisation of the Church is not the Christian religion, but belongs to the world, and like it is to be distinguished from the Kingdom of God (§ 35). And if anyone would be convinced of the necessity of again inculcating the doctrine of σκάνδαλον, which has disappeared from theology since the time of Chemnitz, let him but survey from this point of view the present position of Church parties and their public organs.

§ 42. The notion *sin* expresses a religious and universal-ethical estimate of what is otherwise distinguished, according to a legal or particular-ethical standard, as misconduct, inten-

tional or unintentional wrong-doing, crime, vice, baseness, or
wickedness⌋ On the other hand, the notion *evil*, which even
Schleiermacher (vol. i. p. 507) brings into the closest causal
connection with sin, and which, in its entirety, he designates
as *Divine punishment*, is as such of no religious import. It
is not our relation of subordination to God, but always some
claim born of our freedom, that furnishes a standard for what
we call evil. For since we have experience of our freedom
in the conception and execution of our ends, evil signifies
the whole compass of possible restrictions of our purposive
activity. Now, as these restrictions may arise both from
natural events and from the will of human beings, Schleiermacher divides evils into social or immediate, and natural or
mediate. I leave on one side, in the first instance, the predicates which accompany this division, for they have been
evoked by a combination of the notions of evil and sin
from which I dissent. But⌡the two kinds of evil assumed by
Schleiermacher are not co-ordinate. For all social evil proceeds from the will of others only by operating upon us
through their natural organism. Were the hatred and
calumny of others not natural events, no social evil would ever
come into existence at all. Hence evil is always a natural
event. Its division into species depends on the fact that, as
a restriction of our freedom, it is sometimes merely the result
of mechanical causes, while in other cases it takes its rise in
the will. But in the case of the latter species of evil we must
regard as the ground of possible restrictions of freedom not
merely the will of others, but also our own will, and that too
both in the form of deliberate intention and of carelessness.
For a man's own freedom is limited by natural events not
only when others or he himself wills something which they
ought not, but also when they do not will some definite good
which they ought to will.⌋ An illness contracted by anyone
deliberately or through negligence takes its rise in the will
no less than an intentional or unintentional injury done by
others to his health or honour. ⌊Hence evil is in all cases a
natural event, restricting us in the use of our freedom, and in

the conception and realisation of our purposes. It originates either in merely natural causes, and therefore, being non-purposive, is accidental; or else it has its roots in the will. In the latter kind of evil it is either one's own or another's will that is operative intentionally or negligently. Social evil is thus only a part, though a very extensive part, of the second class of evils.

From the connection between the general notion of evil and the restriction of our freedom, it follows that that notion depends in every case solely on our own judgment. Accordingly, Schleiermacher's distinction of mediate from immediate evil is invalid. According to him, evils arising from mechanical causes, *i.e.* natural evils, are to be reckoned evils because the world appears different to the sinner from what it did to the originally perfect man. But in judging that an accidental fire, or a flood which ruins our property, is an evil, no thought either of sin or of a comparison with the original perfection of mankind is implied, but rather the presupposition that we have need of property, not only as a means of subsistence, but also to enable us to serve our generation in our calling. Social evil, *e.g.* slander, is of essentially the same character. The feeling that our freedom has been violated by it is due solely to our forming a judgment to that effect, since we might quite well judge that the slander of contemptible men does not impair our freedom or our honour. That the notion of evil is subjectively conditioned is also proved in cases which come under the first class, by the fact that one man feels as evils those accidental bodily sufferings which another, through having grown accustomed to them or owing to an effort of will, no longer experiences as restrictions of his freedom. Hence occurrences substantially identical may count as evils to one man and not to another. Finally, the distinction between merited and unmerited evils enters into the ordinary mode of estimating evils, and that in such a way as to affect each of the two principal classes. Evils which arise from mechanical causes are partly unmerited, and partly merited, should it be felt that the possible means of prevention have not been employed. Evils which arise from our own will are always merited, so far at least as that term merely denotes their source, and is not taken as indicating the ethical value of the actions by which the evil has been occasioned. For should a man, *e.g.* a soldier, be compelled by his occupation to neglect his health, or should he draw down upon himself the hatred of other men just through his veracity and advocacy of the good, then the evils which follow are ethically unmerited. Again, evils brought upon a man by himself may be accounted ethically merited, as for instance, should a man ruin his health by intemperance, or evoke the hostility of others by violating their rights. What is alone of importance here is that a man should be practised in forming moral judgments on any given case. Where this is lacking, the very distinction between ethically non-merited and merited evil is not fully made out. But even the judgment that we are personally culpable in respect of certain evils has *per se* no connection with the religious judgment of self, for the guilt in this case is measured merely by reference to the fact that our own will, by commission or omission, is the cause or partial cause of restrictions of freedom which it experiences itself.

Hence the notion of evil has no direct relation to the notion of sin. It is not a religious conception like the latter. For the notion of sin is determined by comparison with God, to Whom reverence and trust are due, and by the religious estimate of the universal moral law ; the notion of evil, on the other hand, by the relative standard of the freedom of the individual. In point of fact the notion of evil is so much a relative one, that evils may be turned into goods or into means towards moral good, which could never be the case with sin. For the limitations which in certain quarters of the globe nature puts upon the preservation of human life and man's instinct to enjoy natural objects, are the cause of that richer and fuller ethical development of humanity which could not be attained in a more favourable environment. In the same way the limitations which arise

23

from social life, and by which men are disciplined or discipline themselves, come to be transformed into benefits. Now these experiences would be altogether impossible were evil an entity as distinct and objectively defined as sin. So far, however, as any relation obtains between the two, it can only be indirect and restricted in degree. It was impossible for the older theology to ignore this way of looking at the subject. For although all evils, as Divine penalties, were from the outset attributed to sin, and though the two were regarded as coincident in extent, yet it had to be acknowledged not only that evils lose their penal value for believers, but also that death no longer wears the character of an evil, but is rather deemed a means of release (p. 44). This exception itself forbids us to adhere to the objective theory of the interconnection of sin and evil as being the rule; while the transformation of evils into goods proves true not only in the case of those who are regenerate in the Christian sense, but even in the case of every energetic and genuine character. Since the fact rather is (p. 46) that the specifically religious feeling of guilt is bound up with our reckoning some particular evil which befalls us as a Divine punishment, that is enough to demonstrate that it is an error to think of evil in its entirety as the equivalent of Divine punishment.

Schleiermacher has not made these relations any clearer, but rather succeeded in confusing them, by blending in a peculiar way his own observation—which does not, indeed, extend far enough—with a complaisant accommodation to tradition. He points out the relative character of, at least, natural evil, though social evil, too, partakes of the same nature. He bases that conclusion principally on the fact that natural evil arises out of the opposition between the world and man, which opposition was originally designed as a stimulus to the activity of the God-consciousness and an incentive to moral resolution, but which, by reason of the impotence of the God-consciousness in a state of sin, now leads to restrictions of life. For otherwise Schleiermacher

adopts in the most unqualified fashion the old doctrine that
all evil is the penalty of sin, in the sense that by God's
dispensation it is bound up with wickedness in the general
order of things.   He modifies the import of this proposition
only so far as to say that the totality of evil is the correlative
of sin considered as the conjoint act of mankind, and is
coincident therewith.   For, as he holds, it is a Jewish and
pagan error, which Jesus Himself rejected, to suppose that
the amount of evil corresponds, in the case of every individual,
to that of sin (vol. i. p. 507).   To this representation I reply
that the entrance of universal sin has in no wise had the
effect of abolishing and neutralising the original character of
the opposition between the world and us, which was to serve
as a restriction, and yet as a stimulus to the development of
freedom.   Thence it follows, therefore, that, as has been laid
down already, the conceptions of evil and sin are not properly
kindred.   To be sure, not merely in the Greek and the
Hebrew, but also in the Christian, religion, it is reckoned that
an opposite religious and moral attitude in men involves an
opposite relation to the world, *i.e.* either lordship over it or
restriction by it, and that, too, at God's instance.   Within
Christianity this is an antithetical inference from the knowledge we have that the good, as the warp and woof of the
Kingdom of God, is the final end of God in the world.   From
this point of view the idea of Divine penalties is legitimate
and necessary.   But the application of this notion in
experience is not so simple as unscrutinised theological
tradition. would lead us to expect.   For evil in general
cannot be known to be a Divine punishment of sin in the
case of an individual or of the entire race. The view of
evils as punishments is conditioned, rather, by the specifically
religious consciousness of guilt; not merely by the judgment
that we have incurred a restriction of our freedom by our
own act, but by the judgment that the act in question has
contradicted the Divine moral law.   Further, the only way
in which we can charge ourselves with guilt for the aggregate
of evils in society, is by judging that by sinful action we

partly help to produce this aggregate, partly adopt it. But let this interpretation of general evils as personal punishment extend the individual's consciousness of guilt never so far, the coincidence asserted between evil generally and punishment for sin still remains unproved. It is true that the feeling of guilt is a sufficient motive for our estimating evils as penalties inflicted on ourselves, but it is not a principle which justifies us in imputing as Divine punishments to others the evils which they experience. Jesus' example shows that the Christian view of the world is distinguished from that which belongs to pre-Christian religions just by the fact that evils, which affect others, are never to be regarded as being connected with their sin. Destructive natural events, such as pestilences, deluges, congenital infirmity, or even acts of military violence, are, in the religious theories of ancient nations, regarded objectively as Divine punishments, people's minds being awakened by such experiences also to careless offences which they might have committed against law or ceremonial duty.   Nevertheless, in consequence of Christ's express declarations (John ix. 1–3 ; Luke xiii. 1–5), a member of the Christian society will decline to have evils of that kind set down to him by others as Divine punishments. When a pastor, whose zeal has found Dogmatics but an evil counsellor, undertakes to make use of such calamities as occasions for castigatory sermons to his congregation, he excites legitimate irritation, and lays himself open to the judgment of Jesus, " Except ye repent, ye shall all likewise perish." For the judgment, that those who are visited by a signal calamity have sinned in a signal manner, is a pagan and Jewish error, and, should it be propounded in Christian society, a proof that a changed heart is still lacking.   True, the acceptance of Divine teleology seems to demand that we should ascribe, though not to evil in every case, at least to a signal and conspicuous instance, the significance of a special Divine intention to punish. "But who has known the mind of the Lord, or who has been His counsellor?"   In such cases the Christian view of the world comes out, rather, when we infer from our consciousness of reconciliation that God is educating us in patience and humility and in manifestation of that sympathy which becomes Christians.[1] But when the notion of educative penalties is employed in this way, we abandon the indiscriminate application of the dubious proposition, that all evils are Divine punishments in a detrimental sense.

This dogmatic prejudice, of which even Schleiermacher was unable to rid himself, rests on the fact that in traditional Dogmatics too narrow a scope is ascribed to reconciliation. For if it is restricted to deliverance from guilt and the penalties of sin, then such a view either demands the assumption that all evils were and are punishments for sin, or it provides the reconciled with anything but a secure and free attitude towards all the evils of life, particularly towards those which experience does not permit us to reckon penal. Where that narrow interpretation of reconciliation is maintained, it leads in practice to people's torturing themselves with the attempt to put a penal construction upon all evils which befall them, lest alongside of the consciousness of reconciliation there should exist in their experience a wide domain shadowed by alien necessity. In theology we should have at the same time the corresponding position—a position which it is impossible to prove from the general notion of evil. But reconciliation is not merely the ground of deliverance from the guilt of sin, and from evils in some way merited; it is also the ground of deliverance from the world, and the ground of spiritual and moral lordship over the world. Through reconciliation, too, we come to cherish a different estimate of self, and are changed in disposition, as well as in our whole attitude of character towards unmerited evils, which are due to the fact that the created spirit is implicated in the organised system of nature—that system being understood in the sense in which it actually forms a precondition of social life amongst men. Since the effects of reconciliation are thus different in degree, the difference between evils recognised in our customary judgments, may or rather must

[1] *Geschichte des Pietismus*, ii. p. 543, iii. p. 68.

be accepted by the Christian view of the world and theology,
to wit, that only a part of them is to be referred, *quâ* punishment, to individual or common sin.] The principle thus
adduced, it is true, has still to be proved. But it had to
be asserted here, partly because it confirms, as a just
presupposition, the distinction—commonly made in spite of
Dogmatics—between the scope of Divine punishment and
that of evils, and partly because the formation of the theological system generally is determined by regard to the ideas
of the Kingdom of God and reconciliation. Otherwise we
expose ourselves to the danger of setting up false premises,
and reaching false conclusions regarding these leading conceptions of Christianity.

[The religious and theological estimate of *death* will likewise have to conform to the explanations now given of the
relation between sin and evil.] Although the older school,
following Paul, held that the universal destiny of death was
the objective result of the first sin, yet it was compelled by
the idea of reconciliation to add that, for those whose sin is
forgiven, death has no longer the value of punishment, but
serves as a means of their release (p. 46). This addition
contains the important implication, that, in the religious view
of the world which prevails in Christianity, death at all events
does not count as the greatest evil, that the estimate which is
formed of it stands in no direct relation to the consciousness
of transgression which even one who is reconciled may have,
that, on the contrary, the destiny of death at most stands in
relation to the power of sin to which men are subject in the
state previous to conversion (Rom. viii. 10, 38). In the case
of the reconciled there is not that fear of death which is an
evidence of the bondage in which mankind lay before the
time of Christ, and which testifies to man's recognition of an
affinity between his own sin and death (Heb. ii. 15). When
the topic of death has to be dealt with in Christian theology,
we must start from the light shed upon it by the authentic
Christian view of the world, and not from impressions native
to pre-Christian religions. It must be added that, viewed in

the light of the certainty of eternal life, which is attached to reconciliation, death may indeed seem hard enough to each individual, but it will no longer appear as the sheer opposite of that purposeful life in which the soul is conscious of its worth (Rom. xiv. 8). As such the pre-Christian nations regarded it, a view which directly corresponds to the deficiency or uncertainty of their hope concerning the restoration of life after death. The Old Testament spokesmen for the people of Israel partly lamented death as a natural fate, and partly connected it with sin, inasmuch as in both cases they chafed at the contradiction it involved to the religious destination of man to communion with God. The Christian and the Old Testament views, accordingly, are opposed to one another and mutually exclusive. They are independent of each other, just as the religion of reconciliation rises above the highest manifestations of that Old Testament piety which strives after reconciliation. For the Psalmists especially chafed at the fate of death, just because the religious thought of Israel had moved them to form a higher estimate of the vocation of man, while yet it afforded them no assurance of reconciliation with God and the world.

Now it is a defect in theology, due to a mechanical use of Scripture, that not the New Testament, but the Old Testament, estimate of death has been employed in fixing the standard conception. For the Christian view of the subject is thereby forced to occupy the position of an exception to that standard. This proceeding is quite analogous to the way in which the legal requital of human conduct has been put forward as the principle of the Divine world-order, while the Christian *régime* of reconciliation and the Kingdom of God, which is of an exactly opposite kind, is linked on to that principle by way of exception (§ 33). True, Paul deduced the existence of the universal destiny of death from the sin of Adam. Nevertheless, the mere fact that this idea was framed by the Apostle does not straightway qualify it to become a theological principle. It is not a necessary element in the Christian view of the world, which, with perfect correctness, decides that death is neither an obstacle to blessedness, nor an object to be feared, since Christ has reconciled men and risen from the dead. Moreover, the Christian view of the world as such does not call for any theory regarding the origin of death. Paul formed his conception of the matter, too, solely by way of inference from the principle of reconciliation and eternal life, his exegesis of the Old Testament record serving him as a medium. But a position which is only related inferentially to the Christian view of the world, cannot claim to rank, as a theological principle, above the essential content of the Christian view. There is now this further fact, that not everyone can convince himself that the theory which Paul arrived at, of the dependence of death upon Adam's transgression, is correct. Are such persons any the less able to adopt the estimate of death which springs from the Christian idea of reconciliation? That cannot be justly affirmed. Nay rather, our judgment, that we must indeed die, but that we die unto the Lord (Rom. xiv. 8), is entirely unaffected whether we regard that destiny as a dispensation of nature, or as the consequence of Adam's transgression. For in both cases the theory is excluded that death is a consequence of our own sin. And that is the point of importance if the expectation of death is not to collide with our consciousness of reconciliation, if the dread of death is not to continue, and cause the reconciled to doubt whether death is for them an ascent to the level of eternal life with God, where we are set free from the burden of the transitory.

For the rest, Paul has expressed his view about the doom of death imposed on Adam's descendants in such a way that it forms no obstacle to the Christian theory, of which he himself is a classical representative. If there is no condemnation to those who are Christ's, not even the condemnation of death, death is in their case only a phenomenon belonging to their life as associated with an earthly body, and their spirit is life unaffected thereby (Rom. viii. 1, 10). This excludes precisely the Old Testament idea of death as the end of personal life, the utter stultification of the created

spirit.   But the point of importance for theology is, that
this latter should not be assumed to be the normal and
universal significance of death in the determinate counsel of
God, since nothing can be theologically formulated as the
determinate counsel and dispensation of God, but what comes
to view in connection with the eternally chosen community
of the Kingdom of God.   Otherwise theology never succeeds
in grasping the unity of the world-order, but can only affirm
two successive and mutually contradictory decrees of God,
the first of which has for its import the universal condemnation of men to death, while the second is directed to the
restoration of a section of mankind to life, and thus has the
form of an exceptional decree.]   Even Paul lends no counte-
nance to a representation such as this.   For he declares that
God has shut up Jews and Gentiles together unto disobedience
that He might have mercy upon them all (Rom. xi. 32).   If
even the judgment of the Jews turns upon Paul's well-known
reading of the character of the Mosaic law, then the similar
judgment of the Gentiles can only be understood in the light
of that more comprehensive Divine purpose which led to the
original sentence of death upon men.   The fact, therefore,
that this action on God's part is described in the Christian
revelation as a means or a precondition of grace, suggests
that the right interpretation of God's earlier economy is to
be found in its connection with His final purpose.

—[It has thus far been granted that the penal purpose of
God is the source of a narrower circle of evils, those, namely,
conditioned by the religious feeling of guilt.]   But this idea
of a Divine purpose to punish requires to be more precisely
defined.   It cannot, of course, be framed where there is no
recognition of a Divine government of the world, or of the
conception of the Divine authority of the moral law. [Still,
in the religions of civilised peoples we do find that certain
evils are wont to be regarded as Divine punishments.   This
way of looking at the matter proceeds upon the idea of a
reciprocal legal relation existing between men and God, an
idea which in the case of the Greeks, the Romans, and the

Israelites derives its origin from the fact that these peoples regarded the State as, even in a religious sense, the highest good. Now, although Christ's express declarations (p. 356) warn us against taking the degree of evil, in legal fashion, as an indication of the degree of transgression on the part of those afflicted, yet the traditional theology is content to set up the characteristic idea of retribution as a perfectly adequate expression of the penal value of an evil. The superficiality of this view becomes manifest in the case of the theologians of the *Aufklärung*, who, while willing to recognise the orthodox representation, yet do not find it corroborated by experience, and hence feel compelled to abandon it, and substitute in its stead the quite differently constituted notion of "educative punishments" (vol. i. p. 403). If this procedure be erroneous, then the error must in part be attributed to orthodoxy, which has never subjected the legal conception of punishment to a critical examination, and hence has been unable accurately to define it in its Christian usage. Now, punishment in its legal sense is a deprivation, entailed by the authority of civil society, upon one who has acted contrary to his legal obligations, in order that the absolute claims of civil society may be affirmed (p. 247). But the Christian religion is not a legal federation between God and man. To apply, therefore, the legal conception of punishment to certain evils within the scope of our religious view of the world, cannot be right.

This want of perspicuity, however, is due solely to the fact that, after all, the Christian religion bears a certain analogy to law—an analogy, however, which does not hold good in respect of all the essential characteristics of the latter. For in point of fact law always involves a contraction of personal freedom, but its object therein is to guarantee the moral independence of each individual in relation to everyone else. The prerogative of every member of civil society consists in the right he has to take full advantage of all permissible, or not legally proscribed, means for the development of his moral personality. Accordingly, the personal

right of each finds its scope in the sphere of what is permissible, which exists alongside of the sphere of legally
prescribed and proscribed activity.   Now the idea of a right,
possessed by men in relation to God, is framed in consideration
of what God permits to them, with a view to their making
good their own proper individuality over against Himself.
At both the stages of Biblical religion there comes out clearly
the conception, that in the fellowship granted or permitted to
men by Divine grace we earn the enjoyment of independent
personality, just as it is in that fellowship that the idea of
God comes to assume its proper form.   It is in this sense of
the word " right " that the Israelites, on the ground of their
having been chosen by God, possess the priesthood, as
representing the right to approach God.   And in the same
sense dogmatic theologians frame the idea of a right of Divine
sonship, as belonging to those who are reconciled in Christ
through the grace of God.   Comparing, then, the implications
of this notion with the characteristics of the general legal
conception, we see that they accord with each other in
expressing personal independence.   But personal right in
civil society has reference to the material of allowable actions,
whereas the right of men over against God depends on the form
of Divine permission, inasmuch as the determining impulse of
Divine grace makes its appeal to their freedom.   Further, in
civil society what is called personal right is the antithesis of
legal obligation, whereas in the religious sphere one's right in
relation to God is also a comprehensive expression which
covers one's whole duty towards Him.   Finally, in civil
society each member is conscious of his personal right as
contradistinguished from every other, whereas the right implied in the priesthood and the right of Divine sonship
are bestowed respectively upon the individual Israelite and
Christian, in virtue of his reckoning himself part of the entire
religious community, and thinking and acting in harmony
with it.   And thus the thought of right in relation to God,
as expressing personal independence, is counterbalanced by
the relations of religious subordination to Him.

Now, if the notion of punishment, which is indigenous to the region of law, is to possess validity in the domain of the Christian view of the world and Christian self-judgment, then, as has previously been inferred (p. 355) from the meaning of the Kingdom of God as the Divine final end in the world, our experiences of evil, speaking generally, will be linked by God to wicked conduct. But since a multitude of evils have the value for men of being means of education and trial, or carry with them the glory of martyrdom, it is not possible for others to determine, in a particular case, which evils have the significance of retributive penalties. We decided, therefore, that a feeling of unrelieved guilt is the only thing which enables the individual, if he thinks about God at all, to recognise his condition as penal, and set it to his own account. Now we find this confirmed when the deprivation of the right of Divine sonship is interpreted as a Divine punishment. To begin with, this form of expression is only the Christian phase of the previously (p. 53) discussed idea of Divine punishment, understood as an experience of separation from God. For the loss involved in such separation is estimated in the light of the right, bestowed upon the Israelites, to approach God. The result of our present inquiry was thus foreshadowed by our earlier analysis of the interpretations of Divine punishment which have become fused in theological tradition. But at the same time our present conclusion serves in several ways both to confirm and to give point to the suggestions we have made towards a definition of the forgiveness of sins. *First*, by means of the comparative or relative notion of the forfeiture of the right of access to God or of Divine sonship, the hypothesis of a graduated series of penal states is confirmed to this extent, that in particular instances it will be easier or harder to regain the privilege of access to God or of Divine sonship. In any case, either the notion of Divine penalties is irrational, or else we must abandon the supposition that all the penalties of God are objectively equal in severity, and that every sin is in itself deserving of eternal damnation. *Secondly*, the above notion of Divine punishment goes to confirm the position that external evils can be demonstrated to be Divine penalties only from the point of view of the subjective feeling of guilt (§§ 10, 11). For the right of access to God or of Divine sonship cannot be thought of as forfeited, unless the forfeiture is consciously recognised as such by the individual affected by it. The sense of having forfeited one's right of Divine sonship, which forces one to regard an experience of external evils as a Divine penalty, is the feeling of guilt that separates from God. Again, then, the accuracy of our previous investigations is confirmed by the idea of Divine punishment here set forth. *Thirdly*, it follows that the unrelieved feeling of guilt is not so much one penal state among others, but is itself actually that of which all external penal evils are but the concomitant circumstances. Even in the older school of theology it was maintained that the feeling of guilt should be connected with Divine penalties, but this supposition it was impossible to prove by the modes of thought to which they confined themselves. But if the forfeiture of rights in the sphere of law becomes real even when the sentence of punishment is passed, and does not require for its existence the execution of sentence by forfeiture of the property or of the customary freedom of the convicted person, then Divine punishment must be constituted precisely by the consciousness of guilt, as being an index of the forfeiture of access to God or of Divine sonship.

These results throw further light on the interpretation, which occurs in Paul's Epistle to the Romans, of the estate of death in which men stand. Hitherto we have had to leave undecided the question as to how far God, in decreeing death upon the descendants of Adam before they sinned, constituted them sinners in relation to Himself (p. 347). While it is impossible that this decree carries with it anything of the nature of mere appearance, we had for all that to forego the more precise determination of the fact denoted by the decree of universal death prior to the sin of individuals. Now, if this doom be called a penal sentence, it is a fair question whether that does

not signify that God, in thus antecedently decreeing death to
Adam's race, apart from the physical aspect of dying, has
really carried out His purpose that mankind should not attain
to access to God and Divine sonship, but should remain apart
from Him with their consciousness of guilt unrelieved. This
would also be the purport of the statement, that in the disobedience of our first parent God has represented the multitude
of his descendants as sinners both by His judgment *and for
His judgment*, has represented them, *i.e.*, as those who ought
not to have any proper fellowship with Him. This conjecture
is corroborated by the parallel statement regarding the significance of Christ's obedience. For the relation of the
justified to God as expressed in terms of that great fact is,
according to 1 Pet. iii. 18, precisely that of vouchsafed
access to God. Hence the penal state of all mankind who
lived before Christ, which Paul recognises in the sentence of
death antecedently passed upon them, and which, arguing
from the conditions of justification in Christ, he infers
as the counterpart of the other, consists in their being
debarred from that fellowship with God which was to be
first rendered possible through Christ. Now, although the
estimate of the religious community of Israel which Paul
adds in his well-known view regarding the design of the
Mosaic law stands, as we see by comparing it with the
Epistle to the Hebrews, in considerable need of amendment,
yet the debarring of the Gentiles from communion with God
is an observation true to fact. The singular element in all
this is to be found in the fact that Paul combines the Divine
intention of it with the sentence of death passed on Adam's
posterity, and that he maintains the existence of a penal
condition previous to the actual demerit of individuals. To
say the least, that is inexact; for personal demerit is necessary
in order that even an evil common to all may be recognised
through the subjective consciousness of guilt as a personal
punishment. But there will be the less need to repudiate
these observations as offending against the incontestable
meaning of the Pauline passage, seeing that Paul himself, in

another reference in the same Epistle, attributes the alienation of the Gentiles from God to their own demerit. Both representations are attempts on Paul's part to place himself in the true attitude to a historical problem which necessarily obtruded itself with special force on the Apostle to the Gentiles ; nor can we take exception to the diversity in his solutions of the problem, for the point at issue does not concern the essence of the Christian religion, but only a derivative question.

§ 43. The older school, with their assertion that all evils are Divine punishments, awaken in our minds the impression of their professing to have a complete insight into all parts of the Divine world-order. But even Schleiermacher, while he rejects, indeed, the distributive evidence adduced for that thesis, has overstepped the bounds of his competence as a Christian theologian in maintaining, as a general principle, that the totality of evil in the world is coextensive with the existence of sin, regarded as a conjoint act of the whole human race. This thesis, for one thing, goes beyond all possible experience, and, moreover, it is explicitly disproved by the very words of Jesus which Schleiermacher has adduced, those, namely, concerning the man born blind. As Jesus' disciples, according to His teaching in this context, we ought in the case of certain evils not to raise at all the question regarding their connection with sin. But as regards this point the Christian theologian, as such, is not differently situated from the individual Christian. That sort of omniscience which the older divines actually claim on this as on so many points, and which is customarily expected of a theologian by believers who have been spoiled by false dogmatic teaching, always serves only to compromise the Christian faith in the eyes of others, who adhere indeed to Christianity, but will not accept a system of words in exchange for religion. A theologian can as little maintain conscientiously the quantitative coextension of all evils with all sins, as he can solve with real success the other classical problems which belong to this region of thought. Who knows, for example, what are the reasons why God permits and endures at all, as a phenomenon extending over the whole human race, the sin which runs counter to His own final end ? And besides, it would certainly be an act of presumption to maintain, with Zwingli, that sin, in its whole extent, is called into existence by God as the necessary presupposition of the redemption which He has decreed from eternity, and as the opposite of the good, by experiencing which men are to acquire the knowledge of, and taste for, the good. If we know that the final end of the human race, or the highest good, is realised through the bringing in of the Kingdom of God, and if we possess in this principle that practical guidance which each Christian man needs for salvation, we must refrain from passing any positive judgment which would imply that God has condemned the rest of mankind, whether as guilty or as innocent—even though this hypothesis appears to be, logically, the reverse-side of the former conviction. As theologians, we are justified in explaining the practical conditions of our spiritual and moral life, on which depends our estimate of its intrinsic content and its relative place in the world, as following by logical necessity from our knowledge of the character of God as revealed in the Christian religion ; but no principle of logic warrants our interpreting the various aspects of the apparently aimless and really adverse phenomena of human life, which surround the luminous domain of our religious and moral duty, by the hypothesis of a positive eternal condemnation of the human race by God (p. 130). On the other hand, the pretended dogmatic omniscience and in-fallibility, which spring from the rationalistic principle which is at the root of all orthodoxy, are fitted only to lead theological knowledge into error, as also to repel the sound religious sense which, resting on experience, repudiates such dogmatic propositions as stand outside of all relation to possible experience.

The assertion that sin is infinite in its nature, even when removed by the redemptive work of Christ, is the result of a purely rational inference. How ill-grounded this proposition is, we see from the way in which Thomas introduces it. " In sin," he says, "there are contained two elements. On the one hand, sin consists in turning away from unchangeable and infinite good. On one side, therefore, sin is infinite. On the other hand, sin consists in unregulated turning towards changeable good. In this respect sin is finite, especially as the act of turning is itself also finite. For the acts of a created being as such cannot be infinite" (vol. i. p. 65). Thomas decides for the adoption of the former of these views of sin, because he likewise measures the worthlessness of sin by the fact that it violates the infinite majesty of God; for even in human affairs, he says, an offence is all the more heinous, the greater the person against whom the offence is committed. This presupposition, the validity of which is also accepted by Protestant orthodoxy, has already been refuted in the most convincing manner by Duns (vol. i. p. 74). For either the "infinity of sin" is to be understood objectively, in which case we land ourselves in Manichaeism; or the idea is a subjective impression, in which case it means only that we cannot with all our efforts of imagination arrive at, nor with all possible intensification of our own consciousness of guilt represent exhaustively, the extent of sin in space and time, and its power to disturb the orderly course of human history. But for that reason sin, as a product of the limited powers of all men, is yet limited, finite, and quite transparent for God's judgment. And, moreover, that that formula of Thomas is indirectly expressed in Paul's leading train of thought, and that the death to which the posterity of Adam are doomed is equivalent to eternal death, can neither be proved exegetically nor brought into harmony with the view of Paul as a whole. For he excludes from the posterity of Adam who are doomed to death the community of those who are to be saved, for whom death is merely a passing experience, and he adds the explicit proviso that, in the case of those who are lost, it is the refusal to believe in Christ which gives death the intensified character of eternal destruction (Rom. viii. 10; 2 Cor. ii. 15, 16). Inasmuch as the σωζόμενοι in Paul's sense can at no stage of their

24

existence and in no respect be conceived as ἀπολλύμενοι, there can be nothing less in accord with his authority than the assumption of a change in the decree of God, such as orthodox Lutheran Dogmatics is guilty of in the proposition : God has in Adam condemned all the posterity of Adam, and afterwards brings some of them to blessedness on account of their faith. As the latter decree is thrown back into eternity, the proposition comes to mean that God eternally resolves to bless those whom in a temporal decree He condemns for ever with Adam. This manifest absurdity is accepted also by the Reformed theology, since the point of distinction between the two theologies—whether or not God's election is conditioned by the faith which He foresees—is here of no account. Quite consistently with his theological dependence on Luther, Calvin has allowed himself to be led into adopting this view, by the fact that for Luther both the doctrine of predestination and that of original sin have value only as evidences for the bondage of the human will—and that as co-ordinate arguments, completely independent of one another. As Luther had no intention at all of constructing a theological system from the point of view of the idea of election, he contented himself with establishing the bondage of the will in relation to salvation by affirming that God in His first decree placed the whole of mankind under the ban of original sin, and in a decree subsequent in time, according to His own secret election, restored a portion of mankind, contrariwise, to blessedness. One who believes that he may proceed thus in theological science of course shuts his eyes to the contradiction which is expressly contained in the above formula. But even Calvin has not clearly grasped the fact that his doctrine of *providentia*, to say nothing of that of *electio*, demands at the very outset a quite different conception of common sin from that which was taken over from Augustine. Just here we can see very clearly that, as I have shown elsewhere on different grounds,[1] the theological system of Calvin was not developed from the principle of the idea of election.

[1] *Jahrb. für deutsche Theologie*, xiii. p. 108.

Mediaeval theology, however, presents a series of classical authorities the tendency of whose views is that the notion of sin can only in a modified way be referred to the elect, or the redeemed, if the unity of the religious view and the connectedness of the theological system are to be maintained.   In this series the place of precedence must be assigned to *Abelard,* in so far as he refutes the idea that redemption through Christ's death means purchase from the power of the devil, by maintaining that the predestined, to whom redemption applies, have, on the very ground of their Divine election, never been under the power of the devil (vol. i. p. 49).   For, inasmuch as the devil represents the extreme, that is, the definitive degree of sin, those persons cannot be reckoned as his who belong by eternal election to God.   *Duns Scotus* accepts the view which was quite rightly formulated by Thomas, namely, that sin, in virtue of its origin from created will, is something finite in its nature, and to this he adds that to maintain that sin is intrinsically infinite would be Manichaean.   But while Duns accepts the terminology of Thomas so far as to allow that the " infinity of sin " may be maintained in a certain external sense, in virtue of its opposition to the infinite God, he explains at the same time that the punishment for deadly sin may be called infinite in the merely external sense, that is, when the will persists finally in sin, but not because God could punish sin in no other way (vol. i. p. 74).   Therefore, the full extent of the penalty of condemnation is reserved by Duns solely for those who persist finally in sin.   And yet for this reason the endless punishment to which they are doomed is not, strictly speaking, infinite, because the final resolve to persist in sin also remains within the limits of created being. All the more evident is it that that sin is finite which finds forgiveness through the intrinsically finite merit of Christ.

The following arguments of *John Wessel* [1] move within

---

[1] *De magnitudine passionum* x.: " Hic dolor debitus noster dolor est, quem si vere agnus dei tollens peccata mundi pro nobis portavit, in tanta mensura portavit,

the bounds of a more concrete theological theory. On the
lines of Isa. liii. 4, he explains the pain which Jesus took
upon Himself, as the Lamb of God, as the penal suffering
destined for us. As such, it is equivalent to the penalty
which each single person has incurred. But as penalty is
always incurred exclusively in one's individual capacity, and
its measure to be determined by the degree of individual
sinfulness, therefore the purpose of Jesus, when He took
upon Himself our penal suffering, must be judged by the
measure of the penalty which is due to each individual. At
the last judgment He will urge against all the damned the
valid charge that He took upon Himself as much suffering
as would suffice in God's judgment for the absolution of their
penalties, but that they despised Him. But for the individual elect, He has undertaken only so much suffering as
serves for the remission of the limited penalties which were
destined for each of them. The measure of this punishment,
it is true, is hidden from the eyes of men. But no one of
the redeemed has of himself merited eternal damnation, seeing
that they have not fallen into the stiff-necked sin of the
despisers of grace, but merely into the sin of weakness and
ignorance, and that their deadly sins are not sins unto death.
In the foregoing exposition, this Augustinian takes no account

quantus districto divinae iustitiae iudicio repositus pro omnibus omnium nostrum peccatis, quos redemit ex morte, languore et dolore. — Superat omnia
divinarum legum necessitas, quibus statutum, nihil finaliter indecorum futurum
in regno destinato. Non iam de suppliciis inferni quis obiiciat. Nullus enim
per Christum redemtus unquam meruit tali supplicio cruciari, quia nullus re-
demtorum in illam obstinaciam obdurati cordis prolapsus est, sed infirmitate
et ignorantia, non obdurata malitia contemtorum lapsorum in profundum.
Licet igitur dicamus, multos mortaliter peccare in hac nostra humana infirmitate, nemo tamen per haec peccat usque ad mortem. Sunt igitur peccata nostra
mortalia, sed non mortua, sicut nos mortales et non mortui. Quae autem
mortalia tantum sunt, quanta poena divinis legibus reposita sit, non puto
cuiquam notum esse mortalium. Iuste ergo in iudicio Iesus contra omnes
perditos causabitur, tantam eius afflictionem pro eis assumptam, ut dei iudicio
ad omnem poenam pro eorum peccatis abolendis sufficere iudicetur, et eos con-
tempsisse. Praeterea pro singulis salvandis tantum obtulit deo, quantum pro
illius voluit abolitione. Voluit autem, quantum apti. Apti autem, quantum
mundi et conformes Christo. Intentio enim Christi erat individua, quia solis
praedestinatis, et limitata, quia praecise tantum, quantum cuique in suum
locum et ordinem."

at all of the absolute worthiness of punishment of original
sin—a principle which also he nowhere else maintains;[1]
rather, he starts from the idea that every punishment is determined by individual guiltiness, and stands in quantitative
correspondence therewith.　Thence he concludes that, if
Christ in His suffering has taken upon Himself the punishment due to all men, even the damned, therefore in His
purpose to suffer He has discriminated the *quanta* of punishment due to every individual man.　That is indeed a piece
of psychological violence, the harshness of which, however,
only shows that the conception of a universal purpose to
endure punishment in the stead of others cannot but make
shipwreck alike on the qualitative and the quantitative conditions of the notion.　But yet it was a profoundly significant
insight into Biblical motives of thought, which led Wessel to
distinguish between the degrees of sin which either admit or
exclude the possibility of redemption.　Quite similar to
Wessel's distinction is that which *Staupitz*[2] has brought out
between the man who is a sinner for a certain time, and
therefore is punished for a certain time, and the man who is
a sinner always, and therefore is punished always.　If now
we recognise as valid the fact of Divine Providence, it follows that the sin of the elect is temporal and not eternal,
and accordingly also to be punished with merely temporal
penalties, which, however, have then the value of educative
punishments, intended to purify the elect from their stains.

In close agreement with these theologians is *Zwingli*,
whose conception of Providence and election stands nearer to
the theological type of Staupitz than can be affirmed of
Luther.　Zwingli,[3] as is well known, defines the inherited
propensity to sin as a malady, not as a condition of personal
guilt.　As, however, he finds therein the source and motive
of all actual sins, he is by no means of the opinion that this
innate disposition plays no part in bringing about eternal

---

[1] Cf. the art. on Wessel by H. Schmidt in Herzog's *R. E.* vol. xvii. p. 742.

[2] *Von der Vollziehung ewiger Erwählung*, §§ 89-93.　Opera, ed. Knaake, i.
p. 156.

[3] *De peccato originali declaratio*, Opp. iii. p. 631 ff.

damnation. But, while he raises the question whether the
malady of original sin delivers all men over to the penalties of
eternal death, he attempts its solution only by bringing out
the interrelations between sin and redemption. In order to
make good the truth of both these conceptions, he opposes
them first of all in this way : by original sin we are all lost,
and by means of redemption we are restored to perfect life.
The latter proposition, however, limits the former. The
former is true only when we disregard the fact of redemption.
This fact, however, being given, those are in error who maintain universal damnation on the ground of original sin. For
the children of Christians are not condemned for original sin.
They are, rather, through the character of the community
established by the promise of grace, the objects of Divine
favour. For Christian believers are only the extended
community of the children of Abraham, Isaac, and Jacob.
Now, in regard to the last-named, whom God elected before
his birth, it follows that original sin could not condemn him.
For he who belongs to God stands to God in the relation of
friendship. If so, then no condemnation takes place on
account of innate qualities of character. Therefore, from the
point of view of eternal election, in the positive community
of salvation the hereditary propensity to sin is not in itself
the ground of eternal damnation ; it becomes such only when
one brings down destruction on oneself by personal transgression of the law, and therefore by one's own guilt of
unfaithfulness towards God. In this statement we have an
indirect admission of the idea expressed by Wessel and
Staupitz, that he who belongs to the number of the elect
practises actual sin only in a temporal degree, or in the degree
of ignorance ; for within this circle one never reaches the
stage of contempt of salvation, or of intentional unfaithfulness. This view, it is true, is incompatible with the
Augustinian representation of original sin as the sufficient
ground of eternal damnation. If, therefore, the assumption
of an hereditary transmission of sin be maintained at all, it
can be understood only in Zwingli's sense.

Johann von Lasco attempts to solve the same problem by the assumption that, within the mass of Adam's posterity who were condemned with him, the grace of God which was proclaimed to men in the *Protevangelium* was imparted from the very beginning, by imputation of the eternally decreed redemption through Christ, to such men as do not reject Christ by their own voluntary contempt of Him ; for He did not undertake His vicarious suffering for those also who prove themselves His despisers.　Lasco, therefore, reckons as dating from Adam not only original sin, but also the existence of the Church of God, characterised by the note of faith in the promised redemption.[1]

Following the same path, I come, finally, upon the Lutheran *von Oettingen*,[2] and that for this reason that, in complete harmony with my own position, he follows the methodological principle that the full extent of sin is recognisable only in relation to the Christian salvation, and possible only in opposition to it.　Proceeding on these lines, Oettingen not only arrives at the principle that, presupposing the revelation of salvation, the degree of sin varies according to the definite capacity of appropriating salvation, but likewise maintains that eternal damnation is limited to the sin against the Holy Ghost, that is, to stiff-necked rejection of grace.　In this assertion it is indirectly admitted that eternal damnation does not inherently depend on original sin ; and thus one of the formal bases of traditional Lutheran as well as Calvinistic Dogmatics is given up.　Oettingen, it is true, fails to draw this consequence.　He seeks, rather, to create the impression that his position, which is an entirely novel one, was already in a certain measure foreseen by Luther.　But the expression which he cites from Luther[3] means only that all non-Christians, who *are* in the state of eternal damnation on the ground of

---

[1] *Ep. ad Bullingerum* (1544).　Confessio ecclesiae Londinensis.　Opera, ed. Kuyper, ii. pp. 587, 298.

[2] *De peccato in spiritum sanctum* (Dorpat, 1856), pp. 49, 146.

[3] *Catech. maior*, ii. 66 : "Quicunque extra Christianitatem sunt—in perpetua manent ira et damnatione.　Neque enim habent Christum dominum, neque ullis spiritus sancti donis et dotibus illustrati et donati sunt."　Cf. Köstlin, *Luther's Theologie*, vol. ii. p. 374.

original sin, *remain* in that state because they are not redeemed from it. Eternal damnation, in so far as it denotes a degree and a duration of punishment, is here attached *a priori* to original sin. From Luther's subsequent comparison between damnation and redemption, we can conclude only that he admits a certain modification in the duration of eternal punishment, according as redemption has been either merely not appropriated or definitely rejected. But in Luther's view the redeemed also formerly stood under the doom of the highest degree of punishment. Oettingen, therefore, is at variance not merely (as he alleges) with several of the Lutheran divines, but also with Luther himself, in limiting eternal damnation, as the punishment of the highest degree and of unbroken duration, to the sin against the Holy Ghost, and in measuring the degree of sin in general by the standard of active susceptibility to grace. Such being the case, I trust no one will doubt that the nature of original sin, if its existence be maintained at all, can be consistently determined only in Zwingli's sense.

Now, it has been ascertained previously (vol. ii. pp. 241–246) that through all circles of thought in the New Testament there runs the idea of the *graduated value of sin*, the idea, namely, that sin, in so far as it can be forgiven or rendered inoperative through conversion, is to be distinguished from sin brought to its full intensity in the form of final decision against the Christian salvation, or that of incorrigible selfishness. This estimate of sin is formed in exact accordance with the gulf which separates sin from the Christian salvation; it stands likewise in analogy with the fundamental principle of the Mosaic law (vol. ii. p. 38), the scope of which is derived from a quite similar standard of value; it corresponds, finally, to the theological method of determining the conception of sin, the validity of which I maintained at the outset. This constant element in the religious view of things, which Jesus recognised as well as the writers of the New Testament, has been rendered ineffective by the Augustinian doctrine of original sin. The time has come at length to restore that principle to its rightful place.

The distinction between sin as ignorance and sin as final decision against recognised good, is thinkable first of all as related to the conception of sin in general. Sin in general is active and habitual opposition to God and to the good— the good which men discern, with some measure either of vague presentiment or of definite knowledge, to be the final end guaranteed by God for the human will. But, as has been argued above (p. 343), the worth or the worthlessness of sin is not determined by the logical notion of opposition, which would involve that the extremest possible opposition to good is realised in every instance of sin, or that all sin is conscious and thoroughgoing wickedness. If the nature of sin were to be determined in this sense, it would indeed have a very limited extent in actual experience. { Sin is, rather, in all instances, opposition to the good, that conception being defined in the ethical sense, so that the least deviation from the good or even the simple omission of the good already forms opposition thereto ; for the good must be unconditionally and completely realised by the will at every moment.) Now ignorance, as experience teaches in the case of children, is a very significant factor in the origin and development of sin. Children when they enter upon the common spiritual life of men, are neither equipped with a knowledge of good or of the moral law, either as a whole or in its special details, nor endowed with an inclination to decide against the good as a whole. Rather, they must first learn to value the good in its special details, and amid the special relations of life in which they stand ; for they are absolutely unable from the very outset of life to comprehend the good in its universal character. But now precisely in the case of children the will enters into the sphere of active operation with the evident expectation that it possesses unlimited influence over surrounding objects and circum- stances. Such being the case, ignorance is the essential condition of the conflicts which arise between the will and the order of society regarded as the standard of the good, and also the condition of the fact that the will confirms itself in its opposition to the order of society. One cannot, it is true, understand how such a result must ensue. Sin has no real end, either for the individual life or for the advancement of the whole. Ignorance, also, is not the sufficient ground for the confirming of the will in sin; for the will and knowledge are not wholly commensurable with one another. Therefore, neither *a priori* nor yet in accordance with the conditions of experience, is it to be denied that there may be a sinless development of life. For it is likewise only by reckoning up the sum total of experiences that we arrive at our conviction of the universal prevalence of sin. With this, theology, too, ought to rest satisfied. For the hypothesis of an innate propensity to sin, even as Zwingli understands the idea, would also have to be established by means of observation; and even supposing the hypothesis established, nothing more would be reached thereby than what ordinary experience ascertains, even without such means of interpretation. And, finally, though the gradation we have recognised in active and habitual sin be regarded as holding good for different men, yet the sin which is inborn in all men could be viewed only under the form of ignorance. That even in this form a propensity of opposition to the good can be developed, experience teaches in the case of children—but then only if we presuppose that their will is put to the test. But how ignorance can be a sinful propensity, prior to all activity of the individual will, is unintelligible. Thus even the possibility of maintaining Zwingli's hypothesis disappears.

The distinction which is made in the New Testament, between sin as ignorance and sin as final and thoroughgoing opposition to good, has a certain analogy to the current distinctions made between unintentional and intentional, and between venial and deadly sin. But the former distinction, unlike the latter ones, applies not to individual actions, but to habitual dispositions of will from which the individual actions proceed. That distinction, moreover, has not the significance of a standard to be applied in forming our judgment of other men, on the basis of a complete experience of the facts, just as the other distinctions with which we have compared it are recognised as standards for the practical judgments of the educator, the judge, and the Catholic father-confessor. For the distinction belongs undoubtedly to the sphere of religious thought, and therefore holds good in the first place as the *standard for the judgment of God.* Now, as we are not called upon as Christians to pass judgment on individual men, corresponding to or even forestalling the judgment of God, the recognition of this distinction signifies anything but the right to judge men as individuals, and to attribute to their sins the one or the other degree. Rather, as an element in the Christian view of the world, the distinction denotes the point of view from which the Divine redemption or reconciliation of sinners is possible, it being presupposed that there also exists a degree of sin which can only expect to be expelled from the Divine world-order. Now, inasmuch as the positive determination of men's capacity for redemption must be reserved for God, we ought to be satisfied with comprehending all these instances of sin under the negative category of sin as ignorance. We cannot, certainly, avoid taking into consideration the fact that there fall under this category those sins, likewise, which present themselves to our human judgment as a thoroughly confirmed habit of hardening (Eph. iv. 17–19). But if we are to maintain our *good faith* that such men are not regarded by God as past redemption, the conclusion which suggests itself is that God looks upon their sin in a different light, namely, as ignorance. This predicate has a quite different importance, when viewed from the standpoint of Christianity, from the presupposition which bears the same name in the Mosaic law of sacrifice. For in the latter case account is always taken merely of individual actions, or of such conditions of bodily uncleanness as we must judge to be morally indifferent. By Christians, on the other hand, the sinful condition of others, in so far as it does not exclude the capacity for redemption, must be left to God's decision, and His estimate of sin as ignorance must be accepted with due reverence. At the stage of Mosaic law, moreover, it remains uncertain how the relation of man to God in consequence of the sin of ignorance stands prior to the sin-offering, since the covenant grace of God still remains in force. On the other hand, as regards the sin which God views as ignorance, in virtue of its finding forgiveness through Christ, it is certain that in its character of enmity against God it excludes the relation of peace between men and God.

⟨ If, now, the question be raised how we have to conceive the relation of God to sin regarded as ignorance, above all one ought not to expect that theological knowledge, as such, will reach further in this direction than religious judgment. In regard to the point before us, our theology is only competent to show that the distinction between the two stages of sin is in harmony with our ruling conception of God. In general, our knowledge of how sin is related to the Divine world-order has very narrow limits indeed. We must guard against describing sin as an operation of God, and a harmonious element in His world-order, for in all instances sin is the opposite of good, and that which runs counter to the recognisable moral end of the world. (It is an apparently inevitable product of the human will under the given conditions of its development, but, conscious as we are of our freedom and independence, is nevertheless reckoned by us as guilt.) Nor can we, with Schleiermacher, mediate between these two lines of thought by holding that God regards sin, not as opposition to good, but merely as hitherto unattained moral perfection, whereas we must regard our imperfection as sin, in order to awaken in our minds the longing for redemption and perfection (vol. i. p. 536). For as our theological view must in nowise diverge from, or run in opposition to the religious view of Christianity, our judgment regarding sin must be in harmony with the Divine judgment. On the other hand, our estimate of sin as opposition to God is indeed a logical presupposition of faith in redemption, yet in itself no real ground for the production of this faith, but just as easily a ground for doubt, or even obdurate indifference.

If, therefore, God loves sinners (§ 39), inasmuch as His thoughts are directed to their redemption, He does not regard sin in general as imperfect good; rather, He regards that special form of sin which does not exclude redemption as an attribute of men which does not exhaust nor finally determine their worth for God./ The question will be raised, whether it is conceivable that sinful men on such conditions should be objects of God's love. Now, love is that will which accepts, as belonging to one's own end, the task of advancing permanently the end of other personal beings of like nature with oneself (§ 34). Moreover, the possibility of love is in nowise bound up with its being reciprocated, that is, with the condition that the loved one also, under all circumstances, recognises the personal end of the lover as a permanent task of life, in the same way as the lover does to him. Rather, in their natural estimate of moral relationships, men are at one in the opinion that the love of a mother to the infant child which cannot respond to her love, and the love of a father to a lost son, represent a higher degree of love than that which is found in mutual friendship. Furthermore, this thought is affirmed in the Christian commandment to love one's enemy (Matt. v. 44; Rom. xii. 20). That commandment would be absurd, were it the expression of the view that we ought to support our enemy in the aims in which he denies or combats our existence or our essential interests. But when we speak specifically of love towards our enemy, this means no more than that we show respect towards him as a moral personality, by maintaining his existence and desiring that his disposition should change. Hence, when Schoeberlein reduces the relation of God to sinful humanity to the respect shown by Him to their personal independence (vol. i. p. 651), what he thereby conceives is merely a modification of love, not something different from love in its nature. His hypothesis, however, is not in harmony with the original expression which is given to the motive of the

Divine decree of redemption. Rather, in His purpose of redemption God loves the world, *i.e.* the sinners who are filled
with enmity towards Him (Rom. v. 8 ; John iii. 16). If, now,
we attempt to ascertain the meaning of this conception through
the analogy of that love towards enemies which is possible
to us, we find that in both cases the love is conditioned by
the fact that we are able to distinguish, whether hypothetically or categorically, between the momentary direction of
will which finds expression in the other's enmity, and a permanent element in his personality which makes him worthy
of love. In human affairs cases are met with in which one
recognises an enemy as a man who is otherwise distinguished
by very estimable qualities of character, as well as cases in
which one can respect an enemy only in view of one's desire
for his complete change of mind. In the relation of God to
men, who as sinners stand in a general attitude of opposition
to the Divine final end, it is evident that only the latter
case holds good. But now the question arises, whether, from
the commandment that men should love their enemies, a competent conclusion can be drawn at all in reference to an
analogous relation of the Divine will towards sinners. For
love towards one's enemies, in the hope of their conversion,
could perhaps be enjoined as evidence of one's own determination to refrain from the judgment that anyone is beyond
conversion. But it is precisely from this point of view that
the doubtfulness of the analogy comes to light. For, supposing that even in countless instances within human experience the act of blessing and interceding for one's enemy
finds no encouragement in the desired result of his conversion,
the commandment of Christ would be useless and ineffectual
as a means of virtue, were it not in the first place a direct
consequence of the religious view of the world which belongs
to Christianity (§ 39). But in the Christian view the love
towards our enemy which we are commanded to cherish, is
necessarily based on the corresponding trait of character in
the idea of God. The love, therefore, which is the expression
of the essential will of God revealed in Christianity, includes

also love towards sinners as the ground of their conversion. For the change of heart, which holds good, in the case of human love towards one's enemy, as a condition which lies beyond our power and therefore can only be kept hypothetically before our eyes, takes in the case of God's love the place of the consequence intended by that love. But now, in so far as the change of heart which is to be brought about by God's love towards sinners must be conceived under the form of freedom of the will, we cannot conceive that result as taking place when sin, regarded as enmity against God, has reached that degree of self-determination at which the will has deliberately chosen evil as its end. Where we can justly suppose such a case, there also we must regard the love of God as impossible. Therefore, the love of God can be conceived in relation only to such sinners as have not fallen into that degree of sin which excludes conversion of the will. It is just this negative relation that is expressed by the predication of ignorance—and nothing more. The presupposition of such a degree of sin in the case of others has just this much practical significance for us, that we ought to esteem them as capable of conversion. Theoretically, however, this assumption of sin as ignorance has the significance only of a standard for God—a standard, therefore, which is conceived only negatively, because its specific application does not belong to us. The thought, therefore, means that the love of God to sinners, as the motive of His purpose of redemption, and as the ultimate efficient ground of their conversion, cannot be extended to those persons in whom the purpose of opposition to the Divine order of good has come to full consciousness and determination. Whether there are such men, and who they are, are questions that lie equally beyond our practical judgment and our theoretical knowledge.

1. Sin, which alike as a mode of action and as a habitual propensity extends over the whole human race, is, in the Christian view of the world, estimated as the opposite of reverence and trust towards God, as also the opposite of the Kingdom of God—in the latter respect forming the king-

dom of sin, which possesses no necessary ground either in the Divine world-order or in man's natural endowment of freedom, but unites all men with one another by means of the countless interrelations of sinful conduct.

2. Of the evils which make themselves perceptible as hindrances to human freedom, those have the significance of Divine punishments—presupposing the Divine government of the world—which each individual, through his unrelieved consciousness of guilt, imputes to himself as such — that consciousness of guilt, as expressive of the lack of religious fellowship with God, being itself already the initial manifestation of punishment as the forfeiture of the privilege of Divine sonship.

3. In so far as men, regarded as sinners both in their individual capacity and as a whole, are objects of the redemption and reconciliation made possible by the love of God, sin is estimated by God, not as the final purpose of opposition to the known will of God, but as ignorance.

CHAPTER VI

§ 44. THE nature of Christianity as a universal religion is such that *in the Christian view of the world a definite place is assigned to its historical founder.* In the two ethnic religions which come nearest to Christianity (though in different degrees), and which have preserved some recollection of their historical founders, namely in the Persian religion and in the religion of Israel, Zoroaster and Moses are indeed acknowledged as the founders and lawgivers of the faith; but there is no need of a personal confession either of the one or of the other, because for the religions which they founded the religious community is the nation, and the nation is the community. In the universal religions, on the other hand, it is through express recognition of the founder of the religion that membership in the religious community is described and attained (vol. ii. p. 13). At the same time, in these religions a certain gradation presents itself in the worth and significance of personal adherence to the founder. In Islam it is enough to name the Prophet alongside of God, because for this religion of law he is merely the lawgiver. Nearer to the religious estimate of Jesus Christ in the Christian religion comes the significance which in Buddhism is attached to Sakyamuni Buddha as an incarnation of Deity. But in this case there is the difference that, whereas what Buddha aimed at was not by any means what his followers believe themselves to have received from him, Jesus, on the other hand, had in view for His own Person essentially that significance which is claimed for it in His religious community. In other words, Buddha had no intention of founding a

25

religion; he did not so much as set forth any conception of God, or any explanation of the world in its relation to God; he did not explain how man is to reach a definite attitude towards the world or a definite position in the world: he merely indicated the direction along which man is to achieve his own redemption from the misery of actual existence, namely, by the ascetic annihilation of personal life. A philosophy or ethic such as this, which addresses itself to human freedom, may be the basis of a school, but not of religious fellowship; therefore, the significance it secures for its author is that of the founder of a school. That it was afterwards associated with the Indian idea of God, and that the corresponding idea of Divine incarnation was applied to Buddha and to his successors, was a result utterly foreign to the view of the antagonist of Brahmanism. It is true that within the Christian community there are those who hold exactly the same view with regard to the purpose of Jesus, and the fate which has befallen the doctrine of His Person in the Christian Church. According to their reading of the Gospels, Jesus taught a lofty morality, but in the exercise of this vocation never transgressed the limits of a purely human estimate of Himself; only through influences that are wholly external have His followers been led to regard Him as an incarnation of the Deity. But this view is historically inaccurate. For beyond all doubt Jesus was conscious of a new and hitherto unknown relation to God, and said so to His disciples; and His aim was to bring His disciples into the same attitude toward the world as His own, and to the same estimate of themselves, that under these conditions He might enlist them in the world-wide mission of the Kingdom of God, which He knew to be not only His own business, but theirs. But this involves the assumption that He Himself means more for His disciples than the passing occasion of their religion or a lawgiver for their conduct, who would be of no more account when once the law which He proclaimed was thoroughly learned. In the case of Buddhism, on the other hand, the system as a system does not secure for its founder any abiding significance. For if Buddha himself has attained to that personal annihilation to which he showed his followers the way, he can be remembered by them only as a pattern of past days, because each one becomes himself a Buddha, an enlightened one, that is, he too recognises the worthlessness of existence, and acts accordingly, with a view to his own annihilation.

In Christianity the case is otherwise. The aim of the Christian is conceived as the attainment of eternal life. This means the consistent realisation of the personal self-end, of which the test is that the whole world does not compare in worth with the personal life, and that by the acquisition of spiritual lordship over the world, this, the true worth of life, is vindicated (§ 27). Now this religious vocation of the members of the Christian community is prefigured in the person of its Founder, and rests upon His person as its abiding source of strength for all imitation of Him, because He Himself made God's supreme purpose of the union of men in the Kingdom of God the aim of His own personal life; and thereby realised in His own experience that independence toward the world which through Him has become the experience of the members of His community. This ideal, the true development of the spiritual personality, cannot be rightly or fully conceived apart from contemplation of Him Who is the prototype of man's vocation. Thus what in the historically complete figure of Christ we recognise to be the real worth of His existence, gains for ourselves, through the uniqueness of the phenomenon and its normative bearing upon our own religious and ethical destiny, the worth of an abiding rule, since we at the same time discover that only through the impulse and direction we receive from Him, is it possible for us to enter into His relation to God and to the world.[1]/ On the other hand, this specific estimate of their founders, even when known, is quite alien to the ethnic religions, because in

[1] By this is meant that the disciples of Jesus take the rank of sons of God (Matt. xvii. 26), and are received into the same relation to God in which Christ stands to His Father (John xvii. 21–23).

these there is not posited as ideal aim the independent development of the personal character to the worth of a whole, as against the natural and particular impulses of life. The genius of an ethnic religion is satisfied if there be participation in the fixed tradition and custom of the nation ; and such participation, when regarded as the supreme standard of human fellowship, imposes on personal independence impassable limits. Because this ideal of self-realisation has not come within the horizon of any of the ethnic religions, therefore in none of these has the founder received a place which can be compared with the significance of Christ. Even in the case of Zoroaster and of Moses, the ideal interests of their religions are so bound up with the natural consciousness of belonging to a particular nation, that the decision of the Parsees for Zoroaster, and of the Israelites for Moses, was the inevitable result of hostility toward the Hindus in the one case, and toward the Egyptians in the other.

There is yet another reason why the Person of Christ maintains its place in the Christian view of the world. Christ founds His religion with the claim that He brings the perfect revelation of God, so that beyond what He brings no further revelation is conceivable or is to be looked for. Whoever, therefore, has a part in the religion of Christ in the way Christ Himself intended, cannot do other than regard Christ as the Bearer of the final revelation of God. At the same time, this point of view is conclusive only in connection with what has already been set forth. For Islam also claims to be the perfect religion, and yet is content with a superficial recognition of its prophet, to whom, under this title, there is actually no place assigned in the Mohammedan view of the world. Thus the claim Christ makes to the perfect revelation of God in Himself is only defined as against the rival claim of Mohammed, by the fact that on the ground of His peculiar relation to God, Christ lived a life of mastery over the world, such as makes possible the community in which each Christian is to attain the similar destiny of the life eternal. Because this goal is not the reward of fulfilling a statutory law,

Christ does not count, like Mohammed, merely as a lawgiver. On the contrary, since the aim of the Christian is to be attained under the form of personal freedom, therefore the twofold significance we are compelled to ascribe to Christ as being at once the perfect revealer of God and the manifest [*offenbar*] type of spiritual lordship over the world, finds expression in the single predicate of His Godhead.

This mutual relation between the *Godhead of Christ* and the raising of the members of His community to mastery over the world as their true destiny, is set forth with greatest clearness in that dogma of the Greek Church which affirms the consummation of the human race in Christ as the Word of God, Who is Himself God. The communication of ἀφθαρσία through the teaching—otherwise the incarnation— of the Divine Word, is regularly described also as θεοποίησις (vol. i. p. 4). Mastery over the world is the content of both these descriptions of the Christian, as well as the motive for defining clearly the idea of the Divine Word. This relation of things is no longer considered in present-day discussions of the meaning of the Godhead of Christ. The Greek Catholic formula, that God became man in order that man might become God, is indeed repeated in the West, because it was adopted along with the Nicene type of doctrine by Augustine. Accordingly we find it used by Thomas Aquinas (P. iii. qu. 1, art. 2), as by Athanasius, to explain the incarnation of the Divine Word. In Luther's hymn, " *Vom Himmel kam der Engel Schaar*," there is an echo of the same thought in so far as by the birth of Christ we are said to have become of the race of God. Also, in the wake of mysticism, not only in the Middle Ages (vol. i. p. 117), but even to some extent where mysticism has found acceptance in Evangelical circles, we find traces of this conception of the deification of man. Nevertheless, the combination has remained on the whole unproductive for the Western Church, because the latter, since Augustine, has pushed into the foreground the human personality of Christ and His corresponding activity as mediator between God and man (vol. i. p. 38). If, at the same time, His Godhead was in traditional fashion stipulated for or assumed, yet it followed that the result of the mediatorial activity of the man Christ could not be described as the bestowal of Godhead upon men. For this reason, the Godhead predicated of Christ suggests always a gulf between Christ and the members of His community, a gulf which no salvation wrought by Christ avails to lessen.

The Latin Church of the Middle Ages no doubt handed on the primitive formula of the one Person in two natures —human and Divine. But neither in the sphere of theology nor of asceticism did the Latins understand how to make a clear and decisive use of Christ's Divinity. In Peter Lombard the interpretations of Christ's redemptive work and the doctrine of Christ's Person stand side by side without any vital connection, and the same is the case with Lombard's theological successors. After all his ingenious inquiries and conclusions concerning the assumption of human nature by the Divine Person of the Word, Aquinas leaves the relation as obscure as before. Or rather, amid all his efforts to establish the dogma, he unconsciously betrays the fact that the only conception he can attain is that of an undefined and indefinable relation between the mutable human nature and the immutable Divine Person in Christ, whereby the human nature is in reality not affected.[1] The God-manhood of Christ is upheld as real, subject to the alteration, that is, the exaltation, which the human nature has experienced through its connection with the Divine. The Godhead thus remains in the background ; and if we would recognise a union of natures according to the strict standard of Godhead, this is rendered impossible by the instruction which Thomas himself gives us, for he bids us conceive the Divine nature as immutable, and involved only through the relation which the

---

[1] *Summa theol.* P. iii. qu. 2, art. 7 : " Unio, de qua loquimur, est relatio quaedam, quae consideratur inter divinam naturam et humanam, secundum quod conveniunt in una persona filii dei. Omnis relatio autem, quae consideratur inter deum et creaturam, realiter quidem est in creatura, per cuius mutationem talis relatio innascitur ; non autem est realiter in deo sed *secundum rationem tantum*, quia non innascitur secundum mutationem dei."

human nature assumes toward it,—*secundum rationem tantum*. To this type of doctrine corresponds the contemplative treatment of Christ's Person throughout the Middle Ages. Nominally, indeed, it is ever the *verbum incarnatum* Who as the Bearer of God's redeeming love is adored by Bernard in all the sufferings of Christ. But in reality the Bridegroom, the fairest of the children of men, to Whom devout souls give back love for love, is nothing more than the ideal man, whose perfectness is manifest in the strength of his self-denial. Thus the Godhead, assumed in theory, is in practice denied, for the Divine majesty is set aside that there may be room, on the footing of equality, for the play of mutual love. What is the worth, then, of a confession of Christ's Godhead, expressed in the formulas of Greek theology, if, in the West, both theology after the most ingenious efforts confesses itself unable to attain any real knowledge of its object, and piety treats Christ as if Godhead did not belong to Him at all? [1]

In Luther we come upon a definite attempt to establish theoretically the old Christology by proving the *communicatio idiomatum*.[2] At the same time, Luther's religious estimate of Christ does not depend upon a rigorous realisation of the theological formula of the one Person in two natures, although on the whole he continues to give to this formula its ancient place. His religious estimate of Christ, as distinguished from his theoretical exposition of Christological dogma, is expressed in his catechetical and to some extent also in his homiletical writings. In his earliest catechetic treatment of the main articles of the faith,[3] it is evident how, through the positing of a new idea of faith, the objects of faith also are transformed. If faith no longer consists in assent to revealed dogmas, but in confidence toward God, then it follows that faith, *i.e.* trust in Jesus Christ and in the Holy Spirit, is a recognition of the Godhead of Christ and of the

---

[1] *Geschichte des Pietismus*, i. p. 49.

[2] *Von Conciliis und Kirchen*, Walch, xvi. p. 2724 ff.

[3] *Kurze Form, die zehn Gebote, Glauben und Vaterunser zu betrachten* (1520), Walch, x. p. 182.

Holy Spirit, since trust of this kind can be given to God
alone. Through this explanation of Luther's the Godhead of
Christ is introduced as a judgment of value. It is the same
point of view which in the Larger Catechism meets us in the
form that God and faith (*i.e.* trust) stand in necessary
relation to each other, so that even in the case of a corrupt
faith that idol becomes our God, to which we offer our highest
and supremest trust (p. 211). To this thought of Luther's,
Melanchthon, at a later date, amid discussions of a scholastic
order, was yet able to give expression.[1]

The estimation of Christ as God, involved in the act of
putting our trust in Him, implies also a change in, or at least
a new interpretation of, those attributes which directly or indirectly are ascribed to Christ in the Creed. Christ cannot
be the object of our trust if the description of Him in the
Creed is meant to be understood in a sense purely objective.
For this reason Luther in his *Kurze Form* adds with regard
to each attribute that it is there " for me." This, however,
is controlled by the preliminary statement : " I believe not
only that Jesus Christ is the true and only Son of God, in an
eternal Divine nature and essence eternally begotten, but also
that all things are subjected to Him by the Father, and that
even in His humanity He is appointed Lord over me and
over all things which with the Father in His Divinity He
created." With this is to be compared, in the first place, the
formula in the Shorter Catechism: " I believe that Jesus
Christ, very God, eternally begotten of the Father, also very

---

[1] *Loci theol.* 1535, *C. R.* xxi. pp. 366, 367 : "Sicut scriptura docet nos de
filii divinitate non tantum speculative sed practice, hoc est iubet, ut Christum
invocemus, ut Christo confidamus—sic enim vere tribuetur ei honos divinitatis
—ita vult nos spiritus sancti divinitatem in ipsa consolatione et vivificatione
cognoscere. . . . Haec officia spiritus prodest considerare. . . . In hac invoca-
tione, in his exercitiis fidei melius cognoscemus trinitatem, quam in otiosis
speculationibus, quae disputant, quid personae inter se agant, non quid nobiscum
agant."—The subject is discussed also by A. H. Francke, *Christus s. scripturae
nucleus* (Halae, 1724), pp. 121–150 : "Ille, de quo omnes dei servi in V. et N.
test. unanimiter testantur, quod omnes homines in eum credere debeant, et
quidem tam excellenti modo, quo sine gravissimo idololatriae crimine in rem
ullam credere nemo potest, ille est cum patre verus vivens ac essentialis deus.
Atqui in Christum talis fides requiritur. Ergo Christus una cum patre est
verus vivens ac essentialis deus."

man, born of the Virgin Mary, is my Lord, by Whom I, a lost
and condemned man, have been redeemed, gotten, and won."
In both cases the predicates of the old Christology are repeated, though in shorter form and less definite outline than
would satisfy the old requirements.   But the *Kurze Form* makes
it plain that the faith which accepts these statements cannot
be regarded as the trust which, properly speaking, is religious
faith.   These predicates are simply taken for granted, and
trust in Christ has for its object His attribute of Lordship,—
that He is Lord over me and over all things.   Both in the *Kurze
Form* and in the Shorter Catechism the recognition of Christ's
Divinity is bound up with this statement.   Should it be
imagined that the traditional interpretation and this new
interpretation of Christ's Godhead mean for Luther the same
thing, or that the latter stands in analytic relation to the
former, such a conclusion has against it the fact that in the
Larger Catechism the word Lord is made equivalent to
Redeemer, and also that it is there declared that the eternal
Word submitted to incarnation and to suffering *in order that*
He might become our Lord.   That Christ is " my Lord "
depends therefore upon the whole scope of His human existence, activity, and suffering, upon the effort " He put forth in
daring to win us and bring us under His Lordship."   If this
train of thought is completed by supplying the missing
statement of the Shorter Catechism, that it is in the Kingdom of Christ as " my Lord " that I serve Him, we can
scarcely suppose that Luther in making Lord equivalent to
Redeemer, disputes the equivalence of Lord and God.   Thus,
while assuming the formula of the two natures, Luther really
connects the religious estimate of Christ as God with the
significance which Christ's work has for the Christian community, and with the position thereby given to Christ at the
head of the Kingdom of God.   According to Luther, the
Godhead of Christ is not exhausted by maintaining the existence in Christ of the Divine nature ; the chief point is that
in His exertions as man His Godhead is manifest and
savingly effective.

Luther here adopts a standpoint which is as manifestly distinct from the Greek method as from the Latin. In the Greek theology, the incarnation of the Divine Word is the complete and saving revelation of the Godhead of Christ ; the teaching of the God-man, and His yielding up of His human life to the death to annul the law of death, are but subordinate proofs of His Godhead for subordinate ends. In the Latin Church, the Godhead of Christ under the form of incarnation is no doubt recognised, but His mediatorial and saving work—the satisfaction rendered and the merit acquired to procure for men the forgiveness of sins—is exhibited only in His human activity as such ; the Godhead in Aquinas comes into account merely as constituting the essential worth for the expiation of sin of Christ's merit and satisfaction ; in Duns Scotus it is not regarded at all. Luther's statements in the Catechisms amount to this, that while the Church formula is retained, it really is in Christ's human achievements that His Godhead becomes for His people manifest, conspicuous, intelligible, winning our faith, not in the form of assent to an unintelligible dogma, but of personal trust for our own salvation.

Luther never dreamed of rejecting the old Christology when he attached to the work of Christ a superior worth as evidence of His Godhead. Nor was this attempt of Luther's without some relation to a thought of the earlier time. For while in the Middle Ages the sufferings of Christ were regarded merely as an attribute of His human nature, the *worth* of these sufferings for cancelling the evil of sin was ascribed by Aquinas to the fact that with the human nature there was united the Divine. It is in keeping herewith that in the sixteenth century those Anabaptists and Scotists who had ceased to regard the redemption of Christ as universal and as the foundation-principle of His Church (vol. i. p. 314), went astray regarding His Godhead. It was therefore to this very attribute of Redeemer that Luther attached his statement of Christ's Godhead, directing toward it the trust of the believer, because it surpasses every other motive for trust. But from this standpoint he seeks, in a way of his own, to throw further light upon the elementary recognition of Christ under the scheme of the two natures, for these he will not relinquish. He is not in the least concerned that the laity, to whose guidance the c techetical writings are devoted, should have before their minds a complete and exhaustive conception of the old interpretation of Christ. For the chief emphasis, as we saw, is laid upon personal trust in the Redeemer and Lord of Christendom. But even apart from any special reference to the laity, Luther has on one occasion [1] sought to show that the opposition between knowledge and faith, always minimised by the Scholastics, is of the nature of a contradiction. While the Scholastics set the one function against the other within the common sphere of the understanding (*intellectus*), Luther withdraws faith from the sphere of the understanding altogether, declaring that the Articles of the Creed anent the Trinity and the Person of Christ are incomprehensible to the understanding, and that "the more we speculate about them the darker and less intelligible do they become." But he closes this discussion by declaring that the trust we put in Christ establishes and recognises His true Godhead, since Christ's Godhead is understood as the power which Christ has put forth upon *our* redemption. It is true that even in this connection Luther has no desire to dispense with the unintelligible formulas; but the very fact that they are pronounced unintelligible forbids their being viewed as other than worthless for the faith which consists in trust. Allusions of a similar kind are to be found in other sermons of Luther's.[2]

---

[1] Exposition of the second Article of the Creed, concerning Jesus Christ, preached in the castle of Torgau (1533). Walch, x. p. 1309.

[2] *Evangelienpostille*: Sermon on the fifth Sunday after Easter: "To believe on Christ does not mean to believe that Christ is a person who is both God and man, *for that will not be any help to any man*, but to believe that this same person is Christ, that is, that *for our sake* He is come out from God, and is come into the world, and then again leaves the world and goes to the Father. It is from this *office* He gets the name Jesus Christ; and to believe this of Him is to be and to abide in His name." Second sermon on Whitsunday: "The

Melanchthon, in his first epoch, interpreted the thought of Luther as meaning that the formula of the two natures in Christ is unimportant so long as Christ is duly recognised in His saving benefits.   Thus, in the *Loci Theol.* of the year 1521 (*C. R.* xxi. p. 85), we read: " Hoc est Christum cognoscere, beneficia eius cognoscere, non quod isti (scholastici) docent, eius naturas, modos incarnationis contueri.   Ni scias, in quem usum carnem induerit, et cruci affixus sit Christus, quid proderit eius historiam novisse ?   An vero medico satis est novisse herbarum figuras, colores, lineamenta, vim scire nativam nihil refert ?   Ita Christum, qui nobis remedii et, ut scripturae verbo utar, salutaris vice donatus est, oportet alio quodam modo cognoscamus, quam exhibent scholastici."   This thought persists also in the *Apology for the Augsburg Confession*, ii. 101 : " Quid est notitia Christi, nisi nosse beneficia Christi, promissiones, quas per evangelium sparsit in mundum ?   Et haec beneficia nosse *proprie et vere* est credere in Christum."   Faith in Christ is under all circumstances the recognition of His Godhead ; Melanchthon, therefore, would have us recognise this attribute in that which makes Christ our Mediator and Reconciler.   Neither in this connection nor where he criticises the invocation of the saints, does Melanchthon employ the formula of the natural Godhead in Christ.   He does not refute the invocation of the saints on the ground that they lack that Divine nature which would justify the invocation of Christ. He gives Christ the advantage over the saints rather on the ground that Christ has laid us under obligation to Himself, which the saints have not.   In this connection we read (ix. 23): " Prorsus aequantur (sancti) Christo, si confidere debemus, quod meritis eorum salvemur."   By these words Melanchthon certainly did not intend to deny indirectly the Godhead of Christ.   Therefore he must be understood to mean that this attribute of Christ is to be found in the ser-

devil can be doing with a sinner who clings merely to the man Christ, he is even content to let folk say and hear the words that Christ is true God ; but one thing he will not suffer—that the *heart* should take such a true and inseparable hold of Christ that Christ's word and the Father's word become one and the same word and will " (Walch, xi. pp. 1251, 1443).

vice He renders, the benefit He bestows, the saving work He accomplishes.

Against the validity of this conception opponents raise two objections: first, that hereby the true Godhead of Christ is denied, and the attribute of Godhead attached to the human Christ only in name; and, second, that Christ is after all only acknowledged as mere man, and so in the end there is a breach of the commandment, Thou shalt have no other gods before Me. With regard to the latter argument, I can shelter myself behind Luther.[1] Also, to say that in the statement of Melanchthon Christ is represented as mere man, is a pure inference of my opponents, to which they have been led by their own conceptions of the matter. They put the alternative—either Christ is the union of Divine and human nature, or else He is mere human nature: now, in such a statement as that of Melanchthon no use is made of the first formula; therefore Christ is declared to be a mere man. In so far as it is attempted by means of this syllogism to prove me in the wrong, I would remark that this cannot possibly be my view of the matter. For by a mere man (if I ever used the expression), I should mean man as a material entity apart from every characteristic of spiritual and moral personality. I am far from regarding anyone even of my opponents as a mere man, for I assume, in every one of them, some good results of upbringing and some measure of moral worth. That I speak of Christ at all only in so far as His personal character as the Bearer of the revelation of God comes into account, surely no one who has read what I have written will deny. At the least, therefore, it is a proof of incompetence and hasty judgment when my opponents

---

[1] *Decem praecepta, Wittembergensi praedicata populo* (1518, *Erl. lat.* xii. p. 5): "Ubi audis, quod Christus pro te passus est et credis, iam oritur fiducia in eum et amor dulcis et sic periit omnis rerum affectus ut inutilium, et oritur aestimatio solius Christi ut rei necessariae vehementer, remansitque tibi nonnisi solus Iesus solus satis et sufficiens tibi, ita ut de omnibus desperans unicum habeas hunc, in quo omnia speras, ideoque super omnia eum diligas. At Iesus est verus, unus, solus deus, quem cum habes non habes alienum deum. Iudaei vero timentes, ne alienum deum haberent, si *hominem Christum adorent*, eo peius adorant alienum deum, scilicet idola cordis sui, quae de deo fingunt."

maintain that I regard Christ as a mere man, and deny His Godhead.

But if Christ by what He has done and suffered for my salvation is my Lord, and if, by trusting for my salvation to the power of what He has done for me, I honour Him as my God, then that is a value-judgment of a direct kind. It is not a judgment which belongs to the sphere of disinterested scientific knowledge, like the formula of Chalcedon. When, therefore, my opponents demand in this connection a judgment of the latter sort, they reveal their own inability to distinguish scientific from religious knowledge, which means that they are not really at home in the sphere of religion. Every cognition of a religious sort is a direct judgment of value (p. 205). The nature of God and the Divine we can only know in its essence by determining its value for our salvation.[1] Let him who denies this see to it how he reconciles his position with the Larger Catechism, and with the fact that we know God only by revelation, and therefore also must understand the Godhead of Christ, if it is to be understood at all, as an attribute revealed to us in His saving influence upon ourselves. We must first be able to prove the Godhead that is revealed before we take account of the Godhead that is eternal. My opponents, however, being bent on getting first an acknowledgment of the latter, imagine that they can establish the Godhead of Christ upon the basis of a scientific idea, that is, through an act of disinterested cognition, previous to all possible experience, and apart from all religious experience of the matter. And as representatives of a scien-

[1] This is the attitude of Theremin in a sermon on the Divinity of Christ, of the year 1818, edited with a preface for 1881 by Kögel. The preacher's desire is to convince his contemporaries of the Divinity of Christ, if only they believe (1) that Christ is a good man, (2) that God is our Father, and (3) that there is a future life of blessedness. "This will suffice us to bring you to the avowal that Christ is the only-begotten Son of God" (p. 7). Compare herewith the following sentences (p. 11): "The confession that Christ is true God lay already involved in your moral sense. . . . Beyond this, then, we will not go. . . . That we should be able to understand and explain in what way the Divine nature unites itself with the human—this God does not ask of us, He has not put it within the grasp of our understanding. But that holiness cannot lie—that we understand, and that may suffice us."

tific conception of the Godhead of Christ, they pursue an impracticable method, inasmuch as their conception of the Word of God, eternally begotten by God before the world, rests only on tradition, detached from all the circumstances of its origin. Accordingly, they would have us make confession of the Godhead of Christ in this particular formula, before ever His Godhead has been proved to us in His saving influence upon ourselves, aye even although the said influence cannot possibly prove His Godhead in the aspects of it here concerned. These teachers must first of all be good enough to tell us what Christ's Godhead in its eternal essence is—what it is in its eternal relation to God; then it will be time enough to discuss whether and in what way this attribute is for us savingly effective and actually revealed. The method of cognition herein applied is false (p. 19), and Luther's warning against teachers who would determine the things of God *a priori*, from above downwards, previous to all definite Divine revelation, holds good for this problem also.[1]

§ 45. Such is the limited order of cognition prescribed for the theologian at this point. So far, however, as the doctrinal system of the Church demands consideration, the preceding discussion has shown that in the Catechisms of Luther and in the *Apology for the Augsburg Confession* there are hints, hitherto neglected, towards a right conception of the Deity of Christ. These hints may· the more readily be followed, since in the doctrine of the two natures the historical and religious conception of Christ finds no place. The supporters of the opposite view must lay their account. with the fact that other men who belong to a different school from theirs, also prove the existence within the symbolic

[1] Compare the remark of Luther on John xvii. 3 (Walch, viii. p. 697): " Observe how Christ in this word weaves into one web the knowledge of Himself and of the Father, so that only through Christ and in Him alone do we know the Father. I have often said this, and I keep on saying it, so that even when I am dead men may remember it, and may be on their guard against all teachers, as devil-driven and devil-led, who begin their teaching and preaching about God up in the heights, altogether separate and apart from Christ, in the way that hitherto in such schools they have speculated and played with His works in heaven above—what He is, thinks, and does in Himself."

books of the main ideas of their own theological position. They might have learned long ago from Philippi that the formulas which they themselves exclusively recognise as the content of the symbolic books do not define the limits of theological knowledge, but are intended merely to prevent those deviations from truth among which is included a curtailing of the problem of knowledge (vol. ii. p. 18).

It is also a false assumption that a uniform *doctrine of the Godhead of Christ* can be exegetically constructed from the New Testament. Strictly speaking, the content of the New Testament books is not doctrine at all. Least of all can we discover in Christ's own words a doctrine of His Godhead. There, indeed, it is not to be expected. For the thought of Christ's Godhead is never other than the expression of that unique acknowledgment and appreciation which the Christian community yields to its Founder. But there meet us in the New Testament two ways of conceiving Christ's Godhead which do not directly correspond. On the one hand, the majority of the apostles connect the name κύριος, which in Jewish usage is equivalent to God, with the lordship over the world on which Christ has entered by His exaltation to the right hand of God (1 Pet. iii. 22 ; Jas. ii. 1 ; Phil. ii. 9–11 ; Heb. i. 3). The frequent application of this attribute to Christ is to be understood in view of the fact that faith has its necessary points of attachment always in the present. Our faith in Christ is not faith in Him as One Who was, but faith in Him as One Who continues to work, namely, under the conditions corresponding to His present mode of existence. This is the starting-point from which the apostles recall even the circumstances of Christ's earthly life, and are confident, because of their faith in Him as Lord, that even His death is an event fraught with blessing to the community. Paul indicates a limit for the conjunction of the name κύριος with the Person of Christ, in so far as he connects the bestowal of this name by God with the exaltation, and puts the earthly course of Jesus' life in the opposite category of an obedience rendered in the form of a servant (Phil. ii. 6–11).

With this, however, must be compared the fact that in Rom. v. 15 Paul associates the specifically Divine attribute of grace with the contemplation of the man Christ, just as Christ in yielding His obedience is at the same time a revelation of God. As Lord over the world, Christ is also Lord over His community. But the latter relation is the primary one, partly because the community acknowledges Him as God, and partly because, in definite statements, the community, of which Christ is head, is made to share His position toward the world.

Whatever in the Epistles goes beyond this practical significance of the attribute κύριος as applied to Christ, and gives to His relation toward the world a wider scope than His present lordship over it, belongs to the sphere of special γνῶσις, —that is, of intellectual cognition, which creates problems rather than solves them. This at least is the case when in 1 Cor. viii. 6 Paul describes the *Lord* Jesus Christ as Him through whom all things have been created or come to be. It is assumed that only God the Father is the Creator of all things, the original source of all that exists: the Lord Jesus Christ, therefore, is the mediate source. But by Lord here must be understood the exalted Christ. Therefore as mediate source of creation we have indicated to us an entity which as such appeared at a given point in time. This is the riddle of which we ought not to get rid by pushing Christ back out of post-existence into pre-existence. For by an exchange of this kind we should invalidate the clear and definite meaning of κύριος. The statements in Col. i. 14–20 also refer to the exalted Christ into Whose Kingdom God has translated the community. If these sentences are in logical sequence, it is a poor exegesis that would interpret them by referring the relative pronouns alternately to the post-existent and to the pre-existent Christ. Most certainly it is the exalted Christ Who is the mediate source of our redemption or forgiveness, which would not be ours if Christ were not risen and exalted. To this are attached the two groups of statements introduced in parallel fashion (ὅς ἐστιν) in ver. 15 and ver. 18*b*. The

26

second group is at the beginning very evidently dominated
by the thought of the risen Christ; but vers. 19 and 20
take us back to the purpose with which on earth Christ
offered the sacrifice of His death; He would have the whole
world come in Him to rest, and to this end would bring all
things into the new way of which He is the goal, and to
peace with each other, through the blood of His Cross. It is
manifest, also, that the first group both begins and ends with
statements about the exalted Christ. It is as the exalted
One that Christ is the image of God and the head of the
community. Now the literal meaning of πρωτότοκος πάσης
κτίσεως and the words πρὸ πάντων have led to the false
assumption that the intervening statements refer to the
temporal pre-existence of Christ before the world, and to
disregard of the fact that up to this point the dominating
conception has been the exalted Christ. But the temporal
priority of Christ before the world cannot be the point at
issue; that would be a barren thought. Superiority over
the world is ascribed to Christ in view of the worth which
belongs to Him in His position as the image of God and the
head of the community. It is as the image and revelation
of the invisible God (2 Cor. iv. 4) that the exalted Christ is
πρωτότοκος πάσης κτίσεως. In this connection πρωτότοκος
can be understood only in the metaphorical sense in which
the corresponding Hebrew word is used, namely, he who is
preferred—the same sense in which it is used in Rom. viii. 29,
and probably also in Rev. i. 5. Christ is He Who is preferred,
Who belongs to God in contrast with creation as a whole,
which is not the image and direct revelation of God. For all
things, so we read, have been created by God in Him, that is
in the exalted Christ. This is the same statement as in
1 Cor. viii. 6. It finds its more exact explanation in the
two following and parallel pairs of sentences. The indefinite
expression " were created " is in these sentences split up into
" have been created " and " consist." That is, first—all
things have been created through and unto the exalted
Christ, and He is before all things. The indefinite formula

ἐν αὐτῷ is here more particularly defined to the effect that
Christ is the mediate cause through which, and the end for
which, all things have been created; and as the *end* of all
things He is before all things. To introduce the idea of
Christ's pre-existence is to make an intelligible explanation
impossible. For only the exalted Lord is conceivable as
the goal of creation. Besides, the preposition πρό applies to
place as fitly as to time, and the former application alone gives
a sentence of weight, in keeping with the new thought εἰς
αὐτὸν ἔκτισται. The second pair of sentences provides the
corroborating conclusion—He in Whom the world as one
continuous whole at this moment consists, is the exalted One,
Who is the head of the community.

The same strain of thought is re-echoed in the Epistle to
the Ephesians. Christ, in Whom all things are to find their
ultimate unity (i. 10), in Whom also the community of those
who fear God was chosen by God before the creation of the
world, is the exalted Christ, through Whom at this present
time all Divine blessings are bestowed upon the community
(i. 3–6). In this twofold relation of Christ to the world
and to the community, the community holds higher rank and
stands nearer to Him; it is filled by Christ, that is to say, it
is the organ of His specific activity, while He fills Himself
in all ways with all things (i. 30), or, in other words, extends
His lordship over the world. From the Divine standpoint,
and in view of the conditions that belong to the very idea of
purpose, these combinations do not present any special
difficulty. For, according to the rule, *ultimum in exsecutione
est primum in intentione*, the ultimate end of a chain of means
exists in the thought and purpose of the agent before the
means, precedes all actual effort, being itself the motive of such
effort, and is present to the agent, from the beginning of his
efforts to the end, as the mediate cause. If, before the creation
of the world, God already recognises or ordains His Son to be
the perfect Lord of the ideal community (1 Pet. i. 20 ; Eph. i.
4), and if it is with a view to Him that the world is created,
then in God's purpose His Son stands above and before the

world as the mediate cause of the same. Here also lies the
explanation of Heb. i. 1–3. In this passage the Son of God
is presented to us first of all in His capacity as Prophet, but
at the same time as predestined by God to be Lord of the
world. Of this Person it is then declared: δι' οὗ καὶ ἐποίησεν
τοὺς αἰῶνας. The context demands that the attribute
expressed in the first relative clause should be recapitulated
in the second relative pronoun—δι' οὗ, i.e. τοῦ τεθέντος
κληρονόμου πάντων, God made the worlds. This is the same
thought as in Colossians; and therefore the third relative
clause in Hebrews refers to the exalted Son of God Who has
assumed His predestined lordship over the world.

Alongside of this group of interpretations of the Godhead
of the exalted Christ stands the twofold statement of John,
that the revealing Word, which is God, has in the Person of
Jesus Christ become a human person, and that the disciples
recognise in Him the manifestation of the only Son of God
by the fact that He lived a life full of grace and truth—a life,
that is to say, exhibiting the characteristics by which God
Himself described His nature to Moses (John i. 14; Ex.
xxxiv. 6, 7). At this point it must be laid down clearly that
the attribute of Godhead thus ascribed to Christ is based on
the personal experience of His disciples. Apart from that relation it is inconceivable. This, and no other, is the ground on
which John ranges the figure of Christ under the wider conception of the revealing Word—a conception which he applies
to the creation of the world, etc., and for which he claims the
predicate God. Thus the two lines of thought which meet
us in the New Testament are wholly independent of each
other, and find their explanation in considerations of a very
different order. The Johannine conception regards the historical manifestation of Christ from the point of view of the
conjoint moral impression made upon the community of
disciples—an impression which agrees with the known nature
of God; the Godhead of Christ as thus established is not
directly associated with the Divine attribute of exaltation
over the world; rather is the underlying assumption the

creation of the world through the Word of God, the Divine worth of Jesus being embodied in the formula that the Word, Which is the universal form of Divine revelation, has in Jesus become a human personality. The representation given by the other apostles connects the Godhead of Christ with the thought of the eternal significance for God of the Person of Christ and the realisation of the same in Christ's present exaltation above the world—also a line of thought which rests upon the view that Christ in the ethical union between Himself and His community is the revealed end of the world.

Both these ways of conceiving Christ's Godhead are distinctively religious, in so far as they describe the significance of Christ for that view of the world which originated with Himself, and for the corresponding self-estimate of the individual. For John must be understood to mean that the life of Jesus produced those same moral impressions which as the chief attributes of God attract to themselves all human trust; and the other apostles regard the present lordship of Christ as the determining motive which lays claim to the whole of human life, and leaves nothing over that dare rule itself by any other motive. Every other standard is relative; however all-embracing any one motive in human life may be, it still leaves room for others. An authority, therefore, which either excludes all other standards or else subordinates them to itself, which at the same time regulates in exhaustive fashion all human trust in God, has itself the worth of Godhead. But these two ways of conceiving Christ's Godhead are of such a nature that each requires the other to complete itself. For what John experienced in Christ cannot be merely an influence wielded by Christ in the past, it must be an influence which still affects the religious view of the world and the religious self-estimate of the individual, if these latter are to be determined thereby. Conversely, the idea of the Godhead of the exalted Christ depends for its convincing power entirely upon whether the marks of this Godhead can be found in His historical existence upon the earth. Paul, indeed (Phil. ii. 9), fixes the precise moment when the Person, Who till then had not been declared God, received the Divine name and the universal lordship. This involves the difficulty that the identity of the one Person in the two forms of existence is not guaranteed. For the marks by which Paul immediately before, and indeed always, denotes the superiority of the man Christ, must surely first be brought into harmony with the predicate κύριος. If the Godhead of Christ, or His lordship over the world in His present state of exaltation, is to be a postulate of the Christian faith, an integral part of the Christian view of the world, then it must be demonstrated to us in Christ's influence upon ourselves. But every form of influence exerted by Christ must find its criterion in the historical figure presented by His life. Therefore the Godhead or universal lordship of Christ must be apprehended in definite features of His historical life, as an attribute of His existence in time. For what Christ is in virtue of His eternal destiny, and what the influence is which He exerts on us because of His exaltation to God, would be wholly beyond our ken if we did not also experience the effects of the same in His historical existence in time. Unless the conception of His present lordship receives its content from the definite characteristics of His historical activity, then it is either a meaningless formula or the occasion for all kinds of extravagance. If, on the other hand, we are to hold fast our faith that Christ is at this moment Lord over the community of the Kingdom of God, and is working toward the gradual subjection of the world to this its true end, then lordship over the world must be recognisable as already a conspicuous feature of Christ's historical life.

Both the Confessional systems of theology which have sprung from the Reformation assume as the formative principle of the whole phenomenon Divine nature with all the Divine attributes, especially omnipotence and omniscience, which are the attributes chiefly concerned in the creation of the world. But in the correlation of the Divine with the human nature, the two systems come into direct

contrast with each other.[1]   The Lutheran doctrine is determined by the consideration that the fulness of the Godhead
is revealed in the human person of Christ; with this in view,
it maintains that through the incarnation of the Divine Word,
or through the union of the Divine with the human nature,
the latter becomes endowed with all the Divine attributes.
The Reformed doctrine is determined by the consideration
that the union of the Divine Word with the human nature
preserves the closest possible analogy with the nature of man
as such; with this in view, it maintains that the Divine Word,
in order to become man, gave up the fulness of His Divine
attributes, more especially those relations in which, as Creator
and Lord, He stands to the world.   Now the Lutheran formula
does not correspond with the historical picture, which the
Reformed doctrine faithfully follows; it requires, therefore,
to be supplemented by the statement that the Incarnate
Word of God during His earthly life regularly refrained from
the manifestation of His Divine attributes ($\kappa\rho\upsilon\psi\iota\varsigma$).   The
difference between the two types of doctrine is specially con-
spicuous in the way in which the ideas of *incarnatio* and
exinanitio are contrasted with each other.   According to the
Lutheran doctrine, the *verbum incarnatum* is the subject of
exinanitio; according to the Reformed, the *verbum sese exin-
aniens* is the subject of *incarnatio*.   That is to say, since the
conception and human birth are the first manifestations of
the *exinanitio*, therefore, according to Lutheran teaching, the
union of the human nature with the Divine, and the transference to the former of all the Divine attributes, are already
presupposed at the entrance of the God-man into the process
of birth, which is the first instance of His hiding His Divine
attributes.   According to the Reformed teaching, the Divine
Word empties Himself of His Divine attributes by entering
into the process of birth—in other words, by entering into
union with human nature.

   What significance, then, have these two explanations for the

---

[1] I refer to Schneckenburger, *Zur kirchlichen Christologie*, 1848; 2nd
edition, 1861.

apprehension and appreciation of the Person of Christ in its historical manifestation ? The Lutheran doctrine corresponds with the historical manifestation only in so far as it is untrue to itself, and, by its assertion of the κρύψις, robs the transference of the Divine attributes to the human nature of all significance for Christ's historical life. It is therefore in direct contradiction to the phenomenon which it pretends to explain. It claims to demonstrate the Godhead of Christ in the peculiar quality of His humanity, in accordance with the line followed by Luther in his Larger Catechism; but the means which are employed to solve this problem do not permit a solution, because they do not rise to the level of the view there set forth by Luther. In this connection there is another point specially to be noted. If the *incarnatio verbi* is assumed to be real because the *verbum incarnatum* subjects Himself to the *conceptio* on which the individual existence of Christ depends, this does not in the very least guarantee that the personality which results from the *conceptio* is co-extensive with the *verbum incarnatum*. It would be equally consistent with the main assumption to suppose that the *verbum incarnatum* manifests Himself only in the completed history of the whole human race. This has actually been maintained, for Strauss in his day declared that the human race in its gradual attainment of religious self-consciousness is the God-man, and corresponds to the idea of the *verbum incarnatum*. It is probably more than a mere accident that this possible heretical consequence of the Lutheran Christology comes from the same theological workshop in which the Lutheran formula itself was put together. On the other hand, the Reformed explanation of the Person of Christ through the kenosis of the Divine Word does certainly remain true to those human and temporal limits within which it perceives the life of Jesus to have been lived; but in the same measure in which it does so, it compels us to refuse the predicate of Godhead to the historical life of Christ. If the eternal Logos, by His conception as an individual man, emptied Himself of those attributes in which His original relation to the world is expressed, and in which He is of like essence with the Father, then in His historical existence He is not the possessor of Godhead. It is in this case impossible to understand why other men also, who in their own sphere are recognised as ideals, should not equally be regarded as incarnations of the self-depotentiating Divine Reason. For this is the possible heretical consequencè of this type of doctrine, which frankly acknowledges that Godhead and manhood cannot be predicated, at the same time and in the same relation, of the Person of Christ—in other words, that the two predicates are mutually exclusive.

Nevertheless, under the pretext that it is the logical outcome of the Christology outlined in the Formula of Concord, the said doctrine has become common among theologians who pride themselves on their Lutheran orthodoxy. The first to tread this way, Gottfried Thomasius,[1] believed himself called on to expand the Lutheran formula of the *communicatio idiomatum*, as the consequence of the *incarnatio verbi divini*, beyond the traditional and one-sided presentation it had hitherto received. It was one-sided that only the human nature should be invested with Divine attributes—omnipotence, omniscience, and the like. In consequence of the *incarnatio verbi divini*, the Divine nature also in Christ must be declared to be the bearer of suffering, want, and weakness, if the formula of the *communicatio idiomatum* was to be valid. This had not been done; nor has it been accomplished by the corrections proposed by Thomasius. The latter falls completely out of line with the system set forth in the Formula of Concord. It is not the *verbum incarnatum* which forms for Thomasius the framework within which he ascribes to the Divine nature of Christ the human attributes of suffering and the like. On the contrary, he maintains that the *verbum divinum*, with a view to incarnation, renounced omnipotence, omnipresence, and omniscience, attributes which bear on the relation of God to

---

[1] *Beiträge zur kirchlichen Christologie*, 1845. Cf. on this point Schneckenburger, *op. cit.* p. 196 ff.

the world, which therefore are for God only relative, and therefore also can be given up by the Divine Logos without abrogating His Godhead. Even if this assumption were on all sides unassailable, it would still be in contradiction to the Formula of Concord. For how can the incarnation of the Logos invest the human nature with those very attributes which the Logos in His union with human nature no longer possesses ? Lutheran, therefore, as judged by the standard of the Formula of Concord, this theory certainly is not. And, what is more, it is self-contradictory. For even if omnipotence and the like are only relative attributes of God and of the Divine Logos, relative, that is, in relation to the world, is not this very relation the limit within which alone any knowledge of God is possible, outside of which God is wholly inconceivable ? Moreover, the conception of the Divine Logos had its origin exclusively in the relation of God to the world. So that we cease to conceive the Logos of God in the way which the conception itself requires, if in any particular case we think away His relation to the world, and therefore His omnipotence, or, in any other relation into which He can enter, leave this out of account as no longer existing. If the Logos, for the sake of His incarnation, emptied Himself of His omnipotence, etc., then He simply cannot be recognised in the Person of Christ as the Logos, eternally begotten of the Father, and of the same essence with Him. This hypothesis serves only to prove that Christ, at least in His earthly existence, has no Godhead at all.

Despite these considerations, even Luthardt teaches : " When the Son of God took upon Him the earthly nature of man, He still retained His Divine nature and the essential and inalienable glory of the same ; but, as concerned His relation to the world, He laid aside in His state of humiliation the Divine conditions of existence, and the corresponding exercise of Divine power, not to assume them again till His exaltation, though then as One who has become man." From the historical notices which accompany §§ 50, 51 of his *Compendium der Dogmatik*, we gather merely that Luthardt

is conscious of propounding doctrine which is the opposite of
what is prescribed to him in the Formula of Concord; but
how to conceive the above statement, or on what grounds
we are to find it intelligible, he does not tell us.   What is
taught under the head of the Kenosis of the Divine Logos is
pure mythology.   Not Luthardt, to be sure, but Gess has
given us the theory in its wildest form.   But the formula is
common to both, and it means a return to the mediaeval
interpretation of the matter.   Acknowledgment is made of a
Divine nature which stands behind the human person of
Jesus, but occupies only a vague relation to it; attention is
then concentrated upon the man Jesus as Mediator, without
any effort to find an indication of His Godhead in His human
life upon the earth.   This way of confessing Christ's Godhead
is a ceremony that has lost its meaning.   On the other hand,
the hints thrown out by Luther and Melanchthon in which
they transcend the limits of Latin Catholicism, and bid us
learn the meaning of Christ's Godhead in Christ our Redeemer,
are for these Lutherans or Pietists non-existent, although
they occur in symbolical books.

Another series of attempts is associated with the dark
saying of Marheineke (vol. i. p. 582), that Christ in His own
person is humanity itself, so far as He presents in Himself
what is common to all individual men.   This statement is
with all celerity exchanged for the other, that Christ in His
own individuality embraces dynamically as root-principle all
human individuals, or, that He represents in personal form
the totality of individuals, and gathers together the original
types or ideal personalities of all separate individuals in
Himself.   That is, the generic idea is conceived in the one
case as an abstract unity, in the other, in nominalistic fashion,
as the collective unity of all the separate individuals.   If
either one or the other can rightly be applied to Christ,
there is an end to His human individuality.   But what have
statements of this kind to do with His Godhead?   In the
characteristics here described, Christ is supposed to correspond
to the idea of the second Adam.   In the same way, then, that

the first Adam, as head of the natural creation, reaches over into the realm of spirit, so Christ, as Head of the spiritual creation, points to *what may be called* a cosmic or meta-physical significance of His person. " And this, then, is the point where Christology borders on the doctrine of the Trinity, and where the statement of Scripture about the Word that was in the beginning finds its fit place." "That point in the cosmos which is the centre of receptivity for God (namely, Christ as the central individual of the human race), is the point where a real world-unity and world-consummation are possible; but its actual realisation comes from the personal self-communication of God. For the idea of the world as it exists eternally before God does not stop short at mere receptivity for God, it includes also the being wholly filled with God, namely in itself and at the point where, corre-sponding to this central receptivity, there takes place the equally central fulfilment." That is to say, for the complete-ness of the world-idea the indwelling of God in the central Man is an indispensable supposition. This theory bears a remote resemblance to that interpretation of Christ's Godhead which Paul derives from the final cause of the world. But if we put the theory to the test, and ask in what features of the historical picture Christ's Godhead appears, we do not find an answer to our query any more than to the reflection that the existence in the Person of Christ of this central individual has never been proved. The reason of this defect lies in the fact that behind this theory a religious interest in the person of Christ is nowhere discernible. To guarantee the completeness of the world-idea may be a philosophical motive, but it is certainly not a religious one; for no relation has been shown between the world-consummation in this central man and any saving good derived therefrom. In short, this idea lacks not merely the requisite scientific maturity, but the religious kernel; it is therefore not a theological concep-tion at all.

The religious estimate of Christ, which finds expression under definite conditions in the predicate of His Godhead,

must approve itself in the connection between Christ's visible
conduct and His religious convictions and ethical motives; it
does not stand in any direct relation to the presumable
endowment of His Person with inborn qualities or powers.
For not in this latter relation but in the former does He
exert an influence upon us. The religious estimate of His
Person will stand related to His moral conduct in so far as
the latter is the test and counterpart of His own conviction
that He enjoys a unique fellowship with God. For this
reason the religious dignity of Christ does not depend upon
the unbroken completeness of His ethical horizon—a completeness which, in fact, does not exist if we compare the
ethical perceptions of Christ with a system of the present day.
In his *Life of Jesus for the German People*, Strauss maintains
that Jesus has only a relative significance for the development
of the moral ideal, since He betrays no sense of the ethical
significance of the family or of the joy of life, no idea of the
moral worth of the State, of trade, of art and science; that,
therefore, His moral code is defective, and requires to be
supplemented. As if the worth for the human race of a
man like Jesus depended on His having a complete view of
all possible applications, both positive and negative, of the
influence which He sought to exert upon human life—a
view that is reached only afterwards in the form of scientific
cognition which lay outside the range of His vocation ! With
the most perfect system of ethics Christ would not have
altered the course of the intellectual world; with any such
system He would long ago have become antiquated. For the
more detailed the programme of any reformation in the
spiritual sphere, the more limited is its field of action; the
more indefinite it is in detail, the wider and more lasting is
its influence. As a matter of fact, Jesus is not concerned to
provide a moral code for the details of life; that is not His
business, and any estimate of His person that has this for its
starting-point is historically unjust. Jesus has the same
right as every other man to demand that He be understood
in the light of His own individuality. That this individuality

is that of the religious man and thereafter of the prophet
and founder of a religion, cannot, of course, be recognised
where, as in the case of the *Life* just mentioned, the thought
of God is simply suspended.   This explains also why in the
end the historical figure of Jesus became for Strauss quite
indistinct.   Would a man who regards all music as a dis-
agreeable noise undertake to write a life and an appreciation
of Mozart?   That were the true parallel to this atheistic
method of writing the history of religion.

Jesus is the bearer of the perfect spiritual religion, which
consists in mutual fellowship with God, the Author of the
world and its final goal.   In the idea of God as the final
goal of all things lies the reason why Jesus recognises as
binding upon Himself for God's sake the widest conceivable
aim of moral effort, namely, the union of mankind through
love; while in the idea of God as the Author of the world
lies the reason why Jesus for His own personal life repudiates
every motive that is individual, worldly, and therefore less
than Divine.   But inasmuch as Jesus desired His own attitude to God to be shared by the rest of mankind, He laid
upon His disciples, as their aim also, the union of mankind
through love, or, in other words, the realisation of the Kingdom of God; and through His own personal freedom in relation to the world, He led His disciples, in accepting their
view of the world from Him, to the assured conviction that
human life is of more worth than all the world.   By making
the aim of His own life the aim of mankind, who are to be
called into the fellowship of His community, He is before all
else the Founder of a religion and the Redeemer of men from
the dominion of the world.   He is the author of a moral code
only in so far as the raising of men above the world, and their
fellowship in this relation, carries with it the ordering of their
conduct towards each other in the Kingdom of God.   But
since this end is served by setting up the universal principle
of brotherly love, it is not any defect in the moral code of
Jesus as such that the ordering of the separate provinces of
moral life is left to the free application of this supreme

principle. Had Jesus directed His attention to the ethical regulation of the separate provinces of human life, the result would have been—since He meant to be the Founder of a community—that He would have drawn up definite legal enactments. Hence the objections of Strauss come in the end to this, that Jesus did not impose upon His disciples a system such as that of Islam. That He did not follow this path marks His unique and incomparable supremacy over all other founders of religions.[1]

If the subject-matter of Christ's life, in pursuance of His purpose to redeem mankind and reveal to men the love of God, serves to render visible His Godhead, then, within the limits of the dogma of the two natures, no one has so aptly stated this connection as St. Bernard.[2] In his *in Cant. canticorum*, sermo vi. 3, we come upon the following: " Dum in carne et per carnem facit opera non carnis sed dei, naturae utique imperans *superansque fortunam*, stultam faciens sapientiam hominium daemonumque debellans tyrannidem, manifeste ipsum se esse indicat, *per quem eadem et antefiebant*, quando fiebant. In carne, inquam, et per carnem potenter et patenter operatus mira, locutus salubria, *passus indigna* evidenter ostendit, quia ipse sit, qui potenter sed invisibiliter secula condidisset, *sapienter regeret, benigne protegeret.* Denique dum evangelizat *ingratis*, signa praebet *infidelibus, pro suis crucifixoribus orat*, nonne liquido ipsum se esse declarat, qui cum patre suo quotidie oriri facit *solem super bonos et malos, pluit super iustos et iniustos ?* " These three sentences speak of the God-man, but to this effect, that the Divine Person of the Logos wears the human nature—the flesh—as the organ of His activity. On these assumptions Bernard develops the *communicatio idiomatum* in both directions, ascribing sufferings to the Divine Person of the Logos, and acts of omnipotence to the human nature of the same. But these acts of omnipotence, which are to be on a level with the creation and governance of the world, Bernard exhibits to us in moral achievements of the

---

[1] Cf. Stephan, *Das heutige Aegypten* (1872), pp. 257–261.

[2] Cf. Lesefrüchte aus dem heiligen Bernhard, *Stud. u. Krit.* 1879, p. 322.

God-man. That Christ overcomes His fate, reveals to us in
Him the Creator of the world ; that He endures indignities
which He has not deserved, of course for the good of men,
reveals in Him the Creator, the wise Ruler, the gracious Pro-
tector of the world ; finally, that He does not withhold His
benefits from the unthankful and unbelieving, that He prays
for those who crucify Him, proves His connection with the
perfect God, who bestows His favours both on the evil and
the good. The God-man has all the Divine attributes ; but, as
Bernard says,[1] He exercises these attributes in the work of
redemption with effort, whereas in the work of creation the
effort does not occur. Further, in the work of redemption,
He exercises these attributes for the salvation of men, and
therefore in the form of moral acts, especially in the effort of
endurance. These activities, having as their aim redemption
and the revelation of love, are more than human activities ;
at bottom, they are Divine. Of the likeness between the
moral activities of the God-man and the omnipotence of
God, we can be assured only if we have already established their Divine worth for our salvation. Luther can
scarcely have known these sentences of Bernard ; yet his
own exposition in the Larger Catechism follows the same
lines. It is as my Redeemer that Christ is my Lord ; what
is said of Him in the second Article of the Creed explains redemption, its manner and means ; that is, how much
it cost Him (*quanti constiterit*) ; and what He spent and
dared to win us and bring us under His lordship, namely,
that He became man, and suffered, and died, etc. etc. And
all this in order that He might be my Lord.[2] The theological

---

[1] *Sermo* xx. 2 : "Multum laboravit in eo salvator, nec in omni mundi
fabrica tantum fatigationis auctor assumsit. At vero hic et in dictis suis sus-
tinuit contradictores et in factis observatores et in tormentis illusores et in
morte exprobratores. Ecce quomodo dilexit."

[2] On this point compare A. H. Francke, "*De magnitudine et maiestate Iesu
Christi (programmata diversis temporibus in acad. Hal. proposita*, 1714), p. 170 :
"Tantus cum esset dei filius, an in carne se manifestantem, humanam naturam
adsumentem *minorem* factum opinabimur ? Absit, ut quem *magnum caritate,
ipsamque caritatem* esse agnovimus, eum minorem putemus in eo ipso, quo
magnitudinem suae caritatis non verbis aut promissis amplius sed re ipsa decla-
ravit, factoque stupendo, ipsis angelis mirabili, hominibus depravatis incredibili

solution of the problem of Christ's Divinity must therefore be based upon an analysis of what He has done for the salvation of mankind in the form of His community.

§ 46. This subject is treated in Dogmatics under the title of the three *functions* or *offices of the God-man*. In the most developed form of the dogma the aim is rightly to distribute among the functions of Prophet, Priest, and King the activities of Christ described in the New Testament, which had for their aim the establishment and ordering of human salvation, and which extend in time over the *status exinanitionis et exaltationis*. This application of Old Testament types to the interpretation of Christ's Person has its first representative in Eusebius of Caesarea; but only since the Reformation has it become a factor in theology.[1] The origin of this threefold type is to be found in the literal meaning of the word Christ, it being regarded as legitimate to refer the anointing with the Holy Spirit not only to the anointing of a king, but also to that of a priest and of a prophet. But in estimating the practical worth of this principle of division, we must take account of the way in which it gradually became current with the theologians of the Reformation. It is well known that the theologians who follow Melanchthon and Luther down to Hafenreffer and Gerhard, treat the saving work of Christ only under the two heads of King and Priest.[2] Attention may also be called to the fact that it was Calvin who added the type of the Prophet (in the *Catechismus Genevensis* and *Institutio*, ii. 15). The school of Melanchthon and

ostendit, comprobavit et ipse ut *caritas* in mundo apparuit." P. 180: "Detinuit nos diutius consideratio *magnitudinis Christi in ipsa morte elucentis*. At cum in hac morte eius, morte inquam Christi, quem mors retinere non potuit, omnis vita et salus sita sit, imo *omnis ex ea fidei victoria* et futura eorum, quos fides ad finem servata coronabit, gloria dependeat, de tanta re ne incepisse quidem aliquid dicere nobis videmur."

[1] For other upholders of this theory, since Eusebius, compare Krauss, Das Mittlerwerk nach dem Schema des *munus triplex, Jahrb. für deutsche Theol.* xvii. (1872) p. 595 ff.

[2] Cf. Heppe, *Dogmatik des deutschen Protestantismus im* 16 *Jahrh.* ii. pp. 209–212. The statement holds of Strigel, Hemming, Hesshus, Homberger, Selnecker, Heerbrand. Hafenreffer, on the other hand, in explaining the name Christ, has first the two titles, and afterwards the three.

27

Luther did not by any means ignore Christ's work of teaching, but the Old Testament type of the high priest seemed to justify its being reckoned part of His work as Priest. Even in Calvin, in the first edition of the *Institutio* (1536), we find only the Kingship and the Priesthood assumed as exhausting the meaning of the name Christ.[1] The working out of the idea brings before us in its full extent the religious view of the world and sense of personal worth which, in the first epoch of the Reformation, accompanied every effort at theological reconstruction. What Christ is *for* us, must verify itself in the transferring of His worth *to* us. The recognition of Jesus as the Christ has for us no meaning unless through Him we know ourselves raised to kingship or dominion over the world, and to priesthood or undisturbed communion with God. Only in relation to these practical ends will even an objective theological discussion of the statements of the Creed satisfy the religious interest. But Calvin's treatment of this subject is derived from Luther's tract *De libertate christiana* (vol. i. p. 182). A comparison of the sentence already quoted with this tract of Luther's proves for one thing that the immense significance of the latter was not lost upon Calvin, and besides, the agreement between Luther and Calvin is a confirmation of the method by which thus far I have endeavoured to pave the way for a doctrine of the Person or saving work of Christ. If, in accordance with this view, the aim of Christ's activity as King and Priest is to secure for us freedom with regard to the world and with regard to sin, and freedom in our intercourse with God, then surely I am in line with the real trend of the Reformation when I bring the specific significance of the Person of Christ for the Christian view of the world and sense of personal worth into relation

[1] *C. R.* xxix. p. 69 : "Credimus et Christum ipsum esse, hoc est, omnibus sancti spiritus gratiis perfusum, ut de plenitudine eius omnes accipiamus, quicunque simul per fidem eius consortes ac participes ; hac denique unctione constitutum esse a patre regem, ut in ipso reges essemus, imperium habentes supra diabolum, peccatum, mortem et inferos ; deinde sacerdotem, qui suo sacrificio patrem placaret ac reconciliaret, ut in ipso sacerdotes essemus, ipso intercessore ac mediatore patri preces, gratiarum actiones, nosmetipsos et nostra omnia offerentes."

with the attainment of our own personal independence over against the world. Finally, the order adopted by Luther— King, Priest—explains not only why the theologians who followed Luther and Melanchthon adhered to this appellation, even after their attention was directed to the significance of Christ's work of teaching, but also why Calvin, when in the *Catechismus Genevensis* he added the type of the Prophet, put it in the third rank, and why, when in the *Institutio* of the year 1559 he gave the first place to the office of Prophet, he still put the office of King before the office of Priest. It is true that in the *Institutio* of the year 1539 he already put the office of Prophet in the forefront as evidence of Christ's anointing. But this does not mean that he sought to attach to it the same importance as to the Kingship and the Priesthood, the former of these being here expounded with somewhat more detail than before.[1]

The complete presentation of the three *munera Christi* in the *Institutio* of the year 1559 (vol. ii. p. 15) marks a change for the worse in this respect, that the practical bearing of the Kingship and the Priesthood of Christ, in the transference of these attributes to believers, has disappeared. Which shows that the religious interest has suffered at the hands of the purely dogmatic method, which treats human salvation exclusively from the side of dependence upon God, without keeping in view the practical consideration that in Christianity our religious dependence upon God is to form the basis of our personal independence. At the same time, in distinction

---

[1] *L.c.* p. 515: "Quantum ad regnum attinet, non terrenum aut carnale est, sed spirituale, quod in coelum magis, futuramque et aeternam vitam respiciat. Deinde talis illi est regnandi ratio, ut non tam sibi regnet quam nobis. Potentia enim sua nos armat et instruit, decore et magnificentia ornat, opibus locupletat, denique in regni participationem exaltat et evehit. Siquidem eius communionis, qua se nobis illigavit beneficio, reges et ipsi constituimur, robore eius ad certamen cum diabolo, peccato et morte depugnandum armati, iustitiae eius ornamentis ad spem immortalitatis vestiti, divitiis sanctitatis eius ad fructificandum deo per bona opera locupletati. — At sacerdotis functionem nihilo minori nostro bono sustinet ; non ideo tantum, quod sua intercessione placatum patrem nobis propitium reddit, sed quod nos quoque in sacerdotii consortium asciscit, ut ipso freti intercessore ac mediatore patri preces, gratiarum actiones, nosmetipsos et nostra omnia offeramus."

from other methods of treatment, it is important to mention that Calvin still gives the same definition of Christ's Kingship, so far as subject-matter is concerned, that he has previously given, namely, that Christ's Kingship verifies itself in our assurance of eternal salvation, in our victory over sin, in our patience in face of the evils of the world.[1]   The scope of the *regnum Christi* in this relation he expressly limits to the *status exaltationis*.   On the other hand, he extends not only the priestly but the prophetic office over both the *status Christi*.   For the satisfaction offered in Christ's sacrificial death is continued in the intercession of the exalted Christ, and the exercise on earth of the office of Prophet in the *continua evangelii predicatio* within the Church through the communication to the Church of the Spirit.   This exclusive reference of the kingly office to the inward perfection of believers occurs elsewhere, so far as I know, only in Amesius (*Medulla,* i. 19. 24, 26); but how far removed Amesius is from the starting-point adopted by Calvin, when he adds, that the prophetic office of Christ admits of being transferred to other men, but not the office of King nor the office of Priest !

While I reserve my right to return at a later point to another interpretation due to Calvin of the Kingship of Christ, the exposition already given justifies the conclusion that Calvin consistently maintained that reference of Christ's Kingship to the defence of believers and their deliverance from sin and the world, which he adopted from Luther's " Freedom of a Christian Man."   Meanwhile, from Luther through Melanchthon there spread among the theologians of the German Reformation another definition of the *regnum Christi sprituale*.   This was the conception of the community of believers, in so far as that community is established, main-

---

[1] Lib. ii. 15. 4 : "Unde colligimus, ipsum nobis magis regnare quam sibi, idque intus et extra, ut scilicet donis spiritus referti ex iis primitiis sentiamus vere nos deo coniunctos esse ad perfectam beatitudinem.   Deinde ut eiusdem spiritus virtute freti non dubitemus, contra diabolum, mundum et quodvis noxae genus nos semper fore victores. . . . Ad aeternam usque vitam nos attolit, ut patienter hanc vitam sub aerumnis, inedia, frigore, contemtu, probris aliisqne molestiis transigamus hoc uno contenti, quod nunquam destituet nos rex noster, quin necessitatibus nostris subveniat."

tained, and governed through the Word of God.[1]   Calvin had
already adopted this as the content of the office of Prophet in
both the states of Christ.   But to show how movable Calvin
was on this point, it is worth noting that in the *Catechismus
Genevensis* he appropriates the above interpretation of the
kingly office, in spite of its inconsistency with the view he
had otherwise expounded; and since the kingly office concerned the *status exaltationis,* there followed the further
change that he limited the prophetic office in this connection
to the *status exinanitionis.*[2]   At the same time this inconse-
quence on Calvin's part has not had any appreciable influence
in his own circle.   On the contrary, the Heidelberg Catechism
adopts the statement of the Catechism of Geneva about the
office of Prophet, and combines under the head of Kingship
the two references acknowledged by Calvin, namely, the ruling
of the Church as such by Word and Spirit, and the defence
as well as maintenance of the standing of believers.[3]   The same
method of statement meets us in Rodolf, the expounder of the
Catechism.   But all the other Reformed theologians accessible
to me retain the double reference of the kingly office proposed
in the Catechism, namely, that of Calvin and of Melanchthon
and Luther, combine with it Calvin's extension of the prophetic office to both the states of Christ, and land themselves
in a double explanation of the origin of the Church, namely,
from the persistence of the prophetic office, and from the
kingly office of Christ.   The Lutherans, especially Gerhard,
Quenstedt, and Hollatz, follow suit; although in Baier we miss

[1] Cf. Köstlin, ii. p. 380 ; Melanchthon, *Loci C. R.* xxi. pp. 519, 920 ; *vid.
supra,* p. 287.

[2] Niemeyer, *l.c.* p. 129 : "Regnum Christi spirituale, quod verbo et spiritu
dei continetur, quae iustitiam et vitam secum ferunt. . . . Propheta Christus
est, quum in mundum descendit, patris se legatum apud homines et interpre-
tem professus est idque in eum finem, ut patris voluntate ad plenum exposita
finem poneret revelationibus omnibus et prophetiis."

[3] *L.c.* p. 457 ; *Cat. Pal.* 31 : "Christus appellatur unctus, quod a patre
ordinatus et spiritu sancto unctus sit summus propheta ac doctor, qui nobis
arcanum consilium et omnem voluntatem patris de redemtione nostri patefecit,
et summus pontifex, qui nos unico sacrificio corporis sui redemit, assidueque
pro nobis apud patrem intercedit, et rex, qui nos suo verbo et spiritu gubernat,
et partam nobis salutem tuetur ac conservat."

Calvin's original reference of the kingly office to the defence of believers. I may mention, also, in regard to the conception of the *regnum Christi*, which originally was not divided into the *regnum potentiae* and the *regnum gratiae*, that after the doctrine of the two natures became prominent, a distinction was drawn in both schools between what was due to the Divine nature, and what to the exaltation of the human nature in Christ. And although here also we find traces of the opposite views held by the two schools with regard to the relation between the two states of Christ, yet this is of small significance for the theory of the three offices. On the contrary, our inquiry has shown that the form in which this dogma was taught in the seventeenth century by both sides alike, was a compound of elements from Luther and Melanchthon on the one hand, and from Calvin on the other.

When the activities of Christ in His two states are divided according to subject-matter among the three offices, the result is a network in which each office appears under both states, and each of the two states displays all the three offices. This method obtains even in the case of those who, like Amesius and Wendelin, begin by making the essential order of the offices evolve itself in the temporal sequence of events, namely, Christ first taught, then offered Himself as a sacrifice, and finally entered upon His lordship. For these theologians, too, recognise the continuance of the prophetic and of the priestly office *in statu exaltationis*—their position being that the effect of what Christ accomplished in His earthly life is brought to bear upon mankind through the continuance of similar activity on His part in His exaltation, whereby, according to the theory in question, the *opus mediatorium Christi* becomes complete. It has been proved by Krauss that in their application of this doctrine the Lutheran theologians lack the necessary precision. For my purpose here I select one instance of this for special notice.

It is a formal weakness in the view under consideration, that its advocates have from the beginning been content to demonstrate the *regnum Christi* merely *in statu exaltationis*, whereas

they make the other two offices hold for both forms of existence. This betrays an ominous resemblance to the Socinian
position, and throws doubt upon the possibility of successfully opposing the latter in the other points connected with
the doctrine of Christ. For, according to Luther's Catechisms
at least, it is the *regnum Christi* which is the direct test of
His Godhead. If the Kingship of Christ fails to approve
itself *in statu exinanitionis,* then the teaching of the highest
Prophet affords so much the less ground for applying to Him
the predicate of Godhead, that His sufferings in the office of
Priest seem directly to contradict the characteristic attributes
of Deity. Many of the Reformed theologians, however, under
the impulse of opposition to the Socinians, have made a brave
attempt to supplement the theory at this point. In Gomarus,
Maccovius, Wendelin, Heidanus, Rüssen, I find the following
adduced as proofs of the Kingship of Christ, namely, that He
was born as King of the Jews, that He was worshipped by
the Magi, that He issued commands to evil spirits, that He
made changes in the law, forgave sins, wrought miracles, and
made a royal entry into Jerusalem. By these things He
declared not only His destination to Kingship in the future,
which the Socinians admitted, but His possession of the right
to the same. In conclusion, the said theologians argue that,
if these are not valid proofs of the active Kingship of Christ,
then that Kingship cannot be dated even from His resurrection, but is established only by the complete subjection of
the world to Him at the last. These arguments have been
appropriated by the later Lutherans Hollatz and Buddeus.
But a makeshift of this sort, compounded of elements wholly
incongruous, is the more powerless to produce conviction that
it betrays complete ignorance of what is universally recognised as the subject-matter of the *regnum Christi in statu
exaltationis.* This consideration, according to the statement
supplied by Krauss, has been regarded by one only of the
Reformed theologians on the European continent, namely,
Wolleb. By him, the effort Christ spent on the formation
of His community, namely, His appointment of the apostles

and His institution of the sacraments, is described as evidence of His active exercise of kingly rights.[1] This assumption is shared by the Helmstedt Lutheran, Hornejus, and it re-appears in Schleiermacher (vol. i. p. 522), who quotes the sending forth of the disciples and the instructions given for their conduct as the historical marks of the Kingship of Christ.

Within the circle of Calvinism, however, even before its contact with Socinianism, there appeared a most vigorous interpretation of the Kingship of Christ in His historical life, an interpretation with independent features of its own. The Puritan exposition of Christ's Kingship has in view the acceptance of Christ as Lawgiver for the Church in its capacity as a visible, organised, and worshipping community. This is a direct departure from the conception of the *regnum Christi spirituale* upheld alike by Calvin and by Luther. The idea attained concrete realisation owing to the special conditions under which the congregations of Dutch and English exiles were forced to dispense with the support of the State, and the English Puritans, like the Scots, had to effect the formation of a Reformed Church in conflict with the civil power. At the same time it cannot be denied that in the editions of the *Institutio* between 1539 and 1554 there is a statement of Calvin's pointing in this direction, which is wanting in 1536, and has again dis-appeared in 1559. This statement, however, Calvin makes, not under the head of the *regnum Christi*, but by way of explaining the title *dominus* in the Creed.[2] The idea was appropriated by John a Lasco, along with Calvin's interpreta-tion of the *regnum Christi*. In the Catechism of the Con-

---

[1] *Christ. theol. compend.* i. 18: "Regium officium in humiliationis statu administravit ecclesiam verbo ac spiritu sic congregando et conservando, ut nihil externae regiae maiestatis in ipso apparuerit."

[2] *C. R.* xxix. p. 516: "Postremo illi domini elogium adscribitur, quoniam hac lege mundo praefectus est a patre, ut eius dominationem hic exerceat. . . . Sic autem significatur, non tantum praeceptorem esse et magistrum, cui auscultandum sit docenti, sed caput ac principem, cuius imperio parendum sit, cuius nutui obtemperandum, cuius ad voluntatem obsequia nostra sint dirigenda."

gregation of Exiles in London (1551), he speaks, on the one hand, of the Kingship of Christ as existing for the protection of believers from every evil, and expresses the thought that believers *ipsius plenitudine in reges atque sacerdotes domino in spiritu consecrantur*. But at the same period, in the *Compendium doctrinae*, following the order *regnum, prophetia, sacerdotium*, he describes the content of the first of these offices as being the communication through Christ of all eternal and unchangeable laws for the Church. This view first finds a distinct echo in the Scots Confession of 1650: "Iesum Christum esse Messiam promissum, unicum ecclesiae caput, iustum nostrum legislatorem, unicum nostrum summum sacerdotem confitemur." Then the founder of English Puritanism, Robert Browne,[1] follows suit with the statement: "The Kingdom of Christ is His office of government, whereby He useth the obedience of His people, to keep His laws and commandements to their salvation and welfare." Also, in the Larger Catechism of the Westminster Assembly of the year 1648, this thought certainly gets the first place, before the other acknowledged attributes of Christ's Kingship: "Christus exsequitur munus regium dum populum sibi ex mundo vocat, eosque officiariis, legibus ac censuris donat atque instruit, quibus eos visibili modo regit et gubernat."[2] These principles reappear in the Puritan theologians of the seventeenth century, and on them is based, in particular, the binding force of Christ's legislation with regard to worship. Yet it is well worth noting that a theologian so influential as John Owen refuses to regard as exhaustive this reference of Christ's Kingship to the external supremacy of the Gospel, as seen in the obedience given to Church officers. He not only recognises that thereby injury is done to the significance of Christ's Divine nature as the basis of His dominion over the world, but, in the spirit of Luther and Calvin, he emphasises the internal and spiritual

---

[1] *The Life and Manners of all True Christians*, 1582.

[2] Ioh. a Lasco, Opera, ed. Kuyper, tom. ii. pp. 416, 430, 304, 306 ; Niemeyer, *Coll. Conff.* p. 345, Appendix, p. 54 ; Weingarten, *Revolutionskirchen Englands*, p. 21.

character of Christ's dominion, as consisting in that rule over souls which alone gives obedience to Christ its worth.[1]

The Puritan view of Christ's Kingship is undoubtedly the source of that flavour of the ceremonial law which obtains in the Scottish Church and in Independency'; it also opens the way for that rejection or limitation of the interference of the State with the Church which is the mark of Independency, and has dominated the ecclesiastical history of Scotland. At the same time, even for this particular circle of Calvinism, the significance of the view before us is far more ecclesiastical than dogmatic. For example, the fact that in the Reformed Churches of the Continent this view is not current, has never been felt by the Puritans to be a ground of ecclesiastical separation. On the contrary, we see in Owen that the directly opposite doctrine of the spiritual nature of Christ's Kingship is maintained alongside of it as the matter of chief concern. No doubt, historically considered Christ's intention of founding a community, and His preparatory steps toward that end, are to be viewed as the material of His Kingship; but the indications in Matthew's Gospel (if the words were spoken by Christ at all), that His community is to assume a constitutional form, have not the force of statutory legislation; the legal element, which is the unique feature of Puritanism, does not come from Christ. The Puritan idea of the Kingship of Christ, therefore, so far as it goes beyond the position of Wolleb and Schleiermacher, need not further be taken into account. Here and there, however, in the Reformed theology we get valuable hints toward a restatement of the dogma of the three offices of Christ. For example, there is the remark of Amesius that

---

[1] *Person of Christ, God and Man*, chap. vii. (*Works*, London, 1721, p. 51): "Some seem to imagine that the kingly power of Christ towards the Church consists only in external rule by the gospel and the laws thereof, requiring obedience unto the officers and rulers, that He hath appointed therein. It is true that this also belongs unto His kingly power and rule. But to suppose that it consisteth solely therein, is an ebullition from the poisonous fountain of the denial of His Divine person." P. 53: "The rule of Christ as King of the Church is internal and spiritual over the minds, souls, and consciences of all that do believe."

in the *statu exaltationis* the Kingship of Christ involves a certain modification of the prophetic and the priestly office, so that Christ *regium sacerdotium et prophetiam regiam exerceat* (*Medulla*, i. 23, 32). Does not this remark apply also to our view of Christ's earthly life ? Does not the prophetic activity of Christ, so far as it seeks the establishment of the Kingdom of God from His own person as centre, also display the note of Kingship ? Besides, have not the Reformed theologians (vol. i. p. 275) made the positive statement that, in discharging the priestly office of satisfaction by His double obedience, Christ acts as *caput ecclesiae*, that is to say, exercises the office of a King ?

The reply to the first question is already given in the statement with which Ernesti (vol. i. p. 521) introduced his objections to the customary definition of the three offices, namely, that if Moses is a type of Christ, then for the latter the kingly and the prophetic office fall into one. This corresponds also to the acknowledged historical facts. For when Jesus, who appeared with the marks of a prophet only, and was so regarded, sought recognition from His disciples as the anointed King, He ranged the material of His prophetic activity under a conception which must in itself have had no relation to it. Hence it is a purely arbitrary analysis of the word " Christ " when theologians find expressed in it both the prophetic and the kingly office. Then the gradual development of the dogma showed that Christ *in statu exaltationis* had to act not only as King but as Priest in establishing the Church ; so that in this connection also the two titles coincide. On the other hand, it follows from the statement of Reformed theologians already referred to, and which has found so wide response in more recent times, that the Kingship of Christ is to be regarded as operative in His priestly ministry also ; which combination we may reasonably understand to mean, in the sense of Ernesti, that Christ, by offering up His life, gives the supreme proof of His Kingship in the interest of His subjects. In any case it follows that, if Christ in His priestly ministry is to be regarded as *caput ecclesiae*, Priesthood and Kingship cannot be set alongside each other as independent offices, but the former must be understood as a particular consequence and application of the latter.   Thus the analysis of the title Christ, which led to the scheme of the three offices, is as amply refuted in argument as it lacks justification in history.   For Jesus is called the Anointed solely to denote His sovereign dignity.   If He is also called Prophet and Priest, it is clear that His prophetic activities afford the material for the exercise of His Kingship, and, in view of the previous discussion, we may surmise that His priestly activity, in freely surrendering His life, must be regarded also as a particular manifestation of His Kingship, conditioned by the special circumstances of the case.   Reformed theologians, *e.g.* Amesius and Wendelin, justify the setting up of the three offices alongside of and in succession to each other, from the *ordo conferendae salutis, qui prius debuit explicari, deinde acquiri, postea applicari.*   But this observation is not of sufficient weight to uphold the linear enumeration of the three offices of Christ against the subordination, already indicated, of the two other offices to the office of King.   For what is here formally and theoretically distinguished, is in actual fact neither co-ordinate nor distinct.   The whole operation, therefore, is of value only in so far as it secures a complete mastery of the material which must be included in determining the significance of Christ as *mediator salutis;* but what that significance is, the scheme of the three offices does not reveal, for the simple reason that complete knowledge must take the form of unity.

While, therefore, in our effort to grasp the significance of Christ's life, we are at liberty to follow the lines of the scheme now before us, yet this much we must regard as proved, that Christ's exercise of His Kingship, which for Himself is the chief thing, seeing He wishes to be recognised as the Christ, will find expression both in His prophetic and in His priestly service.   And since the kingly activity of Christ pertains to the founding and upholding of the religious community of Christ, therefore in the *statu exinanitionis* it is represented by the purpose of Christ to accomplish this end, which purpose pervades His two other activities, and is never out of their view.   On the other hand, the priestly and the prophetic offices refuse to be merged in each other, for the former moves in the direction from man to God, and the latter in exactly the opposite direction, from God to man. The traditional theology, however, differentiates also the material presented to us under these two conceptions.   To Christ's prophetic office are reckoned all His words, to His priestly office all His deeds.   Moreover, as Priest, Christ must satisfy the double legal demand made by God on sinful men, namely, through the conformity of His whole conduct to the moral law in His intercourse with men, and through readiness to endure all possible persecution as the punishment of sin. Now, as is well known, the distinction between active and passive obedience is due entirely to this consideration of the double claim of the law upon sinful men.   Regarded in themselves, the two conceptions are not mutually exclusive. For obedience in suffering is either non-existent or else it exists in the active form of endurance ; suffering which is not at bottom an exercise of moral will would not come under the head of obedience at all.   These considerations apply also to the older Dogmatics, for the latter distinguishes and co-ordinates the two conceptions of obedience only in regard to the satisfaction offered to God, whereas, from the point of view of merit, it combines them in the one obedience to the Divine will.   This means the setting up alongside of each other of two views of. the same matter, one clear and the other crooked, and the question arises not only whether this is in itself conceivable, but especially whether there is evidence for it in the consciousness of Jesus.   I waive the point as to whether God regarded the life of Christ at one and the same time from the standpoint of legal righteousness and from that of loving Providence.   But for the individual consciousness of Jesus it is neither proved nor even probable that He regarded the details of His life at one moment as satisfaction to God, at another as service rendered, at one

time in the light of the distinction between doing and suffering, at another in the light of the subordination of suffering
to doing. Yet this must needs be the case to satisfy the
demands of the traditional Dogmatics. For though, at the
end of Christ's life, His sufferings assumed for Him a form
more intensified in degree, yet in essence they were identical
through all the stages of His public life, being interwoven
with His work from the beginning. Thus the particular
distinctions which have been made in the material of Christ's
priestly office do not stand the test of comparison with the
facts of His historical life.

The same is true of the distribution of Christ's words and
deeds between the two offices of Prophet and Priest. The
deeds of Christ in their conformity to the Divine law are
regarded exclusively as something rendered to God ; but
surely, in the first place, they are something rendered to man,
to the various classes of men with whom Christ comes into
more or less intimate relation. The words of Christ are
regarded exclusively in their prophetic significance for man ;
but His words, equally with His deeds, must submit to be
judged by the standards of the moral law. And therefore
the truth, wisdom, and self-possession that mark the words of
Christ are just as much a part of His moral obedience toward
God, as the " grace and truth," which pervade all His deeds,
are part of His function as Prophet to reveal the will of God
to men. Therefore, just as it proved impossible alongside of
Christ's priestly and prophetic activity to find a separate
sphere for the exercise of His Kingship, so it is equally
impossible to assign to each of these two offices a separate
department of Christ's life. Thus the expectation based
upon the doctrine of the three offices, that thereby we should
reach a true division of the life of Christ, is shown to be
groundless. The kingly office of Christ finds expression only
in His manifest purpose by deed and word to establish the
community of the Kingdom of God and to lead it to its goal ;
and although Christ in His life both reveals God to men and
represents men to God, or brings men near to God, yet in

the light of our preceding discussion we must not expect that Christ's words and deeds as a whole will permit of exact subdivision between these diverse categories. In all these respects the doctrine of the three offices spells failure. If, however, the formal distinction between the kingly Priesthood and the kingly Prophethood of Christ is to be maintained, we must show how this distinction, as a means of apprehending the homogeneous life-work of Christ, is derived from the manifest inward unity of the same. For the older school it might be sufficient that in the New Testament Christ is named Prophet and Priest; for us that counts as a valuable fingerpost to guide our inquiry, but can by no means be taken as the expression of a complete understanding of the life-work and religious worth of Christ.

The superficial formalism of the old method comes out, also, in the way in which the contrast between the two states of Christ is applied to His three official functions. For it is only in theory that there is any contrast between them; in reality, whatever falls within the *status exaltationis* must be conceived as a continuation of the corresponding functions of the *status exinanitionis*, if it is capable of being clearly conceived at all. I have already pointed out (p. 406) that the formula which describes Christ as exalted to the right hand of God, either has for us no meaning, since Christ as exalted is beyond our ken, or else offers an occasion for every form of extravagance, unless regard be had to the fact that between Christ and the community of believers, which He designed by His words, deeds, and patience to establish, there is an abiding relation whereby Christ continues to be the ground of its existence and specific character. If by His kingly Prophethood and Priesthood Christ founded His community, then its present maintenance, through the continued exercise of these functions in His exalted state, can only be rightly judged in the light of what is recognised to have been the content of these functions in His historical life. Indeed, this principle is already systematically applied to explain the attribute of intercession which, in the Epistles to the Romans and to the

Hebrews, is ascribed to the exalted Christ, and which therefore is regarded as a continuation of His Priesthood. It is
understood to mean that what Christ accomplished as Priest
by His sufferings and death for the founding of His community, remains the efficient ground of its relation to God.
The continuance of the kingly Prophethood signifies that the
power of the Gospel of the Kingdom of God, through which
Christ founded His community, is that means for its maintenance and extension which corresponds to the historical dignity
of Christ, and causes His person to be recognised as still
effective for that end. With regard to Christ's earthly life,
we had already found that no material was forthcoming for
the exercise of His kingly office which did not fall in part
under His prophetic, in part under His priestly, activity.
This conclusion is further strengthened when we proceed to
examine more closely the idea introduced by Calvin, that the
exalted Christ exercises His Kingship in the assurance which
believers have of their salvation, in their victory over the
enemies thereof, and in their patience under all kinds of evil.
For it will appear that these are merely such results as are
necessarily involved in His Priesthood, so far as by His
Priesthood He has reconciled us to God.

The traditional scheme of the three offices is only a first
step toward grasping the significance of Christ for the community which believes on Him. It is a mere attempt to
reach as complete a mastery as possible of the material at
our disposal. But, since it offers us only distinctions and
contrasts without reducing these to an ultimate unity, it is
far from being an exhaustive treatment of the subject, which
as such is neither twofold nor threefold, but one. I have
endeavoured to approach the truth by reducing the different
data before us to their inherent unity. From this point of
view it is necessary, first of all, that Christ's activity *in statu
exaltationis* be conceived as the expression of the abiding
influence of His historical manifestation. Further, His deeds
and words must be regarded as the one common material of
His prophetic and priestly activities, and His kingly office

must be included in these as a specific modification of the
same; or, more correctly, His Kingship must be shown to
consist in these very same priestly and prophetic activities
in so far as both are inspired by His purpose to found and
maintain a community of believers.   Only the prophetic and
the priestly activities refuse to coalesce, because in the
relation between God and man they run in exactly opposite
directions.   And yet, just because of this twofold relation,
they form the unity of the *opus mediatorium*.   It will be our
business, by means of further elucidations, partly to sub-
stantiate, partly to complete, this unity of the prophetic and
priestly functions in Christ.   This, however, we can only do
by analysing the purpose which may be seen to pervade
Christ's life as a whole.

In conclusion, another point must be noted, namely,
that the designation of the three " offices " is not free from
objection.   It is quite true that the equivalence in theological
usage of *munus* and *officium* is a guarantee that the old
theologians did not conceive the first expression as contrasted
with the second.   But German usage has given a preference
to the word *Amt*, and offers no equivalent for *officium*.   Now
the word *Amt* denotes a special calling such as contributes to
the existence of a legally constituted community, or an ethical
community existing under legal conditions.   But in the case
before us the circumstances to be dealt with are wholly
different.   For by the Kingdom of God which Christ establishes is meant a community resting, not on legal rights, but
on loving conduct; among its other characteristics is this,
that for love men give up their legal rights, or at any rate
do not bring the standard of right as such visibly into
application.   That Christ's Kingdom is not of this world
(John xviii. 36), can only mean that it is exempt from the
standard of legal rights.   Besides, in the Old Testament
prophecy never was an *"Amt"*; it was always a free religious vocation.   Finally, the Epistle to the Hebrews sets
forth that the Priesthood of Christ is subject to other conditions than the official (*amtlich*) priesthood of the Old

28

Testament. Therefore it is only of the personal vocation of Christ that we have any right to speak in these relations. Accuracy in the scientific use of terms is not a matter of indifference. Although the old theologians had no intention of drawing a distinction at this point between *munus* and *officium*, it has happened all the same that, following in Melanchthon's track, they have introduced as the specific organ of the *regnum Christi spirituale* the official, that is, the duly licensed, preaching of the gospel and administration of the sacraments (p. 289). An inference from that position meets us in the statement of the Reformed theologian Polanus :[1] "Huius regis nostri prorex seu vicarius generalis non est papa Romanus, sed omnes fidi ecclesiae pastores sunt Christi vicarii." This is not consistent with the spiritual character of Christ's lordship, which is manifested in the fact that Gospel and sacraments continue to exist at all in the community of believers. That particular officials are duly licensed to administer Word and sacrament follows, not from the religious character of the community as such, in which, consistently with Christ's vocation as Prophet, all must be regarded as "taught of God," but from the earthly and historical conditions of the existence of the community. If, on the contrary, a duly licensed office as such is the organ of Christ's lordship, then the declarations of Christ Himself, that His Kingdom is not of this world, and that His disciples are not to rule but to serve (Mark x. 42–45), are made of none effect. It is better that Polanus be declared mistaken. But, to remove the occasion for such assertions, and for the hierarchical pretensions which are founded upon them, it is well to withhold from the work of Christ the title of "office" (*Amt*), since this title may lead the holders of office in the Church, because of their formal ecclesiastical distinction and prerogative as compared with the ordinary members of the community, to pose as the representatives of Christ.

§ 47. The religious view of the world is such that God

[1] *Syntagma theol.* vi. 29. p. 443.

is recognised as the efficient cause at work in the significant phenomena of nature and of the human mind.   In the sprouting of vegetation the heathen sees particular gods; in its decay he sees their death; Zeus thunders, and by the hot rays of the sun Apollo slays.   Nor, on this level of natural religion, is any particular need felt for any other formula than that the life of the gods is identical with the life of the corresponding natural objects.   For only to the more exact observation of the scientist does Nature give the impression of possessing in herself a relative independence.   It is otherwise when individual men acquire religious significance, since these produce an unqualified impression of mental independence.   If in their actions there is descried a special interposition of God, as when the Assyrian king inflicts God's judgment on the Israelites, or Koresch is God's servant to deliver them from banishment, then these persons come into consideration as instruments of the Divine action.   In this capacity they stand at a greater distance from God, if it be assumed that the Divine purposes which they serve are to themselves unknown.   Nearer to God stand the prophets; but these, too, in varying degree.   The heathen view of prophecy, for example, assumes a curtailment or cessation of the usual mental independence of the prophet, who is accounted an organ of Divine revelation in the degree in which through ecstasies and mania he has ceased to have control over himself.   But the prevailing Old Testament view of prophecy presupposes both the mental and the moral independence of the prophets, and controls the Divine impulse which is perceived in them by the recognition of their own consciousness of the same, and their convinced assent to the words of God which are given them. At the same time the religious value attached to the prophets and their words both by themselves and their countrymen is this, that they are accounted the instruments or organs of the self-revelation of God.   In no way different is the estimate put by Jesus upon Himself, save only that the essential and ultimate Divine purpose, which Jesus is conscious not only of explaining in word but of realising in deed, involves His placing His own independent personality in a still closer relation to God His Father. His estimate of Himself betrays, it is true, a sort of sliding scale in the way He describes His own relation to God, not only in John, but also in the other Gospels; yet amid this variety of presentation, describing Himself at one time as a mere ambassador who has seen and heard God and executes His commands, and at another time as the Son of God Who pursues God's work and in His own person exercises God's lordship over men for the ends of the Kingdom of God, Jesus attributes to His life as a whole, in the unity which for His own consciousness it possesses, the worth of being the instrument of *the complete self-revelation of God*. This is the purely *religious type of self-judgment*. But the unique feature of the case is, that there is not a trace of evidence to show that Jesus exempts any one relation of His own spiritual life and activity from the standard in question. For even when He expresses Himself in terms of independent human purpose, that purpose is at least adjusted to the ultimate Divine end for men which He is seeking to promote. The difference, namely, does not present itself to His consciousness in the form of a contrast, as in the case of Paul, who says on the one hand that Christ lives in him, and on the other that he lives a natural life, but in the faith of Christ (Gal. ii. 20). And thus John, in seeking to realise the impression made on his own mind of the worth of Christ's life as a whole, was in a position to construct a new formula, which implies more than that Christ was an instrument of Divine revelation. His faith in the Divine worth of Christ expresses itself in this judgment with regard to Him—that the Divine revelation is a human person.

This conception is not framed to suit any system of scientific knowledge, or to embody a statutory explanation of the experienced fact; the context on both sides admits of its being formulated in two different ways. Viewed in the light of the opening words of John's exposition, the statement has this meaning, that the Divine revealing Word constitutes the form, and the human individual the substance, of the Person of Christ. This is what in the end the doctrine of the Greek Church comes to. For the theory of the anhypostasis of the human nature in Christ, the reverse side of the theory that both natures subsist in the unity of the hypostasis, is intelligible only if the Divine Logos is the form in which this human individual exists, outside of which He has no real existence at all. For the form is the basis of reality. The anhypostasis of the human nature in Christ does not mean that the human nature is not individual,[1] or that the human soul in Christ is incomplete ; it means that this human individual only exists in such a way that the Divine Logos is the moving force of all His visible activities, and that His human soul as such has no scope for independent activity as in other men. This also is the thought of Christ which dominates the orthodox exposition of His prophetic and kingly functions. But the interpretation of His Priesthood refuses to be bound by the limits of this theory. In the conception of obedience to God the human soul is operative as form ; the Divine nature comes into account only in so far as it is made subordinate to the power of the individual will of the man Christ, and defines the infinite worth of Christ's obedience in counterbalancing sin. In this respect the Lutheran and the Reformed doctrines of Christ's priestly function have alike failed to transcend the limits laid down by Augustine, namely, that Christ's mediatorship depends on His humanity (vol. i. p. 38). Within the limits of this conception Duns Scotus could even refuse to the work of Christ the infinite worth which Aquinas, in virtue of the union with the Divine nature, had assigned to His human satisfaction. Finally, Melanchthon and the Lutherans, in opposing Stancarus, failed to do more than uphold the position of Aquinas. This doctrine has certainly fallen upon the right method, in apprehending Christ's God-

---

[1] Cf. Schneckenburger, *Zur kirchl. Christologie*, p. 74 ff.

head as the worth to be put on those human achievements
of His which suffice for our salvation.   It is at least wholly
wide of the mark when many theologians of the Reformed
school attempt to refer the conception of Christ's priestly
activity, which has God for its remoter object, back to God
also as subject.[1]   Such utterances are possible only for those
who have not condescended to carry out the notion of
obedience and satisfaction to God into that specific detail,
the propriety of which in other matters they themselves have
acknowledged.

Even the Johannine prologue, after presenting the Divine
Word as the form, and the human individual as the material
of the revelation in Christ, reverses its point of view, and in
the human personality as form bids us recognise as substance
grace and truth, those distinctive marks of Godhead.   Nor is
this method accidental or arbitrary.   For, in the first place,
it corresponds to the self-manifestation of Christ in His words
and actions, that is to say, to the historical reality.   Further,
it follows from a necessity of thought.   For we cannot
surrender the position that the soul which reveals itself in
the spoken " I " is the self-dependent form of all its functions.
If God or the Logos, *i.e.* the universal self-revealing function
of the spiritual God, is permanently assumed as the form of
Christ's Person and its manifestations, then the latter is
reduced to the aspect of a mechanism ; for the form is at the
same time the efficient cause.   But if we regard the life of
Christ as a mechanism, we not only do away with the distinction between Christ and nature, but give the lie to our
own experience of His spiritual personality.   Moreover, we
should only be justified in relinquishing our recognition of
Christ's personal and human independence, if we could permanently, from the Divine standpoint, trace the controlling
presence of God, and the special limitations under which it
works.   But this we are not in a position to do.   While,

---

[1] Schneckenburger, *op. cit.* p. 47, quotes Cocceius, *De foed. et test. dei*, v. 92 :
" Deus sibimet ipsi satisfecit " ; Hulsius, *Systema Controversiarum*, p. 310 :
" Formale principium est natura divina . . . haec obtulit victimam humanae
naturae."

therefore, our religious judgment is to the effect that God is not merely with Him (Acts x. 38 ; John viii. 29), but in Him (John xiv. 10, xvii. 21), that His characteristic activities are the activities of God, that His love to men, as the motive of all His conduct, is identical with the love of God, yet we are compelled to alternate this judgment with others which express the ethical independence of Christ under the category of human freedom. And while we are in a position to understand the sequence of Christ's life from the latter point of view, it is a question whether we may trust ourselves to understand the special conditions of Christ's dependence upon God, however indefinite the formula in which we might express them. The situation is exactly the same as when with Paul, from a religious standpoint, we conclude that God works in us to will and to do (Phil. ii. 13), or, with the Epistle to the Hebrews, that God works in us that which is well-pleasing in His sight through Jesus Christ (Heb. xiii. 21), or with John, that the love of God attains its perfection when we love the brethren (1 John iv. 12)—only thereafter to interpret all these phenomena by the law of human freedom. Moreover, the distinction does not apply here that in Christ the working of God is excluded, because in Him the Divine Word is a human personality. For the Divine Word includes in itself the characteristic working of God, and is simply inconceivable without it—even according to the traditional formula. In that, namely, which is eternally begotten by God, God as the begetter is continuously and effectively present.

A scientific apprehension of the relation expressed in the religious view of Christ appears to be attainable, therefore, only on the assumption that we have grasped the historical manifestation of Christ under the form of the human Ego, that is, have viewed it *in the light of its inherent unity as judged by ethical laws*. The problem lies along the same lines by which it has been attempted to reach a unifying view of Christ's priestly activity ; only it is a problem of wider extent, and we have no assurance beforehand that the distinctions between satisfaction and merit, between passive and active obedience, will be available for its solution.

Both schools of Reformation theology adopt the ethical method of apprehending Christ, in so far as they take note of His obedience to the Divine law, and attach worth to the same. But it is only with a section of the Reformed theologians that this ethical tendency reaches any degree of completeness. In the case of the Lutherans it is traversed at the very beginning by the twofold contention, that Christ for Himself had no obligation toward the law, because as God He stands above the law, and that by fulfilling the law He gained nothing for Himself, because as God He possesses all things. The first of these statements is an after-effect of the nominalism of Luther, under circumstances which make the wholly extraneous and arbitrary character of this element conspicuous (vol. i. p. 277). The other statement Reformed theologians have sought to repudiate, by asserting with regard to the Godhead of Christ the possibility of His earning a *plenior gloriae patefactio;* Alting alone has kept within the lines of an ethical judgment of Christ by employing the argument that Christ merited His glory by completely identifying Himself with the attainment through His own merits of our salvation (vol. i. p. 287). The ethical method is also traversed by the contention of the Lutherans, that the fulfilment of the law, to which Christ was under no obligation for Himself, was meant by Him to make up for the fulfilment of the same by all mankind. For conduct ceases to have any ethical significance when, for the agent, it is not an end in itself at all, but so far as he is concerned is practised merely as a means to some other end. An obedience to the law, by which a man is not seeking to attain the end of his own being, is in no sense a moral obedience. Therefore the only view that remains on ethical lines is the view of the Reformed theologians, that Christ rendered obedience to the law, in the place of the elect, as Head of the Church (vol. i. p. 275). In this special capacity of Christ a basis could be found for maintaining that, what Christ by fulfilling the law accomplished

as the representative of others, He accomplished also for Himself, and *vice versâ*. The ethical method is further traversed
by the distinction and co-ordination of the two kinds of
obedience, active and passive, which, in relation to the twofold demand of the law upon sinful men, serve as satisfaction
to God. For on this condition Christ's sufferings have
assigned to them only an objective, and no personal worth.
The incompatibility of this distinction with the ethical point
of view at once obtrudes itself in the addition made to it by
the older Dogmatics, to the effect that the one obedience of
Christ in deed and suffering, which conforms itself not to the
universal law, but to the special prescription of God, is a
vehicle of merit. This idea is specifically ethical; but it is by
no means an ethical idea of the first rank, and therefore the
application of it to Christ is not above suspicion, either in
itself, or in view of the accompanying circumstances. For
it is bounded by a conception of freedom which is not subject
to the standard of the moral law, or to the universal validity
of moral duty; it originates in the hypothesis of a private
and incalculable relation to God, which is inconsistent
with the other bases of the doctrine. Finally, the older
theology betrays how very limited is the interest it takes in
the ethical apprehension of Christ, by the fact that the prophetic and kingly functions of Christ are never so much as
examined to see whether they too ought not to be interpreted
from this point of view; most of all, however, by the further
fact, that the directly religious functions of Christ, which are
of such significance in His life, namely, His habit of prayer,
and His submission to the dispensations of God, have received
no consideration whatever in the doctrine of His Person. So
far as the first point is concerned, I have already (p. 430)
recalled the fact that Christ's speaking in the place and
power of God must nevertheless be subsumed under the duty
of truthfulness and the virtue of conscientiousness, if as
Prophet He is not to be wholly unlike His Old Testament
forerunners. The traces of His Kingship have not been
followed up at all in His historical life; only unwittingly

did the Reformed theologians, who describe Christ in His
satisfaction as the Head of the Church, take an ethical view
of His Kingship.   But the point at which the older doctrine
completely fails to meet the demands which necessarily arise
from the study of the life of Jesus, is in the interpretation of
everything that presents Christ as Himself the subject of
religion.   For this aspect of His person is easily seen to be
at once the centre and the circumference of all that was
purposely accomplished by Him, with a bearing on others.
And for this aspect of His Person there is no room, either in
the scheme of the two natures or in that of the three offices.
Wherefore, then, this determined opposition to a treatment
of the life of Jesus which obscures His subjectivity, when my
opponents have nothing better to offer in Dogmatics than a
repetition of the old formulas, which likewise obscure the
subjectivity of Christ?

§ 48. The fundamental condition of the *ethical apprehension of Jesus* is contained in the statement, that what Jesus
actually was and accomplished, that He is in the first place
for Himself. Every intelligent life moves within the lines
of a personal self-end. This the old theologians could not
bring themselves to see, for they referred the obedience of
Christ exclusively to the end of representing mankind, that
is, to an end other than the personal self-end of Jesus. Even
Alting could attach validity to the statement *sibi ipsi meruit*
only as an addition to the service Christ had rendered to
mankind. Of course, this dislocation is due in part to the
fact that the two ways of regarding Christ—from the point of
view of His Godhead, and from that of His manhood—were
not kept clearly separate, the latter being always obscured by
the former. At the same time, it cannot be overlooked that
the ethical view of the merits of Christ, as we here find it, is
tinged with a certain egoism, the egoism, namely, of onlookers.
These claim Christ so exclusively for their own salvation,
that they will not concede to Him the honour of existing for
Himself; although, without this, how is it possible to render
any real service to others? And, indeed, this method of

regarding Christ is in contradiction not only with the universal rules for estimating other personalties, but also with the undeniable features of Jesus' presentation of Himself, especially in the Fourth Gospel. In opposition to this view, therefore, it is certain that the human life of Christ must be viewed under the category of His consciously pursued personal end, and with allowance of His right to self-existence, so that thereby His influence and intentions with regard to men may be apprehended as such. For all such ends become criteria of a man's characteristic and personal conduct, only in so far as they are included in His personal self-end. This leads to the inversion of the Altingian formula: Jesus has acquired merit at our hand by identifying our interest with His own, His merit in our behalf follows from the merit He has acquired for Himself. But, since the idea of merit is excluded if the idea of duty is involved, we must state the matter thus—In so far as Christ, by His duly ordered speech and conduct, realises His personal self-end, it follows from the special content of the latter that in this form He also realises the ends of others, *i.e.* has ministered to the salvation of mankind as a whole.

Thus the question falls to be asked, What is the special content of the personal self-end of Christ? As such, the older theology denotes the unbroken obedience of Christ to the Divine law, and His obedience (or patience) under the sufferings which by special dispensation God caused to come upon Him, although in this connection no necessity for these sufferings appears. I do not, of course, mean these two kinds of obedience in the sense of the theory already discussed (p. 269), which assigns their place to the doing and suffering of Christ from the standpoint of satisfaction to God, for in both these aspects the said theory lies outside ethical treatment. By this theory the doing and the suffering of Christ are viewed solely in the light of a certain objective worth, not therefore in the light of their unbroken continuity with His distinct personal life; nor is His conduct in obedience to the law viewed in the light of its relation to

His personal self-end. Here, on the contrary, I am referring to Christ's doing and suffering as the two partial manifestations of that complete personal obedience which is treated by the older theologians from the point of view of the merit of Christ. Under their formula, however, sufficient care is not taken to ensure that the doing and the suffering of Christ can really be understood as partial manifestations of the one obedience. It needs to be supplemented by the observation that the suffering of Christ, through the patience with which it was borne, becomes a kind of doing. For this is the only way in which an ethical value can be got out of suffering at all. Apart from this condition, all suffering is either ethically indifferent, or else it is disease; more especially mental suffering, that is not met with the exercise of self-control and patience, is just mental disease. To Christ none of these cases applies, since His active patience kept pace with His experiences of suffering. By His patience the suffering inflicted on Him is as such made His own; and that, too, without any deadening of feeling, but rather with keen sensitiveness to suffering in every degree and throughout the whole course of His public life. For these considerations room is found in the formula, that the obedience of Christ in doing and in suffering is identical, obedience here being understood to mean activity of the will. The expression is certainly indefinite, but we have no option, for in another respect, also, the unity of Christ's obedience in doing and suffering is not safeguarded by the traditional formula. While, for the necessity on Christ's part of obedient conduct, reference is made to the universal moral law, for the necessity of His sufferings we are referred to the special dispensation of God; and in this connection the special dispensation of these sufferings by God must remain unintelligible, except where it can be explained from the need of paying the penalty for man. For if, as regards the positive fulfilment of the moral law by Christ, the ethical standpoint of universal human obligation, as understood by the Reformed divines, is to be maintained, then, clearly, the explanation of Christ's

sufferings from the special need on God's part of legal satisfaction belongs to a different category, since this explanation
is not derived from any consideration affecting Christ Himself.   The inconsistency can be removed only by the introduction of an idea which was strange to the thinkers of former
days, but which has been applied by not a few theologians
since Schleiermacher.   It is the idea of an *ethical vocation*
(vol. i. pp. 529, 648).

A man's vocation as a citizen denotes that particular department of work in human society, in the regular pursuit of
which the individual realises at once his own self-end and
the common ultimate end of society.   Every civil vocation is an ethical vocation, and not a means of egoism, in so
far as it is pursued under the view that, in society as a whole,
and in the individual, the moral law ought to be fulfilled, and
the highest conceivable goal for the race attained.   The
varieties of ethical vocation, according to their natural origin,
divide themselves in manifold fashion into vocations which
have their origin in the family, vocations which are concerned
with the production, manipulation, and distribution of the
means of physical life, vocations connected with the State
and with religion, vocations in the sphere of science and art.
Their manifoldness consists in this, that they attain ethical
distinctness in part directly, in part, like the last-named, only
indirectly; that several of them can exist compatibly with
each other in the same individual, while others cannot; that
some are of a public, others of a private nature.   Rightly
understood, every ethical vocation falls within the scope of
the moral law; but inasmuch as each man's vocation forms
for him the special sphere within which he regularly fulfils
the universal moral law, it follows that each man, in the
ethical exercise of his own vocation, at once attains his own
ethical self-end and renders his rightful contribution to the
ethical end of society as a whole.   For the particular is the
logical means of reaching systematic knowledge of universal
laws, and of the subsumption of the individual phenomenon
under the law.   In the sphere of will, the form under which

the objective unity of the individual will with the universal
law of conduct is realised, and the condition of that realisation, is that the ethical activity of the individual forms a
whole.   This is borne out, in the first place, by the fact that
men without a civil vocation, and without its ethical standard,
succumb in one degree or another to egoism ; further, by the
fact that any individual judgment of duty (namely, that on
this particular occasion of acting, the action must needs be
in keeping with the moral law) is reached through the intermediate idea of a man's distinct vocation, or through the
analogous judgment that in this particular case he is called
to obey the behest of love ; finally, by the fact that a man's
ethical vocation, in the narrower as in the wider sense, begets
those ethical principles in which a mature and conscientious
character specialises for itself the moral law, and regulates at
the same time the personal attainment of virtue.   For conscientiousness not only follows as a single virtue from the
significance of a man's vocation for the development of moral
character ; it guarantees also the acquisition of the other
virtues, in so far as the particular vocation forms the uniting
link for the universal and the individual conditions of ethical
existence.

The idea of an ethical vocation serves also as a criterion for
the public life of Christ as a visibly connected whole.   When
Christ presents Himself as the Bearer of God's moral lordship
over men, through Whose unique speech and conduct men
are impelled to submit themselves to the power which proceeds from Him, and in the direction which is indicated by
Him, He understands the name Christ as the expression of
His individual vocation.   His conduct within this sphere is
as certainly in harmony with the universal moral law, as the
end of the Kingdom of God, which He pursues in His special
vocation as its Founder, is the supreme end out of which the
moral law arises.   At the same time, His conduct in pursuit
of His vocation, being a particular line of conduct, is one-
sided, and excludes personal participation in other vocations.
Indeed, this exclusiveness of Christ's vocation goes further

than in other cases of a similar kind. Old Testament prophets could at the same time discharge a civil vocation;
other founders of religions were at the same. time heads of
families and heads of tribes, and waged war; Christ had no
civil vocation, at least not after He entered on His public
work; He detached Himself from His family without founding a family; if He ever occupied Himself in any systematic
fashion with the sacred learning of the Jews, it cannot have
been by way of a vocation, as was the case with Paul. In
short, Christ combined no other vocation with that to which
He was conscious of being called. This fact is explained by
the range of the vocation to which He devoted Himself. For
the vocation of the kingly Prophet, to realise God's ethical
lordship, is the highest of all conceivable vocations; it aims
directly at the ethical as a whole; and if this aim was to be
pursued as the special business of life, and firmly fixed before
the mind of Him who pursued it, it had to be separated from
all subordinate aims, which otherwise are meant to find a
place within the whole. To fix His vocation as Christ firmly
before him, Christ had to forego all those natural conditions
in the stability of which other vocations find a guarantee of
their own stability—a fixed dwelling and means of support,
attachment to a family, the confidence of fellow-citizens.
He depended only upon the personal devotion of friends and
followers, and built up about Him the circle of His twelve
disciples in the view that His vocation demanded the formation
of a separate religious community. On the other hand, He
adopted a neutral attitude toward all the other interests of
human society, toward law and State, industry and science;
He was even inwardly indifferent toward the religious usages
of His countrymen (Matt. xvii. 24–27), and did not suffer
Himself to be shaken in the constancy of His aim by the
presentiment that, in the nation to which with scrupulous
conscientiousness He had exclusively devoted himself (Mark
vii. 27), this aim would fail to be realised (Matt. viii.
11, 12). Equally far was He from allowing His clear
consciousness of the universal scope of His mission to be

impaired by the fact that He was called to work only among
the Jews.

Regarded as a consequence of His loyalty to His vocation,
Christ's patience under the varied sufferings due to the
opposition of the leaders and rulers of His nation becomes
intelligible.   For not suffering in itself, but suffering as the
occasion and test of patience and steadfastness, is what comes
into account from the ethical point of view.   To the contradiction between Christ's purpose of reform and the authoritative position of the Pharisaic scribes, were due all the
affronts, secret and open, to Christ's personal honour, and the
danger to His personal safety, and all these brought in their
train temptation for Him.   The more intense realisation of
these temptations in the soul of Jesus immediately before the
final catastrophe, was only the climax of what had occurred
in each case of open persecution which He had had to endure.
In every such case He must have experienced in one degree
or another a conflict between the impulses of self-preservation
or personal honour, and of loyalty to His vocation.   But, till
then, it had cost Him less effort to put the claim of His
vocation before the claims of ordinary existence and the
natural joy of living—so little effort, perhaps, that He may
never have made clear to His own mind the actual state of
the case with regard to these constantly recurring temptations.   Had He succumbed to one such temptation, it would
have meant that, to preserve the tranquillity of His individual
existence, He had renounced His vocation.   But, on the contrary, all the sufferings that befell Him, and especially those
He was ready to bring on Himself by His appearance in
Jerusalem, He steadfastly endured, without once proving
untrue to His vocation, or failing to assert it.   Therefore
these sufferings, which, by His enduring of them even to the
death, He made morally His own, are manifestations of His
loyalty to His vocation, and *for Christ Himself* come into
account solely from this point of view.   This connection of
things is the more transparent, since Christ faced the climax
of His fate neither rebelliously, nor with callous indifference,

nor in any fanatical self-deception, but under the impression that, just as His appearing in Jerusalem was an unavoidable discharge of His vocation, so also His violent death was destined under God's appointment to serve the same end.

In this latter statement, the delineation of the ethical connection between the sufferings and the vocation of Christ already gives place to *the religious view* of the same, apart from which view Christ Himself was not conscious of His unique and independent position among men. The business of His vocation was the establishment of the universal ethical fellowship of mankind, as that aim in the world which rises above all conditions included in the notion of the world. The historical connections of this idea may be left out of account; in which case it becomes all the more evident that a vocation of this kind can only be conceived under the guiding idea of one supramundane God. But for this reason Christ not merely recognises the business of His vocation to be the Lordship or Kingdom of God, He also recognises this vocation as the special ordinance of God for Himself, and His activity in the fulfilment of it as service rendered to God in God's own cause. Since His consciousness of His vocation adjusts itself to these conditions, He is led to frame a conception of self-preservation which is not at variance with that consciousness but in harmony with it, and therefore is fitted to throw light upon His bearing under suffering. The saying in John, which carries in itself the proof of its genuineness, " My meat is to do the will of Him that sent Me, and to finish His work " (iv. 34, cf. xvii. 4), applies to His particular vocation; for $\theta \acute{\epsilon} \lambda \eta \mu a$, in other applications also, usually refers to the particular. The task assigned to Jesus, therefore, is a course of conduct in which the content is conceived as the work of God Himself, because the aim represents God's innermost purpose. The execution of this purpose serves Jesus as meat, that is, as the means of self-preservation, and therefore as satisfaction. The joy He has in it, the sense of harmony with God and with Himself (xv. 11 ; xvii. 13), follows inevitably from the lively experience of the worth of His vocation for

29

Himself.   He found in it a spiritual self-preservation, which approved itself in the clear anticipation of continuance after death (x. 18), and thus, even when the hope of restored life retreated before the actual terrors of death, He still could not be swayed by any value attaching to the preservation of the natural life.   The above saying, moreover, likewise displays the characteristic feature of the consciousness of a vocation wherever found, namely, that the more general content of the vocation is always embraced within the category of the personal self-end, and lends to the spiritual self a support which makes it more or less independent of the conditions of natural existence in the world.   Every degree of moral loyalty to a vocation overcomes the world, inasmuch as it evokes patience to endure the opposing influences that come from the world, that is, the evils of life—in other words, to subordinate these unavoidable experiences to our own personal freedom.   But it is in Christ that we perceive the widest application of this, and our perception of it in Him is the source from which we draw the corresponding principle.

And thus what Christ says in that sentence from John would approve itself as valid for Him, even although we sought no other light upon His life than what is afforded us by the idea of vocation in general, and the vocation of Christ in particular.   But the present investigation was undertaken with the view of obtaining the correct ethical judgment upon the Person of Christ, in so far as the ethical point of view is taken in formal opposition to the religious.   We have found, however, that an ethical judgment of Jesus in the light of His unique vocation to establish the Kingdom of God, if it follow His own judgment of Himself, runs out into a religious judgment, namely, His religious judgment of His own Person. Therefore, also, in our own thinking on this matter, the religious estimate of Christ must not be set over against the ethical, but added to it, as that without which it would not be complete.   The question arises as to what is implied in this view.   If the life-work of Christ is the work of God, this involves the assumption that the personal self-end of Christ has the same content as is contained in the self-end of God, which content Christ knew and adopted as such, in accordance with the fact that He was already known and loved by God Himself as the Bearer of the Divine self-end. This statement, which essentially coincides with Matt. xi. 27, is inevitable, if we hold to the position that a universal ethical Kingdom of God is the supreme end of God Himself in the world, if we admit that historically this idea first received shape through Christ, and if we are not satisfied with the vague conception of a wholly accidental relation between God and the world, especially the moral world.   Now the freedom and independence of a man's conduct in pursuit of the supreme end of the Kingdom of God is proof that at bottom, and in a way suited to the human spirit, we are dependent upon God (p. 293); therefore Christ, in the exercise of His particular vocation, must certainly be regarded, not merely as independent of all the world, but as upheld by God.   Since, however, as the Founder of the Kingdom of God in the world, in other words, as the Bearer of God's ethical lordship over men, He occupies a unique position toward all who have received a like aim from Him, therefore He is that Being in the world in Whose self-end God makes effective and manifest after an original manner His own eternal self-end, Whose whole activity, therefore, in discharge of His vocation, forms the material of that complete revelation of God which is present in Him, in Whom, in short, the Word of God is a human person.

The problem here presented to theology is solved when we have shown that there is no contradiction between the ethical and the religious apprehension of Christ, that the former finds its necessary complement in the latter, and that there is nothing here inconsistent either with the Christian idea of God, or with the complete conception of moral freedom.   The origin of the Person of Christ—how His Person attained the form in which it presents itself to our ethical and religious apprehension—is not a subject for theological inquiry, because the problem transcends all inquiry.   What

ecclesiastical tradition offers us in this connection is obscure
in itself, and therefore is not fitted to make anything clear.
As Bearer of the perfect revelation, Christ is given us that
we may believe on Him.   When we do believe on Him, we
find Him to be the Revealer of God.   But the correlation
of Christ with God His Father is not a scientific explanation.
And as a theologian one ought to know that the fruitless
clutching after such explanations only serves to obscure the
recognition of Christ as the perfect revelation of God.

§ 49. On the other hand, we find our results verified in
certain aspects of the life-work of Christ, which already
incidentally have come more or less within our view.   The
Kingdom of God, the realisation of which forms the vocation
of Christ, signifies not merely the correlate of the self-end of
God, but also the goal that constitutes the highest destiny of
man.   Christ, therefore, would not have rightly or fully
apprehended His vocation if He had not known that He was
under obligation (Mark x. 42—45) to serve those whom, as
the new religious community, He undertook to train for that
destiny, and that this *obligatory service*, this obedience toward
God, is the specific form of that *lordship* which He both
acquires and exercises over men.   Now in the idea of obligation the moral law is identical with the moral self-determination of the individual.   For the sense of obligation—the
subjective judgment that, in a particular and definitely limited
case, it is necessary to act in accordance with the moral law,
or some particular moral principle—is as much due to the
moral disposition of the individual, as it is derived from the
universal law.   If, then, Christ was conscious that, in the
exercise of His vocation, even in the resultant sufferings and
voluntarily endured death, He was under obligation to serve
men for their highest good, it follows, further, that here He
obeyed love as His impelling motive.   For love is the abiding
disposition to further spiritual personalities in regard to their
proper self-end, under the condition that in so doing we
recognise and are seeking to attain our own self-end (p. 277).
This condition is evidently present in the case of Christ, since

He could never have adopted as His vocation the founding of the Kingdom of God, if He had not regarded the loftiest possible destiny for mankind as the goal of His work, which He pursued for His own sake.   And indeed the whole picture which has come down to us of the life of Christ reveals the loftiness of His love, and His lordship over friends and foes alike is made the more conspicuous by the fact that, even in the circle of those who stood nearest Him, He found no fitting help or support from any reliable or constant love toward Himself.   In a certain quarter of theological speculation, we are met by the principle that perfect love requires the similar mutual relation of two personal wills.   In so far as love is the principle of perfect fellowship between two personal beings, this may be true.   But the perfect love, as motive power and guiding principle of the individual will, is independent of responsive love (Matt. v. 46); on the contrary, just there, where it meets with no answering love, perfect love proves in every possible case its peculiar sublimity. Such a case is the experience which befell Christ when those to whom He devoted His service, and whom He sought to save, on the one hand repelled Him in every possible manner, and on the other hand so imperfectly understood Him, that even the devotion of His most devoted disciples brought Him no return for the strain upon His own spririt.   I do not need to complete in any further detail the picture of Christ's life to elicit the admission that the formula offered us by John—" grace and truth "—reflects most aptly the impression made by the personal conduct of Christ.   For this is the type of love which reaches far beyond all possible return, and in the face of every rebuff persists unchanged.   Inasmuch, then, as the love of Christ maintains its supremacy in all possible service, and even in the face of every hindrance, bent ever on the realisation of the Kingdom of God—that goal in which is attained, so far as God is love, God's own self-end—it follows that the " grace and truth " in Christ's whole activity is the specific and complete revelation of God.   This result not only corresponds with the reflection of John, but also makes

clear that the revelation of God in Christ, when referred
to the technical notion of the Divine Word, surpasses those
revelations which are given in creation, in the illumination of
the nations, and in His presentation of Himself through the
name Jahve.. For in the characteristic activity of Christ in
the discharge of His vocation, the essential will of God is
revealed as love, since Christ's supreme aim, namely, the
Kingdom of God, is identical with the supreme end of the
Father. At the same time, however, we must understand
John to mean that the exhaustive comprehension of Divine
revelation in one human personality reckons on no other test
than this "grace and truth," which, according to Old Testament standards, expresses the essential will of God. If these,
then, are the criteria by which the conception of Christ's
Godhead is framed, it follows that John does not mean us
to seek in Christ for the Divine attributes of omnipotence,
omnipresence, and omniscience, which, it is said, ought also,
or even first of all, to occupy our regard. In so far as the
Divine Revelation or Word of God is active in this personality,
or is to be conceived as the form of its activity, the point at
issue is clearly the definition of God's being. Since the being
of God is spirit, and will, and above all love, it can therefore
become effective in a human life, for human nature as such is
laid on the lines of spirit, will, and love. On the other hand,
the relation of God to the world, in so far as God creates and
rules the world, could not be brought to direct manifestation
in a human life, which is itself part of the world.

This remark, however, is confronted by the statement of
Jesus that all things have been delivered unto Him of the
Father (Matt. xi. 27), a statement which does not, it is true,
denote an inborn omnipotence, but which does describe *power
over the world* as something the possession of which Jesus
claims for Himself, in virtue of Divine bestowal. This
declaration cannot be got rid of by saying that it sounds
too Johannine to be authentic. For on the whole it stands
on no loftier level than when Jesus declares His intention to
exercise that lordship of God over the people of Israel which

till then had been looked for in vain. With the appearance
of the lordship of God there is bound up, in the prophetic
vision of the future, the further prospect of a transformation
of the natural world. As the expectations of the prophets
were the norm by which Jesus formed His own conception
of His vocation, it is a logical consequence that He should be
convinced of a unique relation of His own Person to the
world. The religion of the Old Testament represents the
one spiritual God as the Creator and Ruler of the whole
world; since the religious community of Israel obeys God
and serves Him, it knows itself called not only to lordship
over the other nations, but also to the unfettered enjoyment
of natural good, which is protected through Divine appointment from the ordinary experiences of the opposite. This,
however, betrays an inconsistency in Israel's view of the
world, an imperfection in its very nature. For while the
Divine purpose in the world is bound up with the naturally
conditioned unity of the Israelitish nation, the position of
this nation in the world is made dependent upon legal and
political conditions and material advantages, which as such
are of a mundane order, and do not correspond to the supramundane position of the one God. Thus there was forced
upon Israel the necessity of always postponing to a future,
which never became present, the reconciliation between its
position in the world and God. Jesus rose above this standpoint, and introduced a new religion, by setting free the
lordship of the supramundane God from national and
political limitations, as well as from the expectation of
material well-being, and by advancing its significance for
mankind to a spiritual and ethical union, which at once
corresponds to the spirituality of God, and denotes the
supramundane end of spiritual creatures. But since Christ
in this achievement of His life is at once the Revealer of
God in the full sense, and also a man who according to
His knowledge of God worships God and serves Him, it is
a logical consequence that He asserts for Himself a position
toward the world which corresponds to the idea of the one

God and to the worth of God's spiritual Kingdom. If this
latter, in the way Christ began to realise it, is the final
aim of the whole world, it follows that the whole world is
subject to Christ. The peculiar character of the religion
founded by Christ depends, therefore, of necessity upon the
fact that He whom God knows, and Who has perfect knowledge of God, asserts supremacy over the world.

But the correctness of this assertion must be further
tested by the definite content of Christ's life; for a mere
claim upon the future would not be commensurate with
the gravity of this assertion. As a matter of fact, it does
not prove to be true in the sense that Christ had the whole
fixed system of things at His arbitrary disposal. For the
support of His material existence He was dependent on all
the fixed conditions of human life. Even His power of
miracle did not go so far as to make trial of itself in any
alteration of the great mechanism of the world, such as
the expectation of the prophets had associated with the
setting up of the Kingdom of God (Matt. xvi. 1–4). The
miraculous power of which He was conscious (Mark vi. 5, 6),
and which He reckoned part of His equipment for His
vocation (Matt. xii. 28), is exercised within a much more
limited sphere. But even if this fact were less evident than
it is, the narratives are not of a kind to allow us to discover any rule as to how far the supremacy of Christ's
will over external nature actually extended, the more so
that we have no similar experiences at our command to
disclose to us the psychical and physical grounds of Christ's
miraculous power. Not in itself, but because of the enforced
lack of the means of explanation, this is a sphere which
does not lend itself to scientific investigation.

However, the significance of the supremacy which Christ
asserted over the world is not affected thereby, nor is our
comprehension of this attribute rendered impossible. If, as
we cannot but assume, this attribute stands in connection
with the religious destiny of man, as that destiny was first
realised by Christ Himself, we may expect that Christ's

position of supremacy toward the world finds application
also to other men, who, within His community and in
accordance with the view of the world which He proclaimed, enter into that relation to God which was His
aim for them, and which has been made possible to them
through Him. This expectation is met by the statement
in Mark viii. 35–37. This statement reveals the *supramundane* worth, that is, the worth as against the whole
world, of the spiritual life of each individual man, and
shows the way in which this entirely new perception
attains objective reality. For the assuring of life against
death, even when for Christ's sake life is renounced, is a
specific test of that supremacy over the world upon which
we enter through Christ, since death is our most painful
experience of the instability of all the elements of this
world, among which, from the natural point of view, each
human individual is reckoned. The practical echo of this
rule is supplied by the triumphant conviction of Paul—" All
things are yours; whether Paul, or Apollos, or Cephas, or
the world, or life, or death, or things present, or things to
come; all are yours; and ye are Christ's; and Christ is
God's " (1 Cor. iii. 22, 23); "I am persuaded, that neither
death, nor life, nor angels, nor principalities, nor powers,
nor things present, nor things to come, nor height, nor
depth, nor any other creature, shall be able to separate us
from the love of God, which is in Christ Jesus our Lord "
(Rom. viii. 38, 39). This independence of the religious
consciousness over against the world, and the supremacy
over the world which is to be realised within the sphere
of this religion, are identical. Every expression of independence is an evidence of supremacy in one particular
department of life. Now, in this positive freedom of the
Christian, which is derived expressly from fellowship with
Christ and subordination to Him and to God, the real point
is not power to effect material changes in the mechanical
stability of the world and in the fixed conditions of the
social order, but a changed estimate of all the relations of

natural and historical life.   For, since the Christian life is
determined by the supreme supernatural end of God, all
other possible motives and impulses which, in the order of
nature, and amid the ordinary and natural conditions of
human society, can affect human life in the way of creating
dissatisfaction, are either rendered powerless or are made
subordinate to that supreme motive.   Thus the Christian
in this present life, in spite of his lowly, helpless, suffering
state, has experience through his faith of an exaltation and
riches (Jas. i. 9), which are to be understood as a position
of supremacy and an amplitude of power, inasmuch as reconciliation with the supramundane God is consummated by
a power over the world akin to His.

Our dependence on the world under the natural conditions of moral existence is such that our horizon is bounded
by our own family and our own nation, for we adjust and
attach ourselves to the prejudices and customs which in
these circles have come down to us.   As for Jesus, His
connection with the Chosen People had for Him the greater
significance, because the peculiar character of this people,
its religion, its institutions, and more especially its hopes,
were the necessary historical presupposition of His own
vocation, and because, in the exercise of that vocation, He
saw Himself confined to this one people (Mark vii. 27).
But although He was bound to His nation by the most
passionate sympathy (Matt. xxiii. 37), He not only freed
Himself from the Old Testament preconceptions as to its
political destiny, but also made it known that He did not
regard Himself as inwardly bound by any of those ceremonial
ordinances in which spiritual adhesion to the Chosen People
was required to find expression (xvii. 25—27).   Even if
for Him it was not difficult to oppose the conditions of
the new religious family to the claims of the natural family
(Mark iii. 33—35), yet by so doing He certainly renounced
the support of the family relation ; He also overcame the
natural sympathy that bound Him to His nation, despite
the powerful religious motives in its favour, through the

fixed anticipation that He would not complete His vocation among the Israelites; that, on the contrary, the other nations of mankind would succeed to Israel's destiny (Matt. viii. 11, 12, xxi. 43). In spite of this, He confined the actual discharge of His vocation to the Chosen People, and never apparently had to resist the temptation to extend His activity before the time to other peoples. Thus, although it was only as a born Israelite and in connection with His own nation that Jesus could fulfil His vocation, yet He raised Himself above these particular or earthly limitations of His existence, not only by the width of His horizon which embraced all mankind, but by His religious judgment of Himself, which was independent of all Old Testament standards. This instance of Christ's supremacy over the world is the more characteristic that the Apostle of the Gentiles never attained a like measure of inward freedom from the preconceptions of Judaism. Paul remained so staunchly loyal to the distinctive position assigned by the Old Testament to his race, that, in spite of all contrary considerations, he preserved unshaken the hope of the ultimate conversion of Israel to Christ (Rom. xi. 25). In this respect he not only falls short of Christ's inward freedom, but comes into direct collision with the expectation of Christ. The aforesaid attitude of Jesus is at the same time an evidence of the degree in which He realised in His own person that universal human nature which is required by the idea of His vocation. The fact of His belonging to one particular nation in reality only serves Him as a means of fulfilling His vocation; inwardly He is untrammelled by any constraint of earthly prejudice reflecting the narrow spirit of the family or the nation.

Inconspicuous enough is this exercise of supremacy over the world, and I can imagine that even those who accept the exposition here given of the loftiness of Christ's judgment of Himself, may yet regard the present inquiry as an uncalled for digression. They may be inclined, that is, to rest content with the expedient of previous theologians, that Christ possessed supremacy over the world as right and might, but in His existence as a human individual would on no account exercise this supremacy, postponing it to the future, when, at the right hand of power, He should wield it through His community (Mark xiv. 62). But I have already shown (p. 406) that this exercise of supremacy by the exalted Christ is intelligible only if, in His life on earth, it is not confined to a mere claim of right or an unexercised endowment. For how can we prove the existence of such attributes unless by some corresponding activity of the earthly Christ? Moreover, Christ's exercise of power upon His community, and through His community upon the world, is anything but a fact of objective and palpable experience. The phenomena in which many seek the real proof of the might of Christianity, namely, political influence and the legal authority of Church officials and ecclesiastical institutions, are the very things that come under strong suspicion of falsifying the intention of Christ; indeed, it is only a really strong faith in the invisible that, amid the miry abominations and miserable trivialities of Church history, can trace the advancing power of Christ over this world at all. Finally, the power over the world which Paul ascribes to the Christian, and which must serve as our guiding analogy in interpreting the original assertion of Christ, falls entirely within the sphere of the spiritual, and cannot become palpable or evident in any corresponding degree. If, therefore, our concern be to find in the historical portrait of Christ other proofs than those already quoted of His characteristic independence of the spirit of His nation, the inconspicuous character of these proofs cannot afford any ground for doubting the correctness of the result.

What I mean is, that Christ's *patience under suffering*, which has already come under notice as a consequence of His loyalty to His vocation, is the real test not only of His constancy in this regard, but also of His unique power over the world. For the individual impulses of self-preservation, avoidance of pain, and the keeping inviolate of personal honour

—impulses which in every case He subordinated to the consciousness of His vocation—imply as their correlative term the world as a whole. No doubt, more immediately, it is the hostile human world which evokes the collision between Christ's life-work and His material and social self-preservation, and it is only a very narrow section of the world of men with which He comes into painful contact. But since Christ recognised His life-work as the cause of God, His immediate opponents represented for Him the whole world of mankind, so far as it revolts against God's ruling of the world. Wherefore He declares that, by His determination to submit patiently even to the probable issue of its opposition to Himself, He has overcome the world (John xvi. 33). When in steadfast loyalty to His vocation He refuses to bring the motive of physical and social self-preservation into harmony with the claims of His opponents, who represent the ungodly tendency of the human world, He demonstrates in their case His power over the world. For unless this human society had tongues wherewith to slander, and hands wherewith to strike, it would not be an object of fear at all, or an occasion of victory. But as every evil is a natural event (p. 351), so any suffering imposed by human society can affect us, and become at once a temptation and an occasion of victory, only in so far as it represents at the same time the opposition of the system of nature as a whole. The pain of soul caused by slander, as by blows dealt to the body, denotes the collision of the whole fabric of the material world with the personal sense of worth in the individual spiritual man. For the whole mechanical and organic connection of the individual man with the world is involved, when we are aggrieved by a physical blow, or an uttered slander, as effects of human ill-will. This connection of things is not, as a rule, present to our mind, but we can easily understand that Christ was in a position to take this view of the matter, since He drew the sharpest possible contrast between Himself, as the Bearer of God's peculiar purpose in this world, and the world itself.

Under this assumption He knew not only that power over the world had been given Him, but also that by the patient endurance of all suffering, as the test of His loyalty to His vocation, He was overcoming the seductive opposition of the world. This view is involved in the idea of God on which Jesus based His religious conception of the world and His judgment of Himself, and it is just this worth assigned to patience in His own person which forms an essential part of that view of the world which He has brought to light.

A valuable confirmation of this result is afforded by the words which occur in Matthew (xi. 28—30), in immediate connection with the declaration of Jesus that all things have been delivered unto Him by His Father. The central point of this utterance, which, as a rule, is not rightly understood, is the description of Jesus as one who, despite His inherent righteousness, is, like the righteous men of the Old Testament, in a state of oppression and suffering, but who willingly accepts the same. For the predicates πραΰς καὶ ταπεινός appear in the LXX as equivalent to the Hebrew עָנִי, and this word, or rather the equivalent Aramaic word עַנְוִי, is the only word Jesus can have used. Now this word is the conventional designation of the righteous man in view of the consistent oppression which he has to endure at the hands of the godless; which circumstance is certainly included here, since it is the reason why Jesus compares Himself with those who labour and are heavy laden. The addition τῇ καρδίᾳ, which is equivalent to עֲנַו־לֵב, is not inconsistent with a state of external oppression, but represents the latter as that in which, because of His righteousness, Jesus acquiesces. He thereby distinguishes Himself from the men to whom He offers His help, but also from the righteous of the Old Testament, who always regard their oppressed condition with complaint and longing for deliverance. Here, therefore, we see the advance upon the Old Testament made by the righteousness of Jesus in its attitude to the world. By acquiescing in the obstructions of the world as a dispensation of God, Jesus subordinates to Himself the relation between Himself and the world, in consequence of the mutual knowledge subsisting between the Father and the Son, even as on this same account He recognises His sufferings to be the yoke by which He is led of God, by Whom He, the Son, is first recognised. Wherefore, when He calls to Himself those who would fain carve out their own fate and are succumbing under the obstructions to their freedom, His aim is to lead them to see in their burdens dispensations of God; on these terms the said burdens will become light, because, by the patience which springs from the religious motive, men lift themselves above their misfortunes and the world. From this point of view their sufferings even become for them a helpful yoke, which brings them experience of the guiding of God. This is the proof Jesus Himself offers us of the supremacy over the world which belongs to Himself through the mutual knowledge existing between Himself and God. It forms the material also of the view summed up by Bernard (p. 415) in the predicates *superans fortunam* and *passus indigna*, as the distinctive marks of the world-controlling Divinity of Christ.

According to the hints given us in the New Testament, the grace and truth (faithfulness) manifested in the discharge of His vocation, and the loftiness of His self-determination as compared with the particular and natural impulses which spring from the world, are the features in the earthly life of Christ which are summed up in the attribute of His Godhead. Nor are these two elements, when more closely examined, really different. For the patience in suffering, which proves Christ's power over the world, is at the same time a manifestation of His faithfulness toward men; and His persistent faithfulness to the Jews, despite His anticipation that His work among them would be fruitless, is the proof of His inner freedom and victory over the external circumstances of His life. From the human point of view, this patience and faithfulness, as the purpose pervading Christ's life, have their source in the desire, inspired by His vocation and sustained by His unique knowledge of God, to set up the Kingdom of God among men as their supramundane final end. Viewed from the Godward side, this human life falls to be regarded as the perfect revelation of God, because the supreme end of the world, to which Christ's life is devoted, rests upon the self-end of God, that is, on His essential will of love. The notes of Christ's Divinity, therefore, have only such scope as is provided by His life-purpose, in so far as that purpose is the Divine end for the world, and the correlate of the self-end of God. To the creating and sustaining of the natural world this attribute cannot directly, at least, be referred; though it may be so indirectly, in as far as God creates and sustains the world with a view to its final end, as realised through the special work of Christ. This connection of ideas is indicated by Bernard, when he finds in the predicate *passus indigna* a special instance of God's wise government of the world. The expediency of innocent suffering endured for the good of the community is synonymous with God's wise government of the world for this reason, because the Christian community is God's supreme end in the world. A complete definition of the Godhead of Christ must therefore take account of the fact that Christ's grace and truth and world-subduing patience have had their effect in the existence of the community of the Kingdom of God under corresponding moral attributes. For to Him Who wields the lordship of God, or Who, to borrow Luther's phrase, is in virtue of His redeeming work " My Lord," we must reckon all those to belong who experience this same lordship in themselves ; in this connection the community of the Kingdom of God must be regarded as such, in so far as its members, through conduct prompted by universal brotherly love, and through the various possible manifestations of supremacy over the world and independence of the same, display in themselves the successful issue of Christ's peculiar work. Here also is the explanation of the fact that the conception of Christ's Divinity, or the application to Christ of the Old Testament Divine name, first arose in the Christian community; Christ Himself was never in the position thus to describe Himself. Therefore this attribute can be rightly appraised by theology only when Christ is conceived as the living Head of the community of God's Kingdom. For we must bring Christ into relation to His people, before we are in a position to recognise that in His own order He is unique.

That this is so, the religious consciousness of the Christian community assumes as certain. And hitherto theology has done nothing more than accept the assumption; she has never proved it. All forms of the doctrine of the Incarnate Word are imperfect, because none of them faces the question whether incarnation took place once and for ever in the Person of Jesus, or whether it may not be supplemented or repeated in the persons of others. I have already had occasion to point out (p. 408) that, neither in its Lutheran nor Reformed nor modern pietistic form, does Christology provide against the possible inference, that the God-man can be realised only in the race of mankind as a whole, or that His appearance may be repeated in each of the several spheres of moral and intellectual life. But our present line of thought makes it clear, that only in the sphere of the ethico-religious life, viewed from the standpoint of the Kingdom of God, does the God-man find His place, because that Kingdom, and nothing else, is the direct correlate of the Divine self-end. It follows, therefore, that, as the historical Author of this communion of men with God and with each other, Christ is *necessarily unique in His own order*. For if a second could be produced who, really, was on a level with Christ in grace and truth, in world-conquering patience, in scope alike of purpose and of achievement, he would yet stand in historical dependence upon Christ, and therefore, logically, would be subordinate to Him. Hence, as compared with those who succeed Him in the realisation of the Kingdom of God, the fact that this end is the self-end of God has for

Him quite a different meaning. For the members of Christ's community come to take this attitude as those who have had within them, originally, another bent of will; whereas the figure of Christ cannot be understood at all unless it is His original and distinguishing characteristic, that He finds His own personal end in the self-end of God. If Christ is thus the personal revelation of the will of God as essentially love, then certainly, from the point of view of degree, the love of God finds its perfect revelation in the fact, that the members of the Kingdom of God fulfil the law of brotherly love (p. 291); but from the point of view of kind, these manifestations of brotherly love in their widest extent must be regarded as the intended result of the Divine lordship introduced through Christ in grace and truth and spiritual freedom over the world. Similarly, the position of power which the Christian community occupies in the world, the transformation through the principle of love of the public conscience, the intrench-ment of the same in public institutions, the progressive liberation of the human mind from the dominion of nature, and the corresponding subjection of nature through knowledge and application of her laws to human ends, must also be reckoned results of the Divine lordship among men, and ascribed to its historical Author. In this estimate of Christ, the Christian faith approves itself as the view of the world which corresponds to the recognition of God as Spirit and as Love.

The exposition here given of Christ's Divinity it has been thought to disparage by the remark, that the attribute of Divinity is proved only of the will, but not of the nature of Christ, and that therefore, even in the case of the will, it remains unexplained. Whence the further inference is drawn, that Christ's Godhead is by this method not really recognised at all, but rather denied. Now this distinction between nature and will is not religious but scientific, although our opponents, as a rule, are not aware of the fact, and make the dispute to be about religious truth. If they are really the religious men and the experts in religion which they claim to be, let them prove it by showing that, even when they treat religious and scientific knowledge as one, they are capable of distinguishing between them; else they will not be able to maintain their claim to be the most competent judges in matters of religion. In all other cases we estimate character on the supposition that its essence is manifest in the will. Excellence of character is that state of the will in which the natural impulses are so restrained and governed as to be sub-ordinate and subservient to the good and unselfish end which the will pursues. For the created spirit has as his allotted task to take the inborn propensities of his soul, which corre-spond in some way to his physical equipment, and are known as his natural disposition, and, through the development of his will, to transform these into his obedient instruments. It is by his measure of success in this achievement that we judge the character of a fully developed man; and it must appear to us odd if a strong personality in his more mature years is judged by the natural disposition which he manifested in his youth, as if the latter were his real nature. It would be a parallel case to this if, in estimating the character of Christ, we were compelled straightway to disregard every trace of Divine lordship over the world, on the ground that this constitutes nothing essential in Him, but is only, as it were, the outward manifestation of the natural endowment with which He was born of Mary; for this, they tell us, is the correct description of His nature. But the will for good is never the simple mechanical result of the natural endowment within which it comes into being. Given a natural disposi-tion the most favourable, from a moral point of view, that can be imagined, it must still be educated, and therefore transformed, by the ends which it adopts at the bidding of a will bent on good. The latter would cease to be a will for good, if it had to be regarded as the mechanical result of an assumed natural endowment. This is the absurd idea suggested to us by our opponents, when they require us to find the essential nature of Christ, not in His world-conquering will, which marks Him as the God-man, but in

His physical origin, which has never yet been reconciled with His historical appearance, and never can be.   If Christ is to be judged by categories that are applied to no other object than Himself, then He is rendered unintelligible.   Or, if it is not beyond me to see from within the working of my opponents' minds, I should say that they regard Christ's will as a mere appendage of His nature, in the same way that acceptance of the idea of God as the Absolute reduces what is His essential characteristic, namely, His love, to a mere appendage of His nature.   If, as my opponents make me responsible for conclusions which they, with their alien ideas, have drawn from my statements, I in like manner seek to make intelligible to myself the distinction they draw in the case before us between nature and spirit or will (p. 238), then I find myself compelled to insist that this distinction of spirit and nature depends on the material constitution of the latter.   Even in my conception of the Divine nature, I cannot get away from this characteristic.   Therefore I conclude that, when my opponents will not allow Christ's good and 'world-conquering will, under the other characteristics already discussed, to be regarded as His true essence, because they do not believe in the independence of the good will as against all nature, they have fallen into a materialistic mode of thought.

When we investigated the Kingdom of God as the correlate of the thought that God is love, it appeared that this organisation of men can be construed as the object and end of God's love, only in so far as it is conformed to the type of its Founder, the Son of God.   The harmony with God and likeness to Him which the Kingdom of God must maintain in order to be understood as the objective of God's love, attaches to the said Kingdom only in so far as it is called into being by the Son of God, and bows to Him as its Lord (p. 281).   In other words, it is on the Son of God that in the first place the Father's love falls, and, only for His sake, on the community of which He is Lord.   Moreover, if these relations are eternally involved in God's will of love (p. 301),

it follows from our recognition of this fact, that the special
significance Christ has for us is by no means exhausted in
our appreciation of Him as a revelation conditioned by time.
On the contrary, it is implied that, as Founder and Lord of
the Kingdom of God, Christ is as much the object of God's
eternal knowledge and will as is the moral unification of
mankind, which is made possible through Him, and whose
prototype He is ; or rather, that, not only in time but in the
eternity of the Divine knowledge and will, Christ precedes
His community.   Of course, to this statement a certain
qualification must be added.   For whatever belonged to the
natural and generic limitations of Christ, more especially His
individual natural endowments and His Jewish nationality,
cannot be taken as the object of the eternal will of God,
since these things are by their very nature bound up with
the world, consequently can be fore-ordered, even by God,
only through a volition in time.   But Christ, we know,
reduced the significance of these limitations to mere means
toward His own spiritual life, in particular toward the apprehension of His own religious fellowship with God, and the
carrying out of the vocation He had embraced.   Sharing the
religious and moral customs of the Jews, He yet knows Himself, as the Son of God, exalted above them ; in discharging the
duties of His vocation toward His countrymen, He knows
His work destined to be fruitful, at the same time that He
distinctly foresees its fruitlessness among the Jews ; in His
own life-conduct, that universal human morality of which the
Kingdom of God shall be the perfect realisation so markedly
preponderates, that we fail to notice in Him those traces of
individual temperament which are wont to count for something even in the most perfect of men.   Yet Christ's life was
not a mere abstract presentation of universal human morality ;
for He gave the whole wealth of personal devotion to the
universal content of His vocation.   Rather is He Himself
the prototype of that life of love and elevation above worldly
motive, which forms the distinguishing characteristic of the
Kingdom of God ; and this as the deliberate result of His

vocation to be the Founder of that Kingdom, not in any mere
application of the principle of the Kingdom to the separate
details of human life, which is the source from which other
men derive their ethical vocations.   If, therefore, the Kingdom
of God as the correlate of the Divine self-end is the eternal
object of the love of God, this is so because Christ as the
prototype and inspiring force of that union of the many in
one, in other words, as the Head and Lord of that Kingdom,
is the eternal object of the love of God, so that in this special
form the Kingdom of God is present eternally to the Divine
knowledge and will, while its individual members are objects
of the knowledge of God in time (p. 122).

The congruity between the Son of God and God as His
Father, by which the conceivability of this eternal relation
must be determined, reaches, however, still further.   For if
the idea of love is necessarily confined to beings of a like
order, then, of course, it cannot be applied to God in any such
way that the thought of God must be subsumed under some
higher genus.   Rather must everything that is compared
with God be first regarded in the light of the distinction
between being and becoming.   Here theological tradition
comes to meet us with the thesis that no being shares in the
aseity of God.   Yet the distinction between God and all
forms of being is specific, in so far as it can just as little
be got rid of or dispensed with in actual life as can the
distinction between two members of a species.   On the other
hand, the individual spirit is marked by every possible
characteristic we think of as existing originally in God.
Therefore we may use the idea of species in order to compare
spiritual beings with God, provided we make the reservation,
that everything we class in the same species with God comes
ever from God, while God, in regard to what He is, does not
become, but everlastingly is, and that nothing we compare
with God ever attains the character of aseity.   With this,
theological tradition in so far corresponds, that, in affirming the Divinity of Christ, it expressly excludes aseity, and
by asserting the eternal generation of the Son, applies the

category of becoming, as distinct from being, to that Existence which is to be denoted as the eternal object of the Divine love. Under this condition, the view expounded above—that the eternally-beloved Son of God, on the ground of the like content of His personal will, and of the uniqueness of the relation He holds to the community of the Kingdom of God and to the world, is to be conceived under the attribute of Godhead—accords with the traditional theology. Of course our time-conditioned view of things cannot get rid of the antithesis between God's eternal decree and the realisation of the same in the empirical phenomena of time, just as our conception of the community of the Kingdom of God is bound up with the antithesis between the calling in time and the choosing before the foundation of the world. At the same time we must premise that this relation does not mean for God that there is in Him any want or need ; rather is His self-sufficiency everlastingly satisfied in what to us, in the long series of preparatory stages, looks like the expression of a want (p. 299). For this reason the eternal Godhead of the Son, in the sense here described, is perfectly in-telligible only as object of the Divine mind and will, that is, only for God Himself. But if at the same time we discount, in the case of God, the interval between purpose and accomplishment, then we get the formula that Christ exists for God eternally as that which He appears to us under the limitations of time. But only for God, since for us, as pre-existent, Christ is hidden. Inasmuch, then, as God's stand-point is impossible for us, we shall be wise if we content ourselves with this formal proof of our religious estimate of Christ. Only this, too, may be added by way of conclusion, namely, that by the same line of reasoning the Spirit of God, as the Holy Spirit, also becomes intelligible. The Spirit of God is the knowledge God has of Himself, as of His own self-end. The Holy Spirit denotes in the New Testament the Spirit of God, in so far. as the latter is the ground of that knowledge of God and that specific moral and religious life which exist in the Christian community (p. 273). Since the community has for its conscious purpose the realisation of the Kingdom of God as the Divine self-end, it is correct to say, that the practical knowledge of God in this community which is dependent upon God, is identical with the knowledge which God has of Himself, even as the love of God is perfected in the fact that within the community love is practised toward the brethren.   But if in His Son God loves eternally the community that is like His Son, in other words, if the community is *eo ipso* the eternal object of God's will of love, then also it is God's eternal will that His Spirit should be the Holy Spirit in the community of the Kingdom of God. In the form of this eternal purpose, the Spirit of God proceeds from God, inasmuch, namely, as He is destined to enter into the community which enjoys the perfect knowledge of God.

§ 50. The ethical view of the life of Christ in the light of His vocation found its appropriate sequel in the religious estimate of His life as the revelation of the love of God, and of that freedom which, as the characteristic power over the world, is the mark of Godhead.   This discussion has followed essentially the point of view expressed in the kingly Prophethood of Christ; it diverged from the traditional interpretation of that title only in this, that the whole moral conduct of Christ, as the presentation of the Divine grace and truth, was included in Christ's activity as Prophet. It remains to be seen whether and how the ethical view of the *priestly character*, which was at the same time claimed for the life and sufferings of Christ, may in like manner be turned to account from the religious point of view.   Under the head of Priest the old theology attempts only an ethical, not a religious interpretation, for the priestly character of Christ has for its content His obedience, that purely human and voluntary achievement.   The estimate of this obedience under the aforesaid title never for a moment leaves the lines of ethical, *in specie* forensic, judgment, nor does it issue in any distinctively religious attitude.   Only indirectly does the interpretation of Christ's priestly work fall within the view of religion, namely, in so far as it was initiated by God and is recognised by Him ; but a religious significance for us is secured to the content or result of this priestly work only through its being taken up into Christ's prophetic activity, and through the corresponding proclamation in the Church of how Christ has determined God to the grace of forgiveness. This formal inconsistency with the representation given of the prophetic office becomes the more painful in view of the fact, that the forensic interpretation of Christ's priestly work conflicts in every respect with the religious interest of the Christian.   For, as standards of conduct, law and religion are in Christian experience diametrically opposed, and the assumption that in God righteousness and grace work in opposite directions is in so far irreligious, that the unity of the Divine will forms an inviolable condition of all confidence in God.   Therefore, the introduction into the theology of Protestantism since Töllner of the fundamental position of Abelard is a distinct advance upon orthodoxy.   There only remains the question whether the thought of Christ's priestly work can be duly and logically combined with the religious value already attached to His life.   It is true we cannot in this case avoid a complete remodelling of the traditional doctrine of Christ's priesthood and sacrifice.   But this step is forced upon us, on the one hand by the established facts of Biblical theology, and on the other by the ethical consideration that what Christ in any way achieved for others must be included in what He thereby achieved for Himself.

It is unbiblical, then, to assume that between God's grace or love and His righteousness there is an opposition, which in its bearing upon the sinful race of men would lead to a contradiction, only to be solved through the interference of Christ.   The righteousness of inexorable retribution, which would be expressed in the sentence *Fiat justitia, pereat mundus,* is not in itself a religious conception, nor is it the meaning of the righteousness which in the sources of the Old and New Testaments is ascribed to God.   God's righteousness is His self-consistent and undeviating action in behalf of the salvation of the members of His community ; in essence it is identical with

His grace (vol. ii. p. 102). Between the two, therefore, there is no contradiction needing to be solved. It is unbiblical to assume that any one of the Old Testament sacrifices, after the analogy of which Christ's death is judged, is meant to move God from wrath to grace (vol. ii. p. 184). On the contrary, these sacrifices rely implicitly upon the reality of God's grace toward the covenant people, and merely define certain positive conditions which the members of the covenant people must fulfil in order to enjoy the nearness of the God of grace. It is unbiblical to assume that the sacrificial offering includes in itself a penal act, executed not upon the guilty person, but upon the victim who takes his place. Representation by priest and sacrament is meant not in any exclusive, but in an inclusive sense. Because the priest draws near to God when he brings near the gift, therefore he represents before God those in whose behalf he is acting ; it is not meant that because the priest and the sacrifice come near to God, the others may remain at a distance from God. These relations hold even when it is sins of ignorance which give occasion for sacrifices ; in the latter case forgiveness results from the fact that, with the sacrifice, the priest has indirectly brought the sinners also into the presence of God. Lastly, it is unbiblical to assume that a sacrifice has its significance directly for God, and only under certain other conditions also for men. On the contrary, the sacrificial act is just what combines these two relations.

The ethical conditions of a satisfactory theory are not met by the orthodox doctrine of Christ's priesthood, in so far as the latter has no regard for the distinct expression in the historical portrait of Christ of this fact, that *Christ is first of all a Priest in His own behalf* before He is a priest for others. The traditional theology overlooks this, since it conceives the idea of priest solely in the derivative sense of official priesthood, that is, as the mediation in behalf of others with God. But whoever is regarded as wielding an influence in this direction, must surely in the first place be a priest in his own behalf, that is, must possess and exercise the right of drawing near to God (Num. xvi. 5). Is that, then, a complete doctrine of Christ which has not one word of explanation for the fact that Christ prays regularly to God, and desires to transmit to His disciples His own religious fellowship with God expressed thereby ? The appreciation of this feature of Christ's character is obscured by the material conception of His Godhead, although surely it is evident that all specific action of God upon Christ, in virtue of which Christ reveals the Father and accomplishes His work, depends upon that spiritual interaction which appears in Christ's intercourse through prayer with God as His Father. The error in the interpretation of Christ's position as Prophet may be allowed to pass, since in this case the needful amplification and correction is easily supplied; but every interpretation of Christ's activity as Priest is for us distinctly incomplete, which is not based upon the fact that Christ is in the first place a Priest in His own behalf, that is to say, that He is the subject of personal religion, or, more definitely, that He is the subject of that true and perfect religion, compared with which no other has been able to bring men to the desired goal of nearness to God. For since Christ was the first to possess complete and exhaustive knowledge of God, He is therefore also the first who was qualified in the true and final manner to exercise that fellowship with God which was the aim of every religion, and to experience in Himself in its fulness the reciprocal and saving influence of God. If with the attitude adopted by Christ we compare the method of the Old Testament sacrifices, then these latter as separate transactions fall short of the constancy, and as ceremonial transactions of the spirituality, of Christ's nearness to God, and since they express only an indirect and material approach to Him, necessarily fail to effect for any man that personal attitude to God which pervades the consciousness of Jesus (Heb. x. 1–4). A nearer analogy is presented by the religious practice of the Psalmists, but in this case with an effort the success of which is not at every moment assured, but as a rule is rather anticipated for the future. Besides, there is the further difference, that the piety of the Psalmists does not as such possess the power of establishing a community, whereas Christ lives in the intention of transmitting to His disciples His own fellowship with God; and that we ourselves are able to institute these inquiries at all is only possible because this intention of Christ has had success in us.

If, then, Christ is to be thought of as Priest, the fundamental form for this priestly activity is contained in each moment of His unique consciousness, that as the Son of God He stands to God as Father in a relation of incomparable fellowship, which is realised in His knowledge of God, in the surrender of His will to God's providential guiding, and in the security of feeling which accompanies the same. When, in prayer especially, He collects Himself for this fellowship, He asserts the nearness of God, and assures Himself of the love of God as the ground of His own position as God's Son (John xv. 10, 11). At the same time this function is not exercised outside His consciousness of His vocation and the activity resulting therefrom, but of necessity opens out to include the whole range of this activity, even as it receives thence in return stimulus and support. For Christ recognises His vocation, and exercises it, as the direct work of God; the aim of His own efforts is known to Him as the very aim of God; His conduct therefore is intelligible to Him as a service rendered to God, which in its own way brings Him just as near to God as prayer itself. Thus the particular instance of loyalty to His vocation to which the circumstances led, namely, His readiness to die, served as really to support His conviction of the love of God toward Himself as did the consciousness He enjoyed of fulfilling God's commands as a whole (John x. 17, xv. 10). Paul has framed the twofold conception, first, that the fruit of his own efforts in his vocation, namely, the converted heathen, are a· sacrifice to God in the offering of which he renders priestly service (Rom. xv. 16); and, on the other hand, that that personal sanctification, which makes the body the fit instrument of the God-honouring life of the soul, is the spiritual sacrifice which each believer is to offer to God (xii. 1). Regarded in this light, Christ's activity in His vocation and His consistent personal virtue also fall within the view of His priestly approach to God.

But under what conditions are we to understand that Christ's loyalty to His vocation as a whole, and more especially His willingness to endure death as a consequence of that loyalty, have the significance of *priestly service for others?* It is true that this extreme instance of obedience to His vocation is the only one which is directly viewed by Christ Himself under the aspect of sacrifice, namely, in His words at the Last Supper, to which the less distinct references in John (x. 11, 17, xii. 24, xv. 13, xvii. 19) add nothing that is specific. The inclusion of this active obedience in the priestly work of Christ for others does not rest on any direct statement of the New Testament. At the same time, the value thus attached to the active conduct of Christ, so that His patience in suffering and willingness to die are included along with it under the one conception of His meritorious obedience, is the one point in the traditional interpretation which comes nearest to the truth. It is not the mere fate of dying that determines the value of Christ's death as a sacrifice; what renders this issue of His life significant for others is His willing acceptance of the death inflicted on Him by His adversaries as a dispensation of God, and the highest proof of faithfulness to His vocation. Thus it is impossible to accept an interpretation of Christ's sacrificial death which, under the head of satisfaction, combines in a superficial manner His death and His active life, while at bottom it ascribes to the death of Christ quite a different meaning, namely, that of substitutionary punishment. I have shown how alien this interpretation is to the whole Biblical idea of sacrifice as rightly understood, also how little the only utterance of Paul which points in this direction (Gal. iii. 13) has to do with the idea of sacrifice, how exactly rather it corresponds with Paul's apocryphal conception of the Mosaic Law, a conception which cannot as such be theologically binding (vol. ii. p. 248). I have shown that the asserted necessity of a penal satisfaction to God as a condition of the exercise of His grace has no foundation in the Biblical conception of God; on the contrary, it is an intellectual inference from the principle of Hellenic religion that the gods practise a twofold retribution, a principle further supplemented by the assumption that the original adjustment of the relation between God and man is to be interpreted in terms of a legal ordinance (§ 32). It only remains, therefore, to show that the idea of a penalty borne for others in the manner in which this is here asserted, is as inconsistent with the conditions of moral life in the individual as it is foreign to the words of Christ.

The sufferings of Christ in His death are said to have been equivalent to the penalty which through sin the whole human race has brought upon itself. This proposition is based, not upon the ground that in the two cases the exact amount of suffering is the same, which is incapable of proof, but on the ground that there is an equivalence in quality and worth, in so far as Christ by the immeasurable worth of His Divinity counterbalanced the immeasurable worthlessness of sin, and consciously accepted as the punishment of sin the evils that befell Him, in other words realised momentarily in His own experience eternal damnation. Certainly this latter supposition is the indispensable condition of any value as satisfaction attaching in the sight of God to the sufferings of Christ. A punishment which is not felt as punishment lies beyond the horizon of a theology which regards legal retribution in its strictest form as the fundamental order of the world. But we have seen that the idea of punishment is not complete when it regards merely these objective conditions of legal order; to render it complete, the evils inflicted by public authority, in consequence of unlawful actions, must be accompanied by the sense of guilt in the person concerned (§ 14). Apart from this, the individual does not feel or reckon the punishment as punishment, but as an unpleasant interlude, perhaps, or even as an injustice done to himself.   Now the doctrine of a penal satisfaction rendered by Christ stands in so direct a relation to this imperfect conception of punishment, which is due to inaccurate observation, that this fact alone is fatal to its validity. For Christ had no sense of guilt in His sufferings, consequently He cannot have regarded them as punishment, nor even as punishment accepted in the place of the guilty, or in order to deter men from sin.   It may well be that an innocent man, who is a member of the same community with guilty men, shares the experience of evils which the guilty have brought upon themselves as punishment.   But whether the innocent man, because of his innocence, finds such evil consequences of others' guilt the easier or the heavier to bear, he at least cannot feel them as punishment, seeing he is himself wholly innocent, or, at any rate, not a partner in their guilt.   Crell has rightly remarked against Grotius, that when God afflicts a family or a nation for the crime of its head, and thereby causes even innocent children to suffer, the evil for the latter is *afflictio*, not *poena* (vol. i. p. 339).   In the same way Christ, Who was conscious of not deserving any punishment when He encountered death as a consequence of faithfulness to His vocation, cannot possibly have regarded as punishment the sufferings which, through the fellowship with sinful humanity attaching to His vocation, He brought on Himself as the consequence of man's hostility to good—even although He cherished the compassionate purpose of contributing by His death toward the removal of this guilt.

While this theory of Christ's sufferings has resulted from certain arbitrary assumptions anent the original Divine order of the world, assumptions not Christian but legal and Hellenic, yet, as a matter of fact, a certain religious interest has come to attach to the same; the question is whether the theory has thereby become the more convincing.   In this connection, two different arguments are presented to us.   On the one hand, von Meyer and Beck (vol. i. pp. 626, 630) maintain that the penal value of the sufferings of Christ is reflected and confirmed in the similar experience of believers, when the latter

are crucified with Christ.   But the alleged similarity is
contrary to fact.   Even the old theologians perceived that for
the believer all evils are disciplinary in character, and serve to
purify and try the soul (§ 9).   In other words, if the " cruci-
fixion " of believers is to be understood as an inward process,
then it means the transformation of the old man into the
new, which transformation takes place through self-discipline
and the attainment of virtue, and each act of dying to the
flesh is immediately recompensed by the bliss of living to the
spirit.   These experiences of the believer have no resemblance
whatever to simple retributive punishment.   Granting that
they resemble the sufferings of Christ, the only conclusion we
can draw is the one already arrived at, namely, that for Christ
His sufferings served as a means of testing His faithfulness
to His vocation—this and nothing else.   The religious
interest attaching to the penal value of Christ's sufferings has
been expressed in another form by Philippi (vol. i. p. 626).
Philippi makes his conviction of the truth of Christianity
rest upon the consideration, that Christ, by the penal satisfaction He offered to God, proves Himself his surety against
the wrath and retributive justice of God ; but for this, Philippi
would have been quite content with the religion of his fathers.
Here the question arises, by what means is the individual to
know that Christ, in offering a general satisfaction, is surety
also for him ?   He could be assured of this only if Christ suffered
the particular punishment which, as regards quantity and
quality, would correspond to his own personal transgressions.
But these are by no means the lines on which the doctrine
championed by Philippi is actually laid.   Just as the assumed
conception of original sin obscures the particular guilt of
individual men, so the penal satisfaction offered by Christ is
made the equivalent of the eternal damnation due to all
mankind, and is by no means fitted to counteract the sense
of guilt of each separate individual.   However much we may
widen it out into sympathy with the common guilt of men,
the fact remains that the personal aspect is the point of least
concern to the orthodox dogma.   The latter appropriates the

sense of guilt so pre-eminently for · original sin that an individual sense of guilt cannot arise, because all separate transgressions are represented merely as unavoidable consequences of original sin, and add nothing to its guilt. In the same way, therefore, that the conception of original sin admits no distinction of individual sin, so the worth of the satisfaction offered by Christ for hereditary sin as a whole provides no guarantee that He is surety for the particular sins of the individual, which the latter distinguishes from original sin. To bridge the gap here disclosed is logically just as impossible as it has proved for Lutheran theology to establish a logical reconciliation between the universal promise of grace and its application to the individual believer (§ 24). One would need to know beforehand that he is himself elected.

But yet another defence might be offered. I recall, with this view, the remarkable position of Wessel (p. 371), who distributes Christ's penal satisfaction over the various amounts of punishment merited by each individual, whether elect or reprobate, and makes room for all this punishment in the consciousness of Christ, Who is represented as having made satisfaction for the separate penalty due by each individual. It has been pointed out that this view of Wessel corresponds with the fact that he ignores altogether original sin; at the same time it is due to a far more exact appreciation of the individual sense of guilt than was possessed by the Reformers, whose own intention it was to deepen this sense of guilt to the utmost. In this interest they adopted Augustine's doctrine of original sin; but there is no doubt that thereby the sense of individual responsibility, which we must regard as one of the strongest motives of the Christian religion, has in part been weakened and in part perverted. Wherefore also the religious interest which Philippi here manifests is clearly inconsistent with the theology which he describes as the theology of the Church. What a pity that Luther did not devote some attention to the theory of Wessel, and discuss the bearing of his own doctrine upon it ! For that it stands in some direct relation to the emphasis needing to be laid on the individual sense of guilt, is confirmed to me by a communication I have received from a pastor, who, without knowing anything of Wessel, was led by his own experience in dealing with men, to the very same view. If, namely, the individual sense of guilt is to be met by the thought of the penal satisfaction offered by Christ, then nothing is left us but the hypothesis that Christ in His sufferings had a distinct and separate experience of the amount of punishment due to each separate individual of all mankind. The impossibility of this supposition is at once apparent, for there is as little evidence in the history of Christ's life, as there is room within the range of His human consciousness, for an omniscience of this kind; so that we have here a conclusive reason against the interpretation of Christ's sufferings as the conscious experience by Him of the punishment due to all mankind.

Christ's Priesthood, therefore, is a well-grounded expression of the fact that, as the subject of the perfect spiritual religion, Christ stood in the highest possible relation of fellowship with God, and exercised this fellowship at each moment of His life, since every act and word of His vocation arose out of His religious relation to God. The union of mankind through the motive of universal love, He regarded as the Kingdom of God; in bringing about this union He was conscious of exercising in His own person the lordship of God; and this association of His own moral ideal with the thought of God is only possible as the result of His consistent religious attitude, whether in His view of the world, in His apprehension of Himself, or in His worship of God. In other words, the certainty He enjoyed as to His own particular vocation of necessity presupposes that His apprehension of Himself as the Son of God is ever attained through the exercise of His religious relation toward God, that is, through the adoration of God as His Father. Therefore, when we have placed the one common material of Christ's life, His speech and conduct as well as His patience in suffering, under the two separate categories of prophetic and priestly activity, we exhaust the significance of His person as Bearer of the Divine lordship, or founder of the Divine Kingdom. Inasmuch as at each moment of His life the same historical material affords confirmation of His religious character as subject of the perfect religion, and of His personal vocation as the ambassador of God, He hereby displays His specific and unique significance for those who through His kingly Prophethood are led to enter into the same religious attitude to God, so as to adopt as the supreme aim of their own life the realisation of God's Kingdom. To what extent the priestly relation which was exercised by Christ in His own person becomes also significant for others, forms the theme of a later discussion.

1. In order to determine the specific significance of the Person of Christ in Christian thought, whether as regards our view of the world or our judgment of ourselves, account must be taken of the whole range of Christ's activity, and of these two essential considerations—first, that the Christian religion is not a national religion; and, second, that the Christian religion, as the perfect and complete revelation of God, has this object, namely, to render men, in virtue of their relation to the supramundane spiritual God, free and independent with regard to the world.

2. In so far as the speech and conduct and patience under suffering, which make up the life of Christ, arise out of His vocation to exercise the moral lordship of God and realise God's Kingdom, and are the perfect fulfilment of this vocation, even to the extent of His willingly and patiently enduring the pains of death, it follows from the relation of this purpose of Christ to the essential will of God, that Christ as the kingly Prophet is the perfect revelation of God; that, in virtue of the motive which inspired Him, namely, love, and the lordship which in His estimate of Himself and in His patience He exercised over the world, He is equal to God; and that He is the eternal object of the Divine love, and as such also the ground of

the eternal election of the community of the Kingdom of God.

3. In so far as the unbroken faithfulness of Christ to His vocation not only exhibits in detail the religious relation of the Son of God to God as His Father, but always arises out of this relation, Christ maintains in His whole life His priestly relation toward God. If, therefore, His Priesthood is to be regarded as availing for others, it can only be in virtue of this fact.

CHAPTER VII

§ 51. THE necessity of the Divine forgiveness of sins affirmed in the Christian religion is always, in theological systems subsequent to the Reformation, viewed in the light of the relations assumed to obtain between the authority of God on the one hand, and the destination of men for blessedness and the significance of their moral action on the other. Our historico-critical preparation for the decision we have to arrive at on this subject must limit itself to those expositions of Christianity which sprang out of the movements of the sixteenth century, for the inconsistent tenor of the Roman Catholic scheme of salvation offers a twofold answer to the question. I refer to the fact that Thomas (vol. i. p. 93), under the influence of statements of Paul, at the outset follows Augustine in defining *iustificatio* as *transmutatio a statu iniustitiae per remissionem peccatorum*, but, when expanding this conception, regards the forgiveness of guilt as the completion of making righteous (*Gerechtmachung*). And yet, in opposition to this dogmatic principle, there stands the individual's religious judgment of self—asserted in Catholicism too—which regards all merit as the effect of Divine grace, and therefore traces blessedness, or acceptance into the community of the perfected saints, back to the factor of grace, which, in contrast to the perpetual imperfection of conduct in general, is described as the grace of pardon (vol. i. p. 136). According to the first view, forgiveness is found necessary to supplement that actual righteousness which exists through the grace of God, a righteousness which properly determines a man's standing before God and his blessedness. According to the other view, Divine forgiveness of sins is found necessary as the basis in principle of the attainment of blessedness; for all actual human righteousness is imperfect and therefore unfit to determine our relation to God, and, so far as it possesses any perfection, dependent on grace. Thus it becomes plain that the question of *the necessity of forgiveness* receives no clear answer in Catholic Christianity, for we are always referred alternately from the one view to the other.

Now, these two heterogeneous conceptions come to be set in opposition the one to the other, inasmuch as the first is adopted by Socinianism, the second by orthodox Protestantism, though of course the explanations given of either by these two parties are accompanied by modifications. Catholicism, by its oscillation between the two, betrays an endeavour to interpret and to realise Christianity as something which wavers in equilibrium between law and redemption. Orthodox Protestantism makes the significance of Christianity as law subordinate to its significance as redemption; Socinianism does the opposite. The latter system, accordingly, goes on the principle that man owes his standing before God and the prospect of blessedness to his fulfilment of the Christian law. Accordingly, the forgiveness of sins is regarded merely as compensating for the imperfection of his legal performances; it is formulated by God in the judgment that a good intention to render the obedience of faith is equivalent to complete performance, and that therefore the penalties due for its infraction by sin, which would prove an obstacle to blessedness, are not exacted. This result, it is true, is entirely based on the free will of God, as attested by Him in His promise; still, the application of God's redeeming will is made dependent on the presence of the active obedience of faith to the law. The meaning of the Socinian scheme of salvation, consequently, is that forgiveness, as an equitable (*billige*) interpretation put by God upon the good will perfectly to fulfil the law, and as remission of penalties, is necessary in order to compensate for the imperfection of moral action, and to maintain the principle that blessedness follows from moral action.   Under these circumstances, forgiveness is interpreted as an accident of the Christian life, inasmuch as in principle the standing of men before God is reduced to legal perfection or the endeavour to reach it (vol. i. p. 325).   Now, although in this system an explicit basis is found for the religious factor in Christianity expressed by the conception of forgiveness— man being represented as attaining a supernatural destination in accordance with the Divine promise—yet more recent theories of an analogous character have become more indifferent to this consideration (vol. ii. p. 49).   For when once Christianity is regarded as essentially a system of scholastic ethics or a legal mode of life, it is immaterial how much or how little attention is given to those characteristics of its original form which prove it to be a religion.

The orthodox Dogmatics of the Lutheran and Reformed Churches states the ground of the necessity of the forgiveness of sins in general much in the same way as Socinianism does. Forgiveness, or justification by God's grace, appears as necessary because *the fulfilment of the law in the state of grace* no less than in the state of sin is *imperfect*, and therefore unfitted to determine the relation of man to God, or to render his blessedness possible.   Here we have, therefore, the reservation that, if man's conduct had not been disturbed and restricted by sin, on it would have depended his acknowledgment by God and his blessedness.   But as forgiveness is regarded as necessary to the end which, under the reign of sin and its after-effects, is not attainable by moral action, the imperfection of that action is viewed not, as by Socinianism, merely in its quantitative, but in its qualitative aspect. Thence it follows that the forgiveness of sins is recognised, not as a substitute for fulfilment of the law, but as the sole criterion, as the principle of man's standing before God, and as the sufficient ground of his blessedness.   In judging ourselves subjectively, it is demanded that, when asking whether

we are justified, we should look away from all our own
activity in what is good, and turn to the grace of God alone.
To this corresponds the common Evangelical doctrine that
blessedness is subject to no other condition than that which
determines justification.   For on this point there is really no
significant divergence between the two Evangelical confessions.
Even though on the Reformed side no occasion presented
itself for formulating this principle so antithetically as is
done in the Formula of Concord, Art. 4, yet a quite clear
distinction was made between the tenets that blessedness is
solely the effect of Divine grace, and that God at the same
time has so ordained the way to blessedness that we shall
practise good works according to His law.[1]   With no less
decisiveness the Lutheran doctrine holds that, when in a
soul justification by faith is effectual to salvation, the Holy
Spirit at the same time supplies the power to fulfil the
Divine law.   But however much in earnest one may be in
believing that good works merely exist synchronously alongside of justification by faith, without having any share, not
even that of a concomitant cause, in producing salvation as
a result, yet it will be difficult to avoid involuntarily dis-
torting this relation into a causal one, unless some explanation of the necessity of good works in the life of the justified
person is found which shall give the clearest possible expression to the quite different place they really occupy.   This
is not done, for instance, in St. Bernard's phrase, repeated
by Evangelical theologians—*bona opera via regni, non causa
regnandi.*   It may be that a man has attained to the position

---

[1] Calvin, *Inst.* iii. 14. 21 : "Quod praeterea bona fidelium opera scriptura
causas esse ostendit, cur illis dominus benefaciat, stat inconcussum, effectum
nostrae salutis in dei patris dilectione situm esse, materiam in filii obedientia,
instrumentum in spiritus illuminatione. Istis nihil obstat, quominus opera
dominus tanquam causas inferiores amplectatur, sed unde id? nempe quos sua
misericordia aeternae vitae hereditati destinavit, eos ordinaria sua dispensationae
per opera bona inducit in eius possessionem. Quod in ordine dispensationis
praecedit, posterioris causam nominat." *Conf. Helv.*, post. 16 : "Nos sentimus
per opera bona nos servari, illaque ad salutem ita esse necessaria, ut absque illis
nemo unquam sit servatus. Gratia enim soliusque Christi beneficio servamur ;
opera necessario ex fide progignuntur. Ac improprie his salus attribuitur, quae
propriissime adscribitur gratiae."

of lordship not through merit, but through grace; still, if in that position he must practise good works, then they can hardly be anything but conditions, in other words, concomitant causes, of his maintaining his lordship. This consideration is so irresistibly urgent that it becomes exceedingly important for the correct formation of the doctrine to discover in what motives the Evangelical confessions base the necessity of good works in the Christian life.

They do so by assigning two pairs of reasons. First, the necessity is real because God prescribes good works, and because as tokens of the Holy Spirit they follow from true and living faith. Again, good works arise from the desire to promote God's glory, in particular, in order to show gratitude for justification, and from the desire to attain subjective assurance of salvation.[1] But the very plenitude of these reasons, which no theologian has undertaken to bring into relation with one another, betrays some uncertainty as to the position. For if the question were put why God, Who attaches blessedness to justification by faith, prescribes good works and wishes to be glorified by them, it would be impossible to conceal the arbitrariness of such an arrangement. Practically the same answer would have to be given to the questions, on what ground the gift of the Holy Spirit coincides with justification, since the latter is not mediated by Him; and how faith, which in the case of justification is merely receptivity for Divine grace, can at the same time be an efficacious power acting on our fellow-men. Finally, it is not altogether obvious that good works should serve every believer as a ground for believing in his justification. The position that they must do so rests on the belief that both are effects of Divine grace. But here again the question arises, What have justification and good works in common even from this point of view? If nothing save justification by faith secures eternal life, if therefore good works do not, how is the assurance of justification and of eternal life to be gained from them, in so far as they are effects of Divine grace? And there is this further point. Our

[1] *Apol. C. A.* iii. 68, 155; *Form. Conc.* 4; *Helv.*, post. 16; *Catech. Pal.* 86.

consciousness of justification expressly involves that in virtue of their continual imperfection we must look away from our good works as a criterion of our standing before God (p. 164). But now, it is maintained, should our faith in our justification be weak, we are to find the authentic ground for our consciousness of being justified in the fact that good works are present in some degree. Will a man really attain to that peace which justification ought to ensure to him, if placed between these two contradictory estimates of his moral action, both of which he is to accept simultaneously? Schneckenburger at least has asserted that such a supposition is intolerable to a Lutheran. But Schneckenburger is mistaken in supposing that the above-mentioned principle is alien to the creed and Dogmatics of Lutheranism.[1] His view is correct only so far as the tendency to look for verification of the justified status to the moral struggle which is going on simultaneously, does not make its influence felt in the practical religious methods of Lutheranism until Spener. Otherwise, Spener himself could not have affirmed this principle as something novel and decisive in character. On the other hand, under the Reformed system this method of self-examination is partly encouraged by the conception of *perseverantia gratiae*, and partly rendered tolerable by the counterbalancing idea of election.

Within the domain of Lutheranism, self-examination of this kind, ever since it was recommended by Spener, has become the source of a widespread change in religious life, and at the same time the occasion of a dubious alteration in the doctrine of justification. On the one hand, Spener's principle led to the Illumination (*Aufklärung*), *i.e.* to the result that people spared themselves the roundabout path of justification by Christ, and relied before God upon any performance of good works they could claim (vol. i.

---

[1] *Comparat. Dogmatik*, i. p. 42 ; cf. *Apol. C. A.* iii. 155, 229, *vide supra* pp. 143, 144. Further, Quenstedt, P. iv. cap. 9, thes. 8, not. 2 : "Per bona opera iustificatio nostra quoad nos a posteriori confirmatur." Hollatz, P. iii. sec. 2, cap. 7, qu. 22 : "Quicunque legem divinam, quantum in hac vitae infirmitate fieri potest, sincere servat, is fidei suae certus est."

pp. 360, 372). On the other hand, in the Pietistic circles devoted to sanctification, a heightened enthusiasm for good works, and especially an ascetic aversion to secular life, was beyond all doubt originally fostered with the idea of find-ing in these marks of the state of grace assurance of justification through Christ. But such sanctification was not viewed directly as an effect of Divine grace, but as an object to be attained by personal effort, while at the same time it was conceived as the ultimate saving purpose of God. Either, now, the saintly activity which was to serve the believer as an evidence of his justification came to be re-garded as possessing equal worth in God's sight, or the high value placed upon sanctification lessened the attention given to justification, or both tendencies appeared together. This result comes out clearly in the theology of Bengel's school. While referring the reader to my previous exposition of the views of Oetinger, Menken, von Meyer, and Beck (vol. i. pp. 608 ff., 623 ff.), I may describe as the interpretation of redemption common to them all that it consists in the communication of the positive power of a moral, sinless life, and as their view of justification, that it is God's acknowledg-ment of the effectual obedience of faith, as a factor of real value even though requiring to be supplemented. The agree-ment between the leaders of Arminianism and this school, which in the case of Beck actually approximates to Catholic doctrine, is in the last resort to be explained historically by the fact that the teaching of the Reformers did not precisely settle the relation between justification and good works. The influence of this "sanctification"-pietism, however, left its mark likewise on the dictum of Schleiermacher, repeated by Nitzsch and Martensen, that justification and conversion are the aspects to be distinguished in regeneration (vol. i. pp. 531, 550). This view may possibly express merely the temporal coexistence of the two as conceived by the Re-formers. This is the turn which Schweizer, at least, gives it.[1] But with Schleiermacher the dictum really expresses

[1] *Christliche Glaubenslehre*, ii. 2, p. 135.

the dependence of justification on conversion. But the inevitable result of this is to encourage the idea that the purpose of justification is to make sanctification possible and real, which is the declared tendency of the Catholic doctrine of justification (*Gerechtmachung*).

The distortion of the idea of justification in the schools of Bengel and Schleiermacher is the worst error brought about by the obscurity of the positions held by the Reformers regarding the necessity of good works. Without going so far, another distortion of the idea meets us close at hand in practical teaching. For, hardly anywhere, even in that preaching which is most faithful to the standards, does one discover thorough agreement with the Formula of Concord in asserting that salvation depends solely on faith. Rather, in order to guard against Antinomianism, the performance of good works is insisted on as a condition of salvation, *i.e.* good works are admitted to be a concomitant cause. This conjunction of the two, common in popular usage, is thrown into sharp relief in Kant's treatment of the problem of the forgiveness of sins (vol. i. p. 456). For he draws attention to the fact that the hope of salvation is attached to two conditions, that our transgressions be cancelled before the Divine Judge, and that we walk in a new and dutiful life. Both conditions must of necessity hang together, and this is sought to be proved, says Kant, by deducing the one from the other. The two possible combinations between them, however, bring Kant to an antinomy of reason, *i.e.* to a contradiction between the orthodox and the rationalistic theory. For, to begin with, forgiveness appears as the necessary precondition of a good life; on the other hand, one cannot appropriate for one's own forgiveness the penal satisfaction rendered by another, unless one devotes oneself to an amended walk and conversation. This contradiction is not theoretically so insoluble as Kant supposes; and therefore that we must decide practically for the second alternative—that the forgiveness of sins is dependent on reformation—is not so inevitable as he represents. For in life one may, indeed, begin with what we ought to do—that is the principle of all education; but the certainty of Divine forgiveness apprehended later is not therefore necessarily produced by one's own activity. Rather, it may quite well be viewed as the insight we gain into the determining ground of our own activity, and as the condition of its merely relative worth. In that case, however, the question always recurs, how it can be proved that forgiveness, as the essential basis, makes moral activity possible, and, on the other hand, how good works can add anything further, if forgiveness has been fixed upon by God as the sufficient ground of eternal life. For one would think that if the specific result of justification or forgiveness is the capacity to lead a new life, then the Catholic or the Pietistic reading of justification as "making righteous" (*Gerecht-machung*), or real purification from sin, is indicated as the true one. On the other hand, if we cannot thoroughly believe the proposition that eternal life or blessedness is, under the conditions posited in Protestantism, coincident with justification, then the demand for good works as concomitant causes of blessedness can only be understood as due to the silent influence of the idea of merit.

If, on the other hand, the Reformers' conception of justification or forgiveness is rigorously held to, and if the necessity for it is to be seen from the comparison of justification with good works, then what we come to is nothing more nor less than the principle that the forgiveness of God is necessary for the salvation (eternal life, blessedness) of believers, because works are inadequate to this purpose, owing to their imperfection. At the beginning of the Reformation, this position supplied the argument of most practical importance for stimulating religious self-examination as opposed to vulgar Catholicism; but the principle is really very far from furnishing a positive proof of comprehensive range. For the assertion that justification is necessary to eternal life is, in this connection, merely the obverse of the negative judgment that good works do not suffice for eternal life, because—it being presupposed that even the believer is relatively a sinner still—they are always imperfect. Thus the principle is held in reserve that, if good works were performed in perfect measure, they would suffice to establish a legal claim on God to eternal life. This principle, drawn from the dispensation assumed as original, implies that the relation of men to God, expressed in the Christian conception of religion, is properly a legal one (§ 33). But this position is not merely proved untenable in point of fact by the universality of sin ; it is a logical absurdity to conceive the necessary dependence of man on God in respect of his destiny, as being at the same time a relation involving reciprocal rights. Since, then, even as a mere matter of fact, justification by faith and not the legal claim conferred by good works leads to eternal life, the proof which establishes the first view by the untenability of the second implies the more general truth that man's highest destiny, fellowship with God, is the result of God's entering into religious relations with him, for it cannot arise from a legal reciprocity between them. But either this is a tautology, or the logical sequence of these propositions must be reversed. The positive proof, therefore, that justification or forgiveness leads to eternal life, must be led otherwise than by the mere negation of the methods furnished by vulgar Catholicism, with which Luther tortured himself in vain, since at bottom they were absurd. Not until the proof of the connection between justification and eternal life has been formulated entirely anew, shall we also be able completely to refute the Socinian view that forgiveness is merely a supplement to the active obedience of faith, which in its turn has its roots in the free resolve of the individual. Under no circumstances, however, can the positive proof of the necessity of forgiveness be derived from its teleological relation to sanctification or good works, which, indeed, are taken into account in the Catholic doctrine of justification (*Gerechtmachung*) as the aim of the latter, but never in the Evangelical doctrine of justification (*Gerechtsprechung*). But this is not to be taken as foreclosing the question whether justification, even as conceived Evangelically, is not to be regarded as a precondition of good works and their right performance. But, according to the Evangelical interpretation, decisively as it is to be distinguished from the Catholic, justification is certainly not the direct means to that end.

§ 52. But why must so much circumlocution be expended in establishing as a general thesis *the teleological relation of justification to eternal life?* Not only is this connection between the two so directly suggested by statements of Paul (Rom. v. 17, 18); it is proclaimed by the whole Reformation. How often and how strongly does Luther emphasise the truth that life and blessedness are directly bound up with justification![1] Why has this connection not been kept in sight with sufficient clearness to ensure its predominating influence in theology? In the contrary fact—in the fact, that is, that any answer rather than Luther's is given as to the purpose of justification—I find a singular token of uncertain tradition. And this uncertainty goes pretty far back, at least on Lutheran ground. The Formula of Concord, it is true, testifies to the connection between justification by faith and eternal life no less staunchly than Luther's Catechism and the *Apology of the C. A.*[2]; but one seeks it in vain either in the *C. A.* itself or in Luther's Articles of Smalcald. Moreover, while we certainly find it in Chemnitz and Hutter, the later theologians, who partly have no sense for teleological relations, and partly force the treatment of the doctrine of justification into the mould of controversy with Romish teaching, subsume the prospect of eternal life merely under the *effecta iustificationis*—that is, under a particular heading, and without distinguishing it specifically from other *effecta*, especially sanctification (active moral renewal).[3] Thus the connection between justification and eternal life has not had that decisive weight given to it in Lutheran tradition which would have sufficed to repel the perpetual temptation to make sanctifica-

---

[1] Köstlin, ii. p. 461.
[2] Cf. *supra,* p. 67; also *C. A.* iii. 11, 75, 176, 199, 226. *Catech. Min.* v. "Where the forgiveness of sins is, there is also life and blessedness."
[3] Cf. vol. i. pp. 276, 292; *supra*, p. 72.

tion or the good life the end of justification. Besides, theologians were content simply to enumerate the effects of justification—known to be such from passages in the Bible—without considering their significance or their mutual relations. Have then peace of conscience with God, free access to God, Divine sonship, and the hope of eternal life, nothing in common with one another, or are they ideas which require no explanation whatever? It has been shown that a group of Reformed theologians analysed justification into the forgiveness of sins and the bestowal of eternal life or adoption (p. 76); they thus recognised the extremely close relations between the two, to which the Reformed symbols likewise testify. Nevertheless, all this did not bring about a more favourable state of the inquiry. And though Schleiermacher adopted the distinction which the Reformed theologians had made in the idea of justification, yet he never came to see the full meaning of it, for he regarded Divine sonship as the guarantee, not of eternal life, but of sanctification.

But how are we to explain the fact that the sense for the teleological aspect of justification indicated above should have become so enfeebled that a wholly apocryphal connection between it and sanctification came predominantly to the front, though without ever attaining to clear consciousness? In my opinion, this is due to the projection of the idea of eternal life entirely into the next world, and the demarcation of the thought of it from all the relations of our present experience. Luther, indeed, did not view the matter in this light; yet he never devoted to the subject the theoretical consideration which it demanded. But Melanchthon and Calvin have already lost altogether that freshness of insight into the connection indicated, without which a correct theoretical representation of it simply need not be attempted. While justification has bound up with it the hope of, or as in Calvinistic circles it is called, the right to eternal life, yet this latter blessing itself was divested of every relation to the possible experience of the present, and its importance put in the shade. There co-operated further

in the same direction the characteristically Catholic interpretation of eternal life which is derived from Augustine (vol. i.
p. 117), and survives in both Confessions—the view, namely,
that eternal life consists exclusively in the vision of God.   If
God, according to the Neo-Platonic view, has no relation to
the world, then eternal life, attached as it is to cognition of
Him, has no relation either to the world or to the common
life of men, nor could it enter into any connection with the
circle of our present experiences.   Or, so far as it did so,
either there came to the front the significance of good works
as concomitant causes of eternal life, or in both Confessions
a return was consistently made to the methods of Mysticism,
by which Catholic piety anticipates even in this life that
union with God which consists in separation from the world.
But if religion is not only faith in God, but always a view of
the world as well, then the Christian conception of eternal
life must include not only the perfecting of fellowship with
God, but also the specific attitude of the individual to the
world.   If our Reformation is really epoch-making, it must
also supply the elements of another conception of eternal life,
or blessedness, than obtained at the preceding stages of
Christian history.   In the notion of ἀφθαρσία the Greek
Church merely perpetuated an idea of blessedness derived from
the Hellenic mysteries.   By its conception of the knowledge
or vision of God the Latin Church merely gave its sanction
to the aims of the Neo-Platonic philosophy.   If the Reformation has no better and more Christian idea of eternal life
and blessedness to offer, then those mystics belonging to
the Evangelical Churches who revert to the Catholic view
are not to be blamed.

But if we take our bearings from the New Testament,
then, besides the vision of God (Heb. xii. 14), there enters
into the content of eternal life also the exercise of a royal
lordship (Rom. v. 17 ; 1 Cor. iv. 8 ; Col. iii. 3, 4 ; Jas. ii. 5 ;
Heb. xii. 28).   It is all the more worthy of note that Faustus
Socinus has given expression to this idea, since he makes no
further use of it in his system.   For recognising the chief

32

characteristic of the Divine Being is His *dominium absolutum*, and holding that the Divine image in man relates to his lordship over earthly things, Socinus concludes that the perfecting of the latter in the next life will consist in complete lordship over the refractory forces of the world.[1] But Luther had already claimed this attribute, as a consequence of justification, for the Christian life here and now: " Christianus homo omnium dominus est liberrimus, nulli subiectus." In the pages of his tract on Christian Freedom, the triad *iustitia, vita, salus* re-echoes so powerfully throughout, that one receives an impression not merely of their necessary connection, but almost of their identity. For Luther is so thoroughly conscious of life and salvation through fellowship with Christ, and in consequence of justification by faith, that for him the whole present is filled with the sense of security against death and hell. This negative aspect, however, is not the whole. But " as the Kingship of Christ is repeated in the believer, he possesses the spiritual power which reigns in the midst of foes, and is strong in the midst of afflictions. For as strength finds in weakness its uttermost test and trial, in every case we obtain salvation, so that suffering and death are forced to serve us and to work together for our salvation. This is the Christian's priceless power and freedom" (vol. i. p. 182). The one feature in this picture to which objection must be taken is the conjunction of the statements of our priesthood in the " Christian Freedom" with these statements of our kingship. Luther, commenting on 1 Pet. ii. 9, has developed the attribute of kingship before that of priesthood, clearly under the influence of the verbal sequence βασίλειον ἱεράτευμα, though he analyses this combination into *sacerdotium regale et regnum sacerdotale*. The transition to the priesthood of Christians, now, he makes thus: " Nec solum reges omnium liberrimi, sed sacerdotes quoque sumus in aeternum, quod longe regno excel-

---

[1] *Praelectiones theol.* cap. iii. (B. F. P. i. p. 539) : "Imago divina, quam in altero seculo habituri sumus, in eo constituta est, quod omnibus inimicis nostris et morti ipsi atque infero plenissime dominabimur, nec aliquid in deo praestantius est, quam cunctarum rerum dominatus atque imperium."

lentius; per sacerdotium enim digni sumus coram deo apparere, etc." But he ought to have demonstrated this pre-eminence by showing that that spiritual lordship over the world must also be subordinated causally to the unimpeded fellowship with God which is gained through justification. For if lordship over every evil is a consequence of justification by faith, then the bestowal of priestly rights and justification are identical. Luther remained oblivious of this, because he adduced the fundamental idea of priesthood—the right to appear before God—merely as the precondition of intercession on others' behalf, and of assuming the duty of instruction in Divine things. But here, as elsewhere, he is under the influence of the confused idea that the universal priesthood implies the reproduction in each individual of the official priesthood, which, however, cannot be the case. In priesthood, as a common attribute of believers, the whole stress lies on this, that each believer stands near to God, or in fellowship with Him, without the intervention of any other, save Christ ; that we employ this privilege in interceding for others is only to be regarded as a remoter consequence.

The question regarding the necessity of justification or forgiveness can only be solved by conceiving eternal life as the direct end and aim of that Divine operation. But if the idea of eternal life be applied merely to our state in the next life, then its content, too, lies beyond all experience, and cannot form the basis of knowledge of a scientific kind. Hopes and presentiments, though marked by the strongest subjective certainty, are not any the clearer for that, and contain in themselves no guarantee of the completeness of what one hopes, or has a presentiment of. Clearness and completeness of idea, however, are the conditions of comprehending anything, i.e. of understanding the necessary connection between the various elements of a thing, and between the thing and its given presuppositions. The Evangelical article of belief, therefore, that justification by faith establishes or brings with it assurance of eternal life, is of no use theologically, so long as this purposive aspect of justification

cannot be verified in such experience as is possible now. It
is true, the predominant tone of the writers of the New
Testament tends to project eternal life, under the form of
hope, into the next world, just as they limit the idea of the
Divine Kingdom to the stage of its consummation (vol. ii.
p. 295). But they point out clearly that the elements of the
future life are to be found in our present experience of joy,
blessedness, and the feeling of elevation (Jas. i. 9–12 ; 1 Pet. i.
5–9 ; Heb. vi. 5 ; cf. for Paul the use of καυχᾶσθαι, vol. ii.
p. 343) ; and just as clearly Paul reckons joy in the Holy
Ghost as part of the present reality of the Kingdom of God
(Rom. xiv. 17). But Paul also asserts definitely the present
existence of a specific life as the consequence of justification,
as indeed the connection between the two is essential. " If
Christ be in you, the body indeed is dead because of sin, but
the spirit is life because of righteousness," *i.e.* because of
justification through Christ (Rom. viii. 10). Therewith agree
the Johannine statements (1 John iii. 14, 15, v. 11–13),
which, it is true, mention no special mediation as leading to
this result, but for the same reason, too, express no divergence
from Paul in this regard.

The religious significance of " life," at both stages of the
religion of the Bible, depends on the peculiar value of this
attribute for God. The " living " God is the comprehensive
expression employed in opposing the true religion to the
natural religions, which admit sensuous representations of the
gods, or dead idols, because in them the Divine Being is not
opposed to nature. The living God, therefore, is the spiritual,
self-determining Will, which is supreme over its ends and its
creatures, and consequently must be distinguished from them
all. Life, as the religious end of the worshippers of God, is
accordingly conceived as the purposefulness of existence
attained by abiding in dependence on God under the conditions which He has ordained, and directing our path steadfastly
towards Him. These conditions are given by positive revelation. For, so far as concerns the religion of the Old Testament,
it holds fast to the universal primitive assumption that to

approach God uninvited leads to destruction; we must therefore be invited, or possess God's verbal assurance of grace, or conform to the laws of sacrifice, in order to retain life when in proximity to God (vol. ii. p. 201). At the stage of Christianity the assurance of life attaches itself to the dispensation of revelation, *i.e.* to the acknowledgment and appropriation of the end represented by the Son of God. In the Hebrew religion the belief is dominant that life in proximity to God, or under His express protection, involves the political and economic welfare of the chosen people, and, for its individual members, the harmony of happiness and merit; all the restrictions of life due to irreligious adversaries are therefore felt by the Psalmists as a deprivation of their proper life. On the other hand, the spiritual character of the Christian view of the world and self culminates in this, that those relations which fall within the compass of outward self-preservation are not reckoned as essential to the determination of "life." "Whosoever will save his life shall lose it, and whosoever shall lose it for the gospel's sake shall save it" (Mark viii. 35). The conditions of the life guaranteed by God do not even include the political intactness of the Christian Church; on the contrary, the persecutions, the menaces by which the life of the community or the individual may be assailed, are regarded rather as subjects for rejoicing (Matt. v. 11, 12; Jas. i. 2; 1 Pet. i. 6; Heb. x. 34; 1 Thess. i. 6; Rom. v. 3).

These ideas, so opposed to men's ordinary claims to life, show us that life in fellowship with God, at peace with God, and under God's protection, simply cannot be construed religiously without at the same time taking into account the relation between it and the world. In Christianity the worshippers of God know the Creator and Lord of the world as their Father, but yet regard themselves in their given individual character, especially in their corporeal endowment, as parts of the world; it is therefore to be expected that some positive principle should be set up, according to which life with God includes independence of the ordinary outward conditionedness of existence. This principle is indicated by Jesus immediately after the precept cited above : " What shall it profit a man if he should gain the whole world and lose his own life ? for what is a substitute or equivalent for his own life ? " (Mark viii. 36, 37). In this connection " life " means that state of spiritual self-determination which we distinguish from the conditions of bodily self-preservation, by relating it to common ends which are considered more valuable than bodily self-preservation. But inasmuch as voluntary fellowship with God, Who is Spirit, is regarded as the proper consummation to be reached in the line of these spiritual aims, it follows at once that the life of an individual has a higher worth than " the whole world." For God, with Whom we enter into full fellowship in religion, is high above the world, as its Creator and as He Who makes the Kingdom of God the world's one aim.

At this point the Christian view of the world exhibits a most violent paradox. The individual man is a part of the world ; and as what is individual, in its reciprocal relations to multiplicity, forms the element of the created material world, so likewise the individual created spirit can never conceive himself as outside the compass of the world or of divided existence. And therefore the idea we have of our spiritual individuality can never be separated from the idea of our bodily organism. Now, if the spiritual individual has a higher worth than the whole world, then, in such a statement, he is no longer regarded as a part of the world, but as in himself a totality which can stand being compared with the world. To make this clear, it must be observed that it is as a spirit that the individual realises the character of a whole in his own order, whereas the world, as the value of divided existence, is conceived as belonging to nature. To nature belong not merely natural objects proper, but likewise all the social institutions of spiritual life ; for all the spiritual commerce known to us is mediated through nature. Now the Christian view of the world is so constructed as to view the world as a whole from the standpoint of the Divine idea, for this enables us to raise ourselves above the world through fellowship with the Divine life (§ 27). Although even man, finding himself embedded in nature, regards himself as a limited portion of the world, yet, in virtue of his spiritual constitution and his Christian destiny, his life is a struggle to reach a position above the world. For while neither knowledge nor moral will gives him the means of reaching this goal, religion as such is the function by which the tension can be resolved between the given situation of the created spirit and his claims against the natural world. In Christianity, however, the idea of the universally human, moral Kingdom of God is posited as the final end of the world in such a way that all the natural and particular conditions of human fellowship are transcended, and humanity is raised above the world as a spiritual totality. This characteristic of the Christian religion of itself secures that each individual member of the Kingdom of God is from the first offered the possibility of becoming a totality in his own order, *i.e.* in a qualitative sense; for in the moral world, as a totality, each individual member, so far as he comes to possess moral character, is endowed with the worth of a totality. By holding out this prospect, Christianity satisfies the universal religious impulse which at previous stages fell short of its aim. But that which is prescribed, in the idea of the Kingdom of God, as the kind of moral activity proper to man, takes, in the conception of eternal life, the form of a corresponding view of the world and self, namely, that in actual fellowship with the true spiritual God the Christian feels himself as a whole raised above the world, inasmuch as he proves the spiritual worth of his individuality through his dominion over all possible restrictions arising from the divided world of nature. This attitude, which is held out as a prospect to men in the Christian religion, was deliberately and actually exemplified by its Founder (§ 49). It is intelligible, therefore, in view of the mediatorial position between God and man occupied by Jesus, that He should prescribe that one must be ready for His sake to sacrifice natural life for the maintenance of personal life or the attainment of that life, conceived as eternal life. For in that lordship over the world which He exercised, as representative of the Divine final end of the world, through His independence of all human authority and His willing acceptance and patient appropriation of suffering, He realised directly in His own person that eternal life which is opposed to the changes of natural things. By attachment to His person, and by appropriation of His aim, the same possession of eternal life is gained and Christ's attitude towards the world assumed by others also. The worth of this attitude of spirit as superior to the divided and changing world of nature is thus all the more clearly brought out by the enjoined surrender of the natural conditions of our creaturely existence. The willing acceptance of this consequence of attachment to Christ is the highest proof of that freedom, prescribed and rendered possible by Christianity, which belongs to the spiritual life as capable of perfection in its own order.

I do not know that there is any view of the world which attributes a higher value to individual human life, or any form of life of a social kind which offers a more adequate satisfaction to the universal human endeavour to transcend the natural limitations of spiritual existence. When men have sought to outdo Christianity in freedom of thought (*i.e.* surely, in appreciation of the freedom of the individual), by the method of Pantheism, or have even thought to surpass Christian freedom of thought by adopting the materialistic view of the world, they have really, as Strauss has most recently done, set in comparison with the new wisdom a merely derivative or imperfectly formulated representation of Christianity. But in its true form Christianity is directly adapted to secure the spiritual freedom of the individual, and to attain the goal that each man, in his spiritual idiosyncrasy, should become a whole ; for by connecting this, the destiny of man, with the perfect revelation of the supramundane God, that is, with the revelation of the universal final end of the world, the spiritual lordship of the members of the Divine Kingdom over the world, and their eternal life, are established. Now the principle which Jesus enunciated, and which He was

the first to realise, finds a unanimous echo in the testimonies
given by the writers of the New Testament.   By directing
our wills to God as the unchangeable Father from Whom
comes every good and nothing but good (Jas. i. 17), Who, as
the Father of our Lord Jesus Christ, claims our firm trust
unbroken by any wavering of aim (i. 5, ii. 1), we raise ourselves above the world.   For the elevation of soul, in which
the Christian glories even in his lowliness, *i.e.* in the midst of
persecution, marks him off from the real lowliness of the man
who is rich in the world, who passes away like grass before
the scorching wind (i. 9–11).   Faith, moreover, which is im-
movable and firm, and includes in itself a treasury of riches,
i.e. a peculiar amplitude of power, raises itself above the traditional conditions of worldly society, the precedence of the rich
over the poor (ii. 1–5).   What are these statements but descriptions of eternal life, in so far as it sets itself, as consisting in
a steady direction of the will towards God's end, in opposition
to the standards involved in the changeableness of worldly
life ?   For eternity, as a specific attribute of God, signifies
the permanency of the direction of His will to His personal
end (§ 37).   The same conclusion follows from Paul's assurance that the revealed love of God makes us conquerors over
the evils which come upon Christians for God's sake, because
the change from life to death, the tension between present
and future, the force, too, of natural and social institutions
personified in the angelic powers, exercise no determining
influence on the life of the Christian when compared with the
permanency of the Divine love as revealed in Christ (Rom. viii.
35–39 ; 1 Cor. iii. 21–23).   It is specially worthy of remark
that Paul makes the status of Christian teachers subordinate
to the independent powers of believers as such, although
the latter owed to the former the fact of their being Christians
at all.   Yet Christians are represented as the superiors even
of Peter and Paul, in so far as the estimation in which the
apostles are held as party-authorities might pave the way for
schism ; since believers are rather taught to find an experimental realisation of their power over the world in the unbroken

union of the religious community. For, as James testifies
again (iv. 1-4), it is by schismatic controversy that love to
the world, which is enmity against God, and therefore unworthy dependence on the world, make their way into the
Christian community. And all Church history is a confirmation of this truth.

This *potestas spiritualis*, as Luther calls it, cannot be judged
by ordinary sensible standards. On the contrary, as the
Christian community, by its universal and spiritual tendency,
roused its Jewish and heathen environment to suppress it by
force, its members, as Paul expresses it in the Psalmist's words,
were accounted as sheep for the slaughter (Rom. viii. 36), *i.e.*
as things most transitory and devoted to imminent destruction. The representatives of the Christian community, however, exhibit the power over the world which springs from
peace with God by their reversal of the common verdict upon
these evils, as upon evils in general. That which in the
ordinary view is a restriction of freedom (§ 42), and proves
itself such by exciting the feeling of pain, is invested, through
the joy which springs from peace with God—through this
expression of the harmonious feeling of life—with the precisely opposite value of a means which ministers to freedom
(Rom. viii. 28). For when these experiences of evils do not
become the occasions of apostasy from the Christian faith,
when, as temptations, they still do not lead to bodily and
social self-preservation being preferred to the duties of the
Christian vocation, then their utility actually comes to be that
of stimuli to endurance in the Christian faith, *i.e.* means to
the assertion of freedom against the world (Jas. i. 2, 3 ; Rom.
v. 3). In this way confirmation is given of Christ's verdict
that the amount of affliction is not the measure of the sin
present, and that every conspicuous calamity is not, as was
assumed by antiquity, a Divine punishment. The evils of
persecution are rather, as no feeling of guilt exists, accepted
simply as means for testing the Christian's endurance in
the faith. But from the assurance of peace with God possessed by the Christian community there arises, even in the

case of single transgressions, the habit of regarding certain evils, even persecutions, as educative punishments, which, derived as they are from God's fatherly goodness, are intended to purify practical conduct, but for that very reason imply no forfeiture of rights as regards fellowship with God (1 Pet. iv. 17–19 ; Heb. xii. 4–11 ; 1 Cor. xi. 32).   It cannot be doubted that all these characteristics of eternal life enter into Paul's conception of the freedom wherewith Christ has made us free (Gal. v. 1), and of which Paul himself was conscious in the manifold relations of social existence (Gal. ii. 4 ; 1 Cor. x. 29, ix. 1, 19).   Therefore too, conversely, the consummation of eternal life, when it is openly confirmed by God's final judgment, is described by God as the liberty of the children of God, which is called ἐλευθερία τῆς δόξης because it will be specifically acknowledged by God, and thus receive a guarantee of its consummation (Rom. viii. 21).

The result of this argument, finally, is that the combinations, which the Lutheran standards exhibit, of the idea of justification by faith with eternal life on the one hand, and with faith in God's providence on the other (§§ 18, 25), are mutually equivalent, and that the exercise of the latter faith forms the content of the status of adoption by God, while it is just under the attribute of eternal life that that content must reveal itself at first.   In the same way the faith in providence which dominates the world coincides with eternal life ; for the most general conception of life comes to this, that one thing uses other things as means to its end.   Accordingly eternal life, in the Christian sense, is that spiritual independence, possible in the realm of Divine grace, which, in harmony with God's providence, subdues all things to itself, so that they become means to blessedness, even when viewed externally they run counter to it.

§ 53. If, now, it is thinkable at all that freedom and spiritual power over the world should be mediated through *good works*, this cannot be true in the sense that they merit eternal life.   For the very fact that God calls eternal life in men into being by opening to them fellowship with Himself, excludes every consideration of law and equity (*Billigkeit*). The acquisition of eternal life has a meaning only in a religious connection; for us Christians, however, law and equity are not forms of the religious relation. Still, are not good works possibly concomitant causes of eternal life? Even this hypothesis is, to say the least, infelicitous; and to decide upon it we require a more accurate definition of our ideas. It is characteristic of Luther that in the tractate "On Christian Freedom" he should give the negative reply he does to the question. For he declares the realm of moral action to be the opposite of freedom and blessedness, so far as in good works we manifest our servitude and slavery to other men to whom we are bound by life in the body. The latter circumstance, indeed, is not an adequate argument for moral fellowship; but Luther's remark is so far quite accurate, as good works set up a connection between us and other men, who, to begin with, confront us merely as parts of the world. Viewed at this angle, good works, notwithstanding their origin in faith, and although the impulse to which they are due is spontaneous in form, occupy a position directly opposed to freedom and blessedness in God, have so far nothing in common with Him, and therefore cannot be conceived as even concomitant causes of these blessings. This truth is also verifiable by the following observation. If we intend good works pre-eminently to have an effect upon others, if, that is, we count on their being thereby stimulated to moral concord and led to enter into moral fellowship with us, we shall find, in the vast majority of cases, that the best will has no power over the result, but that in this respect we are limited by the independence of others. In such cases of reaction on the part of the world, however excellent our intention may be, we experience anything but freedom and blessedness; and if, nevertheless, we were to persevere in the method of doing good works for the sake of the expected results, we should involve ourselves in passionate impatience, and therefore also inwardly become slaves. Good *works*, therefore, when this aspect is emphasised, cannot be regarded even as concomitant causes of eternal life ; for the intention aimed at the result is fitted neither to maintain freedom nor to increase it.

Nevertheless, conceived as *good* works, they have too clear an affinity with the religious direction of the will towards God, and with the freedom over the world springing thence, for any surprise to be caused by the statement that a man is blessed in his morally good action (Jas. i. 25). To be sure, Lutheran doctrine seems to have as little room for this universal experience as for the connection, also asserted by James, between law and freedom. Luther having once for all planted his foot on the Pauline assertion that law and faith are mutually exclusive (vol. ii. p. 309), which he did not understand in its originally limited reference to the Mosaic law, but referred to the Christian life also, Lutheran theology consistently arrived at the position that action in the Holy Spirit, which is normal in the Christian sense, is not mediated by any subjective reflection upon the moral law. Here we must make allowance for the fact that Luther never arrived at the distinction between moral law and civil law, and that he always included the latter in his conception of the former, while yet he exhibited a justifiable horror of applying a legal standard either to the religious or to the moral life, to justification or to the value of good works. Thus, although good works, as fruits of the Holy Spirit, are in merely objective harmony with the law, and are not regarded as implying any subjective reflection upon this standard, they are stripped of every relation to blessedness. According to Lutheran doctrine, the experience of blessedness has no relation, either objective or subjective, to the law ; good works, which the regenerate soul as such performs, are in agreement with the law at least objectively ; in other words, they contribute nothing to blessedness. On the other hand, by the Christian law James means the law of freedom, in so far as personal disposition and attention and fidelity are devoted to it. Blessedness for him, therefore, is a feature which accompanies the fulfilment of the moral law under these conditions; for it springs from free acquiescence in God's final end. James, therefore, holds to freedom in the law, while Luther always finds freedom in the removal of the law, or at least in subjective abstraction from it. Nevertheless, Lutheran teaching approximates so closely to James' line of thought, that one cannot but think it arbitrary that it should omit the final conclusion, that one is blessed in good works. For, under the title of Christian freedom, Luther has also brought in the voluntary character of moral obedience, which realises the ends of the law apart from any legal compulsion. This idea [1] is very precisely expressed in the Formula of Concord, where it is said that believers, as regenerate, have, according to the Holy Spirit, taken the law into their hearts, and that their voluntary fulfilment of it is a life in the law.[2] It does not, indeed, exactly serve completely to elucidate this idea of voluntariness that it is compared to the motion of the sun, regular with the necessity of natural law. For a disposition which regularly issues in obligatory moral action without the necessity of forming a distinct judgment of duty for each separate act, does not therefore stamp itself as a blind natural force. But it is astonishing that the direct identity of this temper in moral conduct with the freedom and blessedness indicated by Luther was not perceived, and that not even the citation of passages from the Psalms, which express the blessedness of the study of the law, should have led to the recognition of the fact that this blessedness extends also to action arising from an unselfish disposition. The result is that, however closely Lutheranism may ap-

---

[1] Luther, *De libertate christiana*, p. 226, and Melanchthon, *Loci theol. C. R.* xxi. p. 1039, are less clear than Calvin, *Inst.* iii. 19. 4 : "Altera forma libertatis est, ut conscientiae, non quasi legis necessitate coactae, legi obsequantur, sed legis ipsius iugo liberae voluntati dei ultro obediant."

[2] *Form. Conc.*, Epit. vi. 5 : "Fructus spiritus sunt opera illa, quae spiritus dei per homines renatos operatur, et quae a credentibus fiunt, quatenus renati sunt, ita quidem sponte ac libere, quasi nullum praeceptum unquam accepissent. Et hoc modo filii dei in lege vivunt, et secundum normam legis divinae vitam suam instituunt." *Sol. decl.* vi. §§ 4, 5 : "Justificati in lege divina quotidie exercere se debent, sicut scriptum est : beatus, qui lege domini delectatur et in lege eius meditatur die ac nocte, . . . Lex divina cordibus ipsorum inscripta est."

proximate to the lines of the principle affirmed by James, it never comes to an agreement with him.

To solve this antinomy—that good works should be, on the one hand, an evidence of the bondage of men to their fellows as parts of the world, and on the other the medium of the experience of blessedness or freedom—we must put the question, *Why morally good action is necessary in Christianity at all?* What we want here is a theory in which the two pairs of reasons affirmed by the Reformers (p. 489) are combined. The universal ground of all moral conduct towards our fellow-men is that the Christian religion has for its end the Kingdom of God. This association of mankind, of the most comprehensive nature both extensively and intensively, cannot be realised otherwise than through works, concrete action, and speech. These works are good in so far as they are directed towards the universal end which guarantees the usefulness of all the members of the fellowship. Now, the moral law is the system of those ends, dispositions, and actions, which necessarily arise out of the universal end of the Kingdom of God. Love is the pervading motive of this organisation of law-determined action ; but it is also the impulse which leads to the knowledge of all those ends which are comprehended in the moral law. Now, in the Christian view of the world, the Kingdom of God is the supramundane final end of the world, an end which at the same time is fixed, by the conception of God as love, as the content of the Divine personal end. Here, therefore, the arguments put forward by the Reformers, that good works are necessary from respect to the Divine commandment and to the end of glorifying God, find their deeper unity. The two other arguments, that good works are necessary as the fruits of faith and as proofs of one's standing in grace, might also be reduced to this one. For we believe in God or trust in Him perfectly just in so far as we find our own most personal end in realising His Kingdom. However, we ought not to hide the fact that such a conclusion does not express the Reformers' meaning. At most they merely touch upon the idea of the ethical King-

dom of God, but never grasp it seriously. So that, by the
faith which produces good works and is evidenced by them,
they understand faith in redemption and reconciliation, the
faith which appropriates justification, and possesses assurance
of eternal life, to begin with, apart from good works. This
theory is transcended in the solution I have set forth. In
order to prove that solution true, we must turn our investigation of the idea of the Kingdom of God to yet one more
of its aspects.

The Kingdom of God, as God's supramundane final end
in the world, is superior, of course, to all motives which in
any way may be reckoned as belonging to the natural world.
The law of universal love transcends not only the motives
arising out of the physical self-preservation of the individual
and of the human species as such, but also the aims of
spiritual self-preservation in the particular realms of moral
fellowship, the family, civil vocation, social position, the State.
In moral action, the goodness of which is measurable by these
differentiated social ends, we are always dependent on the
natural conditions of spiritual existence in the world. This is
shown by the fact that, in all these provinces of life, with the
relative goodness of action there may also be bound up occasions
of sin. For apart from cases of purely individual selfishness,
pride of family may set itself in opposition to the moral
interests of friendship, and the interests of class in opposition
to the aims of civic existence, while national vanity and love
of power may militate against the humane recognition of the
rights of other peoples. But the principle of universal love
to men abstracts from all natural conditions and limitations
of spiritual life in common, and therefore can give no stimulus
to selfish emotions. But now the universality of the Kingdom of God as final end is proved by our having to take it
up into our particular moral aims. It operates as supreme
motive even in the conduct through which is realised fellowship with one's family, with friends, with those of the same
class, with one's countrymen. Thus we enjoy freedom from
the world, meaning by the world all those determining

motives of lower rank which constitute the dependence of spiritual life upon the elements of the natural world.[1]   For the principle of universal love, as the law both subjective and objective of the Kingdom of God, rests on the fact that men, as spiritual beings, are equal and of equal worth, while all other relations by which our spiritual life is interwoven with nature show such marks of heterogeneity that we can only in a limited sense predicate equality of them.   In the circumstances described, therefore, the acknowledgment of the Kingdom of God as the final end in the world involves the supramundane character of the motive of universal love, and carries with it the principle that conduct animated by universal love constitutes freedom over the world.

This idea is, to begin with, not unrelated to that conception of freedom in which the human spirit as such finds the essence of its self-distinction from nature.   Freedom, as independence of natural causes, as itself the cause which breaks the chain of natural causes operating upon us, we feel to be real when, by the universal conception of an end, we stop and deprive of their power those impulses to action which arise from the correspondence between individual propensities and the " goods " of the world, and which represent one element of natural necessity.   The higher experience of freedom consists in this, that through the conception of a personal end we completely moderate and order our particular impulses in general, so that they are allowed free course only in the degree and at the time that they serve as a means to the final end we have in our mind.   This stage of freedom, however, is not the highest, for the personal end by which the several sensuous or spiritual impulses are controlled may be bad as well as good.   The different species of vice or of systematic selfishness, in which the personal end is

---

[1] On this point we have a controversy with Catholicism of the following kind. In the Catholic form of Christianity, the universal Christian morality of the Kingdom of God is realised in monasticism, *i.e.* outside the natural and particular provinces of the family, friendship, fellowship in civic vocation, and the State. The consequence is that the universal morality of Christianity becomes in monasticism a barren or even a pernicious particularism. For it is in the particular, not alongside or outside of it, that the universal finds its realisation.

confined to the satisfaction of a single propensity, and the different stages of a morally good character, which are devoted to social aims, are identical in the feature mentioned. The highest stage of freedom, therefore, will be that at which the supremely universal end of the association of mankind is made the personal end, and brought into relation with narrower forms of fellowship; for from an end such as this there can arise no stimulus to selfishness, whether coarser or more refined. Accordingly, that freedom over the world as a system of nature, which is manifested in practical life in the Kingdom of God, not merely lies in the line of that conception of freedom which can be affirmed in general, but forms the climax which freedom must of necessity be conceived as reaching if we are to have a complete idea of it at all.

The demonstration just given is a refutation of Kant's position regarding the intelligible and non-empirical sense of freedom. Freedom is not merely an idea which we employ to judge our action—action, however, which experience shows not to be free, but determined at every step; freedom is itself experience. And while each act is motived, and springs from its motive necessarily, yet in varying measure those actions are free whose motive is the universal conception of an end which lays a restraining hand on the very impulse it has aroused. Kant's conclusion was not merely theoretically unsatisfactory, in so far as it left unsolved the contradiction between the subjective claim to be free and the objective fact that action forms part of the causal nexus; it was practically useless as well, for it left no possibility open of action's guiding itself by the law produced by freedom. On the other hand, this very connection asserted by Kant between freedom and the moral law is confirmed by the highest form of freedom as set forth above. The moral law, as the system of those dispositions, intentions, and actions which follow necessarily from the all-embracing end of the Kingdom of God and from the subjective motive of universal love (§ 32), cannot be codified so as to decide, in each possible case of morally good action, that such action is necessary. This is a consequence of the divergence which exists between the character of the disposition and the form the particular action may assume, a divergence which cannot be removed.   For an objective regular norm may quite well be found for the general disposition in those correct inferences which follow from the ends comprised in the Kingdom of God; but no provision is contained therein for prescribing when we must act in accordance with this disposition, and when not.   And so, whether in a particular given case it is necessary and a duty to act according to the general disposition indicated by the moral law, needs to be settled by a judgment guided by the particular circumstances. The formation of the idea of duty, accordingly, is conditioned not merely by the general disposition to obey the moral law, but also by the special virtues of conscientiousness, wisdom, and circumspection.   But since the idea of duty represents the ramification of the general moral law into particular actions, the result is that freedom in this sense is the basis of the moral law, in other words, the basis of the application of the general principle to the particular cases of necessary action. Without the acquisition of moral freedom in the form of a good general disposition and of a development of special virtues, therefore, the moral law not only cannot be carried out, but cannot even in its whole range be known and objectively fixed.   It is further to be considered, however, that the variable element in moral existence does not consist merely in those particular cases of action, as contrasted with which the virtue and disposition acquired might be viewed as unconditionally immutable.   On the contrary, the contrast is merely relative.   Even virtue, even the general moral disposition, is variable; they may be falsified, and they may be injured, if at any stage they are regarded as mechanically complete. They continue to exist only in so far as they are being perpetually reproduced.   But this takes place only when the will, bent upon the universal moral end, ever anew actually produces for itself knowledge of the moral law, and therewith the law itself; for the law does not exist for us apart from our knowledge of it.

In these respects the autonomy claimed by Kant for the will which aims at the moral law is vindicated. The same autonomy proves to be a quality of the Christian law, although Kant himself regards Divine authority as a mark of heteronomy. But in the Christian view, Divine authority is very far from involving necessarily a statutory and merely objective form of the moral law. For the principle of universal love to man does not claim acceptance originally in the form of an objective rule, but is at work in the subjective disposition of the Founder of our religion. It was capable of being expressed as an objective formula because Christ regarded it as the law of the Kingdom of God He was going to found, and as the motive of the action He devoted to it, and because He took for granted that the members of the community of Christ, believing in God as their Father, consistently resolve likewise to obey the Lord of the Kingdom. Now the grade and the character of the moral law are shown by the fact that the final end, from which it receives its form, transcends the natural and particular, in other words, the secular conditionedness of the spiritual life. In the principle of universal love to man, the motives of natural relationship in family and nation, and the natural alliance arising from the relations of class and vocation, are limited so far that they do not militate against the fellowship of spiritual life or the true dignity of man which is in question. Or rather, while we regularly move and have our being in intercourse with our family, with those who belong to the same class, and with our fellow-countrymen, our limited natural goodwill towards them is idealised by our universal regard for the human dignity common to all. In social action for the final end of the Kingdom of God, too, no validity belongs to forms of egoism which might, owing to the struggle for pleasure and rewards, have the effect of forcing good action into the position of means to an alien end. Ideally interpreted, therefore, action for the supernatural final end of the Kingdom of God does not admit that other mark of heteronomy which is excluded by Kant from his conception of the absolute moral law.

The voluntariness of action for the end of the Kingdom of God, however, which properly should pervade our conduct in all the narrower provinces of life, is homogeneous with the manifestations of our religious freedom over the world. The final end, by which such action is guided, is as much supramundane as the attitude taken up by one whose general mood is so little affected by the opposition between happiness and suffering, by the changes of surrounding things, and the possible demands of human authority, that it preserves its identity in spite of them. The homogeneity of both aspects of the Christian life rests, too, upon a single ground, namely, on the commanding importance of the idea of God as supramundane, gracious, and benevolent. Since, therefore, eternal life and blessedness are experimentally enjoyed in this elevation of the feeling of self over the world, the motivation of action by the supramundane end of the Kingdom of God is necessarily reflected in blessedness.   James, therefore, is not quite right when he says that the man who fulfils the law of freedom is *blessed in his deed*.   But what he does express quite precisely in these words is the truth that blessedness accompanies a good deed which springs from the supreme motive, and not from a calculation of the result.   For by acting in the latter way we should impose upon ourselves a limitation of freedom, and so far experience not blessedness, but its opposite.   Finally, we gain here still another argument against the view that good works can merit eternal life.   For if good action, under the conditions prescribed above, produces blessedness—in such a way, namely, that it is to us an experience of eternal life—the two cannot enter into experience in the form of the legal equivalents, service and reward.

The homogeneity which has been proved between the content of the self-feeling of the Christian as free from the world, and action from the supramundane motive of the

Kingdom of God, serves to demonstrate the principle followed by the Reformers, that the Divine revelation given in Christianity both guarantees reconciliation with God, or liberation from the world, or eternal life, and imposes the duty of good works. Only when the homogeneity of both aspects is recognised can we justify the formula which adds the one to the other. But we certainly now gain also a criterion by which to test the proposition that good works are not to be taken as concomitant causes of eternal life. This, of course, is not true, if it is meant as coming under the category of merit and reward. But still good works and eternal life are not so unrelated to one another as Lutheran doctrine strives to make out. As the disposition which finds its motive in the supramundane end of the Kingdom of God itself comes within the compass of eternal life, therefore *good* works are, for one thing, manifestations of eternal life; but further, according to the law that the exercise of a power serves to strengthen and maintain it, they are organs of eternal life. Thus is proved the truth of St. Bernard's dictum : *non causa regni, sed via regnandi.* Moreover, the homogeneity of both sides is shown by their peculiar interaction or mutual conditionedness. On the one hand, the action which finds its motive in the supramandane end of the Kingdom is necessarily subject to the influence of the experiences yielded by Christian freedom. In order to impress this final end vividly on the disposition, and to act in accordance with it, one needs that joyous feeling which removes the disabling and confining sense of evils, one needs freedom from care about the future, independence of social prejudices, and superiority to the fascination of success. On the other hand, action for the end of the Kingdom of God is necessary in order to prove, through the experience of blessedness which it yields, that eternal life, even in the directly religious feeling of self, is no passive possession, but that the Divine bestowal of this religious freedom over the world is really the only thing which makes possible the independence of one's personal spiritual feeling.

All these discussions, however, are not sufficient to remove the impression that Christianity issues in two ideals for man, of which the one cannot be reduced to the other. It does not seem possible to get beyond what was assumed in this respect in our provisional description of the Christian religion (§ 2), namely, that it has for its aim the spiritual freedom, and the most comprehensive moral fellowship, of men. But while Luther, in his tract on Christian Freedom, affirms this two-sidedness, though in a somewhat harsh form, he offers at the same time another view of the matter, when with all his successors he adopts the affirmation of Paul (Gal. v. 6), that love is the necessary consequence of reconciling faith. For that implies that the determination to act for the final end of the Kingdom of God finds its sufficient ground in the fact of reconciliation with God. Now this position is not directly obvious when brought into comparison with Luther's view, that in faith we address ourselves to God, and in action to men. It deserves to be opposed for this further reason, however, that the attainment of that freedom over the world, which is involved in faith in our reconciliation with God, makes each single believer appear as a whole in his own order, while in action for the Kingdom of God he possesses the significance merely of a part of the whole. How, then, is a sufficient basis to be found for this converse relation in the religious self-feeling, that as a whole in his own order a man is worth more than the whole world?

On the other hand, we must remember that the relation of the individual to the fellowship of the Kingdom of God, for whose good he acts, is not exhausted by the distinction of the part and the whole. Rather, it follows from the very nature of an ethical organism, that within it every properly articulated part counts as a whole. Any activity of a part in the service of the whole is a means of furthering the welfare of the whole, only when the aim of the whole is present in the mind as the motive of action. The individual subject, however, who in his special vocation acts from a good disposition for the promotion of the whole, himself acquires, through his thus conditioned development in moral character, the significance of a whole in his own order. Now in the morally good character there must be reckoned, not merely the permanent self-determination to act in accordance with the supramundane final end of the Divine Kingdom, but also that religious independence of the world through which a man first becomes conscious that in worth he is superior to the world. Independence of the world, then, or the Christian freedom which religious faith enjoys, must at the same time involve the power of bringing into play the supramundane motive of universal love to man, *if* what is called for is the practical exercise of fellowship with men. But just this side of the matter is unprovided for in the faith of the individual, who through his fellowship with God has experience of eternal life. Love, therefore, follows from faith in reconciliation only because the God in whom we put our faith has for His final aim the union of men in the Kingdom of God. Even thus, therefore, we fail to transcend the twofold aspect of Christianity.

To attain this end, perhaps we should have to introduce yet another consideration. On the one hand, the common moral end posited in Christianity is embraced in its religious aspect; for in the Kingdom of God, as God's most personal end, what we do is, ultimately, to serve God; on the other hand, freedom from the world, or eternal life as experienced in faith, is likewise adapted to the intercourse and fellowship of men within the Kingdom of God. Reconciliation with God, too, and our corresponding freedom over the world, are not merely a uniform characteristic of all individuals alike, but the common quality through which a plurality forms a whole. But in order to secure this end, in order that each individual should experience reconciliation and Christian freedom over the world, not merely for himself but in his feeling of unity with all others, and in order that these common experiences should be truthfully expressed in prayer, it is necessary that mutual union should be sought

by means of action in every direction from the motive of
universal love to men. Whoever, accordingly, is by faith
assured of his reconciliation, and at the same time desires
to experience it as a possession of the community, has here
a motive for seeking, by the exercise of love, union with
those whom he needs to complete his social feeling of reconciliation. On this presupposition we can understand the
statement that faith in reconciliation operates through love.
But were we to follow out the line of this proposition, we
might possibly come to the conclusion that we do good in
order to enjoy the common blessedness. Such a conclusion
would not violate the principle that the Kingdom of God
must always be conceived as the final end. For that Kingdom
proves itself to be the highest good by the fact that in the
realisation of it we and all others are blessed together. The
above proposition, therefore, must not be regarded as inadmissible ; still, it does not exhaust the matter. Rather must
action for the end of the Kingdom of God be directly deduced
from the truth that we acknowledge this final end of God
in believing in the Father of Jesus Christ. What we gain
thereby, however, is not a simple subsumption of the ethical
under the religious aspect of Christianity. And this conclusion, finally, is confirmed by the following consideration.

The Pauline formula, that faith worketh by love, ought
not at all to be understood in the sense of a simple logical
deduction, or in the sense of mechanical necessity. Belief
in such a connection between love and faith is refuted not
only by the fact that an obvious lack of love to man may be
accompanied by an eminent degree of faith in reconciliation,
but also by the consideration that love appears in the form
of a personal resolve which is not as yet present in faith in
reconciliation. For after all the direct relations of the two
are different : faith faces towards God, and love towards man.
So far, however, as faith in reconciliation seeks in reconciliation fellowship with others by manifesting loving action
towards them, this forms a more secondary motive, which
is no substitute for the special resolve to exercise love.

Thus, love to men and good works do not follow directly from faith in so far as faith experiences reconciliation with God as an individual and social possession; rather do they follow from faith in so far as it appropriates the final end of the Kingdom of God, as the personal end of the God with whom we know ourselves reconciled. But if in conscious faith these aspects are accompanied by different feelings, namely, feelings of peace and of stimulus, then we cannot get beyond the difference and the alternation of the religious and the moral effects of Christianity. The moral impulse, though ultimately it is based on the thought of God, is not exhausted by the religious experience of reconciliation and of freedom over the world. The ethical necessity of love engendered by faith, which is the only necessity that can be affirmed, still retains the peculiar character belonging to the moral resolve by which the man who is reconciled to God accepts the task of the Kingdom of God. The moral necessity of this connection, however, follows from the fact that the same God both guarantees reconciliation and freedom from the world, and bestows the impulse to help in realising the Divine Kingdom. The heterogeneity of the two aspects of the Christian life, however, is balanced in the subjective result—that we are blessed in the experience that all things serve for our good, and that we are blessed in doing good. This feeling is therefore the same in both cases; for, in the experience of Christian freedom, as in action prompted by the motive of the Divine Kingdom, we occupy a position superior to those natural and particular conditions of life which are comprised in the conception of the world. When Luther adopted the maxim of Paul, that where faith reigns love likewise developes, he could not accept this rule, which it is impossible always to verify empirically, without indirectly admitting also the truth of James' saying, that we are blessed in doing good. Consequently, the authors of the Formula of Concord, following in his track almost arrived at the same principle; and this truth failed to receive public recognition at their hands, only because they thought there was a greater danger of its being misused.

§ 54. The question regarding *the necessity of the idea of justification* or forgiveness points, *first*, to that combination of it with eternal life which is accepted not only by Luther, but also by the Socinians;[1] *second*, to the position which is given to this operation of Divine grace [justification], as the principle of the entire Christian life, by Luther and his followers as against the Socinians. In order to determine the conception of eternal life, Luther gathered together, under the conception of Christian freedom, all those indications used by New Testament writers to describe the true elevation of believers about the world; and at the same time he demonstrated the presence in the believer of a freedom or voluntariness of moral action which is homogeneous with that freedom. Calvin also gives expression to the latter idea.[2] In the circle over which his influence extended, however, they failed to reach that more special formulation of this truth which is given in the Formula of Concord (p. 510), namely, the autonomy of moral action. By the special emphasis which it laid upon the duty of sanctification within the community, Calvinism was led to give the regulation of moral action the impress of statutory law. It never sought to bridge over the gulf between this and the recognition of the voluntariness of action which rises out of faith and the Holy Spirit,[3] though more accurate thought would soon make clear the incongruity of these two views. Nay more, in Puritanism the pedantic conception of statutory law, which was most characteristically evinced by the prohibition of images and the Sabbath law, was carried still further in the principle that it

---

[1] *Catech. Racor.* 453: "Iustificatio est, cum nos deus pro iustis habet, quod ea ratione facit, cum nobis et peccata remittit et nos vita aeterna donat."

[2] *Inst.* iii. 19. 4: "Conscientiae legis ipsius iugo liberae voluntati dei ultro obediunt."

[3] *Conf. Helv.* post. 16: "Docemus vere bona opera enasci ex fide viva per spiritum sanctum et a fidelibus fieri secundum voluntatem et regulam verbi dei . . . Diximus autem antea, legem dei, quae voluntas dei est, formulam nobis praescribere bonorum operum."

is essentially as Lawgiver that Christ exercises His kingly office (p. 425). As compared with Calvinism, Lutheranism attained to deeper knowledge on this point, in that it identified the voluntariness of moral action due to the Holy Spirit with the taking up of the law into the disposition. But this principle has not been developed theoretically, and from other considerations the idea that the form of the law is statutory still remains firmly established in Lutheran orthodoxy also. We ought not, therefore, to exaggerate the difference between the two Confessions on this point, as though it were possible to prove a qualitative distinction between them in ethical temperament. Calvinists and Lutherans are at one in acknowledging in principle the voluntariness of moral action springing from the Holy Spirit and from faith in reconciliation; in this view they are united against the Socinians. The proof I am going to attempt of the Reformers' conception of justification requires that, first of all, the leading features of Socinianism should be contrasted with the Lutheran and Calvinistic doctrine.

The Socinian system likewise testifies to the closest relation between justification and eternal life. The latter blessing is made dependent on the condition of faith, and thus derived from God's free bounty in such a way that human merit is excluded. But eternal life is not merely limited to the next world; in accordance with the view of the Middle Ages, it is also represented as man's supernatural goal, and this in such a way as to give it no place in the conception of created human nature. Moreover, the obedience which consists in fulfilling the law is reckoned as part of the faith which attains eternal life. But the forgiveness of sins, or the removal of the penalties which have been incurred, is, as a condition of eternal life, at times distinguished from it, at times combined with it, in order that the deficiency of imperfect fulfilment of the law may be raised to the level of the perfection of eternal life. For the Socinians find Christianity objectively in its perfect commandments and its perfect promises of eternal life and the Holy Spirit, Who implants the hope of life eternal, provided that the Divine commandments are fulfilled, at least so far as the power of the individual will allow.   These principles of Christianity, viewed as an ethical school which still admits certain accidental religious features, mark out good action as the principal thing. But good action is kept firmly to the lines of statutory law. And this law is not construed as possessing merely genuinely moral contents: it is viewed as containing also the ceremonial commandments which inculcate the worship of God by means of the Lord's Prayer and the Eucharist.   Now, between the fulfilment of this duty and the supernatural goal of eternal life, no necessary and material relation, no point of identity, is demonstrated.   The two are just as unrelated to one another as, in the Socinian theory, the nature of God and the nature of man; they are only conjoined with one another by the arbitrary will of God.   Even the adoption in Ethics [1] of the Aristotelian idea of virtue is not sufficient to annul or to counterbalance this eudaemonistic conjunction of good conduct and blessedness.   What becomes clear, rather, is that this predominantly ethical representation of Christianity is a system of heteronomy, just as certainly as its roots are to be found in purely mediaeval motives. As regards the chief point, too, it falls very far short of the Lutheran doctrine that, as subjects of Christian faith, we live in the law and continually reproduce the law for ourselves through the Holy Spirit, inasmuch as we voluntarily act for the common final end marked out by love.

But without departing from these lines, other features of Christian freedom, far richer and more complete, have been drawn from the New Testament sources.   The human will, which in Christianity is directed to the final end of the Kingdom of God, which transcends all natural or particular motives of moral action, proves itself to have attained the highest conceivable level of freedom, both by the independence of its motive from the natural texture of both indi-

---

[1] Ioh. Crell, *Ethices seu doctrinae de moribus prolegomena.   Ethica christiana*, B. F. P. tom. iv.

vidual and social life, and by the fact that it is guided by a
free knowledge of the moral law, through which it perpetually produces that law.   For the moral law exists completely
only as a network of those judgments of duty which determine the necessary form of good action in each particular
case; the judgment of duty in this sense, however, is always
the product of an independent application of the universal
law, through particular moral principles, to the individual's
situation at the moment in the moral society.   This moral
autonomy, however, is necessary for this special reason, that
the law of universal love to our neighbour is altogether
incapable of being drawn out into a statutory series of
general commandments, for it is addressed, in the first place,
not to our actions, but to our disposition.   Now the meaning
of this truth comes out in the distinction between legal and
moral action, and serves to mark off the moral law from all
kinds of civil law, both in conception and in practical
application.   For the principle of autonomy not only holds
good within the circle of the universal moral law as such ;
we likewise act autonomously in each particular province of
life, even in that of law and of the State, in so far as we
deduce the principle of obedience to the statutory law, and
the judgments of duty which embody it, from the validity of
the universal moral law.   On the other hand, even Divine
authority does not imply the heteronomous character of the
Christian moral law, for it lacks the statutory quality on
which that character depends, and excludes all egoistical
regard for purely individual pleasure or reward.

   This freedom of action, of which the believer becomes
capable as a member of the Kingdom of God, is homogeneous
with those religious functions through which he gives effect
to the attitude of superiority to the world rendered possible
to him in Christianity (p. 516).   Both sides belong together,
as certainly as Christianity is *par excellence* the ethical
religion.   The separate elements of the two sides, on closer
observation, likewise display features of interaction (p. 518).
But at the same time it becomes clear that, as a whole

and in principle, the religious functions—trust in God, humility and patience, thanksgiving and petition to God— through which the believer, according to the teaching of Luther, maintains his position against the world, take precedence of the series of moral functions in which we devote ourselves directly to man.   For, in the first place, Christianity as a whole is a religion; in particular, it is the specifically moral religion.   The religious functions peculiar to it, therefore, are the organs of the Christian life, which assume control of our moral actions.   Now, since the latter are characterised by the fact that their motive lies in the idea of the Kingdom of God, no one can make this conjunction save he who sets his trust throughout in God as his Father ; for this is the form in which he first really believes in the Kingdom of God as the destiny which rightly is his.   Moreover, connected moral action in this province requires that we should be assured of our position as against the world, so far as this is possible, in view of the human weakness which still remains to us.   We cannot with confidence undertake that self-abnegation and patience and long-suffering towards men which form a chief part of moral duty, unless through religious trust in God's guidance we are a match for, or rather superior to, those obstacles, small and great, which nature and human society present.   That an action is good and beneficial to the person whom it concerns, depends not only on our good disposition and intention, but also on the gladness which, through trust in God, we extract from our circumstances, which for the most part run counter to such a tone of feeling.   Stephan Praetorius has given striking expression to this thought: " It is impossible that a strong and glad temper, thanksgiving, and a willing new obedience can follow where blessedness does not precede, and the Spirit of Christ is not present.   This basis must be laid ere good works can be brought forth and built up in us." [1]   Nay more, experience proves that through diligence

---

[1] *Morgenröthe evangelischer Weisheit*, vol. i. p. 789, of the collection of treatises cited vol. i. p. 532 of this work.

in a good life-work, in the exercise of a calling that furthers
the common weal, we can banish hindrances to joy which
harassed us when at the beginning of the day we entered
on its duties.   But as a whole, the statement of James needs
to be supplemented to the effect that we are already blessed
in doing what is good, because we greet the law of freedom
with that joy which, in principle, is a possession of the
Christian in his situation amid the temptations of the world.

Despite the homogeneity which characterises the supramundane nature of the morality of the Kingdom of God,
and dominion over the world through trust in God and
patience, these religious functions have the precedence, for
they condition the correlative moral posture of the mind.
Thus the primary content of eternal life or blessedness is
to be found in those religious functions which dominate
the world.   Why, now, is the forgiveness of sins by God,
the removal of guilt, necessary to this end ?   The answer
must be sought along the lines of the theory set forth in
the *Apology of the Augsburg Confession* (§ 25).   Sin is unrighteousness, crime, etc., viewed in their wrong relation to
God.   This relation may be measured either by the contradiction between the action, the intention, the disposition, and
the law of God, or by the contradiction between these
and the authority which God exercises over man through
His providence or care.   Now this alternative, it is true,
is a false one.   For the validity of Divine law always presupposes the recognition of the authority which God acquires
as man's Benefactor and Provider (vol. i. p. 200).   Thus
the basal form of sin, in which it offends against religion,
is the lack of reverence, or indifference towards God, and
the lack of trust, or positive distrust of God.   These two
marks of sin which, in the Augsburg Confession and its
Apology, Melanchthon undertakes, though vainly, to prove
the basal form of sin even in the case of original sin
(p. 341), shade off from one another, and therefore have
no place in original sin, which is posited as in all cases
identical.   For a lack of reverence towards God always

includes as well a lack of trust in Him ; but, on the other hand, there may be a lack of trust in God coexisting with reverence towards Him. This distinction, on the whole, coincides with the distinction which relates to guilt against God. For in the first case we must allow for a dulness in the feeling of guilt, while in the second case that feeling is present, perhaps even in an accentuated degree. But when there is added to it a lack of trust towards God, what we have then is just that complicated condition of guilt, that separation from God, that bondage to the world, against which man cannot assert himself with his own resources, for it supplies him with all the motives which impel him to act and strive. If, now, in place of this condition there is to come its exact opposite, trust in God, not audaciously and arbitrarily and prematurely entertained, but pervaded by reverence towards Him—trust, moreover, which introduces the soul to the promises and the tasks of the Kingdom of God, and thus brings his will to direct itself to God's end, and which, finally, makes the motives which spring from the world subordinate to the Divine final end—then his sin must be forgiven, and his guilt removed. And indeed we must here go back to the judgment of God, which makes it possible for one who, by appropriating the Divine judgment, becomes a believer, to form the corresponding estimate of himself. For a material, mechanical transformation of the sinner is altogether unthinkable, and is out of place, where what is at issue between him and God is his guilty relationship to God. For this relationship is simply *not* taken away when the sinner is made righteous mechanically—that is, say, through the infusion of love. Through the remission of guilt, through pardon, however, the sinner who appropriates it obtains the right, in virtue of his trust in the God whose authority he thus acknowledges, to approach Him, and to set himself above the world, which is no longer for him his ultimate source of impulse. And thus the argument carried on in the Augsburg Confession and its *Apology*, on lines suggested by Rom. v., is proved true and necessary.

34

This proof, it is true, is nothing but a demonstration of the harmony of the ideas which are bound up together in the Christian view of the world and the Christian estimate of self. The man who altogether rejects this system of ideas will find this proof meaningless too.   A refutation of contrary views, or an indirect proof of the necessity of forgiveness, cannot be undertaken unless the opponent concedes at least one element in the Christian view of the world and of self.   Such a concession he makes, when with Kant he finds in the moral union of men by the law of human worth the final end which is in the world and above the world, and recognises in freedom the volitional cause which out of itself produces the absolute law, independently of motives arising from natural causes.   For these ideas are valid in Christianity also, or rather it was on Christianity that Kant modelled them.   But just in so far as they ignore the supramundane worth of moral fellowship, the correlative authority of the moral law, and its correspondence with the specific conception of freedom, Socinianism and the *Aufklärung* and ordinary Rationalism remain entirely unaffected by an indirect proof of the validity in principle of the forgiveness of sin.   The statutory law in Socinianism is always concerned merely with the action of the individual, and its acknowledgment of the lordship of Christ does not imply any idea of moral fellowship as a totality.   Here there is no perception of the full importance of the law, for the form given to it is statutory, and no necessary relation is shown to exist between obedience to it and the eternal life which is promised.   Under these circumstances, even the forgiveness of sins which is acknowledged serves only to weaken the obligatory character of the law.   For if forgiveness implies that God, with eternal life in view, regards the imperfect obedience of each individual as perfect, this seems only a roundabout way of reaching the principle of the *Aufklärung*, that God demands no more from anyone than he is in a position to render in virtue of his individual endowments and his particular situation in life (vol. i. p. 393).   This maxim, however, is a direct consequence of the fundamental tenet of the Wolffian Ethics—that the individual subject as such has for his task the perfecting of his own being in harmony with the law of nature. If this be our starting-point, it is likewise impossible to discover the possibility and the necessity of moral fellowship as a whole in its own order and a possession of supreme worth ; and therefore the necessity in principle of the forgiveness of sins can never be proved to the subject who is thus thrown upon his own resources, and condemned to seek a merely relative morality.

The general necessity of the religious idea of forgiveness or justification thus results from the presupposition which appraises sin as guilt, and as indifference and mistrust towards God ; as also from its teleological relation to eternal life, or that freedom over the world which is possible when man, instead of being separated from God and perpetually opposing His end, comes to cherish trust towards Him, and to have his will positively bent upon the promotion of His end. This radical change involved in reconciliation with God religious knowledge can derive from God alone, and that, too, in the most general sense, from the gracious will of God, the originality and autonomy of which is expressed in the form of the synthetic judgment :—the sinner is right with God, he belongs to God, he is brought near to God. As expressions of objective knowledge these propositions would be absurd, even if used by God Himself ; as expressions of His will, the religious estimate of self can never conceive them apart from the result, that the sinner justified by God, or reconciled with Him, is brought to seek the Divine end. But under the circumstances described, this change in aim means, in the first instance, nothing but this, that human life, for the sake of God and of salvation, is to be raised above the motives which spring from the world. The application of this result to the conduct of life in particular, to the liberation of self-feeling from the restrictions of the world, to the acquisition of patience, further to the liberation of the moral disposition from sinful impulses and from the statutory interpretation of the moral law, to the production of a facility in moral action prompted by universal love to one's neighbour—this is not attained without strain and inward conflict, and not without manifold intermediate causes. The moral necessity of these experiences of personal freedom, due to the Divine act of religious deliverance, is certain ; but it is subject to still other conditions than is the logical synthesis by which our theoretical knowledge attaches these consequences to the Divine end, which the sinner appropriates as his own in undergoing the experience of justification or forgiveness by God.

Reference has been made (vol. ii. p. 355) to the fact that Paul deduces Christian freedom — the experimental content of which coincides with what is meant by eternal life — from the same act of Christ to which elsewhere he ascribes justification or forgiveness (Gal. v. 1), but that in other passages he brings freedom into connection with the Spirit of God as the Holy Spirit (Gal. iii. 14, iv. 5, 6 ; 2 Cor. iii. 17 ; Rom. viii. 2, 14–16). It has also been remarked that the conjunction of the Spirit of God in believers with their freedom does not imply that the nexus is a causal one. The co-operation of the Holy Spirit does not in this case involve any obscuration of the fact that freedom is derived from the act of justification dependent on the work of Christ. But since, nevertheless, the influence of the Holy Spirit and the fact of freedom cannot be unrelated to one another in the experience of the same subject, we must look for light to another combination of ideas employed by Paul. The hope of eternal life which issues from justification (Rom. v. 2) is witnessed to within us by the working of the Holy Spirit (viii. 13, 23). Thus the Holy Spirit, and our exercise in Him of self-sanctification, is the ground whereby we know the certainty of eternal life. Now, as a matter of fact, no distinction can be drawn between this certainty and the practical expression of Christian freedom over against the world. Thus the Holy Spirit, which coexists with freedom, is conceived by Paul precisely as the ground of our knowledge of freedom, not as the real ground of its existence. But

now, what is meant by the Holy Spirit ?   The determination
of this idea has been neglected by theology to such an extent
that I cannot here, as we rapidly pass on, overtake the work
which the question demands.   Neglect of the subject has had
this unfortunate practical consequence, that theologians either
abstain from using the idea altogether, or understand by it a
kind of resistless natural force which runs athwart the regular
course of knowledge and the normal exercise of the will.   In
Paul's usage of the idea, he identifies the knowledge—
common to Christian believers—of God as their Father, Who
proves His love to them through Christ (Gal. iv. 6 ; Rom. viii.
15, v. 5 ; 1 Cor. ii. 11, 12), and their knowledge of His Son
as our Lord (1 Cor. xii. 3), with the function of self-knowledge
peculiar to God Himself, because the knowledge of God
which is possible to Christians is at one with the knowledge
which God has of Himself.   Accordingly, the Holy Spirit is
described by Paul as the power, common to all Christians, of
righteous conduct and of self-sanctification, or the formation of
moral character (Rom. viii. 4, 13), which finds its motive in
that perfect knowledge of God (p. 22).   Although in this
reference he points to the involuntariness of our knowledge
of God as Father as a regular feature of it, yet he represents
its ecstatic mode as neither the only nor the highest form of
the knowledge of God.   For if the whole of moral practice
is derived from the Holy Spirit, this implies that the
knowledge of God as our Father acts as the motive of
the disposition from which spring righteousness and sanctification.   This, however, is consistent ; for the Christian consciousness that God in Christ is our Father necessarily
includes the practical recognition of the final end of the
Kingdom of God.

Under these circumstances, it would cause us no surprise
whatever were freedom over the world in religious experience
also causally connected with the Holy Spirit of God.   For
this freedom follows from our reception, through justification,
into the fellowship of God, in such wise that in common we
find in God our Father and in His love the ultimate ground

of our attainment of freedom.   To think of the influence of
the Holy Spirit, in this connection, as a resistless natural
force is absolutely forbidden; for freedom over the world,
under all circumstances, must be learned, acquired, fought for.
The above view, indeed, has yet another ground to recommend
it.   Our knowledge and invocation of God as our Father
in the Holy Spirit is the effect of our reception as children
of God through the judgment of adoption; our freedom over
the world is the effect of the Divine judgment affirming our
justification by God our Father in Christ.   These judgments
passed by God are in point of fact identical (§ 18); thus,
too, our knowledge of God as our Father, and our freedom
over the world, are related to one another simply as the
different sides of the same experience.   And as, nevertheless,
freedom over the world is dependent on our union to God in
Divine sonship (Rom. viii. 21), so its basis, too, may properly
be placed in the Holy Spirit.   We should be forbidden to
take this view only if the influence of the Holy Spirit had
always to be conceived as applying to moral action.   For
experiences of freedom over the world are not related to the
course of moral activity as its consequences, even though they
are conditioned by the proper exercise of that activity (§ 53).
Thus, the freedom over the world enjoyed by believers, on the
ground that their fellowship with God has been established
through justification by God, likewise issues from the Holy
Spirit, for justification is at the same time the reception of
sinners into Divine Sonship, and it is in the power of the
Holy Spirit that we give expression to our common acknowledgment of God as our Father.

   1. Justification, or the forgiveness of sins, signifying as
it does in principle that the relation of men to God is
changed from the separation due to the feeling of guilt and
mistrust, and from the opposition or enmity of sin, into the
fellowship of trust and peace with God, has for its immediate
end the introduction of men into the enjoyment of eternal life,
which is present in our experiences of freedom or lordship over
the world, and in the independence of self-feeling both from

the restrictions and from the impulses due to natural causes or to particular sections of society.

2. Although no part of the direct aim of justification, or the forgiveness of sins, is the production of morally good action—for the latter finds its proximate motive in the supra-mundane final end of the Kingdom of God—still the freedom of the moral disposition from statutory law, a freedom which manifests itself in the continual production of the moral law in the form of special principles and particular judgments of duty, is a function similar in kind to religious freedom over the world, in the exercise of which without regard to result there is also given an experience of eternal life ; in this respect, therefore, the course of moral action is conditioned by justification or reconciliation.

3. Justification, as the reception into God's fellowship of sinners conscious of their guilt and formerly destitute of trust in God, and reconciliation, as the directing of the hitherto sinful will to the universal final end of God Himself, are, as the fundamental precondition of the Christian life, necessary in order to explain the fact that believers, through trust in God, humility, and patience, occupy that position of supremacy over the world which constitutes eternal life, and in which is experienced that blessedness which is in harmony with the God Who rules over the world as our Father through Christ.

CHAPTER VIII

THE NECESSITY OF BASING THE FORGIVENESS OF SINS ON
THE WORK AND SUFFERING OF CHRIST

§ 55. THE validity of the Divine forgiveness of sins is recognised as a necessary element in Christianity in some sense or
other by all Christian and theological parties. It was the
Socinians who first and most clearly disputed *the relation
between the forgiveness of sins and the death of Christ*, which
had been taken for granted in the Church tradition, although
it had been interpreted in various ways in the course of time.
The controversy stands in immediate connection with the
point already discussed—that every Church theory assigns
to forgiveness an essential significance for the Christian
life, Socinianism only an accidental. At least it is at the
outset analogous to say that all Church theology connects
forgiveness with the judgment of the universal or exclusive
value of Christ's Person or whole achievement, whatever be
its outcome, Socinianism with His prophetic dignity, which
He shares with others. In Church theology, before the appearance of the Socinians, it is either the infinite value of
Christ's Godhead and the perfection of His satisfaction or His
obedience, or the merit of the unfettered voluntariness of His
action in God's service, in short, something which belongs to
Him alone, to which the general ordinance of forgiveness is
referred. The Socinians derive the forgiveness of sins merely
from Christ's spoken word, which they represent as independent of His personal virtue, inasmuch as the same benefit
is promised by other prophets to the same extent, and also
by God immediately, without any necessary kind of mediation
having to be ascribed to men. In particular, they call atten-

tion to the fact that, as Christ repeatedly gave the assurance of forgiveness by His spoken word (Mark ii. 10, 11; Luke vii. 48), this effect is not necessarily and exclusively bound up with His death.

This statement is in a measure justified as against all those estimates of Christ's death which place that event, even in so far as it is subsumed under Christ's determination or voluntariness, in a relation opposed to the estimate of His active life as a whole. The fact that Jesus pronounced the forgiveness of sins in those cases really refutes all those theories which are designed to show that Christ, by His death as a satisfaction for human sins, succeeded in making God willing to forgive, while they either view His morally normal life as being the expression of His duty, or regard it as enhancing the effect of His voluntary death. Nevertheless, the two cases adduced do not harmonise with the positive Socinian view, that Christ as a Prophet announces the forgiveness of sins in general on the condition of the active obedience of faith. This view amounts to saying that Christ in general gave men a knowledge of the Divine law of forgiveness; His prophetic commission the Socinians interpret in the sense of the vocation of a theoretical teacher. On the other hand, it must be remembered that Jesus, even if we refer His procedure to His prophetic dignity, receives individuals through forgiveness into the same communion with God in which He stands with God as the Son of Man, and from which He derives His correct judgment of particular cases. Moreover, the condition of the active obedience of faith which is laid down by the Socinians is not fulfilled in any of these cases. But when it is acknowledged that Christ here acted in virtue of His prophetic right, this signifies for Him not only an assertion of the truth of the words He spoke in God's name, but the agreement of the whole course of His life on the one hand with the grace and truth of God manifested by Him, and on the other with His religious relationship to God as His Father.

Viewed from this standpoint, the forgiveness of the para-

lytic, associated as it is with his cure, keeps to the lines of
the expectation made current by the Old Testament. For
the removal of material punishment is regarded on Old
Testament ground as the necessary proof of the restoration
of Divine favour (vol. ii. p. 60). It is clear, however, that
Jesus here accommodates Himself to the intelligence of the
people around Him. But the case of the sinful woman is of
a different kind. It may, indeed, be maintained that she too
is freed from the punishment which corresponds to sin like
hers. For the expulsion from respectable society which she
had brought on herself is made invalid by Jesus, at least as
regards His own Person, by His allowing the woman, to the
astonishment of the Pharisee, to approach Him, and by accepting the tokens of her trust and repentance. Still her social
position was not thereby fully restored; it is to be presumed
that other people continued to hold aloof from the woman.
That, however, makes it all the clearer what Jesus understands
by the forgiveness He addressed to her. Recognising as He
does her penitent faith in God in her sincere and humble trust
in Himself, He makes the Divine forgiveness of sins actual by
the very fact of His allowing the woman to come near Him.
For just in so far as she has been attracted by His elevation
and benignity, Christ gives her access to God's grace by admitting her to that intercourse with Himself which is described
in the story. Representing, as He does, in His Person both
the grace of God and the normal communion of men with
God, He removes the obstacle to her communion with God
arising from her sin, in so far as the impression of His personality had overcome the sinful woman's natural distrust
and habitual wantonness. In this connection, then, altogether
different considerations force themselves on our attention from
those which come under our notice in the Socinian theory.
We shall therefore from the outset have to modify our confidence in other views of Socinian origin.

If the Socinians and the theologians of the *Aufklärung*
still insist that no necessary connection is to be assumed
between the forgiveness of sins and the historical position of

Christ, this view depends as usual on certain assumptions, and not on a careful consideration of historical facts.   The former thinkers lay stress on God's equity, the latter on His love, as the permanent ground for expecting forgiveness to be, properly speaking, a matter of course between God and men.   Now what the writers of the *Aufklärung* understand by God's love is distinguished from the equity asserted by the Socinians merely by the fact that the latter is deduced from a special resolve of God, while the former is presupposed as God's natural attitude.   But that positive assertion and this natural presupposition both stand as much out of relation to a moral order of the world as they conflict with all the historical conditions under which religions exist.   There is no religion that is not positive, and there has never been ; natural religion, so called, is an imagination.   Every social religion has been instituted.   For not only must every social and regular cultus be referred back to special causes and the authority of individual men, but even the myths of the gods are special combinations of natural phenomena with the idea of God—combinations which were first made by individual men and recognised by others on their authority.   The general ideas of God—that He is not the world, that He is absolute Power, that He is the mild and indulgent Will, that He is the Lawgiver who imposes universal duties—are products of scientific knowledge, which as such are also subject for their production to special conditions, and have gained a special currency through the consent of men ; but they are neither innate in each individual human mind, nor necessary results of reflection upon our position in the world.   These ideas came into vogue as substitutes for the religious knowledge of God, when the understanding of the positive religions had become obscure.   However general the adoption of these ideas in such circumstances has become, their vogue as a kind of religion is proved to be surreptitious by the very fact that they have led to no kind of common cultus.   The Socinian assertion, that God by a counsel of equity treats men created without rights as possessors of relative rights in reference to

Himself, is so far from being self-evident that it is merely a modification of the scientific hypothesis current in the theology of the Middle Ages. The *Aufklärung* assumption of the love of God is the expression of a habituation to the Christian idea of God, under the peculiar circumstances in which philosophical naturalism and religious and moral individualism paralysed the persuasive power of the statutory Dogmatics. If, therefore, God's love or equitable forbearance is recognised as the ground of forgiveness, it is indispensable, with a view to historical fulness of conviction, to connect the latter with the personal activity of Jesus in His vocation as the necessary intermediate cause. To this has to be added the fact that both the Socinians and the theologians of the *Aufklärung* always relate the forgiveness of sins and the moral order of life merely to single individuals as such. This conception of the religious and moral life, however, conflicts with the general rule that the individual acts in these relations only as a member of the family, the tribe, the nation, the spiritual humanity, and with a more or less clear consciousness of this principle. The latter also regulates the history of the positive religions in so far as they have become a cultus, and in so far as they have become operative as a standard for the valuation of all kinds of social and political institutions. Finally, the existence of the *Aufklärung* itself is an example of the same principle, for it has a persuasive power merely as a tradition in certain strata of national culture, and not as necessarily produced by an independent knowledge of each individual as such.

Against the necessity of attaching the forgiveness of sins to the personal work of Christ, the Socinians further appeal to the fact attested by the Old Testament, that God also communicated forgiveness in former times without this means, simply according to His free resolve. We see here a peculiar overestimate of what is indefinite and imperfect in its kind, as against the definite and perfect. And indeed this judgment is again determined less by a full historical consideration of the facts, than by the Socinian view of God as in

trinsically indeterminate Will. No doubt in the religion of
the Old Testament a certain exercise of Divine forgiveness
is statutorily defined in the offerings for sin and guilt; still
the personal moral craving for forgiveness is not satisfied by
such an institution, all the less because the idea of sin which
accompanies it is generally confined to unavoidable bodily
uncleanness, and involuntary violations of theocratic rights.
In part, however, the individual petitions for Divine forgiveness in the Psalms stand out of relation to those acts of
worship; in part, the prayers of the Psalmists and the prophetic promises of universal forgiveness count on the restoration of personal prosperity, or of the political integrity of
the nation, as the proper evidence of Divine favour (vol. ii.
p. 58). If, then, we recognise in cases of the latter kind,
particularly in Jeremiah's promise of the new covenant, a
distinct tendency to assure oneself of forgiveness as a general
dispensation belonging to the higher stage of the development
of the religious community, the similar prayers of individual
Psalmists appear, according to the standard already found in
the Old Testament, as the first and less perfect attempts to
reach that goal. But the imperfection of both phenomena in
comparison with Christianity is shown by the very fact that
the restoration of outward prosperity, protection from the
injuries of persecutors, in general, equilibrium between the
unfettered use of nature and spiritual purity, is anticipated
as the necessary consummation and proof of inward holiness.
According to this standard, the Psalmists can, of course,
scarcely ever have reached the conviction that their prayer
was fulfilled; and the promises of the prophets were fulfilled
through Christ only by their expectation of outward prosperity for the Chosen People being transformed into the
idea that all sufferings have to be patiently borne for the
sake of the forgiveness of sins. Thus the Socinian appeal
against connecting forgiveness with the work of Christ
would be valid only if the Old Testament anticipations were
verified—the anticipations, namely, that spiritual reconciliation with God would be accompanied by material deliverance

from all the ills of life, or would be followed by deliverance
from the material penalties of sin. For the change of the
sinner's relation to God must be verified by his position relatively to the world. But as experience never furnishes this
proof of forgiveness which was expected by the men of the
Old Testament and again by the Socinians, and as the formal
change of position relatively to the world which is asserted as
the consequence of forgiveness in the Christian sense is neither
clearly expressed in the Old Testament nor looked for by the
Socinians, the Socinian assumption of a general order of Divine
forgiveness which should be independent of Christ is out of
all relation to experience and utterly void of meaning.

On the other hand, the particular cases in which Christ
bestows forgiveness result from His consciousness of standing
in the closest conceivable relation to God, and of being called
to receive others into the same relation in such a way that
their sins shall present no obstacle to their trust in God
and God's communion with them. In comparison with this,
it is a matter of indifference whether the punishment due
to definite personal sin is materially removed, in accordance
with the Old Testament expectation, by Christ's healing
power, or whether the estimate of it is formally changed.
This personal method is not inconsistent with the fact that
the representatives of the Christian community attach the
general validity of forgiveness to Christ's death, especially as
the idea of doing so was suggested by Christ's own discourse
at the Supper. For the new covenant which He announces
that He is about to conclude by His sacrificial death unites
the new community with God, in accordance with Jeremiah's
prophecy, on the basis of forgiveness. Now, if we reflect
that the fulfilment of Christ's task in His vocation, through
His willingness to die for its accomplishment, constitutes the
highest proof of His personal communion with God as His
Father (§ 48), and that this position of His also establishes
Christ's right to bestow forgiveness on individuals in those
cases which occurred previously, it is but logical to connect
with Christ's death the forgiveness provided for later genera-

tions. For Christ's death, as it must be explained by His previous obedience, is, in the view of the Apostles, the summary expression of the fact that Christ maintained His religious unity with God and His position as the Revealer of God throughout the whole course of His life. As an indication of His personal perfection in the life-destiny which fell to Him, and which was recognised in His intention to found a new covenant-community, Christ's death, with forgiveness as its purpose, merely represents the religious value of Christ's Person, fully exhibited in its nature, for later generations. If we ascribe the cases of special forgiveness by Christ to His ordinary authority, as His words in Mark ii. 10 require us to do, the reference in the Supper discourse, which Matt. xxvi. 28 appropriately supplements, can be explained in harmony therewith only provided we do not conceive the purpose of Christ's death under any principle which would be opposed to the purpose of His life. But if we still suppose that the purpose of Christ's death is to be interpreted as penal satisfaction, we see ourselves compelled to exclude the previous cases, contrary to the words of Scripture, from Christ's ordinary authority, or we should have to force on these utterances of Christ the meaning that He made them beforehand in view of His vicarious penal suffering. This, however, would be no exposition, but a violent importation, which theological caprice cannot allow itself without pronouncing its own condemnation.

§ 56. As Christ connects the bestowal of *forgiveness* with the prophecy of Jeremiah, forgiveness is to be regarded as the common fundamental *attribute of the community to be founded by Him*. This goal quite distinctly transcends the sporadic and casual form of the blessing of forgiveness, from which the Socinians and the theologians of the *Aufklärung* borrow their standard for judging the matter. Their representations therefore set at nought the specific character of the Christian religion. Forgiveness, as an attribute of that Christian community, implies that in that community men may enjoy fellowship with God in spite of their sins and in spite of

the *intensifying of their sense of guilt*. For this peculiar
antithesis, to be found in men's religious self-judgment and
feeling, has to be taken into consideration in a full account of
the matter in hand.   Just as forgiveness on God's side does
not mean that He forgets men's sin and arrives at a judgment
which would belie the facts of the case (§ 13), so on men's
side the assurance of forgiveness cannot be supposed to imply
that they forget their sins as something indifferent, and pay
no regard to them in their own judgment of themselves.   On
the contrary, the impression of the value of forgiveness is
the first thing that will keep the sense of the unworthiness
of our own offences properly awake.   For the more highly
the Divine grace in this bestowal of forgiveness is prized,
the more keenly must the contrast between our offences and
our reception into God's fellowship make itself felt.   This
fact is not made quite clear by the ordinary doctrine of
poenitentia, which Lutherans owe to Melanchthon (vol. i.
p. 200).   This doctrine posits the idea that the greatest
intensity of the sense of guilt, arising from a comparison
of sin with the Divine law, precedes the act of faith which
embraces forgiveness; and the consequence would be that in
peace of conscience even the recollection of former guilt
would be able to cause no disturbance of feeling.   This
doctrine, in analogy with the Catholic sacrament of penance,
is based on the assumption that a loss of grace, and consequently an interruption of the consciousness of forgiveness,
has taken place, and that grace is to be recovered by *contritio*
and *fides*.   This principle, however, would not only deny all
coherent development of Christian character, but it is also
opposed to Luther's Reformation principle that the whole of
life is a repentance.   The culture of Christian character is
secured by the fact that faith in Divine grace is always the
motive and not the end of *contritio*, since all self-examination
and self-discipline through the Divine law originates in that
love of the good which is based on the turning of the will to
God, that is, on reconciliation with God.   This is in keeping
with the other principle that it is just by the gospel of

forgiveness that we recognise our sin (p. 160). For as forgiveness does not remove the sense of guilt for past sins, but only its power of separating us from God, or that distrust of God which attaches to it (p. 60), so the assurance of forgiveness is confirmed by the very fact that it intensifies the sense of guilt for sins which we commit, and in general awakens a sensitive dread of transgression. For if a fall from the state of grace as such can be made out, it would hold good of such a sin as a man did not immediately repent of, but excused and palliated and refused to acknowledge as sin at all. In so far, then, as forgiveness is experienced in Christianity by every individual as the common foundation and presupposition of the communion with God which is experienced in faith, it necessarily has associated with it the continuance in the memory of the previous sense of guilt, and the intensifying of the sense of guilt for subsequent cases of sin. But this has no longer the significance of Divine punishment attached to it, since the confidence which lays hold of God's promise is associated with these phenomena, and excludes the unhappiness of the previous state. A want of tenderness of feeling accompanied by the assurance of forgiveness would prove the latter to be surreptitious, and indicate a state of religious hypocrisy (vol. i. p. 465).

If, however, the abiding assurance of communion with God, which is attained in spite of the fact that we have sinned and do sin, is bound up with the Fatherly love of God, and if we are conscious of this position relatively to God as one which is common to many, and if even the Socinians and the writers of the *Aufklärung* will not deny that it is just in the Christian community that we exercise this relation, this result will have to be referred to the action of Christ by which He became the Founder of that community. This is different from the case of Jeremiah, who, as a prophet, anticipated the forgiveness of sins, under certain objective and subjective conditions, for a future state of human affairs which was independent of himself. Rather does the admission of the members of the Christian community to communion with God in

35

spite of their sins and their sense of guilt, which is expressed in forgiveness, find its typical standard and historical ground in Christ's communion with God, which He maintained in the whole course of His life, especially in His willingness to suffer for the sake of His vocation, and in the patience which He exercised even unto death. Now, though the material of His vocation is one and the same, yet in it Christ may be compared both to a prophet and to a priest. In the course of His life He in the first place demonstrated to men His Father's love, grace, and truth, by exercising His Divine vocation, to found the Kingdom of God, from the same motive of love to men which constitutes God's proper will for the realising of their happiness. At the same time we must remember that He exercised the love of God in the form of obedience to God's commission, and that He accomplished this task by faith in His Father and by prayer, in such a way as to continually assure Himself in this form of His activity of the ground of His existence as the Revealer of God (John xv. 10, x. 17, 18). This achievement of His life, from this point of view, is also intelligible as being not only for His own sake, but for the purpose of introducing His disciples into the same position towards God. If Christ assures Himself by the obedience indicated of His nearness, His priestly relation, to God, that includes the intention that the existing and the future community should reach the same position. That is to say, Christ as a Priest is the representative of the community which He brings to God through the perfect fulfilment of His personal life (xvii. 19—26). This use of representation is inclusive, not, as it generally is, exclusive. The meaning of the idea is not that what Christ does as a Priest, the community does not require to do ; but rather that what Christ as a Priest does first in the place and as the representative of the community, there the community itself has accordingly to take up its position. But the community of Christ is composed of sinners, who as such are aliens and strangers to God. Their effective union with God is therefore to be thought of as the forgiveness of their sins, as the ending of their separation from God, as the removal of that sense of guilt which is associated with distrust. This special means of founding the Church also originates in Christ's whole conduct of His life, viewed in the light of His double relation to God. For in so far as our aim is to understand forgiveness as proceeding from the loving will of God the Father, Who permits sinners to draw nigh to Himself, this will is manifested as the grace and truth in which Christ represents God for men. On the other hand, when what we want is to see forgiveness become operative as the attribute of a community, this aspect of it is guaranteed by the community's Representative, Whose inviolably maintained position towards the love of God, which is distinctive of Him, is imputed by God to those who are to be accounted His (p. 71). Because Christ kept Himself in the love of God by His obedience even unto death, God's forgiving love is thereby secured beforehand to those who belong to Christ's community. Their guilt is not taken into account in God's judgment, since they are admitted in the train of God's beloved Son to the position towards God which was assumed and maintained by Him. The verdict of justification or forgiveness is therefore not to be formulated in such a way that the community has its relationship to Christ imputed to it, but in such a way that the community which belongs to Christ has imputed to it His position towards the love of God, in which He maintained Himself by His obedience.

This argument is related to the line of thought which is indicated in Christ's discourses in John. Of equal value with this train of ideas are Christ's parables of the flock for which the shepherd cares and lays down his life, of the vine which bears the branches and keeps them alive. In both of these figures He brings His saving, life-preserving work into relation to the community of His disciples as a whole. In the same way it is the unmistakable meaning of the Supper discourse that the result of Christ's priestly offering or sacrificial death is designed for the disciples, in so far as they are the community of the new covenant to be founded on forgiveness. The Apostles attach themselves to this covenant in that they regard Christ's death partly in accordance with the pattern of the covenant sacrifice, partly in accordance with that of the yearly sin-offering, both of which are related to the Israelitish community. Empirically the community always comes into existence as a collective unity of individuals. But in so far as the individual determines by faith the meaning of the community in the Christian view of the world and of life, he must regard the community as the whole which, without regard to enumeration of members, is founded by Christ in consequence of God's purpose of salvation, and which the individual always finds already existing as the body within which, as a believer in Christ, he will meet his own kind. If we are to explain forgiveness, in accordance with the teaching of the Church, by the purpose of Christ, we inevitably think of it as addressed to the community for the present and the future, and not to the twelve individual disciples and the multitudes who should follow them; for no human intelligence is capable of grasping the latter idea.

The introduction of the community into the idea of forgiveness as a benefit to be derived from the love of God and the mediation of Christ (p. 110), was planned by Luther and carried out in the theology of Calvin and his followers (vol. i. pp. 205, 308). The idea is also advocated by Lutheran ascetics and Pietistic theologians. On the other hand, it is not current in Lutheran Dogmatics, as Melanchthon never adopted Luther's idea. Through Melanchthon's influence the assumption became prevalent in the Lutheran theology that the individual is the direct correlate of justification in God's purpose, and this has bound up with it the expectation that the assurance of justification can be obtained immediately, i.e. without the mediation of the idea of the community. At the same time this gives rise to the supposition that the view for which I contend denotes a return to Catholicism (vol. i. p. 313). This objection is no doubt very closely connected with the formula in which Schleiermacher expressed the contrast between Catholicism and Protestantism, namely, that the one makes the relation of the individual to Christ dependent on his relation to the Church, the other his relation to the Church on his relation to Christ (vol. i. p. 520). This formula, however, is inconsistent with the very principle with which Schleiermacher enters upon the doctrine of redemption, namely, that the consciousness of redemption through Christ is referred to the mediation of His religious fellowship (vol. i. p. 511). It was only because Schleiermacher was unable to develop this idea (vol. i. p. 519) that he lapsed into the opposite formula in the introduction to the *Glaubenslehre*. This formula, however, is false. For even the Evangelical Christian's right relation to Christ is both historically and logically conditioned by the fellowship of believers ; historically, because a man always finds the community already existing when he arrives at faith, nor does he attain this end without the action of the community upon him ; logically, because no action of Christ upon men can be conceived except in accordance with the standard of Christ's antecedent purpose to found a community. This position, however, is distinguished from the Catholic view by the fact that it pays no regard to a *legal* organisation of the community of believers.[1] For the idea of the Church which the Catholic doctrine foists in as a necessary medium between Christ and the individual is the *ecclesia repraesentans*, the legally privileged clergy, whose members are deemed fit for that purpose even if, *ex hypothesi*, they do not belong to the community of believers at all, but, as Möhler says, are on the way to hell, or, as Melanchthon has it, are *membra satanae*. He who cannot distinguish between the legal and the religious idea of the Church is not qualified to pronounce a judgment on this subject. Schleiermacher's formula, moreover, is merely the reflection of that Pietistic disintegration of the idea of the Church which was rendered possible from the outset by the vagueness in which the Lutheran Dogmatics left the idea of the Church in the order of individual salvation. But this form of doctrine cannot lay claim to clearness and

[1] In this sense even Calvin (iii. 2. 3) admits : "Fides in dei et Christi cognitione, non in ecclesiae reverentia iacet," despite the fact that in § 35 he says : "Huc redit summa, Christum, ubi nos in fidem illuminat spiritus sui virtute, simul inserere in corpus suum, ut fiamus bonorum omnium participes."

completeness till it is supplemented by the introduction of the idea of the community. It is a Lutheran principle that the justification of the individual is necessarily conditioned by the proclamation of the Gospel. Now this cannot be regarded as the function of Church officials, otherwise we reach no antithesis to the Catholic view, and the religious texture of the exposition is broken. The proclamation of the Gospel, by which the justification of the individual is conditioned, must rather be thought of as the necessary function of the community of believers, *cui claves principaliter traditae sunt*. If, therefore, this principle of Melanchthon's tractate *De Potestate Papae* 24 must be incorporated in the ordinary doctrine of justification, we are bound to admit that the community of believers precedes the justification of the individual. For how shall we regard the community as the original subject of the Gospel, unless we consider it at the same time as the original object of the justifying grace which continues to operate in the Gospel! If, then, we duly supplement those parts of the doctrine which shrivelled up in the hands of the Lutheran divines, we must develop their view into the formula, expressed by Luther, of the justification of the community by Christ. Unless we do so, the inevitable supplement will end in the *ministerium verbi divini* becoming the precondition of the justification of the individual; and it would then be impossible to point out any essential difference upon this point between Lutheranism and Catholicism (vol. i. pp. 311). But if we are prevented by all kinds of reasons, particularly by the comparison with Luther's idea of the *regnum Christi spirituale* (§§ 35, 46), from regarding this supplement as genuine, there is only the other left, which corresponds with the Reformation principle of Lutheran Dogmatics.

In Christ's purpose, then, the guaranteeing of a general forgiveness to humanity, and the founding of the community whose members recognise in God as His Father their Father also, are equivalent ideas. And in the acknowledged result of His work, our assurance of forgiveness, *i.e.* of a communion with God which is possible in spite of our sin—and our belonging to the community of those who believe in Christ, are identical. Only on the understanding that these are equivalents it is possible to establish the necessity of the connection asserted between the forgiveness of sins and the personal life of Christ, particularly the completion of His life in His sacrificial death. Now Christ is the Mediator of these coincident effects just in the twofold position which He occupies with the identical material of His life. He is not the Mediator of forgiveness, because, as Head and Representative of humanity or of the community contemplated by Him, He exercises a determining influence upon God to be gracious to men. For His priestly position towards God is subordinated to His displaying, as the Revealer of God, the grace and truth—the love of God to sinners, which purposes their reconciliation without having first to be evoked by the human merit of the Mediator. But in so far as Christ's obedience includes an effect upon God, Whom Christ Himself at the same time represents, instead of the "merit" with which Christ is supposed to win something from Him, I must again remind my readers that Christ by obedience keeps Himself in the love of God, and further point out that in doing so He at the same time represents His community before God that it may be the recipient of the forgiveness which God first guarantees by Christ's grace and truth. This achievement has for God the value that by its means humanity, entering into the community of Christ, is brought to the goal of the Kingdom of God, which is God's own most personal end.

The Kingship of Christ, however, while it includes under His prophetic and priestly work one and the same material of His life, has not the same value in both. Patience in suffering is the possessor of dominion over the world ; it is in this respect the mark of Christ's Godhead and His solidarity with the Father. It is at the same time the mark of the perfect obedience which enables Christ as Head of the community to represent it before God for the receiving of forgiveness. But in the former relation it is Christ's dominion over the world, in the latter His much closer dominion over the community that comes into view.   Now this gradation is just the right order of the relation.   For unless the dual position of Christ in His mediatorship is to lead to a contradiction, His priestly quality must be subordinated to His prophetic so as even to be embraced in it.   This, however, cannot be maintained unless the supreme, that is, the kingly dignity assumes a wider meaning when Christ is regarded as the Revealer of God than when He is a Representative of the community.   No revelation of God is complete apart from recognition of the believing community.   If, however, the Christian community views the revelation of God in Christ as perfect, it must in some way or other be capable of being combined in thought with Christ, it must find its own position prefigured in the course of the revelation in Christ.   Now this takes place when, along with His quality as a Revealer, and with reference to the same material of His life, it likewise recognises Him as its foregoing Representative, Who as the Receiver of revelation represented it before it gained its special historical form.   This also shows that Christ as Lord and King of the Church has not the directly cosmical significance which is expressed in His Divine dominion.   It is only indirectly that the latter also has to be considered in His relation to the community, in so far as His obedience exalts Him above the world, and in so far as the community by its endowment with the forgiveness of sins has received the capacity for life and blessedness.

The only question is whether this exposition is complete. It will have to be tested in view of such New Testament data as have not been specially considered, and may be regarded as traversing the rounded conception of Christ's vocation. It will also be necessary to allow for the claims of individual religious experience, which partly opposes the principle that it can assure itself of justification only within the framework of the community, and partly connects with Christ's achievement expectations which cannot be biblically verified.   I am the more willing to discuss these objections because the author [1] of them agrees on the whole with my expositions, and merely endeavours to supplement or deepen them. If I rightly understand the starting-point of this undertaking, it is the method of the Pietists, which is at once to long for the forgiveness of sin, and to struggle against the simple appropriation of it from the promise of God. It is to this phenomenon that Häring alludes when he brings into prominence the twofold nature of the consciousness of guilt, as being at once the state of Divine punishment, properly so called, and the condition of God's forgiveness. He bases on this an objection to the reference of forgiveness to the community and to the individual in it. For he thinks that this combination of ideas affords no adequate solution of the problem how the individual becomes conscious of justification, and that this is a question which cannot be evaded. Still, the doctrine which I have set forth coincides with the view which prevailed from the time of Luther (*Cat. major*, iv. 41, 44) till that of Spener inclusive—the view that as members of the Church we are to determine the reference of forgiveness to ourselves by the baptism which we have received. When Luther made this statement he knew from his experience in the Catholic Church the same difficulties as the Pietists feel in their striving after the assurance of salvation. Therefore I no more require to be guided by these arbitrary endeavours to reach assurance of forgiveness than did Luther.

For the satisfaction of the Pietists, however, who are never done with their confession of sin and repentance, in order that they may bring forgiveness in Christ into relation to themselves, what more is to be assumed in Christ's vicarious work ? According to Häring, the point is that the imperfect repentance wrought by men is completed by an analogous work on Christ's part. This does not imply that Christ Himself repented of sin ; for as he had no personal experience or knowledge of sin, this work is not to be imputed to Him.

[1] Theodor Häring, *Ueber das Bleibende im Glauben an Christus*, Stuttgart, 1880.

But Häring thinks it may be assumed that Christ's consciousness in His vocation included the painful knowledge of the
opposition of all sin to God, and thus realised the purpose
of punishment, which sinners with all their sense of guilt do
not perfectly realise.   I admit in general that in Christ we
have to count upon the purest and tenderest sense of the
contrariety of sin to God; but if such a value is to be put on
that as is done by Häring, I expect Scripture proof to be
adduced.   I regard a construction which entirely dispenses
with the latter as unreliable; it arouses the suspicion that
the picture of Christ is being touched up at one's own
pleasure.   The various cases in which Christ showed His
grief for the obduracy of certain classes (Mark iii. 5; Matt.
xxiii. 37) are no sufficient proof for the statement that Jesus'
sensibility was regularly excited by reflection on sin in
general or as a whole.   On the contrary, He always regards
sinners in their gradation as redeemable and hardened (vol.
ii. p. 38).   It was Paul who paved the way for a general
and identical idea of sin, such as appears in the doctrine of
original sin.   It was, moreover, in the asceticism of the
Middle Ages, from Anselm onward, that this idea received the
explanation which Häring regards as self-evident; and Pietism
follows the latter because it carries on the mediaeval mode of
thought.   The Pietist aspires to embrace the sin of all men
in his repentance, although, as may be observed in Arndt's
True Christianity, it is rather a mere aesthetic aversion—
disgust—which is set forth, than a real imputation of guilt.
For we are responsible only for our own sin.   It is therefore
a mistaken tendency which gives rise to the requirement of
the Pietists, for the sake of which Häring postulates that
supplementary work of Christ.   As the attribute of guilt
cannot be proved to belong to original sin, it is a delusion
to expect our own repentance to make itself responsible for
sin as a whole.   But if it cannot do that, we must not look
for any supplement in Christ's infinite grief for sin, which,
being in any case different in kind from repentance, can in
no way serve as a supplement.   People must rather be shown

that they are expecting of themselves something which cannot be realised. I therefore reject the proposed deepening of my exposition as something which is not based on Scripture, but called forth by a use of the doctrine of original sin which has its home in the practice of monasticism. But I also reject Häring's assumption because it is inconsistent with the blessedness of Christ. We may form an idea of the latter by bringing it into line with the fact that we count it all joy to be surrounded with persecutions. In order to fulfil this precept, we must, according to the example of Christ, be filled rather with sorrow for than indignation against those who by unjust persecution tempt us to retaliate. If, however, to prove our reconcilability, we were to fix ourselves in sympathetic grief for the obduracy of our adversaries, little room would be left for the joy which we have to derive from persecutions. There is no reason to transfer to Christ the Pietistic sentimentality which never comes to full joy and pure blessedness, because the effort from which it springs is spurious.

It affords me satisfaction that Häring has withdrawn this attempt to improve upon my doctrine.[1]   Only he does not rest there, but brings forward what purports to be a supplement of another kind. He agrees with me in believing that Christ's passion is not the punishment for the sins of men. He says: "Christ awakens repentance essentially by the mysterious (?) fate of His passion; the Cross is the powerful sermon-in-action, telling of the inviolable earnestness of the Divine love, which makes Him to be sin Who knew no sin. He Himself, however, given up to this dark fate, accepts it in humble obedience, because He knows the Divine purpose to show the guilty in this way *how earnest God is in condemning sin.*"[2]   Häring appeals for support to Dorner, Kähler, Gess, and others. I need only point out that the idea here expressed is that of penal example, which Grotius first introduced under a mistake; and if the theologians named meant to express something weighty and significant in this

---

[1] *Zu Ritschl's Versöhnungslehre*, Zürich, 1888, p. 39.
[2] *Op. cit.* pp. 40, 41.

way, it will no doubt afford them satisfaction to find themselves on the path taken a century ago by Semler, Gruner,
Michaelis, and other adherents of the supernaturalistic
school (vol. i. pp. 336 ff., 414, 420 ff.).

§ 57. The exposition of the connection between justification as an attribute of the Christian community, and therefore
of its members, and the completion of the work of its Founder
in His vocation, is conditioned by two considerations, namely,
by the positive idea of forgiveness or justification, and by the
equally positive estimate of the value of Christ's suffering as
the occasion of His patience, and the test of His fidelity in
His calling, and steadfastness in His faith.   In this our exposition is in harmony with the positive aim of forgiveness or
justification or reconciliation, namely, that freedom of believers
in communion with God which consists in dominion over the
world, and is to be regarded as eternal life (§§ 52, 54).
This result, however, must still be tested on various sides.
First of all, it seems to stop short of the requirement that
there should be derived from Christ not only a changed
relation of men to God as regards the status of sin, but also
an *actual removal of sin* in believers.   That is what the saying
in 1 Pet. ii. 24 points to in its own way (vol. ii. p. 258).
Now the assertion of an effective deliverance of believers
from sin seems to require to be reached, partly that Christ's
moral action upon believers may remain in equilibrium with
their religious emancipation by Him, partly that the mediating
position of the community for the latter purpose may be preserved unimpaired.   For the truth already ascertained regarding
this position seems to be threatened if we must conceive that
the community of believers continues to live and move in
active sin ; for this fact, if admitted, appears to detract from
the genuineness of their religious knowledge of the truth, and
from the power of the religious impulse which individuals in
the community receive.   Certainly this latter consideration
is discounted when Oetinger and especially Menken teach that
Christ, by Himself resisting all temptations to sin, made
human nature sinless, or destroyed the source of ever fresh

guilt in believers. Menken declares that this effect must be attributed to Christ, in addition to the removal of guilt (vol. i. p. 613). But this is an ill-considered antithesis. For the removal of guilt must be defined in a positive sense, as meaning that there comes to exist communion with God in which the person reconciled with God directs his will to God as his universal final end. Now as this is the opposite of the sinful direction of the will, the effective removal of guilt becomes the basis of the positive possibility of a life no longer sinful as a whole. But this theory is far from coming up to Menken's view. For the general direction of the will to the Divine final end which is included in the idea of reconciliation, does not exclude the possibility of fresh guilt. This possibility lies for every individual in the fact that the general motive to sin is complicated in each man with special inclinations and impulses. If Menken, then, intends to affirm that Christ directly and immediately changes believers in this respect, he affirms something which is contrary to experience, and which at the same time we know to be impossible. As a matter of fact, evil inclinations are always got rid of solely by the cultivation of contrary good inclinations; but in so far as this requires special resolves, these never attain their end except where the development of good character is undertaken as a whole. Although the general direction of the will to God—the direction received in reconciliation—becomes operative as the principal motive for the development of good character, there are still required the special moral resolves and decisions which do not logically or of themselves result from the faith of reconciliation, but must always be apprehended by the will as special. By the general assurance of reconciliation or the general purpose of conversion alone, no special vice is uprooted; we cannot thus evade that special conflict with each vice which consists in the fulfilment of the contrary resolutions. These processes, however, which serve for the effective removal of new offences, necessarily fall within the sphere of the self-active moral will which is to be explained by grace. For this reason, sinful depravity, which is not only a common but also a special depravity in every man, cannot be removed at the outset and immediately by the universal atonement of Christ. We may make experiment upon those " believers " who with a very vigorous consciousness of their reconciliation and a life in many respects virtuous, combine arrogance and dogmatism in religion, and a want of respect and charity for those who think differently from themselves. Such men proceed in this way as if their honest zeal for God's glory protected them without more ado from sins or errors. For I do not suppose that such persons, if we could subject them to serious cross-examination, would palm off those vices as virtues, or as their special licence. Probably the fact of the matter rather is, that they repose too exclusive confidence in the general good will which they have, through reconciliation, in their being directed toward God and the end of the Kingdom of God, just because it is God who guarantees them this good will. But as the idea of a genus does not lead to a knowledge of the species without special observation of the latter, no more does the application of the will which is good on the whole to special cases follow of itself from the presence of the general disposition. On the contrary, the will, which in the latter form is thought of as the general ground of the corresponding activity, must begin to work anew in every special resolution. In so far, then, as sin has its activity in every man in a special form, reconciliation through Christ implies anything but an actual deliverance of believers from sin.

Menken's statement may, however, be understood in another sense, if we consider the formula, which is also advocated by Oetinger, that Christ, by resisting the temptations of the devil, made human nature sinless. What is expressed here is not the idea of single individuals as sinners, but the idea of that which is common to them all. In this sense, therefore, human nature, as it belongs to every individual, denotes the fact that our moral endowment has for its end the moral destiny of the race. Every individual, however, oversteps this circle of attributes by his special endowments

and his peculiar moral activity; the latter may even bring
about changes in the subject. Now, if sin, or, as in Christ, the
possibility of sin, is presupposed as a general affection of
human nature, it is conceivable that human nature should
be altered by moral activity, and thus raised above the
temptation to sin. This result can be conceived, however,
only in so far as the subject has human nature in himself.
On the other hand, in so far as human nature belongs to
other subjects, the assertion that this endowment is changed
simply by the normal moral conduct of another, is altogether
worthless.

Menken's view, however, in the form of it already criticised, appears to be re-echoed in the fundamental formulae of
Schleiermacher (*Glaubenslehre*, §§ 87, 88): "We are conscious
that all approximations to the state of blessedness which
occur in the Christian life are grounded in a new divinely-
produced common life, which counteracts the common life
of sin and the unhappiness developed therein." " In this
common life, which goes back to the activity of Jesus,
redemption is effected by Him through the communication
of His sinless perfection." It is necessary to come to an
understanding with these principles; the more so as Schleiermacher here emphasises the importance of the community of
redemption in a way, the absence of which could not but be
felt in his special definition of the ideas of redemption and
reconciliation (vol. i. p. 517). Now, if the sinless perfection
of Christ, which He communicates in redemption or in the
common life founded by Him, were to be understood as active
moral righteousness, it would have to be objected that such
communication was altogether contrary to experience, and inconsistent with the necessary conditions of moral righteousness.
However much, even from the religious point of view, must
be regarded as divinely communicated, and however distinctly
all our ethical endeavours presuppose the reign of Divine
grace, we still experience the formation of our moral character,
and the separation of it from the impulses of sin which are
peculiar to us, as an act of our own will. But Schleiermacher's

purpose in choosing the above expression is not to be understood in Menken's sense. As he defines the idea of sin as the restriction of the God-consciousness (§ 66), so the sinless perfection of Christ denotes in his sense nothing else than the absolute potency of the God-consciousness. That this consciousness may be communicated, and that it must be specifically represented as communicated and received, follows from the fact that we necessarily conceive our relation to God in the form of God's action upon us. Since, then, we can think of ourselves as children of God only in the community founded by Christ, in all our consciousness of the activity which corresponds to the Divine sonship we regard this status itself as something received from the historical action of Christ, something appropriated from Him. Schleiermacher, however, raises for himself the objection that the Christian community as a whole, and particularly in certain periods, is seen to participate so largely in the general sinfulness, that we cannot help becoming doubtful of its fitness for the mediation of salvation which is entrusted to it. This circumstance also demands a special consideration in view of the doctrine above developed (§ 56).

The reconciliation of the individual has been connected with the whole life-work of Christ in His vocation thus, that the individual who knows himself reconciled finds himself in the community founded by Christ, and reckons himself as belonging to it, in so far as Christ has established for it the right to see in sin which, as such, is repented of, no hindrance to fellowship with God, but rather to assert the Divine sonship in spite of sin. The Christian community, however, in the course of its history, has carried with it so much actual sin, that the question must be raised whether it has not altogether forfeited the relation of Divine sonship bestowed upon it through Christ's work of reconciliation, and accordingly become unfit in any sense to mediate for the individual the religious benefits which proceeded from Christ. Is it not this doubt which gives rise to the claim that the Church fulfils its commission to mediate salvation only if from Christ we rightly derive not only reconciliation but effective deliverance from sin, or when the reconciled community is limited in sectarian fashion to those members who have in the strength of reconciliation attained a recognisable degree of special sanctity ? The first alternative, however, is impracticable, and the other is, to begin with, at least suspicious. For the moral and the religious aims of Christianity do not absolutely coincide. Good conduct, prompted by the final end of the Kingdom of God, is indeed the *conditio sine quâ non* for the authentication of Divine sonship, so that doubt is cast upon the genuineness of the religious factor where flagrant sinfulness is found along with the profession of Christian truth. But the experience of our Reformation teaches that the discovery of prevalent immorality and superstitious perversity in the Christian Church may be the very means of directing the attention more closely to the redemptive power of the Christian religion. On the other hand, the sectarian type of Church has no succour to offer, partly because the principle of sectarian Christianity guarantees no continuity of moral education, partly because the legal kind of sinlessness aimed at in the sects usually leads to the sin of hypocrisy.

What other means, then, are left us to escape these difficulties ? Schleiermacher rightly showed the way out of them in essential harmony with Reformation and orthodox theology. He points to an experience which is possible in the Church in spite of its prevalent entanglement with sin. In this he distinguishes a personal and a common element. "The former consists in the fact that the individual still receives from the image of Christ, which exists in the Church as a common fact and a common possession, the impression of the sinless perfection (the absolute potency of the God-consciousness) of Jesus, which gives him at once the perfect consciousness of sin and the removal of unhappiness ; and this in itself is a communication of that perfection. The other consists in the fact that in all those confusions in the Church, be they never so like the sinful common life of man, there is

nevertheless a settled tendency proceeding from Christ's perfection—a tendency which in all its manifestations, yes,
even in the assertion of the ideas of the true and the good,
more or less has to yield to the eclipse of sinless perfection,
but in its essence or as an impulse is worthy of its origin ;
and this equally with the first element is a true and real
communication of the perfection of Christ." The first point
determines the way in which the mediation of Christ's reconciliation by the community is to be correctly defined. On the
one hand, we should have no experience and no knowledge of
an operation of Christ upon later generations, unless a community of the children of God existed due to His impulse,
and propagated itself throughout all the changes of time.
Yet, on the other hand, the connection of the spiritual life is
of such a kind that the Author of Divine sonship is operatively
present in every genuine case of faith in God as our Father;
and His presence is not so merged in these manifestations
and their connection that the knowledge of the Founder of the
Church can ever cease to be indispensable for the existence
and maintenance of Divine sonship. On the contrary, the
religious possession of Divine sonship must always take its
bearings from the Archetype and Founder of this state, just
as it is always called forth in the individual by the idea of
Christ. The orthodox doctrine expresses this truth by
saying that the preaching of Christ in the Church is the
indispensable condition of justification and the awakening of
faith, and thus of the Divine sonship of individuals. But
even though the psychological scheme which the old theology
uses makes it appear as though this mediation of salvation
were restricted to the form of theoretical teaching, yet nobody
will question the fact that the Christian religion is not
propagated and awakened in individuals in this way alone.
All kinds of aesthetic and moral motives of education are
required even to unfold the meaning of the image of Christ
to the understanding, still more to use the impression of this
image for the awakening of childlike trust in God. But
although the manifold stimulus of the piety of other men, of

morale and discipline in the family and the school, is required
to lend weight to religious instruction and preaching, yet the
independent assurance of Divine sonship can completely stay
itself on nothing but the standard of the living Figure of
Christ, even as fundamentally it springs from the power of
that Figure.   This moulding of piety on Christ will meet
with modifications of the most diverse kinds ; but in any case
it proves the necessity of including the estimate of Christ as
the Founder and Archetype of Christianity in the completed
system of this religion (§ 44).   I intentionally choose these
wide and indefinite expressions in order to remind my readers
at this stage of the fact, that an inexhaustible series of different kinds of religious estimate of Christ owe their existence
to the diversity of ages, sexes, temperaments, and types of
Christian confession.   Who, then, will take it upon himself,
by setting up an exclusive theoretical formula, to decide
between the impressions of Christ's Person, which, in various
degrees of clearness and fulness, with more or less design,
provide a standard for every form of piety which is of
Christian origin ; and to decide between them in such a way
that one part of such phenomena would be declared to be
absolutely false !

Here we already touch the other experience noticed by
Schleiermacher, which is not indeed very clearly expressed
by him, but is to be understood, I think, in the following
way.   Though in large departments of the Christian Church
the God-consciousness made operative by Christ is so much
hindered by sin that even the standards of Christian truth
and goodness are vitiated, yet it is always to be placed to
the credit of such phenomena that the hope of realising
true Christianity is working in them as their hidden impulse.
This way of looking at them is certainly the expression
of a charitableness which at present, perhaps, is scarcely
intelligible.   Still, it does not exclude a very decided
judgment of the errors by which Christianity, in large or
small groups of its adherents, is theoretically and practically
distorted.   This view, however, is the only right basis of

polemical theology, so that if religious or theological controversy forsakes this standing-ground, it descends to the
mean gratification of party spirit and dogmatism. For if
we deny to any Christian party the wish to attain a right
understanding of Christianity, we can neither rightly estimate the extent of the error they have committed, nor
contribute to removing it.   Schleiermacher's opinion, on
the contrary, is not only logically and experimentally
correct, but also in a religious aspect the only seemly one.
It is a principle to which Augustine, for example, is led
almost against his will in his judgment of sin, that everything evil has the condition of its reality solely in the
secret obligation of the will to the good. No theoretical
and practical perversion of Christianity, then, can as such
be conceived, unless there is assumed at the same time
a wish, however dim it may have become, to realise Christianity as such, and a working of this purpose, however
incalculable it may be in amount, towards the desired
result.   This explains not only the striking phenomena
of reformations which break forth from a state of general
corruption, for these have but a limited area, but the phenomena, certainly much more frequent, of Christian humility
and moral purity which appear in the midst of a general
state of perversion of Christian Churches.   Finally, however,
apart from all correctness of dogmatic knowledge, it shows
nothing but a want of trust in God, or despair as to the
extent of the spiritual influence of Christ, when a polemical
theologian does his best, either by direct expression of
opinion, or indirectly by his style of controversy, to represent this action as limited to the party to which he
himself is attached.

§ 58. Further objections to the basing of reconciliation
upon the above explained connection between Christ's
value as a Revelation and His purpose to propagate His
peculiar reverence for God as His Father in a community
of the children of God, are to be expected from the fact
that people are generally in the habit of interpreting *the*

life-work of Christ by a negative formula. Certain features
of the theological tradition have a strong tendency in this
direction, all the more because they are liturgically fixed.
The standing designation of Christ as the Redeemer, the
interpretation of His peculiar achievement as being the
propitiation for our sins, the image of the Lamb which
bears the sins of the world, disclose a different view of His
saving work from the one developed above, and that, too,
with the assumption that the whole truth is completely described by these formulae, and may be correctly and adequately
developed within the framework they offer. Here I leave
out of account the fact that the delineation of the Servant
of God by the Old Testament prophet, and the formula
of the expiation of sins, are usually understood in the
sense of vicarious penal satisfaction.   For there is no
ground for this interpretation either in the words of the
prophet or in any Biblical connection of ideas.   The
Scriptural idea is that the sufferings which the Servant of
God has not merited, but which He experiences on account
of His fellowship with the guilty people, and which He
takes upon Himself the more patiently and therefore the
more completely on account of His righteousness and fellow-
feeling, impel the rest of His countrymen to repentance
after they have clearly perceived the fact of the Sufferer's
innocence and their own guilt (ii. p. 61).   According to
this analogy, it is not wrong to say that the sufferings
which Christ brought upon Himself, without any demerit,
through the fulfilment of His vocation to His people, are
the form in which the sinless Son of God completely demonstrated His fellowship with sinful humanity, for the purpose
of moving them to repentance so soon as His innocence and
the morally necessary fellowship in suffering on the part
of the Innocent with the guilty should be understood by
the latter.   It is questionable, however, whether this formula
should have so great importance attached to it as sometimes
happens, since there is no more indication of it in the
discourses of Christ than in the words of the Apostles.

Certainly Christ traced His sufferings, and the measure of them which He might expect, not merely to the pragmatical circumstance that He came into conflict with the traditional claims of the Jewish theocracy, but to the more general principle that the righteous man suffers through his connection with the unrighteous world (Matt. xi. 28–30, p. 462). Nevertheless, He did not accept His sufferings as an independent task, the meaning of which was to be sought in an idea of sin in general or as a whole (p. 554), but bore them as the accident of His positive fidelity to His vocation. The idea of innocent suffering as the form in which the sufferer enters into sympathetic fellowship with the guilty, implies in the prophet's words that this association with the guilty becomes operative through their being shamed into repentance. The effect of this association is thus thought of as the *moral* change of the individuals who belong to the already existing community, and who let themselves be. brought by shame to their right mind. This goal, however, is a different one from the *religious* reconciliation of men with God which Christ had in view, when He purposed to make a community of forgiveness possible for the first time by the fulfilment of His vocation in the suffering of death. In the allusions and discourses of Christ bearing on this subject, the purpose of bringing His adversaries to repentance by the sense of shame which His sufferings would awaken in them, is not so much as casually mentioned. Finally, the discourses in the Acts of the Apostles connect the impulse to repentance and entrance into the Christian community, not with a peculiar explanation of the sufferings of Christ, but with the fact that He whom the Jews have crucified has been by God installed as Lord (ii. 36–39; iii. 13–19; v. 30, 31).

Most nearly akin to this view is that meditation upon the sufferings of Christ which was elaborated in the Middle Ages, and continued with slight changes by Luther and his followers. There exists a Latin sermon-sketch of Luther's of the year

1519,[1] in which the way the Catholic preachers had of evoking a sympathy with Christ which ended in superficial emotion is first dismissed; and then three principles are brought forward: that in Christ's passion the wrath of God is manifest and compensation is made for the sins of the beholder; that in Christ's readiness to suffer there appears God's gracious will or love to sinners; and finally, that we have to take an example from Christ's patience, humility, and self-denial. This line of thought on the part of the individual Christian naturally presupposes the doctrine of redemption; it involves both the principles of the doctrine of redemption, Christ's satisfaction and God's love, but in the opposite order to that in which they appear doctrinally; and it ends in the application of the pattern of Christ, which goes beyond the doctrine. Now in this sketch Luther has on the whole followed the mediaeval models; he also appeals to Bernard and Albertus Magnus. Only, in the first part, by bringing in the wrath of God he has given an edge to the motive for shame; and he has set aside that distribution of the sufferings of Christ in which the meditation of his predecessors deliberately indulged. The men of the Middle Ages intend, on the one hand, methodically to evoke sympathy and responsive love; on the other hand, in doing so they follow out the idea that Christ's sufferings are remedies against sins, and the sufferings of the particular parts of His body means for the restoration of our corresponding organs as organs of righteousness. This combination of ideas suggests the prevalent custom of painting the blood and wounds of Christ.[2] Luther makes no use of this in the

---

[1] *Opp. var. arg. ad hist. reform. pertin.* iii. p. 410.

[2] Anselm, *Cantuar. Oratio* ii.: "Intuere dulcem natum toto corpore extensum, cerne manus innoxias pio manantes sanguine, et remitte placatus scelera, quae patraverunt manus meae. Considera inerme latus crudeli perfossum cuspide et renova me sacrosancto fonte illo, quem inde fluxisse credo. Vide immaculata vestigia, quae non steterunt in via peccatorum, sed semper ambulaverunt in lege tua, diris confixa clavis; et perfice gressus meos in semitis tuis, facque odio habere benignus omnem viam iniquitatis. . . . Candet nudatum pectus, rubet cruentum latus, tensa arent viscera, decora languent lumina, regia pallent ora, procera rigent brachia, crura pendent marmorea, rigat terebratos pedes beati sanguinis unda. Specta, gloriose genitor, gratissimae

above-mentioned sketch for the meditation of Christ's passion. Nevertheless the mediaeval models have again come to exert an influence in the Lutheran Church since the seventeenth century, and have been imitated, sometimes with more, sometimes with less, taste in poetry and prose. Among the most valuable hymns of this kind used in the Church are Johann Heermann's " *Herzliebster Jesu, was hast du verbrochen* " and " *Jesu, deine tiefe Wunden*," and Paul Gerhardt's " *O Haupt voll Blut und Wunden.*" The last, as is well known, is a translation of the seventh hymn of Bernard's *Rhythmica oratio ad unumquodlibet membrorum Christi patientis et a cruce pendentis.* Both of Heermann's hymns are composed after passages from pseudo-Augustinian writings; through this channel the second *Oratio* of Anselm is their source.[1] In the first hymn the same arrangement may be observed as that sketched out by Luther. Now the beauty of these hymns is beyond all question, and I do not mean to take any exception to their use in the Church on Good Friday, though they were not composed for that purpose. But as meditations of the individual they do not express that by which Good Friday must be signalised as a *Festival*—the praise of reconciliation in general, and the founding of the community of reconciliation. In accordance with Catholic models, they keep to the lines of the idea of Good Friday as a day of mourning, mourning being referred both to Christ's sufferings and to men's sins. The combination of comfort and good resolutions with which they close is treated, in keeping with the character of meditation, quite individually, and fails to stir the Christian and Churchly common feeling which should be directly excited at a Festival.

Another formula of negative meaning appears in the statement that Christ *expiated sin* by His passion. Current as this formula is among many theologians of the present day, it has very little warrant in the Biblical circle of

---

prolis lacerata membra, et memorare benignus, quae mea est substantia . . . Vide redemptoris supplicium et remitte redemti delictum."

[1] *Geschichte des Pietismus*, ii. p. 64 ff.

thought. For the German word *Sühne*—expiation—came into use in this department merely through imitation of the false Greek translation of the Hebrew formula of sacrifice (vol. ii. p. 199). In itself this word signifies either punishment or peace. Now, if the formula is used to express the idea that Christ suffered the punishment for the sins of humanity as punishment, I repudiate this view absolutely, because it stands out of all relation to the Biblical idea of sacrifice, and, besides, does not fit the facts of the case. It is still more unsuitable to use that word in the interpretation of Christ's death as a penal example. The question remains to be considered, then, whether it yields an admissible sense to say that Christ by His passion established peace in relation to the sins of humanity. If we are not playing with words, we must not confound this thought with the content of the idea of reconciliation which we have hitherto been expounding. When Christ reconciles sinners with God, He establishes peace for them Godwards, and does it in such a way that they enter His community. This is a very different thing from the literal exposition of that formula, namely, that Christ reconciled God with the sins of pre-Christian humanity, brought Him into a state of peace with their sins. For God did not enter into the relation of peace with pre-Christian humanity, but humanity, in the form of the community of Christ, attained to peace with God. Therefore Christ's expiation of the sins of humanity, or, as Hofmann following Collenbusch expounds it, His making men good by the counter-working of His obedience against the entire sin of mankind (vol. i. pp. 611, 618), can have no reference to God. Thus the proposition that Christ expiated the sin of humanity can be understood only in reference to our human, Christian way of looking at the matter. The compensation for the entire sin of mankind made by Christ's personal goodness, and that, too, through the proof He gave of His goodness by voluntary suffering, as also through His demonstration of loving fellowship with an apparently lost race, reconciles us to our participation in the fate of our race. That, however, is

an aesthetic judgment, not a necessary religious idea. Therefore we look in vain for traces of this view in the New
Testament. But seeing that the idea has been once formed,
I am far from disputing its truth in its own sphere or its
value. For it serves as evidence for the general normality of
the Christian view of the world, that the event which denotes
the authoritative revelation of God should at the same time
satisfy our aesthetic and moral interest in the destiny of our
race. Accordingly I understand the formula to mean that
our tragic participation in the apparently aimless, and therefore vain development of the human race, is brought into
harmony with our aesthetic sense of justice by the fact that
perfect human goodness not only appears in the Person of
Christ, but also displays itself in that condition of suffering
which falls to His lot in accordance with the law of history
that no established form of life willingly renounces its power.
The destruction of Him Who is lawful Ruler in the sphere of
the good, through the tenacity with which the powers which
had hitherto been dominant maintained themselves, serves to
reconcile us aesthetically even with this despotic manifestation
of sin, because in the very sacrifice of His life we discern
Christ's victory. In this connection it is evident that the
aesthetic satisfaction derived from the drama of Christ's death
presupposes the religious recognition of His worth ; but
this recognition is not expressed by the above theory. The
formula, then, denotes no religious knowledge properly so
called, and therefore is not a proposition forming part of
Dogmatics.[1]

A definition of expiation (*Sühne*), which was introduced
by Stahl [2] to support the theory of penal satisfaction in the
suffering of Christ, is to be assigned to the same aesthetic
form of theory. Stahl, indeed, would permit us to apply
this idea of expiation only to the interpretation of Christ's
death; but if expiation is to be distinguished from passive

---

[1] The view of Hülsmann (*Beiträge zur christlichen Erkenntniss*, published by
Hollenberg, 1872, p. 427 ff.) also goes on the lines of aesthetic reflection.

[2] *Fundamente einer christlichen Philosophie.* I derive my knowledge of this
work from Philippi, *Kirchliche Glaubenslehre*, iv. 2, p. 216 ff.

punishment by the fact that it expresses the voluntariness of the endurance of punishment, this sense of the word is also applicable to the case of a criminal who does not receive his merited punishment passively, or at all unwillingly, but consents to its infliction upon him. Stahl's interpretation therefore narrows the ordinary idea of expiation. For expiation means punishment in general, whether the criminal consents to it or not. If, however, we regard a case of crime as a drama in which the criminal's positive guilt excites our tragic sympathy by reason of its complication with the common guilt of the society around him, yet, as soon as the criminal acknowledges his personal guilt and the justice of his punishment, a different impression is left from that received in the opposite case. We have a feeling of reconciliation in so far as the criminal imputes to himself and takes upon himself the culpable influences of society. On this presupposition it follows that both the possible meanings of expiation are embraced in the definition of the word given by Stahl. The punishment which the criminal willingly takes upon himself awakens the sense of aesthetic satisfaction in the sympathetic observer, in so far as it forms the moral conclusion of an immoral development of life. I would add, however, that such a case as this has no connection whatever with the interpretation of Christ's fate. On the contrary, our very sense of aesthetic justice would be offended if the unmerited suffering of the Righteous were estimated by the value of a vicarious penal satisfaction.

The predominantly negative mode of defining the saving work of Christ is favoured, in the last place, by the fact that in Protestant Dogmatics and ascetic literature the problem of sanctification is generally treated in the negative sense of the renunciation of sin and the world. By this negative definition of the principle of ethics I think I may explain the fact, that Oetinger and Menken make their entirely positive estimate of Christ's personal righteousness subordinate to the negative purpose that human nature may thereby be made sinless. Regarding the barrenness of this assertion, I need add nothing to the previous discussion (§ 57). But in the theological circle which follows Bengel and Oetinger, the latter's idea of the *conflict of Christ with the devil and the wrath of God,* which goes farther back to the authority of Luther, is wont to be understood in an essentially negative sense. Now, assuming that we understand the opposition of Christ's adversaries to Him better if we interpret it as a specific action of the devil, we may still inquire how much light this casts upon the valuable content of Christ's life. Christ did not come into contact with God's wrath; Luther's utterances pointing in that direction are based on a misunderstanding. But in what does a spiritual conflict with the untruthfulness and wickedness of others consist, but in a man's speaking the known truth and doing his duty in accordance with his vocation? The idea of Christ's conflict, therefore, does not carry us a step beyond the judgment of the value of His fidelity in His vocation, but shows that we were right in determining precisely by the latter our estimate of the significance of Christ for salvation. Even the polemical discourses of Christ, by which the idea of His conflict with Satan must be measured, denote nothing more than the application of His knowledge of the true religion — the knowledge implied in His vocation—to the judgment of the characteristics which belong to the false religion and its adherents. If the idea of a conflict is attached to this because the discourses are so pointed and therefore so humiliating, and because the absence of all passion and exaggeration, and of all violation of the truth contrasts so strongly with the loathsome calumny which constitutes the most characteristic mark of Satan in the adversaries of Christ and everywhere, yet Christ's conduct, even in this situation, only gives expression to the fact that He was maintaining the position called for by His vocation.

The idea of a conflict of Christ with the devil is not, however, confined to these relations, but is supposed to be proved by the fact that Christ, throughout His whole life, offered resistance to all kinds of ever-recurring temptations, and precisely in this way fought and conquered the devil, who wanted to make Him unfaithful to His task. This conception also would issue in the maintenance of His fidelity in His vocation being affirmed, but would modify the idea of His fidelity in a peculiar way. It is therefore necessary to examine the statement more closely. Temptation is a cause of possible sin, originating in an impulse, the satisfaction of which appears on first thoughts to be in itself legitimate. The excitation of an impulse which appears from the outset to be unlawful, and so evil, does not give rise to temptation, but is a phenomenon of sinful propensity. It is therefore a signal mistake to refer the well-known saying of James (i. 14, 15), as is generally done, to evil desire. Christ was also exposed to temptation, simply because a temptation is always bound up with an inclination which is at the outset morally legitimate or permissible. It was the impulse, in itself lawful, of self-preservation which led to Christ's desire to be spared the suffering of death. But this gave rise to a temptation to sin, because the wish collided with His duty in His vocation. Christ, however, did not consent to this temptation. He renounced His self-preservation, because He assented to the Divine disposal of the end of His life as a consequence of His vocation. If Christ, then, before His entrance upon His public work was tempted by Satan, the idea that the temptations which affected Him were entangled with the kingdom of sin cannot have been His first impression of them. For no man of moral worth will find a temptation in a situation in which he from the outset recognises Satan. Those experiences of Christ must therefore be understood to mean that the impulses which became temptations to Him, because they at first appeared legitimate, were in due time condemned by Him because their satisfaction would entangle Him in the kingdom of evil. Now, the more mature the moral character is, the more comprehensive and penetrating the insight into one's position relatively to the world, the surer one's judg-

ment of the possible relations of the momentary situation—
then the more seldom does temptation occur, and all the
easier will the decision against it prove.

On the other hand, an inward conflict sets in under
these circumstances, if we swing round, and, under a painful
sense of want of freedom and decision, bring before our
minds the possibility of our adopting resolutions of an
opposite moral tendency. Is it supposed, then, that this
was the regular course of Christ's inner life before He
arrived at good and dutiful conduct, and courageous utterance of the truth, and open censure of His adversaries?
For this is the only form in which I can conceive a continuous inner conflict with Satan. Now he who makes
this assertion, even if but indirectly, in the first place
imports into the Evangelical story aspects of which it
betrays just as little trace as it does of that development of
Christ's consciousness of Himself and His vocation which
others seek in the sources. Further, this assumption of an
ever-recurring vacillation between extreme moral opposites
shows but a small degree of understanding of, and esteem
for, Christ's character, a degree which is least of all compatible with pretensions to a peculiarly believing mind and
exclusive orthodoxy. If anything in the Evangelical story
is authentic, it is the impression of Christ's tranquil and
steadfast character, withdrawn into itself from the vacillation
which commonly prevails, remote from all passionate and
painful excitement; and if on occasion the perfidy of His
adversaries moves Him to indignation, yet this is ennobled
by sorrow for their hardness of heart, and balanced by the
perfect goodness of His disposition and by His Divine
patience. What do people mean, then, by asserting a conflict
of Christ with Satan, more than is expressed by affirming
His positive fulfilment of His vocation, with uninterrupted
fidelity to that vocation, with the conduct and speech which
are worthy of it, with inviolable patience under all the
suffering, even the most intense, which was allotted to Him
in consequence of His vocation, and which He willingly

accepted as the expression of Divine providence! In this way Christ demonstrated for Himself His Father's relation to Him as His Son and Revealer; in this way He made possible the community of the children of God, who share His nature. If Christ, however, at the same time vanquished the devil for Himself by withstanding all the temptations which, had they taken effect, would have dragged Him down into the kingdom of sin, yet that does not in any way secure the community founded by Him against the possibility of a countless number of its members falling away to Satan, and even of certain undertakings in the Church being drawn directly into the service of the devil. How, then, can it be asserted in the face of Church history that Christ by His victory over the devil altogether withdrew His believing followers from the latter's power?

Hofmann's view of reconciliation also contains no reference to Christ's conflict with Satan. " Christ's life, which manifested itself in His obedience in His vocation even unto death, is itself reconciliation, because in that life God carried out without interruption His loving fellowship with the one sinless member of humanity, and because Christ passed through this experience not for Himself, but in His destiny as the Beginner of the new humanity which is His community " (vol. i. p. 618). This is a thoroughly positive conception of the matter, in which the value of Christ's life is quite positively defined. But the agreement between Hofmann and myself has its limits. If we ask what constitutes the new relation between God and humanity which is brought about by the perfecting of Christ's obedience in His vocation, Hofmann's readers always stumble upon the negative formula that this relation is no longer, like the previous one, conditioned by sin. He, too, has failed to observe that this formula, which primarily exactly suits the idea of forgiveness, requires to be supplemented by the positive idea of eternal life, or the freedom of the children of God over the world. As he did not derive the latter datum from the source of his theology, and did not extend his investigation of Scripture to this point, his incomplete account of reconciliation leads to an effort to extract from Christ's passion still another meaning than that it is the occasion of a special proof of His obedience in His vocation. This is how we are to regard Hofmann's formula, that in Christ's life and suffering God manifested not only His will of love towards humanity, but also His hatred against sin, since the creative beginning of a new relation between God and humanity did not take place without the corresponding conclusion of the previous sin-determined relation. The question has to be considered whether Hofmann himself, in his view of Christ's life, has carried out the intended co-ordination of both the points of view—God's loving will towards humanity and His hatred of sin.

We may actively manifest our hatred or abhorrence of sin, if we have the power and ability to do so, in either a legal or a moral way. We may, if we have the power, deprive sin of its pretended rights by punishment. Or we may, if we have the ability, show our abhorrence of it by the practice of the good, to which there pertain as accidents censure of sin, its contrary, and readiness to suffer under the sin of others rather than acquiesce in it. Hofmann himself would not have the first case applied to Christ's death. The second case he asserts, inasmuch as he embraces all the valuable phenomena in Christ's life under His obedience in His vocation, an obedience which exhibits God's fellowship of love with Him, and at the same time represents the beginning of the new humanity. Now, in knowing as in willing, every position established in a certain direction is the denial of the opposite direction. It is therefore impossible to see how God's hatred against sin could be manifested in Christ's work of living and suffering otherwise than in the setting forth of the good by His perfect obedience in His vocation, an obedience which includes acquiescence in the sufferings inflicted by the representatives of sin. Hofmann himself, now, is not in a position to escape from this line of thought ; he cannot conceive the circumstances of Christ's suffering such that they would be to him an exhibition of God's hatred of sin apart from their subordination to Christ's positive obedience in His vocation.   For he says that Christ gave Himself up to God's wrath against men and to Satan's power over them in order *to perfect His obedience* by subjecting it to the severest trial which could befall it, and in order so to experience the consequences of sin that His last and extremest suffering should also be the *consummation of His obedience.*[1]   Hofmann's doctrine, then, may appear to enjoy the advantage of having proved that Christ's passion comprised not only His positive achievement towards reconciliation, but in addition to that a negative operation of the Divine hatred against sin ; but while he did, indeed, attempt to create this impression, yet in reality he kept to the lines of that positive view and interpretation of Christ's achievement towards reconciliation which alone is fitted to establish the positive inference of eternal life.

§ 59. The individual, too, can pronounce forgiveness or justification, reconciliation and adoption into Divine sonship, to be his possession, only in virtue of his attaching himself to Christ's life-work as a whole.   For we have this possession only as members of the religious community of Christ, as the result of the incalculable and mysterious interaction between our own freedom and the determining influences of fellowship ; and this fellowship is possible in its own order only through Christ's unique life-course in its well-known double aspect, and its continuous action through all the ages.   The condition of faith, through which the individual knows himself to be justified by Christ or reconciled with Christ, alters nothing in the connection of ideas which I have set forth.   Certainly there is in no case either a mechanical or a logical necessity laid upon individuals to join themselves in faith to the existing Christian community.   Faith begins in harmony with the law of freedom.   It cannot be calculated beforehand whether Christ will find faith, and the fact that He found it was no more

[1] *Schutzschriften*, Pt. i. p. 9.

determined beforehand than the purpose in general guarantees the result.   But after, in this case, the result has happened, the guiding purpose of its Author provides the standard by which it is to be judged.   The individual can experience the peculiar effect which proceeds from Christ only in connection with the community founded by Him, and on the pre-supposition of its existence.   The assurance of Divine grace is bound up with this economy, and with nothing else. This is also the meaning of the 5th and 7th Articles of the Augsburg Confession.   For religion is always social.   Christ did not aim at any action upon men which would merely be a moral instruction of individuals.   On the contrary, His purpose in the latter direction was subordinated to the creation of the new religion.   The individual believer, therefore, can rightly understand his position relatively to God only as meaning that he is reconciled by God through Christ in the community founded by Christ.   The fellowship with God through Christ which is thus conditioned is the intelligible and valuable content of the faith which is specifically conscious of itself.   Now if, on account of Rom. iv. 5, we are to adopt the formula that faith is counted for righteousness, this proposition can be understood in harmony with our leading line of thought only as meaning that we esteem faith as the subjective manifestation of fellowship with Christ.   For it is just Christ's value for God, and the determining influence of Christ's fellowship with him upon the subject, which forms the ground on which the latter is justified, *i.e.* admitted in spite of his sins to fellowship with God.[1]   On the other hand, the proposition would not be understood as Paul himself meant it, if *faith* were interpreted *as a self-activity, with a content due to the subject himself.*

Repeated reference (vol. .i. pp. 359, 626 ; *supra,* pp. 84, 107) has been made to the fact that this perversion of the Reformation view was brought about in the circles of Pietism.

---

[1] As often as the formula that faith justifies occurs in the *Apology of the Augsburg Confession,* we see clearly that it is an inexact expression, which has to be supplemented and corrected by the ideas expressed above.

Now just as the phenomenon of Pietism was possible at all in the Lutheran and the Reformed Church only on the presupposition that the teleological relation of the idea of justification to eternal life as consisting in freedom over the world had been forgotten, so that distortion of the conception of justification is to be explained especially by the fact that more attention was directed to the efforts of the subject after a lively and sensible faith than to the object, which was for the Reformers the principal thing. According to this view, the believer is justified [1] on account of his resolve to believe, as subject of the principle of the sinless life. This result is also partly due to the circumstance that the idea of righteousness, which as an attribute of the believer is derived from the judgment of God, is understood, in accordance with orthodoxy, as equivalent to moral perfection. The tacit assumption that God can have communion only with the morally perfect (§ 14), led to the interpretation of justification in the sense that God imputes the moral perfection of Christ to believers, and therefore regards them as perfect though they are not so. This mode of arriving at the judgment of God is abandoned in Pietistic circles, but in its place there is constructed the formula that God imputes to the believer the moral perfection which is contained in faith as the principle of the new life that is beginning; and Oetinger and Rothe at the same time asserted that God in this way anticipates His judgment upon the course of the believer's moral life (vol. i. pp. 552, 610). We can here perceive how much this divergent account of justification is dominated by that definition of the idea which prevails in the school from whose doctrines in other respects these very writers desire so widely to differ. This, however, is a phenomenon of frequent occurrence in theology, that the most glaring inconsistencies are connected with the fact that we unconsciously take over from our opponent the very point on which they turn.

It is still necessary to subject to criticism this Pietistic

---

[1] [*Gerechtgesprochen*, pronounced righteous.]

theory in a modernised form. Sulze [1] expresses himself as
follows : "In repentance the power of Divine grace which
entered our soul at our enlightenment and was received by
us in faith, *i.e.* with trust, fights the decisive battle with sin.
The power of sin is thus broken at its centre. Certainly
that does not yet make us perfectly righteous and sinless.
The development of life in us, of which God is the Author,
has only gained a vigorous beginning in us. God in His
grace regards this beginning as the completion, for indeed He
is the Author of it. God Himself best knows the omnipotence of the Divine love which is now in us. Therefore
He can have full confidence regarding us, that the completion
will not fail the beginning. On the ground of this assurance
He regards us as righteous though we are not yet so. We
believe in this judgment of God, and therefore also regard
ourselves as righteous, and have the full joy of our sanctification just as if we were already righteous. Thus, on both
sides, faith is a representation of the future as present."
The rights of religion are claimed for this interpretation as
against the traditional view that justification is brought about
by God, because we believe in the satisfaction of Christ, which
He made to God for us and by which the tension between
justice and love in God is removed. For this historical
knowledge has as such no religious value and no trustworthiness. Further, the need of satisfaction before forgiveness is provided for by the fact that in our earnest repentance
the Spirit of God, Who is in us through regeneration,
innocently suffers for the sin of the old man, and by doing so
testifies that by the rule of Divine justice punishment follows
guilt, though punishment as such is now removed. Justification, however, is bound up with Christ, since humanity
as a whole first becomes acceptable to God in Him as its
Head, and then the Divine life of the individual believer,
which God regards as righteousness, is awakened by Christ.

---

[1] *Die Hauptpunkte der kirchlichen Glaubenslehre mit den Worten der
Bekenntnisse dargestellt und an der heil. Schrift und den Forderungen des
Glaubens geprüft,* 1862, p. 87 ff.

Conformity to the image of the Lord is of course brought
about, not by the inculcation of a system of doctrine regarding Him, but by free and unconstrained love to Him, and
in this way, through the righteousness of Christ, there is
wrought in us the righteousness which justifies us.   In particular, the death of Christ serves to beget in us the new
life, through the power which this event exercises upon
the heart, inasmuch as by it sin is broken at the very heart
of the life of this world.

The same principle, exhibiting the same opposition between the religious and moral interest and the juristic form
of the traditional doctrine of reconciliation, is asserted by
Hanne [1] as an expression of the " modern " religious view :
" That we may stand as righteous before God, that is, that
we may get rid of the burden of sin and the condemnation
felt in our conscience, we ought no longer to remain sinners,
but must become quite other men.   This takes place when
we turn the whole heart to God and receive Christ inwardly,
that with Him and through Him, God's Son, we ourselves
may become children of God.   When we have become one
with Christ by faith, that is, when we begin to strive with
all our energy to become children of God, we appear before
God as such—as His children whose sin He graciously
forgives in view of the future complete dominion of the
Christian spirit in us.   For we are not, indeed, perfect
forthwith ; but we have in us the power which irresistibly
changes us and necessarily brings us in the end to perfection.   In view of this certain event in the future God
declares us righteous, and removes from our conscience
the burden of sin.   The fact that we are for the present
still weak in the new life, and imperfect beginners, is not
taken into account in view of the future, which must be
entirely different, and which has already planted in us its
shoots and sprouts, from which the full flower is slowly but
surely developed.   Thus it is only by actually receiving
Christ into our inner life that we arrive at peace of conscience

---

[1] *Der ideale und der geschichtliche Christus,* 1871, p. 15.

and blessedness. By this path of religious and moral renewal alone does the sinner, according to the modern view, become a Christian and receive true salvation."

Now this line of thought is not in truth so very modern ; for it is as a whole the creed of Böhme and Dippel, who regard the imitation of Christ's death and resurrection in continual repentance as the righteousness which is by faith. The mystical background of this theory is also indicated clearly enough by Sulze, when he makes the life of God in the believer the central idea, and indirectly by Hanne, when he emphasises at the cost of moral freedom the necessity and irresistibility of the principle working in the believer. But the direct descent of the accordant formulae of Sulze and Hanne can be traced back through Rothe and Schleiermacher to Oetinger, and in particular to Kant. Exegetical proof from the New Testament can be claimed for this doctrine, only if we assume that the contents of the sixth chapter of the Epistle to the Romans and Paul's other utterances to the same effect do not indicate a secondary line of thought, but the central point of his view of Christianity. But I at least cannot believe that (vol. ii. p. 226). In this theory the moral transformation of the individual is in itself set forth as the proper purpose of Christianity, and the religious factor is taken into account only in the sense that God recognises beforehand the effect which the spiritual action of Christ will have upon the formation of the believer's good character. The need for this judgment of God is explained by saying that it is the condition on which the conscience is delivered from the burden of guilt, and the true joy of sanctification called forth. Now when the individual as such is compared with Christ and brought into connection with Him, Christ's action upon him is supposed to mean that he receives Christ into himself as his ruling ideal, and gives up the sinful direction of his will by a free resolution, the possibility of which depends upon the conception that Christ admitted no sin into His own soul. For this idea has still to be supplemented if we are to understand the power which the death of Christ must exercise upon the heart, in so far as that death effects the destruction of sin as a whole.

The advocates of this view are justified in emphasising the opposition between their theory and the traditional theory of the Evangelical Church. For they exalt the interest of the individual's moral transformation above the religious interest of Christianity, no less distinctly than the orthodox doctrine is calculated to exalt the common religious transformation above the moral renewal of the individual. Thus we see that the modern theory is analogous to Socinianism, though it generally uses means which are derived from " holiness "- Pietism. This judgment is confirmed in particular by the way in which the Divine sentence of justification is interpreted. For the principle of the new life, which in spite of its imperfect working out in the believer is to be regarded as factually identical with individual moral perfection, is equivalent to the practical obedience of faith which, according to the Socinian doctrine, God regards in spite of its defects as empirically perfect. Now, if the advocates of this theory urge against orthodoxy that the imputation of the moral righteousness of Christ to the individual would indicate a self-deception on God's part, and that it is impossible to see how this assumption serves for the appeasement of the conscience and for moral impulse—I too am unable to understand how the assumption of a Divine judgment upon the new life of the believer, which does not correspond with the believer's judgment of himself, can have any value for the latter. It may be true that God knows the individual man more thoroughly than it is possible for him to know himself, and in particular that God for the moment regards the man as precisely the opposite of what he appears to himself to be, in good as well as in evil. But what will the result be if, in addition to denying the conditions of freedom, we inculcate upon ourselves a faith in our own perfection on the ground of the theoretical persuasion that God, in accordance with conditions of His knowledge inaccessible to us, regards us as perfect? Will the appeasement of the conscience and the joy of sanctification keep their proper limits on these terms? I should imagine that if this were the case it would be very accidental. It is therefore probable that a mistake has been committed at this point, the more so as along with the intention to oppose orthodoxy there goes the admission of the idea— not clearly discarded by orthodoxy—that in justification the question at issue is the recognition of our moral perfection.

The same dependence on the form of doctrine which is regarded as orthodox Lutheran—namely, that justification has reference to the individual as such—leads in the case of another representative of modern Christianity to the thesis that the action of Christ is to be appropriated through the imitation of His religious and moral uniqueness. Christ's decisive and permanent value for humanity consists, according to Schwalb,[1] in His being our example; and he says it is no innovation, but the practice of faith from the earliest times, to strive after likeness to Christ in His Divine Sonship, i.e. His peculiar consciousness of God as His Father, and, further, to copy His moral purity. Now this preacher is certainly right in saying that his programme of the imitation of, or assimilation to, Christ is nothing new; it is in truth the formula of practical Christianity in the Middle Ages, which coincides with the monastic endeavour to renounce the world. It will have to be shown later how this task was modified in the Protestant sense (§ 68); but in any case this change in the idea is not adverted to by Schwalb. He can only appeal to the way in which the example of Christ is developed in the *True Christianity* of Johann Arndt, as the standard of all the relations of life. Likeness to Christ is set forth in certain statements of Paul as the end of life in the Christian community (2 Cor. iii. 18; Rom. viii. 29). If Schwalb, however, according to his principle of the typical character of Christ in His God-consciousness and moral purity, makes it the Christian's duty "to become like the Lord Christ,"[2] the

[1] *Der alte und der neue Glaube an Christus*, 1868.
[2] So Hanne, *op. cit.* p. 42: "He who strives with full earnestness to appropriate the ideal Christ, and to become like Him, cannot succeed in doing so without the historical Christ."

question remains how this is to be done. Now among the
theologians of this group it is, indeed, constantly being said
that " we receive Christ into our hearts," or that " we give
up our hearts to Him," and so it is possible that what they
mean is not exhausted by the phrase that Christ is our
example. But whatever relation the vague and vacillating
expressions of these theologians may have to the claim they
make to be " modernising " Christianity, it concerns our interest
to determine how far imitation really goes, for the idea of
imitation suggests itself as correlative to the pattern character thus asserted to belong to Christ alone.

Imitation has but a very limited scope in mental life.
It is a regular form of mental acquisition in childhood; as
the form assumed by evil habits, it extends into the years of
riper youth; if it appears further as the predominant form
of mental appropriation, it is the mark of mental narrow-
ness or approach to idiocy. For imitation extends only to
particular relations of mental life, and these, too, such as are
very apparent to the senses. It is therefore quite impossible
to imitate a person's character as a whole, even though it
expresses itself never so strongly and clearly in his demeanour. If it is possible to regard a son as the spiritual
image of his father, similarity of natural disposition is the
principal motive of his sympathy with his father's manner,
the appropriation of which in childhood and in the father's
presence is assisted by the imitation of externals, but is in
truth brought about by the incalculable aesthetic attraction
which the father's well-defined character exercises upon the
similarly constituted son. If imitation were the form in
which likeness to the father's character was to be reached,
the child would have to understand how to separate and to
combine again in thought all the particular virtues as such
in which character consists; but this goes beyond the knowledge which is possible in childhood. Harmony of characters
is often found, too, outside the hereditary fellowship of the
family, between juniors and seniors, between scholars and
teachers; this, however, is the case only in consequence of

their free recognition of the same life-purpose, and the normal special means employed for its personal inculcation. But pre-eminent men, the master-minds of history, cannot be in any danger of being matched by imitation; for all agreement of character with them, the more widely it extends, is the more markedly accompanied by a sense of the dissimilarity that remains behind, all pointing to the fact that these great men are originals, and matchless in their own order.

No man, I suppose, was ever more in earnest about the imitation of Christ than St. Francis; but he laid hold upon the outwardly perceptible circumstances of Christ's life of poverty, and exaggerated them. Yet this method was dominated by that submission to Christ which is of a general and inward kind. Not only did he assume that he was subject to Christ in virtue of redemption, but the resolution to imitate Christ's poverty was bound up with the fact that Francis conceived his Model not only in His relation to God, but also in a relation to the world, which implies that the Bearer of the perfect religion renounced the world, inasmuch as He withdrew Himself from all the natural ways and arrangements of life. On this assumption, that religion reflects itself in a definite attitude towards the world, the imitation of Christ in the features of poverty and renunciation of the world seemed possible. This whole field of course lies quite outside the horizon of the "modern" theologian, who looks upon Christianity as exhausted in the reproduction in men of Divine sonship, and thus sets aside the idea of redemption or reconciliation by Christ, not only in a definite doctrinal form, but in every form, or limits its validity to the voluntary act of the individual's self-conversion. But how do we come at all to imitate Christ's Divine Sonship? Does this task possess no special features which would be worth discussing? Is it so much as intelligible without any special presuppositions? What reply can be made if I again call attention to the fact that the imitation of great men in their distinctive character is an impossibility, not to judge it more severely? But certainly the utterly unpractical attitude and the

emptiness of the programme of " modern " Christianity is not
to be urged solely against the representative of the standpoint
which I am at present criticising. On the contrary, the
error which is primarily observable in this school rests upon
a tradition to which people usually surrender themselves
without criticism.

For since Schleiermacher raised the problem of the
peculiar psychological character of religion, German theology
has never grown weary of occupying itself with it afresh.
Nobody, indeed, has been able to maintain the conception of
feeling in the sense asserted by Schleiermacher, as the
function of absolute dependence upon God; on the contrary,
psychological investigation has always been led on to other
lines. In one respect, however, Schleiermacher's precedent
dominates all subsequent attempts, namely, in the fact that
religion is always represented simply as a relation to God,
but not at the same time as a relation or attitude of man to
the world (p. 28). Schleiermacher was able to disregard
this latter requirement because his dialectic led him to
include in the idea of God neutrality towards the world,
the indifference of undivided unity towards the manifold of
existence. Certainly he satisfied that requirement in so far
as he taught that the feeling of dependence on God fills up
a moment of time, only when it is combined with an act of
sensuous feeling or with acts of ideation or volition which
relate to the world. But this view has had no effect upon
his followers, who, in spite of their proposed alteration of
psychological theory, have regarded the contents of religion
only as related to God and never at the same time as related
to the world, though the historical appearance of all religions
actually demands the latter view. People reflect on the
relation of religion, especially the Christian religion, to the
world only when they want to determine the way in which
moral conduct is related to religious faith. But as in doing
so care has to be taken not to confound the two, their
attention is never drawn to the fact that there is another
relation of man to the world, the regulation of which must

be directly provided for in the idea of religion. I mean that in Christianity we are not religiously dependent upon the supramundane God without at the same time experiencing our religious freedom relatively to the world, and actively manifesting our religious dominion over it in our view of the world and our personal tone of feeling.[1]

What, then, do exhortations to imitate the God-consciousness of Christ or to awaken the assurance of Divine sonship in ourselves signify, unless it is at the same time taught that this form finds its material in all those relations of man to the world in which, according to the natural view of things, he is dependent on the world, while this form becomes operative in the material indicated when our judgment regarding these relations and the tone of feeling they produce changes the impression we have naturally into that of dominion over things? But if the Christian God-consciousness is conceived, as it must be, in such a way that spiritual dominion over our situation in the world is the obverse side of our Divine sonship, then it is at least a dubious formula which prescribes the imitation of the God-consciousness of Christ. For those relations to the world in

---

[1] I have before me two popular theological treatises of recent date, the one from the field of critical, the other from that of apologetic theology. It is noticeable how little their formulae regarding justification and Divine sonship differ from one another, but at the same time how little practical fruit they yield, because neither of them embraces the Christian goal of dominion over the world. Brückner, *Was ist die Rechtfertigung aus dem Glauben?* (Heidelberg, 1872) pp. 30, 32: "All religion is a feeling of dependence on God. Freedom in God is its end and aim. The phrase *sola fide* makes that dependence on God absolute, to the exclusion of every other temporally conditioned, humanly mundane, mediation or authority; at the same time, however, it conditions the true ideal freedom of the spirit and conscience by the idea of the omnipotence and love of God. . . . The idea of Divine sonship manifests itself in Jesus Christ in its truth and perfection, through the power of the satisfaction and blessedness which it is capable of giving; it shows in Him as the Founder and Pattern of Christianity how absolute dependence on God, the Father of love, is one with absolute freedom in God." Pfeiffer, *Das Gotteskindschaftsbewusstsein* (Bern and St. Gallen, 1873), p. 74: "The right filial relation of man to God, according to the teaching of Jesus, is the unconditional surrender of the soul to God, and, as the result of acceptance through grace, the consciousness of receiving the continual communication of the Spirit from the Being of the Father and of being blessed in this communication of life."

which Christ experienced His God-consciousness and made proof of it for Himself and for God, are so distinct from those in which the members of His community stand, that Christ is withdrawn from all direct imitation. The maintenance of Christ's God-consciousness in His relation to the world is especially expressed in the patience which He brought to bear on His sufferings, which were the outcome of the situation called for by His vocation and of the antagonism to it felt by the ruling society. His vocation, however, is unique in its kind ; for its special character is directed to the general moral task as such, in other words to the founding of the Kingdom of God and the community destined for this task (§ 48). Therefore nobody can directly imitate Him ; and an imitation which selects particular visible aspects of His life-course would still be no imitation of Christ. For this reason what even St. Francis presents is by no means a satisfying, but rather an unsuccessful copy of his Master.

If Christ's pattern character is nevertheless to be used as a standard of the Christian life, what it yields is nothing but fidelity in the moral vocation which is assigned to everyone as the special field of his contribution to the Kingdom of God.[1] But before we can assert this idea as valid for ourselves, we must remember that owing to the difference between Christ and us we have primarily no right to that consciousness of Divine sonship in which we might copy the God-consciousness of Christ. It has been possible for Schwalb to disregard this fact because he has not clearly and fully described the position of those whom he exhorts to imitate Christ. The fact that it gives us no difficulty, or that we look upon it as a matter of course, to set our trust on God like children, is due to our having grown up and having been educated in the Christian community. This circumstance, however, must be expressly recognised in a theory of the Christian religion, and must be declared to be the given presupposition of the desired imitation of the God-

[1] *Apol. C. A.* xiii. 45-50.

consciousness of Christ. Apart from this practical social foundation for every exercise of Christian piety, we must at the outset confess that through our participation in the sin of society we stand far away from God. We are justified, however, in the assurance of Divine sonship, in spite of our sense of guilt, because we belong to the community which is founded by Christ as the community of reconciliation with God—founded through the fulfilment of His vocation, and under circumstances such as to surround the idea of our imitating that vocation with the most important limitations. On these presuppositions, and following the impulse of reconciliation, we may, without any intention of imitating Christ in all the situations of life in which a natural dependence on the world is expressed, prove our Divine sonship by a frame of mind which changes the sense of dependence into its opposite. In the assurance that all things work together for good to them that love God, because God's love is manifested to them in reconciliation through Christ, we may exercise the same dominion over the world which Christ exercised by the assertion of His consciousness of God. But we shall do this all the more surely, the less we propose to imitate Christ in this relation, and the more we extend our confidence in our reconciliation with God through Him to trust in the Fatherly grace of God in all our experiences. Without this positive supplement given by the independence of our self-feeling over the world, the formula of our freedom in God obtained for us by Christ is certainly as empty and meaningless as the task set us to imitate His God-consciousness. For without that content freedom in God is the formula of world-renouncing mysticism, which attains its end only with that renunciation of spiritual personality after which it also strives (vol. i. p. 122). The latter, however, must rather be preserved unto eternal life in Divine sonship, and the lordship over the world corresponding thereto.

§ 60. The statement that it is inside the community of believers that experience of reconciliation through Christ is to be had, corresponds to the general experimental truth that every spiritual acquisition is brought about by the incalculable interaction between the freedom of the individual and the stimulating and guiding impressions which he receives from fellowship with others. That statement does not, however, imply that the value which inheres in the personal work of Christ for our reconciliation is superseded by the existence of Divine sonship in the other members of the community, and pushed so much into the background that we might disregard Christ as the Author of our reconciliation. Still less can it be maintained that Christ's work of reconciliation is bound up with the privileges of an order in the Church, and transmitted *ex opere operato* through their sensible actions. Christ comes to act upon the individual believer on the one hand through the historical remembrance of Him which is possible in the Church, on the other hand as the permanent Author of all the influences and impulses which are due to other men, and like in nature to Himself; and this necessarily takes place in a personal, and not in a material form. Accordingly, the result of reconciliation appears in its normal completeness in subjective *faith in Christ*. Here it is only necessary to repeat and to bring in what has already (pp. 101, 142) been set forth as the view of the Reformers and as the inevitable result of observation. To believe in Christ implies that we accept the value of the Divine love, which is manifest in His work, for our reconciliation with God, with that trust which, directed to Him, subordinates itself to God as His and our Father; whereby we are assured of eternal life and blessedness. Faith in Christ is neither belief in the truth of His history nor assent to a scientific judgment of knowledge such as that presented by the Chalcedonian formula. It is not a recognition of His Divine nature of such a kind that, in affirming it, we disregard His life-work and His action for the salvation of those who have to reckon themselves as belonging to His community. In so far as trust in Him includes a knowledge of Him, this knowledge will determine the value of His work for our salvation. This value is to be decided by the fact that Christ, as the Bearer of the perfect revelation of God, through His solidarity with the Father, in the right exercise of His love and patience over the world, demonstrated His Godhead as man for the salvation of those whom, as His community, He at the same time represented before the Father by His obedience, and still represents. In this way He awakens the trust in Himself which, as passionate personal conviction, overcomes and subordinates to itself all the other motives of life, using as it does the tradition of Christ propagated in the Church, and thus putting itself into connection with all those who believe in Christ. The recollection of guilt which has been forgiven us, and is daily forgiven, combined as it is with faith in the Redeemer, and suffused with penitence, does not hinder us from asserting a distinct self-feeling over against the world, which no longer dominates us or separates us from God. Faith, if it is derived from Divine grace, will also overcome the disturbances which arise from temptations due to the world. For either these temptations can be repelled, or, if we fail to do so, the sins which we commit afresh are, in our readiness to repent through trust in Christ, subordinated to His forgiving grace. As this comes to be a question of the rule of the Christian life, the view of the world which befits the believer in Christ is designed to enable him to assume, throughout the whole of the world created and governed by God, the position guaranteed to him by Christ. For in Christianity a direct claim is made for the personal feeling of self by the assertion that, on the ground of reconciliation with God, each man has, not the significance of a dependent part of the world, but the value of a whole—a value which proves itself by spiritual dominion over the individual and particular motives which are contained in the world. But the key to every conception of an actual whole lies in the knowledge of the special conditions under which a universal end may, in accordance with law, be realised in a complex of particular phenomena. According to this rule, personal conviction of the Christian view of the world, in which the corresponding self-feeling is assured of its validity, depends on faith in the Divine worth of Christ. For His historical appearance denotes not only the organising centre of the world - whole within which the spiritual self - feeling of Christians receives its permanent and specific satisfaction, but also the absolutely sufficient ground of knowledge by which we make that view of the world our own. We make this very view of the world, and the self-judgment corresponding to it, valid for ourselves when we become personally convinced of the value of Christ as the Revealer of the Divine purpose of the world, and the Founder of the community reconciled with God by Him. At the same time we affirm the value of the view of the world guaranteed by Him by making it the supreme motive for our exercise of will, and that in the direction both of reverence for God and of moral activity devoted to the final end of the Kingdom of God. For these reasons, faith in Christ is the full and clear expression of our subjective conviction of the truth of His religion.

Faith in Christ and God falls within the compass of the idea of love already defined (p. 277). It is that continuous direction of the will to the final end of God and Christ, which the believer maintains for his own sake. In this sense Thomas rightly decided that love to God is the essence of faith, since it raises the intellectual act to the worth of a religious function (p. 103). Now in the New Testament, in spite of the commandment of love to God, a very sparing use is made of this idea (vol. ii. p. 100), and love toward Christ is not expressed except in John xxi. 15, 16. There is good reason why it is otherwise in the Epistles of the New Testament. As a generic idea love to Christ is more indefinite than faith in Him. The former term leaves the point undecided whether we put ourselves on a level with Christ or subordinate ourselves to Him. But faith in Christ includes the confession of His Godhead and His dominion over us, and thus denies the possibility of equality with Him. This is the evident purpose which leads the Reformers to elaborate the idea of faith in Christ. If Christ takes the place of God, faith in Him is necessarily a kind of obedience (Rom. i. 5). Nevertheless the demand for love to Christ occupies an exceedingly large place not only in the Middle Ages, but also in the Churches which sprang from the Reformation. Advocates of this trend of feeling have declared that my exposition of faith, which has kept to the line of the doctrinal standards of the Reformation, is antiquated. I affirm, on the contrary, that the Reformation antiquated that "love to Christ" which is here in question. For love very distinctly implies the equality of the person loving with the beloved. St. Bernard (vol. i. p. 116), who gave to the world the pattern of this species of piety, expressly states that in intercourse with the Bridegroom awe ceases, majesty is laid aside, and immediate personal intercourse is carried on as between lovers or neighbours.[1] And these features recur wherever love to the Lord Jesus is expressed in the terms of the Song of Songs. Now in the Latin Catholic Church this form of devotion and its excitement by sympathy with the sufferings of Christ are logically consistent. For that Church's view of Christ is dominated by a complete breach between His Godhead and manhood (vol. i. pp. 38, 47, 56). In the traditional formulas the Godhead which forms the background of the man Christ is confessed, but a living interest attaches only to this latter Being, Whom Augustine designated as the Bearer of mediation with God, as the Representative of God's love, and in Whom later writers further reverence the Ideal of human destiny, the fairest of the sons of men, and Whom by the play of fancy upon Him they clasp in their arms. In the Latin Middle Ages people purchased, by the verbal confession of Christ's Godhead, freedom to love Him as a mere man, to imitate Him as such, to bring Him down to their own level, to play with Him (p. 391). At that time they attached a practical idea to His Godhead only when they thought of His Judgment. The latter idea, however, held good for a class different from those who cultivated familiar intercourse with Him ; or if such became alarmed at this prospect, then all love-play

[1] *Geschichte des Pietismus*, i. p. 49.

with the Lord Jesus was forgotten. The Reformers transcended these fragmentary and incoherent views, inasmuch as by faith in Christ they expressed reverence for the God-man, and taught men by trust in Him to banish their terror at the Judge. These conditions of Protestant piety correspond to the efforts of the Reformers to show that His Godhead is present precisely in the mediatorial achievements of His earthly life (p. 394). It was therefore a reaction from the clearly recognisable purpose of the Reformation when the Mediaeval material of devotion was again admitted into the Lutheran Church soon after the settlement of the Book of Concord, and later into the Reformed Church.[1]

If, then, it is claimed that the Reformation conception of faith in Christ is transcended and superseded by familiar intercourse with the Saviour, I must assume that this pretension has behind it all those strainings of the fancy with which I am familiar all the way from Bernard to Spangenberg.[2] In my *History of Pietism*, however, I have given reasons why they mark no improvement upon the attitude of faith in Christ described by the Reformers. The principal reason against the above contention is that the excitement of the fancy and the effort after a more or less sensuous feeling of pleasure usually end in the opposite result of desertion and dulness of feeling. This method accordingly brings unhappiness in its train, whilst blessedness is guaranteed by faith in Christ when rightly understood. Perhaps this objection does not apply to the assertion which is made by many of my theological opponents—that an immediate personal relation to Christ and to God is the kernel of the Christian life. But if they demand that theological doctrine shall expressly justify this practice of theirs and determine its conditions, the following facts have to be considered. Every religious judgment, and so every devout consideration of God's leadings and claims as well as of Christ's benefits,

---

[1] *Op. cit.* i. pp. 129, 281, ii. p. 48, iii. pp. 94, 212.

[2] Spangenberg (*Idea fidei fratrum*) first develops the doctrine of grace in relation to faith, but in addition to that prescribes love to God as a contemplative exercise (*op. cit.* iii. p. 454).

is due to our regarding God and Christ as present. But we find ourselves placed immediately over against that which we view as present. In this sense Melanchthon designates the intuition of Christ, or of the promise of grace of which He is the Bearer, as the regular means of impressing upon ourselves the forgiveness of sins or the assurance of salvation (p. 142). Now this method of devotion may keep wholly within its own special rights, even when theology, having as a science fully and clearly to determine the inner texture of religion, is obliged to point out that such acts of religious imagination proceed from a series of mediating causes, the consideration of which is overleapt in the moment of contemplation. If those who are intent on the practice of an immediate personal relation to Christ also possess theological culture, they will not, I hope, deny that their contemplative presentation to themselves of Christ as their Redeemer and Lord is possible only because they have been brought up in the Church, have in it become believers, and in it have been furnished with the right knowledge of Christ; and they will not, I hope, gainsay Calvin's statement that Christ, even as He is represented in devotion, can be rightly conceived only as invested with His Word (p. 113). One who understands physiology and psychology acts like every other man on the assumption that in his sense - perceptions he stands immediately over against things. But in his scientific estimate of such occurrences the .physiologist and psychologist points out that these include a very complicated process of mediation, in which the judgment of the beholder modifies the physical impressions of light on the eye so as to determine the size and distance of things in the way which we think a matter of immediate perception. In the same way the theologian is obliged to trace back the immediate contemplation of Christ in the exercise of devotion to all the historical presuppositions of that act, and to remind his readers of these, in order that devotion may not be taken up with arbitrary distortions of the picture of Christ.

For this purpose theology has to insist that the con-

templation of Christ which befits the Evangelical Christian
shall have mixed up with it none of the elements of the
Song of Songs, that is, no love-play on an equal footing
with the beloved. For this whole domain lies outside the
Word with which Christ is invested when He presents
Himself to contemplation. But that also implies that the
contemplation of Christ should not be practised for the
purpose of deriving from it direct feelings of happiness.
For this, too, is merely a Catholic and not an Evangelical
method; what is sought in this way is merely aesthetic
enjoyment, and not religious strength, which as such we
prove by vindicating our reconciliation with God through
our attitude towards the world. What befits the Evangelical Christian in this respect may be seen from the
prayers which in the *German Passional of our Lord Jesus
Christ* (Nürnberg, 1548) are subjoined to the sections into
which the story of Christ's suffering is divided.[1] Here the
petitions are attached to the contemplation of the suffering
Christ in its separate acts—that "Thou wouldst for Thy
Passion's sake protect us from every snare of the devil and
from all the assaults of sin"; that "I may be strengthened
to overcome all afflictions, sufferings, and sickness in Thy
Passion"; that "I may entirely surrender all my will
to Thy most perfect will, so that my walk and life may
ever be found in Thy service"; that "I may not be
moved by wicked slander, but may possess my soul in
Christian patience." And if it is the bestowal of eternal
blessedness which is sought in the majority of these prayers,
that goal is not conceived save as including the joy of victory
over all enemies.

Faith, marked by the above described characteristics, is
an expression for the whole position which the individual
assumes towards Christ as the Bearer of reconciliation and
the Representative of God the Father. Now, not every
moment of the Christian life is occupied by the distinct

[1] They will be found in the Prayer-book published by the Evangelical Book
Society (Berlin, 1849), pp. 384–410.

appearance of all the characteristics contained in faith. In particular the emotion which attaches to faith is excited only by special adverse circumstances, when it is necessary to emphasise the weight of believing conviction. What Calvin meant by that characteristic (p. 101), and what follows from the worth of God and Christ and salvation (p. 211), is at the same time subject to the limitation that all education is designed to set bounds to our feelings and emotions (p. 165). It follows that our normal experience of the Christian religion, which in the highest sense relies on education, and is unhealthy without it, comes to us through that moderate state of feeling which makes continuity and equilibrium possible. The fact that the temperature of this feeling will be different in individuals according to their temperament, need merely be indicated here; for the whole series of these cases eludes scientific examination. In the full compass of its characteristics faith in Christ marks the beginning of the Christian life, if it is attained through sudden conversion. This case presupposes that a man has lived in vice or in antichristian convictions, and thus that the Christian education expended upon him remained fruitless. But if, amid the surroundings of Church life, education is the normal form in which individuals attain to faith in Christ, it is not to be expected that faith should be called forth in its definite peculiar character, in the totality of its characteristics, prior to the operations of God's grace in the sphere of moral discipline and action. Education is always designed to deprive evil inclinations of their power by particular impulses to moral activity, and thus to attain the cultivation of character as a whole. Accordingly, the arousing of the right religious estimate of self can only be brought about by education indirectly, inasmuch as the practice of goodness ought not to be accompanied by self-complacency, but must be accompanied by humility. Out of the practice of humility and trust in parents and teachers the right sense of guilt in relation to Christ and trust in Him will arise in the maturer period of life. Accordingly that which proves itself the comprehensive motive of the Christian life in the later period can neither be directly understood nor experienced in childhood. Others, certainly, are of a different opinion as to this. Because faith in Christ is represented in systematic theology as the supreme motive of all good conduct, the attempt is made in certain circles to produce in young children a love for the Saviour, and to use this argument systematically in guiding their education. It may be granted that in childhood love to the Saviour is analogous to faith in Christ. The latter, however, is something very serious; the former is playful, for otherwise it would not be within the reach of a child. But moral education, which is a serious business even in nonage, the successes or failures of which must be taken equally seriously, can hardly be inculcated upon a child in the right way by means of a playful idea. The mental development of a child is not brought about by the instillation of general ideas into his mind, in order that by their means he may come to understand what is special and particular. Just as little does education in Christianity and for Christianity depend upon imparting to the imagination a general motive of obedience and good conduct, in order that the requirements of obedience may thence be deduced. The books which represent children of this kind as patterns for others are useless and injurious both from the paedagogic and the Christian point of view. Faith in Christ can be expected only in maturer life. As the general attitude which corresponds to reconciliation, it embraces all the particular acts of reconciling faith, patience, and humility, by which our standing in grace is put to the proof. These are not something alongside of faith in Christ, or something which merely results from it, but are the forms in which faith in Christ is applied to the life which the believer leads in the world.

§ 61. One who, as a believer, is no longer controlled by natural impulses—impulses, that is, at once self-seeking and world-loving—which bear the chief mark of sin in their indifference or mistrust towards God, is in the *state of regeneration*. Now justification or reconciliation is also contained in faith in God through Christ. The question arises, accordingly, how the idea of regeneration is related to these two. It is apparently very easy to decide the point if we only attend to the connections of Biblical phraseology. For on the assumption that God receives us as His children when He reconciles us with Himself through Christ, reconciliation is equivalent to adoption, and the possession of justification or reconciliation is equivalent to Divine sonship (§ 18). Now if the figure of generation is applied to the establishment of the latter status through God's judgment of grace, and this spiritual generation is compared to the antecedent natural generation, it follows that adoption, which is equivalent to reconciliation, may be designated as regeneration by God. Since, further, no natural conditions are included in this idea, it can only be understood in the same sense as adoption, namely, as that for which man is destined by the Divine will of grace, and that, too, in such a way that the believer conforms to God's final end as revealed to him. Since this destination of man, which takes effect in regeneration, is mediated by the revelation of God's Fatherly grace, the Word of God is compared to the generative seed, but is at the same time contrasted with the material means of natural generation as the incorruptible seed (1 Pet. i. 23). Thus regeneration, or, as we inaccurately say, the new birth, cannot as a predicate of the individual believer be materially distinguished from effectual justification or reconciliation or adoption. In this sense Melanchthon, in the *Apology of the Augsburg Confession* (ii. 45, 72, 78, 117), treats *justificare, regenerare,* and *justum efficere* as synonymous (p. 173), because in the connection he is expounding he has in his eye precisely the production of the religious virtues of trust in God, patience, etc., as the goal of justification [*Gerechtsprechung*] or regeneration or sanctification [*Gerechtmachung*] (*justus* being equivalent to *acceptus*, p. 72).[1] For those functions are just the new life which formerly did not exist, and is now awakened by the sin-pardoning grace of God. The fact that this conjunction

[1] Eichhorn in *Stud. u. Krit.* (1887) pp. 425, 460.

of ideas has not been handed down in theology is due to the
action of disturbing influences.

It has been shown (vol. i. p. 303) how vacillating the
usage of *regeneratio* is in such a theologian as Baier. Among
the different interpretations of this idea we find Melanchthon's
view that *regeneratio* is equivalent to *justificatio, qua confertur
jus filios dei fieri.* Yet this conception is not asserted as
normative against the other interpretations ; on the contrary,
he chooses to distinguish them thus, that *regeneratio* is
coextensive with the *donatio fidei,* and precedes it as the
condition of *justificatio.* Now, if this relation is to be interpreted not only theoretically, but operatively and temporally,
we must remember that regeneration as the awakening of
faith also includes the bestowal of the Holy Spirit. Though
Baier makes a restriction here by saying that what is meant
by regeneration is not the special powers of good conduct, but
only the capacity *ad credendum in Christum vitamque adeo
spiritualem inchoandam,* yet other theologians have not been
able to accept this limitation, but have regarded regeneration
through the communication of the Holy Spirit as the actual
turning-point in the life of the believer, which the Divine
judgment of justification must appropriately follow. It
is beyond question that an approximation, though an unintentional one, is here made to Catholic doctrine. It is
therefore a fitting thing that we should try to reach a
decision by examining the latter.

While the Catholic doctrine takes *justificatio* in the Latin
sense as a " making righteous " by God, and regards the
recognition of this operation by the Divine judgment as a
subsequent event, it includes the assertion of a material-
istically conceived means, namely, the infusion of love to
God. By this process is meant that the contrary tendency of
the will is displaced from the seat of the will, as a lighter
substance gives place to a heavier—for instance, air to water,
when the latter is poured into an open vessel. In itself the
application of the idea of space to express various functions
of the mind is unobjectionable, as it is the indispensable form

of our intuition of differences in any unity. Accordingly, we
believe ourselves to be also right in saying that the good
will subordinates to itself the impulses working in the mind;
we even use from this point of view the metaphor of weight,
when we say that the good will suppresses the movement of
the impulses to evil.   But we employ this method of looking
at the matter with the reservation that the will directed to
the good end is, on account of the universal character of this
latter idea, a power of a different kind from the impulses,
each of which only strives after something particular—which
are therefore in themselves indifferent to the universal good
and the universal will, but may be raised to be means of the
evil as well as the good will.   If, then, in ordinary speech we
judge many phenomena of a moral kind according to the
difference of weight between the good will and impulses
which are inclined to evil, we do not put this quantitative
estimate of the factors of moral conduct in the place of its
qualitative opposite ; we make the full understanding of these
phenomena dependent upon the latter. This reservation,
however, is not operative in the Catholic account of justification.   On the contrary, as the infusion of love to God is
meant quite literally, it is precisely the quantitative difference
of good from evil that is here represented.   Under this
category, love is thought of in the first instance as a substance different from the impulses.   Assuming, however, that
the qualitative opposition to a given sin exerted by love to
God is taken into account, yet it follows from the quantitative
view, which is reckoned the higher, that love to God is still
co-ordinated with the subjective impulses which are the
channels of sin, i.e. it is itself viewed as a special impulse
alongside of the latter.   That this interpretation is right is
proved by the ascetic view of the Christian life which
prevails in Catholicism, and with which the dogma in question
must have some connection.   For this asceticism implies that
the particular impulses can assume no positive relation to the
good end, that the special goods to which they are related
have no validity within the highest good, and thus that the will

is directed to the latter only when it renounces the special goods of human life, and therefore also the activity of the impulses connected with these. If, then, justification (*Gerechtmachung*) by God proves itself in this way the principle of independent action, the infusion of love to God can only mean that a special and therefore qualitatively determinate impulse becomes operative as a quantum, the beneficial expansion of which has to displace the impulses, not only as channels of sin, but in every form, from the seat of the will.

Now the approximation to the Catholic doctrine of justification which appears in the exaltation of regeneration above justification, is occasioned in the case of Evangelical theologians by the vagueness with which they hold the conception of the *Holy Spirit*, which is associated with regeneration. Indeed, scarcely any part of the Christian theological view as a whole has been so steadily neglected as this conception. In well-known statements of Paul, the Holy Spirit is brought into connection with Divine sonship, so that in particular the involuntary invocation of God as Father is traced to the Spirit of God (Rom. viii. 15 ; Gal. iv. 6). Now as regeneration leads to Divine sonship, so again Dogmatics has represented the Holy Spirit as the Divine means whereby regeneration is brought about. That, however, not only distorts Paul's thought, which represents the possession and the characteristic utterance of the Holy Spirit as the accompanying mark of Divine sonship, but unintentionally makes this Factor appear as if He were to be conceived as a hyperphysical natural force. True, this conception does not for the most part assume a distinct form, especially as Church teaching, with sound tact, usually avoids suggesting the practical application of so vague an idea. But sectarian or half-sectarian practice customarily appeals to the Holy Spirit just in so far as thereby justification is supposed to be found for passionate zeal, or pathological experiences, or forced, vague, aimless efforts to reach passive assurance of salvation. The idea here expressed is that this Divine Factor moves man with a kind of natural necessity. If, then, the Holy Spirit is appropriated as a particular something which manifests itself directly, He is brought into the closest analogy to the natural powers of the mind, which, apart from the counteraction of the will directed to a universal end, work like natural forces; but in that case He simply cannot act as a counterpoise to egoism.

I think that these phenomena of sectarian Christianity throw light upon the meaning of the idea of regeneration through the Holy Spirit, which ecclesiastical Dogmatics also affirms. For if that process is to be distinguished from justification, which expresses the formal character which belongs to the believer by and for the judgment of God, regeneration by the Holy Spirit can only be understood as a material change. That is to say, there is thought to be awakened in man by the Word of God a supernatural and quantitatively mightier motive, which aims in general at pleasing God and in particular at everything good, and therefore counteracts the old impulses to sin. Now, the important point would still be that God declares a man righteous for Christ's sake, and his conviction of his acceptance with God would depend primarily on this Divine act. But as this judgment of God is conditioned by faith, which forms the comprehensive manifestation of an altered kind of life, and as it appears that God's formal decision regarding a man in justification (*Gerechtsprechung*) must find a reason for it in the man himself, the placing of regeneration before justification recommends itself. This is the way in which the theory arose to which Baier gives the preference. This theory, however, stands in distinct contrast to the Catholic doctrine, for the material change in the individual, which is indicated in the *donatio fidei*, has no independent value assigned to it apart from formal justification (*Gerechtsprechung*), in the sense that no material is real in its kind apart from the form. On the other hand, no weight is given to this consideration in the Pietistic and modern use of the formula that justification is the Divine judgment upon the material change of the believer; that change is rather regarded as a reality in the form of the subjective spirit, which would still have to be subjected to the Divine determination of form by justification.

The Holy Spirit, however, cannot be regarded as a substance, nor is He represented in the New Testament as the Divine means of the regeneration of the individual as limited to the beginning of the new religious life. If this remark seems to be inconsistent with John iii. 5, Tit. iii. 5, I would add that both of these passages refer, not to the Christian baptism of the individual, but to the renovating consummation of the common life of the people of Israel which Ezekiel (xxxvi. 25 ff.) proclaims. If, therefore, the symbolising of the Spirit of God by purifying and refreshing water makes it appear as though He were represented as a substance, theological usage must not be tied to this appearance. On this point we must be guided by the richest and most distinctive conception, which Paul supplies. The Spirit of God, or the Holy Spirit, Who in relation to God Himself is the knowledge which God has of Himself, is at the same time an attribute of the Christian community, because the latter, in accordance with the completed revelation of God through Christ, has that knowledge of God and of His counsel for men in the world which harmonises with God's self-knowledge. The Holy Spirit, however, as the power of the complete knowledge of God which is common to believers in Christ, is at the same time the motive-power of the life of all Christians—a life which, as such, is necessarily directed to the common end of the Kingdom of God (1 Cor. ii. 10–12; Rom. viii. 2–4; Gal. v. 22–26). If, then, in harmony with this exposition of Paul, the state of regeneration or of the new life is in the Reformation system of doctrine brought into immediate relation to the Holy Spirit, that is to be understood as meaning, not that each individual is changed by the specific power of God in the form of a natural force, but that he is moved to patience and humility, as well as to moral activity in the service of the Kingdom of God, by that trust in God as the Father of our Lord Jesus Christ which is common to all Christians. For this reason it is not permissible for any man to determine his relation to the Holy Spirit by observation of himself, in which he isolates himself from all others. In that case there would be reason to fear lest spiritual movements, the course of which is guided by laws of freedom, might be referred to some mechanical power, and be made the occasion of fanaticism. The New Testament witnesses to a series of ecstatic phenomena as operations of the Holy Spirit; and even Paul, when he interprets such phenomena, indulges in mechanical distinctions and interactions between the Spirit of God and the spirit of man, e.g. in Rom. viii. 1 ; 1 Cor. xiv. Now, while we may leave it to sectarians to judge themselves according to these models of ancient times, it is advisable to restrict ourselves in formulating the doctrine of the Holy Spirit to the definition that He, as the power of the complete knowledge of God, bases the co-operation of all individuals in the Christian community upon trust in God as our Father, and upon the realisation of the Kingdom of God. This suffices, too, for practical instruction in Christianity. For if we thought we had to employ the idea of the Holy Spirit in our practical judgment of individual Christians, such an attempt would hardly deserve commendation. For it can be proved from 1 Cor. iii. 1–4 that factious Christians are not to be regarded as possessors of the Holy Spirit. Now, if we point out that so-and-so are factious, and draw the conclusion that they have not the Holy Spirit, we should hardly succeed in convincing them, but should rather increase the evils of controversy which are rife enough in the Church. We must not, however, admit into Dogmatics anything which cannot be employed in preaching and in the intercourse of Christians with one another. In that case we may rest satisfied with an interpretation of the Holy Spirit, which every one can and should put to the test by fostering in every way the Christian sense of union, in self-judgment and in conduct, in pain felt at the pernicious practices of the factious, in restraining or even in giving vent to righteous indignation against them, and at the same time in the fear lest we should contribute to their hardening.

Regarding the justification and regeneration of the individual, then, nothing further can be objectively taught than that it takes place within the community of believers as a result of the propagation of the Gospel and the specific continuous action of Christ's personal character in His community, through the awakening in the individual of faith in Christ as trust in God as Father and of the sense of union rooted in the Holy Spirit, by which are dominated our whole view of the world and estimate of self, despite the continuance of the sense of guilt. How this state is brought about eludes all observation, like the development of the individual spiritual life in general.[1] Rules for the objective operation of Divine grace upon individuals are not to be found, the less so as the relations between men and God always manifest themselves in experience solely in the form of subjective self-consciousness. Thus the relations of the grace of God to believers can be conceived only in the most general forms, as the presuppositions of that which presents itself to observation in the framework of subjective experience.

1. The forgiveness of sins or reconciliation with God, as the common and permanent determination of the relation of men towards God, is not recognisable and operative outside the community founded by Jesus Christ, and dependent upon His specific action.

2. If forgiveness or reconciliation is understood as the right of this community to place itself, in spite of sin and a lively sense of guilt, in the relation towards God of children to their father, it is indispensable to trace forgiveness to Christ in the sense that He, as the Revealer of

---

[1] I take the liberty of calling the attention of certain readers to the fact that I, too, recognise mysteries in the religious life, but that when anything is and remains a mystery, I say nothing about it.

God, through His whole conduct inspired by love to men, manifested God's grace and truth for their reception into God's fellowship, and, with the intention of creating a community of the children of God, proved His religious fidelity to God by the faultless discharge of the task of His vocation; and that God vouchsafes to sinners who are or shall be Christ's disciples, that position relatively to Himself which Christ thus maintained.

3. While it is only as a member of this community that the individual becomes assured of his reconciliation with God and his Divine sonship, this connection does not serve as a means to that spiritual acquisition in such a way as to render superfluous his conscious subordination to Christ as the Reconciler; on the contrary, the conviction of faith in Christ, within the community which shares the same faith, is the permanent form of the individual's reconciliation and Divine sonship, in the sense that the community both is the medium of our clear remembrance of Christ, and, in spite of all defects of knowledge and of religious and moral practice, exerts an impulse to the religious estimate of self which corresponds to the specific action of Christ.

CHAPTER IX

THE RELIGIOUS FUNCTIONS WHICH SPRING FROM RECONCILIATION
WITH GOD, AND THE RELIGIOUS COMPLEXION OF MORAL
ACTION

§ 62. *The lordship over the world possessed by believers*, which
is the aim of reconciliation with God in the Christian sense,
has its limits. For in so far as we are individually endowed
with a corporeal nature, we are parts of the world and
dependent on it as a system. But even " when the earthly
house of this tabernacle is dissolved," the Christian hope of
the survival of the spiritual life in an appropriate body is
an evidence of what is an indispensable assumption, that as
individual members of the race of spiritual beings we can never
escape from the environment of the world (p. 278). Lordship
over the world, therefore, in the empirical sense, can be
attributed neither to the individual nor to the human race as
moulded by Christianity. No one can alter the mechanical
conditions of sensible existence as such, no one can create new
organic species ; each, to secure his preservation within the
system of the phenomenal world, must submit to the laws
of mechanism and of organisms, laws which are valid once
for all. Only within a limited range, and in harmony with
the known laws of nature, can man use nature's forces, or
artificially alter the given form of matter. Within this
province the inventive faculty of the human mind and the
exertions of conjoint labour may result in an extended range
of power, the importance of which is not decreased by the
fact that certain species of animals also exhibit a capacity
for work of an artificial character and for division of labour.
The manifoldness of his work, the discovery of ever new

39

objects and new methods, still constitutes the specific difference between man's spiritual lordship over nature, and the industrial instincts of social animals. The individual's field of labour, however, is limited; just as in the application of his powers to it he has to depend on all the others performing their special part, and thus each supporting the other. But even if the individual were to claim for himself this whole system of dominion over the world, because he participates in it through his labour, yet such a view is utterly inadequate to counterbalance the impressions received from the multitude of natural forces which man cannot tame, and the multitude of hindrances which he has to tolerate from those on whose support he is reckoning. However many portions of the world, therefore, man conquers by labour, no one need hope to conquer the whole in this way, even though in moments of elevated feeling he identifies himself with the advancing forces of human civilisation. But man does make a comparison between himself and the whole system of nature when, in his spiritual feeling of self, he apprehends himself as a being who stands near to the supramundane God, and claims to live in despite of the experience of death. This religious estimate of self was not called into existence for the first time by Christianity; in every higher religion it breaks forth as an aspiration, or as a question addressed to the secret of existence. Christianity has only unfolded that view of the world in which this aspiration finds its confirmation, and the question about eternal life is answered.

The final end of the Kingdom of God posits a system of united human action, the motive of which transcends the natural conditions of spiritual existence. Universal love to man, by which distinctions of nationality, position, and sex are reduced to subordinate ethical motives, is a principle which transcends the world, so far as by the world is understood the system of divided and naturally-conditioned existence. But as the motive of universal love to man operates likewise in connection with those who belong to the same country, or vocation, or family, not merely are all these special provinces of moral action combined in a single whole, but the individual, through his corresponding formation of a good character, becomes conscious that he is a whole to whom the special qualities of his family, his vocation and position, as well as of his nationality, are subservient as means. This estimate of self, however, does not rest exclusively upon this moral activity. On the contrary, if it merely related to this, it would be liable to doubt. For the formation of a good character is not only exposed to hindrances which have their roots in an actually present wrong relation between the powers of the will and the tasks appointed it; it is likewise liable to so many disappointments in its expectation of results from moral action, that they outweigh the conviction that the self is a whole in its own order. But these experiences of suffering are counterbalanced by the directly religious view of the world—the certainty, in other words, that the government and care of God, of which we are the objects, has for its aim our attainment of the supramundane goal of life. By this thought, that for those who love God and are loved by Him all things must work for good, the sense of all natural and social evils is changed into the tone of feeling in which we exercise lordship over these experiences. So long as the view is held that certain restrictions of our freedom are evils unconditionally, our dependence on natural and partial causes, that is, our dependence on the world, is admitted. But when we change our feeling as to the value of evils, not merely do we attain freedom from the particular things in which these evils take their rise, but freedom from the world as such. For not only do particular evils represent just those aspects in which the whole world is a restriction on our freedom, but the counterbalancing thought, that we are the objects of Divine care, implies that each of us, as a spiritual whole, has in God's sight a higher value than the whole world of nature. This is the reason why a man, when by patient endurance of suffering he rules himself, likewise rules the whole world, which is the correlative of the suffering and unhappy Ego.

The lordship of the spirit over the world, in other words, over the system of the natural and particular motives of life, is connected in Christianity with the task of the Kingdom of God, as well as with that religious freedom in which evil in its many forms is employed as a test and purifier of character. The task of the Kingdom of God, however, includes likewise all labour in which our lordship over nature is exercised for the maintenance, ordering, and furtherance even of the bodily side of human life. For unless activities such as these are ultimately to end in anti-social egoism, or in a materialistic overestimate of their immediate results, they must be judged in the light of those ends which, in ascending series, represent the social, spiritual, and moral ideal of man. Otherwise civilisation, which embraces the intellectual and technical species of mastery over the world, is placed in contradiction to the religious and moral species. In that case, however, the farthest advance of civilisation were likely to bring in its train only moral and intellectual barbarism.

Recently a theologian has undertaken to point out a way of escape from the aimless and confused animosity of theological parties—against which he makes the complaint that with one accord they are striving to reconcile Christianity with culture—by maintaining that at bottom the outcome of Christianity is merely *negation of the world*.[1] As establishing this view he claims that monasticism, with its negation of the world, occupies the first period of the existence of Christianity, covering a space of fifteen hundred years; that everything that was great in that period was achieved by monasticism; further, that the early Christian anticipation of the end of the world can only be interpreted as expressing the principle that between Christianity and the world there is an incompatibility; lastly, that not only in the principles of Paul, but also in the words of Christ in Matt. xix. 12, the demand for ascetic negation of the world is laid down. But if it does no more, the original opposition between Buddhism and Christi-

---

[1] Overbeck, *Ueber die Christlichkeit unserer heutigen Theologie. Streit- und Friedensschrift*, 1873.

anity may well continue to determine our opinion of the two as views of the world. I am far from underestimating the significance of monasticism for Christianity as a counterpoise to its Byzantine secularisation.[1] But in monasticism itself we find two species, of which the Oriental comes little short of Buddhism in its negation of the world, but for that very reason is of no more value than the secularised Church life of the Byzantines. The Occidental species of monasticism, however, so long as it retained a general value in history, acquired that value because, while resting on a basis of certain world-negating motives, it applied itself to ordered labour in many forms, *i.e.* to the task of world-mastery in the sense of technical and intellectual culture. The anticipation of the end of the world in the apostolic age would have had to be interpreted as a mark of world-negation in principle, if the inference which certain Christians in Thessalonica allowed themselves had been drawn from it universally. But not only did Paul, on the contrary, enjoin that whoever, influenced by this anticipation, did not work must not look to his fellow-members for support, but there is not a trace in any of the New Testament writings which serves to legalise beggary, which is the basal form of Buddhistic world-negation. Hitherto we have been accustomed to regard the early Christian expectation of the nearness of the world's end as belonging to the shell and not to the kernel. And there the matter will rest, for that anticipation has not acted prejudicially on any of the positive social duties which follow from Christianity. That Paul should deprecate marriage, in view of the calamities heralding the end of the world, goes along with his special estimate of the marriage state, which is anything but the view common to Christians. This follows directly from the saying of Christ adduced, which merely describes exceptions which directly imply the general normality of marriage. The fact that some refrain from marriage for the Kingdom of God's sake indicates a principle which, under

---

[1] Adolf Harnack, *Das Mönchthum, seine Ideale und seine Geschichte*, 2nd edit. 1882.

certain circumstances, makes a similar sacrifice a duty in any public vocation.

Thus there attaches to Christianity only so much world-negation as belongs to world-mastery. What is denied is just the dominion of the world over man ; for the reverse relationship is set before us as our prospect and our task. Christianity favours pessimism, too, only from the unfavourable view it takes of man's situation as subject to the dominion of the world or of sin. On the other hand, its faith in the purposiveness of suffering in testing and purifying character proves that its view of the world is opposed to that of pessimism. For the rest, I need not enter here upon a special elucidation of pessimism, for it is a view of the world which can only be directly refuted through the personal feeling of its representatives. For the charm of superior knowledge, by which the pessimistic theory is accompanied, is an outcome of the rule that every creature strives after well-being, and, if it be possible, a well-being which transcends the measure attained by others. While general optimism, therefore, must, as a permanent self-deception, be reckoned as part of the badness of the world, pessimism in itself denotes the possession of a truth which is thought to give one a more favourable position relative to reality than that occupied by optimists. This, however, is simply to satisfy man's need of well-being, only in a peculiar fashion.

§ 63. The lordship over the world which Christianity bestows upon men, is not to be taken in an empirical sense. So that it is of no consequence what position the planet, with which our existence is bound up, occupies in the universe. True, the opinion is to be met with that the Christian view of the world has been invalidated by the refutation of the hypothesis that the earth is the centre of the universe, and that the sun was directly intended to give light to its inhabitants. I do not consider it the task of theology to attempt to prove as against this view that, of the planets of our solar system, the earth alone is suited to the development of a spiritually-endowed race of organisms. For the materials for such a proof are wanting; and even granting that on this question more were possible than a probable conjecture, there does not exist the slightest evidence to prove that no other astronomical system would furnish the conditions necessary for the development of spirits. Thus it is possible that the earth is not the only scene of the history of created spirits. But it is impossible to perceive how this should invalidate the estimate of self which Christianity leads man to form. The above-mentioned possibility or probability, which we must concede to natural science, has nothing whatever to do with the view we take of our practical attitude towards the natural world, partly because we cannot increase this possibility to any degree of actual knowledge, partly because the estimate we hold of ourselves as spiritual personalities is quite uninfluenced by our knowledge of natural laws. The man who, as an investigator of nature, keeps ever so clearly before his mind that our earth is an extremely insignificant part of the universe, behaves exactly as people did before Copernicus. Practically he behaves as though the earth were the firm foundation of his existence, as though the sun were intended to give him light and warmth, as though all nature, inclusive of the mechanical conditions of the boundless universe, existed simply for him. For these are the tacit presuppositions of our spiritual existence, in which we all in some degree manifest the feeling that we are the purpose of the world, and have the right to be lords over it. This fact indicates that our spiritual life is subject to laws which are not related to known natural laws as their consequences, but come under an exactly opposite category. The universal moral law, when it really deserves the name, represents the thought that the moral fellowship of the human race is the final end of the phenomenal world, the end supreme over all nature. The religious view of the world is, in general, a normal function of the human spirit which, in its Christian form, has for its aim to make possible the supernatural independence of the spirit in all its relations to the world of nature and to society.

Collisions between religion and science, especially natural science, arise only when laws which are valid for narrower realms of nature or spirit are erected into world-laws, and used as a key to open up a view of the whole. But to proceed thus is simply to introduce an apocryphal religious interest into scientific investigation; it can claim none of the rights of science (p. 207). On the recognition of this truth depends the prospect of appeasing the controversy between faith and knowledge. It would be out of place to devote closer attention to this prospect here. But it must be possible to harmonise the scientific study of nature and the Christian view of the world in the same mind; therefore I wish to notice one objection which it is customary to make to the possibility of such a combination. This is the assertion that the teleological and especially the miraculous character of the Christian view of the world is intolerable to one who on principle confines himself to the mechanical consideration of the world. If, now, this issues in the further contention that the scientific view of the world can get along without the conception of end, and without the assumption of miracles, this is a self-delusion. Miracles, in the sense of effects which are not produced according to law, are assumed in every philosophical or scientific theory of the universe; for no such theory is without gaps; and these gaps are discernible whenever such effects are affirmed as are not mediated by any known law. Moreover, without the conception of end it is simply impossible to essay the explanation of organisms, or of nature as a whole. If any man professes to have divested himself of this conception, it is easy to show that it is still tacitly operative in his thinking. But if it be declared untrustworthy in the interpretation of nature, because it denotes a presupposition of spiritual life, in particular of conscious will, which ought not to be applied to nature, neither is the principle of efficient cause abstracted from our experience, but is a presupposition of our thought without which experience is impossible, so that it likewise ought not to be applied to the changes of natural phenomena, if in their interpretation we have no right to employ the conception of end. Accordingly, a view of the world which is teleological, and in detail even miraculous, which answers to man's need of religion, which guarantees to him his position as a spiritual and moral whole in his connections with nature and human society, is—as compared with our knowledge of nature and its laws—anything but irrational; or, if it is so, then the delusion to which we submit in religion is repeated likewise in every investigation of nature, even when conducted solely in accordance with the law of efficient cause. If, finally, it is sought to throw suspicion on the trustworthiness of the religious view of the world by urging that it arises merely from a need of the human heart, let it be remembered that all, even the simplest, study of nature guided by the law of efficient cause likewise proceeds from a need of the human reason, and that its cogency is liable to the same suspicion that the human observer finds something, which he is conscious of in his own will, behind phenomena only because he wishes to find it. Lordship over the world, accordingly, though it is not technical and empirical, but ideal, is not therefore unreal. For the will which exercises religious dominion over the world is the real; and it is at the same time as much ideal as real. Moreover, the spiritual activity which so operates as to secure to the spirit its independence, cannot be something merely imaginary. The truth is, if everything with which we are here dealing were justly condemned as subjective imagination, then every spiritual activity which evidences the self-distinction of spirit from nature would fall under the same fatal judgment.

Now, in general, the form in which religious lordship over the world is exercised is *faith in God's providence*. For that unified view of the world, the ruling idea of which is that of the supramundane God, Who as our Father in Christ loves us and unites us in His Kingdom for the realisation of that destiny in which we see the final end of the world, as well as the corresponding estimate of self, constitutes the realm within which come to be formed all such ideas as that all things and events in the world serve our good, because as children of God we are objects of His special care and help. This faith appears first of all in the form of a definite and distinct judgment, that is, as an act of knowledge. We judge that a particular restriction of freedom, which for the first moment is felt as a special evil, is or has been rather a benefit, in so far as it has promoted the development of the character to its highest quality as a whole within the whole of the moral order. But the conditions under which faith in providence makes its appearance as a species of knowledge, distinguish it from every other species. In it we are guided not by observation of the attitude towards the world occupied by others as well as ourselves, but solely by our own experiences. For observation of the fortunes of others would offer as much occasion—or even more—for dismay, as for confirmation of our own conviction. Often enough so much that is untoward is to be found in the lot of others, that one who felt himself called upon to estimate such facts in the light of the idea of God might easily feel himself tempted to adopt the notions, suggested by the Greeks, of Envy, or the indifference of the gods to mankind. But faith in providence affirms the general truth of the Divine goodness not as a law of phenomena discovered inductively, but as the personal conviction of each individual, drawn from the nexus of the experiences he has made of himself (§ 60). If, on the other hand, we will accept the validity of this conviction only on condition that it be tested by the lot of others, or if we even abandon it altogether because we find that the unfavourable experiences in the case of others are more numerous than the favourable in our own—this is to miss the distinction between the claims due to the nature of theoretical cognition, and the conditions of this religious knowledge of self and the world. Theoretical cognition of general laws, and of truths which are comprehended under such laws, is in itself indifferent to the worth of the individual, and is not sufficiently comprehensive to take in the whole of the world; in cognition which arises out of faith in providence, the individual's desire is to master his own special position relatively to the whole of the world in which, as a Christian, he himself possesses the value of a whole.

The rejection of the rationality or the validity of faith in providence is combined either with the affirmation or the negation of the peculiar worth of spiritual personality. In the latter case, Strauss sees himself helplessly entangled in the monstrous world-machine, with its iron-toothed wheels, its heavy hammers and presses. While, as the prophet of the new faith, he confesses the horrible impression made on man by this situation, he adds the comforting consideration, that while the wheels of the world-machine move round mercilessly, yet they are lubricated by a mollifying oil. Under this figure he recommends us to convince ourselves of the necessity and rationality of the movements of the world-machine even when they crush us, and, through the kindly influence of custom, to accommodate ourselves to those imperfect features of our situation which are disclosed by our experience of the world. The obscurity of the figures which Strauss employs is most significant of the impossibility of his view of the world. If in the world-machine mollifying oil is poured upon us, then men are merely parts of the machine; then they have, as such, no consciousness of the whole or of their relation to it as parts; then they require no comfort when, after having become useless, they are replaced by other parts. Or men are distinguished from the world-machine as intelligent observers, but at the same time are conceived as being such that they are crushed by its movements. Then, truly, it is no alleviation and no comfort, if, before they are crushed, they have a dash of rancid oil poured over them; if, *i.e.* by being reminded of the inevitable necessity of their annihilation, they are robbed of that sense of worth which they draw from the fact that, as observers of the machine and as understanding its structure, they are superior to it. Strauss has not clearly realised either the one or the other position thus possible to man. But while his intention is to deny that man can be superior to the world and at the same time

entangled in it, contrary to his intention his testimony goes
to prove man's superiority. The confusion of the figures
which he employs proves that if men are actually what he in
his new creed insists they are, he must persuade them to
abandon altogether their craving for comfort regarding their
unconditional subjection to the world. If, on the other hand,
this craving is ineradicable, he ought to spare them the
alleviating oil of resignation to necessity and kindly custom;
for, while machine-oil is useful for the parts of a machine, it
does no good to lookers-on.

These discussions, it is true, bring clearly before our
minds the difficulty which faith in God's providence solves.
Man is a part of the world, and that not merely in his
bodily limitations, but also as an individual spirit. And yet
as spirit he distinguishes himself from the world, gains
through the conception of God the idea of his worth as
against the world, and rises in the Christian religion to the
self-feeling that the worth of his spiritual personality transcends that of the whole system of nature. For this estimate
of self is the basis of the horror to which Strauss testifies at
the fact that, as a spectator of the system of the universe, one
is likewise in danger of being drawn, as though by an
unavoidable giddiness, between the wheels of the world-
machine and there pulverised. Thus the self-feeling of man
over against the whole world must be accepted, even though
unwillingly, as a fact on which every merely mechanical view
of the world makes shipwreck. But now if, simultaneously
with the assertion of this standpoint, faith in God's providence
is set aside as unjustified and baseless, it is very improbable
that such a position can be permanently or sincerely maintained. As I understand this position, the denial of Divine
providence springs from the scientific knowledge and estimate
of the law-governed system of all nature, this knowledge being
kept before the mind along with the certainty that as a
spirit man is an independent part of the system of the world.
Now in this case there is indicated a degree of care for the
preservation of one's own life which is fitted only to blunt that

feeling of worth by which, in the midst of the incalculable system of nature, this care is called forth. If one is in earnest with the scientific study of nature in the name of which Divine providence is denied, the consistent outcome of such a view of the world ought to be despair of that value of personal life which we destroy in ourselves by the wakeful care of every moment. If this result does not actually follow, however, that is a proof that the scientific view of the world is not taken so seriously as the negative inference would lead us to expect. And this would only be an example of the ordinary experience that scientific knowledge and practical conduct usually have very little to do with one another. If the same thing should possibly appear likewise in the realm of ethics, that is really intelligible only if what is involved is a scientific knowledge of natural phenomena which does not in itself comprise the conditions of spiritual life. The champions of Pantheism, who regard each spiritual individuality merely as a transient manifestation of the world-soul, or as a function of universal reason, to which, therefore, every kind of theoretical or practical friction between different men ought to matter nothing, take nevertheless a very lofty view of their personal honour, as expressing the permanent worth of the spiritual individual in distinction from all others. The champions of the theory of natural descent, who do not recognise as original the specific differentiation of spiritual life and nature, nevertheless conduct themselves as though this very distinction were the fundamental rule of their existence. And rightly, too. For the feeling of self, which expresses the incomparable worth of the personality as against all other personalities and the whole system of nature, is also the basis of all scientific study of nature, and cannot be neutralised by its results, whatever their character may be. It is thus a delusion to suppose that, by attaching importance to a scientific theory of the world, it is possible to suppress the original feeling of the worth of our own personality and the inferences which naturally follow from it. And it is likewise only an error in cognition to make scientific knowledge of nature as a system a reason for declaring invalid that faith in Divine providence which springs from our religious valuation of our spiritual personality, as contrasted with our relative dependence on the world.   Here, rather, there comes to light a law of our spiritual life which is no less valid than the laws of thought and the laws of nature.   Men are so easily deceived about these matters, because, in estimating those clear ideas and conceptions which are put forward as valid in science, they often forget that our practical behaviour is often ruled more by obscure ideas than by those which are clear.

Now this is exactly the case with regard to faith in Divine providence.   We believe it to be true, not because we can follow or demonstrate its course clearly and completely, in other words, objectively ; but we commit ourselves to it all the more decisively, the less we expose ourselves to the possible danger of falling into uncertainty in our knowledge of it through instituting a scientific kind of inquiry into its grounds.   For to become certain of our own Ego we do not need a scientific analysis of its grounds and conditions, or an empirical explanation of its origin.   We are certain of our Ego, even when we have present to our mind no clear idea of it ; and the professional psychologist is not practically conscious of himself as an Ego in a different way from anyone else.   The feeling of pleasure and pain in which the Ego grasps itself, whether what happens be a sense of our in-dependent activity or an experience of restrictions upon it, is, indeed, always related to the surrounding world, and therefore, too, is always accompanied by ideas.   But so far as these ideas are not clear, the self-feeling of the Ego is represented by good humour or dissatisfaction, according as the sense of self-activity or of restriction predominates.   Accordingly, even *faith in Divine providence* is normally a *tone of feeling* which develops into the form of clear ideas and judgments, only if those hindrances to our feeling of self which arise from the world appear in a quantity which depresses the ordinary

amount of spiritual energy. The normal amount of good
spirits, in which the feeling of self and the sense of power
manifest themselves, is sufficient in the case of many men to
make them feel a certain amount of hindrances no evil at all.
One does not need to be a Stoic on principle in order to face
certain physical pains or social trials with momentary indifference, without having to call up the definite thought of
God's providence and without having to convince one's self
that such evils are intended to test us or to make us better.
The energy used in overcoming pain, and the justifiable self-
confidence which is felt in opposing certain antagonists,
actually lead men of strong character to put aside for the
moment the definite thought of God's help, however much
they feel their dependence on it as a rule. For in certain
circumstances that thought may make us feel as though the
degree of self-activity which duty calls for at the moment
were being impaired.

Now, it may be said, the amount of confidence which
most people possess is only the result of a custom which owes
its existence first of all to the child's ignorance of the hindrances that may arise from the surrounding world, which
lasts until the individual has gone through his own special
experiences, and which either reconstructs itself out of these
experiences if he is a man of force of mind, or, in the reverse
case, gives place to harassing care. As an anxious attitude of
mind is frequently caused by bodily weakness, so, it is argued,
confidence in face of possible evils and in spite of evils which
have been experienced, has no necessary connection with faith
in Divine providence, even though it were granted that this
religious estimate of self is capable of strengthening one's
confidence in life. Of course no demonstration is of any use
against such a view; for the necessity of a religious self-
estimate and world-view is never connected with the
experience of the individual as such. But history, which
shows us men associated together, by no means confirms the
view that confidence in face of possible hindrances due to
nature or human society, and cherished without presumption

or moral perversity, is a matter of course. A great tract of feeling among heathen peoples is dominated by the fear of nature, and there was nothing which the most pious Israelites found it so hard to rise above as troubles due to other men. Must not a completely different feeling, full of confidence in face of nature and unassuming towards men—a feeling which the individual, guided merely by his own experience, regards as due to nature or custom—be the product of Christian education ? Must it not be dependent on the fact that Christianity as a matter of principle excludes the fear of nature, and declines to make it a necessary test of our feeling of self that our worth should be recognised by men ? If we are reminded that the fear of nature not only continued to possess men's minds in mediaeval Catholicism, but was corroborated even by the Reformers, and that to this day it is strengthened by various kinds of belief in devils, still it does not thence follow that it is an original element of Christianity. The theology of the *Aufklärung*, from which this feeling received its death-blow, is not thereby proved to be a culture-promoting force which surpasses Christianity, but rather a mere element in culture, the influence of which in the realm of ecclesiastical Christianity has, in this respect, justified itself. There is really no common element in the spiritual life of men which is rooted merely in nature and not rather in history. The semblance of being the product of nature clings to certain convictions and feelings, only because we are both familiar with their historical connection and not specifically conscious of it. When, therefore, bound up with a direct denial of Divine providence based upon the scientific conviction that the system of nature is governed by necessary law, there is to be found a self-feeling of personal worth, and when withal there is cherished, not a perpetual fear of annihilation by the powers of nature, but a modest confidence in life— then I believe I am justified in asserting that we have here a case of the faith in God's providence which is gained from education working on still as a tone of feeling.

The obscurity which surrounds this point, however, is in

an eminent degree due to orthodox theology itself, in so far as it represents faith in God's providence as an element of natural religion (p. 181). In consequence of this, theological naturalism declares that we can dispense with positive Revelation, which seemed to furnish this natural piety with no more distinct motive. What wonder if men of science, having demonstrated the fallaciousness of the teleological argument, for that reason likewise assert the invalidity of the religious use of this formula, seeing that theologians, whether of the Right or the Left, put forward faith in Divine providence as the result of popular or scientific knowledge of nature? But the confidence with which, whether in favourable or adverse positions in life, men cast themselves on the guidance and help of God, regarding themselves as enjoined by Him to seek the one highest goal, dominion over the world in the fellowship of the Kingdom of God, is in reality a product of the Christian religion. For the God Who is the Lord over the world and our Father, Who cherishes no envy and wrath against His children, gives them the assurance that all things serve for their good. And this truth stands firm only when based upon our reconciliation with God.

§ 64. Nevertheless, faith in God's providence is subject to a difficulty which arises from the religious conception of God Himself, and finds precise expression in the statement that the judgments and ways of God are unsearchable (Rom. xi. 33). This statement of Paul, however, is not meant to annul the significance of God's revelation. The apostle does not affirm that God is absolutely unknowable; for that would contradict the certainty of His saving revelation. But he affirms that the knowledge of God's general saving purpose, which we possess in virtue of His revelation, does not imply an antecedent knowledge of the special methods by which God guides to salvation particular bodies of men or particular individuals. This special side of God's government of the world remains concealed beforehand, and can become clear to anyone only from experience, as the course of the world takes

40

shape. On this point the attitude of the Christian theory is precisely the opposite of that of pre-Christian religions. In the latter we find men forming very decided judgments on events as manifestations of Divine punishment, while at the same time uncertain about the disposition of God or the gods as a whole. But in Christianity the full revelation of God implies that we can hardly comprehend the application of God's saving will to our own destiny, or its intertwining with the history of particular groups of men or of the whole of humanity, and that least of all may we, by our prayers and counsels, exercise an influence on the Divine dispensations. Indeed, even subsequent reflection on historical events, though guided by the idea of the Divine government of the world, is not protected from error by the desire to acknowledge that idea. It is a common enough experience to find egotistical obstinacy mingling even with this practical exercise of religion, while all the time seeking to justify itself by the misuse of Scripture. How soon partisans are ready to pronounce an opinion in God's name on events which are in process of development, just as though they had known the mind of the Lord, or been His counsellors! How rash they are in exaggerating the guilt of the one party and minimising that of the other, speculating, according to the side they take, on the help or the vengeance of God, and deciding how much is merely the work of man and what the cause of God! Cases of this kind furnish really terrible proofs of the weakness of the Christian faith of those who are loudest in their professions. True, the subjection of natural phenomena to their laws is made out by a more or less limited range of observation, and by logical judgment; for all phenomena of this kind are found in space, and the characteristics of natural objects clearly reveal the species to which they belong. But the historical events of human life are likewise in time, and the nature of their mutual intertwining is obscure, for it is always subject to the interference of human freedom. Who, now, will assert that he has at his command a range of historical observation sufficient for forming a judgment on God's special designs; and who is conscious of being so free from personal guilt that he can decide what group of human actions possesses, in God's judgment, the character of pure right or pure wrong? Infallible people, who are in the habit of judging as though they claimed this, profess to occupy a standpoint as far removed as possible from that of "unbelieving" scientists; in reality, they treat the Divine government of the present and the most recent past as though it were simply an object like the objects of natural science!

There are no organs other than those of patience and humility, by which all those experiences of life which lie nearest—those which are most special as well as those which are common—may be comprehended under general faith in God's providence. They yield that prudence which answers to the providence of God, and that religious tenderness of feeling which is rendered possible by the Christian estimate of self. Every logical judgment is incisive, as the word (*Urtheilen*) itself directly indicates; a religious judgment on our experiences of life is light of touch, tender in feeling, pliant. There is no gift for scientific theology, no capacity for ecclesiastical office, which could make any difference here, or ensure such an infallibility as belongs—granting right processes—to mathematical or logical conclusions.

The feeling which views especially the evils of life in the light of Divine providence is *patience*. It is that attitude of soul which, even apart from religion altogether, withdraws the sting from those lasting evils which afflict us. Patience is quite different from apathy. For when the latter is demanded of the Stoic as a duty, whether in reality it is attainable or not, it implies that the pain due to the evil, the emotional sense of restraint, is altogether suppressed. But patience in suffering implies that the pain continues. If it be possible to get rid entirely of the sense of pain, whether by Stoical effort or by the deadening of our spiritual force, there remains no basis for patience. Wherever, therefore, this feeling is called for, it decidedly implies the continuance of the sense of the evil as a restriction of freedom. But by patience the evil is reduced to a relative degree, in so far as patience itself is a specific application of freedom. True, the range of freedom, in the form of patience, is limited in the first place to ordering the relation of sensations to the personal feeling of self, or, more precisely, to the subordination of a particular restriction of freedom to the general feeling of freedom. But patience, as an act of freedom, never confines itself to the inward domain, but always in varying fashion issues in outward manifestation, at least in negative effects. Otherwise we should not become clearly conscious of it. That patience which we have to exercise in the training of children will show itself in a consecutive and positive counteraction of their faults and defects, which we perceive with pain because they restrict the freedom of our intercourse with them. On the other hand, patience under bodily suffering may, perhaps, display itself merely in our refraining from expressions of pain by an exertion of the sense of honour. Between these instances of patience there lie an immense number of possibilities, which represent the reaction of the general feeling of self and personal worth against restrictions of freedom, of which we are specially conscious only under special circumstances.

These general conditions of patience hold good likewise for the Christian form of this temper as a religious virtue. The elevation of the general human exercise of patience into its special Christian form depends on the fact that man's feeling of self and of personal worth, by being combined with the thought of the supramundane God Who is our Father, and guarantees to us salvation through dominion over the world and participation in the Kingdom of God, is raised above all natural and particular motives, even when they are the occasion of troubles. This still admits of evils being felt with pain even by the Christian.[1] True, he is raised to such

---

[1] Calvin, *Inst.* iii. 8. 8 : "Neque ea requiritur a nobis hilaritas, quae omnem acerbitatis dolorisque sensum tollat ; alioqui nulla in cruce esset sanctorum patientia, nisi et dolore torquerentur et angerentur molestia." 10 : "Haec eo dicere volui, ut pios animos a desperatione revocarem, ne studio patientiae ideo

a height that he can glory in the afflictions and persecutions which he undergoes for Christ's sake (Jas. i. 2 ; Rom. v. 3), while the Stoic, who resigns himself to the course of the Cosmos, deadens his sensibility to the feeling of evils. But if we apparently have to infer from the series of New Testament injunctions to rejoice in suffering (vol. ii. p. 350), that pain should not form part of a Christian's sense of social afflictions, yet we can quote against any such position, not only the explicit confession in Heb. xii. 11, but also the example of Jesus and Paul. For while joy in the midst of persecutions is expected from Christians, yet, from the equally clear commendation of patience (ὑπομονὴ καὶ μακρο-θυμία) it follows that joyousness in suffering, while compensating for the feeling of pain, is not to exterminate it. The consciousness of reconciliation with God places the assurance of personal worth firm above all the special motives which arise from the world; and therefore the pain which springs from their oppressive action can be subordinated to the joy which, in our feeling of self, denotes the incomparable worth of Divine sonship. But in the case in question, joy would not last; rather, it would veer round into indifference, unless underneath the joy the pain still continued. Moreover, the truth of the Fatherly care of God for His children suggests to us not only the inference that no evils arising from the world can overbalance the blessing of fellowship with God, but also this further application, that these evils, as tests of our fidelity to God, are elevated into relative blessings. And this comes about just through the exercise of patience as the peculiar and proper manifestation of Christian freedom. Finally, so far as a general or special feeling of guilt accompanies experience of evils, that experience is elevated through faith in God's Fatherly providence

protinus renuntient, quod naturalem doloris affectum exuere non possunt. Quod necesse est evenire iis, qui ex patientia stuporem, ex homine forti et constanti stipitem faciunt. Sanctis enim tolerantiae laudem defert scriptura, dum ita malorum duritia afflictantur, ut non frangantur nec concidant : ita amaritudine punguntur, ut simul perfundantur spirituali gaudio, ita premuntur anxietate, ut dei consolatione exhilarati respirent."

into the idea of educative punishment. For experience of evils has a bettering influence only when it is looked at in the light of the truth that the goodness of God leadeth us to repentance (Rom. ii. 4). The goodness of God is not one ground of repentance, and punishment another; rather, it is the general principle under which even Divine punishment is to be brought. The idea of legal retribution no more carries with it the impulse to improvement than does the thought of experiencing Divine wrath. It is therefore an error to regard the preaching of an angry God as a necessary element in the Christian ordering of life. Those who *ex hypothesi* are overtaken by the wrath of God, are nothing bettered by having the prospect foretold them.

Resignation to God's will, which elevates patience in suffering into a religious virtue, is not to be acquired by sober reflection or by the exertion of the imagination. One who is suffering from a great sorrow which pierces deeply into his life, can hardly in that way make the religious truth which he acknowledges so to operate upon his feeling as to banish the disabling power of pain. Patience under such suffering, drawn from the acquired conviction of God's love, is exercised most surely when it is supported by labour in our vocation, for all the true impulses of the Christian religion can be appropriated, not in inaction and effortless meditation, but only when brought into touch with our regular work; and for this reason activity in our moral vocation, as well as patience in suffering, is an integral element of Christian perfection (§§ 67, 68). In the case in question, the significance of work for the acquisition of patience is evident from the fact that both are united in the conception of the worthy exercise of independent freedom. As the point of importance in patience is that a man should hold firmly to his freedom as a counter-weight to the restriction of suffering and its consequences, though the sense of suffering neither can nor should be removed, work serves as a means of testing our free activity as such, and thus furthers the end of maintaining ourselves even against the

disabling power of pain. This process is not to be understood as though through work ideas were excited which
suppressed the ideas which cause pain. This may, indeed,
be the case with many. They will be in a position to work
out for themselves indifference to the cause of their pain;
but in that case they lose the enrichment of soul which is
the outcome of the struggle of patience with pain, and
remains real even when the latter is still felt only as a
gentle sadness. For the former reduction of pain to
indifference, though it may often succeed, is yet far from
ethically satisfactory; and inasmuch as patience, not indifference, is a religious function, the case described is
mentioned at this point only as exemplifying an aberration
which had to be noted as well as the true principle.

Even from the standpoint of deliberate Christian faith,
resignation to God's will will be found easier in the relations
of private life than in respect to those cases of mutual interest
in public life in which we may be involved on one side.
Here appear the difficulties described above in which, as has
been said, patience and humility must decide what is to be
regarded as appointed by God. In this realm there exists a
great danger of error, when, for example, a man does not
maintain the necessary distinction between his Christian and
his political convictions. This error is palpable in the case
of those Roman Catholics who identify the continued existence and the validity of Christianity with the supremacy of
an infallible Pope. Should they, though from no failure of
Ultramontane intrigues and acts of violence, be disappointed
in their desire thus to amalgamate religion and the lust of
power, they preach all the more passionately the imminence
of Divine judgments upon their adversaries. Quite analogous
phenomena, however, confront us even in the case of those
professors of Evangelical Christianity who think they are
serving it best by making its ecclesiastical administration an
item in their political party programme. If the latter is
shipwrecked, they invoke God's protection upon it, and
shrink from no injustice in representing their political

opponents as the enemies of God. They are clearly altogether unaware of the fact that Christian patience has for
its field of exercise not only the subjection of private life to
the guidance of God, but also the cautious criticism of the
history of the present.

§ 65. *Humility* is the current rendering of the Hebrew
word עֲנָוָה. In the few cases in which it occurs, it denotes
literally the condition of the עָנִי. The epithet " suffering,"
however, became the positive description of the man who
experiences oppressions and troubles as a worshipper of God
and a person of moral righteousness. Since, therefore, the
suffering and wretched are regarded as those who seek God
and walk uprightly (Ps. ix. 11, 13 ; xxv. 9 ; xxxvii. 11 ;
lxix. 33), עֲנָוָה really coincides with righteousness (Ps. xlv. 5 ;
Zeph. ii. 3) and the fear of God which is the beginning of
wisdom (Prov. xv. 33 ; xxii. 14), and in this reference it
denotes the opposite of pride of heart and scorning, *i.e.* of
godlessness (Prov. xviii. 12 ; iii. 34). In the New Testament
the place of these words is taken by the conception ταπεινός.
Apart from the meaning " meek " (2 Cor. x. 1 ; cf. Num. xii.
4), this adjective denotes a humble position in life just in so
far as it includes worthiness in God's sight (2 Cor. vii. 6 ;
Luke i. 52), ταπεινοφροσύνη (Acts xx. 19), that temper, inclin-
ing to the service of God, which accepts resignedly an oppressed
and wretched condition. Accordingly, the expression in part
includes the whole compass of the practice of the Christian
religion as opposed to those who are high-minded (Jas. i. 9 ;
1 Pet. v. 6 ; Rom. xii. 16), in part it points to that subjection to God which is attested by prayer for the forgiveness
of sins (Jas. iv. 10 ; Luke xviii. 14), in part it indicates
Jesus' religious subordination to God, manifested in His
obedience to His vocation (Phil. ii. 8). Lastly, in Jesus'
saying about Himself (Matt. xi. 28–30 ; cf. *supra,* p. 462),
πραΰς and ταπεινός are synonymous, for both words are used
in the LXX for עָנִי. Jesus calls to Himself the suffering,
while He describes Himself as a sufferer. But by His
description of His own suffering, differing from the descrip-

tion He gives of that of others, and further by the addition
of the words τῇ καρδίᾳ, He indicates that He is reconciled
to His suffering because He accepts it for God's sake; this
gives Him calmness, as well as a sense that His burden is
light. Therefore He can invite those to learn of Him who
load themselves with an intolerable burden of care, under the
impression that they can fashion their destiny by their independent exertions. This group of terms, accordingly, has in
any case a thoroughly religious colour, while on the other
hand ταπεινός and ταπεινοφροσύνη denote also modesty in
relation to men (Matt. xxiii. 12; Luke xiv. 11; Col. iii. 2;
Eph. iv. 2; Phil. ii. 3; 1 Pet. v. 5), and in the last two
passages this is done in such a way that its close analogy
with humility before God comes out. Lastly, ταπεινοφροσύνη
(Col. ii. 18, 23) denotes an ascetic worship of God, marked
by a degradation of the bodily life, which is foreign to
Christianity.

The predominating impression we receive from the
Biblical idea of religious lowliness is this, that humility is
represented only in connection with undeserved suffering.
Nevertheless, even in the Old Testament this is not the
case throughout. One could not expect, indeed, that the
rule of goodness (Mic. vi. 8), namely, "to do justly, to love
mercy, and to walk humbly with God," should contain the
suggestion that action of this kind will be accompanied by
adversity. But the delineation of the king in Ps. xlv. 5
emphasises eulogistically the lowliness—which is righteousness—*i.e.* the humility, by which he is characterised, even
when the marks of suffering disappear. Nevertheless, the
usage of the New Testament proves that the idea of
religious lowliness or humility still maintains itself exactly
in its original meaning, namely, as involving undeserved
suffering. However, we find the conception of humility in
the circle of New Testament ideas beginning to be detached
from the presupposition that it implies outward misery.
True, in Jas. i. 9, 10, the view which obtains in the Old
Testament appears again as distinctly as possible. The

Christian is as certainly regarded as occupying a miserable
and oppressed position in outward life, as the rich man is
regarded as godless. But in another aspect this statement
differs from the form predominantly given to the idea in
the Old Testament. The lowly and humble Christian does
not merely expect his exaltation in the future, but is assured
of it as a present inward possession, while in the Old
Testament this feeling is devoid of influence even when the
believer momentarily claims peace-bringing fellowship with
God (Ps. lxxiii. 25–28 ; Mic. vii. 8). The idealisation of the
notion of humility makes its presence felt gently, though
clearly, in the words of Jesus Himself (Matt. xi. 28, 29).
For here the additional words τῇ καρδίᾳ are designed to
express the acquiescence of a pious mind in His lowly
position, as in the phrase πτωχὸς ἐν πνεύματι ; while the
connection of the words shows that deliberate submission to
God is the power which makes any situation of suffering
tolerable. Thus in the idea of the lowly and the wretched,
the emphasis is laid on that attitude of soul which finds
compensation for every burden of life in deliberate acceptance of God's dispensations, and therefore bears such burdens
patiently. This comes out, too, when Paul (Rom. xii. 16)
represents the lowly as the opposite of those who "mind
high things." The conception of "lowly" is thus indirectly
limited to this—that one strives after lowliness, i.e. subjection to God, and stamps it on his own heart. This
inward self-abasement before God is vividly represented in
the parable of the Publican (Luke xviii. 14), in his prayer
for God's forgiveness, and in Jas. iv. 10, in the repentance
which likewise requires outward attestation. Finally, it is
demanded in 1 Pet. v. 6 in respect to all God's unavoidable
dispensations, just as in Phil. ii. 8 witness is borne to it by the
consideration that Christ chose His path in obedience to His
vocation, and therefore submitted willingly to the fate of death.

These indications point to deliberate submission to God's
dispensations as the common meaning of them all. To
be sure, in most of the cases adduced the occasion for this

temper of soul is furnished by the sufferings of life, or the social pressure under which we stand against our will. But this occasion falls out of sight in both the instances of self-abasement in order to secure Divine forgiveness; and Jesus' self-abasement in obedience even unto death represents not merely this lot of suffering, but the whole range of His moral activity in the vocation which He undertook and freely carried out. But if His resolve to fulfil His moral vocation coincides with His resolve to submit to God's ordinance, we have opened up to us the prospect of a view which transcends the original conception of humility. For if Christianity even approximately corresponds to its destiny of spiritual dominion over human society, then either we may reckon on it that moral fidelity to one's vocation will have no hindrances to undergo, but in some degree will obtain the recognition it deserves; or, since all evil is conditioned by our judgment upon it, the believer, by his humble estimate of the fidelity with which he discharges his vocation before God, will rise above the hindrances due to society as though they did not exist. We thus retain the inner essential quality characteristic of the suffering and oppressed, from the manifestation of which the Biblical usage is derived, if by humility we understand the resolve to submit ourselves to God. This resolve, indeed, is not always present to us as a conscious decision, but all the more does it appear in a tone of feeling and a sense of pleasure, which we can only explain by the obscure influence of that resolve. For where you have a distinct determination to be humble, it is rather a proof that it has met with restrictive opposition in ourselves. Humility, as one would wish to exercise it, is, as Scriver strikingly says, the eye which sees everything except itself; true humility knows not of its own existence. In this form, however, humility in the Christian sense does not at all necessarily involve straitened outward circumstances, or troubles due to society.

A more exact knowledge of this conception, and at the same time a confirmation of it, is supplied by the importance

which, even for the men of the New Testament, belongs to
" the fear of God." This tone of feeling may seem to be alien
to Christianity (Rom. viii. 15 ; 1 John iv. 18), but that holds
true only of that pain at the thought of God which clings to
Pharisaic and ceremonial piety. In the Christian sense, however, it is the impulse, accompanied by blessedness, to an open
acknowledgment of God's glory, as in the Old Testament.
For the rest, in Phil. ii. 12, 1 Pet. i. 17, the fear of God
signifies the acknowledgment that we are dependent on God
throughout the whole range of our moral activity, so far as
He is Judge and Father, *i.e.* so far as He guides our life to
the securing of our moral rights as opposed to other men,
according to His especial grace. Now this feeling, as religious lowliness or humility, is opposed to highmindedness or
false independence (Rom. xi. 20 ; cf. xii. 16 ; Col. iii. 22).
While, therefore, in the New Testament it assumes the form
of one special motive of action or self-education alongside of
others (1 Pet. iii. 2 ; 2 Cor. v. 11, vii. 1), it is properly to be
comprehended under the conception of humility. But this
makes it clear once more that humility may be discerned not
merely in relation to the prevalent depression of our outward
circumstances, but also throughout the whole extent of our
conscious moral activity.

This presupposition of our resignation to God depends no
less distinctly on the fact that we know Him as our Father,
and use our freedom to realise His end, than on the fact
that our freedom has its dark side, and God's ways in detail
are unsearchable. Humility equalises contending feelings in
these respects just in so far as it is a tone of feeling,
and the feeling of pleasure predominant in it testifies indirectly to our ruling intention to submit ourselves to God.
Now ascetic writers, *e.g.* Scriver, when dealing with the contrast, which humility overcomes, between the lowliness of
man and the sublimity of God, normally take into account
also the feeling of guilt against God. This, however, is not
one of the essential conditions of humility, for we know that
humility was also an element in Christ's character. Still,

their conception of the matter gives rise to the idea that humility is properly the whole of religion as found in man. For in so far as religion, in all its species and stages, is the acknowledgment—concentrated in feeling—of our subjection to God, humility—granted the omnipotence and grace of God and our reconciliation with Him—will be subjective religion itself. Now this is correct, in the sense that humility is the Christian religion in the form of religious virtue. But patience must be added to it as the other religious virtue. In other words, patience is religious feeling as lordship over a refractory world, and is supplementary to humility as the feeling of submission to God. Humility and patience, however, come under the conception of virtue because they are acquired frames of feeling, and at the same time powers, inasmuch as they move and rule the will. Finally, the compass of both is such that they both accompany moments of special activity, and give to compulsory experiences of suffering their importance as elements in our active character. The test of both forms of feeling will have to be made, perhaps, with more intensity along the line of moral action than in connection with unavoidable suffering. For successful action brings with it the danger of our repudiating humility ; and our patience is menaced when action brings with it no visible result, even though it does not involve us in actual suffering. To sustain patience in the absence of success, and humility in its abundance, is a quite specific test of Christian piety. In cases of an opposite kind, impatience betrays a lack of religious independence of the world ; while, on the other hand, arrogant assurance of success betrays such an irreligious independence in the world as, for all one's desire to defend God's cause, is exposed to nothing so much as the danger of gross errors in the knowledge of God's purposes.

As humility is not necessarily connected with unavoidable suffering, so it does not necessarily involve any definite outward manifestation. It is true, the language of the New Testament itself indicates that there is an affinity between this religious virtue and *modesty* towards men, which, there-

fore, will be found to be a regular feature of it.   Modesty is
a principle of respect for other persons, which rests on the
fact that for one thing we are bound together with one another
to work for a higher common end, and on the presupposition
that in this system each person has a place of his own, and in
himself represents to us the worth of moral fellowship.   Now
humility, which emphasises the obligatoriness of our joint
moral tasks and our responsibility to God, normally calls forth
likewise modesty towards men.   But the validity of this
principle of duty, like all others of a similar kind, is limited
by circumstances.   One is not obliged to be modest towards
insolent people.   Of course one is not obliged, nor has one
the right, to be insolent towards the insolent.   But since we
are bound to be sincere towards them, this may perhaps relieve
us of the duty of modesty.   Insolent people, therefore, who
are so because they profess as universal ends which are really
particular, get into the attitude of regarding as insolent and
arrogant opponents who in reality are humble, but who, in
consequence of that very virtue, can only act in such a way
as to offend their opponents by their candour.   In this
respect the collection of Jesus' sayings in Matt. xxiii. is
worthy of our consideration as an instructive model.   For the
humblest and most patient of men there tells the insolent
representatives of a narrow religiosity nothing but the truth ;
while the Pharisees lived in the belief that they were the
legitimate custodians of God's law and the dispensers of His
salvation, and therefore could count on the deference of all
their fellow-countrymen.

Even in ascetic forms of worship there is no particular
form of expression necessary to humility.   Asceticism as a
whole, which found its way into the Catholic Church from
the realms of alien religions, strives to commend itself as an
expression of humility.   For if the contrast between human
and Divine nature—for which, it is considered, humility
makes up—is reduced to the opposition between impure and
pure, then humility must be identified with abstinence from
such relationships and activities as appear to defile man.   But

the assumption that certain foods and marriage are impure is rejected in the Epistle to Titus and the First Epistle to Timothy, while in the Epistle to the Colossians Paul passes the severest criticism on the position that abstinence from the enjoyment of wine and flesh is necessary, as being a ταπεινοφροσύνη which possesses, as a means of serving God, the value merely of a capricious device, and leads to arrogance. That this latter judgment should be so overwhelmingly confirmed by monasticism everywhere, is easily intelligible. As ascetic legalism represents the surviving influence of the last forms assumed by developing Hellenism, so no two things are more alien to one another than on the one hand the free resolve of the Christian accompanied by his feeling of humility, accommodating itself to all the different experiences of life, and on the other hand a statutory list of scruples touching abstinence, and of outward acts of worship. One who chooses such media to express his humility will be seduced into arrogance by the inward contradiction there exists between the means and the end, and by his externally separating himself from those Christians who are content with what he pretends is a life of defilement. If now, still further, humility towards God is taken to mean that one should place himself, like a corpse, at the disposal of the Superiors of an Order, the consequence is that his sense for truth is falsified all round, a result which needs no special commentary.

Nevertheless, similar misconceptions of Christian humility have been called forth by Calvinism and Pietism. They are connected principally with a more or less distinct feeling of suspicion regarding the "impurity" of aesthetic culture, and of the time-honoured means of social recreation. Originally, therefore, they have nothing in common with the after-effects of non-Christian religions on Christianity at its Catholic stage of development. Both tendencies may be excused on the ground of the historical situation of the Christian Church in which they appeared. For in the Middle Ages the secularisation of the Church was inevitable, since the Church was held to be the legal form of Christian society, embracing within

itself all other forms of life.   Calvinism, in imposing the duties
of sanctification on the entire Christian society in the name
of the Church, acknowledged the principle that the Church
is the framework of everything that is Christian, even of the
State.   In Lutheranism, on the other hand, there was directly
perpetuated the mediaeval, *i.e.* relatively secularised, conception of the Church, until Pietism appeared in this domain in
the same fashion as Puritanical Calvinism, with the result,
however, of narrowing the significance of the Church, and, in
many cases, allowing Christian society to escape from its
framework.   Following a narrow-hearted interpretation of
Old Testament ordinances, both tendencies in part cherished
the belief that no Divine sanction could be found for social
recreation, the misuse of which had led to moral corruption,
and in part restrained the artistic impulse by making public
worship as plain and bare as possible, as the Second Commandment seemed to prescribe.   Where the customs of the
people have been determined by these principles, they give no
occasion to individual revolt.   But when they are combined
with a sectarian tendency, the result is that some strive to
mark themselves off from their otherwise-minded neighbours
by abstention from social joys and the rejection of artistic
pleasures, in order thus to give expression to the religious
complexion of their mind, that is, their humility.   I do not
say that the conscious and deliberate expression of humility
in the way described is a necessary characteristic of Pietism
which holds good in all cases.   But I must say I have found
that when Pietists lay stress on these practices of theirs in
contrast to other Christians, and with open or tacit condemnation of the unbelief of others, they fall into the error
of thinking that a specific manifestation of humility is possible
or necessary.   This error, however, where it obtains, is accompanied for the most part by all those perversities by which,
in Catholic monasticism, arrogant humility is characterised.

§ 66. In statements by the Reformers,[1] cited above, we

---

[1] Cf. p. 169. Calvin, *Inst.* iii. 20. 1 : "Postquam fide edocti sumus, agnoscere quidquid nobis necesse est, nobisque apud nos deest, id in deo esse ac

have a recognition of the truth that *prayer* stands in the
closest connection with faith in Divine providence, and that
the understanding of prayer, as well as faith in Divine
providence, issues directly from our reconciliation with God
through Christ. In every religion, prayer, or, what is equivalent to it, sacrifice, is originally the product and the proof of
man's resolve to recognise his subjection to God in whatever
character He may be believed in. Accordingly Evangelical
theologians do not take a very profound view of the subject
when they find no other ground for prayer than God's
command (vol. i. p. 351). Such an hypothesis arises simply
from attending merely to the statutory stage of the development of religions. This stage, however, presupposes everywhere an original freedom of action in giving shape to the
common forms of worship. The original form of prayer,
therefore, can be understood only from the resolves of
particular persons, as indeed it is in this limited sphere
alone that it is open to observation. What is given as
a description of prayer in Heb. xiii. 15 holds good for
every religion—that it is the sacrifice of praise, the fruit
of lips which acknowledge the name of God. The variety
of prayer in different religions depends on the relations of
the Divine will to us and to the world, which are included
by thought in the name of God. Where prayer is regarded
as an equivalent for tangible gifts, we find also, to begin
with, an agreement between both forms of worship—that
is, a definite resolve to adopt outward action. The resolve
to dedicate tangible property to God is the characteristic
which gives value to all sacrifice in the ordinary sense ;
the resolve to praise God calls forth the equally sensible
phenomenon of prayer, inasmuch as it either interrupts
ordinary profane business, or breaks off the soul's feeling
of uncertainty and doubt. The name of God as our Father,

domino nostro Iesu Christo, in quo scilicet omnem suae largitatis plenitudinem
pater residere voluit, ut inde hauriamus omnes, superest, ut in ipso quaeramus,
et ab eo precibus postulemus, quod in ipso esse didicimus." Petrus Martyr
Vermilius, *Loci comm.* iii. 13 : "Hoc est ingenium filiorum dei, ut quam fre-
quentissime orationibus vacent ; nam illud est dei providentiam agnoscere."

Whom in prayer we resolve to confess, embraces the attributes of almighty love and grace towards us, whose salvation God has in view in His entire government of the world. Thus prayer in the Christian sense is, on the one hand, a special manifestation of the faith in the Fatherly providence of God, which springs from reconciliation; on the other hand, a special manifestation of the resolve to be humble, which is distinguished from the ordinary tenor of that virtue by the fact that the resolve, which is present as an obscure idea or as a tone of feeling, is brought to clear representation. The basal functions of the human spirit are all participant in each of these religious acts. It is not the fact that faith in Divine providence is a kind of knowledge, humility a kind of feeling, prayer a kind of willing. That faith rather includes the resolve of the will to submit to God, together with feeling as pleasure or as pain; humility is a continuous feeling of pleasure in submission to God only because it springs from the corresponding resolve, and is accompanied by an idea—not a clear idea, it is true—of God's power and grace; prayer, as a resolve of the will, finds its material in our knowledge of Divine providence, and attests itself by the attainment or the increase of joyfulness which accompanies the act itself. All that can be maintained is that in each of these religious functions the leading and dominant place is occupied now by knowledge, now by feeling, now by willing. Silent devotion and the feeling of humility, finally, rise into prayer from two motives—first, in order that these religious functions may be exercised by many in common and in accord; and, further, that the individual may ensure his faith in providence and his humility against those hindrances which arise, partly from contact with the secular world, partly from causes which lead him to doubt the security of his own religious convictions.

This discussion is guided by considerations other than those which dominate Schleiermacher's doctrine of prayer. He says (§ 146, 1): "Relatively to the fact that success is never the result solely of our independent activity, but also at the same time the result of the Divine government of the world, our God-consciousness in respect of those present possessions which are the result of previous efforts is either resignation or gratitude; while in respect of those which are still undecided, it is prayer, *i.e.* the combination of desire directed to the best success with our God-consciousness." This limitation of the conception to cases of petition directed to God is not in harmony with the original sense of προσευχή, in idea or in practice, at either stage of the religion of the Bible. Undoubtedly, what predominates in the latter conception is just that acknowledgment of God by thanksgiving and by devotion which balances the tension of desire. The representation given by Schleiermacher, which excludes from prayer precisely this kind of acknowledgment of God, appears to have a closer affinity to that preference for petitionary prayer which has its home in Pietistic circles, and there manifests itself in a didactic interest in the hearing of prayer, the truth of which people seek to demonstrate empirically by numerous examples. This one-sidedness is presumably due to the fact that, apart from German usage, which designates the general conception (of prayer) by the name of a particular species [*Beten*], the discourses of Jesus on the subject are concerned almost exclusively with petitionary prayer and God's hearing of it. The model prayer for Jesus' disciples, too, is simply a collection of wishes. The popular instruction of the Church, accordingly, which is based upon this model prayer, recognises thanksgiving, indeed, as a second kind of prayer alongside of petition, but only as of the second rank, as though we had to thank God only after ascertaining that He has heard our petitions. Against this, however, are to be set two characteristic utterances of Paul. In one (Phil. iv. 6) he desires that in every petition their requests should be laid before God with thanksgiving (vol. ii. p. 346); further, he gives with strong emphasis the precept (1 Thess. v. 16–18), "Rejoice evermore; pray without ceasing; in everything give thanks: for this is the will of God for you revealed in Christ Jesus." This last binding consideration refers to all the three precepts with which it stands connected. Now, these two utterances of Paul yield the conclusion, that for the Christian Church *thanksgiving as an acknowledgment of God stands higher than petition*, that thanksgiving is not one species of prayer alongside of petition, but rather the general form of prayer, while petition is merely a modification of thanksgiving to God.

This certainly takes for granted that in consequence of reconciliation we Christians rejoice alway, even in distress and persecution; otherwise the injunction of Paul is unintelligible (vol. ii. p. 344). But in joy we have no wishes, no intense desire for anything not yet attained; or if wishes do arise, we have them in joy without the pain which springs from their delayed fulfilment. Thus we are in a position to present them to God with thanksgiving, with an acknowledgment, reassuring to ourselves, of His power and goodness. It must be confessed that this attitude of soul is not present at every moment even in the most sincerely pious, and that often it must first be brought forth in prayer by a conflict with a reluctant or crippled frame of spirit which is opposed to it. But if Christianity has true reconciliation to offer, then joy must be recognised as the normal accompaniment of humility and patience. According to Paul's principle, then, it is the rule of prayer in the Christian community that in our joyful assurance of peace with God arising from reconciliation, we should give thanks to God in every case and under all circumstances, and only ask something when thanking Him at the same time. Thanksgiving always combines the whole circle of our own transitory experiences with the thought that, within this realm, God is guiding us according to His wisdom and grace. Were anyone to attempt to make a distinction between this and the praise or the blessing of God, by urging that in the latter case we abstract from the relation between God and the special causes of our need or our satisfaction, such an idea would not stand the test of examination. For there is no religious acknowledgment of God which cannot be applied to the situation of the man who is praying to God. While, therefore, in praising and blessing God, the benefits of salvation may be touched upon only in their most general aspect, yet for that reason such praise shows itself to be thanksgiving.

As regards petition, however, its range is more narrowly limited by the assumed certainty of reconciliation than appears in the religion of the Old Testament. If in the Christian community, or in a vocation devoted to its furtherance, we find ourselves thwarted by prejudice, mistrust, or calumny, it is not for us to follow the prevailing practice of the Psalmists and call upon God to vindicate our rights and slay our foes, so that we may then be able to thank Him. When more closely examined, even the Lord's Prayer is very far from being an example of one-sided petition. For as the invocation of the Father stands at the head of all the particular sentences it contains, so all the petitions in it are subordinate to the thanksgiving which forms the content of the invocation. Further, the wish uttered for the hallowing of the Father's name is only an expression of the certain expectation that the Father will everywhere receive thanks. Finally, the petition for our necessary food is rather an expression of thanks to God, if on the one hand it be assumed that God is ready to grant the necessaries of life before we ask them (Matt. vi. 8), and on the other that we earn what is needed for life by our own labour But simply as a model of what should be prayed for in the name of Jesus, i.e. in view of the revelation of God present in Him, it serves to limit the promises of the hearing of prayer given by Jesus in Matt. vii. 7—11. Our prayers ought to be directed not to every conceivable kind of blessing, such as trouble the minds of the heathen (vi. 31—34), but to the benefits of salvation in all their possible relations to blessedness. To this refers the saying that God hears us if we pray according to His will, so that we immediately experience the fulfilment of our prayer (1 John v. 14, 15). For Jesus proves by His own example that not every petition is justifiable (Mark xiv. 36). Since, then, there exists a danger that we should pray for blessings which it is not God's will that we should receive, the ultimate resting of the soul in the contrary will of God is a manifestation of that thanksgiving by which every petition ought to be ruled and, according to circumstances, limited. Granting this presupposition, prayer is the expression of humility and patience, and the means of confirming oneself in these virtues. But if this view holds good for every uttered prayer, of the individual as well as the community, it is singularly corroborated by Paul's injunction to pray without ceasing. For this denotes that transformation of prayer back into the voiceless feeling of humility and patience, which, as accompanying the whole active life, is equivalent to prayer as the normal form of the worship of God. On this presupposition, all the believer's action, especially so far as it exemplifies the principle of patience and modesty towards one's fellow-Christians, serves the glory of God (1 Cor. x. 31; Phil. i. 11).

§ 67. These religious functions, springing from reconciliation with God, are to be assigned to the elements of Christian freedom as affirmed by Luther (§ 25), thus—faith in God's fatherly providence and patience correspond to the kingly dignity, humility and prayer to the priestly dignity, of the Christian. The believer, however, occupies a position of lordship over the world, in the religious sense meant here, because he stands so near to God, and belongs so peculiarly to God as to ensure his independence of all the elements of the world. That independence is determined by his adoption of the end of the Kingdom of God, which is seen to be the end of the world and at the same time the most personal end of God Himself. These functions are the proper manifestation of the reconciliation and the Divine sonship accomplished in Christianity; where they appear, they represent our personal realisation of Christianity as a religion; they are a guarantee that it is not merely a doctrine of morals. But at the same time they constitute the norm which should determine whether other religious functions—or what are practised as such—possess merely the subordinate value of auxiliary actions, or no value at all.   In this respect it is of practical importance to observe that the Augsburg Confession not merely testifies that faith in God's fatherly providence and prayer are the expression of our consciousness of reconcilia- . tion, but also that these functions, together with humility and the moral activity proper to one's vocation, are the expressions of *Christian perfection*.[1]   The phrase " Christian perfection " is employed here in a sense not directly furnished by the New Testament.   What we have there, rather, is two other aspects of the idea.   First, for all His followers Christ places the task of perfection in the fulfilment of the command to love our enemies (Matt. v. 48); on the other hand, Paul describes a particular stage of the development of moral character in Christianity as the stage of " the perfect," among whom he reckons himself (1 Cor. ii. 6 ; Phil. iii. 15 ; cf. Heb. v. 14 ; Jas. iii. 2).

The language of Catholicism adopts this distinction, but in such a way as to substitute a quite different content.   For monasticism makes it its aim to realise a religious and moral perfection which contrasts with that imperfect kind of Christianity which conforms to the world, by alienating its devotees from civil callings and from the family, and at the same time violating personal independence by the prohibition of private property and the limitation of personal honour by its superiors. Since, now, this cast a semblance of defilement upon moral life in civil callings, there was added as a kind of compensation the tenet that the religion of the laity must at least approximate to the perfection of the monk by practising

---

[1] *C. A.* xx. 24 : " Iam qui scit, se per Christum habere propitium patrem, is vere novit deum, scit, se ei curae esse, invocat eum, denique non est sine deo sicut gentes." xxvii. 49 : " Obscurantur praecepta dei et verus cultus dei, cum audiunt homines solos monachos esse in statu perfectionis, quia perfectio christiana est (1) serio timere deum et rursus concipere magnam fidem et con- fidere propter Christum, quod habeamus deum placatum, (2) petere a deo et (3) certo exspectare auxilium in omnibus rebus gerendis iuxta vocationem ; interim (4) foris diligenter facere bona opera et servire vocationi.   In his rebus est vera perfectio et verus cultus dei, non est in caelibatu aut mendicitate aut veste sordida."   Cf. xvi. *Apol. C. A.* iii. 232, viii. 61, xiii. 37, 45.

as strenuously as possible the ascetic usages of the ceremonial law.[1] This is the tendency of the reform of ecclesiastical life set on foot by St. Francis. Now, when the Reformers hold, in opposition to the pretended perfection of monasticism, that faith in providence, humility, and patience and faithful activity in any calling, represent Christian perfection,[2] they mean this no longer in the sense of a stage superior to a Christian imperfection which is unavoidable and therefore permissible, but as an injunction incumbent on all Christians. They revert, that is, from the line of the apostolic usage to the line followed by Jesus in His demand for perfection. For the perfection meant by Jesus is that which distinguishes the Christian life in general from the imperfection to be found in other religions. Now that is the meaning of the Reformers' principle too; it is meant to exclude every possibility of two kinds of Christianity. Now the Reformers, it is true, place a number of religious and moral functions under the heading of perfection which Jesus did not conceive as such. But still they describe precisely the content which really constitutes the proper character of the Christian life, in other words, the attitude which is rendered possible by reconciliation through Christ. But they have likewise the full right to go beyond the usage of the New Testament in this

---

[1] *C. A.* xxvi. 8–11 : "Christianismus totus putabatur esse observatio certarum feriarum, rituum, ieiuniorum, vestitus. Hae observationes erant in possessione honestissimi tituli, quod essent vita spiritualis et vita perfecta. Interim mandata dei iuxta vocationem nullam laudem habebant, quod paterfamilias educabat sobolem, quod mater pariebat, quod princeps regebat rempublicam ; haec putabantur esse opera mundana et imperfecta et longe deteriora illis splendidis observationibus. Et hic error valde cruciabat pias **conscientias**, quae dolebant se teneri imperfecto vitae genere, mirabantur monachos et similes, et falso putabant illorum observationes deo gratiores esse."

[2] *De votis monasticis Lutheri iudicium* (1522). *Opera lat. ad reform. hist. pertinentia*, tom. vi. p. 254 : "Perfectionis status est, esse animosa fide contemtorem mortis, vitae, gloriae, et totius mundi et fervente caritate omnium servum." P. 261 : "Haec est vera via salutis subdi deo, in fide ei cedere et silere, ponere tumultum praesumtionis operum, quibus quaerunt impii eum invenire, et sese ductilem praebere, ut ipse in nobis operetur, non nos operemur." P. 344 : "Melior et perfectior est obedientia filii, coniugis, servi, captivi, quam monachi obedientia. . . . Igitur si ab imperfecto ad perfectum eundum est, ab obedientia monastica ad obedientiam parentum, dominorum, mariti, tyrannorum, adversariorum et omnium eundum est."

respect; for the historical situation in the midst of which the Reformers had to indicate the true inferences which follow from the Gospel, did not exist in the original circumstances of the Church, and therefore could not be foreseen by Jesus or the Apostles.

The Catholic view of Christian perfection, indeed, is influenced for one thing by the fact that the ascetic motives of the later Hellenism were adopted in the Catholic form of Christianity (§ 65). Nevertheless, the monastic, and in general the statutory, form of Catholicism had, in a formal respect, still another root, which, when it is pointed out, frees the contradiction in question from the appearance of chance. I have shown (p. 177) that the topic of Christian freedom, with which coincide perfection in the Evangelical sense and the status of Divine sonship, has its Catholic counterpart in the *timor filialis*, as that conception is developed by Thomas. The fear of God, which corresponds to the Catholic view of the Divine sonship, is made to consist in perpetual contemplation of the guilt which we should incur by violation of obedience to God. Now, if the feeling towards God answering to the status of a Christian is the perpetual terror of disobeying the Divine commandments which confront the soul in all their statutory multiplicity, and for that very reason confuse the memory and distract the attention, here lies the impulse to withdraw into monasticism from life in the world, and cut off those relationships in life which are attended by the most pressing danger of transgressing Divine commandments. Since, therefore, monasticism is the general expression in history of this Catholic fear of God, the ideal set up by the Reformation of humble and trustful reverence before God is the true opposite of pretended monastic perfection. This, however, carries with it likewise the assurance that every one who in his moral vocation acts according to the law is not confronted by the statutory multiplicity of the Divine commandments, but follows the inward law of freedom, and thus is freed from the terror of missing the mark at every moment, from the uncertainty of his knowledge of the

Divine will. In reserving this point for more accurate discussion, let me add that the Thomistic interpretation of
timor filialis is not at all analogous to the Biblical idea of the
fear of God. For the "fear of God" which Old Testament
experience proves to be the beginning of wisdom, is itself
something quite different from terror lest at any moment we
should violate a commandment of God, even though it be
against our will. For the saints who strive to act in the fear
of God and to follow God's ways, come to know the duties
incumbent on them through their disposition and not through
a statutory law. Even those infrequent appeals to the fear
of God which occur in the New Testament, and have been
interpreted above as referring to humility (p. 636), reflect the
sublimity of God—in other words, that side of His ways or
purposes which is inscrutable *a priori*, but are not guided by
the consideration that we are continually in peril of offending
God. Accordingly reverence towards God is indicated as an
expression of soul equivalent to humility, a feeling of the
qualitative distance between man and God which certainly
limits the natural feeling of self, but not in such a way that
the impression of the Divine authority awakens first and
foremost a thought of the guilt one would incur by offending
God. The interpretation of childlike fear given by Thomas
is a significant example of the method—very common in
theology—of affirming a sense which the words may possibly
bear, without considering whether it really suits the various
relations involved. But this cowering terror of offending
God's Fatherly authority simply does not accord with the
religion of reconciliation, and the trust in God arising thence,
represented by the Apostles. All the more, of course, does
this "childlike terror" agree with the view that Christianity,
in its first aspect and its last, is to be regarded as statutory
law. This childlike fear, therefore, reappears wherever in
Protestantism the standpoint of the law of freedom is exchanged for the predominant recognition of statutory law.

The perfection, however, which is set up as an ideal in the
Evangelical view of Christianity, is a conception which was

not called forth merely accidentally by the misinterpretation of it in monasticism, but is necessary to the completeness of Christianity. It must be asserted, despite the many imperfections we perceive in our religious functions and our moral actions. The destination of men for perfection in Christianity may likewise be seen in the exhortation to rejoice amid all the changes of life which, in the New Testament, accompanies instruction in the Christian faith (vol. ii. pp. 344, 350). For joy is the sense of perfection. In the present case, however, this characteristic has not quantitative but qualitative significance; it marks the fact that in Christianity man is destined and is enabled to be a whole in his own spiritual order (p. 502). Now there is no contradiction between the qualitative sense of Christian perfection, and the fact that we still continue to be conscious of the quantitative imperfectness and defectiveness even of those functions in which our Christian faith is expressed. The phenomena of hesitancy to put faith in God's providence, of reluctance to submit to His dispensations, of momentary impatience under suffering— phenomena, in short, of weak faith and lack of joyousness in religious life—are well known. Nor can they be explained entirely by the fact that even Christian perfection is a growing thing; rather do they express often enough an unexpected revolt of the natural man in the Christian against his religious purpose; nevertheless, in this respect they are not necessarily phenomena of sinful egoism, but phenomena of temptation. But the reactions which are provoked in us by these vestiges of religious instability are themselves an evidence, in their own order, of Christian perfection. For every organic being which in its order forms a whole, can bear a certain amount of defects without destruction. The spiritual life, however, is a whole in this sense that its freedom—directed to the final end of the good—is prepared at every moment to restrain, to order, or to overcome the spiritual impulses which arise from the relation of the spirit to its own individual nature and to the surrounding world. So far, therefore, as restrictions and disturbances spring up in

the proper functions of the religious life, the perception of
these hindrances as such, if combined with a determination to
overcome them, is itself an evidence of imperfection merely
in a quantitative respect, while in a qualitative aspect it is
really a manifestation of religious perfection. The faith
which breaks forth in the prayer, " Lord, help mine unbelief,"
is perfect in its own kind.

Faith in the Fatherly providence of God, which maintains
a right feeling with God through humility, and with the
world through patience, and which expresses and confirms
itself through prayer, forms in general the content of the
religious life which springs out of reconciliation with God
through Christ. For in the human mind clear trains of
knowledge are interwoven with states of feeling in such a
way that conscious and intentional acts of submission to God's
will, and the attaining of the continuous feeling of self to
humility and patience, condition each other mutually. These
phenomena, combined as they are in normal fashion with the
disposition to obey the moral law and with good action in
one's calling, are sufficient evidence, to the man himself who
is the subject of them, of his being in a state of salvation.
There is no other way of persuading ourselves of our reconciliation with God than by finding reconciliation experimentally in active trust in God's providence, in patient
submission to sufferings sent by God as a means of testing
and purifying us, in humble attention to the nexus of His
dealing with our fortunes, in the sense of independence of
human prejudices—and that, too, just in so far as they set
themselves up as a rule to religion—and, finally, in daily
prayer for the forgiveness of sins, on the understanding that
by the exercise of a forgiving spirit we prove that we have a
place in the community of God (vol. ii. p. 34). These acts
are not to be understood in the sense that we reconcile
ourselves to God through them by the power of our own
determination, but in the sense that, as springing from
Christ's reconciliation of sinners, they prove us children of
God who trace back our standing before Him solely to the

grace of God revealed in Christ. Thus these religious functions are already characterised even by Melanchthon in the
Apology of the Augsburg Confession as the evidences of
reconciliation (p. 169). While, therefore, in the fellowship
of the Church, out of regard for unavoidable statutes and out
of consideration for the needs of others, we may aim ever so
much at accommodation and submission, yet in the personal
sanctuary of the unique knowledge of God, the view of the
world and estimate of self which belong to Christianity, consisting as they do more in tones of feeling than in reflections
of the understanding, we stand absolutely independent of our
fellow-men—otherwise, we have simply not attained to the
enjoyment of reconciliation at all. We shall not succeed,
however, either in helping others or enlightening ourselves in
this respect, if we employ the methods for attaining assurance
of salvation which have been criticised above (p. 153). They
come to this, that we should derive our individual assurance
of salvation inferentially from the general article of faith of
the forgiveness of sins through the merits of Christ, instead
of ascertaining it directly from the subjective effects of reconciliation. That a method of logical inference was devised, in
which the *terminus medius* is either assumed as given or is to
be produced by a categorical exhortation to strong faith, is
certainly not to be excused by pleading that the only
functions of the human mind with which its authors were
acquainted were knowing and willing, while they as good as
knew nothing of feeling, or its intertwining with indistinct
ideas, or its significance for the excitation of the will. But
as we cannot now divest ourselves of those discoveries which
assure us that personal life possesses a richer fulness than
men were aware of in the age of the Reformation, Löhe's
proposal (p. 157) merely to enforce anew the old dogmatic
directions which had never been proved by experience, has
neither a claim to success, nor any prospect of it. For if it
comes to this, that we must really secure assurance of salvation, then Gerhard was right in comparing this demand of
Protestantism to that other—that you must be able to

prove that you are a man and not a ghost.[1] Now, if we
reach certainty in the latter case by exercising human
activities as human beings, so in the Christian community
we experimentally attain the certainty of pardon by exercising the confidence of a child towards God as our loving
Father, and submitting with humility and patience to His
dispensations, be they stimulating or depressing. And though
in these exercises we perceive in ourselves never so many
defects, yet in combating them we have always this to be
thankful for, that we are living and moving in the domain of
God's grace opened to us through Christ. But just as one
does not attain the consciousness of being a man by testing
himself by a list of the characteristics of manhood to find out
whether he possesses them all, or by straining himself to
produce them completely, no more is it practicable for a man
fully to attain to a certainty of his salvation by the path of
consistent inference from the general truth of the promise of
grace, or for this end to produce in himself a special sense of
strong faith in that truth. Dogmatic theologians, following
the steps of Melanchthon and Calvin, have come to take this
view only because they have forgotten, or never were aware
of, the functions of Christian perfection, and especially their
consistent harmony with the facts of forgiveness and providence, to which testimony is given in the Augsburg Confession
and its *Apology*. All the more significant is it that Calvin,
when describing *fiducia* as the completion of faith, involuntarily expands the special relations of dogmatic faith into
the general relations of Divine providence.[2] But when,
further, on the soil of Pietism, Methodism, and the Baptist
movement, assurance of salvation is made dependent on one's
being able to supply the date and the exact circumstances
of his regeneration in correct order, the demand becomes just

[1] *Loc. theol.* xvii, § 87, ed. Cotta, tom. vii. p. 109. Cf. vol. i. p. 354.

[2] *Inst.* iii. 2. 16 : " In summa, vere fidelis non est, nisi qui solida persuasione
deum sibi propitium benevolumque patrem esse persuasus de eius benignitate
omnia sibi pollicetur, nisi qui divinae erga se benevolentiae promissionibus
fretus indubitatam salutis exspectationem praesumit. . . . Fidelis, inquam,
non est, nisi qui suae salutis securitati innixus, diabolo et morti confidenter
insultet, quomodo ex praeclaro illo Pauli epiphonemate (Rom. 8. 38) docemur."

as absurd as to say that one cannot rightly consider himself
a man unless he is conversant with the fact and the laws of
his own procreation.

In the Catholic system the right and the ground of
individual assurance remained undecided (§ 23). Assurance,
it is true, is a consistent result of the line of thought founded
upon grace which we find in St. Bernard. So far, therefore,
as the influence of this original element of mediaeval Catholicism survives, as it does in the above-named contemporaries
of the Reformation and the Council of Trent, even in the
Romish Church men may experience their own individual
salvation in patience and humility and submission to God's
will. So far, however, as these virtues are elucidated under
the heading of hope (p. 37), Thomas attaches them, as an
antecedent condition, to the exercise of love toward God and
men. His interpretation of *timor filialis*, accordingly, goes
to prove that for the most part he recommends uncertainty
about our own salvation (p. 177). But yet, just in champions
of the Romish Church, we meet with an assurance of salvation
of the strongest kind, especially in the form of denying salvation to all who hold a different faith. Here the case is
altogether different. For what appears here is an unexpected
acknowledgment of the importance of numbers, as though
quantity could ever take the place of quality. Under the
wing of the Church of the multitude, men feel quite certain
of salvation, for that Church, in their opinion, must rule the
world because it includes within itself all salvation ; and thus
the question of the right of the individual to assurance is
overborne. Just as, until a few years ago, each Catholic bishop
was by himself liable to dogmatic error, but all together
in Council were held to be infallible, so each Catholic is
bound, in *timor filialis*, to cherish doubts of his own salvation, but collectively they are the exclusive possessors of
salvation. Now, the spokesmen who have to maintain this
claim always come forward with the kind of courage which
draws its power from assemblages of the masses. This form
of infallible conviction, therefore, always has about it an

odour such as one is not accustomed to meet with in good
society.

It is no mere accident that the Reformers' notion of
Christian perfection, this expression of the reconciliation with
God which operates in believers, was constructed in opposition to monasticism. For monasticism had reintroduced
into Christianity the religious error of Pharisaism (vol. ii.
p. 275). The Reformation of the sixteenth century would
not have excelled all preceding Reformations of the Church,
had it not at this point decided against the greatest corruption possible of the Christian religion. It is to be regretted,
however, that the theologians of the Reformation were unable
to keep clearly in sight the connection which has been shown
to exist between Christian perfection and the idea of reconciliation. In the 4th Article of the Augsburg Confession,
the statement of justification by faith is not accompanied by
the explanation that its purpose is to be found in the functions
of Christian perfection ; this relation is touched upon merely
incidentally in the 20th Article, and only in view of its abuse
drawn out in Article 27 (p. 647). Apart from the *Apology
of the C. A.*, the Confessions of both branches of the Reformation have preserved nothing of all this ; and, as has been
demonstrated above (vol. i. p. 350), the problem has been
neglected in Dogmatics, and thereby the doctrine of justification which it contains has been mutilated. The practice of
faith in providence, humility, and patience has not therefore
died out in the Lutheran Church ; it has always been duly
nourished by the literature of asceticism and by hymns suited
for use in the Church. But the piety which grows up on
this soil often stands in tense opposition to the " Churchly
theology " of those who hold the office of teaching, and to their
claims to guide the Christian knowledge of the community.
These unfortunate relations are entirely due to the " Churchly
theology," which possesses among its dogmatic media of tradition no theory of the connection between justification by faith
and the functions of Christian perfection. This circumstance
helped to produce a century ago the rationalistic decomposi-

tion of Evangelical Christianity. The reactionary theologians
of this century have not been able thoroughly to annul this
development, and therefore are not in possession of the means
of overcoming the *Aufklärung*.

It is worthy of note, therefore, that the opposition which
Luther brought out between Christian freedom and the piety
of the ceremonial law, has a wider range than is indicated
merely by its application to the criticism of monasticism or
any similar feature in Catholic Christianity. In themselves,
ceremonies are no more absurd than doctrines held in common ;
they become useless and a hindrance to religion only when
the significance which they possessed at their original creation
has become unintelligible. Then, even ceremonial custom
becomes an alien law which, from the point of view of the
Evangelical faith, may indeed be observed as a matter of fact,
but only as a concession to fellow-members of the Church
who have not yet discovered the merely human and relative
worth of such practices as ordinances of the Church.[1] Luther
made this admission at a time when he had not yet conceived
the thought of separation from the Church of the ceremonial
law. He supplements this teaching, however, by the assertion that in our intercourse with unbending champions of
ceremonial we should rather offer them opposition, and by
transgressing ecclesiastical ordinances should seek to excite
them to sin and put them in the wrong.[2] These rules, how-

---

[1] Luther, *De libertate Christiana*, tom. iv. p. 247 : "Si quis scientiam (de
iustitia fidei) haberet, facile se posset gerere citra periculum in infinitis illis
mandatis et praeceptis papae, quae aliqui stulti pastores sic urgent, quasi ad
iustitiam et salutem sint necessaria, appellantes ea praecepta ecclesiae, cum sint
nihil minus. Christianus enim liber sic dicet : ego ieiunabo, orabo, hoc et hoc
faciam, quod per homines mandatum est, non quod mihi illo sit opus ad
iustitiam aut salutem, sed quod in hoc morem geram papae, aut proximo meo
ad exemplum faciam et patiar omnia, sicut Christus mihi multo plura fecit et
passus est, quorum ipse nullo prorsus egebat."

[2] P. 251 : "Occurrunt pertinaces obdurati ceremoniistae, qui sicut aspides
surdae nolunt audire veritatem libertatis, sed suas ceremonias tanquam
iustificationes iactant, imperant et urgent sine fide (Rom. 14. 23). His oportet
resistere, contraria facere et *fortiter scandalisare*, ne opinione ista impia
plurimos secum fallant." The word *scandalisare* must here be understood in
its original sense ; for it is impossible to see how the production of genuine
offence in the minds of the opponents described would deprive their assertions

42

ever, are not merely significant for the position which Luther
then occupied, but may be applied to every case in which a
collision is indicated between the religious aims of the Church
and any of its legal forms.   In relation to ceremonies, says
Luther, the righteousness of faith is always in peril ; but
religious faith must always be confronted with this danger
so long as legal ordinances have to be used to maintain it.[1]
It is just this which makes the position of the Christian
religion under the legal ordinances of the Church so tragic,
that the end which they ought to serve as means may be as
easily threatened as promoted by them.   Now I do not find
that this relation has been perceived by those who, for the
past generation, have put themselves forward as custodians
of the " Churchly theology," as champions of the legal ordinances of the Church, especially of the Church's confession,
and quite recently likewise as defenders of " the rights of
the Church " against the powers which in Germany since the
Reformation have rightly belonged in the constitution of the
Church to the nobility.   The ground of this want of perception, however, lies partly in the fact that Dogmatics, by which
these " Churchly theologians " mean the Confession of the
Church, especially the Augsburg Confession, has lost the connection between the doctrine of justification and the duties
of Christian freedom and perfection, partly in the fact that
the Pietism of this century, from which confessional ecclesi-
asticism springs, has been from the outset guided by a
ceremonial interest in the imperfect Dogmatics of the seventeenth century.   In the " Revival " not only do aesthetic and

of the power to deceive others. This result is attained, however, if they let
themselves be tempted by open resistance into doing what is clearly wrong.

[1] P. 253 : "In summa, sicut paupertas in divitiis, fidelitas in negotiis,
humilitas in honoribus, abstinentia in conviviis, castitas in deliciis, ita
iustitia fidei in ceremoniis periclitatur. Numquid ait Salomon, ignem quis in
sinu gestare potest, ut non comburantur vestimenta eius ? Et tamen ut in
divitiis, in negotiis, in honoribus, in deliciis, in epulis, ita *in ceremoniis id
est in periculis versari oportet*." Cf. Luther's hymn, "Ye Christians, now
rejoice together," with its conclusion—

>" Of men's opinions be thou ware,
>   They'll rob you of your treasure fair,
>   This warning be my ending."

moral motives of revolt against Rationalism prevail over
intellectual interests, but in this spiritual movement a *sacrificium intellectus* is performed just as a proof of earnest
obedience to Christ.　Moved by this ascetic impulse, people
regard the confession of certain dogmas—as these have been
handed down in that forbidding and unintelligible form
which neither displays any relation to a common end, nor
presents a complete practical outline of Christianity—as
the condition and chief guarantee of Christian perfection.
At the same time, there may be heard from these circles
depreciatory judgments regarding the piety in which, as the
Augsburg Confession testifies, Christian perfection consists,
and which draws its continuous nourishment from those
hymns, dear to the Church, in which the healthiest tradition
of Evangelical Christianity is expressed.　In Pietistic circles
people have the appearance of regarding faith in providence
as something inferior,[1] simply because that faith was the
purport likewise of Rationalism, and it ought not to be
conceded that Rationalism contains a sound element of
Christianity.　There is no difficulty in understanding how,
with the mass of Evangelical Christians, faith in providence
has no clear connection with Dogmatics; for in this century
theology has never taken to heart the truth that, according
to the Augsburg Confession, this faith ought to be regarded
as the proof of reconciliation having been experienced ; and
the teaching of the Church, so far as my observation goes,
is not directed to this truth.　What wonder that in Evangelical Christendom at present, just as in the Middle Ages,
there should exist two forms of religion, the lay Christianity
of undogmatic faith in providence, and the perfect piety of
faith in dogma, which, unless we add a circle of Tertians,
male and female, is represented only by the clergy, or at
least expected of them.　Such a state of matters is intolerable, for it runs counter to all the principles of Evangelical
Christianity.　The interest of the laity in the Church is

---

[1] A friend informs me that Hengstenberg once spoke to him with scorn of
the "Commit-thou-all-thy-ways" Christianity of a third person.

always growing weaker, for they find a surer basis for their
Christianity in their private convictions than in dogmatic
preaching, which contributes nothing to a better understanding of what is involved in Evangelical perfection.   Christians
who are dogmatically perfect, however, are always becoming
less fitted to rule in the Evangelical Church, partly because,
owing to the ceaseless agitation of Church politics necessary to maintain their influence, they become secularised,
partly because their hierarchical aspirations carry them
along the lines taken by Jesuitism.   Do those on this side
really think that it is possible and necessary to impart a
dogmatic temper to the laity, in order that what only exists
to guide the teaching of the Church's ministers should become
operative as the confession of all Church members?   One
would expect that, if dogmatically correct views are to be
insisted on, at least women would be spared, for they, though
without clear dogmatic knowledge, mostly know how to
practise Christian perfection in exemplary fashion.   For
ladies who strive to make themselves perfect in dogmatic
faith, and in criticising the faith of others, hardly please God
any more thereby than they please men.   I am quite aware
that those who are interested in the ecclesiastical particularism
which is fenced round by the claim to render the most
genuine and the truest worship, will protest in the most
vehement way against these remarks, and all the more
vehemently that their party cannot deny that I have the
Augsburg Confession and Luther's most original views on
my side.   Nevertheless, I ask them to consider that the
Church, quâ legal institution, belongs to the world; and
separate Churches, in so far as they are characterised by
legal ordinances, are the most worldly of all.   The interest
which attaches to these Churches exclusively or predominantly, is secular and a motive to secularisation.   True, we
are called on to live and work in a particular Church.   But
the same rule holds good as was laid down by Paul for
marriage as a worldly condition (1 Cor. vii. 29), "Let him
who has his particular Church be as though he had none!"

§ 68. In the Augsburg Confession *moral action in one's civic vocation* is reckoned as one of the features of Christian perfection, and this is intelligible from the opposition felt to monasticism.   On the other hand, such a conception seems to be entirely out of relation to the New Testament.   It is true, our civic vocation receives a peculiar sanction from Paul's words, that men should not seek to escape from slavery because of Christianity, but should remain in this or any other vocation in which their calling to be Christians found them (1 Cor. vii. 20, 24).   But this feature does not appear to find a place among the marks of perfection, whether we understand that ideal in the sense Jesus gives it, or in the particular distinctive form it receives from the Apostle. Besides, the position of the Augsburg Confession has against it the assertion, always emphasised in Evangelical doctrine, that even in the state of grace we must always be mindful of the imperfection of moral action, that we may base our salvation, not on good works which always come short of the law's demands, but only on faith in Christ.   This doctrine, with the relations in which it stands, must first be more closely examined.   Attention has already been drawn to the difficulty of making a practical application of it when taken rigorously (pp. 164, 489).   For we are told that we must look away from our good works on account of their imperfection, so as to base our salvation upon faith in Christ; but in order to have the assurance of faith we must conclude from our good works, in spite of their imperfection, that we stand under the influence of grace.   Either this leads to an endless series of alternating judgments of opposite content, or it is an error to estimate our works by the standard of the law. For although the consciousness of imperfection, which every day we find within, may serve to emphasise faith in Christ as the condition of salvation, yet the perpetual consciousness of imperfection in our good works is no slight obstacle to enthusiasm in discharging the moral tasks of Christianity· It is certainly no just reproach against the Reformers that by the assertion of justification by faith they render men indifferent to the tasks of moral activity; but from their assertion of the continual imperfection of such action and of the inevitable inaccessibility of its goal one might easily draw an inference of that kind. For if we know ourselves unconditionally condemned beforehand to imperfection in any activity, the impulse to discharge it is crippled. The possibility of perfection must be held out in prospect if we are to expend our industry on any branch of action.

Now the conception of good works, such as are measured by the statutory law, expresses a task which not merely is impracticable if sinfulness be presupposed as still operative, but which it is impossible to combine in thought with the attribute of perfection. Perfection is the attribute of a whole (§ 67); on the other hand, good works, as related to the statutory law, cannot be conceived as a whole. Not only do they form an endless series in time; they have likewise at every moment of time to occupy an indefinite expanse in space. For the law, as we conceive it, claims the will simultaneously for all the possible ends which fall within the compass of the good. In order to do one good work, however, one must simultaneously leave unattended to all other demands for good action and the furtherance of good ends, for a single action is all we are capable of at one point of time. So that sin, whether as evil will or as indifference, is not essential to the thwarting of a quantitatively perfect fulfilment of the moral law; such fulfilment is impossible *per se*, as judged by the statutory form of the law. Therefore the duty of good works, unlimited as it is in time and in space, and the duty of perfection, namely, to realise moral action as a totality, are mutually exclusive. The unpractical rigorism, in which both demands are combined, has also avenged itself in history. For in the theology of the *Aufklärung* this dogma has veered round into the contrary assertion, that God demands from every man only such and so many moral services as from his endowments and his circumstances he is capable of rendering (vol. i. p. 393). Nor did this laxity in conceiving the moral task usurp the place of the orthodox doctrine by a sudden reversal of judgment, in the form, *i.e.*, of a declension from truth ; nay, we meet with the above principle in the official conduct of pastoral work even in the halcyon days of orthodoxy (vol. i. p. 418). Confirmation of this view is to be found in the argument urged by Calvin, that with Divine sonship there is combined the confidence that God will judge imperfect moral deeds not after the strictness of the law, but with leniency according to circumstances.[1] And although for God this rule is balanced by the fact that to believers so judged He imputes the perfect righteousness of Christ, that does not touch the practical self-estimate of the believer in the light of this rule. But how, I ask, does this principle of God's leniency towards the believer's imperfect moral action differ from the view put forward by Socinianism and the theologians of the *Aufklärung*? The impossibility of quantitative perfection in good works, which is admitted, always carries with it likewise a limitation of the validity of the moral law.

In still another respect the rubric of good works, current in orthodox theology, is unsuitable as a comprehensive designation of the ethical side of Christianity. To state our task so excludes the perfection of moral achievement in any sense, and is thus at the same time a denial that in moral relations the believer can ever become a whole in his own order. But now the Christian religion has it for its aim that through reconciliation and the spiritual dominion over the world which answers thereto, the believer should gain and display the value of a whole. And so it would indicate an incongruity in Christianity were the state of the believer, in religious and

---

[1] *Inst.* iii. 19. 5 : "Qui legis iugo adstringuntur, servis sunt similes, quibus certa in singulos dies opera a dominis indicuntur. Hi enim nihil effectum putant, nisi exactus operum modus constiterit. Filii vero, qui liberalius et magis ingenue a patribus tractantur, eis non dubitant inchoata et dimidiata opera, aliquid etiam vitii habentia offerre, confisi suam obedientiam et animi promtitudinem illis acceptam fore, etiamsi minus exacte effecerint quod volebant. Tales nos esse oportet, qui certo confidamus, obsequia nostra indulgentissimo patri probatum iri, quantulacunque sunt et quamvis rudia et imperfecta. Neque haec fiducia nobis parum necessaria est, sine qua frustra omnia conabimur ; siquidem nullo nostro opere se coli reputat deus, nisi quod in eius cultum vere a nobis fiat. Id autem quis possit inter illos terrores, ubi dubitatur, offendaturne deus an colatur opere nostro."

moral respects, necessarily subject to contrary conditions. In the New Testament, however, the rubric of good works is never used as though meaning that it is an exhaustive expression for the essential practice of morality ; the expression rather occurs as a description of the normal phenomena of that moral action which, in important statements in the apostolic Epistles, is differentiated from good works by being entitled the one all-inclusive good work of life (vol. ii. pp. 292, 371). On the other hand, moral perfection is to be regarded not merely as something demanded by Jesus, but also as a fact attested by Paul (p. 647). When, therefore, in Methodism [1] the perfection of sanctification is directly aimed at, this idea, altogether apart from any relation to the statutory law, is related to the perfect character of love to God, which excludes sin, and in its own order represents a whole, despite the weaknesses and imperfections which accompany it. This representation, it is true, is partly obscure, and partly bound up with dubious associations. For what it really describes is not at all the moral, but simply the religious character, and this, too, only in its most general expression. But how perfection of love to man is included in perfect love to God is not shown. Moreover, it is sought to confirm the statement by arguing that it is possible not to sin even when actually doing wrong to others. But the casuistical contention that error of this kind stands in no relation to sin, deserves no more notice than does the remark that not every transgression of the law is sin. For this betrays an effort once more to conform Methodist perfection to the statutory law, from which, to begin with, it had been withdrawn. Thus the standard of possible perfection is not clear. For perfection of the ethico-religious character demands under all circumstances a moral sensibility which guides self-examination otherwise than according to the coarse lines of the moral law, conceived in a statutory form ; on the other hand, Methodist positions lead to the view that the character of personal sinlessness is to be attained by laying all sorts of restrictions on moral sensibility.

[1] Cf. Jacoby, *Handbuch des Methodismus* (2nd edit. 1855), p. 254 ff.

The conception of moral perfection in the Christian life ought on no account to be associated with the idea of a fruitless search for actual sinlessness of conduct in all the details of life. It rather means that our moral achievement or lifework in connection with the Kingdom of God should, however limited in amount, be conceived as possessing the quality of a whole in its own order. For these are the conditions of the matter described by Paul. At the same time it is clear that Paul regards the life-work as a totality, because he conceives it as limited by our special vocation. For it is as mediated by the species that a multiplicity of phenomena, directed to a common end and through it regularly connected, constitute a whole. And so Luther, even though without thinking Paul's self-estimate (vol. ii. p. 365) worthy of any special consideration, helped to express a true thought when, in his " Address to the Nobility of the German Nation," he maintained that every Christian in his civil vocation, of whatever nature it might be, exercised the character of a spiritual personality ; and congruous with this is the thought that activity in our calling is to be reckoned part of the Christian's perfection.[1] Now, in spite of the authority of the Augsburg Confession, this truth, while remaining operative in the practice of Protestantism, has not received its proper weight in public teaching. The predominance of a negatively ascetic conception of morality in the era of orthodoxy, indeed, made it possible for Johann Arndt, in his *True Christianity*, to judge our civil vocation merely in the light of the principle that the heritage and goods of the Christian are not in this world, and that therefore they should use temporal things as aliens to the world. Of course, if we conceive the example of Christ, as did the Middle Ages, as the ideal of abstract self-abnegation, we shall miss the truth that we have to seek in Christ no special moral pattern other than that of perfect fidelity to our calling.

While referring back to the analysis I have given of the

[1] Cf. also *Apol. C. A.* iii. 71, viii. 25, 48–50 ; further, Calvin, iii. 10. 6 : " Satis est, si noverimus, vocationem domini esse in omni re bene agendi principium ac fundamentum, ad quam qui se non referet, nunquam rectam in officiis viam tenebit."

idea of " vocation," which was made in order to explain the
religious value of Christ (§ 48), I repeat that each individual
acts morally when he fulfils the universal law in his special
vocation, or in that combination of vocations which he is able
to unite in his conduct of life. This excludes every moral
necessity to expend good action on such ends as do not fit
into the individual's vocation. Such good action, however,
as is incumbent, but is not directly determined thus, may be
viewed as obligatory, on condition that by a judgment of duty
it can be construed analogously to our vocation, that is,
provided that after consideration of all the circumstances one
is called to discharge it as an extraordinary duty of love.
True, even when the fulfilment of the moral law is confined
to one's calling and what is analogous thereto, the series of
good actions which are incumbent is still infinite in time ; but
there falls away thus the chief ground of the imperfection of
good works as measured directly by the universal moral law.
The fact that good action is conditioned by one's calling
invalidates the apparent obligation we are under at each
moment of time to do good action in every possible direction.
But, further, just here it becomes plain that the significance
of our moral calling for good action in general supersedes the
statutory idea of the moral law, on which depends the intolerable, because boundless, demand for good works. The autonomy
of moral action (§ 53) is realised in general whenever we find
in our moral vocation the proximate norm which specifies for
each individual the action which the moral law makes
necessary. Our special calling, in fact, is seen to be the field
of moral action to which we are summoned, because we
appropriate it as subordinate to the universal final end of the
good, or as an integral part of the Kingdom of God. On this
presupposition, a universal statutory moral law is unthinkable,
for it would have no point of contact with the moral significance of special vocations. Rather, out of the moral disposition
which, in the field of a special vocation, takes shape in action
for the highest common end, we have to evolve those principles
by which we regulate particular groups of moral action, and,

in harmony therewith, form particular judgments of duty affirming that it is necessary in a given case to realise the final end of the good. Under these circumstances and in this form the individual, out of his freedom, produces the moral law, or lives in the law of freedom.

It is under these conditions, too, that the individual's moral achievement becomes a whole. The realisation of the universal good within the special limited domain of our vocation, and in such a way that all extraordinary actions are regarded as essential from their analogy to our vocation, is the reason why the multiplicity of good works, in which action manifests itself, forms an inwardly limited unity, in other words, a whole. But even to conceive the whole thus does not yet show it to us as a magnitude which is also limited externally. Even if the spatial unlimitedness of good works, as measured by a universal statutory moral law, be set aside, yet the temporal series of actions necessary in one's moral vocation appears to be infinite. Here, therefore, a self-torturing self-scrutiny might insert its lever, and throw back the discussion on to the lines of the idea of good works from which we are trying to escape. Does not an impression of perpetual imperfection, even in the discharge of our calling, follow from the fact that every omission of an action possible in this domain is to be reckoned as guilt? How can we ever satisfy ourselves, even in this domain, and how can it ever be right to yield to the impression that what we are achieving is a whole in its own order? But against this I set the experience that though we may have scruples about many omissions of actions possible in our calling, there comes later the knowledge that the relaxation which we have allowed ourselves to take has served to increase our activity in our calling. Moreover, the omission of possible useful actions is not wrong, but only the omission of actions which are morally necessary. Besides, the conception of a whole does not depend so much on quantity as the above objection presupposes. True, a whole, too, must be a *quantum*, in the present case, as in all cases. But a whole does not require as one of its conditions a quantitative extension *ad infinitum*, which, indeed, renders a whole impossible. And he who in the moral fulfilment of his vocation is more indefatigable than his neighbour, merely makes the whole possibly greater, while he also possibly imperils its existence ; and prudence counsels us not to put an excessive strain on our powers. But, finally, this circumstance brings before us the fact that a fulfilment of our vocation, though quantitatively more limited, certainly possesses the value of a whole, if at the same time we attain, in producing it, moral character as a whole. The Apostle Paul already perceives this when he makes the practice of moral righteousness relative to the end of self-sanctification (Rom. vi. 19 ; vol. ii. p. 287). For this signifies nothing but the formation of virtuous character, which we cannot attain by a negatively ascetic elaboration of our previously existing defects, but only by embarking on a positive and broadening course of action. But according to the laws of the will, good action for all the ends of society works reflexly in such a way as at the same time to produce personal virtue.

Moral action in our calling is, therefore, the form in which our life-work as a totality is produced as our contribution to the Kingdom of God, and in which, at the same time, the ideal of spiritual personality as a whole in its own order is reached. Thus freedom in the law is realised. But this is homogeneous with the religious functions of faith in providence, patience and humility, and prayer, through which the believer assures himself that he possesses, in virtue of reconciliation, the value of a whole in contrast to the world. These aspects mutually condition one another in such a way that no one of them can occur in an authentic form without the others. One cannot practise action motived by the law of freedom without, in the religious functions, attesting his freedom over the world ; and one cannot assure oneself of forgiveness, without exercising love in deed and in truth (1 John iii. 18, 19 ; vol. ii. p. 348). All this goes to fill out the extent of Christian freedom ; so also it forms the content of Christian perfection. As in the religious functions which spring from reconciliation we attain our ideal lordship over the world and are blessed therein as in doing good, so the goal of the moral formation of character is eternal life (Rom. vi. 22). Personal assurance of the indestructibility of spiritual existence always attaches itself to those experiences of the worth of the religious-ethical character. But, finally, Paul is also right in maintaining that the ultimate standing of a person in the Kingdom of God depends on the goodness and the rounded completeness of the life-work he achieves in his moral vocation (vol. ii. p. 367). Although this thought is expressed by the idea of a reward, yet it plainly differs from the meriting of blessedness by good works. The latter combination of ideas is formed on the mould and measure of the law, and even so is unintelligible ; for no inner mutual relation can be shown between blessedness and good works. On the other hand, what is posited as result in Paul's assertion is only what is already produced in the production of a good life-work (Gal. vi. 7, 8). For in doing good we are blessed, and the performance of our vocation assures us of our standing in the Kingdom of God, and that, too, so far as it is the fellowship of blessedness. But this is related to reconciliation as a consequence ; with the appropriation of reconciliation, too, the will receives a direction towards the final end of the Kingdom of God. There is, therefore, no contradiction between the assertion that in reconciliation eternal life is bestowed by God through Christ, and completed consistently with the grace of God thus manifested, and the assertion that we reach the consummation of salvation through the development of the religious-moral character, and through the life-performance —perfect in its own order — of our vocation. For we are blessed not only in fellowship with God, but also in fellowship with all the blessed. For the former we have only God to thank ; the latter we produce through our personal contribution to the common weal of the Kingdom of God. Thus is evaded the erroneous view that the measure of forgiveness in the case of each individual is determined by the measure of his loving activity (vol. i. p 645). For that much is forgiven to a particular person implies that he had to be brought to God from a greater distance, but not that he is brought nearer to God than another. In forgiveness all are brought near to God, but no one nearer than his neighbour. But the intensity of love and common feeling in the work of life which is provided for in the possible perfection of each individual, is the condition of fellowship with all those who gain the prize of eternal life. Finally, when Paul speaks of the perfect as such, whom he distinguishes personally from others, he does not mean thereby to set up a specific class-distinction; he only indicates the fact that, in accordance with the conditions of growth, all members of the Christian Church do not reach simultaneously that stage of religious and moral formation of character to which all are called.

1. Religious dominion over the world, which constitutes the immediate form of reconciliation with God through Christ, is exercised through faith in the loving providence of God, through the virtues of humility and patience, and, finally, through prayer, and through this last likewise receives common expression.

2. In the exercise of trust in God in all situations of life, in the production of humility and patience—these inward activities, too, supported by prayer—the believer experiences his personal assurance of reconciliation.

3. The freedom of action in the form of a special moral vocation which, motived by the universal final end of the Kingdom of God, imposes a law upon itself by the production of principles and judgments of duty, and serves to confirm the appropriation of reconciliation, forms, together with the foregoing religious functions, that perfection invested with which each believer must show himself to be a whole or a character who occupies a permanent place in the Kingdom of God and enjoys practical experience of eternal life.

INDEX